THE CONTEXT OF MEDICINES IN DEVELOPING COUNTRIES

CULTURE, ILLNESS, AND HEALING

Editors:

MARGARET LOCK
Departments of Anthropology and Humanities and Social Studies in Medicine, McGill University, Montreal, Canada

ALLAN YOUNG
Department of Anthropology, Case Western Reserve University, Cleveland, Ohio, U.S.A.

Editorial Board:

LIZA BERKMAN
Department of Epidemiology, Yale University, New Haven, Connecticut, U.S.A.

RONALD FRANKENBERG
Centre for Medical and Social Anthropology, University of Keele, England

ATWOOD D. GAINES
Departments of Anthropology and Psychiatry, Case Western Reserve University and Medical School, Cleveland, Ohio, U.S.A.

GILBERT LEWIS
Department of Anthropology, University of Cambridge, England

GANANATH OBEYESEKERE
Department of Anthropology, Princeton University, Princeton, New Jersey, U.S.A.

ANDREAS ZEMPLÉNI
Laboratoire d'Ethnologie et de Sociologie Comparative, Université de Paris X, Nanterre, France

THE CONTEXT OF MEDICINES IN DEVELOPING COUNTRIES

Studies in Pharmaceutical Anthropology

Edited by

SJAAK VAN DER GEEST

Anthropological-Sociological Center, University of Amsterdam

and

SUSAN REYNOLDS WHYTE

Institute of Ethnology and Anthropology, University of Copenhagen

KLUWER ACADEMIC PUBLISHERS
DORDRECHT/BOSTON/LONDON

The Context of medicines in developing countries.

(Culture, illness, and healing ; v. 12)
Includes index.
1. Materia medica--Developing countries.
2. Pharmaceutical industry--Developing countries.
3. Medical anthropology--Cross-cultural studies.
I. Geest, Sjaak van der, 1943-   . II. Whyte,
Susan Reynolds.   III. Series.
RS153.C74 1988   306'.4   88-3273
ISBN 1-55608-059-X

Published by Kluwer Academic Publishers,
P.O. Box 17, 3300 AA Dordrecht, The Netherlands
Kluwer Academic Publishers incorporates the publishing programmes of
D. Reidel, Martinus Nijhoff, Dr W. Junk, and MTP Press.

Sold and distributed in the U.S.A. and Canada
by Kluwer Academic Publishers,
101 Philip Drive, Norwell, MA 02061, U.S.A.

In all other countries, sold and distributed
by Kluwer Academic Publishers Group
P.O. Box 322, 3300 AH Dordrecht, The Netherlands

About the cover

The cover illustration is taken from a flipbook used for educating people in Bangladesh on essential drugs. The text below the illustration reads: "Always ask when and how many medicines to take".
The flipbook was prepared by PIACT/PATH Bangladesh and funded by the WHO Action Programme on Essential Drugs. The illustrations are by Kamrun Nahar Rashid.

All Rights Reserved
© 1988 by Kluwer Academic Publishers
No part of the material protected by this copyright notice may be reproduced or utilized in any form or by any means, electronic or mechanical, including photocopying, recording or by any information storage and retrieval system, without written permission from the copyright owner

Printed in The Netherlands

TABLE OF CONTENTS

PREFACE	vii
CH. LESLIE / Foreword	ix
INTRODUCTION	1
S. R. WHYTE AND S. VAN DER GEEST/Medicines in Context: an Introduction	3
THE TRANSACTION OF MEDICINES	13
Introductory Note	15
A. FERGUSON/Commercial Pharmaceutical Medicine and Medicalization: a Case Study from El Salvador	19
I. WOLFFERS/Traditional Practitioners and Western Pharmaceuticals in Sri Lanka	47
A. UGALDE AND N. HOMEDES/Medicines and Rural Health Services: an Experiment in the Dominican Republic	57
H. KLOOS, B. GETAHUN, A. TEFERI, K. GEBRE TSADIK AND S. BELAY/Buying Drugs in Addis Ababa: a Quantitative Analysis	81
K. LOGAN/'Casi como doctor': Pharmacists and their Clients in a Mexican Urban Context	107
S. VAN DER GEEST/The Articulation of Formal and Informal Medicine Distribution in South Cameroon	131
A. F. AFDHAL AND R. L. WELSCH/The Rise of the Modern *Jamu* Industry in Indonesia: a Preliminary Overview	149
THE MEANING OF MEDICINES	173
Introductory Note	175
P. U. UNSCHULD/Culture and Pharmaceutics: Some Epistemological Observations of Pharmacological Systems in Ancient Europe and Medieval China	179

L. K. SUSSMAN/The Use of Herbal and Biomedical Pharmaceuticals on Mauritius — 199

S. R. WHYTE/The Power of Medicines in East Africa — 217

A. NIEHOF/Traditional Medication at Pregnancy and Childbirth in Madura, Indonesia — 235

C. H. BLEDSOE AND M. F. GOUBAUD/The Reinterpretation and Distribution of Western Pharmaceuticals: an Example from the Mende of Sierra Leone — 253

C. MACCORMACK AND A. DRAPER/Cultural Meanings of Oral Rehydration Salts in Jamaica — 277

R. BURGHART/Penicillin: an Ancient Ayurvedic Medicine — 289

N. L. ETKIN/Cultural Constructions of Efficacy — 299

CONCLUSION — 327

S. VAN DER GEEST/Pharmaceutical Anthropology: Perspectives for Research and Application — 329

LIST OF CONTRIBUTORS — 367

INDEX OF NAMES — 371

INDEX OF SUBJECTS — 377

PREFACE

Western pharmaceuticals are flooding the Third World. Injections, capsules and tablets are available in city markets and village shops, from 'traditional' practitioners and street vendors, as well as from more orthodox sources like hospitals. Although many are aware of this 'pharmaceutical invasion', little has been written about how local people perceive and use these products. This book is a first attempt to remedy that situation. It presents studies of the ways Western medicines are circulated and understood in the cities and rural areas of Africa, Asia and Latin America.

We feel that such a collection is long overdue for two reasons. The first is a practical one: people dealing with health problems in developing countries need information about local situations and they need examples of methods they can use to examine the particular contexts in which they are working. We hope that this book will be useful for pharmacists, doctors, nurses, health planners, policy makers and concerned citizens, who are interested in the realities of drug use. Why do people want various kinds of medicine? How do they evaluate and choose them and how do they obtain them?

The second reason for these studies of medicines is to fill a need in medical anthropology as a field of study. Here we address our colleagues in anthropology, medical sociology and related disciplines. Researchers working in non-Western cultures have concentrated on 'exotic' forms of therapy, and on the ways people choose between treatment by biomedical specialists and indigenous healers. They have tended to overlook self-care by medications, even though this is the most common form of therapy and even though pharmaceuticals are in many ways the real 'hard core' of biomedicine. This gap cannot be filled by a single book, but we can make a beginning by pointing to some of the analytical problems that deserve attention. These include the individualization of therapy made possible by buying medicines, and the implications of pharmaceutical pluralism for people's changing perceptions of 'indigenous' medicines. We are confident that this collection of papers can be used as a textbook in courses of social pharmacy and medical anthropology, focusing on the use of medicines in developing countries.

The book is divided into two main sections. The first part, on the transaction of medicines, deals with pharmaceuticals as commodities that are produced, sold and consumed. The roles of drug company salesmen, pharmacists, street vendors, and 'traditional' practitioners are examined. Detailed descriptions show how drugs are exchanged and used outside the control of Western professional medicine. The second section examines the meaning of medicines. Western pharmaceuticals are understood in terms of local concepts of healing. Their 'foreignness' and 'high tech' modes of packaging and application (capsules, injections) imbue them with special power and efficacy. There is a short introductory essay by the editors and each of the main sections is preceded by an introductory note, which characterizes the contributions for the convenience of 'shoppers'. The concluding chapter is an overview, which sums up five themes in pharmaceutical anthropology, proposing lines for further research, and ends with a discussion of the practical relevance of the field.

In preparing this collection of articles, we have been helped and encouraged by many people. We would like to thank the contributors for their enthusiastic response and particularly Robert Welsch, who did also some editorial work. Cor Yonker and Rimke van der Geest kindly assisted us with the index. Martin Scrivener, of Kluwer Academic Publishers, saw the importance of the endeavor from the beginning and was supportive through it all.

SJAAK VAN DER GEEST
SUSAN REYNOLDS WHYTE

FOREWORD

This collection of essays deals with the ways people in the developing world today select and use their medicines. The book offers a view from the grassroots, where people are actually taking medicines – not only those of the trans-national companies, but also commercially produced indigenous medicines and locally made remedies. It is pharmaceutical *anthropology* because it seeks to explore the social and cultural contexts in which medicines are produced, exchanged and consumed.

The emphasis on context is the special contribution of the present volume, yet the problem addressed – drugs in the third world – has been of concern for several decades. The role of western pharmaceutical companies has been at the heart of the discussion up to now; little attention has been paid to the manufacturers of non-western medicines. In order to understand the significance of pharmaceutical anthropology and the contributions of the present volume, it may be useful to review some of the issues and developments in the debate about the proliferation of medicines in the developing world.

The modern period of commercial production is often said to have been initiated by German chemical companies in the 1880s, but the manufacture of brand name and patent medicines began in the 17th and 18th centuries, and became a conspicuous and highly profitable market in the 19th century. Muckraking criticism of patent medicines in the United States led to the Pure Food and Drug Act of 1906. The debate has included such things as H.G. Wells' novel, *Tono Bungay*, and in the United States, the highly publicized hearings conducted by Senator Kefauver in the 1940s.

Antibiotics after the Second World War were new 'miracle drugs' that promoted a period of rapid expansion in the international pharmaceutical industry, and the world-wide prestige of injections. Anthropologists began to report this phenomenon in the 1950s, and Clark Cunningham coined the term 'injection doctors' for practitioners that he observed in Thailand in the 1960s. The danger of untrained practitioners prescribing and administering antibiotic injections was immediately apparent, and this initiated the concern among anthropologists and health professionals about the effects of the international pharmaceutical industry on health care in developing countries.

However, nationalist thinkers in at least some Asian countries were concerned about international pharmaceuticals at an earlier time. For example, in India the cost of importing British medicines and other manufactured goods began to be criticized a century ago, and contributed to the Swadeshi movement to buy Indian products. Entrepreneurs who initiated the commercial production of Ayurdevic medicine in the 1880s argued that imported drugs drained the Indian economy, while indigenous preparations were better suited to local conditions. Similar arguments were advanced by medical revivalists in other parts of Asia, culminating with Mao's endorsement of traditional Chinese medicine and the advent of barefoot doctors.

The post World War II advances in chemotherapy and expansion of the pharmaceutical market are the immediate setting for the current debate on how multinational companies affect health care in developing countries. Since socialist enterprise has contributed almost nothing to modern chemotherapy, the charge is that a few companies in the United States, Western Europe, and Japan dominate the world market. Because most of their sales are in the industrial capitalist world, they design their products for this market. They are said to avoid competition by patent control, or to proliferate useless or marginally useful products which they sell by competitive advertising rather than by lowering prices. Thus, approximately 50,000 brand names are used to sell about 700 generic drugs or chemical agents, yielding an average of 70 different market names for every useful product. These market distortions are most severe in developing countries, where the need for cost-effective therapy is greater because resources are more limited (see Gereffi 1983). Additionally, the companies are charged with selling prescription drugs without regard to problems of regulating their distribution, with dumping obsolete prescription drugs in third world countries, and with having experimentally tried out new drugs in these countries. They are said to use misleading promotional materials, and so on. (These charges have been answered by representatives of the companies – cf. Taylor 1986.)

A task force of United Nations agencies addressed these issues and its report, 'Pharmaceuticals in the Developing World: Policies on Drugs, Trade and Production', was adopted in 1979 as a policy statement by the Conference of Non-Aligned Countries meeting in Havana. Also, in 1977 and 1979 the World Health Organization published a list of approximately 200 essential drugs which would cover 90% of the medical problems in developing countries. The purpose was to provide a standard for rationalizing the production and importation of drugs.

Responding to journalistic criticism, the outrage of international health professions, and the threat of governmental actions, the International Federation of Pharmaceutical Manufacturers' Associations publicized a voluntary code of practices in 1981. The code was concerned with providing information about the effects of drugs, labeling, and other forms of sales promotion. It did not consider the way prices are set for drugs and how they are distributed, nor did it consider issues of research, development and technological transfer.

All of this discussion has been very much oriented around the international role of Western pharmaceuticals. One important contribution of the present volume of anthropological essays is that it makes us aware of the absence in the debate of data on the commercial production of Chinese, Ayurvedic and Unani medicines, and on the international market for them. The *jamu* pharmaceutical companies in Indonesia, and the Nigerian companies whose medicines are widely marketed in West Africa, have been previously overlooked as well. Partly, this is because the critics were big game hunters, and these were small fry by comparison to the allopathic drug companies. But the absence is curious because at the same time that the debate on trans-national pharmaceutical companies ripened in the 1960s and 70s, the Chinese model of primary health care publicized the use of indigenous drugs, and the World Health Organization and other agencies sponsored conferences and initiated projects to study the pharmacopeia of traditional medicine for alternative or supplemental forms of therapy.

Helga and Boris Velimirovic were close observers of this activity, and in 1980 published a skeptical article entitled, 'Do Traditional Plant Medicines have a Future in Third World Countries?' Their answer was no, not much. They wrote that traditional phytotherapy would continue to be used for self-limiting, psychological or incurable chronic illnesses, and that the cultivation of plants used in cosmopolitan medicine could be promoted to supply raw material for industrial production, but that nothing was likely to come from ethnobotanical research. They pointed out that between 1958 and 1970, 93.6% of the 466 new drugs introduced into the world market originated in Germany, Switzerland, the United States and England, and that only one, coming from Mexico, originated outside of highly industrial countries. Their advice was that the priority of third world countries should be (1) to limit the production and importation of allopathic medicines to the WHO list of essential drugs, (2) to encourage the transfer of technology where this is feasible, and (3) to regulate the distribution and quality of drugs, and develop strategies to reduce prices.

Sri Lanka adopted a rational program of state controlled importation of allopathic drugs in 1972, but it was resisted by a large segment of the medical profession which was convinced that brand name drugs were superior, and became a major political issue. The law was compromised by an illegal market, and was eventually modified. Meanwhile, the commercial production of Ayurvedic medicine has flourished.

More recently, Bangladesh adopted similar priorities to those pioneered by Sri Lanka. The importation and manufacture of allopathic medicine was limited to a list of 150 essential drugs for primary care, and 100 supplementary drugs for tertiary care. The 1982 law required the withdrawal of 1700 drugs as the existing stocks were exhausted, and put an immediate ban on 237 drugs that an expert committee considered harmful. The Expert Committee reported that in 1981 the people of Bangladesh spent about $75 million on allopathic drugs. This was about 60% of health expenditure, yet the committee estimated that 70% of these drugs would be described as therapeutically useless by authorities in Great Britain or the United States. Only 10% of drugs sold were purchased by the governmental health services; the remaining 90% were taken up by the private sector, distributed by fee-for-service physicians and 14,000 retail pharmacies. Eight multinational companies produced 70% of these allopathic drugs, with an additional 15% produced by 25 medium sized companies among the remaining 158 licensed manufacturers.

Unani, Ayurvedic and homeopathic companies had been exempted from governmental control in Bangladesh. The Expert Committee asserted that they manufactured some "unethical, harmful and uncertain quality products", but it seemed to ignore them when it estimated health care expenditures. In 1982, a WHO consultant reported that 20 Ayurvedic pharmaceutical companies in Bangladesh sold approximately $30 million worth of medicines annually. This figure was only an educated guess; nonetheless an estimate of $75 million for allopathic drugs and $30 million for Ayurvedic drugs indicates that the commercial production of indigenous medicine was a significant part of health care in Bangladesh. This is comparable to the finding of Ahmad Fuad Afdhal and Robert Welsch in the present volume that the companies manufacturing traditional *jamu* medicines in Indonesia control approximately one-third of the total pharmaceutical market of that nation.

In India, by 1972, the Ministry of Health reported that approximately 900 companies manufactured indigenous medicines, with nearly 300 of them reporting sales of 500,000 rupees or more. The products of these companies could be purchased in various African, Asian, South Pacific and Caribbean countries; I have even bought Ayurvedic soap in Manhattan. Chinese pharmaceutical companies have a similarly broad international market.

Several thousand Asian pharmaceutical companies manufacture many thousands of tonics, pills, capsules, salves, powders, teas and cosmetics. Some products follow ancient or medieval formulations, others are new medicines based on humoral traditions; even the soaps, toothpastes, and hair oils have humoral uses or associations. I cannot read the literature published by these companies without thinking of 19th century patent medicines in Europe and the United States. Such a variety of aphrodisiacs, and preparations to enhance and prolong sexual powers! So many panaceas, laxatives, and cures for diarrhea! The Velimirovics would not approve, and the Bangladesh Expert Committee recommended banishing products of this kind, including Vicks Vaporub, which is marketed as an Ayurvedic medicine in South Asia.

The bottom line in the discussions by these and many other specialists is how much choice people in poor countries should have in spending their pennies. Of course health care planners believe that they should not buy tonics to prevent premature ejaculation, or to make their sons more intelligent. They should deal realistically with the terrible problems in their countries, with malnutrition and infectious disease.

The perspective of this book is somewhat different. The emphasis of these contributions is less on what people *should* do, than on what they *do* do. The articles show how people choose their medicines, where they get them, and what kind of guidance they seek and receive. In order to understand what people are doing, it is necessary to take seriously the question of what they think they are doing. What meanings do the different varieties of medicines have for people in various cultures? How do they perceive the efficacy of imported pharmaceuticals and the difference between them and indigenous medicines? Answers to these kinds of questions provide the missing context for the debate about pharmaceuticals. That context is first of all the local one of cultural meanings and face-to-face transactions. Important as global considerations are, they leave many issues untouched. In addressing these other issues of what medicines mean and how they are used in local contexts, the editors and contributors to the present volume have initiated a new field of anthropological research. This field has much to contribute to the great debate about drugs and health care in developing countries.

REFERENCES

Gereffi, Gary
 1983 The Pharmaceutical Industry and Dependency in the Third World. Princeton, NJ: Princeton University Press.
Institute of Medicine
 1979 Pharmaceuticals for Developing Countries. Washington, D.C.: National Academy of Sciences.
Patel, Surendra J. (ed.)
 1979 Pharmaceuticals and Health in the Third World. Special Issue, World Development 2 (3).
Taylor, David
 1986 The Pharmaceutical Industry and Health in the Third World. Social Science and Medicine 22 (11): 1141–1149.
Velimirovic, Helga and Boris
 1980 Do Traditional Plant Medicines Have a Future in Third World Countries? Curare 3 (3): 173–191.

CHARLES LESLIE

INTRODUCTION

SUSAN REYNOLDS WHYTE AND SJAAK VAN DER GEEST

MEDICINES IN CONTEXT: AN INTRODUCTION

This book is about medicines – substances used in the treatment of sickness. Because medicines are material objects (we speak of *materia medica*) and because there is a 'natural science' of medicines (pharmacology), they appear to be natural aspects of the real world. And so they are. But like every aspect of human experience, they always exist within particular cultural and social realities. Various systems of cultural understanding endow them with specific qualities and powers; that is to say, they have culturally defined meanings as well as bio-chemical properties. As objects, medicines are produced, distributed and appropriated through institutions and interactions of various kinds. They are socially transacted from the time they are gathered in the bush or produced in a factory until they are rubbed on by a concerned mother or injected by a helpful neighbor. If we want to understand how medicines are actually used, we must go beyond the bio-chemistry of the substances themselves, to the situations in which the substances are perceived and applied.

The term 'pharmaceutical anthropology' may serve to distinguish the approach we advocate here from that taken in what has come to be known as 'ethnopharmacology'. The latter is concerned with the 'natural' biochemical properties and effects of indigenous medicines. We wish to emphasize the '*context*' of medicines, by which we mean the constellations of cultural meanings and social relations within which medicines exist in a given time and place. While ethnopharmacology concentrates on 'indigenous medicines' of Third World people, pharmaceutical anthropology is concerned with the co-existence of Western and indigenous medicines and with the issue of how each affects the perception and use of the other.

MEDICINE AND MEDICINES

Medicines have come to be perceived as the most typical representation of the therapeutic enterprise – so much so that they have given their name to the totality of therapeutic interventions: medicine. Both patients and curers generally regard the use of medication as the most crucial part of therapy. So it is important to ask what is so special about medicines and how they differ from other modes of dealing with suffering.

We suggest that there are two distinctive qualities of medicines. The first is that they are substances. The second is that they are believed to contain in themselves a power to transform the human condition. Drugs have a greater concreteness than most other types of therapy. In medicines, therapy is reified; a *thing*, a healing token is passed from one person to another and applied directly to the suffering body. The substance itself is perceived as efficacious, allowing therapy to be separated from the skill and knowledge of the therapist.

As substances, medicines can become objects of exchange. As things, they have a *life*. We can speak of the biography of a drug: its production, distribution, marketing, interpretation and use. The life of a drug often involves transaction from one context of skill, meaning and control to another. The assumption that some substances contain an innate power seems to be very widespread and it is an important reason for the diffusion of medicines from one culture to another. Yet even though people of different cultures share the basic idea that a medicine is powerful, the specific nature of that power may be conceived quite differently. The characteristics that indicate potency, the expectations about how a medicine works, notions about suitable uses of a medicine's power – all these are culturally shaped in various ways.

We have used these two central characteristics of medicines to organize this collection of papers into two parts. The first section on the transaction of medicines emphasizes pharmaceuticals as commodities that are produced and distributed. The second section deals with the meaning of medicines as powerful substances. We must stress however that these two aspects of medicines – transactability and meaning – are inextricably linked. People produce, sell, desire and buy medicines because, like all commodities, they have culturally ascribed meaning and value. Sick people do not acquire particular drugs simply because they need them only in the 'natural' sense – the mysteries of biochemical effects are remote for us all. The need for medicines which is the basis for their production and transaction is evident – but it is equally evident that this need is in part culturally constituted. We learn what to need, and it makes no sense to consider the commercial aspects of medications without recognizing this basic point. On the other hand, the meaning of medicines cannot be appreciated without considering the ways in which they are transacted. Typically a drug is not valued simply because it works, but also because it came from a certain source – witness the difficulty in getting people, or governments, to buy 'generic'. It is part of the meaning of a medicine that it was recommended by an authoritative doctor, or manufactured in Switzerland, that it was expensive or that it was advertised and packaged in a particular way. A striking example of how people are taught to need new products from special sources is provided by MacCormack and Draper in this volume. They tell how Jamaican mothers are urged to use imported 'medicine' to treat diarrhea, instead of the herbal tea and coconut water they used to give.

As tangible substances imbued with healing power, medicines raise a very central issue for medical anthropology. They require us to consider the matter of self-care by means that are not self-produced. Other forms of therapy are administered by specialists (surgery, exorcism) or they are created and administered by the sick person or family (meditation, rest, loving attention). But medicines do not require a therapeutic relationship to a practitioner; they permit autonomy. One can acquire and use them independently, thus assuming responsibility for one's own health. (In the Third World, this even holds for prescription drugs, as various contributions to this volume show.) At the same time, insofar as medicines are commodities, one must obtain them through transactions. Most people are not self-sufficient in the medicines they use for self-care. When those medicines are pharmaceuticals manufactured under technologically specialized conditions, according to principles very few of us understand, another type of dependence is created. Instead of intimate dependence on therapists, the user of medicine has a more impersonal and distant dependence upon the market. This is the paradox of self-care by medications. It implies greater self-reliance in one sense, and less in another.

A number of the papers in this volume describe the way that medicines, especially Western pharmaceuticals, are acquired and used for self-care quite outside of what we usually think of as therapeutic institutions and relationships. People reflect upon symptoms, talk to neighbors and drug vendors, and obtain the substance they find appropriate. This is probably the most common form of treatment in both Western and non-Western societies – and the least studied. Pharmaceutical anthropology requires us to shift our gaze from the relation between patient and healer, to the popular sector of the health-care system, where people treat themselves by substances they believe have particular effects.

THE TRANSACTION OF PHARMACEUTICALS

The term *pharmaceutical* relates to the preparation, dispensing and sale of drugs. According to the *Oxford English Dictionary*, it means 'pertaining to or engaged in pharmacy', which is defined as: 'the art or practice of collecting, preparing and dispensing drugs, especially for medicinal purposes'. If the word seems to imply Western manufactured medicines, it is no doubt because it emphasizes medicines as products which are made to be sold – and Western drugs are commercial products par excellence. But because medicines are things, any medicine, whether chemically synthesized or herbal, may be transacted.

Pharmaceuticals are commodities of a very special kind. They are goods which have the capacity to affect the person in a direct way – a power which is at once beneficial and potentially dangerous. The Greek root of the word pharmaceutical referred to poison and witchcraft as well as healing medicines; this double image of medicines is also found in many African cultures, as Whyte's article in this volume suggests. In a somewhat different way, this point about the double potential of medicines runs through much of the discussion of the distribution of pharmaceutical commodities. As powerful substances, medicines are always potentially dangerous; they can always be misused. The issue of *control* is central in analysing transactions of medicines. The question in the minds of policy makers is: How can the dangerous potentiality of drugs be limited? The question in the minds of users is: How can I appropriate the beneficial potential of drugs most directly?

There has been very little published concerning the ways in which Western pharmaceuticals are actually disseminated in the Third World. Therefore we feel that the case studies from the Dominican Republic, Mexico, El Salvador, Ethiopia, Cameroon, Mauritius and Sri Lanka are important as descriptions of the contexts in which people obtain drugs. They describe the ways the Western pharmaceuticals are exchanged outside the clinical institutions of Western biomedicine. The roles of drug company salesman, pharmacists, shopkeepers, and 'traditional' practitioners are elucidated. An important theme here is how information is conveyed about the dangerous and beneficial powers of drugs. How do distributors understand the qualities of pharmaceuticals and what explanations about use accompanies the transaction? It is clear that the instructions worked out by manufacturers often do not reach users. Other kinds of information and cultural understandings are transmitted instead.

THE MEANING OF MEDICINES

However capitalistic the production and marketing of drugs may be, we cannot understand the way they are used in purely economic terms. We must assume that people consume goods as signs and symbols. They attribute meaning and value to differences in products and to different ways of utilizing them. They make choices on the basis of what such differences mean for them as members of a particular cultural milieu. This is as true of the use of medicines as it is of clothes, rock music, and household furnishings. And it is as true of the use of herbal medicines as of manufactured pharmaceuticals. The fact that medicines are applied to the distressed body makes it particularly important to be alert to the ways they carry meaning and mark identity for the sufferer. They are consumed more intimately – and in more stressful situations – than most other kinds of products.

There is no simple strategy for uncovering the meaning of medicines. In the chapters presented here, several approaches are used to examine the ways people seem to understand medicines. One approach is to look for attempts to relate substances to conceptions about the nature of health and the causes of disease. Unschuld does this in showing how the classification of *materia medica* in China and classical Greece was conceptually related to the classification of forces and elements whose imbalance caused disease. A number of the other chapters also suggest that people think about medications in terms of their ideas about disorders and their causes – cough medicines for coughs and cooling medicines for distress caused by too much heat.

We have suggested that a central characteristic of medicines is that they are thought to have the power to produce an effect. Thus one important part of the meaning of medicine is its efficacy. The term efficacy may seem unproblematic enough within a natural science framework. But an awareness of cultural context calls for an examination of the ways people in different situations actually perceive efficacy – what effects they look for and how they evaluate them. This is the task which Etkin takes upon herself, criticizing the biomedical standards with which ethnopharmacology has measured the effects of medicines and reminding us that efficacy, like other aspects of medicines, is culturally constructed.

Another way to approach the meaning of medicines is to focus upon their relation to other kinds of therapy. Whyte suggests that in East Africa medicines may be constrasted with the ritual adjustment of relationships – a form of therapy that necessitates dealing with spiritual and social situations. In Western culture, this kind of meaning is recognized when it is said that people 'pop pills' instead of dealing with the real social and psychological causes of their distress.

Finally, people give meaning to particular qualities of medicines in terms that are generally significant in other realms of culture. For example the color or taste of medicines may be meaningful because of connotations of particular colors and tastes in a given culture. Yellow pills are suitable against depression in Europe; red capsules are appropriate modes of strengthening the blood among the Mende of Sierra Leone. As Bledsoe and Goubaud point out, such qualities of medicaments may be reinterpreted as transactions are made across cultural boundaries.

Because this book focuses upon Western pharmaceuticals in the Third World, special problems in the analysis of meaning arise. Many researchers report that commercial packaging, and 'high tech' modes of application, especially the hypodermic needle, have a particular appeal. Obviously the meaning of medicines is not a simple matter of consistency with established patterns of 'tradition'. Plastic capsules in two bright colors and slick, shiny products can be just as meaningful as time-honored potions and secret herbal recipes. Buying factory-made products may be a way of identifying oneself as 'modern'. More than that, conceptions of power and efficacy may be tied to 'foreignness' and elaborate processing. Provenance and packaging seem to be important dimensions of meaning for many people. The fact that medicines have been produced in distant places or unfamiliar ways may add to their value. (The *Oxford English Dictionary* gives an obsolete meaning of the word 'drug' as 'spices and other commodities, brought from distant countries, and used in medicine, dying and the mechanic arts'.) What one cannot make oneself may be able to accomplish what one cannot do oneself. The expectation that remote peoples have extraordinary knowledge that can be harnessed for therapy is a theme in Western cultures as well as in many others.

METHODS FOR CONTEXTUALIZING MEDICINES

In their efforts to examine medicines in context, the contributors to this volume have employed a variety of methods. Context implies a whole of which something is a part; but holism is a myth, not a method. Choices must always be made as to what aspects of a context to examine. Those choices determine what methods are appropriate.

Participant observation is usually regarded as the most important tool for the working anthropologist. It involves living in a local community, interacting in whatever ways one can, and observing the situation (and oneself within it). The idea is to be an insider and an outsider both. As an insider, one should try to grasp 'the native's point of view' about medicines, the particular cultural meaning and type of social transaction that seems 'natural' to the people involved. As an outsider, one should attempt to 'de-naturalize' medicines by translating, and comparing those conceptions and arrangements to others.

For the study of pharmaceuticals, the important point is the presence of the researcher on the local scene and the effort to involve oneself enough to be able to describe how medications are transacted and interpreted *there* in (implicit) contrast to elsewhere. In the chapter by Burghart, we sense the researcher involving himself with one member of another community. In the one by Bledsoe and Goubaud, interactions with many members of a community are described. Both are examples of the rich potential of participant observation for the study of pharmaceuticals. Because the distribution of Western pharmaceuticals is often 'informal' if not illegal, living in the local community may be the only way to learn what is really going on.

Contexts have both a qualitative and quantitative character. Survey methods are necessary to illuminate patterns and frequency of pharmaceutical use and expenditures involved. A number of the research projects reported here relied, in part, on the use of questionnaires to collect information about who uses what type of medicine when. Logan's study of pharmacists and their clients in a Mexican city shows the usefulness of quantitative methods, as do the studies by Kloos et al., Sussman and Ugalde and Homedes. In all of these studies, the local context of pharmaceutical choice is described in numbers as well as in more qualitative terms.

The context of pharmaceuticals is not only that of the local community however. National cultural contexts also provide settings for the distribution, use and understanding of medicines. In order to examine these contexts, other methods may be used – such as the examination of popular written material, as Afdhal and Welsch have done. Cultural historical contexts, which provide the general framework for a great tradition's conception of medicines, require a study of the scholarly literature of distant times – of the sort Unschuld has undertaken.

All of these methods synthesize rather than analyse medicines in the sense that they place them together with relevant ideas, historical processes and social relations, rather than separating them into constituent 'natural' elements.

WESTERN PHARMACEUTICALS AND ANTHROPOLOGICAL AWARENESS

The impetus behind this book is the surge of interest in Western drugs on the part of Third World people being 'invaded' by them, policy makers attempting to control them, and researchers trying to grasp what is going on. People familiar with local communities in the Third World are aware that many kinds of Western pharmaceuticals are easily available in markets, from local vendors and even from 'traditional healers'. Drugs that are supposed to be 'prescription only' are obtainable over or under the counter. It is evident that one part of the technology of biomedicine, the medicaments, has been separated from the knowledge and practice in which it developed and is being diffused and used rather independently. There are clearly big commercial interests in this diffusion; profits are to be made from this extensive use of medicinal commodities. Governments and international organizations have discussed ways of regulating the situation; the most systematic and far-reaching attempt is the World Health Organization's Essential Drug Programme. It is against this background that anthropologists and their colleagues from other disciplines, who work in Third World societies, are concerned to make their research relevant and available to national and international policy makers. They are beginning to come forward with their local contextual perspectives on the 'pharmaceutical invasion'.

The issue is timely. But the very timeliness of the anthropological interest in pharmaceuticals in developing countries should give us cause to think. Why were we not aware of this phenomenon before? Western drugs have been present in most Third World societies rather longer than social scientists have been. And medicines in the more general sense have always been there. We believe that one important reason for this neglect of medicines can be found in the exotic bias of the anthropological enterprise. The study of foreign cultures involves an examination of how they are *foreign* – and a concomitant blindness to the elements which are familiar. This has meant overlooking the use of aspirin for headache while noticing the use of elephant dung for dizziness.

The exotic bias and the neglect of medicines as cultural constructions is related to the peculiar ability of culture to define what nature is. In Western culture medicinal substances are perceived as having natural properties which affect the human body in ways amenable to 'hard' scientific observation. Medicines belong to the domains of pharmacology and biomedicine, while anthropology has concerned itself with the more spiritual aspects of healing – the symbols, rituals and conceptions which are not only exotic but clearly cultural. One of the challenges of the present situation is to confront Western notions of the naturalness of medicines and to place the study of medicines squarely within the cultural science of medical anthropology.

Just as anthropology itself grew out of the colonial encounter, so medical anthropology grew out of the spread of Western biomedicine to other cultures. The situation of medical pluralism raised the issue of cultural difference in the understanding and treatment of sickness. It brought us to consider conceptions of etiology, notions of therapy, interactions between patients and healers and the ways in which one set of medical institutions and traditions influences another. In the same way 'pharmaceutical pluralism', the presence of Western drugs in other contexts, focuses our attention on the issues of how medicines are conceived and exchanged in other cultures. It forces us to 'de-naturalize' our view of medicines – to reflect upon our own culturally determined assumptions as we try to appreciate others.

In situations of pharmaceutical pluralism, Western and indigenous medicines provide contexts for one another. People understand the one in relation to the other – whether they emphasize similarities or contrasts. Thus Sussman reports that Mauritians see Western pharmaceuticals as fast-working and potent, characteristics which make them suitable for the relief of acute disorders. Herbal medicines are perceived as slower and milder, better for chronic and recurrent conditions, and without the strong side effects associated with Western medicines.

However, the co-existence of different types of medicines is not simply a matter of division of pharmacological labor – assigning symptoms to one or another type of therapeutic substance. Processes of influence and change are under way; medicines are constantly being re-interpreted, channels of distribution are transformed, 'traditions' are re-worked. Afdhal and Welsch's description of the rise of the *jamu* (traditional medicine) industry in Indonesia is an instructive example of this aspect of pharmaceutical pluralism. The introduction of Western medicines created a new context for *jamu* medicines and presented new models for production, packaging and marketing. On the one hand, indigenous medicines were contrasted with Western pharmaceuticals and took on new meaning and value as an Indonesian tradition. On the other, they were made similar to Western medicines by being processed and packaged for greater convenience, and by being produced and marketed for mass availability. In her study of the use of traditional medication in connection with pregnancy and childbirth on the Indonesian island of Madura, Niehof provides another perspective on pharmaceutical pluralism. She elucidates the conceptions which underlie the continued utilization of indigenous medication in a pluralistic context, but notes that the packaged *jamu* purchased in shops may be used as an alternative to some of the 'homemade' preparations.

In situations of pharmaceutical pluralism, terms like 'traditional' and 'modern', 'indigenous' and 'Western' medicines are almost unavoidable. So are the quotation marks around these terms. There is an uncomfortable sense that they are misleading, since the pluralistic context transforms both imported and native medicines. Thus we find 'modern' medicines being distributed by 'traditional' healers and utilized in ways never imagined by the manufacturers. Penicillin may become an ancient Ayurvedic medicine. And we see 'indigenous' medicine being manufactured on an enormous scale, advertised on television, and exported to other countries. Genuine *jamu* from Indonesia can be purchased in Europe. The nuances involved here may serve to remind us once more of the care needed in the use of terms like traditional and Western medicine.

In offering this collection of articles on Western pharmaceuticals in their Third World contexts, we have two objectives. The first is the relatively practical one of providing descriptions and analyses of a variety of local situations to policy makers, planners, health professionals and concerned citizens. We hope that they will be stimulated by these essays to examine other local contexts with more understanding. Our second objective is to contribute to a discussion within anthropology. We believe that there is much to learn from the ways in which Western pharmaceuticals are incorporated in other cultures. Here we have the opportunity to confront our ethnocentric notions of medicines as simply 'natural' substances with biochemical properties. We may correct the bias which has led anthropologists to study 'exotic' phenomena and the therapeutic practices of experts, while neglecting the seemingly familiar and prosaic activities of lay people. We hope that the concern with Western pharmaceuticals may serve to focus the anthropological gaze more steadily upon medicinal substances in general as cultural phenomena. An anthropology of Western pharmaceuticals may be a first step towards an anthropology of medicines, whose scope will include all powerful substances produced, exchanged, and used in order to achieve an effect upon human conditions and human projects. Then we may understand more clearly how the transaction and meaning of efficacious *things* fits with the rest of the therapeutic enterprise.

ACKNOWLEDGEMENTS

The editors would like to thank Michael A. Whyte for his suggestions regarding the introduction and also Margaret Lock who kindly sent her comments.

THE TRANSACTION OF MEDICINES

INTRODUCTORY NOTE

This section focuses on how medicines move from production, through marketing and distribution, to consumption. The next section contains papers that discuss the cognitive aspects of these transactions. But no paper deals exclusively with transactional or cognitive aspects of medicines. It is obvious that the two cannot be separated.

An important theme running through this first section is that the transaction of medicines in developing countries is not a neatly controlled process that obeys formal rules. All contributions show contradictory aspects of these transactions and emphasize the intertwining of formal and informal activities. Manufacturers do not always follow the code of good marketing practice they have set for themselves. Drug representatives sell their products to clients who are not supposed to deal with pharmaceuticals. Medical doctors overprescribe. Pharmacists become doctors and sell prescription drugs without prescription. Unauthorized drug vendors distribute medicines. But the most conspicuous lack of control is found at the end of the transaction line: self-medication is the most common way of using medicines in most Third World situations.

Ferguson's contribution is a classic case study of the pharmaceutical invasion in a town in El Salvador. Her paper, originally published in 1981, was the first attempt to link the role of the pharmaceutical industry to local transactions in a Third World community. Following Illich she describes changes in people's drug use as a process of medicalization, a growing dependence on externally produced medical substances. At the same time this is a commercial process – Ferguson speaks of 'commerciogenesis' – with cultural, social and clinical implications. Her paper contains extensive case material concerning self-medication and the informal sale of medicines in local pharmacies.

Wolffers points at a significant development in the marketing and dispensing of medicines. 'Ayurvedic' practitioners in Sri Lanka increasingly treat their patients with Western pharmaceuticals. Wolffers' case study in two communities shows that salesmen for pharmaceutical firms regard these practitioners as regular clients and that the practitioners rely on the salesmen for their drug information. Wolffers' paper provides a snapshot of an ongoing process of change in indigenous medical practice. The most remarkable aspect of it is the seemingly unlimited syncretism in the practitioners' acceptance of alien therapeutic substances. The author views this development as the logical outcome of commercialization and competition. Practitioners resort to prestigious Western medicines in order to keep their patients.

Various publications suggest that such developments of medical syncretism take place in many other developing countries. The alarming consequences of this process for public health and health care are obvious.

Ugalde and Homedes describe the first year of an experiment in rural health care in the Dominican Republic. To meet poor peasants' demands for affordable medical help and medicines a communal pharmacy was set up where essential drugs could be purchased for a low price. The fact that medicines became continuously available increased the utilization of the local health center. Previously, 'free' medicines were immediately used up, so that patients had to buy more expensive medicines elsewhere. The authors conclude that, paradoxically, the dispensing of 'free' medicines proved more expensive for the local people than the low-priced essential drugs. Another important observation refers to the influence of external features of drugs (price, form, package, etc.) on people's handling and perception of medicines.

The chapter by *Kloos and others* looks at various aspects of drug purchasing in Ethiopia's capital city. The paper is based on a wide variety of research methods, the most important being: questionnaire interviews with 1,143 clients in two government pharmacies, interviews with 220 clients by personnel in the same pharmacies, open interviews and observations of sellers and buyers of drugs in various private shops and pharmacies, and a health survey of a representative sample of 284 households comprising 1,775 people, in four locations in the city. The authors complement their predominantly quantitative data with ten brief case histories that exemplify the complexity of therapy seeking from the patient's point of view.

The authors show that the most common reactions to health problems are: 'doing nothing' and buying drugs from a pharmacy. If, when and where people buy medicines is related to socio-economic factors, educational level and the distance they have to travel to get the medicines. The research shows that buying medicines is done in a context of mutual family and neighbor assistance and is often combined with other activities that have to be carried out in the neighborhood of the pharmacy. The authors further provide information on disease prevalence, deviant use of medicines and local perceptions of illness and medicine. Interestingly, government pharmacies are reported to function more satisfactorily than private ones. The paper ends with suggestions for applying the data in practical health care policy.

Logan carried out a survey among 48 women in a Mexican city and interviewed and observed pharmacists selling medicines. The mothers were asked about their first reaction to five common health problems: headache, stomach ache, cough, diarrhea and *susto*. She found that self-medication with drugs obtained at a pharmacy was the most common reaction to the first four problems. For *susto* the women resorted to local home remedies. The study shows the overwhelming importance of the pharmacy as a first health resort in everyday health problems. Pharmacists were found to play a doctor's role;

they diagnosed their clients' problems and advised them on the best cure. The author concludes with some practical suggestions as to how doctoring pharmacists could be helped to function more effectively.

Van der Geest studied the distribution of medicines in the southern part of Cameroon. His research covered medical institutions dispensing medicines, pharmacies, and unauthorized drug vendors. He shows that the formal and informal (illegal) distribution of medicines are closely intertwined, at the wholesale as well as at the retail level. The informal sale of medicines has become an indispensable part of Cameroon's health care system. It fills the gaps in the formal distribution, but it also helps to maintain those gaps. The author views the situation as a process of 'articulation'; two apparently competitive systems merge into one, to their mutual benefit. There is much evidence, both within this volume and in other publications, that this articulation occurs worldwide. However, this observation has hardly been taken into account in actual health policy.

Afdhal and Welsch, finally, provide an overview of the history of *jamu* in Indonesia, from about the beginning of this century to the present day. *Jamu*, a traditional and locally prepared plant medicine, has undergone a shift to Western-style production and marketing. *Jamu* is now sold on a large scale, in the form of powders, creams, pills and capsules. Packaged *jamu* has become an immense industry; 350 modern factories produce over five million doses per day, a part of which is exported to other Asian countries and to Europe.

The modernization of *jamu* is strikingly paradoxical. On the one hand it is conceived as an indigenous element of Indonesian culture and has become an important symbol of national identity. On the other, its successful marketing is in large part due to emulation of imported Western pharmaceuticals. Its appeal lies to a great extent in its packaging. The authors remark that this face-lift of *jamu* has led to a conceptual break with the past. *Jamu* is losing some of its more general cosmological associations as it is increasingly understood simply in terms of notions of physiology. They regard the modernization of *jamu* as a part of the medicalization of present Indonesian society. The paper illustrates how indigenous and Western medicines constitute one another's context.

ANNE FERGUSON

COMMERCIAL PHARMACEUTICAL MEDICINE AND MEDICALIZATION: A CASE STUDY FROM EL SALVADOR

INTRODUCTION

Multinational pharmaceutical firms and the products they manufacture have been the subject of considerable recent investigation. The majority of these studies focus on two issues: (1) the consequences for human health of the companies' promotional and sales practices (Silverman 1976, 1977; Ledogar 1975; *Mother Jones* 1979; Hellegers 1973; Sesser 1971); and (2) the effects of the pharmaceutical invasion on pharmaceutical industries and public-sector health budgets in Third World countries (Gish and Feller 1979; Lall 1974, 1977; Lall and Bibile 1977; WHO 1977; Evans 1979; Bertero 1972; Segall 1975). Relatively little attention has been paid to the effects of these pharmaceutical industries on alternative medical traditions or means of coping with illness. This paper, using a case study from El Salvador, describes a popular sector of medical care that has developed in response to the ways in which the products of multinational and national pharmaceutical firms are distributed and sold. This had given rise to a form and process of medicalization that differs from that of most developed countries.

The article first provides some initial formulations regarding the commercial pharmaceutical sector of medical care and its role in the process of medicalization in many parts of the Third World. These general propositions are followed by a case study examining the role of the commercial pharmaceutical sector in the delivery of health care and the resulting form of medicalization. The information for the case study is drawn from fieldwork conducted from August 1978 through July 1979 on the use of pharmacies as a source of health care advice and treatment in the town of Asunción, El Salvador.[1]

A brief review of the literature on the health and economic consequences of the pharmaceutical invasion is necessary as background to this investigation.

THE MULTINATIONAL PHARMACEUTICAL INDUSTRY IN DEVELOPING COUNTRIES: HEALTH AND ECONQMIC CONSEQUENCES

The availability of medications manufactured by large scale and sophisticated pharmaceutical companies is one of the most salient developments in health care in recent decades. The production of these medications is concentrated in a few countries and, within these countries, in a small number of firms.

France, the Federal Republic of Germany, Italy, Japan, and the US produced roughly 80% of the total output of medications in 1970; and in 1974, exported approximately 60% of the total value of medications transported in international commerce (Gish and Feller 1979: 4). In 1976 it was estimated that only 25 firms located in the major pharmaceutical producing countries supplied 50% of the total world shipments of pharmaceutical products (Gish and Feller 1979: 9). Although precise figures are not available, marketing surveys indicate that developing countries account for approximately 20% of world pharmaceutical consumption. Reliance on these medications varies considerably from one region to another. Drug consumption is significantly higher in Latin America and Asia, for example, than it is in Africa (Gish and Feller 1979: 3).

Multinational pharmaceutical firms have also established production and some research facilities in developing countries (Evans 1979). These areas are attractive because they offer a cheaper labor pool and often have less stringent regulations regarding the testing and marketing of new products than do the developed countries. Regardless of geographic location, however, the majority of these firms tend to manufacture medications designed to meet the health care needs of populations in the developed countries (Ledogar 1975; Gish and Feller 1979).[2] It has been reported that many of these products are promoted in Third World countries in such a way as to have adverse effects on health. Multinational firms have been found to export medications considered unsafe for use in the home country, to exaggerate the indications for use of many products, and to minimize their counterindications and warnings (Silverman 1976; Ledogar 1975; *Mother Jones* 1979). Although statistics on drug-induced illnesses and deaths are rarely available in developing countries, investigators in these areas report that such occurrences are not unusual (Sarasti 1970; Hellegers 1973; Ledogar 1975). Medical authorities have voiced repeated concern about the inappropriate use of medications, especially antibiotics. The misuse of these products leads to the development of drug-resistant strains of infectious disease and it is conceivable that epidemics comparable to those of the pre-antibiotics era may occur (National Academy of Sciences 1979).

The money spent on medications in many Third World countries is a significant drain on scarce financial resources. The World Health Organization Expert Committee on the Selection of Essential Drugs reported that drug expenditures account for more than 40% of the available public-sector health funds in some developing countries. In 1977, the committee published a guideline listing approximately 200 drugs regarded as sufficient to treat the majority of illnesses in developing countries (WHO 1977). In Brazil, however, there are over 30,000 different products for sale; in Mexico there are possibly as many as 80,000 (Gish and Feller 1979; Silverman 1976).

It is estimated that 80% of today's major preparations have been developed in the last 20 years (Kewitz 1976). Unlike some of the older, biologically derived products, the majority of these new chemically synthesized drugs can produce harmful side effects, and the benefits and risks involved in their use must be carefully considered. In the Western developed countries, the use of these medications is usually limited by laws which regulate sale and require certain products to be employed under the supervision of physicians or other licensed practitioners. These prescription medications represent one of the major healing strategies employed by Western biomedical personnel and are integral components of the Western biomedical tradition.

Although many developing countries have modeled their official health care systems along Western lines, the articulation of elements in this health care tradition had not been replicated in all cases. In particular, in many Third World countries Western biomedical practitioners do not exercise the degree of control over the use of prescription drug products that is characteristic in the developed countries. Throughout Latin America, for example, prescription medications, usually manufactured by multinational pharmaceutical firms, often can be purchased over-the-counter in pharmacies, shops or from medicine vendors. In this context, the Western-style health care delivery systems has undergone a process of disarticulation and uneven penetration. The link between healer and healing resource is not always present and the products are frequently available in the absence of physicians or other Western trained practitioners.

THE COMMERCIAL PHARMACEUTICAL SECTOR AND ITS ROLE IN MEDICALIZATION

The term 'commercial pharmaceutical medicine' will be used to refer to the popular sector of medical care that has developed in response to the penetration of Western manufactured drug products and the disarticulation of elements in the Western biomedical tradition. The concept was developed by Carl Taylor (1976) in an article treating the role of the indigenous practitioner in the delivery of health care in India. Taylor reported that Punjabi practitioners relied heavily on modern medications in treating their patients and concluded that: 'It showed that when we used the term "indigenous practitioner", we were really talking about indigenous practitioners of medicine, and not practitioners of indigenous medicine' (1976: 787) Although Taylor was concerned primarily with indigenous practitioners' use of modern medications, here the concept of commercial pharmaceutical medicine is expanded to include a variety of practitioners whose philosophies of disease causation and cure represent popular variants of Western and alternative medical traditions. Although these practitioners' philosophies differ, they share a reliance on Western medications as an important healing strategy. In addition to alternative curers who employ these products, the popular sector includes two other groups: (1) pharmacy owners and clerks, shopkeepers and medicine vendors who, as part of their business, often prescribe modern medications to their customers; and (2) shot-givers, hospital and clinic workers, pharmaceutical company sales representatives and medical school drop-outs whose work or experience is related to the Western medical establishment and who often serve as important sources of advice and treatment.

Included in this medical sector are several important sources of health care that have received little attention in the medical anthropology literature. In the Western biomedical framework, pharmacy clerks, shop owners, medicine vendors, pharmaceutical company sales representatives, and the like have limited and largely supportive roles in the delivery of health care. They are owners of, or employees in, health related enterprises, not medical practitioners *per se*. In many developing countries, however, trained Western medical personnel are scarce, and these individuals often function as primary source of advice and treatment. They are neither indigenous nor Western practitioners, but rather popular sector representatives who combine alternative and Western knowledge of disease process and cure and whose practices bridge the medical and business sectors of society.

These and many indigenous practitioners share a reliance on modern pharmaceutical products in treating their patients and, in many cases, share a similar training in their use. Indigenous curers frequently rely on advice from pharmacy personnel about the use of medications (Taylor 1976; Cosminsky and Scrimshaw 1979). These individuals in turn, depend on information from package inserts included with products or on the pharmaceutical company sales representatives who are themselves usually minimally trained (Ledogar 1975; Taylor 1976). A system of education has thus developed that serves to integrate modern medications with lay and alternative conceptualizations about the nature and treatment of illness. While the integration of Western and alternative medical practitioners into a unified system for the delivery of health care has received considerable attention, other forms of integration have been overlooked. It is suggested that medical practitioners from diverse traditions have already achieved a degree of integration in their healing strategies through shared reliance on drug company sales personnel and their products.

As an outgrowth of the commercial pharmaceutical sector, a form and process of medicalization different from that of the developed countries has occurred in many parts of the Third World. In his work *Medical Nemesis* (1979), Ivan Illich used the term medicalization to refer to the growing tendency in Western society to define problems of living in medical terms and to seek solutions by consulting licensed medical practitioners. He suggested that the iatrogenic (physical or medical system induced) consequences of this dependence appeared whenever Western biomedicine gained a predominant position in society. To combat the various forms of iatrogenesis produced by this medical system, Illich called for the deprofessionalization and demonopolization of the health care establishment and a return to individual and community autonomy in defining and treating illness.

The commercial pharmaceutical sector, as discussed above, has produced in many developing countries a type of medicalization that is only tangentially linked to the presence of professional Western biomedical practitioners. In this context, no one type of healer or medical tradition exercises the degree of control over defining what constitutes illness or how it should be treated that characterizes physicians in the developed economies. In countries like El Salvador, the health care sector is neither monopolized by one kind of healer nor completely professionalized. Instead there is a growing dependence on a particular form of therapy: prepackaged medications, usually manufactured by multinational firms, and a consequent reliance on a range of agents and institutions that make these products available.[3] Since this dependence is channeled through practitioners representing a variety of medical traditions and is ultimately tied to the business firms that manufacture, promote and sell the products; its cultural, social and clinical manifestations will be referred to as forms of commerciogenesis.[4] This perspective casts doubt on Illich's analysis of the causes and his proposed solutions to the problems of medicalization and lends support to previous critiques of his work by Navarro (1976), Berliner (1977), and Waitzkin (1976).

To explore these propositions regarding the effects of the penetration of multinational pharmaceutical firms on the health care sector and on health seeking behavior, the case of Asunción, El Salvador, will be examined. Attention will focus first on the role of commercial pharmaceutical practitioners in the delivery of health care, and second on the form of medicalization that has resulted from the manner in which access to pharmaceutical products is mediated.

THE CASE OF ASUNCIÓN

The town of Asunción is located in western El Salvador in the Department of Sonsonante. This predominantly mestizo community of approximately 11,300 inhabitants functions as a municipal seat and commercial center for the surrounding rich agricultural region. The community was selected as the research site for two reasons: (1) it offered a diversity of health care resources to its population; and (2) since its pharmacy owners relied on different distributional networks for their stocks of pharmaceutical products, comparisons could be drawn regarding the impact of different marketing networks on health seeking behavior.

The major representatives of the commercial pharmaceutical sector were the town's four pharmacies, mediums at spiritist centers, medicine vendors and *idoneos* (pharmacy clerks, many of whom have established private medical practices run from their homes).[5] All of these practitioners used prepackaged pharmaceutical products as an important healing strategy.

Also available in Asunción was a government sponsored Health Post staffed full-time by a medical student completing the required year of social service, a dental student and assistant, a public health inspector and assistant, three nurses, a secretary, and a receptionist. Another physician worked part time at the Health Post and also ran a private practice in the community. The Health Post was open six mornings a week and offered free care and medications.[6] A public hospital and an additional twenty-two physicians were located in the nearby town of Sonsonante. Other sources of care in Asuncíon included a small number of indigenous healers (*sobadores*, *curanderos*), midwives and an array of Protestant churches in which healing sometimes took place.

A central concern in this investigation was to determine patterns of reliance on these sources of care by different socio-economic strata.[7] Initially, a census of every fourth dwelling, or 525 households, was conducted to gather standard socio-economic and demographic data. These households were scaled on the basis of four criteria: house type, possessions, household head level of education, and household head occupation ranked by a panel of five community members in terms of prestige. On the basis of total points, they were then divided into four socio-economic strata.

The two lower groups, representing 18.7% and 45.9% of households interviewed, lived in homes that by community standards were regarded as poor. These dwellings were constructed of straw, wood, scraps of metals or adobe, had hard-packed dirt floors, and frequently lacked potable water and electricity. In most cases, household heads had attended school for less than three years and worked as day laborers or vendors or in small-scale trades such as carpentry, shoe making and repair, and tailoring. Underemployment in these two strata was substantial. Agricultural day laborers reported being able to find steady work only during coffee, cotton and sugar cane harvest seasons. Large landholders in the area seldom paid the government stipulated wage of C4.50 (US $1.80) per day to their employees, and the average annual income for households dependent on this type of employment was calculated to be C798 (US $319.20).[8] Incomes for those household heads employed in the trades sector were slightly higher, but again there was substantial underemployment. Many individuals, unable to find jobs locally, commuted daily or weekly to work in the large cities of Acajutla, Sonsonante, and San Salvador. At the time of this investigation, a small number of men had contracted to work on building projects in Saudi Arabia. Others entered the United States illegally in search of jobs. Together the two lower strata comprised 64.6% of the households interviewed and will be considered as the community's poor.

A middle class, representing 24.0% of the population, was composed of owners of larger commercial enterprises, school teachers, and other administrative personnel and their families. In addition, some of these families owned urban and rural properties. Household heads in this strata usually had between four and twelve years of education. Most families lived in adobe or brick homes that had tile floors, running water and electricity, and many owned consumer goods such as televisions and stereos. The upper strata in the community, comprising 11.4% of those interviewed, usually owned medium to large agricultural properties and household heads generally held high school or university degrees. These families often traveled and educated their children abroad. They owned a wide range of consumer goods and one or two motor vehicles.[9]

While official health statistics do not provide information on the frequency of illnessess and deaths as they are distributed among the various socio-economic strata in the municipality, they do reflect the conditions of poverty is which the majority of the population live. Of the 220 deaths recorded in the municipality for 1978, 65 (30%) occured in infants under one year of age and 29 (13%) in children one through four years of age. The leading cause of death was gastro-intestinal disorders (22%), followed by upper-respiratory infections, other infectious processes and old age (each 14%).[10] Health Post records for the months of January and May 1979 provide an indication of the most prevalent illnesses. Of the 1,656 patients who consulted at the clinic during these two months, 655 (40%) were diagnosed as suffering from upper-respiratory infections, 363 (22%) from gastro-intestinal disorders and 245 (15%) sought care for uro-genital infections or family planning measures. One out of every three children under the age of five seen at the Health Post was diagnosed as showing signs of some degree of malnutrition.[11]

The role of the commercial pharmaceutical sector in the delivery of health care

To determine patterns of reliance on the various sources of medical care, an illness episode survey was designed and conducted over a four-month span. A sample of 84 families was selected, representing the four socio-economic groups interviewed in the census, and asked to participate in the survey. Twelve of these households either refused to participate or had moved. Because these households were evenly distributed among the four strata, they were not replaced. A total of 72 families took part in the survey: 16 households from the lowest socio-economic strata, 22 from the second, 19 from the third, and 15 from the upper strata of the community population. Wives or companions of household heads or (in cases where the household head was a single male or female) household heads, were interviewed initially once every two weeks and then once a month regarding illnesses experienced by household members and sources of care sought during the two weeks preceding the visit. Because of the sample size and the relatively short time span covered in the interviewing, the total number of illnesses reported was small. Therefore, in making comparisons of use patterns, distinctions will only be drawn between the two lower and two upper strata.

A total of 186 cases of ilness was reported in the survey. The three most frequently reported conditions werer upper-respiratory infections (87 cases),

TABLE I
Health care resource employed by lower and upper strata households in treating illness

Strata	Total number of illnesses reported	Total number self-medication or lay illness referral	Total seeking care from medical practitioners	Western biomedical practitioners			Commercial pharmaceutical practitioners				Other practitioners	
				Private physician (% of those seeking care)	Hospital	Health post	Pharmacy	Idóneo	Vendor	Spiritists center	Mid-wife, *sobador*
I & II (poor)	109	62	47	10 21%	4 9%	6 13%	18 38%	3 6%	4 9%	1 2%	1 2%
III & IV (middle & upper)	77	35	42	27 65%	2 5%	3 7%	8 19%	1 2%	1 2%	0	0
Totals	186	97 52%	89 48%	37 42%	6 7%	9 10%	26 29%	4 4%	5 6%	1 1%	1 1%
	100% of 186			100% of 89								

gastro-intestinal disorders (24 cases), and other infectious processes (16 cases). Three illnesses resulted in death: one baby died of an upper respiratory infection; one adult suffered a stroke; and another adult had a heart attack. Table I presents health care resources employed by lower and upper strata households in treating the 186 cases of illness.

In 52% of the cases, families relied only on self-medication or on lay illness referral networks to treat the condition. That is, they used products they were accustomed to or remedies and medications recommended by friends or family and sought no other source of advice or treatment. Forty-eight percent of the families in the sample, however, sought treatment from health care practitioners. The sources of care used most frequently by the two lower strata in the community were the pharmacies. Thirty-eight percent of these families relied on the pharmacy as their first health care resort, 9% on medicine vendors, 6% on *idóneos*, and 2% on the town's spiritist centers. In other words, 55% of the lower strata families relied on commercial pharmaceutical practitioners as their primary source of health care. Twenty-one percent of these families sought care from private physicians and only 13% relied on the Health Post. Families in the two upper strata showed an inverse pattern of reliance on sources of care. Twenty-three percent of these families relied on commercial pharmaceutical pratitioners, 65% on private physicians and 7% on the Health Post.

The results of this survey indicate that, while commercial pharmaceutical practitioners are an important source of treatment for all strata in the community, they are the primary source of care for the two lower strata, the community's poor. Studies carried out in Mexico (Brown 1963), Guatemala (Woods 1977; Cosminsky, Scrimshaw 1979), El Salvador (Harrison 1976; Murray 1977), Brazil (Ledogar 1975) and Colombia (Press 1971) report a similar reliance among the urban and rural poor on pharmacies and alternative practitioners who use modern drug products in treating their patients. It is likely, then, that the commercial pharmaceutical sector provides a major portion of health care advice and treatment to populations in many Latin American countries.

Although there are studies examining the impact of the Western biomedical tradition on alternative medical traditions, most treat the Western biomedical system as an integrated system rather than as the disarticulated social formation postulated here, and many focus on changes in healing roles induced by contact with Western trained practitioners.[12] Relatively little is known, however, about how modern prepackaged pharmaceutical products are integrated into alternative medical traditions or what types of products commercial pharmaceutical practitioners use in treating their patients. While there is some indication that these products are integrated into traditional categories of hot and cold (Logan 1973), this was not the case in Asunción. Also, little information exists on type of medication used by clients and practitioners. In Asunción, although practitioners used both over-the-counter and prescription medication, information gathered in the illness episode survey suggests that they more frequently employed prescription products.

To give an indicaton of the types of remedies employed, one condition known in the town as *atacado del pecho* (roughly equivalent to chest cold) will be discussed briefly. The symptoms include cough, nasal congestion and sometimes fever. Fifty-four cases of this condition were reported in the survey, mostly among children. Table II presents type and source of medication used by the two socio-economic strata for this illness.

Of the twelve people who sought care from commercial pharmaceutical practitioners, nine received a prescription medication, usually an antibiotic or sulfa product. All of those who sought care from a private physician were from the two upper strata, and in every case a prescription drug was recommended. Because government sponsored hospitals and clinics in El Salvador do not inform patients of the name or type of medication they are prescribed, it was not possible to tabulate these cases.

The number of families who used prescription medications recommended by friends or kin, or prescribed by health practitioners for previous episodes of the same illness, was also significant in this and other illnesses. Four of the seven upper strata families purchasing pharmaceutical products to treat colds bought prescription medications. Three of the fifteen lower strata families did likewise. Prescription medications were also used as preventive measures.

TABLE II
Type and source of medication employed by lower and upper strata households in the treatment of chest colds

Strata	Self-medication				Western bio-medical practitioners				Commercial pharmaceutical practitioners				Other practitioners	Total
	Behavioral change only*	Used herbs and teas only	Purchased OTC medicines	Purchased prescription medicines	Physician OTC	Physician Prescription	Hospital	Health Post	Pharmacy OTC	Pharmacy Prescription	Idóneo OTC	Idóneo Prescription	Midwife Herbs	
I & II (poor)	5	2	12	3	0	0	1	4	1	8	1	0	1	38
III & IV (Middle & upper)	0	1	3	4	0	6	0	0	0	1	0	1	0	16
Totals:	5	3	15	7	0	6	1	4	1	9	1	1	1	54

* Eliminated foods considered as cold and stopped bathing.

Two women reported that they gave a teaspoon of *Pantomicina* (tetracycline) to their children each day to prevent colds. (Tetracycline is counter-indicated in pregnancy and in children under the age of eight.) In one of the town pharmacies, a pharmaceutical company sales representative strongly recommended to the investigator and to the pharmacy personnel that we take one *Bactrim* (sulfamethoxazole and trimethoprim) anytime we felt a cold developing. (This drug is also counter-indicated in pregnancy, not effective in treating colds and, in Asunción, was expensive. One tablet cost C1.00 [US £0.40]). Two of the best selling products in the town pharmacies, Bayer's *Campolon B 12* (a vitamin product) and Abbott's *Pedralyte* (an electrolyte solution used for treating dehydration), were frequently used as nutritional supplements by families in the sample. Information gathered during the illness episode survey, then, suggests that prescription medications are often prescribed by commercial pharmaceutical practitioners in treating their patients and that these and other brand-name products are used in self-treatment and preventive regimens.

The use of prescription medications and other prepackaged products by alternative healers in treating their clients fosters pluralism in the health care sector of many developing economies. Because commercial pharmaceutical practitioners combine local beliefs regarding etiology, diagnosis and treatment of illness with reliance on modern medications, they are often viable competitors with private physicians and sometimes are preferred over public health facilities. In Asunción, for example, commercial pharmaceutical practitioners were relied on more heavily than the government sponsored Health Post, even though the Health Post offered free treatment and medications. Families interviewed complained about the long waits and rude treatment, especially from nurses, that they encountered at the Health Post.[13] Some clients interviewed at the Health Post stated that if they had had enough money, they would have preferred to go to one of the local pharmacies or *idóneos* to be treated. Service from these sources of care is faster and in many cases, both the care and the medications provided are perceived to be superior. Many townspeople stated that the brand-name medications sold at pharmacies and often dispensed by alternative healers were more effective than the unlabeled medications provided free of charge at the Health Post.[14]

In El Salvador, as in most Latin Amercian countries, over-the-counter sale of prescription drugs and prescribing of these products by other than licensed health care practitioners is technically illegal. It appears, however, that some governments have opted to permit the development of a two-tier, or parallel, delivery system for medical care (Ledogar 1975). In Asunción, for example, those who can afford to pay have access to private physicians' advice and treatment and to any medications they wish to purchase and use. Poorer families in the community, on the other hand, rely heavily on commercial pharmaceutical practitioners for care, information, and access to pharmaceutical products. In this context, the commercial pharmaceutical sector represents an alternative personal service system for the delivery of health care. It provides access to a powerful treatment resource of Western biomedicine without the State having to underwrite the costs of delivery or to improve or extend its public sector health services.

The form and process of medicalization in Asunción

In Asunción, the impact of the penetration of multinational pharmaceutical firms is channeled in large part through the major retail outlet for drug products – the pharmacies. Because they are an important source of health care advice and treatment and because they are often an important source of information about medications and products used by alternative practitioners in treating their patients, pharmacies play a central role in the process of medicalization.

Although pharmacy owners in El Salvador are legally required to hire the services of either a licensed pharmacist or certified *idóneo*, these trained personnel are often not available for consultation in the shops. In many cases pharmacies are run by owners or clerks who have received no formal training in the use of the products they prescribe and who frequently have little formal education. Of the seven pharmacy clerks employed in the stores in Asunción, for example, four had received a sixth grade education in local schools, two had completed the third grade, and one had never been to school. Two of these individuals were illiterate. In one of the stores, the owner's 10-year-old nephew often prescribed and dispensed medications. Of the four pharmacy owners, one was a licensed pharmacist who had graduated from the National University, but due to other business interests, he left the running of the store entirely to his wife and two hired clerks. Another owner was a physician, but as result of a stroke had been bedridden for years and also relied on his wife to run the shop.[15] The two other owners of pharmacies in Asunción had completed the fifth grade in the local schools. The pharmacies, then, were staffed and run by individuals whose knowledge about medications was gained from first-hand experience in their use rather than from formal training.

Pharmacy owners and clerks had few sources of information available regarding the use of the products they prescribed and dispensed. At the time of this study, many multinational pharmaceutical firms in Central America had eliminated the package inserts they used to include with their prescription products. Reportedly, this represented an effort to reduce the over-the-counter sale of these medications. These inserts contained the companies' suggested indications for use, counter-indications, warnings, dosage and formula. In some cases doses and formula plus general indications for use were printed on the drug carton or package, but in others no information was provided. For example, Pfizer, S.A.'s *Terrabron* (tetracycline and nystadin) and *Terramicina* (tetracycline), Abbott's *Pantomicina* (tetracycline) and *Pedralyte* (electrolyte solution) MKesson's *Diazepam*, Searle's *Dramamine* (dimenhydrinate) and Squibb's *Steclin* (tetracycline), all popular medications in Asunción, contained no information on the counter-indications and warnings and only very general information regarding indications for use. Most multinational pharmaceutical firms package prescription pills, capsules and tablets so that they can be sold on an individual basis. The only information included in these cases was the name of the product and the manufacturer. National Salvadoran firms were more likely to include inserts with their products. In many instances, however, these inserts make no effort to alert the buyer to the risks involved in using the medications and, therefore, must be considered as promotional devices. The insert included with Laboratorio Lopez's *Palmicetina* (pediatric cloramphenicol), for example, did not indicate that there were any dangers involved in using the product, although this medication is known to cause aplastic anemia in some patients and should be used with caution.

Another source of information about the use of medications – the *PLM* or the Central American drug reference guide similar to the *PDR* in the United

States – that was formerly dispensed free to pharmacy owners, had to be purchased from the publishers in Mexico. Only one pharmacy owner in Asunción bought this handbook. As Silverman (1976) has pointed out in his work *The Drugging of the Americas*, the information found in this guide and in package inserts is of questionable value. Many pharmaceutical firms exaggerate the indications for use of their products and minimize the counter-indications and warnings. Furthermore, what little information is available to owners and clerks in pharmacies is written in biomedical jargon and is difficult, if not impossible, for non-physicians to understand.

The owners of the two pharmacies in town who purchased their medications from distributorships and pharmaceutical firms relied heavily on information provided by the companies' sales representatives. Interviews conducted with seven of these sales representatives, however, revealed that most had received little training in the uses of medications. *Visitadores*, sales personnel whose primary function is to sell products to physicians but who also sell at pharmacies, were generally better educated than *viajeros*, sales representatives who sell at pharmacies. The three *visitadores* interviewed had received some college education. Two of the four *viajeros* had completed high school and the two others had gone through the ninth grade. While most had attented short courses sponsored by the companies whose products they sold, the sales representatives reported that these classes stressed sales and promotional considerations. The incomes of *viajeros* and *visitadores* are largely dependent on their volume of sales. *Viajeros* interviewed reported earning an average monthly salary of only C300.00 (US $120). *Visitadores*, because they were better educated, earned on the average of C1000.00 (US $400) per month. *Visitadores* stated that they were usually able to more than double their monthly salaries through their sales commissions, while *viajeros* reported increasing their regular monthly incomes by six to seven times through their sales commissions. The minimal training in drug use, plus the financial incentives these sales representatives have to sell products, makes the information they provide pharmacy personnel of dubious quality.

Partly because of the lack of reliable information, prescription and over-the-counter products have become integrated into lay conceptualizations regarding the use of medications. In a sense, pharmacy personnel in Asunción serve as interpreters between different medical care traditions, gleaning what they can from information they receive regarding Western medications and relying to a large extent on shared cultural understandings of the nature and treatment of illness.

This integration is well illustrated by the case of chest colds, discussed above. Pharmacy personnel and most townspeople felt that this condition was caused by the weather (often the north wind which stirred up dust and produced lower temperatures), usually coupled with a failure of the sufferer to comply with expected role obligations or responsibilities. Women interviewed in the illness episode survey frequently explained their colds by saying '*me serene*' meaning that they had lingered outside their homes at dusk longer than they should have. Children's colds were often said to have resulted from a *descuido*, a carelessness on the part of either those responsible for their care or the children themselves. The most common form of *descuido* reported was children being given or sneaking cokes or popsicles on particularly warm days. Although many people had heard of microbes, there was little understanding, especially among the poorer strata, of contagion or of exactly how microbes produced illness.

Pharmacy owners and clerks shared in these attitudes regarding the nature of this illness and combined Western medications with popular treatment strategies in the advice they offered their clients. In the case of colds, patients were reminded to avoid foods or drinks considered cold (fruits, cold drinks) and not to bathe until their symptoms diminished. In addition, they were usually prescribed tetracycline which was regarded as best for illnesses of the chest and throat. Other broad spectrum antibiotics, such as cloramphenicol, were preferred to treat stomach conditions and diarrhea. Again, these medications were combined with advice regarding foods or behaviors to be avoided until the patient improved.

Quantity and presentation (liquid, pill, injection) of a medication recommended to clients in the four pharmacies reflected both practical considerations and shared understandings regarding the treatment of illness. During periods of pharmacy observations conducted over a three month span, 171 cases of illness were treated in the four stores. In 131 of these cases it was possible to gather information on the form of medication recommended to the client and age of the patient. In the four pharmacies, presentation of medication was found to be related to the age of the patient and the perceived seriousness of the complaint. Because they were easier to administer, injections and medicines in syrup or liquid forms were usually prescribed for babies and small children. Injections were also recommended for adults or older children whose complaints were regarded as serious or who had not responded to previous administrations.

Quantity of a medication was related to the manner in which products were packaged and to the customer's ability to pay. Customers buying liquids, syrups or injections were required to buy the entire bottle; these products were not dispensed in small quantities in any of the pharmacies. Pills and tablets, on the other hand, were sold individually from the bottles or, as noted previously, came conveniently packaged in the unit dosage form.[16] Customers purchasing pills and tablets generally bought no more than four, regardless of the nature of the complaint or the type of medication. Pharmacy owners and some clerks were aware that small quantities of drugs may not be sufficient in treating certain complaints. Because many customers could not afford to buy in large amounts, however, pharmacy personnel recommended that they buy in small amounts and return to purchase more if the patient did not improve.

These practical considerations were usually supported by cultural preferences and beliefs. The most frequent number of pills or tablets prescribed and purchased was four, a number of ritual significance in the community possibly dating from preconquest times (Westheim 1965). It was also commonly held that injections were more powerful than pills or liquid medication, that once a patient felt better there was no reason to continue taking medicine, and that if a patient did not respond promptly to a drug, it was ineffective. Many customers who were prescribed, or purchased on their own, small quantities of medicine and experienced no relief concluded that the product was ineffective and bought another small quantity of a different drug. Drugs manufactured by foreign firms were considered to be of higher quality, more effective, and fresher than products made by Salvadoran firms.

While some of the patterns of prescribing in the pharmacies reflected the integration of Western medications and lay beliefs, others grew out of the different pressures exerted on pharmacy owners by their suppliers. These patterns reflect in a different manner the impact of the pharmaceutical invasion and its role in the process of medicalization in Asunción. Owners of two of the pharmacies purchased all of their stock from the sales representatives of distributorships and pharmaceutical firms who visited the stores monthly. The two other owners purchased their medications directly from large wholesale pharmacies located in Sonsonante or San Salvador. Since large wholesale pharmacies generally do not employ sales representatives to visit small towns, the pharmacy owners themselves were responsible for placing their orders and arranging to have the medications delivered.

Pharmaceutical firms and distributorships made available to their clients certain sales incentives not offered by wholesale pharmacies: *bonificaciones*, a system whereby a pharmacy owner who purchased a certain quantity of a product was given another quantity free of charge; and *vinetas*, money-back box-top offers (money back to the pharmacy owner in this case, not to the customer). Large companies such as Bayer usually have a number of products on special at all times. Other companies have permanent *bonificaciones* on some of their medications. Often new products are launched with these sales offers to get them established on the market. Pharmacy owners who took advantage of these sales offers on the product *Gesterra* (for menstrual irregularities), for example, stood to make 68% more on the sale of the product than those owners who did not have this option available to them. The system of *bonificaciones* and *vinetas* encouraged pharmacy owners in the two stores that relied on distributorships and pharmaceutical firms to purchase large quantities of medications and often new and more expensive products.

These differences in distributional networks were evident in the prescribing patterns of clerks and owners in the two groups of stores. Pharmacy personnel in those shops that purchased from distributorships and pharmaceutical firms consistently recommended more expensive medications to clients who asked

TABLE III

Total amount spent by illness category and average amount spent per customers by illness category in groups of pharmacies

Illness categories	Pharmacies purchasing stock from pharmaceutical firms and distributorships			Pharmacies purchasing stock from wholesale pharmacies		
	Number of customers	Total spent	Average spent	Number of customers	Total spent	Average spent
Respiratory disorders	33	C133.55*	C4.05	14	C15.15	C1.08
Gastro-intestinal disorders	16	C62.95	C3.39	10	C13.85	C1.39
Other infectious processes	20	C81.30	C4.07	16	C24.45	C1.53
Nutritional disorders	6	C48.25	C8.04	6	C16.05	C2.68
Rheumatic and body aches	7	C14.85	C2.12	5	C6.50	C1.30
Uro-genital disorders	7	C25.70	C3.67	3	C2.00	C .66
Trauma	7	C12.85	C1.84	2	C2.25	C1.13
Headache	7	C14.25	C2.04	0	C .20	C .20
Dermatological disorders	6	C39.55	C6.59	0	0	0
Psychological disturbances	2	C1.80	C .90	0	0	0
Lacked data to tabulate	2			1		
Total	113	C435.05	C3.92	58	C80.45	C1.41

* C2.50 equals $1.00

for advice and treatment. Table III presents the total amount spent by illness category and the average amount spent per customer by illness category in the two groups of pharmacies.

Patients at stores that purchased their stock from pharmaceutical firms and distributorships paid, on the average, 260% more than those who consulted at establishments that relied on wholesale pharmacies.

Pharmacy personnel in those stores that obtained their stock from pharmaceutical companies and distributorships also tended to recommend that their clients buy greater numbers of medications to treat complaints. Thirty percent of the 113 customers seeking advice at these pharmacies and 19% of the 58 customers seeking advice from shops that relied on wholesale pharmacies purchased two or more different types of medications to treat their illnesses. The differences in number of medications prescribed between the two groups of stores is actually greater than these figures suggest. In those shops that relied on pharmaceutical firms and distributorships, often the customers could not afford to buy the number of medications recommended by pharmacy personnel. These cases, therefore, are not reflected in the above figures. Clerks and owners of stores that relied on the pharmaceutical firms and distributorships, then, used the opportunity presented by customers seeking treatment to unload more expensive, brand-name, and often new medications that were either not selling well on their own or just getting established on the market.

The pressures to sell that grew out of the different distributional networks were also evident in the customer services offered by the two groups of pharmacies. In an effort to increase customer reliance on their stores, owners who purchased from pharmaceutical companies and distributorships offered credit to select customers and administered injections to clients who bought the medicine in their establishments. In none of the shops, however, did pharmacy personnel undertake physical examinations of patients. In some instances the sick person was not present and the client was a family member who related the symptoms to the owner or clerks.

The pharmacies that relied on distributorships and pharmaceutical firms were among the most successful business ventures in Asunción, reflecting both the profits to be gained through this supply network and the townspeople's growing reliance on prepackaged medications. Table I, presented earlier, indicated that pharmacies were the most frequently used sources of care by people in the two lower socio-economic strata. Of the 47 lower strata families seeking care from medical practitioners, 18 relied on the pharmacies as their first health care resort. Of these 18, 15 sought care from those pharmacies that purchased their stock from pharmaceutical firms and distributorships; one consulted at a pharmacy that relied on the wholesale pharmacy supply network; and two used pharmacies located in the nearby town of Sonsonante. Attracted by the lower prices on some of the over-the-counter products and the services (especially the administration of injections) that stores relying on pharmaceutical firms and distributorships offered their clients, the poor were recommended medications that cost substantially more than those prescribed at the other two pharmacies. Although the patterns of prescribing found in the stores that bought from the pharmaceutical firms and distributorships created a dependence upon more expensive, brand-name, and often new medications among all strata in the community, the poor could least afford to spend their small incomes on these types of products.

The absence of reliable information on the proper use of prescription medications, augumented by their over-the-counter sale, their use by commercial pharmaceutical practitioners, and their use by individuals in self-treatment and preventive regimens, has brought about a form of medicalization in Asunción that differs from that found in countries where licensed health care practitioners control access to these medications. In Asunción, the penetration of modern prepackaged pharmaceutical products has fostered pluralism and led to the development of the commercial pharmaceutical sector. The dependence on the sources of supply of these medications has resulted in three forms of commerciogenesis or commerce induced illness. These parallel the cultural, social and clinical forms of iatrogenesis discussed by Illich for the Western developed countries; but, as this dependence is channeled through a variety of medical practitioners, they assume a somewhat different form in Asunción.

Cultural forms of commerciogenesis

The penetration of products manufactured by multinational pharmaceutical firms has altered patterns of reliance on less expensive but, in many cases, equally effective remedies made by Salvadoran firms, by pharmacies themselves, and by people at home. It has also reduced the reliance on medical practitioners who continue to depend on locally made products to treat clients. In the early part of this century, Asunción was a center for traditional healing and some of the local curers were well known throughout the country for their skills. The most famous in recent time was Juana Torres who died approximately twenty-five years ago. She was reported accused by a physician of being a fraud and was called before the national legislature where she successfully defended her practice on the grounds that physicians could not treat conditions such as *males* (hexes or spells cast by witches) since they did not regard them as illnesses. Curers like Juana Torres relied on a range of techniques to treat their patients and often referred them to the town pharmacies with prescriptions for pharmacy-made products. Although a few healers still rely exclusively on traditional healing strategies, in Asunción the majority now also use prepackaged pharmaceutical products. One of the town pharmacies that now buys from wholesale pharmacy outlets was well known in the 1930s and 1940s for its store-made *aguas* (mineral waters), *esencias* (essences), *pomadas* (pomades), and *aceites* (oils) and was an integral component of the community-centered health care system. Although it still stocks these remedies, it has suffered a steady decline as customers and healers have come to rely on prepackaged medications.[17]

In addition to these alterations, new medically related specializations, such as shot-givers, have developed as a result of the ready availability and widespread use of Western style drug products. There were at least five women in the community who supplemented their families' incomes through giving injections. Once was a nurse who worked at the Health Post, but the other four had received no formal training. Although none of these women routinely diagnosed illness or prescribed medications, they provided an important service, administering intermuscular and intravenous injections and sometimes IVs to clients.[18]

The pharmaceutical invasion has brought about a popularization of medical traditions, a decline in some forms of indigenous healing and created new medical specialties. In many cases it appears that these developments have neither necessitated nor produced radical modifications in beliefs regarding etiology and diagnosis. Nor have alternative and lay healing strategies simply been placed by Western therapies. Instead, Western styled medications (and sometime Western disease terminology, dress and other paraphernalia [Woods 1977; Cosminsky and Scrimshaw 1979; Landy 1974]) have been integrated into alternative medical traditions and lay conceptualizations of illness. Considerably more work needs to be done on how modern medications are integrated into the healing strategies of alternative curers, a point barely touched on in this article. The information presented here has focused on the integration of these products into townspeoples' and pharmacy personnel's conceptualizations about the nature and treatment of illness, a process that often has serious social and clinical repercussions, as detailed in the following two sections.

Social forms of commerciogenesis

The growing reliance on modern medications by commercial pharmaceutical practitioners and townspeople often drains away resources without providing any long-term improvements in health or living standards. Dependence on these products, and the agents and institutions that make them available, fosters the notion that the solution to illness resides in the consumption of medications rather than improvements in living conditions. Radio, television, and newspaper advertisements contribute to this belief. Although prescription drugs are not advertised in the mass media, large companies such as Bayer indirectly promote their use by suggesting that the quality and efficacy of their products are superior to those of other companies and that a feeling of well being and health can be obtained by buying their products. One of the town's *idóneos* wrote most of his prescriptions on Bayer prescription forms, thus linking his practice with the company's reputation for quality.

Although vitamins and vermifuges manufactured by pharmaceutical firms may be helpful in treating cases of malnutrition and parasite infestation, the prevention of these conditions awaits a more equitable sharing of the country's wealth and a greater commitment on the part of the government to improved water supply, sanitation, and other public health measures. The heavy reliance on medications to treat colds, parasite infestations, and malnutrition, characteristic especially among the poorer strata of the community population, results here, as elsewhere, in a cycle of disease-treatment-disease that benefits pharmaceutical firms but does not alter the conditions under which people live and which account for their illnesses (Segall 1975; Gish and Feller 1979; Young 1978).

The case of one of the lower strata families visited during the illness episode survey illustrates this cycle. Mr. Musto, the household head, was sporadically employed as a day laborer. His 19-year-old wife worked as a street vendor selling fruits and vegetables in season on commission from neighbors. The family's average monthly income was about C75.00 (US $30.00). Because Mrs. Musto frequently traveled to Sta. Ana or Sonsonante to sell, her two children, ages nine months and two years, were left in the care of her eight-year-old nephew. Her children were sick with upper-respiratory or gastro-intestinal infections on each of the six home visits made during the course of the survey. In the case of the Musto's children, as in similar instances, it was difficult to determine when one illness ended and another began. The children chronically suffered from acute conditions. When Mrs. Musto coud afford care for her children, she generally relied on one of the town pharmacies that purchased its stock from pharmaceutical companies and distributorships. On one occasion, I was present in the store when she came in for advice and treatment with her youngest child and her husband. The child, who had a cold and fever, was prescribed one injection of *Terrabron* (tetracycline and nystadin), *Bactrim* (trimethoprim and sulfamethoxazole) in liquid form and four *Asawin* (aspirin compound) pills. Mrs. Musto, who was suffering from a sty, was prescribed *Stetlin* (tetracycline) ointment. The family also asked for advice regarding vitamin tonics for their children because they were so thin. *Optotonico* (a Merek product) and *Ferrocebrina* (a Lilly product) were recommended. The bill for these medications totaled C30.00 (US $12.00). This represented 40% of their average monthly earnings. Three weeks later, on a regular visit to the home, the child was again sick with a cold.

Although some of the diseases found in communities such as Asunción can be treated effectively through curative services and others will respond to public health vaccination campaigns (McDermott 1980; Foege 1979), the most frequent causes of illness and death – upper-respiratory and gastrointestinal infections, coupled with malnutrition – depend for their solutions on alterations in the socio-political and economic conditions of life and are beyond the scope of purely medical interventions (Smith 1979; Dubos 1952; Segall 1975). McDermott (1979, 1980) has suggested that to address the disease problems in Third World countries a major effort be launched by multinational pharmaceutical firms in conjunction with international health agencies, national governments, universities and national pharmaceutical firms. This recommendation ignores the kind and amount of investment multinational firms already have in these areas, their impact on national pharmaceuticals industries, and their effect on public sector health care budgets. These broader social consequences of the pharmaceutical invasion are detailed in works by Lall (1974, 1977), Bertero (1972), Evans (1979), Katz (1973), Gish and Feller (1979) and were alluded to in an earlier section of this paper. The case of this industry is only one aspect of a broader pattern of economic exploitation by international cartels in the Third World that has serious and direct effects on human health (Ledogar 1975; *Mother Jones* 1979; Castleman 1979). The best known of these is the promotion of infant formulas by large companies such as Nestlé, Abbott and Bristol Myers.

Clinical forms of commerciogenesis

Medication induced illnesses resulting from use of modern medications were fairly common in Asunción. Three cases were reported in the illness episode survey as a consequence of self-prescribed and self-administered medications. One of these, an allergic reaction to an antibiotic, required hospitalization. A woman who gave injections in the community told the researcher that clients sometimes experienced a rash after a shot of antibiotic but that this was nothing to be concerned about. Another case, ending in death, illustrates the possible effects of the integration of modern medications into lay and alternative practitioner beliefs about treatment strategies. The four-month-old daughter of the Martinez's, a middle class family interviewed in the illness episode survey, had suffered from recurring bouts of upper-respiratory infections since her birth. She had been treated by a private physician and at the Health Post for bronchitis. On March 17, the child had difficulty breathing and was taken to the Health Post by Mrs. Martinez, her mother, and her sister-in-law. After waiting two and a half hours to receive care, they left the clinic, and at the urging of the sister-in-law, went to an *idóneo*. He administered a 'strong' injection, prescribed *Binotal* (ampicillin) and *Broncovinotal* (cough syrup), and told Mrs. Martinez that the child should be given only these drugs in order to avoid a possible *choque de medicinas* (a clash of medicines). The baby initially responded to the treatment, but early the next morning was again unable to breathe and shortly thereafter died at home. Although her condition worsened, no other sources of care were sought because of the family's faith in the *idóneo's* advice regarding the strength of the injection and the possible effects if combined with other drugs. Mrs. Martinez's explanation of the illness and death of her child (her third child to die out of five born) combined popularized Western notions of illness and medications with beliefs in witchcraft. She stated that, as the weakest family member, the child had died of bronchitis as a result of a *mal* (hex or curse) sent to the family by an undetermined source.

In the pharmacies, clerks were often confused by the proliferation of identical products with different brand-names and would prescribe products like *Hostacilina* to patients allergic to penicillin, unaware that *Hostacilina* is penicillin. The widespread use of small doses of antibiotics to treat conditions such as colds poses another type of health threat. As noted earlier, the misuse of these products leads to the development of drug-resistant strains of infectious disease, a problem reported in many developing countries (National Academy of Sciences 1979). The lack of package inserts describing indications for use, counter-indications, warnings and doses of medications leads to product misuse. For example, one of the pharmacy owners was hospitalized as a result of an over-dose of *Lisalgil* (no information on product in the PLM or PDR), manufactured by a Mexican firm, to treat a headache. The package contained no information regarding dose, very general indications for use and a label saying it should be sold only with a physician's prescription.

These cultural, social and clinical manifestations of commerciogenesis were found among both lower and upper strata families. Although the two strata shared a reliance on modern prepackaged pharmaceutical products, usually manufactured by multinational firms, this dependence was mediated in somewhat different ways. Among the upper strata of the community, reliance on these medications was often, although not always, channeled through and fostered by the most frequently used sources of care for these families: physicians and other Western-trained practitioners. To refer to the manifestations of this process of medicalization as iatrogenesis (Western biomedical practitioner or system-induced illness) as Illich does, however, is misleading. It confuses instrumental personnel (Western trained practitioners) with causal agents (pharmaceutical firms and governmental policies regarding the pharmaceutical and health sectors). In the case of lower strata community families, reliance on modern medications was fostered by and channeled through commercial pharmaceutical practitioners. In both instances, it is apparent that medicalization is not as dependent on the monopolization of the health sector by any one type of medical practitioner or medical tradition. Rather, the deciding factors are a socio-economic and political structure that facilitates the penetration of modern pre-packaged pharmaceutical products, their use by a variety of medical practitioners, and their use by townspeople in curative and preventive regimens.

SUMMARY AND CONCLUSIONS

In the case of Asunción, the penetration of products manufactured by multinational pharmaceutical firms, coupled with the State's unwillingness to enforce laws regarding the sale of prescription medications and the staffing of pharmacies with trained personnel, has led to the development of a commercial pharmaceutical sector of medical care. This has resulted in a form and process of medicalization different from that found in the Western developed countries. As a parallel system for the delivery of modern medications, the commercial pharmaceutical sector provides townspeople, especially the poor, with access to products and medical care without the government needing to underwrite the costs of delivery. A dependence has been created on a particular form of therapy – modern, brand-name and often prescription medication – and the agents and institutions that make them available in the community, rather than on a particular type of practitioner or medical tradition. In Asunción, this dependence has altered local health care traditions and the means of coping with illness that were previously common in the community, drained away resources without providing any long-term improvement in living conditions, and actually caused illness.

This case study of an urban area in El Salvador has examined the interactions among medical traditions, national policies related to health care and pharmaceuticals, and national and international business interests in the formation of a popular sector of medical care and an alternative form of medicalization. Where medical traditions are different or where access to pharmaceutical products is mediated in other ways, it is unlikely that the specific configurations described for Asunción will be replicated. The processes leading to the formation of the commercial pharmaceutical sector and form of medicalization described here are, however, found in many other developing market economies subject to the pharmaceutical invasion. As noted previously, a number of investigators in Latin America have indicated that pharmacies and alternative medical practitioners who use Western manufactured drug products are important sources of health care. Other investigators working in India (Leslie 1976; Taylor 1976), Taiwan (Unschuld 1976) and Ethiopia (Lundin 1974) report similar patterns. It is likely that, in contexts where the alternative medical traditions are different and where access to prepackaged pharmaceutical products is channeled in another fashion, other configurations of the commercial pharmaceutical sector and medicalization have resulted. Additional research on these topics is necessary among both urban and rural populations in Third World countries.

Investigation of the impact of modern pharmaceutical products on mortality and morbidity rates in developing market economies is also needed. In Western Europe and the United States, mortality from many infectious processes had already declined significantly prior to the discovery of effective medications, due in large part to improvements in nutrition and public hygiene (McKeown 1979; Dubos 1959). The drug revolution that began in the 1930s with the discovery of sulfa products brought about further reductions. In countries such as El Salvador, on the other hand, mortality rates have declined apparently without significant improvements in nutritional status, public health measures, or increases in real income for the majority of the population (White 1973; Durham 1979; see Laurell 1977 on Mexico). Although vaccination campaigns may have played an important role in the decline in mortality from some infectious processes, it is possible that the commercial pharmaceutical sector (as a personal service system for the delivery of modern medications, especially to the poor) has also been a contributing factor. Declines in mortality, however, may also be accompanied by increases in morbidity, much of it unreported in official health statistics, as alternative sources of care are used for treatment. In this context, modern pharmaceutical products may function to keep greater numbers of people alive as the quality of health deteriorates.

ACKNOWLEDGEMENTS

This research was supported by a Pre-Doctoral Traineeship from NIMH grant 5 T32 MH 15132-02 awarded to the Medical Anthropology Program at Michigan State University. Drs. Josep Spielberg, Harry Raulet and Arthur Rubel were especially helpful at various stages in the investigation. The study could not have been conducted without the cooperation of the pharmacy personnel and many families in Asunción, individuals whose insights often surpassed mine. Pharmacy owners requested that the issues regarding the lack of information on the proper use of medications be brought to the attention of a wider public.

This article has been published before in *Culture, Medicine & Psychiatry* vol. 5, pp. 105–134 (1981). The present version has undergone some revision and editing.

NOTES

1. Asunción is a pseudonym.
2. Interestingly, some new products for the treatment of intestinal helminths – a major health problem in many developing countries – were originally developed for veterinary and insecticide use and were afterwards found to be effective in treating human populations. Peters (1979: 73) comments that the market prospects for veterinary products and insecticides are far more lucrative than those for products used in treating poor people.
3. Although figures are not available, it was reported to me in conversations with medical and pharmacology faculty at the National University of El Salvador that the country relies heavily on the importation of pharmaceutical products manufactured by multinational firms and that this reliance, and the consumption of modern medications, has increased substantially in the last thirty years. Similar reports are available for Guatemala (Schieb et al. 1977). Some multinational firms, notably Bayer and MKesson, have established plants in El Salvador. While it was beyond the scope of this investigation to examine the effects of the penetration of multinational pharmaceutical firms on the Salvadoran pharmaceutical industry, it was found that many of the sales and promotional practices of Salvadoran firms parallel those employed by multinational firms.
4. Although both alternative and Western biomedical practitioners promote the use of modern medications, they, in addition to their clients, are often the unwitting victims of the pharmaceutical companies' sales and promotional practices. The origins of the term commerciogenesis are uncertain. It was relayed to me in a personal communication from Ms. Dianna Melrose of OXFAM in Oxford, England.
5. Mediums at spiritist centers in Asunción were consulted for a wide range of problems in addition to illness.
6. Those who could afford it were requested to donate C1.00 (US $0.40) to the Health Post.
7. It was initially planned to include a small number of rural families in the study, but the political situation during the research period made interviewing in the surrounding rural *cantones* unfeasible. The percentages for the socio-economic strata presented here differ slightly from those published in the original article. The data has since been computerized and errors in calculations corrected.
8. Large landowners in Asunción reported that they paid their workers C3.00 (US $1.20) per day. In a study conducted by Concepción Clara de Guevarra (1975), it was estimated that agricultural day laborers in the Department of Sonsonante received a daily salary of C1.50 (US $0.60).
9. In addition, a small number of upper strata families maintained homes in Asunción and large agricultural estates in the region but resided in the capital and returned to town only for holidays.
10. Injuries and deaths resulting from the political turmoil that characterized El Salvador during the research period were less frequent in the western part of the country than they were in the north and east. This may be because western El Salvador, particularly the Departments of Sonsonante, Sta. Ana and Ahuachapan, were the seats of the 1932 peasant uprising that took an estimated 10,000 lives (Anderson 1971: 136). Memories of these events were still fresh in

many people's minds in Asunción, one of the centers of the rebellion. From April through July 1979, however, five teachers, members of the ANDES (the national teachers' association) were killed in the municipality, reportedly by the right-wing terrorist organization *Mano Blanca*. A bomb was set off in the National Guard Post in Asunción at the end of April, injuring a number of children in a nearby home. These types of occurrences have been the leading cause of death in El Salvador since 1978.

11. Public-sector health facilities in El Salvador rely on the index for malnutrition employed by INCAP and based on age and weight of the child. Of the 301 children under the age of five diagnosed as suffering from malnutrition, 197 showed signs of Grade I malnutrition, 82 of Grade II and 22 of Grade III. These figures undoubtedly underestimate the incidence of malnutrition in the town and municipality. They are based only on those families who bring their children to the Health Post and also reflect individual differences in diagnostic categories employed by the two physicians. The medical student did not consider malnutrition an illness and only listed it as a diagnosis when he could find nothing else wrong with the child. The other physician frequently recorded the condition as a primary diagnosis.
12. In many Third World countries, the Western biomedical tradition can be considered a disarticulated social formation in two senses. As Navarro (1974) indicates, the hospital-centered and curative orientation characteristic of this medical tradition addresses the needs of only a small portion of the population and therefore is disarticulated from the wider social context. As indicated here, the Western biomedical tradition may also be considered as disarticulated or fragmented in the sense that its medical practitioners do not control access to one of its major healing resources, prescription drug products.
13. In most cases, patients interviewed before and after their consultation with Health Post physicians had gained little understanding of their illness but had received a Western-style disease label. These types of interactions with physicians may contribute to the popularization of Western biomedical terminology. In the community, for example, the term 'bronchitis' was commonly used to refer to any persistent cough, and 'ulcer' to pain in the region of the stomach.
14. In an effort to reduce the amount of self-medication, public-sector health facilities in El Salvador do not inform patients of either the name or manufacturer of the medication prescribed. Public-sector policies such as this one have difficulty competing with the unregulated private-sector sale of pharmaceutical products.
15. Although it is illegal in El Salvador for physicians to own pharmacies, this doctor was able to circumvent the law. He was trained as a physician in Mexico and, while he practiced medicine in El Salvador for many years, was never formally licensed to do so.
16. This manner of individually packaging pills and tablets has been found to reduce medication errors in busy hospitals (Siler 1977). At pharmacies, however, it allows for the sale of medications on a pill-by-pill basis and may therefore encourage the misuse of certain types of products, in particular, antibiotics.
17. The other three pharmacies in town carry a limited line of pharmacy-made remedies. These medications are sometimes used by townspeople but are more frequently relied on by the rural population. At the time of this investigation the owners of three of the town pharmacies were considering the discontinuation of these remedies because the cost of ingredients had risen substantially and their market appeal had diminished. The wife of one of the pharmacy owners reported that the ingredients used in making the medications were routinely diluted. Some products, in fact, consisted only of food coloring and cooking oil or water. She explained these practices by saying that what cures is the faith the customer has in the medicine, not its contents.
18. In interviews conducted with five shot-givers in San Salvador, the capital, two reported that women sought their services to induce abortions. Products employed for this were: diethylstilbestrol (DES), paranethadione and piperazine.

REFERENCES

Anderson, Thomas
   1971 Matanza. El Salvador's Communist Revolt of 1932. Lincoln, Nebraska: University of Nebraska Press.

Berliner, Howard S.
   1977 Emerging Ideologies in Medicine. The Review of Radical Political Economics 9(1): 116–124.

Bertero, Carlos O.
   1972 Drugs and Dependency in Brazil – An Empirical Study of Dependency Theory. The Case of the Pharmaceutical Industry. Cornell University: Latin American Studies Program, Dissertation Series.

Brown, Jack
   1963 Some Changes in Mexican Village Curing Practices Induced by Western Medicine. America Indigena 23: 93–120.

Castleman, Barry I.
   1979 The Export of Hazardous Factories to Developing Nations. International Journal of Health Services 9(4): 569–606.

Cosminsky, Shiela and Scrimshaw, Mary
   1979 Medical Pluralism on a Guatemalan Plantation. Mimeographed.

De Guevarra, Concepción Clara
   1975 Exploración Etnografica. Departamento de Sonsonante. San Salvador: Ministerio de Educaci.ho.

Dubos, Rene
   1959 Mirage of Health. New York: Harper & Row.

Durham, William H.
   1979 Scarcity and Survival in Central America. Ecological Origins of the Soccer War. Stanford: Stanford University Press.

Evans, Peter
   1979 Dependent Development. The Alliance of Multinational, State, and Local Capital in Brazil. Princeton, New Jersey: Princeton University Press.

Foege, William H.
   1979 Accessibility of Vaccines. In Pharmaceuticals for Developing Countries. National Academy of Sciences, Division of International Health, Institute of Medicine. Washington, DC: National Academy of Sciences; 83–94.

Gish, Oscar and Feller, Loretta Lee
   1979 Planning Pharmaceuticals for Primary Health Care: The Supply and Utilization of Drugs in the Third World. Washington DC: American Public Health Association, International Health Programs Monograph Series, No. 2.

Harrison, Polly
   1976 Contexto Socio-Cultural de Prestaciones de Salud en Areas Rurales de El Salvador. San Salvador, El Salvador: USAID Contract 519-127.

Hellegers, John F.
   1973 Chloramphenicol in Japan, Let it Bleed. Bulletin of Concerned Asian Scholars 5: 37–45.

Illich, Ivan
   1976 Medical Nemesis. The Expropriation of Health. New York: Pantheon Books.

Katz, Jorge
   1973 La Industria Farmaceutica Argentina: Estructura y Comportamiento. Buenos Aires: Instituto Torcuato di Tella.

Kewitz, H.
  1976 Drug Utilization The Role of Medical Schools. *In* Clinical Pharmacological Evaluation in Drug Control, Report on Symposium. Copenhagen: WHO Regional Office for Europe.
Lall, Sanjaya
  1974 The International Pharmaceutical Industry and Less Developed Countries, With Special Reference to India. Oxford Bulletin of Economics and Statistics 143–172.
  1977 Medicines and Multinationals: Problems in the Transfer of Pharmaceutical Technology to the Third World. Monthly Review 28: 19–30.
Lall, Sanjaya and Bibile, Senaka
  1977 Political Economy of Controlling Transnationals. Pharmaceutical Industry in Sri Lanka, 1972–76. Economic and Political Weekly 23 (33&34): 1419–1436.
Landy, David
  1974 Role Adaptation: Traditional Curers Under the Impact of Western Medicine. American Ethnologist 1 (1): 103–128.
Laurell, Asa Cristina and Blanco Gil, Jose, et al.
  1977 Disease and Rural Development: A Sociological Analysis of Morbidity in Two Mexican Villages. International Journal of Health Services 7(3): 401–424.
Ledogar, Robert J.
  1975 Hungry for Profits: US Food and Drug Multinationals in Latin America. New York: IDOC.
Leslie, Charles
  1976 Asian Medical Systems. Berkeley, California: University of California Press.
Logan, Michael
  1973 Humoral Medicine in Guatemala and Peasant Acceptance of Modern Medicine. Human Organization 32(4): 385–395.
Lundin, Stig
  1974 The Rural Drug Vendor, A Survey of the Situation in the Province of Arussi. CADU Publication No. 95.
McDermott, Walsh
  1979 Historical Perspective. *In* Pharmaceuticals for Developing Countries. National Academy of Sciences, Division of International Health, Institute of Medicine. Washington, DC: National Academy of Sciences; 9–27.
  1980 Pharmaceuticals: Their Role in Developing Societies. Science 209: 240–245.
McKeown, Thomas
  1979 The Role of Medicine: Dream, Mirage, or Nemesis? Princeton: Princeton University Press.
Mother Jones
  1979 The Corporate Crime of the Century. Mother Jones (November).
Murray, Gerald
  1977 Traditional and Modern Strategies of Health Delivery Among Peasants of El Salvador. San Salvador, El Salvador: USAID Contract la-c-1186
National Academy of Sciences, Institute of Medicine
  1979 Pharmaceuticals for Developing Countries. Washington DC: National Academy of Sciences, Division of International Health, Institute of Medicine.
Navarro, Vicente
  1974 The Underdevelopment of Health or the Health of Underdevelopment: An Analysis of the Distribution of Human Health Resources in Latin America. International Journal of Health Services 4(1): 5–27.
  1975 The Industrialization of Fetishism or the Fetishism of Industrialization. A critique of Ivan Illich. International Journal of Health Services 5(3): 351–370.

Peters, Wallace
    1979   Drugs Against Parasitic Diseases. *In* Pharmaceuticals for Developing Countries. National Academy of Sciences, Division of International Health, Institute of Medicine. Washington DC: National Academy of Sciences; 59–82.

Press, Irwin
    1971   The Urban Curandero. American Anthropologist 73: 741–756.

Sarasti, Hernando
    1970   To the Editor. Chloramphenicol in South America. New England Journal of Medicine 282(14): 813.

Schieb, F.
    1977   Analysis del sector salud Guatemala. Vol. 1. Guatemala City, Guatemala: Agencia de los Estados Unidos en Guatemala para .le Desarollo Internacional a Guatemala.

Segall, M.
    1975   Pharmaceuticals and Health Planning in Developing Countries. Brighton, England: Institute for Development Studies at Sussex, No. 119.

Sesser, Stanford
    1971   Special Dispensation. Peddling Dangerous Drugs Abroad. New Republic 164: 16–17.

Siler, W.
    1971   Death by Prescription. Nashville, Tennessee: Sherbourne Press.

Silverman, Milton
    1976   The Drugging of the Americas. Berkeley: University of California Press.
    1977   The Epidemiology of Drug Promotion. International Journal of Health Services 7(2): 157–166.

Smith, C.E. Gordon
    1979   Major Disease Problems in the Developing World. *In* Pharmaceuticals for Developing Countries. National Academy of Sciences, Division of International Health, Institute of Medicine. Washington, DC: National Academy of Sciences; 30–48.

Taylor, Carl
    1976   The Place of Indigenous Medical Practitioners in the Modernization of Health Services. In Asian Medical Systems, Charles Leslie, ed. Berkeley: University of California Press; 285–299.

Unschuld, Paul
    1976   The Social Organization and Ecology of Medical Practice in Taiwan. In Asian Medical Systems. Charles Leslie, ed. Berkeley: University of California Press; 30–316.

Waitzkin, Howard
    1976   Recent Work in Medical Sociology. Contemporary Sociology 5(July): 401–406.

Westheim, Paul
    1965   The Art of Ancient Mexico. Garden City, New York: Doubleday Anchor.

White, Alastair
    1973   El Salvador. London: Ernest Benn Limited.

Woods, Clyde M.
    1977   Alternative Curing Strategies in a Changing Medical Situation. Medical Anthropology 1(3): 25–54.

World Health Organization
    1977   The Selection of Essential Drugs. WHO Technical Report Series 615.

Young, Allan A.
    1978   Rethinking the Western Health Enterprise. Medical Anthropology 2(2): 1–10.

IVAN WOLFFERS

TRADITIONAL PRACTITIONERS AND WESTERN PHARMACEUTICALS IN SRI LANKA

Studies on the distribution of pharmaceuticals in developing countries have focused on prescription (and over-prescription!) by doctors, and the sale practices of pharmacy workers and informal vendors (Cunningham 1970; Ferguson 1981; van der Geest 1982a, 1982b; Greenhalgh 1987; Hardon 1987; Logan 1983; Melrose 1982). But there is still another type of distributor that deserves attention: traditional health practitioners. Landy (1977) has argued that traditional healers must adapt to processes of modernization in health care if they want to survive. One very effective adaptation seems the inclusion of Western pharmaceuticals within their therapeutic arsenal. Reports about the use of modern pharmaceuticals by traditional practitioners come from Africa (Good et al. 1979), Central America (Ferguson 1981), Bangladesh (Sarder and Chen 1981) and Sri Lanka (Waxler 1984).

Most studies on this subject come from India, however. Ramesh and Hyma (1981) claim that two thirds of the traditional practitioners exclusively use indigenous medicines, which implies that about one third of the traditional practitioners use modern pharmaceuticals – at least occasionally. Takulia et al. (1977) claim that 80–90% of the Indian traditional practitioners prescribe modern pharmaceuticals, alone or in combination with traditional herbs. Knowledge of these modern pharmaceuticals is obtained from the medical representatives of various drug companies and salesmen from wholesale drug suppliers. Bhatia et al. (1975) report that 90% of the Indian traditional practitioners make some use of modern pharmaceuticals, and 10% use them exclusively. In their survey it appeared that the use of injected pharmaceuticals was very popular. Only 14% of the traditional practitioners in their sample said they did not give injections at all.

These figures are impressive, but more specific information is lacking. Neumann et al. (1971), who did a survey in two Indian states, found remarkable differences between various traditional practitioners in their use of modern pharmaceuticals. In Kerala 62% of the healers would not use any modern pharmaceuticals, while in the Punjab this figure was only 24%. It was assumed that traditional medical culture was better organized in the South Indian state than in the Punjab.

Criteria for describing the activities of practitioners using modern pharmaceuticals are rarely well defined. It makes a great difference if a healer only uses vitamins or iron, applies simple over-the-counter painkillers, prescribes antibiotics, or treats people with corticosteroids and sedatives. Another important question is whether healers use modern pharmaceuticals exclusively or in combination with traditional herbs. In a survey among traditional practitioners in Sri Lanka, I tried to standardize these differences (Wolffers 1987a).

One of the major influences on traditional medical systems is the fact that a well developed network of distribution for easily usable symptomatic modern drugs brings products for self-treatment to remote areas. Their strongly-promoted influx has drastically changed the health-care scene. Western medicines have found a place in people's conceptual framework. Patients often demand them from their traditional practitioners. Bhatia et al. (1975) report that traditional practitioners in India begin using allopathic medicines for fear of losing patients.

It seems indeed likely that commercial considerations play a major role in the adoption of Western pharmaceuticals by traditional practitioners. We shall return to that momentarily.

THE HEALTH-CARE SYSTEM OF SRI LANKA

Sri Lanka is one of the few developing countries where a low-income economy combines with favorable health indicators. Infant mortality and maternal death rates show a steady decline over the years (see Table I).

The dramatic fall in maternal death rate and infant mortality between 1945 and 1950 was caused by the elimination of malaria in 1947 with the use of DDT for vector control. The success in the following years is in part a result of the public health care policy of successive Sri Lankan governments. Already in the 1930s the famous Kalutera Experiment with Public Health Nurses, Public Health Midwives and Public Health Inspectors was implemented. These preventive health workers form the link between the villagers and the modern health care institutions of Sri Lanka. The curative modern health care system is also well organized and of good quality. The facilities are free and within easy reach. Within 0.8 mile there is always some source of medical care, and there is a Western facility at least within 2.5 miles (Simeonov 1975). Moreover, the island is relatively small and a good and cheap public transport system insures that within a few hours one can be in the capital or one of the other major cities. This has caused large-scale bypassing of the lower health care levels and increased medicalization; for example 79% of all deliveries in the country are institutional (Nichter 1986).

The free curative health care system proved a heavy financial burden for this poor country, and over the years the government's expenditure on health care could not keep up with the rising costs. Since the change of government in 1977 a different policy has been followed with more privatization of health care facilities; a detoriation of the quality of the public facilities has been the consequence. Sri Lanka still has the reputation of a country with a reasonably good public modern health care system, but those who can afford it prefer

TABLE I
Maternal death rate and infant mortality rate in selected years

Year	Maternal death rate	Infant mortality rate
1945	16.5	140
1950	5.6	82
1955	4.1	71
1960	3.0	57
1965	2.4	53.2
1970	1.5	47.5
1975	1.0	45.1
1980	0.9	34.4

Source: Annual Health Bulletin Sri Lanka 1983.

private facilities, that always have medicines in stock, and are not understaffed.

Traditional medicine for its part has always played an important role in the country's health care. Sri Lanka is the only country in the world with a special minister for Indigenous Medicine. There are several public traditional facilities, though the majority of the traditional practitioners work privately. Their importance in the national health care system is reinforced by the gaps in the modern medical system in rural areas, which lack doctors. In the whole country there are about 1,800 modern doctors and 900 Assistant Medical Practitioners. Of these 1,800 doctors, 544 can be found in the capital Colombo. Waxler (1984) concludes that in Sri Lanka modern doctors and traditional practitioners do not find themselves in a competitive situation because they are working in different areas, not only geographically, but also in terms of social background and career aspirations.

The indigenous medical system in Sri Lanka, Ayurveda, is not the same as the Ayurvedic medical system of India. Ayurvedic medicine in Sri Lanka is synonymous with indigenous medicine, and covers practitioners of Unani, Siddha, Ayurveda and folk medicine (Wannaniyaka 1982).

There are two important training institutes that have been in existence since 1928. The biggest is the Institute of Indigenous Medicine in Borella (Colombo), the other is the private Gampaha Institute (40 km East of Colombo). Training is also available from famous priests and healers who assemble students around them. The *paramparika* are practitioners who have been trained by their fathers; they have to pass an exam to be registered. Most traditional practitioners are now registered.

Students who want to enter the Institute of Indigenous Medicine need high school at least. The Institute is supposed to be comparable with Medical School, and receives many young people who have been turned down at the University. These students, who were basically interested in a career in

Western-style health care, have a more cosmopolitan attitude than the students at Gampaha Institute, who originally chose to study indigenous medicine.

THE TRADE IN PHARMACEUTICALS

Before taking a closer look at the place of modern pharmaceuticals in the work of traditional practitioners, the legal aspects of drug distribution will be described. Prior to 1970 many different small agencies were responsible for importing drugs. This changed when the State Pharmaceutical Corporation (SPC) was set up. One central state organization made orders on the world market and accepted the best offer. By centralizing imports and purchasing in bulk, the authorities were able to bring the costs of modern medicines down by 60% (Lall and Bibile 1977). At the same time the government tried to do something about the number of different drugs in the country. In the 1960s the number of drugs was reduced to 2,100 on the recommendations of a drug subcommittee. At that time no action was taken against brand-names for the same products. This was done in a later stage and a list with 700 different drugs was the result. Sri Lanka was one of the first countries with a restricted list. Though there was considerable resistance to it from transnational companies, prescribing doctors and urban elite groups, the policy was considered a success. Due to pressure from industrialized countries and a change of government, however, the drug policy changed in 1977. More possibilities for privatization were introduced, and gradually the products which were banned in the 1970s returned to the market. The public health care service is still working with the restricted drug list, but as the stocks of the public facilities are mostly insufficient, people are partly dependent on private pharmacies. Moreover, the growing popularity of these private facilities diminishes the effects of the limited drug list (c.f. Balasubramaniam 1985).

The State Pharmaceutical Corporation (SPC) is the sole importer for the public sector and in 1986 30% of the private sector requirements were supplied by the SPC (Fernando 1987). The distribution and promotion of pharmaceuticals in Sri Lanka by private companies and importers does not differ from that in most other developing countries. Eight major transnational companies operate in Sri Lanka and a number of importers are active selling products of other transnational companies. Numerous drug representatives visit doctors, pharmacies and traditional practitioners for promotional purposes. Some companies have their own representatives, who receive 2% on their turnover. The smaller companies sell their products to salesmen who travel in vans, reselling to pharmacies, doctors and other drug distributors. The salesmen offer products from different manufacturers.

The following case presents an example of a very small producer of pharmaceuticals:

Mr. N. runs a pharmacy in a suburb of Colombo. He has no qualifications as a pharmacist, although the former pharmacy owner did. When we enter the pharmacy, Mr. N's niece is present. She is a trained nurse, who earns more by suturing, wound-treatment, bandaging and injecting in her uncle's pharmacy than in the public hospital. Patients pay a bit less here than in one of the private clinics. The pharmacy-owner has been working in this pharmacy for twelve years. Before that time he was employed as a clerk by a company that imported Italian pharmaceutical products. There he learned something about modern pharmaceuticals. For the past few years, he has been producing some products himself at the back of the pharmacy in his wife's batik workshop. He makes Whitfield ointment, an analgesic balm, benzyl benzoate ointment, Kaolin Pectin Mixture against diarrhoea, an expectorant and Henley's toothache remedy. These are all medicines for external use made of mixtures which can be produced rather easily. One can find Mr. N's products all over Sri Lanka, especially in the smaller boutiques. They are distributed by three salesman, who also work for other producers.

Mr. N.'s cousin in London sent him a book titled *How to make pills* and after reading it, he started to make acetylsalicylic acid and acetominophen tablets, the two most popular simple painkillers in Sri Lanka. He has bought an old volkswagen engine at the junk-yard and intends to use the exhaust for drying the granules.

He is a self-taught man and uses the British Pharmacopeia. Presently he is experimenting with an ointment against burns. It contains chloramphenicol, an antibiotic which can have serious side-effects if taken internally, and which can also cause an adverse reaction of the blood producing system if applied externally.

Mr. N. is not an exception in Sri Lanka. Pharmacies are often run by people with insufficient pharmaceutical training. A survey in Colombo has suggested that people working in pharmacies lack a basic knowledge of pharmaceuticals more often than not. It appeared that the personnel in pharmacies is almost entirely dependent on the information given by the pharmaceutical companies (Wolffers 1987b). At the same time, self treatment with ready-made modern pharmaceuticals is increasing in Sri Lanka, especially among the literate urban middle class (Abosede 1984). One of the people working in a pharmacy in Colombo said: 'The patient knows what he wants. I know what it costs, and I don't see the need for any additional information'.

The following case shows the situation of a drug representative:

Mr. S., 32 years old, married with two children, works for Glaxo. He was born and still lives in Colombo and belongs to the urban middle class. He got a job as a drugs representative and started work after two months' training by the company. He has a car and visits modern doctors, pharmacists, shop-keepers and others who dispense modern pharmaceuticals. As he receives 2% commission on his sales in addition to his salary, he is motivated to sell as many products as possible. When I ask if he ever visits traditional practitioners, he hesitates. His superior, the sales manager, who is present at the beginning of the interview, states that it is not the policy of the company to approach them, but if the traditional practitioners ask for it, the compnay will visit them. Mr. S. explains that he is constantly looking for new selling points, and it does not matter if these are modern doctors, pharmacies or traditional practitioners. "If I don't go there, somebody else will, and in that case it is better that I have the profit." He gives examples of well-known traditional practitioners who need 10,000 tablets of acetominophen and 2,000 capsules of ampicillin per week. In one of the villages he visits, he deals with two practitioners who compete with each other and have become rather demanding. They ask for stronger medicines to be more powerful than the other and often buy corticosteroids.

TRADITIONAL PRACTITIONERS AND MODERN PHARMACEUTICALS

Waxler (1984) writes that 50% of the traditional practitioners in Sri Lanka use modern pharmaceuticals, and that these practitioners are the most successful in business. Elsewhere (Wolffers 1987a) I have tried to analyse in more detail how traditional practitioners make use of modern pharmaceuticals, and what their specific background is. In one village, 50% of the practitioners used modern medicines. The ones who did not had an average age of 61 years, while the others were 42 years old on average. Most of the practitioners using modern pharmaceuticals were trained at the Institute of Indigenous Medicine in Borella (Colombo), while those coming from the Gampaha Institute were very strict about not using modern medicines. The practitioners using modern medicines usually had a busier practice and charged higher fees.

A closer look at the practitioners dispensing modern medicines reveals different patterns. Of the practitioners dispensing modern medicines 28.6% restrict themselves to simple painkillers and rely mainly on herbal treatment. In this group, the *paramparika* (the practitioners without formal education but trained by their fathers) were found. Another 21.4% dispense also antibiotics, whereas herbal remedies played a minor role in their treatment, and 17.9% would go as far as dispensing the whole range of modern medicines, including corticosteroids and sedatives, while refraining from herbal remedies. These results are summarized in Table II.

More or less the same was found in a village closer (12 km) to Colombo: 40.7% of the general traditional practitioners used modern pharmaceuticals. They were younger, had a busier practice, asked higher fees and had studied at the Institute of Indigenous Medicine.

We turn now to a discussion of how modern pharmaceuticals are used in specific situations. It appears that traditional practitioners who prescribe an antibiotic in an acute situation like cough and fever, stick to herbal treatment in the case of a catarrh. This treatment seems to reflect a general pattern of treatment choice in Sri Lanka (Wolffers 1988). Our survey suggests that patients with acute complaints tend to go to the modern doctor, those with very serious diseases to a modern facility, those with chronic non-

TABLE II
Traditional practitioners' use of modern pharmaceuticals in a rural community

Kind of medicine	Number	Percentage
No modern pharmaceuticals	14	50
Using modern pharmaceuticals	14	50
a. Only painkillers	8	28.6
b. Only antibiotics + painkillers	1	3.6
c. Corticosteroids + antibiotics + painkillers	5	17.9
Total	28	100

incapacitating complaints to a traditional practitioner, those with chronic incapacitating complaints to both at the same time or in succession (shopping), and those with mental problems to a traditional practitioner. The traditional practitioners who prescibe modern pharmaceuticals attempt to cover, as it were, the gamut of possible therapeutic choices. In the case of a chronic complaint like rheumatism, for which people try out different treatments, many of the traditional practitioners combine elements of modern and traditional therapy. They advise diets, give herbal treatment and prescribe antibiotics simultaneously. One of the traditional practitioners we interviewed expressed this rather clearly saying: 'It depends on the patient. If he has patience and can wait I will treat him in the Ayurvedic way, but if he is restless and comes back within a few days I will treat him with modern medicine.' A fragment of our interview with one of these 'modern traditional practitioners' may illustrate the situation.

Doctor S. was trained at the Institute of Indigenous Medicine right after the Second World War. He also followed an obscure course in Great Britain. He himself talks about a training in pharmacy, but others in the village call it a training for medical analyst. Doctor S. has a successful practice. Many patients consult him, and he is one of the three most popular private general practitioners in the village. His patients see him as a modern doctor, though he does not use modern pharmaceuticals exclusively. When asked what he is, he answer 'I am both, and I use both methods. Every patient needs different treatment. One needs modern pharmaceuticals and the other Ayurvedic treatment. But you cannot combine the two systems. Either you do it in the modern way, or you do it in the Ayurvedic way. It is a different way of thinking. In Ayurveda for instance, there is a disease called "Whateroga" (translated as "windy pains"). The disease is caused by too much air in the body, especially in the abdomen. Any Ayurvedic doctor will recognize it immediately. In modern medicine however you have to know what causes the pain in the abdominal system. It may be due to worms, gastritis, indigestion of food, abdominal obstruction, abscess, gastric ulcer, pregnancy, labour pains, abortion, tumor, or an actopic pregnancy. As a doctor you have the responsibility to look at these things. A diagnosis like "whateroga" is not sufficient. There are of course very good medicines against "whateroga", like Hingua Steca in tablet or powder form, but panadol (acetominophen) is also very effective. Sometimes you can satisfy the patient by giving him panadol as well as Hingua Steca. In the old days people worried a lot about the right treatment. The prescriptions were complicated. There are now many drugs which makes the work of a practitioner much easier. In acute diseases I will always use modern pharmaceuticals for immediate result'.

When I ask him about the treatment of rheumatic complaints he says: 'My patients never complain about my treatment. I give them indomethacine. They never use it for a long time, because after a while they will go over to Ayurvedic treatment'. Asked about the information from the pharmaceutical salesmen he says: 'They are a great help for me. I do not know where I could otherwise obtain my information. Every week they come and talk for about 5–10 minutes. Last week they gave me some samples of imodium (loperamide). I will give it to all my patients with diarrhoea, and if that does not have effect within two days, I will prescribe antibiotics'.

THE REACTION OF THE AUTHORITIES

These developments are recognized by those who are responsible for health care in the country. In 1978 a Committee was appointed by the Department of Ayurveda to make recommendations about the synthesis of the indigenous and the modern medical system. This committee was to examine the present status with regard to teaching and to recommend reforms. Concerning the use of modern pharmaceuticals by traditional practitioners the report of the committee says: 'Such practices were described by some as being out of step with the fundamentals of Ayurveda and other indigenous systems. Others have expressed the view that modern scientific methods of treatment would be acceptable as long as they were not in conflict with Ayurvedic principles'. The report concludes: 'In fact no medical institute training of indigenous practitioners should include instruction on western drugs in its curriculum' (Ministry of Health 1978).

The committee advises against further synthesis, but does not propose concrete measures to change the present situation. The problem is probably too sensitive. The traditional practitioners form a considerable pressure group and rely on important political support. Nobody can prohibit their use of modern medicines or enforce legal restrictions. Moreover, the modern traditional practitioners have become an important facility of modern medicine in those areas where doctors are scarce. In this way the modern health care system of Sri Lanka experiences a considerable increase of its manpower, whose training moreover is not as costly as that of modern doctors. These practitioners are private facilities, with no cost to the government. Waxler (1984) even claims that the quality of their work is often not worse than that of modern doctors. Everyone seems 'satisfied'.

CONCLUSIONS

Modern pharmaceuticals have become important ingredients in the treatments of many traditional practitioners, and their importance increases steadily. The stereotype of the traditional practitioner working with herbal remedies and the modern doctor using modern pharmaceuticals is no longer true in many developing countries, certainly not in Sri Lanka.

Sri Lanka seems a clear example of a country that tolerates the uncontrolled distribution of potent modern pharmaceuticals, since it cannot fill the gaps in health care delivery in another way. The informal supply, prescription and distribution of pharmaceuticals should be understood as a financial and commercial phenomenon. The commercial process takes place at two levels.

Manufacturers of pharmaceuticals – from transnational industry to local producer – not only respond swiftly and indiscriminately to demands for medicines, but actively create such demands by employing drug representatives who promote their products. Our exploratory investigations suggest that Ayurvedic practitioners constitute an increasing proportion of their clientele.

The dispensing of modern pharmaceuticals by Ayurvedic practitioners is no less commercial. These practitioners should be regarded as entrepreneurs in Barth's (1963) sense of the term: People who take initiatives in administering resources and pursue an expansive economic policy. By their willingness to take risks for the sake of maximizing their profits, entrepreneurs act as innovative cultural agents. They introduce new products, new ideas and new demands. Ayurvedic practitioners, as we have seen, not only initiate medical treatment with modern pharmaceuticals but also respond to their patients' demands. The adoption of modern pharmaceuticals is both innovation and survival strategy. Practitioners who do not administer modern pharmaceuticals are likely to lose clients to those who react more readily to clients' demands.

Any attempt, by the government, international health organizations or consumer groups, to control the present pharmaceutical situation in Sri Lanka (or elsewhere) should take into account the extremely commercial context of this phenomenon. Any policy to change the situation will have to deal first with the commercial character of medical practice.

REFERENCES

Abosede, O.A.
  1984 Self-Medication: an Important Aspect of Primary Health Care. Soc Sci & Med 19: 699–703.
Balasubramaniam, K.
  1985 The Neglected Solution. HAI News 24, August 1985, 1–2.
Barth, F.
  1963 The Role of the Entrepreneur in Social Change in Northern Norway, Bergen: Universitetsforlaget.
Bhatia, J.C., Dharam, V., Timmappaya, A., and Chutani, C.S.
  1975 Traditional Healers and Modern Medicine. Soc Sci & Med 9: 15–21.
Cunningham, C.E.
  1970 Thai 'Injection Doctors': Antibiotic Mediators. Soc Sci & Med 4: 1–24.
Ferguson, A.E.
  1981 Commercial Pharmaceutical Medicine and Medicalization: a Case Study from El Salvador. Cult Med & Psych 5: 105–34 (also in this volume).
Fernando, J.
  1987 Drug Situation in Sri Lanka, 1987. Paper presented at ARDA meeting Bangkok 1987.
Geest, S. van der
  1982a The Illegal Distribution of Western Medicines in Developing Countries: Pharmacists, Drug Pedlars, Injection Doctors and Others. A Bibliographic Exploration. Medical Anthropology 6: 197–219.
  1982b The Efficiency of Inefficiency: Medicine Distribution in South Cameroon. Soc Sci & Med 16: 2145–53.
Greenhalgh, T.
  1987 Drug Prescription and Self-Medication in India. An Exploratory Survey. Soc Sci & Med 25: 307–18.
Good, Ch. M., Hunter, J.M., Katz Selig, H., and Katz, S.S.
  1979 The Interface of Dual Systems of Health Care in the Developing World: Toward Health Policy Initiatives in Africa. Soc Sci & Med 13D: 141–54.
Hardon, A.
  1987 The Use of Modern Pharmaceuticals in a Filipino Village: Doctors' Prescription and Self Medication. Soc Sci Med 25: 277–92.

Lall, S. and Bibile, S.
  1977 Political Economy of Controlling Transnational Pharmaceutical Industry in Sri Lanka, 1972–1976. Economic and Political Weekly, special number, August 1977, 1419–36.
Landy, D.
  1977 Traditional Curers and the Impact of Western Medicine. *In* D. Landy (ed.) Culture, Disease and Healing, London: Macmillan Press. pp. 468–81.
Logan, K.
  1983 The Role of Pharmacists and Over-the-Counter Medications in the Health Care Systems of a Mexican City. Medical Anthropology 7: 68–89 (revised version in this volume).
Melrose, D.
  1982 Bitter Pills. Oxford: Oxfam.
Ministry of Health of Sri Lanka
  1978 Report on the Committee on the Synthesis of the Indigenous Medical System and the Western Medical System. Committee appointed by the Minister of Health Mr Gamini Jayasuriya on 7th August 1978.
  1984 Annual Health Bulletin Sri Lanka 1983. Colombo.
Neumann, A.K. et al.
  1971 Role of Indigenous Medicine Practitioners of India: Report of a Study. Soc Sci & Med 5: 137–49.
Nichter, M.
  1986 The Primary Health Care Center as a Social System: PHC, Social Status, and the Issue of Team-Work in South Asia. Soc Sci & Med 23: 347–55
Ramesh, A. and Hyma, B.
  1981 Traditional Indian Medicine in Practice in an Indian Metropolitan City. Soc Sci & Med 15D: 69–81.
Sarder, A.M. and Chen, L.C.
  1981 Distribution and Characteristics of Non-governmental Health Practitioners in a Rural Area in Bangladesh. Soc Sci & Med 15A: 543–50.
Simeonov, Dr. L.A.
  1975 Better Health for Sri Lanka. Report on a Health Manpower Study. WHO regional office for South East Asia, New Delhi 1975.
Takulia, H.S., Parker, R.L., and Srinivas, M.A.K.
  1977 Orienting Physicians to Working with Rural Medical Practitioners. Soc Sci & Med 11: 251–6.
Wanninayaka
  1982 Ayurveda in Sri Lanka. Colombo: Ministry of Health of Sri Lanka.
Waxler, N.E.
  1984 Behavioral Convergence and Institutional Seperation: an Analysis of Plural Medicine in Sri Lanka. Cult Med & Psych 8: 187–205.
Wolffers, I.
  1987a Changing Traditions in Health Care, Sri Lanka. Leiden, Dep. of Anthropology: PhD Thesis.
  1987b Drug Information and Sale Practices in Some Pharmacies of Colombo, Sri Lanka: a Research Note. Soc Sci & Med 25: 319–21.
  1988 Illness Behaviour in Sri Lanka: Results of a Survey in two Sinhalese Villages. Soc Sci & Med: forthcoming.

ANTONIO UGALDE AND NURIA HOMEDES

MEDICINES AND RURAL HEALTH SERVICES: AN EXPERIMENT IN THE DOMINICAN REPUBLIC

INTRODUCTION

During the last two decades Western medical services have become much more accessible to Latin American rural populations. Several reasons could be singled out to explain the change:
 (1) Transportation improvements have given rural dwellers the possibility of moving back and forth between countryside and towns with relative ease. When in need, an ever growing number of peasants visit free or low cost urban public medical services and private clinics.[1] They also go to town to buy medicines that cannot be purchased at home.
 (2) Since World War II, rural-urban migration has been phenomenal. Today many peasants have close relatives in the cities and, thus, visits to urban medical services including those which require an overnight stay are facilitated. Visits to town fulfill multiple purposes.
 (3) Since 1970, with the financial assistance of international agencies, many Latin American countries, have developed extensive networks of rural clinics and polyclinics staffed by physicians doing their compulsory year(s) of social service. As will be discussed later, these clinics are greatly underutilized, yet for the first time, peasants find Western medical facilities in their midst.
 It would be exaggerated to say that accessibility of medical services has ceased to be a problem in rural Latin America; in some countries and in regions with scattered rural populations, the problem continues to be severe, but, unquestionably, for a rapidly expanding number of rural dwellers, access to Western medical services has improved greatly in the past two decades.
 Studies in several Latin American countries (Eoff 1980; López Acuña 1980; Menéndez 1981; Martin 1981; Tuñón et al. 1981), including the Dominican Republic (Leshow 1983; Ugalde 1984), indicate that in spite of the new and extensive physical infrastructure and the deployment of physicians, auxiliary nurses and health promoters in rural areas, the utilization and quality of these services are low, while public expenditures in the provision of the services are high. These findings have also been confirmed in some countries in Africa and Asia. For example, Segall (1983: 1948) pointed out that 'PHC is not a cheap option in national terms', and Dunlop (1983: 2020) added, ' . . . one can find a number of examples of underutilized facility and staff in many publicly operated health care systems in Africa'. In her work in rural Philippines, Hardon (1987) found that 'people in the village generally are not satisfied with the treatment in the health center. They prefer consultation of doctors in town'.

At the same time, in part because of the inefficiency of the public sector, out-of-pocket rural health expenditures are also high, and the quality of care purchased by the peasants is questionable. The reasons behind this unfortunate misuse of public and private resources are numerous and complex. Several authors have pointed out the relation between underutilization of rural health services, high public and out-of-pocket expenditures, and the inadequate supply of low-cost essential drugs. One of the first to note this relation was Van der Geest. In his field work in Cameroon (1982a: 2148) he found: 'The most conspicuous consequence of this chronic lack of medicines is the underutilization of health services. Health centres which are known to be without medicines are no longer visited and people seek alternative solutions for treating their ailments: private institutions, the pharmacy in town, illegal medicine vendors who often function as practitioners as well, and of course, traditional medicine. Meanwhile the state continues to pay for the – non-functioning – infrastructure of health centres'. This point was also voiced by Melrose (1983: 183): 'the most obvious consequence of rural dispensaries running out of drugs is that people stop going to them. Meanwhile government facilities that are under-used and paramedics find it doubly hard gaining acceptance as health educators when they cannot deliver essential drugs. This adds to the urgency of improving the availability of essential drugs for primary health care'. Our own research in the Dominican Republic (Ugalde 1984), which will be discussed later in more detail, revealed an almost identical situation.

The issue of drug supply is of particular importance because drugs represent a large percentage of primary care expenditures and because of the dependency that patients, even in rural areas of the Third World, have developed upon modern medicines. According to some estimates (Taylor 1985: Table 3 citing IMS World Drug Marketing Manual), in developing countries the consumption of drugs represents between 30 and 50% of health care expenses, although the figure estimated for Latin America is 21% (Patel 1983: 196).[2] It is well known that for the poor, the purchase of medicines represents the largest out-of-pocket health expenditure, and that the lower the income the higher the percentage of health expenditures in medicines.[3] In our study of a rural health district in the Dominican Republic we found that 58% of out-of-pocket health expenditures were for drugs; (only 10% were for fees, 6% for hospitalization, 6% for laboratory work, and 20% for other expenditures) (Ugalde 1984: 446). The dependency of rural dwellers on modern and expensive drugs, and the reasons behind it, were well illustrated by Hardon (1987) who at the same time described the unnecessary costs and health risks incurred by the use of modern medicines in the rural areas of the Philippines, an issue raised by several other authors (Ferguson 1981; Melrose 1982; Van der Geest 1985). Alland (1970) also showed the adoption of modern medicines even in societies that rejected Western medical practices.

The lack of adequate supply systems for the provision of drugs coexists with the ample availability of modern medicines even in rural areas of the Third World. Many writers have critically discussed the questionable marketing techniques of multinational pharmaceutical corporations and the existence of weak government controls in developing countries (Lall 1981; Melrose 1982; Silverman et al. 1982; Wartensleben 1983; Gereffi 1983). It is well known that many drugs which in industrial nations require a prescription are purchased over-the-counter (Ferguson 1981; Van der Geest 1982b). In the Dominican Republican, as in much of Latin America, little rural stores (*colmaditos*) carry a variety of analgesics and antibiotics (see Appendix 1 for the list of drugs sold at one general store at El Rio) all of which are sold over-the-counter. It is obvious that most Latin American peasants have easy access to a large array of pharmaceuticals. In fact, it is the wide commercialization and penetration of medicines in the countryside which is, in part, responsible for the dependency on drugs, excessive self-medication, improper use and high costs of medicines, and which requires policy attention. In this article, we will discuss the relation between drug availability and the utilization of medical services in a rural health district (*sección*) in the Dominican Republic and the results of an experiment with a communal pharmacy which was designed to solve some of the above problems.

THE SETTING

The Dominican Republic (population 6.2 million in 1985), like many other Latin American countries, has experienced a massive rural-urban migration. The urban percentage of the total population has increased from 24 in 1950 to 52 in 1981 and is expected to reach 68 by the end of the century.[4] Today, many peasants have relatives in the cities. Improvements in transportation during the last 25 years have also bridged the distance between country and city, and placed a large majority of peasants within easy access to towns. As recently as 1974, a national assessment of health care services in the Dominican Republic indicated that: 'The lack of medical resources, especially of doctors in the rural areas, has been especially serious in view of the poor health status of the rural populace' (US H.E.W. 1974: 98). Due to this scarcity, rural dwellers took advantage of the relatively easier access to urban centers and went to the near-by cities and towns for medical care. According to the first national morbidity study of 1974 about one fourth of peasants were receiving modern medical services (Pérez Mera 1978: 220, our estimate from Table 10), and since very few of these services were available in rural areas, we must conclude that the majority were obtained in the cities.

Starting in 1975, the development of the rural health physical infrastructure has been extraordinary. With the financial assistance of US AID, the World Bank, and more recently the Inter-American Development Bank, subcenters and clinics were built: by 1984 there were 341 rural clinics and many additional ones under construction, a remarkable increase over the 59 rural and urban clinics available in 1971 (US H.E.W. 1974: 88). Concomitantly, the law of *pasantía* was approved by Congress. According to the law, all physicians upon graduation had to serve for one year in a rural clinic before receiving certification for practice.[5] The *pasantía* insured the presence of physicians in the countryside. In the rural clinics, the physician assisted by an auxiliary nurse provided free consultations and distributed monthly about 240 pesos of free medicines. National budget allocations to the Ministry of Public Health and Social Welfare (SESPAS) grew likewise, from 17 million pesos in 1970 to 131 million in 1985, or about 9% of the national budget (until 1984 the official value of the peso was equivalent to the US dollar).[6] In sum, in the Dominican Republic the physical accessibility of modern care has greatly expanded in the last ten years and the economic barriers to utilization have been reduced considerably.

Our research was carried out in the health district of El Rio which has approximately 5,500 inhabitants distributed in about 18 hamlets.[7] This is a mountainous region, with small fertile valleys well suited for agriculture, and irrigated by streams and creeks. A mild climate and abundant rain allow for almost year-round agricultural use of the land. A wide variety of vegetables, tubers, tropical fruits, legumes, commercial flowers and coffee beans are harvested at different times of the year. In this part of the country there are many small family farms, but there are also some very large tracks of good agricultural land owned by absentee landlords which are left idle or used for grazing. Typically, households are dispersed, although there are some hamlets along the main road where it is possible to find a concentration around the school, the church and the stores.

From the end of 1982 through 1984 our study had several phases and followed an anthropological approach with field workers residing in the community and spending many hours of conversation and observation in the households. In the first nine months, two sociologists and one physician randomly selected 70 households in eight hamlets, for an in-depth study of their economy, social organization, morbidity and illness management. Household income and expenditures were analyzed meticulously, including income from subsistence crops. Morbidity was studied through the records of the clinic (attended morbidity), through a detailed morbidity survey in the 70 households (reported morbidity) and through a physical medical exam and a laboratory analysis of feces and blood of a 40-household subsample (clinical morbidity). Our study included the estimation of out-of-pocket health expenditures of every illness episode that occurred in each household during the period of six months previous to our interview. We let respondents define illness, and we included within the health expenditures the costs of transportation to and from clinics and hospitals in near-by-towns and cities, and costs of food and lodging for patients and for persons who accompanied them during the visit to urban clinics or hospitals. We also studied the organization of formal and informal health services such as the clinic, health promoters, traditional healers, midwives, and drug sellers. Findings from this study which have been reported elsewhere (Ugalde 1984), were the basis for experimental changes and additional research which will be discussed in the next pages.

During Summer 1984, a team of two health educators, one physician, one social worker and one sociologist studied the role of health promoters and physician-patient relations at the clinic and two health outposts, organized in 1983 in hamlets of the district as part of the efforts to increase the utilization of medical services. Included in this research was the study of the communal pharmacy (opened in January of 1984) focusing on its dispensation of medicines and patients' compliance (Ugalde et al. 1986).

UTILIZATION OF MODERN MEDICAL SERVICES AND AVAILABILITY OF MEDICINES

During the first phase of our study we found a low utilization of the clinic. Two months previous to the beginning of our research (October and November 1982), the daily number of consultations was 14 (based on 22 working days per month). We timed the consultations, and as an average the patient-physician contact was 3 minutes 50 seconds, in other words, the clinic was empty most of the day. The national rural health service statistics suggested that El Rio was not an unusual clinic; 46 percent of the rural clinics had less that 15 consultations per day (see Table I). We also discovered that the utilization of the clinic was very erratic, some weeks there could be as few as 20 consultations and others, more than 150.

We directed our research efforts to understand the reasons behind the poor and unusual pattern of utilization of the services. We identified the following causes: the dispersion of the population, the temporary nature of the appointment of rural physicians due to the system of *pasantía*, very poor managerial practices, low educational levels of providers and users, and a dismal supply system of pharmaceuticals by SESPAS (Ugalde 1984: 443).

TABLE I
Utilization of rural clinics in the Dominican Republic, 1983*

	Number of daily consultations							Total
	<5	5–10	11–15	16–20	21–25	26–30	31+	
Number of rural clinics	8	54	68	60	35	22	32	279
Percentage of clinics	3	19	24	22	13	8	11	100

* Daily consultations were calculated by dividing total yearly consultations by 264 working days or 22 days per month. According to the law rural clinics should be opened on Saturdays but the law is disregarded. In 1983 many rural clinics had more than one physician in residence, therefore the number of consultations per physician is much lower.

Source: Official reports filed at the Office of Primary Health Care.

When the rural health service was organized in the Dominican Republic in the mid-seventies, rural clinics were assigned a monthly subsidy of 350 or 500 pesos (250 or 416 US dollars) according to population. The subsidy was distributed in medicines, supplies for the clinic (cotton, alcohol, syringes, soap, detergent, toilet paper, etc.), all shipped from the national rural storage center located in Santo Domingo, the capital city, via the regional offices. El Rio receives 240 pesos of some forty essential drugs as established by the country's list (which is very similar to PAHO's) many of which are generic, and the rest, up to 350, in clinical and cleaning supplies. In El Rio, and we verified that this was the case in other clinics, the monthly shipments arrives on irregular dates, often two shipments arrived two weeks apart, and other times many weeks passed without a shipment. Every so often a monthly shipment would never arrive. Pilfering of medicines along the distribution route was common. The invoices sent with the supplies did not correspond in quantity or in kind with the content of the shipment: if the physician refuse to sign the receipt, the supplies were not delivered. In theory, rural physicians were supposed to make a monthly request of essential medicines from a list provided by SESPAS, but since the requests were disregarded, most physicians did not bother to fill out the forms. Complaints by rural physicians were routinely disregarded, and because of the temporary nature of their appointment, physicians seldom took enough interest in the rural clinic to persist in reporting administrative deficiencies. We also discovered that the free dispensation of medicines was not contributing to equity; those who had limited access because of distance, age or poverty received fewer medicines or no medicines at all.

Conversations with the clinic's physician and the study of the consultation records suggested that there might be some relation between the disorganized and free dispensation of medicines and the large fluctuations in the number of consultations at the clinic. According to the attending physician, when people knew that the monthly supply of medicines had arrived, they hastened to the clinic, not in search of diagnosis but to request free medicines. In conversations with villagers we found that it was not infrequent to give chickens the antibiotics received at the clinic. The physician at El Rio added that he preferred to satisfy the patients' demand for medicines, even if on many occasions they might not have been needed. He did not want to give the impression that he did not care for them; many had walked one hour or more and would get upset if they knew that medicines were available and not given to them. Within a few days after their arrival, the medicines were gone and the number of consultations declined. The physician's interpretation of the reduction in consultations was that when patients heard that the clinic had run out of medicines they preferred to by-pass the clinic and go to town to private or public health clinics. The same view was expressed by physicians we visited in several rural clinics in other parts of the country. A malevolent observer might think that it was to the advantage of the attending physician to rapidly reduce the stock of medicines, for without medicines there were very few consultations and less work. Thus, rural physicians had a perfect excuse to curtail the number of days and hours of consultation. It was well known at the Ministry that rural physicians seldom kept the official hours, and absenteeism was rampant. A vicious circle of mutual blame was prevalent in the rural health service: SESPAS officials accused rural physicians of irresponsibility and lack of dedication, and the physicians charged their superiors with incompetence, claiming that under the conditions prevailing in the rural clinics it was impossible to carry out their work.

Under these conditions when the clinic was out of medicines, many patients did not think that it was worth their time and effort to go to the clinic only for diagnosis and chose self-medication instead. It should be noticed that the diagnostic capabilities of rural clinics in the Dominican Republic and in other countries in Latin America are limited generally to osculation, and that patients are aware that lab and other clinical tests are required in some cases for adequate diagnosis. For example, during our morbidity study, one of the respondents indicated that she was not feeling well and that she was planning to go to Santo Domingo to have a cardiogram. She thought that perhaps something was wrong with her heart and added: 'I have never had one and it is time to have a cardiogram'. Free medicines were not available in the cities (free medicines were only part of the rural health program), but patients believed correctly, that physicians in towns had more experience than the newly graduated physician in the rural clinic. Besides, when medicines were not available at the rural clinic, patients frequently had to go to town to buy medicines even if they visited the rural clinic, and therefore, by-passing the clinic was a logical decision.

In El Rio self-medication and urban consultations were contributing to high out-of-pocket expenditures. As an average, each household in El Rio spent 126 pesos per year on health (24 pesos per person or 16 US dollars in 1983). As has been indicated earlier, drugs represented 58% of health expenditures. Out-of-pocket expenses for medicines were high because of the following: (1) the relatively high costs of medicines in the little local rural stores, due in part to the small volume of their operation (Thus, one aspirin was sold for 1 cent in the local stores, but the bulk price was one-third of 1 cent); (2) the purchase of me-too-drugs which tend to be more expensive than generic medicines; (3) the purchase of many remedies of doubtful therapeutic value because of self-medication (see Appendix 1 for the list of popular drugs used in self-medication which are not prescribed by physician; these are not traditional remedies and are manufactured by modern laboratories); (4) overmedication – patients buy one medicine, only to buy a second one when they find no improvement after the first; (5) the unnecessary use of drugs in illness episodes which do not require medication such as common coughs or non-severe diarrhoeas; (6) the abuse of medicines to alter behavior, for example, valium was liberally prescribed as a sleeping pill for the elderly; and (7) the

TABLE II

Average cost of medication per illness–episode by prescriber in 70 households, El Rio (Constanza), 1983 (in pesos)*

Prescriber	
Family and self	2.10
Rural physician at El Rio	5.59
Physician other than rural physician	16.92
Traditional healer	10.78
Others (pharmacists, friends)	10.08

* The figures do not include pre- and postnatal care or dental care. One illness episode could be treated by medications prescribed by one or more persons.

lack of concern by many physicians about the cost of the medicines they prescribe; often there are medicines of equivalent therapeutic value which are less costly.

Table II shows the large differences in the cost of prescriptions according to prescriber (the Table is based on the morbidity study of the 70 households where 347 episodes were reported within six months previous to the study). As could be expected self-medication was the least costly, and urban physicians the most expensive. It could be argued that the higher costs of medicines prescribed by physicians outside the rural clinic reflected the higher complexity of the illness treated by them. To verify this point we looked into the nature of each illness treated by physicians outside the rural clinic and found that the majority of them could have been cared for at the primary level. As we have just indicated we interpreted the higher costs of medicines prescribed by urban physicians to their lack of concern about the cost of medicines they prescribed. It should be noticed that, contrary to what might have been predicted, the cost of prescriptions given by traditional healers and those recommended by pharmacists were quite high as well.

ORGANIZATION OF THE COMMUNAL PHARMACY

We wanted to find solutions to some of the above problems, specifically the research team was interested in reducing the out-of-pocket expenditures without decreasing the quality of care. As indicated, medicines were the highest expense, therefore, the priority was to find less costly ways to supply them, as well as to reduce their unnecessary use. The researchers advised the local health team and SESPAS on the organization of an experimental communal pharmacy where medicines would be sold instead of given away. It sounds paradoxical to reduce out-of-pocket health expenses by buying medicines instead of receiving them free, but the following considerations led us to believe that it was possible: (1) if medicines had to be purchased, the tendency to request them without need would decrease and patients would tend to acquire them only when prescribed; as a result, medicines would last longer at the clinic, and patients would not need to by-pass the clinic and go to town, thus saving money by not incurring transportation expenses or physician's fees, and by buying less costly prescriptions received from the clinic (as indicated in Table II prescriptions by the rural physician were less expensive than those prescribed by urban physicians); (2) utilization of the clinic would also produce savings by reducing much unnecessary self-medication that, as mentioned earlier, we had found economically wasteful and in some cases harmful; (3) a positive side effect of the previous points would be the reduction of overmedication and iatrogenesis.

As an alternative, we also considered the possibility of increasing the monthly shipment of medicines from SESPAS to the amount required to insure that essential drugs would be available at the clinic at all times. We decided against this choice because: (1) the elasticity of demand for free medicines could be very high, and, consequently, at a national level this policy could increase substantially SESPAS' expenditures which, as it was indicated earlier, were already 9% of the national budget; (2) more importantly, this policy would almost certainly foster overmedication and iatrogenesis; and (3) we had doubts about the organizational capabilities of SESPAS to guarantee the availability of larger amounts of medicines at all times. As indicated, SESPAS had serious difficulties in adequately distributing small supplies of medicines. We thought that this strategy would only contribute to additional wastefulness without resolving the problem. Van der Geest (1982a) expressed similar fears in his Cameroon study and also considered inappropriate the free dispensation of drugs. It should be remembered that many socialist regimes and socialized health care systems sell essential drugs at cost. We thought that the key issue was to make essential medicine affordable to the community. A conclusion was reached that the sale of essential drugs at a communal pharmacy in the clinic and in the two newly organized health outposts would be a better solution than an increased supply of SESPAS medicines to reduce out-of-pocket expenditures and to increase therapeutic efficacy.

The research team recommended that the communal pharmacy comply with the following policies: (1) no person should be deprived of medication because of his/her inability to pay, this condition responded to the basic principle that access to health care is a human right; (2) the pharmacy should never be without essential medicines, in other words, a supply system had to be organized that would guarantee essential medicines at all times. We wanted to avoid having patients, particularly mothers with small children, come to the clinic from far away only to find out that the prescribed medicine was not available in the communal pharmacy; (3) in accordance with the custom of rural local stores, a tradition that exists in many Latin American countries, a liberal credit system should be established for those patients who might find it difficult to pay in full for the medicine at the time of purchase.

This principle, would also guarantee that patients who did not bring enough money to the consultation would not have to go back home to get additional cash; (4) the pharmacy should be organized and managed by the local health team.

SESPAS authorized the clinic of El Rio to organize the communal pharmacy following the above principles and continued to donate the 240 pesos of essential medicines and the 110 pesos of clinical and cleaning supplies. The clinic (and the pharmacy) remained under SESPAS, but it was given some financial autonomy. The local health team decided to sell medicines at the same price paid by SESPAS to its suppliers plus a 5% surcharge. The pharmacy opened an account in a bank at the near-by town with the two signatures of the physician and the supervisor of health promoters required for withdrawals; these were the two persons responsible for the management of the communal pharmacy. The proceeds of the sales were used: (1) to buy additional medicines directly from manufacturers or wholesalers when the SESPAS supplies failed or were late, as was often the case, or when the stock of some medicines was low. (Ideally, the pharmacy should buy the needed medicines from SESPAS, but at times SESPAS did not have the organizational capabilities nor the flexibility to satisfy the communal pharmacy's needs);[8] (2) to finance the free dispensation of medicines to families considered paupers by the health promoters in each community; (3) to buy a few medicines which were not included among the drugs shipped by SESPAS but needed by some chronic patients such as those with hypertension. Previously, patients had to go to town to buy the drug in local pharmacies, incurring transportation costs, time losses, and higher retail prices; and (4) to supply the clinic with materials, such as paper, folders for clinical histories, working materials for the twelve health promoters, etc. and to repair equipment in order to improve the quality of care. It was expected that the administrative decentralization produced by this economic autonomy would improve the quality of medical care provided by the clinic by breaking the vicious circle of mutual blame.

The communal pharmacy and the new policy of selling medicines began in January of 1984. From October through December 1983 the physician and the health promoters explained the impending change to community leaders, to patients attending the clinic, and to the inhabitants of the health district. During the first weeks of 1984 there was some unhappiness about the innovation. Towards the end of January, the physician met with the leaders of the communities at their request. The meeting was tense, but he was able to explain the reasons behind the change and its purpose: to reduce out-of-pocket expenses for medicines, and to guarantee the presence of essential medicines in the clinic at all times. The leaders accepted the explanation and since then there have been no complaints about the operation of the communal pharmacy. As one of them said: 'From now on, we will eat less medicine'.

By the way of summary of this section, we present the hypotheses that the research team formulated at the time the communal pharmacy was established: (1) the selling of medicines will not affect the number of consultations; (2) the erratic fluctuations in the number of weekly consultations will be reduced, and (3) the out-of-pocket health expenditures will decrease. In the next section we will describe the results of the first year of operation of the communal pharmacy and some of the issues that remain unresolved.

EVALUATION OF THE COMMUNAL PHARMACY

An assessment of the performance of the communal pharmacy can be made with the statistics presented in Table III. As can be seen, the value of medicines sold at the pharmacy was three times that supplied by SESPAS. This figure can give us an idea of the potential demand for medicines in rural primary care, a point to which we will return later.

According to Table III, in 1984 the average cost of a prescription sold at the communal pharmacy was 1.35 pesos. If we compare this figure with those presented in Table II, we can see that the cost of medicines prescribed at the clinic in 1984 was even less than that of self-medication in 1983. This reduction took place in spite of the fact that in mid-1984 the prices of drugs sky-rocketed in the Dominican Republic.[9] Medicines purchased by SESPAS experienced a 55 percent increase, and the medicines sold by wholesalers 99 percent (see Appendix 3). Retail prices increased even more, for as wholesale went up, demand went down, and pharmacies had to increase prices to make up for the sluggish demand. We estimate that the average cost of a prescription sold at the communal pharmacy in 1984 would be about 0.70 cents at

TABLE III
Communal pharmacy of El Rio: selected statistics, 1984

Total medicines sold (pesos)	11,105
Medicines received from Secretary of Health (pesos)	3,353
Medicines purchased by communal pharmacy from manufacturers and wholesalers (pesos)	5,683
Number of consultations	4,319
Cost of medication per consultation (pesos)	2.6
Cost of each prescription[a] (pesos)	1.4
Medicines given free to paupers (pesos)	444
Percentage of medicines given free as of value of medicines sold	4
Number of pauper families that receive free medicines	164
Percentage of pauper families as of total families in the health district	16
Medicines purchased on credit (pesos)	1,614
Outstanding credit at year's end (pesos)	488
Percentage of credit as of value of medicines sold	15

[a] Our own research in El Rio (Ugalde et al. 1985) yielded an estimate of 1.9 prescriptions per consultation.

1983 prices, and, consequently, we can conclude that the communal pharmacy produced major savings to the inhabitants of El Rio. Further saving would be possible if the pharmacy could purchase from PROMESE (see note 7 and Appendix 2).

About 16% of the households (160 families) were classified as paupers by the health promoters and continued to receive free medicines. Generally, these were elderly people without relatives, and large households headed by females. The selection of the families was a relatively easy task; as had been expected some promoters in the first listing included a few blood and ritual relatives which did not fall within the category of poor and the supervisor corrected the abuses without problems. The selection and adjustment of the families entitled to free medicines did not produce any protests; the communities were small and most people were aware of who the paupers were. The amount of free medicines given to them was 4% of the value of all medicines sold at the pharmacy during the year. If the need should arise, free medication could be increased substantially because by the end of the year the pharmacy had accumulated several thousand pesos. Thus, this model could be applied to other communities in the Dominican Republic (and perhaps in other Latin American countries) which are less affluent and may have more paupers.

As have been indicated, a liberal policy of credit was established from the beginning. In order to avoid possible abuses, it was made clear that the credit was expected to be paid back. Table III shows that the credit given during 1984 was 15% of the value of the medicines sold and that most of it was paid by the end of the year. The outstanding credit at year's end was 4% of total sales; much of it was credit given in the last few weeks of the year that was expected to be repaid in 1985. We do not know the precise figure of losses due to bad debts, but certainly it was less than 4%, perhaps as little as 2% of sales, an amount that can be easily absorbed by the pharmacy.

As Figure 1 shows, the extreme fluctuations in the number of consultations that had characterized the clinic in the past, and which presumably were caused by the uneven supply of medicines, reduced in 1984, when medicines were available at all times. The eleven high peaks in 1983 correspond quite closely with the arrival of medicines. Some variations continued to exist in 1984. As we found out, some low peaks responded to holidays, when people tend to go less to the clinic and when the clinic is open fewer days of the week, to the physician's absenteeism, to extreme weather conditions, and other unusual circumstances.[10]

The number of consultations was minimally affected by the communal pharmacy. In 1983 there were an average of 96 consultations per week; this figure went down to 83 in 1984. As can be seen in Figure 1, most of the decrease took place during the first weeks of 1984 immediately after the implementation of the change. The number of consultations during the second semesters of 1983 and 1984 was very similar 2,484 and 2,340 respec-

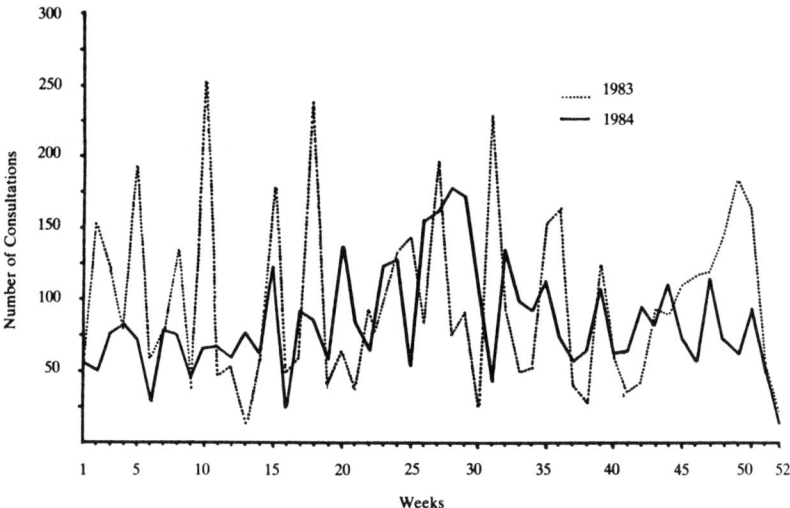

Fig. 1. Number of consultations per week at the rural clinic of El Rio (Constanza), 1983 and 1984.

tively, or a 5.7% decrease. The 1985 figures suggest also that the loss was a temporary one, consultations increased from 1,175 in the first 18 weeks of 1984 to 1,457 during the same period in 1985 (the latest information available at the time of writing). It is logical to suppose that many of the people who in 1983 went to see the physician only to receive medicines ceased to do so in 1984, and to conclude that the 1984 visits to the clinic were more genuine medical consultations than in the past (over-the-counter drugs could be purchased at the communal pharmacy without a consultation, and these visits were not counted as consultations). In other words, in the past the clinic was used primarily as a pharmacy or dispensary of free medicines; now it was used for consultations.[11] In sum, the data from the communal pharmacy of El Rio confirmed the hypothesis that the selling of medicines at low cost was not a barrier to the utilization of the clinic.

The communal pharmacy allowed financial decentralization and local autonomy. Its impact on the quality of care is difficult to assess but for the first time in the history of the clinic, patients' records began to be kept properly, the clinic could supply itself with folders, paper and other office and clinical supplies necessary for the adequate operation of a health care institution. It was able to keep the cold chain without interruptions because it had the resources to refill the gas tanks and repair the refrigerator without having to depend on the Ministry, and it was able to repair and purchase gasoline for the two motorcycles used by the supervisor of health promoters and the physician to visit the hamlets of the health district. During 1984 the pharmacy spent 1,656 pesos on maintenance and operation of the clinic including the purchase of plastic containers for the sale of medicines.

A number of questions emerged during the first year of operation of the pharmacy some of which remain unresolved. One of the issues for which there was no clear answer was the sale of disposable syringes at the communal pharmacy. In the rural areas of Latin America, as in many other parts of the Third World (Cunningham 1970; Alexander 1971; Bhatia 1975; Jones 1977; Wyatt 1984), there is a general belief that injections are superior to other forms of medication, and when a medicine is available in injectable form, the patient prefers it. This is also the case in El Rio. Some patients who lived far away from the clinic and from the health outposts wanted to buy disposable syringes and have the medicine injected by a local midwife or other person in the community. The problem is that the disposable syringes in El Rio, and we suspect in other places as well, are used many times before they are disposed. In fact, we found this practice at the clinic itself, where a disposable syringe was normally used two or three times before being disposed of and the physician considered the practice safe (attempts to find glass syringes in the country failed). Even if disposable syringes are boiled, the advisability of encouraging this practice can be questioned. In rural households, sanitary conditions leave much to be desired and we can assume, as other researchers have documented, that syringes are not sterile (Wyatt 1984: 913 and the many references cited by the author). The health risks of injecting medicines under these conditions are obvious. During our field work, members of the health committee in the hamlet of Arroyo Bonito elected the health promoter because of her experience in injecting. On the other hand, the refusal to sell the syringes would not change the custom, as patients or those who inject would buy them in town at a higher price.[12]

A second problem was the custom of buying medicines in very small amounts. It is traditional in rural areas to go to the store daily and buy only what is needed for the day. Even items such as salt, spices, sugar and matches are purchased in minute amounts; eggs are bought one at a time as needed, and cigarettes are bought by the unit. The same practice applies to the purchase of medicines. Patients may buy one or two aspirins at a time, and they or some member of the family will return to the store the following day to buy the medicines needed for the day. For example, none of the seventy households we surveyed in-depth kept any medicines on hand. Patients who live at a distance from the communal pharmacy are not inclined to walk to the pharmacy everyday to buy the medicines and prefer to acquire them at the little stores along the way even if they have to pay more, and if the stores do not have the medicine, as frequently is the case, the attendant suggests a substitute. The field notes taken by a field worker in the hamlet of Arroyaso, where a branch of the communal pharmacy was functioning under the care of a health promoter, reflect this problem and that of the injections discussed earlier:

They (patients) also go to the little store here where they may buy injectable medicines in smaller amounts (than those prescribed). They then simply buy a syringe from the health promoter. She has noticed that these (the syringes) are not well taken care of (by patients), are used over and over again, and are passed from one person to another without disinfecting them. As far as amounts of medicines dispensed: the syrups and cremes come in containers already mixed and measured by the physician. As for fills and items which the *botica* (communal pharmacy at the health outpost) has in bulk: sometimes the patient requests a certain amount in which case the health promoter simply fills the order, and other times they ask her how much.

Patients who preferred not to return to the communal pharmacy and bought the prescribed drugs at the little local stores incurred higher out-of-pocket expenditures and the risk of taking the wrong medication and/or dosage. Buying small amounts of medication probably encouraged the termination of medication when the conditions of the patient improved before the completion of the treatment. In the case of antibiotics, early termination or use of a different type of antibiotic may have negative health effects. The opening of branches of the communal pharmacy at the two health outposts where the physician had consultations once a week was an effort to bring the communal pharmacy closer to the villagers. Yet, for those peasants in the other hamlets of the health district, and even for those who resided in the hamlets where the pharmacy operated but at a distance from it, the daily purchase of the dosage was a barrier to the full utilization of the communal pharmacy.

A third factor that reduced the utilization of the communal pharmacy was the common belief that low priced medicines were of lower therapeutic quality than more expensive ones. The poor presentation of the medicines sent by SESPAS, and the low quality of packaging at the communal pharmacy for the medicines received from SESPAS or purchased in bulk from wholesalers, tended to reinforce the perception that the medicines sold at the communal pharmacy were of inferior quality. In the Dominican Republic, as in many other countries, if a low-priced product is supplied by the government, the suspicion about its quality is heightened. Furthermore, some patients are acquainted with brand-name drugs that the communal pharmacy did not carry and preferred to pay a higher price for them at the local stores or in town. The more affluent the patient the more the tendency to demand brand-name medicines. To encourage the utilization of the communal pharmacy by all social classes of the community, the physician in El Rio decided to stock the pharmacy with some of the most popular brand name medicines. The research team was not sure about the desirability of this practice but the following observation made by the clinic's physician is worth mentioning to present the problem as perceived by the local health team:

It appears as if there were medicines for each social class. For example, middle class patients come and ask which is the most expensive medicine we carry for influenza. This is common for analgesics, antispasmodics, and other drugs. If the patient can afford it, he/she buys it and goes home most satisfied. I have tried to teach them that they are wasting their money, it has been of no avail. On the other hand, poor patients ask for a good and inexpensive drug. Of all the medicines that patients request, the least solicited are those sent by the SESPAS.

The experience in El Rio suggests that attractive packaging of medicines is important. A regional or national program to provide attractive containers and envelopes to facilitate communal pharmacies' delivery of small amounts of medication to patients could be very useful. The lack of trust of government-supported programs will only fade away in time, after patients find out for themselves that the medicines sold at the communal pharmacy have the same therapeutic value as those purchased at private pharmacies.

CONCLUSIONS

In the last 20 years, many governments have built expensive health facilities in the countryside and staffed them with physicians, nurses and auxiliary personnel. The costs of these services are substantial but unfortunately, their utilization and quality are low. At the same time, and in part because the public services are so inadequate, peasants are incurring relatively large out-of-pocket health expenditures, the majority of which goes to purchase drugs. The reasons for this are complex. In our study of a rural clinic in the Dominican Republic we found that the inadequate supply of medicines was one of the many problems affecting the performance of the clinic. Utilization of the clinic was limited to those times when medicines were available. Because medicines are free, many villagers, whether in need or not, would come to the clinic only to request them. The free distribution of medicines was not contributing to equity, instead it was fostering overmedication and paradoxically, it was increasing out-of-pocket health expenditures. In an effort to remedy this situation, a communal pharmacy was organized at the clinic, under the management of the local health team, where essential and generic medicines were sold instead of given away. The results of the first year of operation of the communal pharmacy confirmed the hypotheses which supported the ideas behind its organization, namely: that the erratic use of the clinic would decline, that the cost of medication would be reduced, that a credit system for users would be feasible, that the number of consultations would not decline to any extent, and that the quality of care would be improved. The experience of the communal pharmacy demonstrated that essential generic drugs were affordable by many villagers and that the medication needs of the paupers could be satisfied with a very small subsidy. It can be suggested that the centralization of the supply of medicines is very positive, and that the main role of the central government should be the mass procurement of essential generic drugs for distribution at cost to regional or local health centers. While finding ways to supply generic essential drugs is urgent, there are other problems which also require immediate attention. One of them is the tendency among villagers to buy in the market brand name medicines or popular medicines of doubtful therapeutic value with the economic wastefulness that these practices entail. A second problem is posed by the extended custom of injecting medicines with syringes that unquestionably imply a health risk. The resolution of these and other issues require educational efforts and controls of advertisement of products whose purchase wastes scarce household resources and often involves a health risk.

The study of the use of pharmaceuticals in El Rio shows that people's attitudes and behavior towards medicines are related to a variety of socio-cultural factors some of which are obvious: social class, accessibility of drug supplies (the clinic, the local *colmados* and urban pharmacies), financial resources of the household, social relations, the marketing techniques of the manufacturers, etc. What perhaps is less evident is the impact of the organization of health services on people's attitudes towards medicines, an area which requires more systematic attention and research.

In this chapter, we have described the first year of an experiment in the provision of medicines to peasants in a district of the Dominican Republic. The account underscores the point that knowing the cultural context in which health workers carry out their activities is indispensable for understanding these activities. In the same vein, we need to know the medical perceptions and socio-economic constraints of those using health care facilities to understand *their* activities. Two observations seem particularly relevant. First, dispensing of free medicines, designed to guarantee an equitable and 'wholesome' distribution, fostered both over-utilization of drugs and financial problems for the many who did not succeed in procuring free drugs. The experiment with low-priced essential drugs showed that – paradoxically – for the peasants, paying for medicines was cheaper than 'getting' them free of charge.

Another interesting observation concerning the context of drug consumption was that external features of drugs can have a considerable impact on people's perceptions and use of medicines. The people of El Rio thought that for medicines, low price meant low quality. They also preferred injectable medicines and were greatly infuenced by the drug *packages*. The role of packaging in the perception and use of pharmaceuticals seems particularly intriguing, as is indicated by several other contributions to this volume. It deserves more systematic research.

In this chapter we have discussed an experiment in applied medical anthropology. The experiences in El Rio show that planning health care improvement demands studying its context.

APPENDIX 1.
Medicines sold at the largest general store in El Rio, 1983

Brand-name	Drug classification and common usage**
Balsamo Bengue*	anti-inflamatory, bronchial dilator
Baralgina	analgesic, antispasmodic
Bronquina*	cold preparation, bronchial dilator
Cloromicetin	antibiotic
Compuesto vegetal Sra. Muller*	used during menstruation
Dramanime	antinauseant
Enlax	laxative
Extracto de Malta*	tonic
Fortimal*	tonic with iron
Irgapirina	antiarthritic, analgesic
Jarabe Sanito*	decongestant, expectorant
Linimento Jacobino*	bronchial dilator
Magnesia	antiacid, laxative
Mejoral	analgesic
Misteclin	antibiotic
Neomelubrina	analgesic, antipyretic
Padrax*	antiparasitic
Pastillas Elva	
Pildoras Dr. Ross*	laxative
Sanicol*	
Vick (pills, syrup and creme)	decongestant, expectorant
Vitapirina*	analgesic
Vivimec*	analgesic
Winasorb	analgesic

* Popular remedies used in self-medication and never prescribed by physicians.
** The use as explained by buyers.

APPENDIX 2.
Price increases between 1983 and 1984 of selected essential drugs in the Dominican Republic, in pesos.

Medicines purchased by SESPAS for rural clinics	Prices		%
	Dec. 1983	1984	Increase
Aspirin (100 tablets)	0.50	0.80 (August)	60
Antiseptic (1 gallon)	6.05	17.09 (Sept.)	182
Ampicillin (100 capsules of 500 mgr)[a]	9.00	29.00 (April)	222
Antidiarrheal (1 gallon)	4.15	7.50 (August)	81
Antispasmodic (1 gallon)	6.30	8.00 (August)	27
Antipyretic (1 gallon)	6.10	11.45 (August)	88
Hematinic (100 tablets)	2.00	2.00 (Nov.)	0
Benzoyl Hexacloride (1 gallon)	18.00	18.00 (August)	0
Milk of magnesia (1 gallon)	4.20	7.50 (April)	79
Antiparasitic (100 tablets)	0.18	0.33 (August)	83
Multivitamin (100 tablets)[a]	1.30	3.00 (August)	131
Ophthalmological solution (one bottle)	0.80	0.95 (August)	19

| Antihypersentive (100 tablets) | 2.00 | | 3.00 (May) | 50 |
| Average increase | | | | 52 |

Medicines purchased from wholesalers by El Rio communal pharmacy			1984	
Aspirin (100 tablets)	0.85	(May)	1.20 (Dec.)	41
Antitetanic (10 blisters)	15.00	(Feb.)	34.40 (June)	129
Baralgina (100 tablets) (antispasmodic and analgesic)	12.40	(March)	32.00 (June)	174
B_{12} complex (10 blisters)	30.00	(March)	55.00 (May)	58
Belladol (1 bottle) (antispasmodic-anticholinergic)	1.50	(April)	3.00 (Sept.)	100
Cheracol (antibiotic) (100 capsules)	10.90	(March)	30.10 (August)	176
Dolo-Tanderil (100 capsules) (analgesic, anti-inflamatory)	24.40	(March)	60.00 (August)	146
Mejoral (analgesic) (100 tablets)	3.50	(May)	5.75 (July)	64
Neomelubrina (analgesic) (100 tablets)	8.50	(March)	18.00 (July)	112
Tylenol (100 tablets)	5.75	(March)	6.90 (June)	20
Winasorb (analgesic) (100 tablets)	11.00	(April)	15.40 (Sept.)	40
Average increase				99

[a] After the initial increase, the prices of these drugs were lowered slightly.

APPENDIX 3.
Comparative prices of selected drugs available to the public through PROMESE and commercial channels, Dominican Republic 1985 (in US dollars)*

	PROMESE price (generic)	Commercial price (brand-name)
Ampicilina 500 mg (capsule)	0.13	0.50
Ampicilina 250 mg (capsule)	0.05	0.22
Cloranfenicol 250 mg (capsule)	0.02	0.30
Eritromicina 250 mg (capsule)	0.08	0.33
Penicilina v-400 250 gr (tablet)	0.05	0.33
B complex (tablet)	0.01	0.13
Diazepam 5 mg (pill)	0.01	0.12
Diazepam 5 mg (injection)	0.30	0.56
Furosemide 40 mg (pill)	0.01	0.15
Acetaminofen 500 mg (tablet)	0.05	0.07
Ergometrina 0.2 mg (tablet)	0.01	0.08
Hidrocortisone 5 gr (creme)	0.37	1.87
Acetil salicilic acid (tablet)	0.01	0.06
Aminofilina 120 cc (syrup)	0.97	1.30
Prometazina 10 mg (tablet)	0.02	0.22
Propanolol 40 mg (tablet)	0.05	0.15
Reserpina 0.125 mg (tablet)	0.10	0.42
Tetraciclina 250 mg (capsule)	0.03	0.07
Insuline fast V-100	5.75	13.00

* *Source*: PROMESE, Medicamentos Genéricos de Venta Aquí, 1985.

NOTES

1. The impact of improvements in transportation on the utilization of health services during the second half of last century in the United States has been discussed by Starr (1982: 65ff). Today in the Dominican Republic, the availability of international transportation makes it possible for many Dominicans of all social classes to receive care overseas. For example, the Dominican Communist Party makes arrangements for an unknown number of Dominicans to receive high technology medical care in Cuba. It is estimated that about 8% of the Dominican population resides in the United States, mostly in the New York area; some Dominicans with the assistance of their overseas relatives also travel to this country to seek care.
2. As Patel (1981) observed these percentages are based on factory prices and do not include the profits of importers, wholesalers and retailers. In the Dominican Republic, retail prices for some medicines could be ten times higher than factory prices.
3. Instituto de Investigaciones Económicas, 1968: 108 for Venezuela; Secretaría de Economía y Hacienda, 1970: 147, 153, 159, 165 for Honduras; Bureau of Labor Statistics, 1967: 44–63 for Puerto Rico; Pérez Mera and Cross Beras, 1981: 70, 79 for Dominican Republic; Katz, 1974: 13 for Argentina.
4. The 1950 figure is from Secretariado Técnico de la Presidencia de la República (1980: 3) and the 1981 from the national census of the same year.
5. In a different study (Ugalde and Homedes: in preparation) that we carried out in all rural clinics (39) of a health region we found that the year of service is not completed at the same clinic. Frequently, within the year a physician is assigned to two or three clinics.
6. The 1970 figure is from (Pérez Mera 1979: 124) and the 1985 is from the Budget Law. Commonly, only part of the approved budget is transferred to SESPAS, the cuts can be as high as 10 or 15% of the approved budget.
7. The precise number of hamlets is difficult to determine in dispersed rural areas in the Dominican Republic. The national census identification of hamlets does not coincide with that of the local population. Local people are not in agreement among themselves: for example, if a group of neighbors decide to change the neighborhood into a hamlet the change may be acceptable to some and not to others.
8. In 1984, due to the exorbitant price increase of pharmaceutical products (see footnote no 9) SESPAS and INESPRE, the government agency in charge of price stabilization, decided to organize a program to procure and import large amounts of essential drugs, many of which were generic. The new program known as Essential Medicines Program (PROMESE) organized non-profit pharmacies in public hospitals, in urban centers and in the government-owned sugar mills. PROMESE's prices were so low (see Appendix 2) that private pharmacies requested the government's permission to buy from PROMESE. The permission was granted and the government established an official rate of profits for the medicines purchased from PROMESE. However, as of this writing, PROMESE had not been able to handle distribution in rural areas. Perhaps in the future, PROMESE could extend its services to rural clinics and lower even more the costs of drugs for the peasantry.
9. The reason for the increase was the removal of the public subsidy that the pharmaceutical imports had enjoyed from the time the peso began its devaluation. The subsidy was removed under pressures from the IMF.
10. We learned too late that two useful statistics on utilization would have been the number of weekly consultations divided by the number of working days in the week, and the number of weekly consultations divided by the number of days worked in the week. The latter would have removed the influence of absenteeism.
11. At the clinic of El Rio, in 1984 the number of yearly consultations per person was 0.8, below the norm of 2 recommended by the Pan American Health Organization. However, the number of yearly consultations should also include referral and self-referral consultations. Our information for 1983 suggests that the number of consultations outside the rural clinic

was higher than those in the clinic, and therefore, the total number of yearly consultations per person in El Rio could be close to the norm. If we take into account the barriers posed by rural dispersion we can conclude that these statistics are very satisfactory.
12. This example raises some doubts about the wisdom of primary health care policies which placed the responsibility of selecting the health promoter within the communities.

REFERENCES

Alexander, C. A. and Shwaswamy, M. K.
    1971   Traditional Healers in a Region of Mysore. Social Science and Medicine 5: 595–601.
Alland, A.
    1970   Adaptation in Cultural Evolution. An Approach to Medical Anthropology. New York: Columbia University Press.
Bhatia, J. C. et al.
    1975   Traditional Healers and Modern Medicine. Social Science and Medicine 9: 15–21.
Bureau of Labor Statistics
    1967   Income and Expenditures of the Families. San Juan: Department of Labor, Commonwealth of Puerto Rico.
Cunningham, C. E.
    1970   Thai 'injection doctors', antibiotic mediators. Social Science and Medicine 4: 1–4.
Dunlop, D. W.
    1983   Health Care Financing: Recent Experiences in Africa. Social Science and Medicine 17: 2017–25.
Eoff, G. M.
    1980   Vista socio-cultural de la salud rural y la entrega de servicios de salud: mito y realidad. United States Agency for International Development, Honduras (unpublished document).
Ferguson, A. E.
    1981   Commercial Pharmaceutical Medicine and Medicalization: A Case Study from El Salvador. Culture, Medicine and Psychiatry 5: 105–34.
Gereffi, G.
    1983   The Pharmaceutical Industry and Dependency in the Third World.
    Princeton: Princeton University Press.
Hardon, A. P.
    1987   The Use of Modern Pharmaceuticals in a Filipino Village: Doctors' Prescription and Self Medication. Social Science and Medicine 25: 277–92.
Instituto de Investigaciones Sociales
    1968   Presupuestos familiares a índice de costo de la vida en la ciudad de Valera. Merida, Venezuela: Facultad de Economía.
Jones, A. D.
    1977   Medical Practice and Tribal Communities. *In* Ciba Foundation Symposium, Health and Disease in Tribal Societies vol. 49: 243–55. Oxford: Elsevier.
Katz, J. M.
    1974   Oligopolio, firmas nacionales y empresas multinacionales. La industria framacéutica argentina. Buenos Aires: Siglo XXI Editores.
Lall, S.
    1981   Economic Considerations in the Provision and Use of Medicines. *In* Blum, R. et al. (eds.) Pharmaceutical and Health Policies. International Perspectives on Provisions and Control of Medicines. New York: Holmes and Meier, pp. 186–210.
Lesbow, R. et al.
    1983   Project Evaluation Summary Specific to the Rural Health Delivery System (SBS) in

the Dominican Republic. Evaluation and Recommendations. Boston: Management Science for Health (unpublished document).

López Acuña, D.
1980 La salud desigual en México. Mexico: Siglo XXI Editores.

Martin, P.
1981 An Assessment of Factors which Affect Community Participation in the Honduran Health System. Washington DC: American Public Health Association (unpublished document).

Melrose, D.
1982 Bitter Pills. Medicines and the Third World Poor. London: Oxfam.
1983 Double Deprivation: Public and Private Drug Distribution from the Perspective of the Third World Poor. World Development 11: 181–6.

Menéndez, E. L.
1981 Poder, stratificación y salud. Análisis de las condiciones sociales y económicas de la enfermedad en Yucatán. Mexico, D.F.: Ediciones de la Casa Chata.

Patel, M. S.
1981 The Global Costs of Primary Health Care. Man and Development 2: 105–129.
1983 Drug Costs in Developing Countries and Policies to Reduce Them.
World Development 11: 195–204.

Pérez Mera, A.
1978 La salud en República Dominicana, primera parte. Estudios Sociales 11: 201–34.
1979 La salud en República Dominicana, tercera parte. Estudios Sociales 12: 119–47.

Pérez Mera, A. and Cross Beras, J.
1981 Patrones de consumo y estructura social en Santo Domingo. Santo Domingo: Fondo para el Avance de las Ciencias Sociales.

Secretaría de Economía y Hacienda
1970 Encuesta de ingresos y gastos familiares, 1967–1968. Tegucigalpa, Honduras: Dirección General de Estadística y Censos.

Secretariado Técnico de la Presidencia
1980 República Dominicana en Cifras 1980. Santo Domingo: Oficina Nacional de Estadística.

Segall, M.
1983 Planning and Politics of Resource Allocation for Primary Health Care: Promotion of Meaningful National Policy. Social Science and Medicine 17: 1947–60.

Silverman, M. et al.
1982 Prescriptions for Death. The Drugging of the Third World. Berkeley: University of California Press.

Starr, P.
1982 The Social Transformation of American Medicine. New York: Basic Books.

Taylor D.
1986 The Pharmaceutical Industry and Health in the Third World. Social Science and Medicine. 22 (11): 1141–50.

Tuñón, C. et al.
1981 Informe sobre el estado actual de los comités de salud. Análisis preliminar y estrategias. Panama: Ministerio de Salud Pública (unpublished document).

Ugalde, A.
1984 Where There is a Doctor: Strategies to Increase Productivity at Lower Costs. The Economics of Rural Health Care in the Dominican Republic. Social Science and Medicine 19: 441–50.

Ugalde, A. et al.
1986 Do Patients Understand Their Physicians? Prescription Compliance in a Rural Area of the Dominican Republic. Health Policy and Planning: 1: 250–259.

Ugalde, A. and Homedes, N.
 (in preparation) The Human Factor: Physicians and the Productivity of Rural Health Clinics in the Dominican Republic.
US Department of Health, Education and Welfare.
 1974 Syncresis. The Dynamics of Health. An Analytic Series on the Interactions of Health and Socioeconomic Development. Washington, DC: Office of International Health. Division of Planning and Evaluation.
Van der Geest, S.
 1982a The Efficiency of Inefficiency. Medicine Distribution in South Cameroon. Social Science and Medicine 16: 2145–53.
 1982b The Illegal Distribution of Western Medicines in Developing Countries: Pharmacists, Drugs Pedlars, Injection Doctors, and Others. A Bibliographic Exploration. Medical Anthropology 6: 197–219.
 1987 Self-care and the Informal Sale of Drugs in South Cameroon. Social Science and Medicine 25: 293–306
Wartensleben, A.
 1983 Major Issues Concerning Pharmaceutical Policies in the Third World. World Development 11: 169–175.
Wyatt, H. V.
 1984 The Popularity of Injections in the Third World: Origins and Consequences for Poliomyelitis. Social Science and Medicine 19: 911–5.

HELMUT KLOOS, BERHANU GETAHUN, ASREGID TEFERI, KEFALO GEBRE TSADIK & SOLOMON BELAY

BUYING DRUGS IN ADDIS ABABA: A QUANTITATIVE ANALYSIS

INTRODUCTION[1]

Since the Ethiopian revolution in 1974 some pharmacies in Addis Ababa and most drug importers/wholesales have been nationalized as part of restructuring the national health care system under the principles of centralized planning and socialism.[2] In addition to price control, there has been a curtailment of the types of drugs private retailers can sell and a prohibition on treating clients in retail shops. The remaining private pharmacies and druggist shops are to be nationalized with further extension of government control over the private sector of the economy. In 1984 we examined the utilization of private and government pharmacies in Addis Ababa by different socioeconomic groups. We found a distinct preference for government retailers, largely due to their lower drug prices and larger inventories. Due to the usual limitations of pharmacy based studies, particularly sampling bias, we recommended that population based studies of drug retailing and utilization be carried out (Kloos et al. 1986a, 1986b). The present paper is based on integrated household surveys in four *kebele* (urban dwellers' associations) and additional pharmacy based studies in December 1984 and April/May 1985. The objective of this study is to examine relationships between disease prevalence, disease perception, decision making in drug selection and geographic and socioeconomic accessibility of retailers in drug purchasing in Addis Ababa. Case histories of pharmacy clients are included to complement the statistical data. Together they allow us to view drug purchasing within its urban context. The paper thus emphasizes the sociogeographical and cultural character of the retailing and use of drugs.

URBAN SETTING, DISEASE AND HEALTH CARE

Addis Ababa has a population of 1.5 million (Office of the Population and Housing Census Commission 1984: 46). It is located at an elevation of 2,400 meters in the humid, temperate highland zone characterized by warm days and cool nights. Founded in the late nineteenth century, Addis Ababa has experienced rapid growth, generated primarily by rural-urban migration. In 1978 nearly half of the population was still reported to have been born in rural areas (Hailu 1982). Rapid urban growth resulted in shortages and deficiencies in housing, social services and environmental sanitation, the improvement of which is given high priority by the socialist government.

In spite of higher income levels and better health facilities in Addis Ababa than in rural Ethiopia, certain ecological and socioeconomic factors create serious health hazards for many urban residents. During the two rainy seasons (March-April and June-September) common colds may reach epidemic proportion. Contamination of the environment, together with enhanced survival of bacteria, viruses and free-living parasites and insect vectors, create additional health hazards (Stinzing et al. 1977, 1981). More than 60% of all dwellings in Addis Ababa were considered substandard (Mulugeta 1985) and mean water consumption per household was less than one-third that of Nairobi households (Shiferaw 1984: 32). The few epidemiological studies show that infectious diseases, particularly intestinal parasitic, viral and bacterial infections, acute and chronic respiratory infections, liver diseases and skin diseases constitute the bulk of cases seen at local hospitals and clinics (Dotsenko 1975; Freij et al. 1977; Tadicheff et al. 1981; Manzur 1981; Lester and Tsega 1976). The influence of urbanization on health in Addis Ababa and other African cities was examined by Parry (1979), who noted a rise in chronic noninfectious and venereal diseases, also indicated by other studies (Haragewoin 1982; Teklu 1980, 1982, 1984; Kitaw et al. 1982; Plorde 1981; Olsson 1979; Osterwald and Gebre Medhin 1978; Friedman and Wright 1977). The relationship between malnutrition and infectious disease has also been well established for Addis Ababa residents (Brown and Gilman 1980; Freij et al. 1979; Gebre Medhin and Gobezie 1975).

Health care in Addis Ababa is pluralistic, as in other African cities. It involves 'modern', 'transitional' and 'traditional' medicine. The modern health care system consists of government (Ministry of Health, Addis Ababa Municipality and other government agencies) and privately owned facilities. Ethiopia's current health policy advocates a primary health care approach, including the provision of health services to the whole population, decentralization and expansion of health services in rural areas, emphasis on disease prevention, community participation and self-reliance (Ministry of Health 1978: 14). The general health services are organized at six levels, with community health services and health stations forming the broad base of this pyramidal structure, health centers and rural/medium hospitals at the middle levels and regional and central referral hospitals at the apex (Ministry of Health 1986: ix). New curricula for the training of health workers have been designed and traditional birth attendants are trained by the Ministry of Health to increase the number of health cadres and to solve pressing health problems in line with the National Democratic Revolutionary Programme. The objective of integrating traditional medicine with the modern health facilities, considered necessary due to the reliance of 80% of the population on indigenous healing methods (Ministry of Health 1978: 14, 16) has not been accomplished. This is largely due to deep-seated antagonism, and conceptual disagreement between Ethiopian healers and Western trained physicians. It has resulted in further polarization and has driven traditional healers underground.

A new Health Sector Perspective Plan (1984–1994) was developed by the Ministry of Health in 1984 as part of the Ten-Year Comprehensive Plan to facilitate health services development. An immediate outcome of that Plan was the creation of new central referral hospitals in four regional capital cities and the reduction of such hospitals to two in Addis Ababa. In spite of the broad decentralization effort by the Ministry of Health, disproportionately large amounts of the national health resources continue to be allocated for the capital city. In 1983/84, 3257 out of 11,296 hospital beds nation wide, 244 of 767 physicians, 101 of 194 health officers, 652 of 1960 nurses, 119 of 217 pharmacists and 75 of 98 pharmacies and drug shops were in Addis Ababa, which represents only 3% of the population. This unequal health service distribution required a health budget allocation of 19.81 Birr (US $10) *per capita* for Addis Ababa, compared to 1.89 Birr for the rest of the country (Ministry of Health 1986: 9–10).

Health services in Addis Ababa also include 120 health stations in schools and other government agencies, and two military hospitals. Community health services accessible to the public have been developed by many *kebele*. They provide immunizations and care for children and mothers (administered by Ministry of Health teams), environmental sanitation (administered by the Addis Ababa Municipality and involving community participation) and health education by *kebele* health committees. Issuance of letters to poor residents permitting them to obtain free medical services, including drugs, and regulation and control of injection doctors and traditional healers are additional functions of the *kebele* health committees. The ten health stations, seven health centers and twelve public hospitals operated by the Ministry of Health provide preventive and curative services to a large proportion of the city population (Kloos et al. 1987). The hospital referral system has been found to be inefficient, however, particularly for patients from rural areas (Meche and Woldeab 1984).

Drug manufacturing, import/whole and retail establishments have increasingly come under government control. The single drug manufacturing firm in Ethiopia and several importers/wholesalers were nationalized and merged in the Ethiopian Pharmaceuticals and Medical Supplies Corporation (EPHARMCOR). Increase in import taxes resulted in the increase of Ethiopia's share of drug production from 18.5% in 1980 to 31.0% in 1983 (Bedassa 1984). By 1986, 26 of the 57 pharmacies (but none of the 18 drug shops) had been nationalized and more government takeovers were expected. Pharmacies are better suited for government expansion of health services than drug shops since they are staffed by university trained pharmacists and are allowed to compound drugs. The 15 rural drug vendor shops which were licenced by the Ministry of Health to sell a few non-prescription drugs in the residential suburbs of Addis Ababa contribute little to meeting the drug needs of the population.

Thirteen of the 24 government pharmacies were operated by the Ministry of Health in hospitals. Six of the remaining eleven government pharmacies were operated by the Municipality and five by the Ministry of Health. These eleven pharmacies apparently sell as many drugs as the 34 privately owned pharmacies, based on the sales volume of several retailers (Kloos et al. 1986a). The greater use of government pharmacies by the public is largely due to a combination of their lower prices (10–20% less than in private shops), the larger number of drugs they carry and their location on major traffic routes. Both the Ministry of Health and the Municipality reduced the profit margin of retailed drugs from 40% to 25%, with further price reductions anticipated in the future. Furthermore, they supplied their own pharmacies with, but prohibited private retailers to sell, certain prescription drugs, including some higher antibiotics, insulin, tuberculosis drugs, several tonics and psychotropic drugs. Government are supplied by the state-owned EPHARMCOR corporation but private retailers depend for some of their drugs on private importers/wholesalers. The latter have come under increased government pressure through taxation and restrictions on the number of brand drugs they can import since the Ministry of Health wants to develop an essential drug list in line with primary health care objectives.[3]

As a result of these developments most private retailers either continue certain sales practices from pre-revolutionary times or resort to new strategies to stay in business. These include the sale of prescription drugs without prescription, sale of large amounts of drugs to individual clients, mostly illegal peddlers and injection doctors (Kloos 1974), employment of family members and relatives, and reductions in sales prices. Illegal sales practices are still rare in government pharmacies, which pay fixed salaries to their personnel, regardless of sales volume and are subject to frequent internal and external audits (Kloos et al. 1986a).

Pharmacies and drug shops, by far the most important sources of drugs for the Addis Ababa population, offer several distinct advantages over hospitals and clinics. In addition to being more accessible to residents because of the fast service they provide and the absence of long waiting lines, they stay open longer hours, their personnel readily advise clients on what drugs to purchase and many of them sell prescription drugs without prescription.

Private, illegal clinics, operated by non-physicians and cut off from wholesalers also depend on retailers for drugs. Registered private clinics operated by physicians or health officers, by contrast, issue prescriptions which their patients can fill in any pharmacy or drug shop. Moreover, as part of the recent emphasis by the Ministry of Health on primary health care, retired health officers, dressers and other health auxilliary workers are now permitted by the *kebele* to give injections and other basic services. They too obtain their drugs from commercial drug retailers.

Traditional healers and midwives are permitted to work only in collaboration with the official health services. However, the still widely used, competitive and culturally deeply rooted traditional healers have shown little cooperation with the official health services. Addis Ababa residents are well aware of the illegal status of traditional health practices by professional *debtera* (church scribe/healers), *woggesha* (bone setters) and *medhaniyd awaki* (expert herbalists) and are thus reluctant to discuss using them. Household remedies, involving a large number of herbs (Kloos 1976), continue to play an important role in the treatment of lesser ailments and as a treatment option for many other illnesses.

'Transitional health care', including injectionists, drug peddlers, 'dressers' and medical technicians working illegally out of their homes also continues to meet some of the health needs of Addis Ababa's population. Thus residents have a wide range of health care options at their disposal.

METHODOLOGY

Data on drug retailer use and drug purchasing behavior were collected from five sources. *First*, an interview questionnaire was administered by university geography student to 1,143 clients of two government (municipality) pharmacies. One is located in the high-density slum environment of the Merkato Market area and the other in the more suburban, socioeconomically mixed Mekakelegna District. Information gathered about clients buying medicines concerned their residence, the place they visited before coming to the pharmacy, level of education, age, sex, type of illness to be treated (in Amharic), type and price of drugs purchased, and reason for purchasing specific drugs. Proprietory and generic names of drugs and cost of purchases were determined by visual inspection of drug containers receipts. *Second*, unstructured interviews were carried out with several local pharmacists, clients (case studies) and officials of the Ministry of Health and Addis Ababa Municipality. *Third*, personnel in the two study pharmacies interviewed 220 clients on what drugs, if any, they had used in the past or knew about for the same illness or disease. This information was used to evaluate drug selection. *Fourth*, direct observations were made of drug purchasing behavior in pharmacies to obtain further information on drug selection and purchasing and on the operation and management of retail shops.

Fifth, a questionnaire interview survey was carried out among 10% random samples of all households in four of Addis Ababa's 285 *kebele* to evaluate the link between illness episodes and use of pharmaceutical drugs in a representative population. A total of 284 households with 1,775 people was studied. In order to control for differences in socioeconomic level and location in the city, one central inner city, two peripheral and one semi-peripheral *kebele* were selected.

The prevalence of acute illnesses and their treatment were studied retrospectively for the 30-day period preceding the survey, and chronic illnesses and their treatment for six months. Disease symptoms were classified into 'possible diagnoses' using the lay health reporting system developed by the World Health Organization (1978) and adapted for Ethiopia (Tekle-Haimanot 1985). This permitted the establishment of relationships between symptom clusters and multiple illness in the same person and treatment behavior, a persistent methodological problem in health surveys (Kroeger 1985).

ILLNESS AND UTILIZATION OF MEDICAL RESOURCES

Table I shows the distribution of households with ill persons by education of their head (for all four *kebele*). The percentage of households with ill persons and number of ill persons per household were similar for all education categories. Differences in illness prevalence among the four *kebele* are not shown in the table, but the lowest socioeconomic classes carry the heaviest disease burden. This is indicated in our sample by the greater prevalence of more severe acute and chronic infectious diseases and malnutrition in poorer families and neighborhoods and the more frequent reporting of the relatively mild but ubiquitous common colds by more affluent households. Relatively greater reluctance of poorer and less educated families to discuss their health problems with the interviewers tended to reduce the differences in actual illness prevalence among the four *kebele*. Repeated probing improved reporting somewhat. Several respondents, when asked about their reluctance to discuss their health problems, answered that this might bring illness upon them and also that many of their illnesses were so common and persisting that it would be useless to discuss them.

When data for the 351 ill persons in the four *kebele* were aggregated in eight illness categories, by type of health resources used, a distinct pattern emerged (Table II). Acute upper-respiratory infections were most common (34.5%), followed by intestinal infections (18.0%, and chronic non-infectious diseases (13.0%), particularly gastritis (*chequara*), heart conditions (*lib dikam*), hypertension (*dembizzat*) and diabetes (*sikuar*). Next in frequency came 'other infections' (10.4%), especially skin diseases (scabies or *ekek*, and ringworm or *chirt*), infectious hepatatis (*yewof bashita*), eye and ear infections and venereal diseases (primarily gonorrhea or *chebt*, and syphilis or *kitign*). These were followed by chronic respiratory infections (7.8%), especially tuberculosis or *samba*, bronchitis and asthma or *assim*, nutritional deficiencies and 'others' (3.7% each). For all major illness categories except acute upper respiratory infections (which were reported most frequently by the most highly educated families), the highest prevalence rates were reported by the least educated groups. Venereal diseases, tuberculosis, leprosy and malnutrition were apparently underreported, as described below.

TABLE I
Households studied, prevalence of illness and drugs stored at home in four *kebele*, by education of head of household

	Education				
	Illiterate or literacy campaign education (n=187)	Grade school (n=91)	High school (n=42)	University (n=31)	Total (n=351)
Total number of households studied	128	92	36	28	284
Percentage of households with ill persons	76.6	68.5	61.1	71.4	71.5
Number of persons in sample	772	612	234	157	1775
Number of ill persons	187	95	38	31	351
Percent ill persons	24.2	15.5	16.2	19.7	19.8
Number of households storing drugs	19	18	9	16	62
Number of drugs stored	32	29	26	57	144
Mean number of drugs stored per household	0.25	0.32	0.72	2.04	0.5

Overall, most ill persons and their families were said to have done nothing in response to illness (22.5%). Failure to seek medical treatment was attributed mostly to knowledge of the transitory nature of the seasonal upper respiratory infections, including influenza (*gunfan*), common cold (*berd*) and tonsilitis (*gororo* or *tonsil*). Lack of money and the widespread view that the use of drugs cannot eliminate nutritional deficiencies were other reasons. A few persons in the slums mentioned lack of transportation to government clinics or hospitals, where they could have obtained free service. Pharmaceuticals purchased either with or without prescription in pharmacies, drug shops, small rural medicine vendor shops, or in small neighborhood shops represented the most frequently used health resource (21.0%), followed by the use of government clinics and hospitals (17.0%), household remedies (12.8%), private clinics (12.3%), holy water (*tsebel*) from churches and holy springs (4.3%), and drugs stored at home, injection doctors, traditional healers and small shops (all less than 2%). Only 5.2% of the 423 contacts with health services constituted combined or successive treatments for the same illness episode, probably due to underreporting. Treatment for diseases carrying a social stigma, particularly venereal diseases and tuberculosis were crossly underreported. Also the seasonal respiratory infections, cultural syndromes, epilepsy and mental illnesses were underreported. Common colds, if treated at all with either traditional or modern medicines, were

TABLE II

Health resources employed by 351 ill persons in four *kebele*, by illness group

Health resources used	Acute UR infections[1]	Chronic respiration infections	Headache	Intestinal parasitics, diarrhea, or stomach ache	Other infectious diseases	Non-infectious diseases	Nutritional deficiencies	Others	Total (percent)
Self-medication:									
Drugs from pharmacies	18[2]	3	24	34	21	22	19	6	21.0
Drugs stored at home	2	0	3	0	0	2	0	6	1.4
Household remedies	16	9	16	17	9	9	0	0	12.8
Nearby shop or traditional medicine shop	1	0	0	0	2	2	0	0	0.9
Government clinic or hospital	8	5	14	13	18	32	31	31	17.0
Private clinic	11	9	5	16	21	9	6	19	12.3
Injection doctor	2	0	0	5	0	0	0	0	1.7
Traditional healer	0	0	3	1	0	5	0	0	1.2
Holy water (*isebel*)	0	21	11	0	9	5	0	0	4.3
Did nothing	40	9	14	7	16	16	38	31	22.5
Combination	6	33	37	76	44	55	16	16	5.2
Total no. of actions taken (percent)	146 (34.5)	33 (7.8)	37 (8.7)	76 (18.0)	44 (10.4)	55 (13.0)	16 (3.8)	16 (3.8)	423 (100)

[1] Upper-respiratory infections.
[2] Percentage of all illness episodes in this illness category; multiple illnesses in the same person are included.

commonly considered to be a minor health problem not worth mentioning. The cultural syndromes *buda* (evil eye) and *zar* (possession), on the other hand, are serious afflictions few people discuss with strangers.

Of the 87 individuals who reportedly used commercial drug retailers, 61 (70%) had used government pharmacies and the remaining 26 private pharmacies, drug shops and rural drug vendors.

Most household remedies consisted of the use of herbs for all types of infections and headaches, and butter for constipation and sometimes cough. The withdrawal of certain foods such as the pepper spiced *wot* (sauce) was resorted to in the treatment of some intestinal problems, including gastritis.

Self-medication with drugs purchased from drug retailers for illnesses that were traditionally treated with household remedies, including all infectious and most chronic diseases, reflects the degree to which pharmaceuticals have made inroads on the lay use of herbal medicines. This effect was most pronounced among the upper education classes. That new remedies are gradually evolving was indicated by the use of gasoline as a disinfectant in wound treatment and abortions and of tetracycline powder (from capsules) mixed with butter for eye infections. Other reinterpretations of the use of commercial drugs include the use of injectable penicilline as eye drops and of oral antibiotic capsules (powder) for external wound treatment. It is not known to what extent these modifications in drug usage reflect economic considerations or cultural perception of these antibiotics.

Small general shops in the neighborhood were used primarily by less educated, poorer people for aspirin, Algon and other analgesics and antipyretics for upper-respiratory infections, headache, fever and rheumatism (*kurtmat*). Although these shops are usually nearer than the official drug retailers, they are seldom used since they carry only two or three drug items, are more expensive than drug retailers and cannot advise clients authoritatively on drug use.

The use of drugs varied for different illnesses and education groups. The highest use rates were recorded for non-infectious diseases, stomach ache, diarrhea, parasites and headache among households with university educated heads (45–67%) and the lowest rates (0–15%) for nutritional deficiencies, headache and acute upper-respiratory infections among the least educated families.

The proportion of households storing drugs and number of drugs stored per household increased sharply with education of household head. Whereas only 19 of 128 (14.8%) households in the illiteracy/literacy campaign category reportedly stored drugs, 9 of 36 (25.0%) households headed by high school graduates and 16 of 26 (61.5%) with university graduates did so. Similarly, mean number of drugs stored per household increased from 0.25 in the former to 2.04 in the latter (Table I). Kitaw (1984a, 1984b) found similarly small numbers of drugs stored by Addis Ababa households and concluded that the problem of drug hoarding, widespread in countries providing free medical services (Van der Geest 1982; Fraser 1985) and in more affluent societies (Slater et al. 1986) does not exist in Ethiopia. Type of drugs stored varied also with level of education. More educated households stored mostly analgesics, expectorants, decongestants and antacids and less educated households, antibiotics. These differences reflect prevailing diseases in different socioeconomic environments together with differences in disease perception and affordability of drugs. The fear that stored drugs lose their potency after several weeks or months and that they may be even harmful was most commonly expressed by less educated households. Concern over old medicines was also expressed in the study of pharmacy preferences of clients. Thus an important reason Addis Ababa residents prefer government over private retailers is that the former have generally fresher drugs due to the more rapid turnover of inventories (Kloos et al. 1986a).

According to Kitaw (1984b) who studied self (lay) care in two rural Ethiopian communities and in Addis Ababa, the major reasons for widespread practice of self-care are the perception that the illness is minor or beyond cure, poverty and urbanization but not the unavailability of modern practitioners. He found that self-care is often the first measure taken in illness, which, if not successful, is usually followed by consultation with a practitioner of modern medicine. This pattern indicates that self-medication will continue to be an important first and last step in illness treatment in Addis Ababa.

THE TRIP TO BUY DRUGS

Information on what transportation means people use, how far they travel to obtain drugs and which retailers they patronize can assist health planners in evaluating constraints in drug utilization and in the location of new retail shops (Kloos et al. 1986a). Most health services used by the study population were located within a 3 km radius of their homes. Preference for nearby facilities indicates the importance of distance constraints on the utilization of modern, transitional and traditional health resources. Our previous studies on pharmacy utilization in Addis Ababa showed that few walked more than 3 km (Kloos et al. 1986a). Trips to more distant hospitals were due to their specialized services and extended trips to some pharmacies and clinics were attributed mainly to daily commuting and shopping patterns of respondents. Other factors included patronization of facilities based on social and ethnic ties to pharmacists, shop owners and practitioners, and contractual credit arrangements between employers and government health care facilities. Type of transportation other than walking did not influence distance travelled but major differences were noted between the low and high socioeconomic *kebele*. Whereas practically all trips in the former were made either on foot or by using taxis and public buses, half of the trips in the latter were made with private cars and nearly all of the others with taxis and buses. In poorer families distance prevented many patients without own transportation means from seeking treatment outside their *kebele*, particularly those who were unable to walk.

According to the results of our pharmacy-based surveys on client travel in 1984, most clients made the trip to pharmacies as part of multiple purpose trips to or from places of employment, shopping or social visits. These places were, on the average, located significantly nearer to retailers than their places of residence. Using the results of the 1984 and 1985 surveys in two municipality pharmacies, these relationships are confirmed cartographically at the *keftegna* level in Figures 1 and 2. Similarly, the larger number of clients using the pharmacy in the huge and very popular Merkato Market and the greater distances they travelled than clients of the Mekakelegna District pharmacy indicate the role of multipurpose trips as a means of saving transportation cost and time.

Distance effect on drug purchasing was also examined by comparing the types of drugs purchased at the two study pharmacies by clients living in the same districts. No significant differences were noted ($p<$less than 0.05) when applying the nonparametric Mann-Witney test. Clients from rural areas, however, purchased relatively more 'other antibiotics' and fewer taenicides than those from Addis Ababa. These differences appear to be due to the scarcity of broad spectrum antibiotics, the lower consumption of beef (and thus presumably lower infection rates with *Taenia saginata*) and the greater use of herbal taenicides in rural areas.

Seasonal variation in the number and type of drugs purchased could be discerned in the same two pharmacies. The consistently greater use of drugs, particularly antibiotics and upper respiratory drugs in May (during an extended rainy season in 1985) than December (dry season) appears to be due primarily to seasonal variation in diarrheal and upper respiratory disease transmission. The decline in the number of clients from rural areas in May may be explained largely by the agricultural calendar which demands that crops be sown and cultivated during the rainy season, leaving little time for travel to the cities. The nearly constant sale of taenicides, in December and May, by contrast, is due to the common use of raw beef (*brindo*) and the customary use of taenicides every two months, a practice that has been described in the earliest travel reports from Ethiopia (Pankhurst 1969). The increasing use of pharmaceutical taenicides, including dichlorophen, Yomesan, Kossopharm and several others has made some inroads on the use of indigenous taenicides, including the flowers of the *kosso* (*Hagenia abyssinica*) tree, the seed pods of the *enkoko* (*Embelia schimperi*), *kechemo* (*Myrsine africana*) and *metere* (*Glinus lotoides*) bushes and the bark of the bisanna tree (*Croton macrostachys*) in Addis Ababa and other urban centers. However, these traditional purges are still widely used in rural areas (Kloos 1976). The periodic use of taenicides is so much a part of the lifeways of the Addis Ababa population that it is hardly considered a medical treatment. This was also

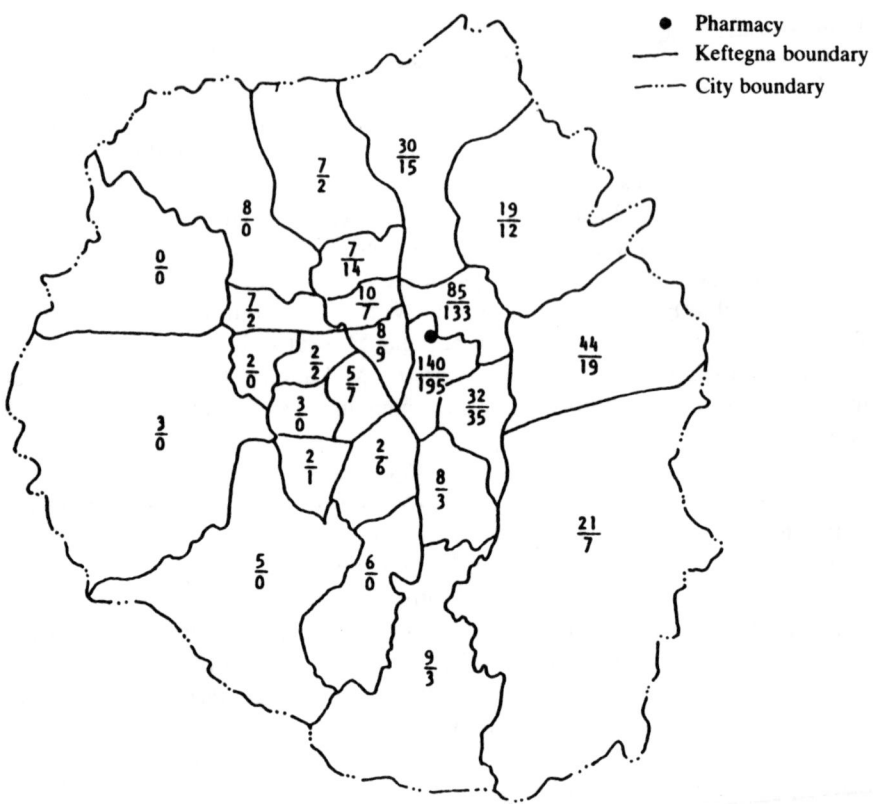

Number of clients living in the individual *keftegna* are shown above the line; number of clients starting the trip to the pharmacy from the respective *kebele* are shown below the line.

Fig. 1. Place of residence and origin of trip to pharmacy, by *keftegna*: Pharmacy in Mekakelegna District.

revealed by the fact that only two households in the *kebele* survey reported having used it.

DRUG SELECTION AND PURCHASING

With increasing use of non-prescription drugs and illegally purchased prescription drugs, Addis Ababa residents are accumulating considerable knowledge of how to obtain information about suitable drugs, how to identify them and how to evaluate them for self-treatment. Individuals afflicted for the first time with an illness may consult a number of sources at different stages of a given illness or concerning different illness symptoms. Decisions on if, when and where to obtain treatment are usually made by the family. If it is decided

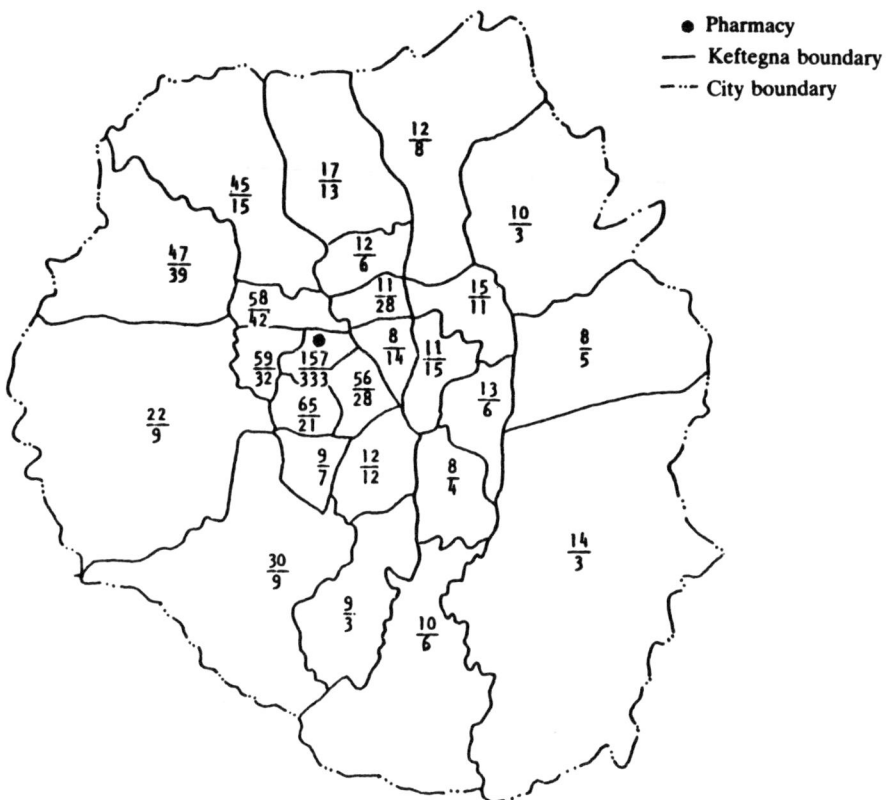

Number of clients living in the individual *keftegna* are shown above the line; number of clients starting the trip to the pharmacy from the respective *kebele* are shown below the line.

Fig. 2. Place of residence and origin of trip to pharmacy, by *keftegna*: Pharmacy in the Merkato Market.

that the most appropriate treatment option is to self-prescribe drugs, and if children are ill, then one of the parents or older siblings usually make the trip to a drug retailer of nearby general shop. Relatives, neighbors and friends may also be involved in drug selection and acquisition, especially if adults are ill and cannot leave the home. Relatives who are considered to have the financial means to assist an afflicted family are often approached for medicines or to pay for hospital and clinic bills. Knowledgable persons, including individuals who previously had the same illness and health officers, nurses, pharmacy personnel, doctor friends and minimally trained persons such as hospital guards and cleaners are consulted in self-diagnosis and drug selection. The type and number of persons consulted is influenced by the severity of the illness, previous treatment strategies attempted, and the range of information sources and treatment options available to the patient and his/her family. Frequently children, neighbors, relatives and friends are sent to drug retailers to obtain drugs for the sick person. They usually rely on oral instructions on what medications to obtain. Drug retailers in turn often give only oral drug dosage instructions. These widespread practices suggest that misinformation and improper drug use are serious problems in Addis Ababa.

Of the 682 clients interviewed in May 1985, 320 (46.9%) purchased drugs for other persons, mostly family members (78.4%), followed by friends (7.2%), other relatives (5.9%), neighbors (4.7%), and co-workers and supervisors (3.8%). Although all types of drugs were purchased for family members, they included few antibiotics for the widespread venereal diseases, largely due to the social stigma attached to gonorrhea (*chebt*) and syphilis (*kitign*), indicating that venereal disease was underreported and information on venereal disease drugs unreliable. This was also evident from the evasive answers of female clients, who commonly referred to venereal diseases as *mahitsen* (uterus disease) instead. Males talked somewhat more freely about the purchase of venereal disease drugs and commonly admitted that they had bought them for themselves or for friends. Discussions with pharmacy personnel revealed that many clients pretending to buy antibiotics for various other infections, actually obtained them for venereal diseases. The secrecy surrounding their purchase is also suggested by a study of rural drug vendors in Wollega Administrative Region. It was estimated that these small retailers saw seven times as many gonorrhea cases as all hospitals, health centers, clinics and health stations combined (Nordberg 1974:30). Multiple drug resistance, an indication of indiscriminate and unregulated use of pharmaceuticals, is common among Ethiopian gonorrhea cases, particularly in Addis Ababa (Gedebou and Tassew 1980; Dodge and Wallace 1975).

Tuberculosis drugs, antispasmodics for asthma, antihypertensive drugs and diuretics, on the other hand, were frequently purchased for family members. Heart conditions are considered particularly serious in Amharic thinking. Over pulsing of the heart as a result of exertion is thought to result in pain, fever, fatigue, mental confusion and occassionally in death (Young 1976). Multi-vitamin preparations were commonly purchased together with heart medications, both with and without prescription, in an effort to regulate and strengthen the heart.

In the selection and evaluation of self-prescribed drugs in Addis Ababa, attention is paid primarily to their efficacy and only secondarily to their side effects. Responses to the question 'Why did you select the drugs you purchased now?' are shown in Table III. Of the 422 (68.1%) clients interviewed who purchased drugs without prescription, 245 (58.1%) responded that they had used them before and found them to be effective or curative; 45 (10.7%) had consulted the pharmacist or dispenser in the same pharmacy where they purchased the drugs; 46 (10.6%) said that they had consulted with family members, friends, neighbors or colleagues at work or were instructed by them

TABLE III
Reasons for selection of specific drugs by 422 clients in two pharmacies
(self-selection of OTC and prescription drugs)

Reason given	No. of clients	Percent
I used this drug before; it was effective or cured me before	245	58.1
The pharmacist or dispenser recommended this drug	45	10.7
I always use this drug because it is effective or curative and has no side effects	32	7.5
I always use this drug because it has no side effects	14	3.3
My family, friends, neighbors or colleagues at work instructed me to purchase this drug for them	25	6.1
Friends recommended this drug	14	3.3
My family recommended this drug	5	1.2
Neighbors recommended this drug	3	0.7
Various people recommended this drug	9	2.1
I was a medical, pharmacy or biology student or had worked in a drug retail shop and I know the properties or usage of this drug	6	1.4
I like the taste of this drug	3	0.7
I do not want any other drug for this illness	8	1.9
Other reasons	13	3.8
Total	422	100

to purchase drugs for them. The large number of clients basing their selection solely on efficacy and the few clients mentioning absence of side effects reflects the concern in Amharic etiological concepts with expelling the disease agent and the associated use of powerful purgatives, emetics and fumatories. Strong medicines are expected to produce violent effects, occasionally resulting in death, and are also associated with pungent smells and unpleasant tastes. The traditional concern over the adequacy of the amount of medicines prescribed (Young 1976) and the practice of taking the whole prescription at once has frequently been associated with side effects. Particularly taenicides are used in this manner and accounts of drug poisoning resulting in death or permanent damage are widely known in the population. These effects have been confirmed by bioassays in the laboratory (Tsega et al. 1978, Arragie 1985; Rokos 1969). Use of powerful antibiotics for illnesses yielding to less potent drugs, represents another health hazard. The pharmacological action of drugs is not known to the average client and oral and written dosage instructions by pharmacy personnel are not always followed; thus children, the very old, pregnant women and drug sensitive patients in particular are at risk. Ascaricides, including Unipar, were purchased for children as young as one year, Metronidazole for a six month old girl with influenza, and codein and penicillin for influenza in three year olds. Chloramphenicol, in spite of its well known side effects (Silverman 1976: 8), was prescribed for a six month old infant with diarrhea and vomiting and for older children with common cold. Nevertheless, the acquisition of drugs with fewer side effects, such as the taenicide Taeniapassin, indicates a concern over side effects by some clients.

In an effort to study the knowledge clients had of different drugs for the same illness they had during the interviews, we asked them what drugs they had taken during previous illness episodes. Less than 40% of 200 clients interviewed had used another drug and nearly all those who did, reported having used only one other drug for the same illness. Many clients were surprised that there existed other drugs for their illness, indicating a lack of drug information in the public and little experimentation with new drugs once clients decided to use a particular one. This is also indicated by the importance of personal acquaintance with specific drugs in the selection process (Table III).

Case histories of ten pharmacy clients and clinic patients are included here to illustrate in greater detail the processes of selecting, purchasing and using drugs. These individuals were interviewed in private and government pharmacies and at their places of work. Although not necessarily representative in a statistical sense, description of their health behavior may contribute to an understanding of the context of drug purchasing and use in Addis Ababa.

Case 1

A 19-year-old male shop keeper with gonorrhea (*chebt*) and stomach ache (*hod makatel*) for the last eight months, took 18 capsules of ampicillin upon the recommendation of his neighbor soon after appearance of symptoms. He purchased the drug from a nearby private pharmacy which sold him this partial dose without prescription. After initial improvement his illness, especially his abdominal pain, became worse. He suspected gastritis (*chequara*) and decided to go to a government clinic, where venereal disease was diagnosed. He was prescribed tetracycline and Optalgin, which he purchased one week later in a government pharmacy upon receiving his monthly salary.

Case 2

A mother, a housewife with literacy campaign education and her one-year-old baby came from a town near Addis Ababa to purchase vitamin drops for the baby's diarrhea (*tekmat*) and poor appetite. She reportedly had taken the baby two weeks earlier to a private clinic in her home town, where she was given Worm Expel, an ascaricide. The diarrhea persisted and the mother went to another clinic in her community. The 'doctor' gave the baby an injection and prescribed the vitamin drops. The woman purchased them in a government pharmacy next to the bus station in Addis Ababa from where buses leave for her home town.

Case 3

A 23-year-old male, with grade school education, a trader in the Merkato Market, purchased the taenicide dichlorophen in a government pharmacy as usual every two months. He had first been infected with beef tapeworm some ten years ago. At that time he had self-diagnosed the infection from the presence of *Taenia* segments in his stool and had been advised by a friend to purchase dichlorophen as the most effective drug without side effects. He claimed that dichlorophen had always cured him and that he never used any other taenicides, either of the modern or traditional types, considering the latter to be too dangerous due to their toxicity.

Case 4

A male high school student 17 years of age had developed diarrhea three days earlier. At the suggestion of his friend he ate a beef dish (*kètfo*) with much hot pepper (*berbere*) in it. The illness persisted and the next day he purchased tetracyclin capsules in a private pharmacy, thus following the usual practice of his family in such circumstances. His severe diarrhea persisted, however, and his father suggested that he go to a government pharmacy, where prices are lower than in private shops, and seek advice from the pharmacist on what specific medicine to take. There he purchased the antidiarrheal drug Lomotil and the amoebicide Entreseptol.

Case 5

A 24-year-old male hotel worker had had vitiglio (*lemts*) for a year. For the first nine months he did nothing, hoping that it would go away by itself. When new areas became depigmentated in his face he self-diagnosed the problem as *mich* and applied the leaf juice of *damakase* (*Ocimum* sp.), a *mich medhanid* (mich medicine), with which he was familiar and which he obtained from a neighbor. For several weeks afterwards he noted some improvement but subsequently the problem worsened in spite of continued use of the medicine. After another month he decided to go to a hospital at the suggestion of a friend. Based on the diagnosis (which the patient did not know) the physician prescribed Multivitaplex Vitamin C. He chose to fill the prescription in a government pharmacy near his work place.

Case 6

A 35-year-old male, a daily laborer with literacy campaign education, developed what he himself diagnosed as gonorrhea as evidenced by burning sensation during urination and the presence of puss (*megel*) in the urine. He had been informed about the symptoms of *chebt* (gonorrhea) by a neighbor friend who had often been infected in the past. This man also advised him to purchase Penacine in a pharmacy since it had always cured him of gonorrhea. He also gave him dosage instructions. The patient purchased this drug in a private pharmacy near his work place.

Case 7

About ten years ago a 50-year-old male high school teacher was diagnosed as having asthma (*assim*). Ever since that time the same physician (the patient's family doctor) regularly prescribed Franol. During episodes of common colds he also prescribed tetracycline and ampicillin, to be taken together with the Franol. During upper-respiratory infections and when working hard physically the patient himself increased the dosage of Franol for comfort, using one tablet daily instead at the two to three day interval. He preferred to buy his drugs in a government pharmacy due to more reliable drug supply and lower prices than in private shops.

Case 8

A 52-year-old farmer from Arsi Administrative Region, who had come to Addis Ababa primarily to visit his son and to purchase some household goods, stopped in at a private pharmacy in the Merkato Market which he had patronized for many years to obtain Worm Expel for a child of his neighbor with ascariasis (*wosfat*). He had brought with him an empty package of this drug, given to him by his neighbor, to assure that he obtained the desired medicine. When told by the pharmacist that this pharmacy no longer carried this brand but that he could sell him an equally effective ascaricide (a generic drug) for a lower price, the farmer refused, saying that his neighbor would not be satisfied with any other drug, particularly since the child had a bad case of *wosfat*, requiring a strong medicine.

Case 9

A middle-aged man, said to be a local 'hakim' (injection doctor) and, according to a pharmacy sales clerk, quite wealthy, purchased under the counter from a private pharmacy two tins of tetracycline, 50 vials of injectable penicillin and five packages of cotton bandages. He refused to answer the questions of the interviewer. Seeing his client's discomfort, the pharmacy owner reprimanted the interviewer, saying that the survey harmed his business by driving away old customers.

Case 10

A 33-year-old university instructor had developed a kidney/urinary infection a year ago. He purchased ampicillin over the counter in a government pharmacy since that had been effective for other urinary infections he had had in the past. He took the normal dose recommended by the drug manufacturer. He obtained no relief, however. After a 'short time' he went to a hospital in Addis Ababa, where the physician prescribed bactrim, which reduced symptoms somewhat. When his family doctor returned from overseas two months later he went to see him in his private clinic. This physician declared that he was determined to cure him and prescribed gentamycin in spite of the expressed concern of the patient over the fact that he had already taken two antibiotics for this infection. The physician injected ten ampulles of gentamycin 80ml intramuscularly at eight hours intervals. Upon completion of the treatment the patient noticed ringing in his ears and low level abdominal pain. Reading the drug manufacturer's literature the patient learned about the possible side effect of ear problems and that he should have been hospitalized during the administration of gentamycin. This prompted him to seek out 'many physicians' for consultation and advice. He had obtained the names and addresses of these urologists and ear/nose/throat specialists from friends. None of these specialists could help him. At last he visited an ear/nose/throat specialist in a hospital who told him that his problem was due to overdosage of gentamycin. Subsequently the patient experienced continous low-level ringing in his ears, which was aggravated by severe headaches whenever he used any type of drugs and even certain foods. He discontinued taking zinc supplements even though they eliminated his abdominal pain since they aggravated the ear problem. Out of fear of additional drug reactions he declined to use a sulfa drug prescribed by a physician when his kidney/urinary tract infection flared up again. Instead he used garlic, with beneficial results. At the end of the study period the patient decided to use homeopathic medicine which he obtained from an Indian colleague, resulting in marked improvements in his overall health without side effects.

COMMENTS

All cases illustrate the functional role of social networks and geographical and ecomonic accessibility in the various steps involved in drug purchasing. Five of the patients had self-diagnosed their illness and self-medicated drugs. In the selection of drug retailers and drugs six patients were influenced by friends, relatives, neighbors and pharmacy personnel. The tendency of patients with a new illness to seek the advice of persons close to them before going to pharmacies indicates the need to discuss and confirm self-diagnoses and evaluate different treatment options with experienced and trusted individuals. Patients repeatedly affected by the same illness had already developed diagnostic and treatment strategies, as evidenced by their use of the same type or brand of drug. That this may occasionally prevent utilization of new brands or generic drugs and thus possibly delay treatment, is suggested by Case 8. On the other hand, user perception of the 'proper' use of drugs may deviate from doctors' prescriptions (Case 3), as in the earlier mentioned modifications in the use of antibiotic capsules. Shopping around for the most effective drugs was illustrated by Cases 1, 2 and 10. The latter also revealed the danger of overdrugging by physicians without the necessary precautionary clinical measures and the beneficial effect of patient education in drug evaluation. Use of pharmacies near bus stops, places of residence or places of employment and homeopathic medicine obtained from a colleague all reflect the effects of social and geographical proximity on the acquisition of information and buying medicines nearby. Preference for government or private drug retailers by patients in different socioeconomic classes and with different illnesses is in agreement with results from this and previous studies (Kloos et al. 1986a). These case studies, then contribute to an understanding of drug purchasing in an urban environment from the user's point of view, by identifying opportunities, barriers and adaptive responses.

CONCLUSION

This study indicates that numerous factors determine if, when and where Addis Ababa residents seek medical treatment. Commercial drug retailers have come to occupy an important position in the city's health care system. In an environment characterized by high incidence of diseases which were traditionally dealt with at home and by professional healers, the utilization of over-the-counter drugs is becoming an acceptable and even preferred health strategy. Recent government restrictions on traditional healers and provision of cheaper commercial drugs through the rapidly expanding government pharmacies appear to have hastened this trend.

The quality of the quantitative data produced by this study varies considerably due to differences in method and research setting. The results of the retrospective household studies are probably least reliable owing to a combination of recall difficulties, unfamiliarity of the population with survey research and the hurry of some student interviewers to complete the interviews. Recall of illness events declines even during the first week (Kroeger 1985). The problem of unfamiliarity of Ethiopians with survey research and resultant misconceptions and biased or wrong information was described by Pausewang (1973). Some interviewees misunderstood the survey as an attempt to determine family income for taxation purposes or to recruit people for *kebele* duties. Others expected the interview team to set up health programs or to construct clinics and pharmacies. Carrying maps and notebooks, the interviewers were also thought to be urban planners and fears were expressed in the slums about the possibility of urban renewal and associated evictions. Whereas these misconceptions could be largely eliminated by explaining the objectives of the interviews, the limited contact between household and interviewer, ranging from 40 minutes to one hour, resulted in shallow answers. The fact that about 10% of all interviewees, especially of the Dorze ethnic group, spoke little Amharic contributed to information loss.

Data from the pharmacy surveys, particularly on type of drugs purchased, type of illness and cost of purchases were generally more reliable due to visual inspection of containers and sales receipts. The health problems reported by clients generally correspond with the type of drugs purchased but information on the specific and appropriate use of antibiotics was unreliable. In addition to the reluctance of many clients to report venereal and other diseases with a social stigma, misdiagnoses, by both patients and clinics, were common. Personal data on place of residence, origin of trip to pharmacies, age and education of clients appeared fairly accurate, judging from the consistent geographic pattern of these variables (Kloos et al. 1986). Comparison of household and pharmacy data, including observed drug purchasing, suggests that the information on drug selection and purchasing is also quite reliable. Lack of time of many clients going to or coming from work or shops and the setting of the interviews in the often crowded pharmacies must have resulted in loss of some information although the refusal rate was only 4%.

One important aspect of drug purchasing in Addis Ababa – prescription practices of physicians – was not studied. Overprescribing of antibiotics, uncritical acceptance of new drugs by physicians and common neglect of the drug evaluations and recommendations by drug manufacturers have been identified as a major problem in Addis Ababa (Minas 1984). The cost of prescription drugs is significantly higher than that of over-the-counter purchases. The additional cost of physician visits and socioeconomic barriers are thought to contribute to self-diagnosis and self-treatment in Addis Ababa (Kloos et al. 1986a).

This quantitative study indicates that survey research may be useful in studying drug purchasing in urban settings, both in the home and in drug retailer shops. This approach, by permitting analysis of extensive illness, behavioral and environmental data, may provide new insights into the interrelation between drug selection, social, cultural and geographic opportunities and barriers to obtaining and using them. The present study indicates that the concept of 'activity space' (Shannon et al. 1985), as defined for different social and cultural groups, is instrumental in understanding different facets of drug purchasing. Sickness, communication, visiting drug shops and selecting medicines occur in spatially, socially and culturally defined systems or communities. The common preference of drug retailers located within convenient distance from home or work place (Gagon 1977; Kloos et al. 1986a) underscores the importance of studying drug purchasing from a contextual point of view.

Important from a public health point of view is the constraint of distance on utilization, as revealed by declining use of drug retailers and other medical services with distance from the residence of patients and the failure of many ill persons in the slums to seek treatment in the absence of transportation facilities. Other areas of public health concern are prevailing drug retail, acquisition and use practices, including the predominance of self-medication, the reliance on oral dosage instructions, the widespread purchasing of drugs for other persons, and the cultural perception of appropriate and economically efficient drug use. Pharmacists and other drug retailer personnel can be instrumental in minimizing misuse of drugs by taking a more active role in educating the public over the counter. Health planners would benefit from information on aspects of drug retailing and drug use as they relate to health needs of the population (based on the prevalence of illness and disease) when planning new drug retail outlets. The plan of the Addis Ababa Municipality to establish drug shops and pharmacies in all *keftegna* lacking drug retailers will have to consider the relatively high health *demands* of the higher socioeconomic groups but also the greater health *needs* of the poorer people.

NOTES

1. The authors are indebted to Mr. Eshetu Wondemagegnehu, Head of the Department of Pharmacy and Laboratory, Ministry of Health, and Mr. Abebe Engedasew, Head of Health and Community Services, Addis Ababa Municipality, for their assistance and stimulating discussions. Thanks are also due to the residents and officials of the study *kebele*, the officials of the respective *keftegna* and the pharmacy personnel for their cooperation and support. The Department of Geography, Addis Ababa University, kindly provided technical assistance.
2. In Ethiopia nearly all studies by social scientists of health services have been confined to traditional medicine (Giel and Workneh 1968; Rodinson 1967; Messing 1958; Mercier 1979; Workneh and Giel 1975; Young 1976, 1977; Kloos and Ahmed Zein 1988). Only one sociological study of modern health care in Ethiopia, examining factors in the utilization of primary care services and injection doctors, paid some attention to pharmaceuticals (Buschkens and Slikkerveer 1982: 53–55, 104). Studies of rural drug shops (Nordberg 1974; Lundin 1974), pharmacies in Addis Ababa (Sekhar 1981; Sekhar et al. 1980, 1981) and national drug distribution (Desta 1971) were concerned primarily with public health aspects. In a preliminary study of the utilization of private drug retailers in prerevolutionary Ethiopia one of us evaluated several factors, including their location, transportation facilities used by clients, size of retail shops and management practices (Kloos 1974).
3. Government pharmacies have larger proprietory and generic drug inventories than private shops. Thus their clients are more successful in obtaining the drugs of their choice (Kloos et al. 1986a). Whereas the great majority of the government pharmacy clients patronized retailers either because of low prices, availability of drugs, or good services, most clients of private shops mentioned their nearby location and their familiarity with them (Kloos et al. 1986a).

REFERENCES

Arragie, Messele
    1983   Toxicity of Kosso (*Hagenia abyssinica*). 1. Acute Toxicity in Mice. Ethiopian Medical Journal 21: 84–93.

Bedassa, A.
    1984   The Ethiopianization of Pharmacies (1935–1983). Paper presented at the 9th Annual Conference of the Ethiopian Pharmaceutical Association, 9–10 November 1984, Addis Ababa.

Brown, K. H. and Gilman, R.
    1980   Ascariasis and Malnutrition: A Study in Urban Ethiopian Children. American Journal of Clinical Nutrition 33: 2698–2699.

Buschkens, W. F. L. and Slikkerveer, L. J.
  1982   Health Care in East Africa: Illness Behaviour of the Eastern Oromo in Hararghe (Ethiopia). Assen (Netherlands): Van Gorcum.
Desta, Asfaw
  1971   National Health Planning in Ethiopia. D.P.H. Thesis, Johns Hopkins University, Baltimore.
Dodge, R. W. and Wallace, Craig K.
  1975   Neisseria Gonorrhea in Ethiopia: Antiobiotic Sensitivity Pattern. Ethiopian Medical Journal 13: 19–22.
Dotsenko, A. P.
  1975   Some Pecularities in Frequency and Clinical Picture of Diseases in Ethiopia. In Collection of Research Works of the USSR Red Cross Dejazmach Balcha Memorial Hospital in Addis Ababa. 7th Issue. A. P. Dotsenko, (ed.) Addis Ababa: Artistic Printers.
Freij, Lennard, Nystrom, L. and Wall, Styg
  1977   Exploring Child Health and its Ecology. Scandinavian Journal of Medicine 12 (Supplement): 1–99.
  1979   (with Meeuwisse, G. W., Berg, N. O., Wall, S. and Gebre-Medhin, M.) Ascariasis and Malnutrition: A Study of Urban Ethiopian Children. American Journal of Clinical Nutrition 32: 1545–1553.
Friedman, P. S. and Wright, D. J.
  1977   Observations on Syphilis in Addis Ababa. 2. Prevalence and Natural History. British Journal of Venereal Diseases 53: 276–280.
Fraser, H. S.
  1985   Rational Use of Essential Drugs. World Health Forum 6: 63–66.
Gagon, J. F.
  1977   Factors Affecting Pharmacy Patronage Motives – a Literature Review. Journal of the American Pharmaceutical Association (New Series) 7: 556–565.
Gebre-Medhin, M. and Gobezie, A.
  1975   Dietary Intake in the Third Trimester of Pregnancy and Birth Weight of Offspring Among Nonprivileged and Privileged Women. American Journal of Clinical Nutrition 28: 1322–1329.
Gedebou, Messele and Tassew, A.
  1980   Neisseria gonorrhea Isolates from Ethiopia. 2. Pair Correlations Between Minimal Inhibitory Concentration Values of Five Antibodies and Frequency of Multiple Antibiotic Response. Bulletin of the World Health Organization 58: 73–79.
Giel, R. and Workneh, Fikre
  1968   Faith Healing and Spirit Possession in Ghion, Ethiopia. Social Science and Medicine 2:63–79.
Hailu, Beyene
  1982   Towards an Understanding of Urban Growth in Ethiopia. In Studies in African and Asian Demography. Cairo Demographic Center, Research Monograph Series No. 11. Cairo.
Haragewoin, M.D.
  1982   Some Clinical Aspects of Hypertension in Ethiopia. East African Medical Journal 59:283–287.
Kitaw, Yayeyirad, Gebray, A., Bushara, B. and Asfaw, B.
  1982   Dental Health Condition of Students in Ethiopia: Findings from the Development Through Cooperation Campaign, 1976–1977. Ethiopian Medical Journal 20:9–14.
Kitaw, Yayeyirad
  1984a   Drug Hoarding and Utilization in a Developing County. Paper presented at the 9th

Annual Conference of the Ethiopian Pharmaceutical Association, 9–10 November 1984, Addis Ababa.
1984b Self (Lay) Care in a Developing Country: A Study of Three Communities in Ethiopia. Unpublished report. Addis Ababa.

Kloos, Helmut
1973 Disease Concepts and Medical Practices in Relation to Malaria Among Fever Cases in Addis Ababa. Ethnomedicine 2: 229–253.
1974 The Geography of Pharmacies, Druggist Shops and Rural Medicine Vendors and the Origin of Customers of Such Facilities in Addis Ababa. Journal of Ethiopian Studies 12: 77–94.
1976 Preliminary Studies of Medicinal Plants and Plant Products in Markets of Central Ethiopia. Ethnomedicine 4: 63–103.
1986a (with Tsegaye Chama, Dawit Abemo, Kefalo Gebre Tsadik and Solomon Belay) Utilization of Pharmacies and Pharmaceutical Drugs in Addis Ababa. Social Science and Medicine 22: 635–652.
1986b (with Tsegaye Chama, Dawit Abemo, and Kefalo Gebre Tsadik and Solomon Belay) Utilisation of Selected Pharmacies and Drugs: a Study in Medical Geography. Ethiopian Medical Journal 24: 105–111.
1987 (with Berhanu Shewarga, Getachew Tafesse, Tadesse Habtamu, Gashew Gete, Mekuria Maquanent and Mogas Kassa) Utilisation of Selected Hospitals, Health Centers and Health Stations in Addis Ababa. Ethiopian Medical Journal. 25: 157–166.
1988 (with Ahmed Zein, Zein) Health and Disease in Ethiopia: a Guide to the Literature 1940–1985. Addis Ababa: Ministry of Health.

Kroeger, Axel
1985 Response Errors and Other Problems of Health Interview Surveys in Developing Countries. World Health Statistics Quarterly 38: 15–37.

Lester, Francis T. and Tsega, Edemariam
1976 The Pattern of Adult Medical Admissions in Addis Ababa, Ethiopia. East African Medical Journal 53: 620–634.

Lundin, Stig
1974 The Rural Drug Vendor: a Survey of the Province of Arussi 1966 E.C. CADU (Chilalo Agricultural Development Unit) Publication No. 95.

Manzur, J.
1981 Skin Diseases in Addis Ababa: Preliminary Review. Ethiopian Medical Journal 19: 123–134.

Meche, Hailu and Woldeab, Mehari
1984 Reaching the People: Issues in the Utilization of Selected Hospitals in Addis Ababa. Ethiopian Journal of Health Development 1: 65–72.

Mercier, Jacques
1979 Approche de la Médecine des Debteras. Abbay 10: 111–128.

Messing, Simon D.
1958 Group Therapy and Social Status in the Zar Cult of Ethiopia. American Anthropologist 60: 1120–1126.

Minas, Mesfin
1984 Utilisation of Drugs in Ethiopia (Panel Discussion). Presented at the 9th Annual Conference of the Ethiopian Pharmaceutical Association, 9–10 November, 1984. Addis Ababa.

Ministry of Health
1978 Utilisation of Health Services in Ethiopia. Addis Ababa: United Printers.

Ministry of Health
1986 Comprehensive Health Services Directory 1976 E.C. (1983/84 G.C.). Addis Ababa.

Mulugeta, Solomon
    1985   Meeting the Housing Shortage in Addis Ababa: the Case of Housing Cooperatives. M.A. thesis, Department of Geography, Addis Ababa University.
Nordberg, E.
    1974   Self-portait of the Average Rural Drug Shop in Wollega Province, Ethiopia. Ethiopian Medical Journal 12: 25–32.
Office of the Population and Housing Census Commission
    1984   Ethiopia 1984 Population and Housing Census Preliminary Report. Vol. 1, No. 1. Addis Ababa.
Olsson, B.
    1979   Dental Health Situation in Privileged Children in Addis Ababa, Ethiopia. Community Dental and Oral Epidemiology 7: 37–41.
Osterwald, R. and Gebre-Medhin, M.
    1978   Westernization of Diet and Serum Lipids in Ethiopians. American Journal of Clinical Nutrition 31: 1028–1040.
Pankhurst, Richard
    1969   The Traditional Taenicides of Ethiopia. Journal of the History of Medicine and Allied Sciences 24: 323–334.
Parry, E. H. O.
    1979   Urban Change and Health in Africa. Ethiopian Medical Journal 17: 127–142.
Pausewang, Siegfried
    1973   Methods and Concepts of Social Research in a Rural Developing Society: a Critical Appraisal Based on Experiences in Ethiopia. Munich: Weltforum Verlag.
Plorde, D. S.
    1981   Sexually Transmitted Diseases in Ethiopia. Social Factors Contributing to their Spread and Implications for Developing Countries. British Journal of Venereal Diseases 57: 357–362.
Rodinson, Maxime
    1967   Magie, Médecine et Possession en Éthiopie. Le Havre: Moutin & Co.
Rokos, L.
    1969   Eye Complications in Poisoning Caused by 'Kosso' (Hagenia abyssinica). Ethiopian Medical Journal 7: 11–16.
Sekhar, C. C.
    1981   Pharmacy in Ethiopia. East African Medical Journal 58: 838–842.
Sekhar, C. C., Raina, R. K. and Rao, P. G.
    1980   Drug Scene in Ethiopia. East African Medical Journal. 57: 44–47.
Sekhar, C. C., Raina, R. K. and Pillai, G. K.
    1981   Some Aspects of Drug Use in Ethiopia. Tropical Doctor 11: 116–118.
Shannon, Garry W. et al.
    1985   Pharmacy Patronage among the Elderly: Selected Racial and Geographical Patterns. Social Science and Medicine 20: 85–94.
Shiferaw, Tesfaye
    1984   Utilisation of Domestic Water in Addis Ababa. M.A. thesis, Department of Geography, Addis Ababa University, Addis Ababa.
Silverman, Milton
    1976   The Drugging of the Americas. Berkeley: University of California Press.
Slater, P. E., Ellencweig, A. Y., Braun, M., Yishai, O., Hozmi, M., Benadiba, E., Benarroch, F. and Yachin, S.
    1986   Drug Hoarding in a Jerusalem Community. Journal of the Royal Society of Health 106 (3): 87–89.
Stinzing, Gudmund, Habte, Demissie, Tufevesson, B. and Back, Erick

1977 Aetiology of Acute Diarrhoeal Disease in Infancy and Childhood During the Peak Season, Addis Ababa 1977: a Preliminary Report. Ethiopian Medical Journal 15: 141–146.
1981 (with Back, E., Tufevesson, B., Johansson, T., Wadström, T. and Habte, Demissie) Seasonal Fluctuations in the Occurrence of Enterotoxigenic Bacteria and Rotavirus in Paediatric Diarrhoea in Addis Ababa. Bulletin of the World Health Organization 59: 67–73.

Taticheff, Sioum, Abdulahi, Yayha and Haile Meskal, Fisseha
1981 Intestinal Parasitic Infection in Pre-School Children in Addis Ababa. Ethiopian Medical Journal 19: 35–40.

Tekle-Haimanot, Makonnen
1985 Two Rounds of a Rural Health Survey in Ethiopia, 1982–1983: Needs, Objectives, Preparations, Data Collection and Evaluation of Quality. World Health Statistics Quarterly 38: 107–126.

Teklu, Baylew
1980 Disease Patterns among Civil Servants in Addis Ababa: an Analysis of Outpatient Visits to a Bank Employee Clinic. Ethiopian Medical Journal 18: 1–6.
1982 Chronic Disease Prevalence in Ethiopian Bank Employees. Ethiopian Medical Journal 20: 49–54.
1984 Hypertension Screening amongst Bank Employees in Addis Ababa. Ethiopian Medical Journal 22: 1–5.

Tsega, Edemariam, Landells, J. and Teklehaimanot, Redda
1978 Kosso Toxicity in Mice. Sinet (Ethiopian Journal of Science) 1: 99–106.

Van der Geest, Sjaak
1982 The Efficiency of Inefficiency: Medicine Distribution in South Cameroon. Social Science and Medicine 16: 2145–2153.

World Health Organization
1978 Lay Reporting of Health Information. Geneva.

Workneh, Fikre, and Giel, R.
1975 Medical Dilemma; a Survey of the Healing Practices of a Coptic Priest and an Ethiopian Sheik. Tropical and Geographical Medicine 27: 431–439.

Young, Allan
1976 Internalizing and Externalizing Medical Belief Systems: an Ethiopian Example. Social Science and Medicine 10: 147–156.
1977 Order, Analogy and Efficacy in Ethiopian Medical Divination. Culture, Medicine and Psychiatry 1: 183–199.

KATHLEEN LOGAN

'CASI COMO DOCTOR': PHARMACISTS AND THEIR CLIENTS IN A MEXICAN URBAN CONTEXT

While doing anthropological fieldwork in Mexican urban areas, I noticed that many people routinely consulted the local pharmacist 'almost like a doctor' (*casi como doctor*). They presented their physical complaints and described their symptoms, expecting the pharmacists to diagnose their illnesses and to prescribe treatment. The pharmacists obliged their clients by labeling their illnesses and by selling them the pharmaceutical preparations they recommended. I also observed that many people self-diagnosed their illnesses and medicated themselves with over-the-counter-drugs (hereafter referred to as OTC's) which they purchased at local pharmacies, often in consultation with pharmacists. Both the practice of consulting pharmacists and that of self-diagnosis and self-medication are made easier in Mexico, as in many parts of the Third World, because few pharmaceutical preparations or patent medicines require a physician's prescription to be purchased. In Mexico, in the early 1980s, only 289 items (such as Dexadrina, Nembutal, and Qualude) needed prescriptions to be sold. It is also common practice in Mexico to buy drugs labeled 'prescription only' without a prescription as I have observed people doing on numerous occasions. When people do have prescriptions, they still rely on self-diagnosis and often trade prescriptions with friends, neighbors, and family members who have had the same symptoms. Because of these practices, many medications are available in Mexico for people to use freely.

The role of pharmacists as quasi-physicians, the practice of self-diagnosis and self-medication with OTC's have been noted but not focused upon by students of Mexican health care. Some studies have referred to the role of Mexican pharmacists as health care practitioners. In a review of rural health care in Mexico, Cañedo (1974: 1133–1134) briefly cites the important role of pharmacists as diagnosticians, healers, and general advisors on health matters. Fabrega and Silver (1973: 84) also mention that pharmacists ought to be considered as *de facto* medical practitioners because they are often consulted by individuals who seek relief from illness symptoms. Similarly, Young (1981: 124–125) in a comprehensive study of health care options in a Mexican village suggests that pharmacists are a health care alternative. Since, however, there were no pharmacists in the community Young studied, he has no data on which to base a quantative analysis of the role of pharmacists.

Some health care studies of Mexico note that people self-medicate with OTC's (Brown 1963: 101; Young 1981: 104, 106; Madsen 1965: 126–127) or consult pharmacists about their illness symptoms and take the medications they recommend (Young 1981: 124–125; DeWalt 1979: 7; Chiñas 1963: 61). Other studies refer to the pattern of medical pluralism that develops when OTC's and traditional healing practices are linked, as Higgins (1975: 35) does when he observes that pharmaceutical products are often used to cure in conjunction with traditional remedies such as herbal teas and massages. Similarly, Brown (1963: 100), in describing how local curers have adapted to the availability of patent medicine reports that *curanderos* have updated their healing arts by incorporating OTC's into their practices. Fabrega and Silver (1973: 44, 84), Kelly (1965: 61), and DeWalt (1977: 8) also state that traditional healers in Mexico have added OTC's to their curing repertoire.

Despite the readily observable importance of pharmacists, self-diagnosis, and self-medication with OTC's in Mexico, these topics have received only passing mention in the anthropological literature. This omission is an illustration of Young's (1981: 6) point that anthropologists studying health care usually center on the exceptional rather than the ordinary. It is the 'ordinariness' of pharmacists, self-diagnosis, and self-medication then that had brought these topics to be side-lined rather than high-lighted in health care studies of Mexico. The near absence of these topics in the literature also demonstrates a central theme of this volume – that anthropologists studying health care have often failed to take account of the use of Western pharmaceuticals in the Third World.

It is the 'ordinary' responses to illness – self-diagnosis and self-medication – that are the most frequent responses. And increasingly in the Third World, self-diagnosis and self-medication incorporate OTC's and consultation with pharmacists. Since this trend was evident in Mexico, it seemed to me that a quantitative study needed to be done to address the lack of data on the role of pharmacists, self-diagnosis, and self-medication with OTC's in that country. Not only were quantitative data needed on these topics but also it seemed to me that a study of the context in which they occurred was necessary, since few studies of the role of pharmaceuticals have provided data of this kind. For these reasons, I did a study of the role of pharmacists, self-diagnosis, and self-medication with OTC's in Ciudad Juarez, Chihuahua, Mexico during the summer of 1980.

RESEARCH SITE

Ciudad Juarez lies in a narrow, fertile valley at the base of two mountain chains at the international boundary between Mexico and the USA, directly across the Rio Grande from El Paso, Texas. Because of its location at the lowest mountain pass for hundreds of miles, the Juarez area has been a transcontinental crossroads since pre-colonial days. With the establishment of the international border in 1848, however, Ciudad Juarez has become even more important as a crossing point. Today the city is a major border crossing for the thousands of Mexicans entering the USA, legally and illegally, to seek employment. Like several other northern Mexican cities such as Tijuana, Mexicali, and Nogales, Juarez is rapidly becoming a major metropolitan area; it now has a population of one million. In its growth, Juarez draws thousands of workers from the interior of Mexico to work in its industrial and tourist sectors. The major industry of the city at present is the 180 in-bond assembly plants that employ some 77,000 workers.[1] Juarez is also a tourist center to which North Americans come for Mexican food, crafts, entertainment, and a taste of a different culture. Visitors also flock to the city to take advantage of lower prices for consumer goods such as gasoline and food or such services as dental care and automobile repair. Some tourists come to Juarez to participate in activities which are either illegal or difficult to find in the USA such as bullfights, off- track betting, dogfights, prostitution, and cockfights. The ambience of Juarez is not only one of vitality and growth but also one of poverty, unemployment, and exploitation.

The general health status in the northern border regions of Mexico where Ciudad Juarez lies is better than in the rest of the Republic (Loewe-Reiss 1978: 255). The area's higher standard of living permits a healthier diet with a greater comsumption of meat and vegetables than elsewhere in Mexico (Leon-Portilla 1972: 112). The greater *per capita* income of the area's residents allows them more economic resources with which to purchase health care and to choose among health care options (Ardón 1978: 22; Loewe-Reiss 1978: 255). Another factor contributing to the city's better overall health status is that the metropolitan northern border areas of Mexico fare better in health care facilities than the rest of the Republic. There are both more physicians and more hospital beds *per capita* in border cities than elsewhere in Mexico (Nolesco 1978: 54–55; Rubel and O'Nell 1978: 195). Also aiding the city's health status is the fact that urban areas in Mexico generally are better serviced by all kinds of medical facilities than rural ones (Cañedo 1974: 1131; Schendel 1968: 250).

Despite higher than national average standards of health and better health care facilities, however, ecological and socio-economic factors create serious health problems for residents of Juarez. Since the city lies in a desert area, there is considerable seasonal variation in temperature and rainfall. During the long, hot, dry season, such problems as dehydration, drownings in the Rio Grande and irrigation canals, poor sanitation because of chronic water shortages and respiratory ailments caused by high dust levels are all health hazards. During the short, summer wet season with its sudden heavy rains, the flooding of low-lying areas and contamination of over-flowing sewage create additional health risks. High density living and poverty exacerbate these environmental health problems. Under these conditions, influenza and pneumonia have become the primary causes of mortality. Enteritis and other diarrhetic diseases have become the second leading causes of death. Common chronic illnesses include tuberculosis, cirrhosis of the liver, diabetes mellitus, heart disease, and vitamin deficiency (Loewe-Reiss 1978: 244–245).

METHODOLOGY

In order to determine the role pharmacists, self-diagnosis, and self-medication with OTC's in Mexican health care, I collected data from three sources. *First*, I directed the administration of an intensive health care questionnaire given to the women of 48 households in an inner city neighborhood of Ciudad Juarez.[2] The responses to this questionnaire supplied data about the treatment of illnesses and the use of health care facilities. *Second*, I conducted interviews with several local pharmacists (including the past and current presidents of the pharmacists' professional organization) who served as key informants. *Third*, I observed the operation of several local pharmacies to get the context of pharmacists' role in health care in Ciudad Juarez.

The availability of medical care (Young 1981: 170; Simoni and Ball 1975: 176) and the expense of treatment (Ardón 1978: 22; Teller 1972: 2, 203; 1973: 218; Polgar 1963: 412; DeWalt 1977: 10) are often mentioned as important determinants of how people choose among health care alternatives. In order to determine what choices people make when many options are available, I selected a centrally located inner-city neighborhood. This area is part of a large residential section of Juarez about 1 1/2 miles from the central business district. Pharmacies, public hospitals and health centers, private physicians, and herbal curers all lie within this neighborhood or within easy walking distance from it. In order to minimize the effect of expense in choice of treatment, I selected this neighborhood because many of its residents enjoy an income which allows them to consider a wide range of health care options. Two-thirds of the families had incomes above the average of US £514 *per capita per annum* reported for Chihuahua (Loewe-Reiss 1978: 252).

Since survey research had previously been done in the sample neighborhood, the residents were accustomed both to the questionnaire format and the teams of researchers. The neighborhood had approximately 480 households so that the 48 households interviewed represented a 10% sample of the area.[3] I obtained a systematic sample of the households by designating every 10th household for interviewing (Pelto and Pelto 1978: 132–133). Each interview took a minimum of 3/4 of an hour; some lasted as long as 1 1/2 hours. The interviews were conducted in the late afternoon or early evening hours, times when women were likely to be at home whether they were housewives or workers outside their homes. Teams of Mexican female students from a private Mexican research agency collected the data on both the pre-test and final forms of the questionnaire.

All of those responding to the questionnaire were women. For the purposes of this study, women were the preferred informants for several reasons. First, women in Latin America have the primary responsibility for family health care (Rubel 1966: 180; Erasmus 1952: 420; Young 1981: 104; Weaver 1970: 143, 144; McClain 1977: 342). Second, Latin American women traditionally take care of children under five years, the age group most likely to be ill (Young 1981: 78). Thus, women are the individuals who make the initial decisions regarding family illnesses and who minister to the ill. Given these factors, women were the preferred sample.

The sample consisted primarily of married, middle-aged housewives who were long time residents of Juarez. Most were either born in the city or had migrated there earlier in their lives from one of the northern border states of Mexico (particularly from the other parts of Chihuahua, the state in which Juarez lies). Almost all had children. They had an average family size of five, two adults and three children, making their families slightly smaller than the average family size of 5.4 reported for the Mexican border states (Loewe-Reiss 1978: 254). Seven of the 48 households were headed by single women.

Some variation in the sample occurred with husbands' occupation, informants' education, and family income. Nearly half of the informants' husbands worked as vendors, construction workers or unskilled blue collar laborers. The other half were office or skilled workers. A small number were retired or unemployed. Half of the informants had some primary school education; the other half had completed primary school or received additional schooling beyond the primary level. Two-thirds of the informants had family incomes above the average for Chihuahua, one third had incomes at or below the average. In this sample, female headed households did not correlate with low income. Since these single women worked in the in-bond plant industries of Juarez, they earned a higher income than would normally be expected for female headed households in Mexico. Thus, their income placed them in the above average range. Single women who headed households were also younger and had fewer children than the rest of the women in the sample.

In the questionnaire, the women were asked to describe and to evaluate their use of health care facilities in Juarez. The health care options included on the questionnaire were selected based on the results from a questionnaire pre-test administered in a neighborhood demographically similar to the sample neighborhood. Only those health care options named by the informants in the pre-test were included on the questionnaire.

Informants mentioned the following health care facilities (in alphabetical order): *Centros de Salud, curanderos*,[4] government dispensaries, household remedies, IMSS, OTC's, pharmacies, private physicians, and the Red Cross. Each is described briefly as follows:

The *Centros de Salud* are government sponsored public health clinics which charge set fees for specific services.

Curanderos are local healers who diagnose, prescribe, and carry out treatment for illnesses. The methods and substances ued in treatment vary and have been described widely in the literature (Kiev 1968; Trotter and Chavira 1980).

Dispensaries are operated by the government and by labor unions that charge set fees for specific services which are similar to the *Centros de Salud*. Fees are usually lower than with a private physician.

Household remedies (*remedios caseros*) include a wide range of substances considered to promote healing. Household remedies mentioned by informants in the sample included herbs (*yerba buena*), mineral elements (*bismuth*), and foods (sugared water, carbonated lemon water, salt, and bread).

IMSS is the Mexican social security system whose services are available only to those with stable, salaried jobs. For this reason, only 20% (Loewe-Reiss 1978: 247) to 36% (Purcell 1981: 45) of the Mexican work force is covered by IMSS. Generally, the poorest people, because they have unstable jobs, are excluded from this system. In this sample 41.7% of the informants were eligible for IMSS, slightly higher than the percentage eligible in the Mexican working population as a whole. This is a reflection of the industrial work force employment of many individuals in the sample neighborhood.

OTC's include a wide variety of medications sold at the 200 pharmacies in Ciudad Juarez.

Pharmacies range from tiny, one person stores selling only pharmaceutical products to large chain stores selling all kinds of retail items in addition to pharmaceutical goods. The largest are in the downtown area; smaller pharmacies operate in neighborhoods. The downtown pharmacies are likely to be run by a university trained pharmacist and to sell many products unrelated to health care (cosmetics, toys, and household furnishings). Neighborhood pharmacies are often operated by men who have apprenticed in a pharmacy and have learned their trade through experience rather than formal education. These pharmacies commonly carry only health care merchandise.

Private physicians see patients at specific times when patients present particular complaints. Patients are charged on a fee for service basis.

The Red Cross operates as a private charity, offering free medical service at a single central city location. Ambulance services are also available through the Red Cross.

On the questionnaire, in order to determine the role of pharmacists, self-diagnosis, and self-medication with OTC's, I asked the informants what course of action they would follow in seeking relief from specific symptoms of illness. I asked them a series of open-ended, hypothetical questions concerning what they would do if someone in their family became ill with each of the following four illness symptoms: headache, stomach ache, cough, and diarrhea. I selected these illness symptoms because they represent common symptoms of the most prevalant illnesses reported for the area. The format for the questions was as follows: 'If a member of your family had a headache (stomach ache, cough, diarrhea) what would you do?' They were then asked a follow-up question, 'If the headache (stomach ache, cough, diarrhea) continued, what would you do?'

Common symptoms of illness rather than specific illnesses themselves (tuberculosis, influenza, or gastritis) were used so that informants could define the illness as they chose and select the kind of treatment they felt appropriate. Phrased in this way, each symptom could be diagnosed by the informants as indicating any number of different illnesses. A stomach ache could be thought to indicate constipation, indigestion, colic, parasites, or *empacho*, an illness defined locally as discomfort caused by food adhering to the stomach wall; diarrhea could be diagnosed as any one of a variety of gastro-intestinal illnesses. Because each of the four symptoms was so commonplace, it offered informants a wide variety of diagnoses possible for each one.

Informants were also asked what they would do if someone became ill with *susto*, defined as an ' . . . ailment in which a startling, frightening, or shocking experience causes some level (from weak to total) of disengagement of the soul from harmonious syncopy with the body' (Trotter 1982: 219). In a recent study of traditional, locally defined illnesses in the Texas-Mexico border area (Martin et al. 1985: 235), *susto* was the common illness of this kind reported to physicians by their patients. Symptoms of *susto* include withdrawal, passivity, insomnia, fatigue, irritability, anxiety, weakness, and loss of appetite. I included *susto* on the questionnaire to elicit data directly concerning responses to a traditional, locally defined illness – although, the other symptoms could also be diagnosed as indicating such illnesses.

The hypothetical method was used in this questionnaire because of its proven utility in other health studies (Young 1978; Weaver 1970; Herskovits 1950). The principle advantage of the hypothetical method is that it allows for the collection of data that would not be easily observed because the topics under investigation are so commonplace that they are taken for granted by informants.

USE OF HEALTH CARE FACILITIES

Tables I and II show the informants' responses to questions about their use of health care facilities. Analysis of the responses as shown in these two tables reveal that pharmacists do play a significant role in Mexican health care.

Pharmacists were the most widely used medical option by the informants with 41.7% stating that they consult a pharmacist at least once a month. Only 10.4% of the informants reported never using pharmacists at all. The 89.6% who report consulting pharmacists are spread throughout the sample. No demographic criteria proved to be significantly related to the use pharmacists – informants in all categories made use of their services.

Informants indicate that they consult pharmacists in conjunction with their use of OTC's. They do not seem to consider consultation with pharmacists and the use of OTC's as discrete forms of treatment. The combining of these two forms of treatment is the reason, no doubt, why pharmacists were not cited separately by informants when they were asked about their initial responses to illness symptoms. (See the discussion in section entitled, 'Response to Illness Symptoms').

Informants' responses to questions about why they use the health care options they do reveal that they consult pharmacists more frequently than other health care providers for a variety of reasons. In an open ended question about how pharmacists were able to help them, the most frequently

TABLE I
Frequency of use (N = 48)

Percent of informants using each of the following	At least once a week	At least once a month	At least once a year	Less frequently than once a year	Never
Centro de Salud	—	8.3	33.3	14.6	43.8
Curandero	—	—	2.1	2.1	95.8
Dispensary	—	4.1	14.6	12.5	68.8
IMSS	—	22	17.6	2.1	58.3
Pharmacist	—	41.7	25	22.9	10.4
Physician	4.2	27.1	20.8	33.3	14.6
Red Cross	—	—	10.4	37.5	52.1

TABLE II
Use of services (N = 48)

Percent of informants using each of the following	Routine illness	Emergencies	Diagnostic tests— preventive care	Pregnancy	Not used
Centro de Salud	4.2	2	50	—	43.8
Cuandero	4.2	—	—	—	95.8
Dispensary	27	2.1	2.1	—	68.8
IMSS	10.8	4.2	6	20.7	58.3
Pharmacist	89.6	—	—	—	10.4
Physician	62.5	10.4	2.1	10.4	14.6
Red Cross	10.4	37.5	—	—	52.1

given reason cited by informants (listed by 22) was the pharmacists' abilities as diagnosticians and prescribers of medicine. Typically, people reported that they go to a pharmacy and describe their symptoms to the pharmacist. He then either asks further questions about the symptoms or begins to select medications that he believes will alleviate them. Through discussion, the pharmacist and client come to agree on which medications the client will purchase. In this way, operating at their best, pharmacies can provide useful information about the OTC's they sell. They give basic information about various medications, describe how they work, and tell what side effects they may have. They also recommend particular medications for specific afflictions and give information to enable people to choose among similar products. Based on my observations, pharmacists seldom seem to push people to buy medications. Their advice seems informative, given in the spirit of providing information rather than trying to make a sale.

Yet not all pharmacists are knowledgeable, well-trained, and willing to give advice about illness symptoms and OTC's. The quality of health care given by pharmacists varies considerably. Some pharmacists I observed were perfunctory in giving advice or information. Some were not well informed about the products they were selling. Nonetheless, pharmacists' effectiveness as health care providers is constantly being evaluated by their clients. If the advice they give and the medications they sell do not prove effective, their clients will consult other practitioners instead.

The second most frequently cited reason (listed by nine informants) for going to a pharmacist was to get prescriptions filled. Since informants report consulting physicians as the second most common response to the four illness symptoms and the most frequent response to persisting illness symptoms (see the discussion in section entitled 'Response to Illness Symptoms'), it is clear that they would receive prescriptions that would need to be filled at pharmacies.

The use of prescriptions links physicians and pharmacists in health care. An interesting side-light to this doctor-pharmacist link as health care practitioners is that some physicians own part interest in pharmacies, especially ones located near offices. The consequences of this linkage for health care delivery need to be explored.

The third most frequently cited reason (given by seven informants) for consulting a pharmacist was a belief in the efficacy of the OTC's they sell. Many people not only seem to think that the OTC's they select cure their illnesses but they also seem to think that they, as patients, are well-informed enough about their illnesses to be able to select them. Especially when the same illness symptoms re-occur, people are very prone to diagnose the symptoms as indicating the same illnesses as they have had before. Thus, they ask the pharmacist to 'give me something for parasites' or 'give me something for conjunctivitis', apparently not thinking that they need to consult a physician or anyone else to diagnose their illnesses. In this way, informants choose to consult pharmacists because this choice allows them to self-medicate and thereby retain control of their own treatment. The use of OTC's with a pharmacist's guidance fits easily into a traditional system of self-treatment that once included only household remedies.

The fourth most frequently cited reason (listed by five informants) for consulting a pharmacist was cost. Pharmacists do not charge for their services as do other practitioners (including some *curanderos*). They are also more economical to consult because they can provide medications without a prescription and thus allow people to bypass costly visits to physicians. In addition, pharmacists are willing to discuss various OTC's in terms of their cost effectiveness. Informants also mentioned that pharmacists save them money by giving them free medications or by selling them medications at a discount. Usually these free or discounted drugs are samples given the pharmacist by pharmaceutical salesmen. Additionally, Mexican pharmacists routinely sell OTC's in small amounts, i.e., it is possible to buy two aspirin rather than having to buy the entire bottle. Pharmacists, then, are less expensive than other health care practitioners.

Their ability to diagnose illnesses, to sell medications, and to fill prescriptions, their clients' belief in the effectiveness of the OTC's they sell, and their provision of low cost treatment were the reasons most often given by informants for consulting pharmacists. Observation suggests several others. Since many pharmacists live and do business in the neighborhoods they service, they may be more knowledgeable about the health problems and living conditions of their clients than other health practitioners. Thus they are perhaps better able to diagnose and treat the most common ailments afflicting their clients. The effectiveness of their care is questionable, however, when they are confronted with complicated or unusual illness conditions. The pharmacists' lack of medical training is a handicap for dealing with the out of the ordinary illnesses their clients may suffer. In these cases, there is always the danger of mis-diagnosis and the prescription of medicine harmful to the client.

Observation also suggests that people select pharmacists because they provide convenient health care. Pharmacies are often located in places easily available to their clients. In some new urban neighborhoods, especially lower-income ones on the outskirts of the city, pharmacists are the only medical practitioners available. In addition, many neighborhoods pharmacies are open seven days a week and for longer hours than other health care services. Another convenience of consulting pharmacies is that it is simply less time consuming to use them than any other health care alternative. There are no lengthy waits; no troublesome forms to fill out.

Informants may also prefer pharmacists because they provide a more comfortable social context for medical care than do other health care practitioners. Consulting a pharmacist involves no interaction with intimidating medical personnel, no lengthy examinations, and no unfamiliar language. Mitchell (1980) reports that in Jamaica many people choose to consult pharmacists rather than physicians because the socio-economic status differences between physicians and patients involve conflicting health beliefs and role expectations. These differences disrupt the physician-patient relationship and make the delivery of effective health care difficult. For this reason, many choose to go to a pharmacist instead. While such a gap between patients and physicians does not seem so important in Ciudad Juarez, given that informants report that they frequently consult physicians, they still prefer to go to pharmacists initially. To them, pharmacists are more social equals than social superiors; individuals who have specialized health knowledge to whom they can turn when they are ill.

Finally, my observations suggest that because pharmacists must please their clients to stay in business, they are perhaps more willing than other practitioners to be amenable to their clients' ideas about appropriate health care. Since many pharmacists are from the same socio-economic background as their clients, they may share the same ethnomedical beliefs and thus offer treatment and prescription more congruent with the health care notions of their clients.

The cultural and legal contexts in which Mexican pharmacists function allow them to flourish as primary health care providers. Since few medications require a prescription and, since it is common practice to be able to purchase 'prescription only' drugs without a prescription, the range and number of medications available for pharmacists to use are large. As one pharmacist noted, the quasi-legal status in which pharmacies function persists because Mexican authorities understand that medical care of this kind may be the only medical care affordable or available to some people.

Other factors in the cultural and legal contexts also facilitate the role of pharmacists as primary health care providers. Mexican law dictates a tiered structure of pharmacies; the first tier pharmacies are headed by individuals who have university degrees training them to be pharmacists; second tier pharmacies are headed by those who have been trained by the practical experience of serving as apprentices in pharmacies. Many more pharmacists learn their profession by serving as apprentices to other pharmacists than by receiving university training. As the head of the pharmacists' professional association in Ciudad Juarez noted, second tier pharmacists are legally permitted to operate only in rural areas because of the scarcity of university trained personnel there. Despite this law, however, second tier pharmacies do operate in urban areas. In Ciudad Juarez, I observed that large, center city pharmacies were usually run by university trained individuals affiliated with the pharmacists' professional association. Pharmacies in neighborhoods were more likely to be run by pharmacists who were trained as apprentices.

Both kinds of pharmacists, however, receive information about OTC's from pharmaceutical salesmen. The accuracy of the information these sales representatives give may be questionable (Silverman 1976) yet their influence on the prescription practices of physicians and pharmacists in the Third World is notable. Since they are vendors and not health care practitioners, they are more interested in selling OTC's than dispensing accurate information about them. Clearly, more needs to be known about their influence on health care, especially in developing countries where their number seems to be very high.

The widespread consultation with pharmacists as though they were physicians raises some interesting points about the appropriate health care role of pharmacists. Observers in the USA have noted that pharmacists there have augmented their duties by offering advice about drugs and their use (Ritchy and Raney 1981). One argument in favor of such an expanded medical role for pharmacists is that the number of pharmaceutical preparations is increasing at such a rate that no single physician can keep track of them and that pharmacists, who because of their training know more about drugs than physicians, should have a greater decision making role in the use of pharmaceuticals (Silverman and Lee 1974: 192). Other observers argue that a third class of drugs be added to the current prescription/non-prescription classification whereby people could obtain medications without prescriptions but with the professional guidance of a pharmacist (Griffenhagen 1976: 30). At its best, this is the system in which pharmacists in Mexico currently operate.

Tables I and II also report the informants' use of health care options other than pharmacies. Private physicians were the second most widely cited medical care option with 27.1% of the informants reporting that they consult them at least once a month. Twenty-two percent used IMSS (Social Security) at least once a month and 8.3% used *Centros de Salud* and 4.1% used dispensaries this often.

One reason why some health care options are elected more widely and frequently than others is that informants report using the options differently. They report using the Red Cross during emergencies, especially when there are accidents or injuries that require ambulance services. They indicate that they use the *Centros de Salud* for preventive medicine (injections), diagnostic examinations (x-rays, blood and urine tests), and to obtain health certificates for school registration. Certainly medical emergencies and the need for diagnostic tests are situations less common than the onset of illness symptoms. For these reasons, informants report using the Red Cross and the *Centros de Salud* less frequently than those health care options dealing primarily with illness symptoms; pharmacists, private physicians, and IMSS.

Informants report that *curanderos* are the least widely and least frequently consulted of all medical care options. In this study, only 4.2% of the informants reported ever going to a *curandero*. Reports from some other students of Mexican health care also cite the infrequent use of *curanderos*. Martin et al. (1985: 235) find a high incidence of traditional, locally defined illnesses in Texas-Mexico border area – precisely the kind of illnesses *curanderos* are thought best to treat. Yet the patients in their study consulted physicians for treatment of these illnesses, not *curanderos*. Similarly, Keefe (1981), Edgerton, Karmo and Fernandez (1970), Teller (1978) and Press (1973) report the decreasing importance of *curanderos* as health care practitioner among urban Hispanic populations.

Yet the findings of others indicate a changing, rather than declining role for *curanderos*. A study by Trotter and Chavira (1980: 431) found that housewives treated common illness symptoms such as those in this study while *curanderos* treated problems regarded as more serious such as ' . . . bad luck in business . . . marital disruptions, alcoholism or alcohol abuse, infidelity, being bothered by supernatural manifestations, cancer, diabetes and infertility' (1980: 433). Therefore, the data from this study do not exclude the possibility that while informants in the sample do not use *curanderos* for the symptoms listed in the questionnaire, they may, however, consult *curanderos* for other problems, as Trotter and Chavira (1980) note. Only further research will resolve the issues of whether the role of *curanderos* is declining or evolving and whether or not it varies among Hispanic populations.

RESPONSES TO ILLNESS SYMPTOMS

Table III shows what informants reported doing if someone in their family had one of the four illness symptoms or *susto* and Table IV shows what they reported doing if these problems persisted. The answers indicate that self-medication, either with OTC's or household remedies, is the most frequent initial reaction to all four illness symptoms and to *susto*. That informants self-medicate as an initial response to illness is often cited in the literature for Mexico (Kelly 1965: passim; Young 1981: 168; Brown 1963: 99); and in the literature for other places as well: Western Malaysia (Colson 1971: 230), Lower Zaire (Janzen 1978: 219), India (Beals 1976: 192), Nigeria (Maclean 1965: 238), Manus (Romanucci-Ross 1977: 438) and the USA (Schaller and Carroll 1976: 196: 204). Yet despite the widespread practice of self-medication, very few anthropological studies have dealt with this topic. They have more often focused on later stages of the illness referral system where treatment is sought from specialists for symptoms that have not responded to forms of self-medication.

What are the consequences of self-medication? It may represent competition for other medical practices, a supplement to others, or dangerous practice in the hands of the unknowing (Dukes 1963: 8). Many people who self-medicate do not think it is dangerous and have great confidence in their ability to treat themselves (Whiteford 1976: 100; Erasmus 1975: 420; Young 1981: 104). Some believe that information about drugs and the availability of drugs should be in the public domain and used at the patient's own risk (Alland 1970: 173). Unfortunately, few ethnomedical studies have systematically investigated the results of self-medication or other forms of indigenous self-treatment (Kleinman and Sung 1976).

OTC's are the most frequent form of self-medication for all four illness symptoms. The importance of pharmaceutical preparations is clear, supporting the observational data that such medications have a significant role in Mexican health care.

Although not asked for specific product names of OTC's in the questionnaire, some informants referred to particular remedies by their commercial brand-names such as: Alka-Seltzer, Breacol, Desenfriol, Kaopectate, Mejorales, Pepto-Bismol, and Tylenol. These informants answered the question, 'It a member of your family had a stomach ache (headache, diarrhea, cough), what would you do?' by saying 'I would give them Pepto-Bismol (Alka-Seltzer, Kaopectate, Breacol)'. It seems, then, that informants not only use OTC's widely but also that some are quite specific about which ones they prefer. Although some informants responded by citing the use of specific commercial brand-name products, no informants responded consistently by naming them for all four illness symptoms.

Table V shows that the naming of particular products most commonly occurred in responses to questions about headaches. Given that informants

TABLE III
Treatment of illness symptoms (N = 48)

Percent of informants doing each of the following	Diarrhea	Headache	Cough	Stomach ache	*Susto*
1. Self-medicate	50	89.6	79.2	50	62.5
a. OTC	(37.5)	(89.6)	(68.8)	(29.2)	—
b. Household remedies	(10.4)	—	(10.4)	(20.8)	62.5
c. Combination	(2.1)	—	—	—	—
2. Private physician	35.4	4.2	12.5	31.3	6.5
3. Pharmacist	2.1	2.1	2.1	4.2	—
4. Other provider (including IMSS, *Centros*, Red Cross, and dispensaries)	10.4	2.1	2	2.1	—
5. Do nothing/don't know	2.1	—	—	6.3	16.4
6. Don't have this problem	—	2	4.2	6.1	14.6

TABLE IV
Treatment of persisting illness symptoms (N = 48)

Percent of informants doing each of the following	Diarrhea	Headache	Cough	Stomach ache	*Susto*
1. Self-medicate	6.3	4.2	6.3	6.3	16.7
a. OTC	(2.1)	(4.2)	(4.2)	(2.1)	—
b. Household remedies	(4.2)	—	(2.1)	(4.2)	(16.7)
c. Combination	—	—	—	—	—
2. Private physician	62.5	68.8	66.7	62.5	25.0
3. Pharmacist	2	—	2	—	—
4. Other provider (including IMSS, *Centros*, Red Cross, and dispensaries)	8.3	8.3	10.4	2.1	—
5. Do nothing/don't know	—	2.1	—	2	8.3
6. Doesn't persist	20.9	14.6	10.4	21	35.4
7. Don't have this problem	—	2	4.2	6.1	14.6

report using OTC's more frequently to cure headaches than any of the other illness symptoms, it is likely that they think they have more knowledge about and have more confidence in these name brand OTC's. Some informants listed more general names for the OTC's they reported using. Nine stated using aspirin as a treatment for headache; two cited analgesics. Twenty-five informants reported using cough syrup for treatment of coughs, without naming a specific brand.

TABLE V
Brand-name OTC's (N = 17)

Number using following brand name OTC's	Diarrhea	Headache	Cough	Stomach ache
Alka-Seltzer		1		1
Anacin		1		
Breacol			1	
Desenfriol			1	
Kaopectate	1			
Mejorales		7		
Pepto Bismol	1			1
Terramicina	1			
Tylenol		1		

Whether or not commercial preparations will replace traditional forms of self-medication as has happened in Jamaica (Mitchell 1980:146) remains to be seen. Informants seldom reported using OTC's and household remedies in combination; they seemed to place them in discrete categories, using either one or the other. Yet, informants incorporate new elements into the realm of household remedies. They reported using such items as cooking oil to salve burns, toothpaste to deaden the pain of burns, and burned paper to stop infection. Household cures are a dynamic part of health care and should not be stereotyped as 'traditional knowledge' with set, unchanging formulae. These data suggest that OTC's have not replaced household remedies but rather that they have been added to the repetoire of medications available at the household level. In a sense OTC's can be viewed as new household remedies.

More informants cited using OTC's than household remedies in response to all four illness symptoms. Nonetheless, the percentage reporting OTC's *vis-à-vis* the percentage using household remedies varied with each illness symptom. For headaches and coughs, OTC's seem to have proven their effectiveness to the informants. Everyone who self-medicated for headaches reported using an OTC; none cited a home remedy. More informants mentioned using OTC's (68.8%) for coughs than either household remedies (10.4%), or private physicians (12.5%). Choice of treatment for headaches and cough did not vary with any of the demographic criteria.

For diarrhea, OTC's were again the most frequently cited form of self-medication (37.5%). Only 10.4% reported using household remedies and 2.1% using some combination of both (the only instance in which they were reported to be used in combination to treat either initial or persisting illness symptoms). In this case, younger informants (25 years or less), those with above average incomes, or more formal education tended to choose private physicians over any other form of treatment, if they did not choose OTC's as the preferred initial treatment.[5] No other demographic criteria were shown to influence choice of treatment.

For stomach pains, 50% of the informants reported that they self-medicated, 29.2% named OTC's and 20.8% household remedies. Nearly a third (31.3%) mentioned seeking treatment from a private physician. Again, younger informants, those with above average incomes, or more formal education chose a physician over other forms of treatment, if they did not initially choose OTC's. Older informants, those with less formal education or below average income tended to choose household remedies over other forms of treatment, if they did not initially choose OTC's. No other demographic criteria were shown to influence choice of treatment.

In summary, it seems that OTC's have widespread acceptance among informants as a means of self-medication. In the informants' view, OTC's seem to have proven useful, especially in treating headaches and coughs. Although still widely used, OTC's were less frequently reported for the treatment of diarrhea and stomach pain. In these cases, the percentage of informants using OTC's dropped while the proportion of informants who reported using household remedies and physicians rose. Young women, those with above average family income or more formal education tended to opt for physicians rather than household remedies to treat diarrhea and stomach pain, if they did not initially report using OTC's.

Since age seems to have affected the choice of treatment of diarrhea and stomach ache, it may be that younger women do not yet have the knowledge of household remedies that older women do and therefore do not employ this form of self-medication as much. It could also be that knowledge of household remedies is not being passed on to younger women.

For treatment of *susto*, 62.5% of the informants state that they would self-medicate with home remedies; none report that they would use an OTC. The same pattern holds for treatment of persisting *susto* – of the nearly 17% who continue to self-medicate, all name household remedies; none OTC's. Clearly, in the informants' view, home remedies, not OTC's, are the appropriate treatment for *susto*. Apparently for many people, traditional, locally used remedies are the most effective treatment for traditional, locally defined illnesses (Whiteford 1976: 104, 105). Nonetheless, Martin et al. (1985: 234) found that people in the Texas-Mexico border area consulted physicians also for treatment of locally-defined illnesses. Thus, they found less insularity between cosmopolitan medicine and indigenous medicine.

As we have seen, for initial treatment of *susto*, the majority of informants report using household remedies. Yet within this treatment choice, variation occurred. While some informants (6) simply cited household remedies as a general treatment category, most others reported employing one or the other of two distinct kinds of cures. On the one hand, of the 24 informants who named a particular household remedy for initial treatment of *susto*, 17 cited a food item which they eat or drink. The following list shows the food items these informants named: sugared water (8); sugar (3); water (2); salt (2); lemon (1); and moistened bread with sugar (1). On the other hand, seven other informants replied that they would 'try to calm' the individual afflicted with *susto*, although none described exactly how they would do this.

Similar patterns of intra-sample variation occurred with informants' responses to questions about treatment of persisting cases of *susto* with household remedies. Nearly 17% state that they would continue to use such remedies. Most report continuing to use general household remedies or to ingest particular food items. One informant chose to continue an undefined 'calming' treatment and another chose to make a ritual sweeping (*barrida*) of the body with a candle (the only informant who mentioned such a cure).

Ingesting food, trying to calm individuals or performing a *barrida* seem to be quite different approaches to treating *susto*. Trotter (1982: 220) also found a variety of treatments for *susto* among the Hispanic population. In his sample of 35 cases of treatment for *susto*, approximately 2/3 reported ingesting food (primarily herbal teas) and 1/3 reported using ritual treatments such as the *barrida*.

Other informants (6.5%) reported choosing physicians to treat *susto* initially and 25% named them for treating persisting *susto*. Among those who chose physicians were two informants who reported that they would go to a psychiatrist to treat persisting *susto*. Perhaps they view *susto* as a psychological illness or they think that having *susto* is in itself reason to suspect emotional problems.

Some informants reported that they do nothing or wouldn't know what to do if they did get *susto* (16.4%). Over a third of the informants report that *susto* does not persist after initial treatment. Nearly 15% state that they don't get *susto* at all. These responses perhaps indicate that for some, *susto* is not a serious illness nor one that affects them. It may also be that some of these people categorize the symptoms of *susto* as indicating some other illness, as Rubel and O'Nell (1978: 150) have found in their research on *susto* in Mexico. They report that what people once diagnosed as *susto*, they now diagnose as tuberculosis, hypertension or diabetes.

To treat *susto*, informants use a variety of household remedies, physicians, psychiatrists, or state that they don't know what they would do, do nothing, or don't get this illness. This variation in responses to *susto* may reflect that informants do not share the same beliefs about its etiology and thus do not share ideas about what constitutes appropriate treatment.

If the variety of responses to *susto* reflects that individual informants have different notions about this locally defined illness and its treatment, it is important to know what factors account for these differences. The data here do not indicate what might be salient factors, since only income level proved to be a possible factor in treatment choice for *susto*. Both the 6.5% who chose physicians initially and the 25% who chose them for persisting *susto* had above average incomes. These informants may select physicians because they can afford to do so or because they believe *susto* to be an illness which can be treated effectively by physicians. Of the nearly 15% who state that they don't get *susto*, all have above average incomes, but showed no other demographic pattern to distinguish them from the rest of the sample.[6]

CONCLUSIONS

'*Casi como doctor*' is a quote from one of the housewives who was interviewed for this study. Her expression encapsulates the idea that many people in Mexico have about the appropriate role of pharmacists; i.e., that they perform many of the same health care functions as physicians. As quasi-doctors, pharmacists diagnose illness and prescribe medicines. To the informants, pharmacists are not only quasi-physicians but also better than physicians in some respects. The health care services pharmacists offer are low cost, convenient, fast, easy, uncomplicated to use, and allow people to retain control over their treatment. It is not surprising that many people resort to pharmacists for relief from illness symptoms.

This study underscores the importance of OTC's as an established form of treatment central to the health care system in Mexico. In this system, pharmacists and OTC's are inseparably linked, since the former give advice about the latter. In the opinion of the informants, the linkage of pharmacists and OTC's produces a kind of health care that functions well to cure the illnesses they suffer.

There are also drawbacks, however. Self-medication as described in this paper may cause considerable health hazards. Misdiagnoses, overdoses, inappropriate medicines, over-reliance on OTC's, out of date and dangerous medications remain potential dangers for those who depend on pharmacists and OTC's for primary care. Azarcon, for example, was readily available in Mexico in the early 1980s and self-prescribed as a cure for stomach illnesses. Unfortunately, it is a toxic lead compound that can cause acute lead poisoning. During the mid-1980s, shortages of OTC's began to occur in Mexico, creating problems for all those who had developed a reliance on them to cure their illnesses.

Given that this kind of health care system is unlikely to be replaced by other health care alternatives, what can be done to make this system function better? First, the important role of pharmacists should be recognized. With this recognition, could come training, particularly for the pharmacists who learn their craft as apprentices, that would teach them to do better what they now already do. Specific courses in pharmacology and symptom diagnosis geared toward application in the setting of pharmacies would enhance the already existent skills of pharmacists and make their diagnostic advice more appropriate and less harmful to their clients.

Second, public service announcements on Mexican radio and television could be made to educate the public about the proper use of OTC's and potential dangers in their use. Such public service announcements already appear on Mexican radio and television about alcohol abuse and child molestation. Another possible means to educate the public about the use of OTC's are the comic book style romantic and adventure *novelas* that people everywhere in Mexico read. Public service advertisements in these *novelas*, like the media broadcasts, would reach a wide audience with helpful information.

The dangers of self-medication are augmented by the marketing practices of pharmaceutical firms. Exporting drugs to developing countries can be profitable business which pharmaceutical firms are unlikely to discontinue voluntarily. By implementing a rigorous essential drugs program, the Mexican government could curtail the sale of useless and harmful medicine and guarantee the steady supply of medicines which are needed in primary care.

In addition to demonstrating the link between pharmacists and OTC's in Mexican health care, this study also casts light upon the relationship between traditional, locally defined ideas and practices regarding illness and health care and cosmopolitan notions and practices. The interaction of these two medical traditions is complex, as the often contradictory results of health care studies show. Some scholars have found the widespread use of *curanderos* (Trotter and Chavira 1980); others report declining use (Keefe 1981; Edgerton, Karmo, and Fernandez 1970; Teller 1978; and Press 1973). This study and others find that people separate the use of the OTC's and local indigenous treatment (Whiteford 1976), but other studies report that *curanderos* mix OTC's with traditional cures (Brown 1963; Fabrega and Silver 1973; Kelly 1965; DeWalt 1977). Responses to *susto* in this study show great variation among the informants ranging from seeking treatment from a psychiatrist, to making a *barrida*, to not getting the illness at all. Other studies also have reported such variation in responses within an Hispanic population (Trotter 1982).

On one hand, then, the traditional, locally defined health care sector clearly persists and intersects with the cosmopolitan. On the other hand, health care choices in Mexico have been much affected by cosmopolitan medicine. Physicians have been found to be widely consulted in Mexico in this study as in others (Ardón 1978; DeWalt 1977). One study reports that people even consult physicians for help with traditional, locally defined illnesses (Martin et al. 1985). People continue to incorporate new, modern elements into traditional household remedies.

These contradictory findings point up the need for research which will analyze how traditional and cosmopolitan medical beliefs and practices intersect in Mexico. Rapid change, variation between and within Hispanic populations, socioeconomic variables, and differences in education all suggest themselves as factors which contribute to the complex interrelation between these two medical traditions, in particular with regard to the use of medicines. The participant-observer approach of anthropology which is geared toward collecting contextual information and getting at community level practices should be very useful at bringing an understanding to this complex relationship.

ACKNOWLEDGEMENT

A different version of this article appeared in *Medical Anthropology* 7(3): 68–69 (1983).

NOTES

1. Established in the late 1960s, the border industries program was set up to provide jobs for the many unemployed workers in the area. With low wages and tax breaks as incentives, multinational companies were encouraged to build plants where the component parts of products (clothing, electronics, toys) could be assembled in Mexico and then shipped out to be sold elsewhere.
2. COMO (*Centro de Orientación de la Mujer Obrera*) students collected the data for the questionnaire as part of their research training.
3. Population statistics were taken from a community study of the area done by COMO
4. Questions about *susto* or *curanderos* are noted as sensitive or controversial to Hispanics (Kay 1977: 89–90; Keefe 1981:46). For this reason, the results of studies on these topics are often questioned. Every precaution was taken in this study to insure the accuracy of the data on *susto* and *curanderos*. The questionnaires were administered in Spanish by native speakers of Spanish; by women to women; and by those of a lower income socio-economic background to those of the some background. The only differences between the interviewers and interviewees was that the former had slightly more formal education and were somewhat younger than the latter. No one in the sample refused to answer questions about *susto* or *curanderos*. None of the interviewers reported embarrassment or reluctance to discuss these topics by those interviewed.
5. None of the tendencies noted here were statistically significant at the .05 level. Because of the small sample size, these findings should best be viewed as indications of possible differences among the informants in the sample.
6. A recent work by Rubel, O'Nell, and Collado-Ardón (1984) breaks new ground in the examination of *susto* and will re-structure the framework for future studies of this illness. They find that *susto* occurs when an individual's capacity to adapt is overwhelmed by a combination of biological disease load and the victim's inability to perform role expectations. With the catalyst of a frightening event at some point in the victim's life, the individual succumbs to *susto*.

REFERENCES

Alland, Alexander Jr.
   1970 Adaptation in Cultural Evolution: An Approach to Medical Anthropology. New York: Columbia University Press.
Ardón, Rolando Collado
   1978 'Rural Medical Care or Rural Organization for Health?' In Modern Medicine and Medical Anthropology in the US-Mexico Border Population. Ed. by Boris Velimirovic. Washington, DC: Pan American Health Organization, pp. 22–30.
Beals, Alan R.
   1976 'Strategies of Resort to curers in South India'. In Asian Medical Systems. Ed. by Charles Leslie. Berkeley: Univ. of California Press, pp. 184–200.
Brown Jack
   1963 'Some Changes in Mexican Village Curing Practices Induced by Western Medicine'. America Indigena 23: 93–120.

Cañedo, Luis
　1974　'Rural Health Care in Mexico'. Science 185: 1131–1137.
Chiñas, Beverly
　1973　The Isthmus Zapotec Women's Roles in Cultural Context. New York: Holt, Rinehart and Winston.
Colson, A. C.
　1971　'The differential use of medical resources in developing countries'. Journal of Health, Soc. Behav. 12: 226–37.
DeWalt, Kathleen
　1977　'The Illnesses No Longer Understand: Changing Concepts of Health and Curing in a Rural Mexican Community'. Medical Anthropology Newsletter 8(2): 5–11.
Dukes, M. N. G.
　1963　Patient Medicines and Anthropology in Society. Den Haag, Holland: Drukkerij Pasmans.
Edgerton, Robert B., Karno, Marvin and Fernandez, Irma
　1970　'Curanderismo in the Metropolis'. American Journal of Psychotherapy 24: 124–134.
Erasmus, Charles
　1952　'Changing Folks Beliefs and the Relativity of Empirical Knowledge'. Southwest Journal of Anthropology 8: 411–428.
Fabrega, Horacio Jr.
　1974　Disease and Social Behavior. Cambridge: M. I. T. Press.
Fabrega, Horacio J. and Silver, Daniel B.
　1973　Illness and Shamanistic Curing in Zinacantan. Stanford: Stanford Univ. Press.
Griffenhagen, G.
　1976　'Is Self-medication emerging from the Dark Ages?' Trial 12: 26–30
Herskovits, Melville J.
　1950　'The Hypothetical Situation: A Technique of Field Research'. Southwest Journal of Anthropology 6: 32–40.
Higgins, Cheleen Mahar
　1975　'Integrative aspects of folk and Western medicine among the urban poor in Oaxaca'. Anthro. Quarterly 48: 31–37.
Janzen, John M.
　1978　The Quest for Theraphy in Lower Zaire. Berkeley: Univ. of California Press.
Kay, Margarita
　1979　'Health and Illness in a Mexican American Barrio'. In Ethnic Medicine in the Southwest. Edward H. Spicer, (ed.) Tucson: Univ. of Arizona Press, pp. 99–166.
Keefe, Susan
　1981　'Folk Medicine among Urban Mexican Americans: Cultural Persistance, Change, and Displacement'. Hispanic Journal of Behavioral Sciences 3 (1): 41–58.
Kelly, Isabel
　1965　Folk Practices in North Mexico. Austin: Univ. of Texas Press.
Kiev, A.
　1968　Curanderismo: Mexican American Folk Psychiatry. New York: Free Press.
Kleinman, Arthur and Sung, L.H.
　1976　'Why Do Indigenous Practitioners Successfully Heal? A Follow-up Study of Indigenous Practice in Taiwan'. Paper presented at the Medical Anthropology Workshop on the 'Healing Process'. Michigan State Univ.
Leon-Portilla, Miguel
　1972　'The Norteño. Variety of Mexican Culture: An Ethnographic Approach'. In Plural Society in the Southwest. Ed. by Edward Spicer and Raymond H. Thompson. New York: Interbook Inc., pp. 77–114.
Loewe-Reiss, Ricardo

1978 'Considerations on the Health Status along Mexico's Northern Border'. In Views Across the Border ed. by Stanley R. Ross. Albuquerque: Univ. of Mexico Press, pp. 241–55.

Maclean, C. M. U.
1965 'Traditional medicine and its practitioners in Ibadan, Nigeria'. Journal of Tropical Medicine and Hyg. 68: 237–244

Madsen, Claudia
1965 *A Study of Change in Mexican Folk Medicine*. Middle American Research Institute. Publ. No. 25. New Orleans: Tulane Univ. Press.

Martin, Harry W., Martinez Cervando, Leon, Robert L., Richardson, Chad and Reyes Acosta, Victor
1985 'Folk Illnesses Reported to Physicians in the Lower Rio Grande Valley: A Binational Comparison'. *Ethnology* 24 (3): 229–236.

McClain, Carol
1977 'Adaptation in Health Behavior Modern and Traditional Medicine in a West Mexican Community'. *Social Science and Medicine* 11: 341–347.

Mitchell, Mary Faith
1980 *Class, Therapeutic Role, and Self-Medication in Jamaica*. Ann Arbor: Univ. Microfilms International.

Nolesco, Margarita
1978 'Health and Disease in Northern Border Area'. *In Modern Medicine and Medical Anthropology in the US-Mexico Border Population*. Ed. by Boris Velimorovic. Washington DC: Pan American Health Organization, pp. 49–59.

Pelto, Petti J. and Pelto, Gretel H.
1978 *Anthropological Research — The Structure of Inquiry*. Cambridge: Cambridge Univ. Press.

Polgar, S.
1963 'Health Action in Cross-Cultural Perspective' *In* the *Handbook of Medical Sociology*, ed. by H.N. Freeman, S. Lewis and L.G. Reeder. Englewood Cliffs, New York: Prentice Hall. pp. 397–419

Press, Irwin
1973 'Bureaucracy Versus Folk Medicine: Implications from Seville, Spain'. *Urban Anthropology* 2 (2): 232–247.

Purcell, John F. H.
1981 'Mexican Social Issues'. In *Mexico-U.S. Relations*, ed. Susan Kaufman Purcell. New York: Proceedings of the Academy of Political Science. Vol. 34, No. 1, pp. 43–54.

Ritchey, Ferris J. and Raney, Marilyn
1981 'Medical Role — Task Boundary Maintenance: Physicians' Opinions of Clinical Pharmacy'. *Medical Care* XIX No. 1: 90–103.

Romanucci-Ross, Lola
1977 'The Hierarchy of Resort in Curative Practices: The Admiralty Islands, Melanesia'. *In Culture, Disease, and Healing*. ed. by David Landy. New York: Macmillan Publ. Co., Inc., pp. 481–487.

Rubel, Arthur J.
1966 *Across the Tracks: Mexican-Americans in a Texas City*. Austin: Univ. of Texas Press, Hogg Foundation for Mental Health.

Rubel, Arthur J. and O'Nell, Carl W.
1978 'Difficulties of Presenting Complaints to Physicians: Susto Illness as an Example'. *In Modern Medicine and Medical Anthropology in the U.S.-Mexico Border Population*. ed. by Boris Velimirovic. Washington, DC: Pan American Health Organization, pp. 147–154.

Rubel, Arthur J., and O'Nell, Carl W., and Collado-Ardón, Rolando
1984 *Susto, A folk Illness*. Berkeley: Univ. of California Press.

Schaller, Warren E. and Carroll, Charles R.
  1976   *Health, Quackery, and the Consumer*. Phila.: W.B. Saunders Company.
Schendel, George
  1968   *Medicine in Mexico*. Austin: Univ. of Texas Press.
Silverman, Milton
  1976   *The Drugging of the Americas*. Berkeley: Univ. of California Press.
Silverman, Milton and Lee, Philip R.
  1974   *Pills, Profits, and Politics*. Berkeley: Univ. of California Press.
Simoni, Joseph J. and Ball, Richard A.
  1975   'Can We Learn from Medicine Hucksters'. *Journal of Communication* 25: 175–181.
Teller, Charles H.
  1972   *Internal migration, socio-economic status and health: access to medical care in a Honduran city*. Ithaca, New York: Cornell Univ. Latin American Studies. Dissertation series.
  1978   'Access to Medical Care of Migrants in a Honduran city'. *Journal of Health and Social Behavior* 14(3): 214–226.
Trotter, Robert T. II.
  1982   'Susto: the Context of Community Morbidity Patterns'. *Ethnology* 21 (3): 215–226.
Trotter, Robert T. II. and Chavira, Juan Antonio
  1980   'Curanderismo: An Emic Theoretical Perspective of Mexican American Folk Medicine'. *Medical Anthropology* 4 (4): 423–482.
Weaver, Thomas
  1970   'Use of Hypothetical Situations in a Study of Spanish American Illness Referral Systems'. *Human Organization* 29: 140–154.
Whiteford, Michael
  1976   *The Forgotten Ones: Colombian Countrymen in an Urban Setting*. Gainesville: Univ. of Florida Press.
Young, James Clay
  1981   *Medical Choice in a Mexican Village*. New Brunswick, New Jersey: Rutgers Univ. Press.

SJAAK VAN DER GEEST

THE ARTICULATION OF FORMAL AND INFORMAL MEDICINE DISTRIBUTION IN SOUTH CAMEROON

The context of medicine distribution in South Cameroon is more complex than I had foreseen when I set out to do anthropological fieldwork in 1980.[1] Perhaps naively, I had expected to find one fairly surveyable field of formal services and another small and rather chaotic one of informal activities where medicines were transacted, purchased and consumed outside professional medical control. This chapter is about my discovery that there are not two fields, but only one in which formal and informal activities are closely interwoven. In a sense one could say that the chaos is not restricted to a delimited informal sector but is found everywhere. But one could equally well hold that there is no chaos at all. What appears chaotic and formless (in-formal) at first sight proves fairly structured when one looks more closely and starts to understand the commercial logic of the whole. That is another discovery on which I shall report in this paper.

After a short discussion of the methodology and a presentation of the research area I will describe what are called the 'formal' and 'informal sectors' of medicine distribution. I will then discuss the products that are purchased through the informal sector and show how these informal (and often illegal) services cater to people's needs. The intertwining of formal and informal is dealt with at the end. Cameroon is taken as an example but it is clear that similar situations exist throughout the Third World.

BACKGROUND AND RESEARCH METHODS

Most social science research directed to medical problems in non-Western societies can be divided into two groups. Anthropologists have been especially concerned with medical phenomena that are radically different from those in their own societies. Undoubtedly, exoticism, which is a characteristic of so much anthropological work, has played a role in this bias. Practically speaking, this means that most medical-anthropological work has been focused on *traditional medicine*, especially its religious aspects, those phenomena which have disappeared from Western medicine. The second group, generally consisting of medical sociologists and epidemiologists, has done research into the functioning of existing *modern medical services*, the prevention and spread of disease, frequencies of infant mortality, etc. This research has usually been highly quantitative, being based on surveys among health workers and/or patients. It is the reports of these researchers which play an important role in the evaluation and planning of governments' health policies. It is also these data which end up in the international reports of the World Health Organization.

Between these two areas of research there is, however, a large fallow area: *informal modern health care*. Medical anthropologists have little bothered with this area because it is, after all, modern medicine. The fact that it is informal was not enough to attract their attention, although they are generally interested in deviant and marginal phenomena. On the other hand, the medical sociologists have not bothered with this area because they found it to be too informal. Perhaps they did not even notice it. It could not be revealed by surveys and, apparently, it was not very important for general policy. It was to this subject that my research was directed.

The fieldwork was carried out in the Division of Ntem in the extreme south of Cameroon. This chapter describes the situation as it was in 1980 when most of the research took place. Ntem has an area half that of the Netherlands, but the population is only 140,000, which gives a population density of nine people per square kilometre. The area falls within the rain forest zone. Agriculture is by far the most important means of subsistence. The main town and capital is Ebolowa with 20,000 inhabitants. It is not only an important administrative center but also one of trade, education, medical care, and other infrastructural services. Most people of Ntem live in villages.

The health situation in these villages leaves much to be desired. There is a shortage of clean drinking water and sanitary facilities. Pigs, goats, and other domestic animals wander freely around; refuse disposal is insufficient; and the housing is often of bad quality (Amat and Cortadellas 1972: 342–356). Certain food habits, such as that whereby the best food is reserved for the adults, especially the men, form an extra threat to child health and are a cause of infant protein deficiency. A survey (RUC 1978) has shown that twenty percent of the children under five years of age in the tropical rain forest area of Cameroon are malnourished and that fifty percent are anemic.

According to Ministry of Health statistics (MSP 1978), malaria and intestinal helminthiasis are the most common diseases for which the people in Ntem consult the medical services (respectively, fifteen and ten percent of all reported diseases). They are followed by skin diseases (eight percent), colds and influenza (eight percent), rheumatic complaints (eight percent), bronchitis (five percent), and gonorrhea (three percent). According to the same statistics, measles is by far the most important cause of death among children, but the actual cause of death is always a complication such as pneumonia, malaria, or encephalitis. Weanling mortality in Cameroon as a whole is estimated to be one hundred and fifty per thousand and infant mortality eighty-six per thousand.

In the Ntem division there are three hospitals with a total of 450 beds. The two largest, with a total of four hundred beds, are both situated in Ebolowa, about five kilometres apart. In addition to this, there are forty-five health centres and only one officially recognized pharmacy. Other medical services, especially primary facilities such as herbalists, traditional midwives, informal medicine sellers, neighbourly help, and of course self-help, cannot be expressed in figures.

The methods used in this research are varied, and some can be characterized by Douglas' (1976) pleonasm 'investigative research'. By this term, Douglas means a detective-like approach to the gathering of information, whereby the researcher assumes that the most relevant information is often being withheld while that which is said is meant to conceal what is of real importance. Obviously, such concealment is most likely to occur when direct answers would be threatening to the informants. This was certainly the case for some unlawful practices in the field of drug distribution. In many interviews I paid special attention to contradictions and subtle reactions which could reveal the more hidden aspects of drug distribution. In order to discover such contradictions, it was necessary to interview a large number of informants on the same subject. In addition, many reports, minutes, accounts, and letters – some of which were confidential – were studied.

I will view the problem of informal medicine trade within the perspective of the concepts of 'informal sector' (Breman 1976; McGee 1978; Van Dijk 1981) and 'articulation of modes of production' (Van Binsbergen and Geschiere 1985). This latter concept implies that certain weak sectors in the economy (and the social formations which are connected to them) are not destroyed by the dominant sector but are preserved because they are useful to the latter. In this contribution, I hope to make clear that this also applies to the medicine trade in Cameroon. The informal trade is intrinsically connected to the formal trade, but this connection has a hierarchical character. By this I mean that the informal sector is subservient to the interests of the formal sector.

THE FORMAL SECTOR

Before proceeding it is necessary to point out that what I will be describing is the *formal* formal sector; that is to say, what that sector looks like on paper, for example in the *organogrammes* which one finds at the Ministry. It is therefore a description of what the formal sector should be. When however, we turn to the question of what it actually looks like, it becomes difficult to distinguish between formal and informal.

In discussing medicine distribution it is possible to distinguish three channels: (1) public institutions, (2) private non-profit institutions, and (3) private commercial institutions.

The *public institutions* are all state-owned facilities concerned with the distribution of medicines. These mainly include hospitals and health centers. These institutions distribute medicines freely. All hospitals and health centers have their own pharmacy. Patients are given prescriptions and referred to this pharmacy, where they receive the necessary medicines. Medicines are distributed to all institutions by the Pharmacie Centrale d'Approvisionnement, a department of the Ministry of Health. Hospitals are allowed, within certain limits, to order the medicines which they require. The smaller centers receive a standard supply once a year, and they have to make this last for the whole year. In anticipation of the argument which follows, it will be useful at this point to remark that this system functions only with great difficulty. All public institutions are short of medicines, and the idea of an adequate supply of free medicines is nowhere near to being realized. This fact is partially illustrated by the existence of a large number of private institutions.

The *private non-profit institutions* are church-related hospitals, health centers, and primary health care projects. The most important difference between the church-related and public institutions is that medicines and medical care in the former are not free of charge. Medicines are distributed in the same way in both types of institution. The patient receives a prescription which he can exchange for medicine, but in the church-related institutions the medicines must be paid for. Although these religious institutions do not have a profit motive, they are forced to make large profits on the sale of medicines in order to finance their activities. Private institutions receive almost no financial assistance from the state whereas the public institutions are totally financed.

All church-related institutions receive their medicines from one communal buying agent, La Fondation Ad Lucem, in Douala, which may only supply religious organizations. Ad Lucem allows various pharmaceutical companies in Europe to apply for the provision of the required medicines. The company which charges the lowest price receives the order. Because huge orders are involved, Ad Lucem is able to purchase for very low prices. Following WHO (1977, 1979) directives, Ad Lucem attempts to purchase medicines which are no longer patented and can therefore be produced more cheaply under generic instead of their brand-name.

The *private commercial institutions* which distribute medicines in the formal sector are the authorized pharmacies run by pharmacists with a university degree. According to the 1983 statistics, there were at that time only seventy-six of these pharmacies, and thirty-four were in the two largest cities, Douala and Yaoundé. The remaining forty-two pharmacies were situated in smaller cities. All pharmacies are therefore situated in urban areas. The reason for this is obvious. Pharmacists are entrepreneurs who only settle in areas with a high purchasing power. Most pharmacists would jump at the opportunity to open a business in one of the two largest cities, but many small rural towns apply in vain for the establishment of a pharmacy; no pharmacist is prepared to move to such a commercially uninteresting location.[2]

The fact that a country, almost twice as large as Great Britain, with a population of 7.5 million, has so few pharmacies does not, however, imply that they have a small turnover. In 1977 the fifty-two private pharmacies sold approximately the same amount of medicines (in value) as the seventy-two state hospitals and 277 public health centers together distributed to their patients. A year later, in 1978, the value of medicines distributed by the commercial sector was fifty percent greater than the public sector (see Van der Geest 1981: 140). It is quite likely that this tendency has continued.

The shortage of medicines in public hospitals and health centers forces the people to go to the pharmacies. Doctors and nurses in these institutions often write prescriptions for medicines which are only available in the private pharmacies. Sometimes patients or family members must travel for hours in order to reach a pharmacy which has the required medicines. The Division of Ntem is a large area. Travelling is difficult due to lack of transport and poor quality of the roads, particularly in the rainy season. With some bad luck it may take villagers a whole day (of waiting) to travel a distance of forty kilometres. The fact that there is only one pharmacy in this whole area is bound to cause problems. The same situation exists in the two neighbouring divisions.

THE INFORMAL SECTOR

Next to and (as we shall see) within this formal sector exists an informal medicine trade which has ramifications into the farthest corners of the region. There are at least five categories of informal medicine sellers. The most important are the shopkeepers who sell general provisions, including medicines. In the capital Ebolowa there are approximately seventy-five shops where one may purchase at least one or two medicines. The second group consists of market vendors who also sell medicines alongside other products. The third group can best be referred to as 'hawkers'. They travel from village to village during the cocoa harvest when the villagers have extra money at their disposal. These hawkers provide a variety of articles in addition to medicines. The fourth group consists of traders who are specialized in the sale of medicines and have a much larger assortment than the previously mentioned three groups. In Ebolowa, I found four such traders. They not only sell medicines but may also give medical advice when asked. One of them even gave injections. The fifth group consists of the personnel of medical institutions. They privately sell the medicines which should be provided to the patients free of charge.

After having shown who is involved in the informal retail trade in medicines, the questions which arise are: where do these people get their products; and what is the nature of the informal wholesale medicine trade? There are three types of wholesalers who supply the informal sector with medicines: those who sell smuggled medicines from Nigeria, official pharmacists, and personnel from medical institutions.

The smuggling of medicines from Nigeria has taken on enormous proportions, but it is impossible to discover the exact extent of this trade. The import and sale of medicines is much more free in Nigeria than in Cameroon. In

Cameroon unqualified sellers may not import medicines, so they are forced to import their products illegally from Nigeria. The medicines are transported by taxi or van and are allowed to pass by customs officials who are bribed. According to some informants, large amounts of medicines are carried over the border by foot or in boats along the coast. In West Cameroon there is a large number of depots where the medicines are stored and from where they are later distributed throughout Cameroon and even to neighboring countries such as Gabon and the Central African Republic.

The second group of wholesalers consists of legally recognized pharmacists. Here it is necessary to mention that the laws governing the exercise of the profession of pharmacist (RUC 1980) are very rigorous. According to these laws, only qualified pharmacists may sell medicines. (This of course is absurd when one considers the fact that there are so few pharmacies and that these are concentrated in the urban centres). In any case, the laws do not change the fact that almost all medicines can be purchased in large quantities and without a prescription in the pharmacies. Informal medicine sellers make use of this opportunity to purchase their supplies from the pharmacies. They pay the normal retail price which means that they have to sell them in the villages for a price which is a good deal higher.

The third group of wholesalers consists of hospital and health center personnel. As I have already mentioned, these institutions receive medical supplies from the Ministry at regular intervals, which they should provide to patients free of charge. I estimate that approximately thirty percent of these medicines do not reach the patients, at least not directly, but are appropriated by the health workers themselves.[3] The health workers then distribute them among friends and relatives, sell them to patients whom they treat at home, or sell them to informal medicine sellers (Van der Geest 1981: 61–86, 1982). It is this last possibility which makes them wholesalers in the informal medicine trade. It is impossible to determine the size of this 'wholesale trade'.

THE PRODUCTS

In the Division of Ntem, I noted seventy different medicines which are sold in the informal sector. The most common were analgesics (thirteen sorts), antibiotics (twelve sorts), remedies for coughs and colds (eleven sorts), laxatives (eight sorts), vitamins (six sorts), remedies for worms (five sorts), remedies for anemia (five sorts), and anti-malarials (three sorts).[4] Most medicine sellers were quite prepared to allow me to interview them about their trade even though it was illegal. Research was easiest at the markets where the medicines were prominently displayed. In the larger shops I was often forced to explicitly ask if medicines were sold. This sometimes caused suspicion.[5]

Most important was the work which I did among the three specialized medicine sellers. Because a large number of unknown medicines were involved, the research required long discussions and extensive note taking. This took place between sales. I was afraid that this situation would be inconvenient, but the three sellers cooperated fully. They did not object to my pulling up a chair and carefully noting all the names, ingredients, prices, and instructions for use of the medicines. They patiently answered all the questions which I put to them about the uses of the various medicines. At my request they allowed me to see receipts for medicines which they purchased elsewhere. One of them regularly asked me to purchase medicines for him during my travels. Because these enquiries were so successful, I was able to gather extensive data on the seventy medicines which I had encountered in the informal sector, but it would be beyond the scope of this article to give an exhaustive exposition of the medical aspects of these findings.[6] However, in order to understand the informal medicine trade, it is necessary to make a few general remarks.

The reactions of Western-trained doctors and pharmacists to the list of seventy medicines may vary. A pharmacist who gives priority to the norms concerning the preservation and prescription of medicines which he has learned during his training and which are applied in most Western countries will perhaps disapprove of their free availability. But anyone who takes the actual health situation in Cameroon into consideration will probably be less critical. The informal medicine sellers are often the only available 'representatives' of modern medicine, and when there is some knowledge as to the correct use of medicines, then self-medication with remedies bought in the informal sector is probably the best alternative in the absence of modern care.

Expert opinion on this matter is only useful if it is realistic; and in order to be realistic it must take the whole social and medical context into consideration. With this in mind, I presented the list of seventy medicines to a physician who worked in the research area and was reasonably aware of the health situation. His opinion was that forty-one of the listed medicines were useful or at least harmless when freely available, but he thought that twenty-four of the medicines should no longer be sold. Because of a lack of data, he could not form an opinion about the remaining five medicines.

The forty-one medicines which the physician considered to be harmless can be divided into two groups. The first group contains medicines which are extremely useful because they are effective against common diseases, they are relatively safe, and their correct application is probably generally known. This group includes analgesics, anti-malarials, and remedies for intestinal helminthiasis and colds. The medicines which fall into the remaining group are of questionable value. The fact that these medicines are freely available is not problematic because they are generally not very potent. They are really superfluous. This category includes vitamins, remedies for anemia, and a number of laxatives.

Of the twenty-four medicines which this physician would like to see removed from sale, twelve are antibiotics. Opinions about the free availability of antibiotics are, however, varied. Opponents point to the fact that misuse can lead to resistence. They see self-medication with antibiotics as exacerbating medical problems. The advocates argue that since doctors are often not available, the free sale of antibiotics is necessary. People living in isolated areas benefit from this sale. In addition, the advocates argue, people are generally well aware of how to apply the antibiotics in question. It seems that this subject will remain controversial for some time to come. Other medicines which this physician would like to see taken off the free market are strong laxatives which may cause dehydration, especially among children, and a number of remedies which only repress symptoms. thereby leading to the postponement of consultation with a doctor and possibly detrimental consequences for the patient.

Here it is necessary to mention a number of additional considerations that make the free sale of medicines problematic.One of these is the method of application. Injections which are generally popular, can be dangerous. When they are given as self-medication, the needles are often not sterile. Storage and the age of the medicines also constitute a problem . Because medicines are stored under unsuitable conditions (temperature, light, humidity, and atmosphere pressure), it is doubtful whether they will remain effective. The labels of a number of medicines state clearly that they should be kept cool, but I have never seen a refrigerator for medicines on the informal market, though I have for beer. Also, no attention is paid to the date of expiry. However, the most important problem is the lack of adequate information. Naturally, information which is normally contained in the doctor's prescription is lacking. But even the information on the package insert usually does not reach the client. There are various reasons for this. The most important is that the inserts are not sold with the medicines because the latter have been removed from the original packages and placed in various bottles and jars to be sold in very small quantities. In the rare case that a client does purchase medicines with an instructional leaflet, the information may be inaccurate, as has been shown by research elsewhere (Silverman 1976; Silverman et al. 1982). Many of the medicines which are produced in Nigeria or in England for Nigerian firms immediately catch the eye because of their extremely tendentious advertizing and sometimes misleading directions for use displayed on the package. Finally, almost all products that come from Nigeria have texts in English, which most people in the French-speaking part of Cameroon cannot read.

Unavoidably, lack of information leads to wrong application. During my research I came across many cases of incorrect use of medicines, some with serious consequences. But even if there are no negative medical effects, the non-medical consequences are bad enough. The fact that people in a poor society spend money on useless medicines means that a scarce resource is withdrawn from items that are necessary for the maintenance of health, for example food, housing, and good medicines. On a larger scale, this wrong use of the medicines forms one of the greatest obstacles for the improvement of health in the Third World. Finally, it should be noted that the ignorance of consumers makes deception by the manufacturer and seller easier. Both types of deceit were seen during my research and both led to wrong use.

It is difficult to generalize about the prices which are charged and the profits which are made in the informal sector. Sales policy is capricious and can vary from one seller to another and from one day to another. Some prices are lower than those in the official pharmacies, but most are higher. It should be noted, however, that in the informal sector much smaller amounts are sold, so that the consumer only spends a small amount of money in each transaction.

The data on the profits of medicine sellers are no less difficult to determine. It was possible to compare the purchasing and selling prices which applied to nineteen products sold by one trader. The profit varied from fifty to 1,150 percent. The average was three hundred percent. This may appear to be high, but it should be remembered that the turnover of most traders is very limited. Medicines are sold in extremely small quantities, sometimes only one or two tablets at a time. In spite of the wide profit margin, most medicine sellers only have a meagre existence, except for some vendors in the markets of big cities. In the rural areas the trade only flourishes in the cocoa season when the people have money to spend. During this season cocoa farmers travel to the city to purchase supplies and fill their medicine chest.

THE BENEFITS OF THE INFORMAL SECTOR

One of the medicine vendors described his function as '*dépanner les petits problèmes*'. The South Cameroonians have a long tradition of self-medication. In the past they used only herbs which grew in the vicinity, but now pharmaceutical products are being increasingly used. This development is made possible by the medicine vendors who bring these products as far as the most isolated villages.

In four respects the vendors have more success in satisfying the needs of the average Cameroonian than the pharmacists; all four are related to availability. First, the vendors are financially more within reach, even though their products are relatively more expensive, because the pharmacists only sell fixed amounts of medicines in standard packages while the vendors in the informal sector sell any amount that is asked for. This makes it possible for a client to obtain which he urgently needs, such as analgesics, cheaply. This is what the medicine vendor meant when he described his work as '*dépanner les petits problèmes*'.

Second, the vendors are literally more within reach. It is always possible to find a medicine vendor without having to travel more than a few kilometres, whereas one may have to travel fifty or a hundred kilometres, or sometimes even further, to reach a pharmacy.

Third, the vendors are available day and night. They only close when everyone has gone to bed, and even after that it is still possible to purchase medicines. If someone urgently needs a medicine during the night, he will not hesitate to wake the vendor. The pharmacies maintain European working hours, to which they strictly keep. It is unthinkable that someone, who does not have some form of personal relationship with the pharmacist, would be sold medicines when the pharmacy is closed.

This brings us to the fourth factor, social distance. The difference between the pharmacist and the vendor can probably best be illustrated by two quotations from my fieldnotes:

28 June 1980

I spent two hours at the market with a medicine vendor, a Nigerian boy of about fifteen. It was Saturday afternoon. I noted the country of origin, price, and if present, instructions for use for forty-two medicines. The boy was very helpful; he knew all the prices by heart and showed me all the medicines about which I enquired. He apparently found it quite normal that I wrote everything down. While I was there many people came and purchased medicines. I did not have the impression that they were disturbed by my presence. A lot of *folkologo*, the local term for Tetracycline (an antibiotic), was sold. People kept asking: "Have you got anything for worms?" or "What's that for?" People who do not know very much about medicines but who do not want to reveal their complaint may be able to find the right medicine in this way. It would be impossible to act like this in a pharmacy.

11 August 1980

I have just spent half an hour sitting with E., an old man who sells medicines at the market. While I was there he was visited by six clients.

A small boy comes and pays 25 francs and E. gives him three Quinacrine tablets (antimalarial). These tablets actually cost 10 francs each, but E. explains that the boy is poor.

Two youths. One of them buys six Tetracycline capsules for 50 francs. A young woman with a child dawdles around and finally purchases six Mintezol tablets (for worms) for 375 francs.

A man of about thirty-five, purchases without hesitation Nivaquin tablets (anti-malarial) and a vial of Bipeniciline (an injectable antibiotic). I ask him who is going to give the injection and he replies: "I am, I'm a nurse.[He then goes on to say that he used to be an *infirmier journalier* (a very lowly qualified nurse) but that he lost his job, after which he became a planter. He now helps his neighbours when they have medical problems. However, he feels primarily responsible for the health of his own family.

A middle-aged woman who speaks in pidgin asks for a remedy for filaria. E. says that he doesn't have anything. He tells her to try the pharmacy. But she complains that she doesn't know which medicine to ask for. . . . Once again, I become aware of the fact that many people are inhibited to go to the pharmacy. You can't casually look around, pick up medicines, and ask: "Have you got anything for filaria?[There are all sorts of people who stare at you, and the people behind the counter are different from yourself. They are not patient and friendly. You do not feel at ease. It is a bit like a hospital.

Although the medicine vendor is more within the reach of most people and satisfies their needs better than the pharmacy, there are also many disadvantages connected with purchasing medicines from a vendor. The consumers are well aware that usually vendors have products of inferior quality, that they offer less choice, and that their knowledge of medicines is limited. The preference for the vendor should, however, be seen in the context of the whole health-seeking process. People who become ill first employ strategies which require very little extra effort, self-medication. Only when this does not succeed do they employ other strategies which require more effort and are more expensive. Now, within this 'hierarchy of resort' (Romanucci-Ross 1977), self-medication and medicine vendors share the first place. It is only when this choice of therapy does not produce the required results that the above mentioned objections to the medicine vendors begin to play a role in the choice of further therapy.

THE INTERWEAVING OF FORMAL AND INFORMAL

The relationship between the formal and informal sectors of medicine distribution has two important characteristics. First, both sectors are closely connected, even complementary. Second, this connection is unequal in nature.

The statement that the formal and informal sectors are intertwined and have common interests may be initially surprising. One is more likely to get the impression that both sectors are at daggers drawn, especially in the medicine trade. Let me give a few examples. In the law governing the exercise of the profession of pharmacist (RUC 1980), it is emphasized that medicines may only be distributed by qualified persons, i.e. pharmacists. It is also forbidden to advertize medicines publicy. The law suggests that the utmost care should be taken to ensure that medicines are used properly. Distribution which does not take place within the formal sector as defined by law is contrary to the basic principle of the profession of pharmacist, which is: the optimal distribution of optimal medicines to ensure optimal health.

Art. 48
The sale to the public of any medicament, product or accessory article as defined under Section 6 above, by the intermediary of commission houses, groups of buyers or any other establishments owned or managed by persons who are not in possession of the diploma of pharmacist, shall be unlawful with the exception of those establishments mentioned under Section 32.

Section 32 refers to the so-called 'propharmacies', small pharmacies which, with special permission, are established near health centers and are run by nurses (see note 2).

Art. 49
Any sale, display or distribution of medicaments on the highway, in fairs and markets, by any persons, even in possession of the diploma of pharmacists, shall be unlawful.

It is not only the official legislation which gives the impression that the interests of the formal and informal sectors of medicine distribution are opposed. The reports and other publications of pharmaceutical firms conjure up the same picture. They suggest that the pharmaceutical industry does its best to supply products which are as safe and as effective as possible. In the International Code of Pharmaceutical Marketing Practice compiled by the International Federation of Pharmaceutical Manufacturers' Associations we read:

> The pharmaceutical industry, conscious of its special position arising from its involvement in public health, and justifiably eager to fulfil its obligations in a free and fully responsible manner, undertakes:
> – to ensure that all products it makes available for prescription purposes to the public are backed by the fullest technological service and have full regard to the needs of public health;
> – to produce pharmaceutical products under adequate procedures and strict quality assurance.

And in connection with the way in which medicines are sold, the same code remarks:

> Information on pharmaceutical products should be accurate, fair and objective, and presented in such a way as to conform not only to legal requirements but also to ethical standards and to standards of good taste. Particular care should be taken that essential information as to the pharmaceutical products' safety, contra-indications and side effects or toxic hazards is appropriately and consistently communicated subject to legal, regulatory and medical practices of each nation. The word 'safe' must not be used without qualification (cited in Health Action International 1982: ii–iii).

On the basis of this statement, one would think that the formal and informal sectors have opposing interests. These strict rules, which the pharmaceutical industry formulates for its own practice, seem to imply that the industry does its best to prevent its prescription-only products from being sold on the free market without a prescription or an instruction leaflet. In the same vein, one would expect that doctors, nurses and pharmacists in Cameroon would take measures to prevent the inexpert distribution of medicines. The reality is, however, quite different. It is true that the rules and statements of the representatives of the formal medicine trade are extremely negative in their judgement of the informal sector. But it has not been sufficiently realized that these rules and statements are mostly rhetorical. They are not applied literally, but rather veil the actual state of affairs or make it appear as if the informal practices occur against the will of the formal institutions. In reality, however, the informal trade exists with the approval of the representatives of the formal sector, and they have a direct interest in its existence.

That both sectors of the medicine trade in Cameroon are intertwined and mutually dependent becomes clear when we look at the origin of the products which are sold in the informal sector. The medicine vendors purchase their products from authorized pharmacies and from personnel in the formal health institutions. The transactions in both cases serve mutual interests. The pharmacist increases his turnover by selling to far-off villages through the vendor.

Health care personnel increase their income by selling medicines which were meant to be provided free of charge to patients. The relationship is more complex in the case of medicines which are smuggled from Nigeria. In that case, the intertwining of formal and informal takes place mainly in Nigeria where the medicines are bought. My research did not extend into Nigeria but there are indications that the medicines are purchased from legitimate institutions there.

This intertwining of sectors is, however, not limited to the origin of the product. There is also a direct connection between both sectors in the distribution itself. The two sectors have unclear 'boundaries' and often tend to merge. I will illustrate this with four examples. Hospital and health center personnel are expected to supply the patient with the necessary medicines free of charge. Instead, they sometimes sell the medicines to the patient, either inside or outside the medical institution. So informal trade occurs within the formal health care institutions; but can we call this 'informal trade'? The transaction may be carried out by a professional health worker, perhaps even within the context of formal health care. The second example of the merging of the two sectors is the fact that patients purchase medicines from vendors in the informal sector and take them along to the health center when they go for treatment. This is a common practice, since people know that the health centers often lack medicines.

I encountered the third example in the hospital where a large part of my research was concentrated. Patients sometimes have to wait a long time before they see a doctor, and treatment is not started until they have been examined. As a result, there is a demand for medicines, especially analgesics, which can be taken during the waiting period. For this purpose, they can turn to the medicine vendor who has set up his stand on the hospital grounds, right next to the polyclinic. The fourth example is related to the pharmacies. In spite of the strict regulations mentioned above and the professional training of pharmacists, there are a number of striking similarities between pharmacies and informal medicine vendors. They have in common that clients can purchase any medicine without prescription or expert advice. Moreover, the pharmacist is usually absent from the pharmacy and difficult to reach. The medicines are sold for him by employees who, as far as their training goes, can hardly be distinguished from the informal vendors. The question thus arises as to what extent one should view the pharmacies as part of the formal sector. These examples, to which others could be added, illustrate the nature of the connection between formal and informal. We shall now see that this relationship is an unequal one; the informal sector tends to be subordinate to the formal sector.

Some anthropologists who study politico-economic development in Africa use the concept of 'articulation of modes of production' to describe the co-existence and symbiosis in which one mode of production, the capitalist, dominates the other. In his study of the Maka society in Southeast Cameroon,

Geschiere (1978: 45), following some French authors, defines articulation as a situation in which:

> ... the capitalist mode of production has become dominant, but where the old, pre-capitalist relations retain some importance as subordinate modes of production. ... [A] mode of production is dominant when surpluses from the old production relations are used for its reproduction (i.e. its expansion. Concretely, ... capitalist expension in Africa has not led to the immediate demolition of the old units of production; on the contrary, the old relations of production were very often consolidated to a certain extent and used for the further development of the capitalist sector.

The concept of articulation also seems to be applicable to the relationship between the formal and informal sectors of medicine distribution in Cameroon. Although at first glance, they appear to compete, in fact they cooperate. This cooperation is not on equal terms however; the formal sector is able to subordinate the informal sector to its interests. I will illustrate this with two examples.

At the beginning of my research I was surprised to find that the local pharmacist, who was quite influential in local politics, had not eliminated the surrounding informal trade in medicines. I still assumed that they were competing. It was only later that I realized that the opposite was true. As we have seen, most clients usually have money to purchase only small amounts of medicines which are urgently needed. It would not be profitable for the pharmacists to sell to these petty clients. As a matter of fact, legislation comes to the pharmacists' help: they are not allowed to open the packages of medicines (and all medicines *are* in packages). Petty clients therefore are not served at the pharmacy, but they can go to the numerous medicine vendors. These vendors purchase part of their supplies from the pharmacy for the normal retail price. The vendors are, in a sense, the pharmacy's retailers. Through them the pharmacist sells medicines to the poorer section of the population without having to spend time serving them. The pharmacist was quite right when he explained to me that it was not in his interest to get rid of the vendors beacuse, as he put it, 'they work for us'.

A similar relationship, though more subtle and more indirect, exists between the medicine vendors and the pharmaceutical industry. As we have seen, the pharmaceutical industry claims to do all within its power to ensure that its medicines are safe and effective. Its measures are supposed to include guaranteeing the best quality of medicines and providing careful information. One would expect that the inapplicability of these measures, once the medicines reach the informal sector, would cause concern in the industry. One would also expect measures to be taken to prevent such developments, but that is not the case. The pharmaceutical firms consider these developments to be beyond their responsibility, and they continue to sell medicines to various countries even when they know that a large percentage of these products will end up in the informal sector, perhaps be wrongly used, and have detrimental effects. Pharmaceutical firms do not voluntarily reduce their sales because this would be better for public health. The informal sale of medicines is in the interest of the legitimate industry. The informal medicine trade in Cameroon may not be very large, but in some other developing countries such as India, Thailand, Indonesia, and Nigeria the informal sale of medicines has taken on gigantic proportions. It would be an enormous loss for the pharmaceutical industry if these markets were to disappear.

I am not suggesting that all pharmaceutical companies consciously promote this informal trade. A conspiracy theory is not necessary to understand the developments which we have described here. The system has an internal logic which ensures that the interests of the strongest party are favoured. One might call this the 'articulation of modes of distribution'.

As I said at the outset of this paper, it is not possible in reality to neatly separate a formal and informal sector. I have only used the terms as analytic concepts, for didactic purposes. The last examples show clearly that a division between formal and informal is indeed analytical and not real. When the formal pharmacist engages in transactions with informal vendors he turns into an informal actor as well.[7]

CONCLUSION

The problems associated with the informal medicine trade are acute in many Third World countries, but they are hardly recognized by researchers concerned with the formal aspects of health care. The formal and informal aspects of medicine distribution are closely interwoven. This applies to both the public and private sectors of the formal system of distribution. The formal/legal medicine trade makes use of the informal/illegal trade. The two cannot be separated. This means that a part of the supply of medicines to official institutions is likely to end up in the informal circuit. This complicating factor is medicine distribution to developing countries is not sufficiently recognized by official health care planners and entirely 'overlooked' by representatives of pharmaceutical firms.

Medicines in the informal sector can be detrimental to health because of insufficient knowledge and information (and sometimes pure deception) about their correct use. In addition, scarce money is often spent on useless medicines instead of food and other means which really benefit health. It should also be noted, however, that the informal sector often provides useful medicines to sections of the rural population which would otherwise go without. Because of this, it can hardly be dismissed.

This means that practical suggestions to improve the current situation should not recommend the liquidation of the informal sector. Such a 'solution' would rob part of the population of its only source of modern medicines. Realistic solutions should therefore aim at maintaining and improving the informal sector. Improvement could perhaps be realized by excluding useless and dangerous medicines from this sector and increasing the knowledge of vendors and clients as to the proper use of medicines. These two conditions can only be fulfilled if drastic restrictions are imposed on the importation of medicines. If the number of medicines is limited to approximately 250 essential and relatively cheap medicines, monitoring the trade would become more feasible and laypeople would learn the proper use of the most common medicines more easily. A number of "dangerous' drugs will undoubtedly be included among those 250 essential medicines, but it should be remembered that the dangers decrease as knowledge of proper use increases. Suggestions for such limitations have already been made by the World Health Organisation (WHO 1977,1979). It is because of resistance by those who have vested interests in the present situation (pharmaceutical companies, physicians, pharmacists, and politicians; see Lall and Bibile 1978; Yudkin 1980) that this obvious political choice is only infrequently made by developing countries.[8]

NOTES

1. The research on which this article is based was financially supported by the University of Amsterdam and the Netherlands Foundation for the Advancement of Tropical Research (WOTRO). It was further facilitated by the assistance of Mireille Visser whose unpublished report (Visser 1980) furnished me with much data. I was assisted by Kosso Félix-Fayard, Bita Jean-Claude, Mbang-Bita'a Nicolas, Robert Rempp, Robert Pool, Susan Whyte, and many others, both during and after my research. Useful comments were received from five anonymous readers. The research was approved by the Cameroon government (DGRST Authorisation No. 288). I would like to emphasize that the critical tone of this article is in no way meant to belittle the results which have been attained in the field of health care in Cameroon. This article is meant as a constructive contribution to the search for solutions to the country's health care problems. A slightly different version of this paper was published in the Canadian Journal of African Studies 19 (3): 569–87 in 1985.
2. It should be noted that the authorities have tried to solve this problem by setting up so-called 'propharmacies', noncommercial, government-supported, small drugstores that sell a selection of essential medicines. Propharmacies are allowed in areas where there is no private pharmacy. Their main purpose is to enable rural health centers to continue functioning even if their drug supply has been exhausted. The nurse at the center simply writes a prescription with which the patient can obtain the necessary drug in the nearby propharmacy. Elsewhere (Van der Geest 1983) I have pointed out that the lack of commercial incentive has proved fatal for most propharmacies. In 1980 only one propharmacy functioned in the whole of the Ntem Division. Experiences with the propharmacy seem to be better however in the West of Cameroon (see Nchinda 1978).
3. It should first be emphasized that the figure of thirty percent is indeed a guess and second that the incidence of unlawful private medicine use will vary extremely in different health institutions. The guess of thirty percent was suggested to me by some knowledgeable informants who also guessed. In one (church-related) hospital I was able to calculate the loss of medicines not accounted for. I found that about thirty percent of all medicines had not passed through the appropriate channels.
4. A distinction could also be made between products confected and or marketed by small Nigerian firms and products from multinational companies. The former are commonly called 'patent medicines' in West Cameroon and tend to be rather harmless, often dubious and superfluous medicines. Many of the multinational products are dangerous 'prescription-only

drugs' which are also available without a doctor's prescription. This distinction is not further discussed in this paper.
5. Apparently someone complained about my activities to the authorities. One afternoon a police car picked me up from the street and took me to the police station where I had to 'explain' once again the purpose of my research (I had done so before when I was granted the research permission). After I had satisfied the chief of police I was brought back to the place where they found me and I continued the visits to the shops.
6. For a complete list of these medicines see Van der Geest 1987.
7. The same applies to the pharmacist in El Salvador who has his 10-year-old nephew prescribe and dispense medications (Ferguson this volume), to the pharmacist in Addis Ababa who sells vials with injectable penicillin to 'injection doctors' (Kloos et al. this volume, and to the pharmaceutical firm that sends its representatives to Ayurvedic practitioners in Sri Lanka (Wolffers this volume).
8. This policy, which would have many economic advantages as well, has been efficiently applied by only a handful of developing countries (see Lall and Bibile 1978; Gish and Feller 1979; Melrose 1982; Muller 1982; Mamdani 1986).

REFERENCES

Amat, B. and Cortadellas, Tonia
    1972 Ngovayang II: un village du Sud Cameroun. Contribution à une étude de la santé en Afrique. Paris: Bureau d'Etudes Coopératives et Communautaires.
Breman, J.
    1976 Een dualistisch arbeidsbestel. Een critische beschouwing van het begrip 'de informele sector'. Rotterdam: van Gennep.
Buijtenhuijs, R. and Geschiere, P. (eds.)
    1978 Social Stratification and Class Formation: African Perspectives. Vol. 2. Leiden: Afrika-Studiecentrum.
Douglas, J. D.
    1976 Investigative Social Research: Individual and Team Field Research. Beverly Hills: Sage Publications.
Geschiere, P. L.
    1978 The Articulation of Different Modes of Production: Old and New Inequalities in Maka Villages (Southwest Cameroon). In Buijtenhuijs and Geschiere 1978: 45–68.
Gish, O. and Feller, Loretta L.
    1979 Planning Pharmaceuticals for Primary Health Care: The Supply and Utilization of Drugs in the Third World. New York: A.P.H.A. Monograph Series No. 2.
Health Action International
    1982 an International Code of Pharmaceutical Marketing Practice. Penang: H.A.I.
Illy, H F
    1976 Politik und Wirtschaft in Kamerun. Bedingungen, Ziele und Strategien der staatlichen Entwicklungspolitik. München: Weltform Verlag.
Lall, S. and Bibile, S.
    1978 The Political Economy of Controlling Transnationals: The Pharmaceutical Industry in Sri Lanka, 1972–1976. International Journal of Health Services 8 (2): 299–328.
Landy, D. (ed.)
    1977 Culture, Disease and Healing: Studies in Medical Anthropology. London: Macmillan.
McGee, T.
    1979 Conservation and Dissolution in the Third World City: The 'Shanty Town' as an Element of Conversation. Development and Change 10: 1–22.
Mamdani, M.
    1986 Essential Drugs in the Developing World. Health Policy & Planning 1 (3): 187–201.

Melrose, Dianna
  1982 Bitter Pills: Medicines and the Third World Poor. Oxford: Oxfam.
M.S.P. (Minstère de la Santé Publique)
  1978 Rapport statistique d'activités des services de santé publique, Année 1978: Taoundé: MSP, SSSD.
Muller, M.
  1982 The Health of Nations: A North-South Investigation. London: Faber & Faber.
Nchinda, T.C.
  1978 The Propharmacy as a Means of Meeting Chronic Drug Shortages in Rural Health Centres in Rural African Communities. Tropical Doctor 8: 255–8.
Nichter, M.
  1983 Paying for What Ails You: Sociocultural Issues Influencing the Ways and Means of Therapy Payment in South India. Social Science & Medicine 17 (14): 957–65.
Romanucci-Ross, Lola
  1977 The Hierarchy of Resort in Curative Practices: The Admiralty Islands. In Landy 1977: 481–7.
République Unie du Cameroun (RUC)
  1978 National Nutrition Survey. Washington: US/AID. 1980 Law. No. 80/10 of 14 July 1980: To Regulate the Practice of Pharmacy.
Silverman, M.
  1976 The Drugging of the Americas. Berkeley: University of California Press.
Silverman, M. et al.
  1982 Prescriptions for Death: The Drugging of the Thirld World. Berkeley: University of California Press.
Van Binsbergen, W. and Geschiere, P. (eds.)
  1985 Old Models of Production and Capitalist Encroachment: Anthropological Explorations in Africa. London: Routledge & Kegan Paul.
Van der Geest, S.
  1981 La pathologie de services médicaux: la distribution de médicaments au Sud Cameroun. Problèmes et suggestions. Amsterdam: Anthropological-Sociological Center.
  1982 The Efficiency of Inefficiency: Medicine Distribution in South Cameroon. Social Science & Medicine 16 (24): 2145–53.
  1983 Propharmacies: a Problematic Means of Drug Distribution in Rural Cameroon. Tropical Doctor 13 (1): 9–13.
  1987 Self-care and the Informal Sale of Drugs in South Cameroon. Social Science & Medicine 25 (3): 293–305.
Van Dijk, M. P.
  1981 De informele sector van Ouadadougou en Dakar: Ontwikkelingsmogelijkheden van kleine bedrijven in twee Westafrikaanse hoofdsteden. Ph.D. Diss., Free University of Amsterdam.
Visser, Mireille
  1980 Geneesmiddelenverspreiding in het Département du Ntem, Zuid-Kameroen: een onderzoeksverslag. Unpublished manuscript.
World Health Organization (WHO)
  1977 The Selection of Essential Drugs. TRS 615. Geneva: WHO.
  1979 The Selection of Essential Drugs. TRS 614. Geneva: WHO.
Yudkin, J. S.
  1980 The Economics of Pharmaceutical Supply in Tanzania. International Journal of Health Services 10 (3): 455–77.

AHMAD FUAD AFDHAL AND ROBERT L. WELSCH

THE RISE OF THE MODERN *JAMU* INDUSTRY IN INDONESIA: A PRELIMINARY OVERVIEW

Jamu is the Indonesian term for indigenous medicines usually prepared from herbal materials such as leaves, bark, roots and flowers. Each of the more than 300 major ethnic groups that make up modern Indonesia has its own repertoire of traditional recipes, preferred ingredients and methods of use for these varied herbal preparations, which were characteristically mixed together as needed by a member of the family or a *dukun* (traditional healer). Some herbal medicines have long been part of the public domain, that is, general knowledge in their respective communities. Others, particularly more elaborate mixtures and concoctions have traditionally been regarded as privately owned knowledge, secret heirlooms passed on by the families of *dukun*'s, the royal courts and nobility, or by ordinary citizens.

In the past 20 years Indonesia has begun to modernize rapidly; nevertheless rural communities continue to rely heavily on locally prepared *jamu*'s made from plant materials. But during this same period, the term *jamu* has increasingly become associated with the rapidly expanding assortment of powders, creams, pills, capsules and cosmetics packaged and manufactured both in small cottage industries and by large factories with increasingly sophisticated equipment. Packaged *jamu* is now a large multi-million dollar industry in Indonesia with over 350 factories, both large and small, producing five million doses each day. Moreover, the industry has begun exporting its products to more than a dozen countries in Asia and Europe.

This essay examines the history and recent growth of this modern *jamu* industry in an effort to understand how an indigenous Indonesian cottage industry emerged so rapidly from a relatively insignificant sector of the non-formal economy to become a powerful element in the Indonesian health care industry. The development we describe illustrates some of the complexities and paradoxes of pharmaceutical pluralism. *Jamu*, conceived as an indigenous element of Indonesian culture, has become an important symbol of national identity; much of its appeal lies in its association with Indonesian 'tradition'. At the same time, its ability to compete successfully on the national market is in large part due to its emulation of imported products. Modern processing, packaging and marketing are also part of the appeal of *jamu*.

WHAT IS JAMU?

Visitors to Indonesia often notice with some puzzlement the ubiquitous presence of both young and old women clad in batik sarongs peddling a variety of murky colored drinks from bottles they carry in baskets strapped around their backs. These women are Javanese *jamu* sellers who can be found in virtually any town or city in Indonesia. They eke out a modest living selling *jamu* drinks door to door to regular customers, or by the side of the road, or from stalls in the market. The Javanese peddlers usually prepare their *jamu*'s at home each morning; in contrast, the *jamu* sellers from Madura mix their herbs to order at their client's doorstep (see Jordaan 1985: 192–194). *Jamu* drinks are usually as bitter as they are murky, reflecting the pungent and bitter herbs, roots and barks that are their major ingredients. *Jamu* peddlers have a general reputation for knowing just what ingredients should be mixed together and in what proportions for particular health problems. One hears nowadays that many of these *jamu* peddlers buy some or all of their *jamu* as packaged products from vendors in the markets, instead of gathering the ingredients themselves. But this does not seem to reduce clientele, for in a very real sense, *jamu* is *jamu*, whatever its form. Indeed, in recent years there has been a growing number of *jamu* vendors at the side of the road that serve ready-to-drink *jamu*, and many of these specialize in serving manufactured *jamu*'s that are readily available throughout Indonesia.

Probably very few Indonesians know the ingredients or even the source of the recipes for the *jamu*'s they regularly consume. Even fewer would have more than a meager knowledge of the particular plants used or the properties attributed to them as medicines, for this is commonly held to be the responsibility and specialization of those who prepare, manufacture or sell *jamu*. In this respect, the Indonesian attitude is very little different from that of an American or European who places considerable trust in the knowledge and expertise of his doctor or pharmacist.

If an Indonesian is asked to define *jamu* he is likely to define it as *obat asli Indonesia* (indigenous Indonesian medicine) and he will probably refer to the *ramuan* 'plant materials' used in its manufacture. *Obat* is the Indonesian for 'medicine' although this term is often used in a much broader sense than the English 'medicine' to refer to many kinds of chemicals and poisons that have little to do with medicine or health in a Western sense.[1] The term *asli* has an even broader set of meanings ranging from 'original', to 'genuine' or 'authentic', to 'indigenous'.[2] Depending upon one's interpretation of *asli*, *obat asli* may refer to locally manufactured medicines of any sort, though few Indonesians would systematically classify most Western-style pharmaceuticals as *jamu* simply because they were made in Indonesia. Although the meaning and significance of *jamu* among the general public generally draws upon all three of these senses of *asli*, it is clear that many packaged *jamu*'s are far removed from their 'original' state – particularly those in pill, tablet or capsule form – and quite a number have rather little to do with any 'authentic', 'indigenous' or 'traditional' recipe.

For the Indonesian public, what seems to be *jamu*'s most important distinguishing characteristic is that it is nearly always made from *ramuan* (bark, roots, leaves, wood, flowers etc.), though *jamu* may contain other ingredients as well (e.g. minerals). This emphasis on the herbal nature of *jamu* seems to be closely linked to two popular images, (1) the potions sold by *jamu* sellers on the streets, and (2) the even more esoteric concoctions prepared by traditional *dukun*'s. Both the 'traditional' and 'natural, unadulterated' aspects of herbal preparations are key themes used by most contemporary *jamu* manufacturers in their advertizing, and it is clear that the Indonesian public is quite sympathetic to both images.

The Indonesian laws regulating *jamu* are based on 'UU No. 7, 1963, concerning Pharmacy' which legally defined 'Obat Asli Indonesia' as 'medicines (*obat-obat*) that are obtained directly from natural materials available in Indonesia, processed in a simple manner based on experience and used in "traditional (medical) treatment".'[3] Public conceptualizations are, of course, in no direct way bound to legal definitions, but it should be noted that this definition is broad enough to accomodate almost anyone's interpretation, since in essence it only stresses the 'natural' ingredients and the 'traditional' uses of *jamu*.

This legal and regulatory definition of *jamu* as *obat asli Indonesia* gives the industry considerable flexibility to develop and market new products in virtually any form and for almost any purpose. In the last few years this has allowed the large firms to expand their products to include tonics, pills, tablets, capsules, skin and body-care lotions, creams, shampoos, cosmetics and Western-style make-up, all of which are marketed either directly or indirectly as *jamu*.[4]

Smaller companies still tend to be more specialized and often their products have a simple, home-made appearance. The least sophisticated of these firms package dried but otherwise unprocessed roots or barks, or finely ground powder-mixtures packaged in plain plastic bags, perhaps with a small slip of paper with the name of the *jamu* and the factory's trade name. But in most shops, sitting next to these simple and extremely traditional looking herbs are attractively designed boxes of tablets, pills, capsules, creams, and expensive cosmetics and make-up, manufactured with sophisticated machines. These represent the two ends of the contemporary *jamu* spectrum, and yet neither are typical of the main line of *jamu* that gave rise to the industry and continues to provide the bulk of the industry's gross sales: *jamu bubuk*, 'powdered *jamu*', sold in inexpensive, single-dose packets.

Jamu bubuk is usually sold individually in single-dose foil envelopes containing a standard 7 grams of finely ground *jamu* powder.[5] The consumer empties the contents of the packet into an ordinary drinking glass, adds boiling water, stirs and the *jamu* is ready to drink. Because of the bitter taste, many consumers add honey or sugar; others routinely drink *jamu* with honey and an egg yolk, both of which are widely felt to be healthful in their own right. Some of the products recommend mixing with lemon juice and honey in their 'directions for use'.

Each of the three largest manufacturers (Air Mancur, Nyonya Meneer, Jamu Jago) have a wide selection of these *jamu* powders (about 100 different kinds each) for almost any imaginable purpose, each numbered, color-coded and given a simple name descriptive of the health purpose for which it is intended. Nearly all of these *jamu* names refer to popular Indonesian folk categories of illness and health problems, typically in Indonesian, though a number of names are derived from Javanese, English or Dutch.[6] The exact dimensions of these packets varies with each manufacturer, though they are all rectangular or square with a colorful photograph or drawing on the front that typically symbolizes the kind of *jamu* inside.

Color-coded, numbered and labeled in vernacular terminology there can be little doubt that these inexpensive packets are aimed at a mass market with minimal education but a wide variety of health concerns. The cost of a single packet varies with each manufacturer and sometimes with the type of *jamu* (presumably because some use more expensive ingredients), but they average about Rp 100 each (less than 10 American cents). In most shops vendors display their *jamu* in racks provided by the manufacturers which proudly bear the brand-name and simultaneously allow the public to see several dozen different packets at once.

To assist their more educated clientele and perhaps more importantly, independent vendors and retailers, every major firm publishes a booklet describing the intended uses and benefits of each of their numbered products. This information is also published on the back of each packet and usually in English as well as Indonesian. To satisfy governmental regulatory requirements, each packet lists the major plant ingredients as a percentage of the total.

The recent expansion of the industry into sophisticated capsules, pills, creams, lotions and cosmetics seems very clearly an attempt to compete with imported pharmaceuticals, beauty products and cosmetics, primarily by producing *jamu* and *jamu*-related products in forms that are identical to imported products. The recent growth of the industry suggests that most manufacturers have been fairly successful in this regard. But in doing so they have had to resolve the central contradiction inherent in their industry: how to be both 'modern' and 'traditional' at the same time.

To meet regulatory requirements as *obat asli Indonesia* manufacturers must produce 'traditional' medicines made from natural ingredients. But to compete successfully with imported pharmaceuticals they must establish themselves as a 'modern' industry and their products must imitate the forms and functions of 'modern' pharmaceuticals and related products. Thus, almost without exception the major *jamu* companies speak of modernizing the industry without altering its basic 'traditional' premises (see, e.g., Simandjuntak 1984; Winarno and Maran 1985; Kristanto 1984; Soedibyo 1984; Tilaar 1985). The brochures and advertizements of many firms resolve this inherent contradiction in the following way:

'AIR MANCUR' Ltd. with its factories in Wonogiri and in Palur, as a modernly organized company, and at the same time the heir of the traditional medicines, has successfully elevated our old medicines to a stage equal to that of modern pharmaceutical products of the West (Air Mancur n.d.).

While many industry leaders promote their new products as if these were the essence of the *jamu* industry, it is clear that powdered *jamu*'s, in numbered, single-dose packets, continue to be the backbone of the industry. In a very real sense it is this line of customary products that legitimates and validates the newer products as 'traditional' *jamu* in the eyes of the consuming public, because when the average Indonesian from any socio-economic class is asked about the manufactured *jamu*, it is almost invariably these little packets of powder that first come to mind.

HISTORICAL BACKGROUND OF THE MODERN JAMU INDUSTRY

When discussing the traditional roots of their modern and increasingly sophisticated industry, most *jamu* manufacturers emphasize that *jamu*'s are Indonesia's heritage of herbal medicines and cosmetics that have been passed down through the generations as a *pusaka* or *warisan nenek moyang* – 'an heirloom or inheritance from early ancestors' (see, e.g., Nyonya Meneer n.d.; Air Mancur n.d.; Mustika Ratu n.d.). Some emphasize the traditional medical philosophy of Javanese or Indonesian health care (e.g., Soedibyo 1984; Tilaar 1985); others the mysterious secrets of the royal courts of Central Java (e.g., Mustika Ratu n.d.; Soedibyo 1984).

While an outsider is tempted to view such claims from manufacturers as simply a clever advertizing strategy, this is only partly the case. Indonesians are genuinely proud of and attracted to such medical traditions, and typically understand *jamu* as a concrete link with the past. This is amply demonstrated by the plethora of medical self-help books about *jamu* that have appeared in the bookshops, bookstalls and arms of street vendors throughout the country in the past decade. This popular literature makes many of the same points when discussing *jamu* and traditional medicinal plants.[7]

It is certainly true that every Indonesian ethnic group has its own traditional repertoire of herbal medicines. Many of these traditional recipes are indeed held as family secrets. And there are many early manuscripts from Java, Bali, Sumatra and Sulawesi which attest to the fact that the early royal courts and ancient nobility were interested in the practical aspects of plant medicines as well as the complicated medical philosophies, mysticism, numerology and the like which made sense of these plants and their uses.[8]

But despite the romantic charm of this popular rediscovery of Indonesia's proud past, the origins of the modern *jamu* industry have rather little to do with royal courts, secret knowledge inherited from ancestors in the distant past, mysterious medical philosophies or the traditional knowledge of *dukun*'s. The history of the modern industry actually begins early in the 20th century when a number of enterprising and innovative entrepeneurs on Java independently began manufacturing simple *jamu*'s in their homes as a small cottage industry.

Not much is known about most of these early *jamu* manufacturers, the specific kinds of *jamu* they were producing, or the sources of the recipes they were using. Although some producers were Javanese or Indonesians from other parts of the colony, the majority seem to have been Indonesian-born Chinese. Certainly most of the old *jamu* businesses that have prospered were started by proprietors of Chinese descent. Thus it is clear that these manufacturers were not for the most part relying on old Javanese recipes handed down from their grandfathers, but were consciously innovating on old principles of herbal medicine.[9] Perhaps the somewhat marginal position of the *peranakan* Chinese in Dutch Indies society allowed them to act as innovators and mediators between different cultural groups.

The inspiration for these entrepreneurs was the flood of imported pharmaceuticals, particularly patent medicines from Europe, and probably from other parts of Asia as well, that found their way into shops throughout much of Indonesia, but especially Java.

It is important to note that up to the 1930s imported Western pharmaceuticals were not the sophisticated antibiotics and synthetic drugs we now think of as modern pharmaceuticals. While a number of European medicines contained compounds of mercury, iodine and numerous other chemicals, many others (perhaps most) were relatively simple preparations often made from plant materials that differed very little in principle from the *jamu*'s made in Indonesia today. Quinine, for example, one of the most important and effective of the imported pharmaceuticals used during this era is, of course, an herbal medicine. Moreover, according to Sastroamidjojo (1967: 5) most prescription medicines during the colonial period had to be prepared to order at an *apotik* (pharmacy), which made patent medicines that were 'ready for use' all the more attractive.

During this period many innovative doctors, pharmacists, Chinese 'apotekers' and other enterprising individuals started manufacturing simple *obat* ('medicines') of various kinds and in various forms. These innovators included what are now classified as *jamu* manufacturers, some of whom are major producers today: PT Tawon Jaya (established in 1912 at Makassar, now Ujung Pandang); Jamu Jago (established by Poa Tjong Kwan in 1918 at Wonogiri, East Java); Jamu Pusaka Ambon (started by C. Kainama in 1928 at Jakarta); Nyonya Meneer (in Semarang); Jamu Iboe (established by Liem Soen Hoo at Ngaglik, Surabaya); Obat Karuhun (a 'rumah obat' in Yogyakarta established by Dr. Abdulkadir who also marketed *jamu* throughout Indonesia) and Simona (established in 1933 at Semarang as 'De Indische Kruiden TGG').

Nearly all of the *obat* manufacturers during the colonial period were small by comparison with today's industry leaders. But one should not underestimate their numbers or their importance in the field. During the Japanese Occupation in 1944, for example, there were 80 Indonesian, Chinese and Indian manufacturers of *obat* (of various kinds, many producing *jamu*) in Jakarta alone (Sastroamidjojo 1967: 8). While there were probably more of these manufacturers in Jakarta than in any other city, the local pharmaceutical industry was probably more dispersed than it is today, since most firms were serving locally based clientele.

The first part of the 20th century was an era of innovation in the field of locally produced medicines in Indonesia. A striking example was the introduction of *kretek* cigarettes. Although these clove cigarettes are now the national cigarette of Indonesia, they were first marketed as a medicine for individuals suffering from asthma and other respiratory conditions.

It is important to note, however, that Indonesian *obat* manufacturers were not limited to herbal products. Bintang Toedjoeh in Jakarta and a number of other similar companies, for example, were actively manufacturing medicines made from chemical compounds that were not unlike many of the European patent medicines. There were even local firms manufacturing medicines that illegally or falsely marketed their products under the trademarks and brand names of foreign manufacturers (Sastroamidjojo 1967: 5).

It is not clear how many of these early *jamu* manufacturers were marketing their products as '*jamu*' rather than '*obat*' and one suspects that up until the 1930s most producers saw themselves as manufacturing and selling '*obat*'.[10] Irrespective of whether these firms were manufacturing herbal products or *obat* made from chemical compounds, their major competition was the imported patent medicines that were both modern and easy to use. Sastroamidjojo (1967: 7) notes that the convenience of patent medicines made them especially attractive to consumers with minor health problems. Moreover, from the many stories now told by *jamu* manufacturers about the origins of their companies, it is precisely this feature of the industry that led most entrepreneurs to begin producing *jamu bubuk* as a 'patent' *jamu*. Customers wanted ready to use products and here lay the possibility of significant profits (see, e.g., Winarno and Maran 1985; Kristanto 1984). It seems likely that most *jamu* producers were trying to compete primarily in the same terms as their major competition, that is to say, by presenting themselves as manufacturers of *obat* rather than *jamu*. Moreover, during the colonial period, as today, many consumers were attracted to new and modern products, including medicines, as something that was better and more effective.

REDEFINITION OF JAMU: FROM THE JAPANESE OCCUPATION TO
GOVERNMENT REGULATION OF THE INDUSTRY

For most Indonesians the Second World War represents an era of extreme hardship and suffering. This is not so much because of military action *per se*, but because the Japanese occupation itself was so harsh. From 1942 to 1945 the Japanese military government in the territory was concerned almost exclusively with provisioning its war effort, and as a result many of the colony's resources, privately owned supplies and local products were taken by the military for its own use. Supplies of imported goods, including such necessities as cloth and pharmaceuticals ceased altogether; livestock, rice and other foodstuffs, and personal possessions were appropriated by the military government, its officers and soldiers, typically without compensation; and toward the end of the occupation most Indonesians faced tremendous shortages of food and other basic necessities. In short, the Japanese occupation was for most Indonesians a period of hunger, sickness and want.

Needless to say, with such hardships there was a greater than ever need for the services of the Indonesian medical community.[11] But as medical needs increased, supplies of imported drugs were running out, with no hope of replenishing stocks of even the most standard and basic pharmaceuticals. The Japanese administrators, particularly toward the end of the occupation, encouraged Indonesian *obat* manufacturers to continue and even expand their production of medicines. But such efforts had little significance in light of such staggering shortages. Moreover, these firms were producing few of the most important drugs. As a result, faced with shortages of necessary pharmaceuticals and growing needs, Indonesian physicians turned to the only medicines available: *jamu*, particularly freshly prepared *jamu*.

Sastroamidjojo's (1967: 1–20) vivid description of the period points out the irony of this tragic situation. Although forced to rely on *obat asli Indonesia* and preparations that could be made from local materials, few Indonesian doctors had any significant experience using these medicines in their individual medical practices. While recognizing the need for *jamu* to treat serious illnesses such as malaria, dysentery, tuberculosis and pneumonia, few physicians had more than a vague idea of which plants to use, in what proportions they should be mixed with other ingredients, or in what doses they should be prescribed. Even for less serious conditions, such as scabies, worms, septic sores and fever, few of these doctors who were born and raised in Indonesia could confidently prescribe medications made from indigenous plants because of their limited experience and information.

This situation, of course, had its roots in the Dutch colonial period, when these Indonesian doctors were trained and enculturated into a modern, Western-oriented medical profession. Sastroamidjojo (1967: 2) laments the fact that at the time virtually nothing had been published of a practical nature that could help physicians in selecting, preparing and prescribing herbal medicines. This he attributes to a general disinterest on the part of Dutch colonial authorities in making clinical observations or conducting scientific research about plant medicines. A number of Dutch scholars had, of course, made collections of Indonesian medicinal plants, documenting in a general way some of their medical uses, but at the time of the Japanese invasion the European medical community was generally quite convinced of the effectiveness and superiority of chemical-based pharmaceuticals. Moreover, during the 1920s and 1930s Dutch physicians in Indonesia were becoming increasingly disinterested or even suspicious of simple plant medicines. Even though a handful of Indonesian doctors were using herbal medicines in their clinics and private practices before the Japanese invasion, the majority seem to have shared the attitudes of their European colleagues toward *jamu*.[12]

With the crisis of the Japanese occupation and the shortages of pharmaceuticals that came with it, Indonesian doctors were forced to find substitutes for the patent medicines and prescription drugs they had grown used to using. As Sastroamidjojo notes, the efforts of Indonesian physicians in the face of this almost Herculean task are noteworthy.

In their hospitals, clinics and private practices, doctors started using *jamu* recipes obtained from any number of sources (these included neighborhood *jamu* sellers, vendors in the markets and *dukun*'s). For the most part, such efforts represented the actions of individual physicians trying to deal as best they could with the health problems and shortages of medicines they confronted. Toward the end of the occupation Japanese authorities began to assist them in this by coordinating research and the publication of clinical results.[13] A number of recipes, complete with information on dosages and usage were even published in the government sponsored magazine *Asia Raya*. In short, by the end of the occupation, herbal medicines were being used by the Indonesian medical community throughout much of Indonesia.

The Japanese occupation (1942–45) and to a lesser extent the Indonesian Revolution (1945–49) were associated with a real change in the attitudes and practices of the Indonesian medical community toward herbal medicines. But it is also clear that this enthusiasm for *jamu* was short lived, for as soon as the crisis was past and imported medicines became available once more, Indonesian physicians quickly abandoned *jamu*'s in favor of *obat moderen*.

It is, of course, true that the imported pharmaceuticals available in the 1950s were considerably improved over those available in Indonesia in the 1930s. Imported pharmaceuticals were more convenient and more reliable for major illnesses than most of the *jamu*'s that had been used during the occupation. Although forced to find substitutes during the 1940s, in the long run Indonesian doctors never seemed to accept these herbal-based medicines as valid, legitimate and reliable. Indeed, one gets the impression that the crisis of the Japanese occupation had the effect of heightening the medical community's perception of the differences between imported pharmaceuticals and *obat asli Indonesia* rather than reducing it.

Jamu manufacturers, of course, continued to produce their packaged products which continued to be accepted by the general public. But within the medical profession the distinctions between *jamu* and *obat moderen* became increasingly well defined, and eventually became legal distinctions when the Indonesian government passed a series of laws intended to regulate health care and pharmaceuticals. The legal definition of *obat asli Indonesia* that was formalized in 1963 (with the passage of Undang-Undang No. 7, Concerning Pharmacy) carefully distinguished these *jamu*'s from *obat moderen* based on the distinctions made by the medical community, which of course advised the government about health matters and regulatory needs.[14]

By the 1960s when Indonesia faced a fiscal crisis and the possibility of restrictions on imported drugs, there were still few herbal medicines that Indonesian physicians accepted as adequate substitutes for imported pharmaceuticals (see Sastroamidjojo 1967: 17). Ironically, one of the main reasons physicians raised for not using *jamu* was that there was too little scientific and practical clinical information of reliable nature available concerning the uses and effectiveness of *jamu*. One of the decisions that emerged during the 1964 'National Seminar to Find Indonesian Sources for Pharmacy'[15] in Yogyakarta was that more scientific research was needed and that in particular the practical experiences from the Japanese occupation and the Revolution needed to be collected and studied! In short, since 1940 the Indonesian medical profession's main concern about *jamu* has been the limited scientific research, yet it has always been the medical community itself that was in the best position to actually conduct such research.

JAMU AS A MODERN INDUSTRY

The 1960s and 1970s represent a period of reorganization and redefinition of the *jamu* industry and of what role it is to play in modern Indonesia. We have seen how the industry was granted formal government recognition with the passage of Undang-Undang No. 7, 1963, Concerning Pharmacy. On the one hand, by distinguishing *obat asli Indonesia* from *obat moderen* this law represents the successful efforts of the medical community and the international pharmaceutical industry to limit the meaning of *jamu* for legal purposes. But on the other hand, this law granted the highly organized *jamu* industry a legally guaranteed continuing role within the larger pharmaceutical industry. In obtaining a legally recognized niche for itself, however, the *jamu* industry was obliged to accept government regulation.

Regulation by the Indonesian Food and Drug Administration has meant increasingly complex forms of registration of companies, products and ingredients as well as growing supervision and inspection. In the early years after UU No. 7, government regulation seems to have been quite minimal and even today the vast majority of small manufacturers (of which there are estimated to be several thousand) are unregistered and their small scale enterprises are effectively unregulated. For the rest, government recognition of the industry has been beneficial, although many of the more than 350 registered companies now tend to see regulations as necessary but increasingly burdensome.[16]

At the same time the *jamu* industry was achieving a revised legal role within the field of pharmaceuticals, it was also being redefined in the eyes of economists and national planners as an industry capable of providing domestic production for some regularly consumed pharmaceuticals. This would in turn offset imports and help Indonesia's adverse balance of payments. Once *jamu* was legally recognized as a pharmaceutical, of course, there was no reason for the government not to support the industry. Moreover, unlike the manufacturers of *obat moderen*, which in most instances are partly owned by foreign investors, *jamu* manufacturers have until very recently been almost entirely owned by Indonesian nationals.

The extreme instability of the Indonesian economy in the 1960s, which was characterized by triple digit inflation, made import substitution and domestic investment all the more attractive. At the same time, of course, economic instability and inflation proved very difficult for many of the existing *jamu* companies and several of today's largest firms almost had to 'roll up the mat' (Winarno and Maran 1985). Suharto's 'New Order' and the economic stability and sustained growth that followed brought stability to the industry in the late 1960s and extremely rapid growth in the 1970s. A number of industry leaders attribute part of their economic strength to the support and assistance of the national government.

While the government was trying to find a role for *jamu* in the national economy, a number of innovative entrepreneurs within the industry started revising their own conception of the industry and its potential as a 'modern' industry. For all the larger firms this meant expanding production from powdered *jamu* to include newer forms of their products, particularly capsules, tablets and pills which began to be available in the 1960s. In the 1970s this expansion has most notably been in the 'traditional cosmetics' field.

Production of pills, capsules and tablets has, of course, required increasingly sophisticated machinery and manufacturing techniques. These new manufacturing processes were and continue to be adapted more or less directly from Indonesian factories producing *obat moderen*, which are largely affiliates of international pharmaceutical companies. Indeed, the modern pharmaceutical industry has been the example and prototype for nearly every aspect of the *jamu* industry's attempts to modernize.

Modernization of the industry has brought new management practices and styles, diversification of products, specialization of products to specific submarkets, and a revolution in promotion and advertising. Although many firms retain family ownership, few of the large and medium-sized companies are operated as their smaller family-based operations were. Moreover, with the expansion, all of the major companies have had to develop a reliable distribution network, which is usually accomplished by appointing an agent in each of

Indonesia's provinces who distributes to retailers throughout their region (see Afdhal 1981).

Competition among *jamu* producers also increased considerably during the 1960s and 1970s. This has led some of the medium sized firms and most of the 'traditional' cosmetics producers to specialize their products.[17] But for many of the *jamu* firms this has led to standardization of their basic products, so that nearly all companies have *jamu*'s for the same health problems and in many instances there is even a close resemblance in the recipes used.[18]

Not surprisingly, the industry's efforts to redefine itself as a modern industry is closely connected with a self-conscious attempt to redefine *jamu* as a modern product in the eyes of the consuming public. It has, of course, been easy to convince the consumers that *jamu* pills, capsules and tablets, not to mention the cosmetics and make-up, are modern products, since their form alone and method of use will inevitably be associated with modern medicines and cosmetics. What has been more difficult has been to demonstrate that their products are no more than modern refinements on traditional *jamu*'s that continue to be a valuable heritage of Indonesia's proud past, particularly as the products themselves have begun to deviate substantially from the traditional *jamu*'s they are intended to replace.

The industry's response to this paradox has been to stress that their new *jamu* products contain all the healthy and healthful attributes of traditional *jamu*, but (1) are easier to use, (2) have none of the mess in preparation, and (3) have none of the bitter taste. The industry often claims that *jamu* in any of its forms has none of the side effects Indonesians often associate with *obat moderen*, although for the most part this is largely an undemonstrated claim (see, e.g., Simandjuntak 1984: 83–84). Until the 1970s *jamu* manufacturers made little if any effort to scientifically test their products to demonstrate the healthful claims made about them, but this has increasingly become an industry concern. Large *jamu* producers in particular have encouraged and even financially supported some phytotherapy research, presumably to gain the recognition and legitimation of the medical community (see, e.g., Winarno and Maran 1985), while others only encourage research to improve the quality and hygienic aspects of *jamu*.

Ultimately such efforts to modernize the industry in the eyes of the public have been a self-conscious attempt to attract a more affluent and better educated consumer who can afford more expensive *jamu*'s and 'traditional cosmetics' but is attracted to modern and sophisticated products. Convincing the public of the virtues of *jamu* has thus meant greater sophistication in advertizing and promotion, and these advertizing styles have changed as the Indonesian public has grown more educated and more sophisticated.

The early *jamu* producers relied almost entirely on word of mouth advertizing, sometimes supplemented with billboards and posters. Jamu Jago claims to have brought the first revolution in promotion when in 1930 it began advertizing with automobiles and vans (Winarno and Maran 1985). But a more significant, and probably more effective, promotional scheme began in the 1960s when Air Mancur, then a small and very young firm, began promoting its products at public markets using hawkers and loudspeakers. It is not clear exactly what role these hawkers played in Air Mancur's rapid growth to become the largest *jamu* manufacturer, although it undoubtedly brought name recognition to most Indonesians. This promotional style can still be found in almost any market in the country, although hawkers now use microphones to attract crowds and onlookers and increasingly these hawkers now tend to advertize for more obscure producers. In the meantime, Air Mancur and other large companies have increasingly relied on advertizing in the print media.

Efforts to modernize the industry have proved quite successful in reorienting the consuming public; production figures in all forms of *jamu* have steadily increased since the mid-1970s. Some sense of the growth in modern forms of *jamu* can be seen in Table I and Table II. The totals for 1984 are incomplete representing 292 of more than 350 registered manufacturers and thus show a net decline in production of tablets and capsules. This is contrary to the claims of manufacturers who insist that production is steadily rising (Winarno and Maran 1985; Simandjuntak 1984). What is clear from these tables is that from a nominal production of pills, capsules and tablets in the 1960s the industry has very rapidly expanded production during the late 1970s. Nevertheless, these categories of *jamu* still make up a very small proportion of the total production, 13 percent of the *jamu* manufactured.

Table III gives some idea of the *jamu* industry's current production, although these data are also incomplete representing only 292 of the more than 350 registered firms. But lacking more complete data, the Table illustrates the relative volume of production for several of the different forms of *jamu* registered by the Food and Drug Administration in Jakarta.

Powdered *jamu* is still the most important product for the industry, making up almost 70 percent of all *jamu* manufactured and generating nearly half of the industry's earnings. While other forms of *jamu* are more attractive to the industry because they bring a much higher unit price – and one assumes a correspondingly greater profit – the industry survives largely on the basis of powdered *jamu*. The traditional cosmetics firms and a few companies that manufacture only pills, capsules and tablets have been able to specialize, but for the most part the industry is still highly dependent upon the classic powdered *jamu*'s.

It is not clear what the government's statistics for 'total value' (Table III) are specifically intended to represent, though they are probably wholesale values reported directly by manufacturers to the Food and Drug Administration. The total value of all *jamu* produced in 1984 listed as $ 33.1 million seems far too low, even for a wholesale price. Moreover, $ 15 million would hardly seem sufficient to cover the cost of packaging and of the 8 million metric tonnes of raw ingredients needed to produce 1,165.5 million packets of

TABLE I
Production of *jamu* in pill, tablet, capsule and parem (solid) form during 1976, 1981 and 1984 (in millions of units)

	Production (in millions of units)		
	1976	1981	1984
Pills	6.1	83.4	98.2*
Tablets	13.5	123.2	95.1*
Capsules	8.3	31.2	24.7*
Parem	0.4	6.4	19.9*
Total (in millions)	28.3	244.2	237.9*

* Incomplete data, 292 of 350 manufacturers.

Source: 1976 and 1981 adapted from Simandjuntak (1984); 1984 adapted from the official records of the Indonesian Food and Drug Administration, Jakarta (Dirjen Pengawasan Obat dan Makanan) but includes data for only 292 manufacturers.

TABLE II
Value (in millions of rupiah) of *jamu* produced in pill, tablet and parem form during 1976, 1981, 1984

	Value (in millions of rupiah)		
	1976	1981	1984
Pills	43.4	1,603.7	2,945.4
Tablets	82.1	1,763.8	2,282.6
Parem	22.9	476.4	1,978.5
Total (Rp. million)	148.4	3,843.9	7,206.5

Source: 1976 and 1981 adapted from Simandjuntak (1984); 1984 adapted from the official records of the Indonesian Food and Drug Administration, Jakarta (Dirjen Pengawasan Obat dan Makanan) but includes data for only 292 manufacturers.

jamu. Clearly, as an estimate of retail value of the *jamu* produced in Indonesia, it is far too low.

No one really knows how much *jamu* is actually being produced in Indonesia today, even from the registered manufacturers (see Krisanto 1984). One survey of the industry estimated the retail sales of *jamu* at $ 310 million in 1984 (Surindo Utama 1984), which seems appropriate. Air Mancur, for example, produces half a million packets of powdered *jamu* a day (180 million per year) at a minimum retail value of Rp 100 (10 cents) per packet with some of their products being more costly. Thus, Air Mancur's products alone bring a retail value of $ 16 million per year, and it only produces 15 percent of the powdered *jamu* listed in Table III.

To appreciate the significance of *jamu* in the Indonesian pharmaceutical

TABLE III
Production and value of *jamu* produced in 1984

Form	Total production (in million units)	Total value (in US$ millions)
Powder (packets)	1,168.5	15.0 (45.3%)
Pills	98.2	2.9 (8.8%)
Capsules	24.7	1.3 (3.9%)
Tablets	95.1	2.3 (6.9%)
Cream/ointment	0.1	.0 (0.0%)
Parem (solids)	19.9	2.0 (6.0%)
Liquid (300 ml units)	9.1	7.7 (23.3%)
Rajangan (fresh *jamu*)	289.7	1.9 (5.7%)
Other	0.5	.0 (0.1%)
Total	1,705.8	33.1 (100.0%)

Source: Data adapted from records of the Indonesian Food and Drug Administration, Jakarta. Data includes the production of 292 *jamu* manufacturers.

industry as a whole, the total retail sales of manufactured *jamu* should be compared with the estimated market volume of modern drugs in Indonesia, $ 600–700 million in 1984 (Surindo Utama 1984). In short, the *jamu* industry controls approximately one-third of the total pharmaceutical market volume. Thus, on the basis of these figures, powdered *jamu* accounts for 15 percent of all manufactured pharmaceutical products!

To achieve this volume of sales has, of course, demanded considerable promotional effort on the part of the manufacturers. One survey suggests that in 1984 the 'big three' manufacturers (Air Mancur, Jamu Jago, and Nyonya Meneer) spent a total of $ 1.1 million on promotion and advertizing, largely relying on printed media, especially newspaper advertizing (Surindo Utama 1984). This same survey estimates that the total promotional budget for *jamu* cosmetics firms was $ 3.1 million. And it appears that this promotional budget has been quite effective in favorably motivating consumers to buy *jamu* products.

WHY IS JAMU SO POPULAR?

Up to now we have discussed the historical background leading up to the increasingly important role of manufactured *jamu* within the Indonesian pharmaceutical industry. But we have said rather little about why *jamu* is such a popular product and one that will undoubtedly remain popular for some time. This is unfortunately a difficult question to answer, if for no other reason than the fact that Indonesia is an ethnically diverse country and no single set of factors is likely to be applicable to all sectors of modern Indonesian society.

Nevertheless certain themes do emerge as at least partial explanations for *jamu*'s popularity, even though an adequate assessment of this question will require more intensive research in a number of ethnic groups.

Jamu manufacturers themselves tend to explain the success of their industry in terms of two major factors: (1) that *jamu* has genuine benefits to health which the Indonesian public recognizes, and (2) that recent growth of sales is correlated with an active, even intensive, advertizing and promotional effort.

While it is obvious that promotion of *jamu* has been important in selling *jamu* in new forms during the last decade, it is not clear what specific advertising message has reached the Indonesian public, and perhaps more importantly what message the public has accepted. Most of the current *jamu* advertising is of a very vague and general nature that does not seem to appeal in terms of specific benefits or attributes. Even the explanations on the backs of *jamu* packets which itemize specific health benefits of particular products tend to be quite general in nature and rarely refer to the physiological, philosophical or theoretical basis for the specific benefits.

From interviews with a number of successful *jamu* vendors in the public markets of Jakarta, one gets the impression that retailers are far more influential in promoting specific *jamu*'s and rationales for their use to individual customers than mass advertising. Moreover, vendors consciously direct their explanations and health advice to individual customers, their specific health concerns and their income. In short, sales of most *jamu* continue to be highly dependent upon informal information networks rather than the advertizing campaigns of large and medium-sized producers. In this aspect, *jamu* seems to differ from patent medicines in both Indonesia and Western countries. Moreover, while advertizing has undoubtedly played some role in modern *jamu*'s recent growth, this may be somewhat exaggerated by manufacturers, since the industry's recent expansion is also closely tied to Indonesia's recent economic prosperity and a substantial increase in the public's disposable income.

As to the benefits and virtues claimed for *jamu*, there is virtually no clinical or scientific research that can support or invalidate such claims. A number of Western observers tend to dismiss *jamu* as ineffective or even dangerous, but such opinions are based on a number of unsympathetic prejudices, which have no greater basis in demonstrated facts than the claims of the more moderate spokesmen for the industry. Many millions of regular *jamu* users, on the other hand, tend to be fairly convinced of the general benefits of *jamu* and the specific benefits of particular products. And these opinions are based on a variety of personal experiences and subjective expectations.

The industry is not unanimous on the question of whether *jamu*'s or their constituent ingredients should be tested for their effectiveness. Nevertheless in the last few years a number of laboratories and schools of pharmacy at major Indonesian universities have begun phytotherapy research.[19] It remains to be seen whether these experimental findings will eventually alter the attitude of the medical community, which still tends to ignore *jamu*, but the fact that such research is being carried out probably adds to the appeal of *jamu* for certain consumers interested in 'modern' products. The attention of government and universities seems to legitimate *jamu* as a modern pharmaceutical that is being taken seriously by the scientific community. At the same time, for the majority of Indonesians the results of such research are of little consequence since they evaluate *jamu* in their own terms and seem more interested in traditional forms of medications than scientific verification.

This illustrates a key characteristic of manufactured *jamu*, that it is widely recognized as both a 'modern' and a 'traditional' pharmaceutical, although the importance of one or the other of these associations seems to vary greatly with different individuals and certainly with ethnic background and education. Indeed, the industry has been successful in cultivating both images simultaneously. *Jamu*'s wide appeal seems to be due to its subliminal association with imported pharmaceuticals on one hand and its differences from them on the other. In the last analysis, this diffuse configuration of associations and symbolizations allows *jamu*, as a category of pharmaceuticals, to appeal to an extremely broad consuming public; in fact, to virtually everyone in a country where the idea of herbal medicines has been around since very early times.

Jamu manufacturers have begun exporting their products to more than a dozen countries in Asia and Europe and would like to export more of their products to Europe and North America, though import regulations have proved difficult (see Simandjuntak 1984). The majority of exported *jamu* is currently sold to Malaysia and Singapore where it seems particularly popular among ethnic Malays rather than ethnic Chinese (see Table IV).

It is almost certainly the case that the popularity of *jamu* in Malaysia is due to essentially the same factors as in Indonesia. In Europe, however, *jamu*'s appeal is often associated with the 'back to nature' movement (Simandjuntak 1984: 77) and thus is attractive as a reaction to modern pharmaceuticals. The appeal of *jamu* in Europe is therefore rather different from that in Indonesia where the general public is attracted to anything modern or imported. Indonesians are not involved in either 'back to nature' or even a 'back to tradition' movement in the pharmaceutical field in any proper sense, which is demonstrated more clearly by the fact that the *jamu* industry's most rapid growth is in the most modern-looking forms of *jamu* and traditional cosmetics. Nevertheless in a number of respects *jamu*'s appeal in Indonesia is related to vague associations with natural ingredients and tradition.

Closely associated with some of these non-specific claims made about *jamu* is the fact that the industry is highly diversified, both in the kinds of products available as we have already discussed and also in the regional character of many firms. Indonesians are highly aware of the ethnic diversity in their country and a number of ethnic groups are well known for their particular stereotyped qualities and benefits of their *jamu*'s. Thus Madura, with its

TABLE IV
Exports of Indonesian *jamu*, 1979–84

Year	Volume (metric tonnes)	Value (US$)
1979	2,646.1	2,551,073
1980	4,707.1	4,627,691
1981	4,490.3	5,847,483
1982	4,043.1	5,682,028
1983	3,638.6	5,770,368
1984	2,432.5	3,222,665

Source: Central Bureau of Statistics of Indonesia, Jakarta.

reputation for sexy women, is known for women's aphrodisiacs; Kalimantan for male products. Javanese *jamu* is often associated with tonic and elixers to encourage strength or even bring out the creative juices, while Achenese *jamu* has a distinctive Arab flair.

Some companies have emphasized these ethnic specialties, prompting a recent ruling by the Indonesian Food and Drug Administration which now prohibits advertizing *jamu* as '*jamu* Madura' or '*jamu* Java' because legally all *jamu*'s must reflect a national Indonesian quality rather than regionalism. Although manufacturers have tried to differentiate their products on the basis of these ethnic stereotypes for many years, it is not entirely clear how important they are for the Indonesian public. Undoubtedly for some segments of Indonesian society, ethnic loyalty to one's 'traditional' *jamu* may be important. For many other Indonesians, however, the distinction may add to the mystique of *jamu* more generally, or the mystique of particular manufacturers, particularly those who sell aphrodisiac *jamu*'s.

Several recent Indonesian commentators have emphasized that much of *jamu*'s current appeal lies in its association with increased sexual performance (see, e.g., Winarno and Maran 1985; Simandjuntak 1984). Certainly, a large number of the 1,572 registered *jamu* products are in some way or another associated with and marketed for improvement of sexual performance. Even the various 'traditional cosmetics' and beauty products can be considered in this light, and certainly their manufacturers do not try to dissuade users from the notion that their products may benefit the user's sex life.[20] On the other hand, several manufacturers claim that *jamu* products for the common cold, influenza, headache, and general aches and pains are their major products.

CONCLUSION

For many people in Indonesia, *jamu* is a powerful medicine with important roots in tradition. For others it is a lucrative commercial hoax. But whether one believes consumers, manufacturers or critics, *jamu* is a legally recognized and economically important type of pharmaceutical produced domestically and satisfying needs recognized by its consumers. With its many forms and many producers, *jamu* is many things to many people and it is difficult to know which of these views is the most adequate way to describe *jamu*. In the words of Sudarmilah Suparto who has published a book on *jamu* and is herself a manufacturer:

> ... many doctors in the Department of Health say that *jamu* is traditional medicine. But that's really incorrect. That definition is not precise because up to now we are not yet able to say that *jamu* is medicine. . . . *Jamu* is *jamu*, full stop (quoted in Winarno and Maran 1985).[21]

However, for the 'outside' observer one conclusion can be drawn from most comments made about modern *jamu*, whether the industry is seen as selling useless aphrodisiacs, simple cold medicines or modern versions of traditionally important medicines. This is the fact that modern *jamu* represents one important conceptual break with the past: the industry almost exclusively associates its products with a physiological notion of health and medications. If we look at the claims made about *jamu*, whether positive or negative, *jamu* is almost invariably evaluated in terms of its presumed effects on basic body processes. There is almost no mention of associated spiritual, metaphysical and psychological concepts that are characteristic – in one form or another – of traditional aspects of health and health care in Indonesian societies. Unlike the traditional *jamu*'s in Indonesia, modern *jamu* is not sold as one element of a more holistic concept of health care and health maintenance, but as a product that deals directly with physiology quite independently of other human processes. It seems that this subtle reorientation is hardly recognized by the manufacturers themselves, however.

Traditional Indonesian societies probably tended to compartmentalize *jamu* medicines as one branch of healing art, but *jamu* never seems to have been totally divorced from the spiritual, mystical, metaphysical, social and psychological aspects of mankind (see, e.g., Jordaan 1985; Suparlan 1978; even Geertz 1960). All of these aspects of *jamu* are disregarded by modern manufacturers – though it does not necessarily follow that they are disregarded by consumers. Manufacturers appear to have accepted a distinctively Western view of health and medicine, patterning their industry on the concerns and preoccupations of the manufacturers of imported pharmaceuticals. Much more research is required on this topic, particularly from the perspective of users, but it does appear that in this sense *jamu* is very much a part of the growing medicalization of modern Indonesian society that began early in this century.

ACKNOWLEDGEMENTS

The authors acknowledge the help of R. Jordaan and the editors in the preparation of their paper.

NOTES

1. See also Poerwadarminta (1984: 682). For example, anti-mosquito incense coils that are extremely popular in Indonesia are generally referred to as *obat nyamuk* ('mosquito medicine') and marketed as *obat anti-nyamuk*. Similarly, one often hears the chemicals used to purify drinking water described as *obat*, probably reflecting the foul smell such chemicals add to the water. In a slightly different sense, the poison sometimes added to standing water to kill mosquito larvae is also called *obat*. Nevertheless, the most common sense of the term is 'medicine' or some preparation for medical purposes. The broad definition of 'medicine' is also reported from elsewhere. See Whyte, this volume.
2. These definitions are from Echols and Shadily (1983: 22). Poerwadarminta (1984:62) gives the following '*yang asal; yang semula; yang sebenarnya (bukan salinan atau terjemahan); tulen (sejati); yang berasal dari daerah (negeri dsb) itu sendiri; pembawaan dari lahir*', ('origin/source'; 'from the beginning'; 'actual (not a copy or translation)'; 'pure/genuine'; 'which originates from the region (country etc.) itself'; 'something brought from birth'). In the case of honey (*madu*), for example, Indonesians are careful to distinguish between *madu asli* and *madu campuran* (honey mixed with some other substance). Thus *madu asli* is unadulterated, 'original' or what in the United States is called 'pure honey', even though it may not be indigenously or locally produced and may even have been processed to some minor extent.
3. Sastroamidjojo (1965: 19) gives the following text from a report of the 'Traditional Medicines Section' of the 1964 National Seminar to Search for Natural Indonesian Sources For Pharmacy, which he claims follows the text of Undang-Undang No. 7, 1963 (Bab II, pasal 2, ayat c):

> "Obat asli Indonesia" ialah obat-obat jang diperoleh langsung dari bahan-bahan alam jang terdapat di Indonesia, terolah setjara sederhana atas dasar pengalaman dan penggunaanja dalam "pengobatan tradisionil".
> Translation: "Obat asli Indonesia" are medicines that are obtained directly from natural materials available in Indonesia, processed in a simple manner based on experience and used in "traditional (medical) treatment".

 Sahly (1983: 18) gives a slightly different version of the *ayat* in question, using the new spelling (see also Winarno and Maran 1984).
4. Regulatory restrictions differentiate *obat asli Indonesia* from *obat moderen* 'modern medicine' according to the kinds of ingredients used. It appears that *jamu* may be made from *simplisia* 'active ingredients' extracted from raw herbs, but may not be mixed with chemicals. The firm Jamu Jago has recently begun manufacturing *jamu tujuh angin* ('7 winds *jamu*') from extracts mixed with menthol, but is legally obliged to register this product as *obat moderen* (Simandjuntak 1984: 78). Although legally *obat moderen*, there is nothing to prevent consumers or retailers from considering it as a *jamu*, particularly since it is produced by a *jamu* manufacturer and probably sits on the shelf next to registered *jamu*'s.
5. Both the *jamu* industry and the Indonesian Department of Health use 7 grams as the standard dose, both for *jamu bubuk* 'powdered *jamu*' and *jamu param*, 'solid form'. Tradition, more than any other factor, seems to be the basis for choosing 7 grams rather than 6, 8, or 10 grams. According to Jaya Suprana (President Director of Jamu Jago), when his grandfather, Poa Tjong Kwan, began manufacturing *jamu bubuk*, he sold it in 7 gram units. He seems to have pulled this figure out of the air with no particular rationale. Since then it has become something of a tradition within the industry (see Winarno and Maran 1984).
6. Most *jamu* names are in simple but medically vague language that refers to symptoms or popular syndrome categories. Most are from Indonesian or Javanese that has almost become popular Indonesian. For example, Nyonya Meneer markets 'Jamu Batuk' ('cough'), 'Jamu

Sakit Kencing' ('difficult urination'), Jamu Kuat Laki-laki ('strong man'); Jamu Darah Bersih ('clean blood'), and Jamu Datang Bulan Tidak Cocok ('period doesn't fit').
7. See, e.g., Dharma (1985); Mardisiswojo and Rajakmangunsudarso (1985); Muji (n.d.); Rianggoro (1982); Sahly (1983); Soeparto (1984). These range the entire spectrum of Indonesian publishers, from Sinar Harapan and Balai Pustaka which publish scholarly works and books accepted as being of high quality for a general audience, to Pustaka Karya which does not give a date or place of publication and is often sold by vendors on the street. A related but somewhat different tradition is represented by Mudakir & Soleh (1984).
8. Soedibyo (1984) refers to the *Serat Centini* written in the 18th century for Kanjeng Gusti Pangeran Adipati Anom, Crown Prince of Solo, which does indeed document medical knowledge and philosophy of health (including plant medicines) (see Adisasmita 1974, 1975; Sumahatmaka 1981). Similar kinds of early writings can be found in Bali, Sumatra and Sulawesi in the early manuscripts written in indigenous scripts. The existence of these early manuscripts, however, does not mean that they are the basis for the modern *jamu* industry, but merely attests to the fact that health was a traditional concern of the literati.
9. This is not to say that these manufacturers were not using old recipes, since the Chinese are also well known for their traditional herbal medicines (see, e.g., Kleinman 1980; Kleinman et al. 1975; and several of the papers in Leslie 1976). Peranakan Chinese, who have intermarried with Javanese, would also have access to old Javanese recipes in addition to Chinese ones. The point here is that whatever the ethnic background of these individual manufacturers, the basic tendency during this early period was to innovate upon basic ingredients and recipes. This tendency has not changed today.
10. It is not clear to what extent the terms *jamu* and *obat* were differentiated prior to the Second World War, although the medical community had certainly started making a categorical distinction between the two at least sometime before 1940 (see, e.g., Sastroamidjojo 1967, originally published in 1948, for a sense of how the medical community viewed *jamu*'s just prior to and during the Japanese occupation.) Similarly, it seems likely that *jamu* may have had a somewhat more restricted meaning early in the century. Gimlette, for example, in his posthumously published *A Dictionary of Malayan Medicine* gives the following definition of *jamu*, based on his experiences in Malay early in the century:

> Preparations which do not exactly serve as medicines, but have the object of maintaining health and excluding mischievous influences. Ridley gives as an example of *ubat jejamu*, a nostrum compounded of over thirty spices, astringents, etc.: it is in the form of a powder to be taken in water after childbirth (Gimlette and Thomson 1971: 89).

This term seems to contrast with *ubat* (Malay form of the modern Indonesian *obat*) which he defines as 'A medicinal drug; a magic simple; a medicine' (1971: 246). Gimlette lists a dozen different kinds of *ubat*, whose usage seems to parallel that of the Indonesian *obat* (see Sastroamidjojo 1967: 10–14).

Indonesian and Javanese during the colonial period may have distinguished these terms in a similar way, which would be another reason for not using the term *jamu* for herbal preparations intended more as a curative medicine than a tonic or elixir. This interpretation remains uncertain since Javanese contained both *obat* and *jamu*; it is not clear how they were being used in the 1920s and 1930s (see Gimlette and Thomson 1971: 174; Suparlan 1978: 207; cf. Jordaan 1985: 192–194, 203–204, 214–216).
11. European physicians were for the most part in internment camps during the occupation; Japanese doctors were busy serving the needs of the Japanese army and navy. This left the health needs of the indigenous community in the hands of Dutch-trained Indonesian physicians (both *pribumi* and non-*pribumi*, as well as pharmacists, other health workers, *jamu* sellers and village *dukun*'s.
12. The best evidence for this is that at the 1940 Congress of the Vereniging Indonesische

Geneeskundigen (VIG) (the forerunner of the Indonesia Medical Association), Goelarso, one of the physicians who regularly used fresh *jamu* in his practice, was asked to give a lecture and a small exhibition of *jamu asli Indonesia* along with their raw ingredients. (Sastroamidjojo 1967: 8). On the one hand, this suggests that the VIG was beginning to take some interest in plant-based pharmaceuticals. But on the other hand, it illustrates how unfamiliar Indonesian physicians were with *jamu* in their medical practices. At the end of the Congress the VIG also passed a resolution supporting increased research into '*obat-dan tjara memakainja, jang masih dipergunakan dalam masjarakat Indonesia*' ('medicines and their methods of use that are still used in Indonesian society').

13. It is not clear from the Sastroamidjojo (1967) just how much support the Japanese offered. They did organize a meeting of all the *obat* manufacturers in Jakarta to discuss the production of *jamu*.
14. Three of the most important laws regulating pharmaceuticals in Indonesia are: Undang-Undang Obat-keras, Stbl. Tahun 1949, No. 419, Undang-Undang No. 9, 1960, concerning basic health, and Undang-Undang No. 7, 1963, concerning Pharmacy. The first, concerning strong drugs was never specifically applied to *jamu*. By implication this has defined *jamu* as a non-dangerous pharmaceutical.
15. 'Seminar nasional penggalian sumber alam Indonesia untuk farmasi' (see Sastroamidjojo 1967: 19).
16. The industry is finding registration to be increasingly cumbersome and complex. The withdrawal of several products which contained Mercury has undoubtedly concerned a few manufacturers and there are major worries about the secrecy of recipes (see Simanjuntak 1984). There is also concern about costly requirements to replant the forests after harvesting tropical plants in danger of extinction (see Winarno and Maran 1985; Kompas 1984).
17. For more details regarding particular manufacturers see Krisanto (1984). Simona, for example, exclusively manufactures tablets rather than powdered *jamu*, and most of the cosmetics firms have a few more traditional looking forms, but clearly their profit comes from modern-looking cosmetics and beauty products.
18. All of the major firms produce a type of *jamu* for colds, for 'languor' etc. This latter even tends to be named by all of the firms with the same name 'Pegal Linu' or some minor varient. The ingredients are often not particularly different, although the proportions vary. See also Winarno and Maran 1985).
19. The most important of these are Universitas Indonesia, Jakarta; Institut Teknologi, Bandung; Universitas Gajah Mada, Yogyakarta; and Universitas Airlangga, Surabaya. See also Kompas 1984.
20. Jordaan (1985: 309) remarks that in Madura '. . . sexuality is the second major field of application of herbal drinks'.
21. 'Tetapi banyak dokter-dokter di departemen kesehatan mengatekan jamu itu obat tradisional. Lha itu sangat salah. Definisi itu tidak tepat karena sampai sekarang kita belum boleh mengatakan jamu itu obat . . . Jamu itu jamu. Titik.'

REFERENCES

Adisasmita, Ki Sumidi
    1974 Pustaka Centini Selayang Pandang. Yogyakarta: U.P. Indonesia.
    1975 Pustaka Centini Ikhtisar Seluruh Isinya. Yogyakarta: U.P. Indonesia.
Afdhal, Ahmad Fuad
    1981 Drug Delivery and Drug Marketing: A Comparative Study Among Southeast Asian Countries. Unpublished manuscript, University of Minnesota.
Air Mancur
    n.d. A Booklet of Indonesian Traditional Medicines for Health Maintenance and Beauty Care. Wonogiri: Air Mancur.

Dharma, A. P.
  1985   Tanaman Obat Tradisional Indonesia. Jakarta: Balai Pustaka.
Echols, John M. and Shadily, Hassan
  1983   An Indonesian-English Dictionary. Jakarta: Gramedia.
Geerstz, C.
  1960   The Religion of Jara. New York: The Free Press.
Gimlette, John D. and Thomson, H. W.
  1971   A Dictionary of Malayan Medicine. Kuala Lumpur: Oxford University Press. (first published 1939)
Jordaan, Roy E.
  1985   Folk Medicine in Madura (Indonesia). Ph.D. Thesis, Rijksuniversiteit, Leiden.
Kleinman, Arthur M.
  1980   Patients and Healers in the Context of Culture. Berkeley: University of California Press.
Kleinman, Arthur M. et al., (eds)
  1975   Medicine in Chinese Cultures: Comparative Studies of Health Care in Chinese and Other Societies. Washington: US Government Printing Office for Fogarty International Center.
Kompas
  1984   Peranan Balai Penelitian Menunjang Industri Jamu. Kompas, 17 December 1984.
Kristanto J. B.
  1984   Industri Jamu, Yang Besar dan yang Kecil Hidup 'Damai' Berdampingan. Kompas, 16 Dec. 1984.
Leslie, Charles, (ed.)
  1976   Asian Medical Systems. Berkeley: University of California Press.
Mardisiswojo, Sudarman and Rajakmangunsudarso, Harsono
  1985   Cabe Puyang Warisan Nenek Moyang. Jakarta: Balai Pustaka.
Mudakir, K. and Soleh, Moh.
  1984   Pengobatan Tradisional Secara Islam. Pekalongan: T.B. 'Bahagia'.
Muji, Musaro
  n.d.   Resep Pusaka Tradisional Madura. n.p.: Pustaka Karya.
Mustika Ratu
  n.d.   List of Jamu & Traditional Cosmetics. Jakarta: Mustika Ratu.
Nyonya Meneer, P. T.
  n.d.   Daftar Jamu, untuk memelihara kesehatan dan kecantikan. Semarang: Nyonya Meneer.
Poerwadarminta, W. J. S.
  1984   Kamus Umum Bahasa Indonesia. Jakarta: Balai Pustaka.
Rianggoro, Krisna
  1982   Pengobatan Tradisional Jamu Jawa. Surabaya: Bina Ilmu.
Sahly, Salim
  1983   Petunjuk Pengobatan Dengan Resep-Resep Asli. Solo: Penerbit & Toko Buku Aneka.
Sastroamidjojo, A. Seno
  1967   Obat Asli Indonesia, Chusus Daripada Tumbuh^{2}an Jang Terdapat Di Indonesia. Jakarta: Dian Rakyat. (3rd edition, first edition published 1947)
Simandjuntak, Edward Soaloon
  1984   Meningkatan Pemasaran Jamu, Menjual Gairah Seks. Prisma 2: 74–84.
Soedibyo, Mooryati
  1984   Traditional Medical Philosophy. Paper delivered at the Second International Congress on Traditional Asian Medicine, Surabaya, 2–7 September 1984.
Soeparto, Soedarmilah
  1984   Jamu Jawa Asli. Jakarta: Sinar Harapan.

Suparlan, Parsudi
   1978   The Javanese Dukun. Masyarakat Indonesia 5 (2): 195–216.
Surindo Utama, P. T.
   1984   Media Monitoring
Tilaar, Martha
   1985   Perawatan Kecantikan Tradisional. Paper delivered at the Seminar Dermatologi, Universitas Sumatera Utara, Medan.
Winarno, Bondan and Maran, Canisyus
   1985   Jamu Tradisional. Tempo 15: 10, suplemen khusus "Pariwara".

THE MEANING OF MEDICINES

INTRODUCTORY NOTE

This section contains eight chapters that focus on the perception and understanding of medicines by those involved in their transaction. For manufacturers as well as for pharmacologists, physicians, pharmacists, drug pedlars and patients, medicines have a meaning that goes far beyond their chemical properties and therapeutic reputation. Medicines are artifacts that can only be adequately understood when viewed in their cultural context.

A recurrent theme in many of these chapters is that medicines are understood – and used – according to local perceptions. Their function and mode of application are conceived in terms of culturally specific notions of the nature of sickness and healing. In some societies the concept of medicine is stretched far beyond the Western pharmacological definition and covers experiences that Westerners would describe as psychological, social and religious.

Another intriguing – and somewhat contrasting – observation is that pharmaceuticals become promotors of greater personal autonomy as they enable people to treat themselves individually rather than within the common framework of relationships to healers, kinsmen or spirits. This, together with the fact that they are seen as 'modern' and exotic, means that Western pharmaceuticals assume the role of vehicles of cultural change. The pharmaceutical invasion that we witness in developing countries is in fact part of a cultural transformation.

Unschuld applies a cultural perspective to a comparison of dominant European and Chinese cognitive dynamics in general and of ancient European and medieval Chinese pharmacological paradigms in particular. In both cultures, at a certain period, empirical knowledge of medicines was combined with theories that had earlier served to provide meaning for illness.

The author discusses the implication of a major cognitive reorientation of China where no one will be left untouched by modern science and technology-oriented culture in the future. While he foresees a continuing application of traditional pharmaceutics for a long time to come, he doubts the survival of traditional Chinese theories as an independent mode of thought.

Sussman carried out a household survey on therapeutic choice among Creoles and Indo-Mauritians in two adjacent villages in the southwest of Mauritius. She reports a growing use of Western doctors and pharmaceuticals. Self-treatment with herbal medicine is also common. Remarkably, the choice of treatment hardly depends on diagnosis. According to the author, Mauritians do not classify illness primarily by their symptoms. Rather they designate causes of illness and choose therapeutic resources in a specific sequence. In most cases the use of biomedical facilities is the first step. The use of Western pharmaceuticals is both treatment and a technique to establish the cause of the complaint. If an illness does not respond to biomedicine it is classified as supernaturally caused, requiring other treatment.

Whyte, doing fieldwork in East Africa, takes a very broad view of medicines: 'Medicine is a substance that transforms something – for better or worse'. She mentions examples of 'treating' hunting dogs, cotton, flat tires, lovers and senior relatives with 'medicine'. She suggests that 'traditional' medicines and Western pharmaceuticals share important characteristics which distinguish them from ritual and relational modes of transforming the human condition. The most important of these is that 'medicines' as substances have an innate power which can be acquired by any individual. This enables therapy to be 'liberated' from the social relationships in which it would otherwise be embedded. Medicines thus become the vehicle of a growing individualism.

Another characteristic of all medicines is that foreign provenance is associated with power. Whyte convincingly argues that both Western and African medicines are often brought from far away and are believed to derive their efficacy from their 'exotic' origin. The pharmaceutical invasion of local African cultures was in process long before Western drugs reached the continent.

Niehof's contribution describes the use of *jamu* medicines in the management of gestation and birth on the Indonesian island of Madura. In contrast to Afdhal and Welsch, she provides a view from below, showing how *jamu* is interpreted within the Madurese understanding of the physiological processes surrounding pregnancy and childbirth, which is dominated by (but cannot be reduced to) the hot-cold opposition.

Niehof's paper shows a 'negative' context of Western pharmaceuticals on Madura. Although Western drugs are available, Madurese women do not perceive them as relevant for this area of health care.

Bledsoe and Goubaud address the 'inappropriate' use of Western medicines as a cultural issue. Among the Mende of Sierra Leone indigenous beliefs about illness and treatment provide the explanatory framework for interpreting Western medicines. People appear to base their treatment decisions largely on local notions of how a drug's shape, color and taste is related to its effects. Consistency with traditional logic and the medicine's reputed success in treating analogous illnesses are also important indicators for use. The authors illustrate their argument by describing people's handling of three common health complaints, fever, worms and 'blood problems', and a concern for health maintenance. This cultural reinterpretation often leads to drug use that is at odds with Western assumptions about appropriate use. The authors point out various implications of their research for local and international health planning.

MacCormack and Draper describe how oral rehydration salts (ORS) are perceived and used by mothers and guardians in Kingston, Jamaica. Packaged ORS are promoted by health care workers to replace good traditional practices concerning children's diarrhea. Three observations seem particularly relevant. The ORS campaign leads to increased and unnecessary dependence on professional help, the opposite of primary health care aims. The economic consequences are unfavorable both on the national and individual level – people are advised to buy from abroad what they already have at hand. And finally, to persuade mothers with sick children to come to the clinic to obtain the ORS, the packets are presented as 'medicine' instead of as food. Ironically, the nurses explain the working of the 'medicine' in one way and many mothers understand it quite differently. This anthropological analysis contains important implications for the improvement of health care policy.

Burghart's paper forms part of a detailed analysis of the clinical practice of one Indian Ayurvedic healer who works near the Nepalese border. As has also been shown for Sri Lanka in Wolffers' paper, indigenous practitioners are increasingly confronted with the presence of Western pharmaceuticals. Burghart looks at the growing popularity of injectable medicines. Although the hypodermic needle and syringe are alien to Ayurveda, their use has become almost standard practice. The Ayurvedic healer in this case study frequently administers penicillin by injection, interpreting its efficacy in terms of the equilibrium theory of illness. Although the healer recognizes that penicillin recently came to South Asia from the West, he nonetheless asserts that it was known to the Brahmanical sages in the past. By claiming that this modern antibiotic was known to the ancients, the autonomy of Ayurveda is maintained. Bughart's example illustrates the most radical form of cultural reinterpretation: appropriation.

In the last paper of this section *Etkin* provides an overview of studies on the efficacy of indigenous medicines. She reveals and criticizes the biomedical bias in most studies of efficacy and proposes instead a culturally relative approach. She suggests that people perceive the effects of medicines in terms of stages in a process. There are different expectations and ascriptions of meaning for each stage. The selection, preparation and actual use of medicinal plants is consistent with the prevailing medical cosmology. The perception of efficacy can not be divorced from 'actual' efficacy; that is, people's understanding affects what happens. Etkin's argument applies equally to the study of the efficacy of Western medicines. The way in which these products are perceived and interpreted in a particular culture determines their selection and uses and helps shape their therapeutic consequences.

PAUL U. UNSCHULD

CULTURE AND PHARMACEUTICS: SOME EPISTEMOLOGICAL OBSERVATIONS ON PHARMACOLOGICAL SYSTEMS IN ANCIENT EUROPE AND MEDIEVAL CHINA

To Professor Rudolf Schmitz
on the occasion of his 70th birthday

AN ANTHROPOLOGICAL APPROACH TO THE COGNITIVE BASIS OF PHARMACEUTICS

The application of drugs, for therapeutic purposes, to an ailing organism predates the emergence of literary sources. All we may surmise, on the basis of early evidence, is that both in ancient Europe and in ancient China – to refer to but the two best documented early civilizations – two formerly separate traditions of drug use appear to have merged in about the first millennium B.C. The earliest written documents of ancient Greece, as well as texts unearthed in the province of Hunan in the early 1970s, suggest that experiences with an external application were combined with knowledge about the internal intake of natural and/or man-made substances to form the therapeutic approach of pharmaceutic intervention.[1]

We do not know what kind of reasoning led early man to cover a sore, a wound, or an aching region of his body with a plant, an animal organ, or with any other item from his environment, and, similarly, we may offer nothing but truisms about why early man may have chosen one or another substance for ingestion when he felt ill. However, by the time prescriptions and individual drugs were recorded as literature, the human desire for explanatory world-views had already touched the realm of pharmaceutics, and manmade paradigms had joined, as well as transformed, pragmatic knowledge gained through experience and observation. As a result, drugs and their usage not only became part of human culture per se, they were integrated, in addition, into far-reaching attempts at conceptualization of a perceived reality. Hence an analysis, by anthropologists, of ideas concerning drug application is as meaningful and important as is an analysis of ideas concerning the emergence, nature, and treatment of illness in general. In fact, if medical anthropology intends to reach a comprehensive understanding of the socio-cultural context of health care, it should include – or be supplemented by – pharmaceutical anthropology.

One of the aims of medical anthropology may be seen as a disentanglement of the closely interwoven natural-environmental, human-biological, and socio-cultural threads forming the behavioral and conceptual network of human responses to the experience of illness. Similarly, pharmaceutical anthropology may focus on an analysis of a specific segment of this network, and attempt to identify the proportions of biochemical (or whatever) reality and human imagination in a particular society's understanding of drugs, drug properties, and drug effects. I have purposely chosen the term 'imagination' here because the cultural-conceptual transformation of the experience of drug effects represents nothing but a transfer of general 'images' of the world – as seen by a society – to a narrow aspect of health care, and it is this transfer of images that should concern cultural anthropology as much as anything else.

In some of my own previous studies on Chinese pharmaceutics I have pointed out how – in a complex and heterogeneous society as China has been for two thousand years – different social groups experiencing different social realities and harboring different ideologies have transferred their respective images of the world not only to their respective understanding of health and illness – corresponding to their respective interpretation of social order and crisis – but also to their interpretation of, for instance, drug hierarchies in prescriptions.

Confucians valued the head of the state as the supreme administrator, assisted in his efforts at crisis prevention and crisis management by ministers, aides, and messengers. Not surprisingly, pharmaceutical thinking based on Confucian values sees so-called 'ruler' (*chün*) drugs as instrumental in the elimination of illness, assisted by 'minister' (*ch'en*), 'aides' (*tso*), and 'messenger' (*shih*) drugs. Taoist oriented pharmaceutical literature used an identical terminology to express an opposite image of an ideal society: here it is the task of the lower ranks of 'aides' and 'messengers', and, to a limited degree only, of 'ministers', to actually cure illness, that is, solve crisis, while the 'ruler' has but the function of guaranteeing harmony by doing as little as possible.[2] It should be noted that during the Cultural Revolution in the 1970s, publications appeared in the People's Republic of China adapting the former ruler-minister-aides-messenger terminology in Chinese pharmaceutics to the social ideology dominating then. The four hierarchical levels were redefined as *chu* (as in *chu-hsi*, 'chairman'), *fu* ('helper'), *tso* ('aide'), and *shih* ('messenger').[3]

It should have become obvious in recent years that we can no longer speak of Chinese Medicine as a system of medical ideas and practices representative of Chinese culture, when we refer, for instance, to such facets of traditional Chinese medicine as the medicine of systematic correspondence, based on the yin yang and Five Phases doctrines, or when we speak of traditional Chinese pharmaceutics or demonology. Rather we will have to acknowledge the fact that different social groups in Chinese history, experiencing different social realities and harboring different world views, developed and adhered to, or adopted from abroad, different conceptual systems of health care. These different systems were pursued, to a certain degree, separately by the respective social groups supporting them, but they were also linked to a highly syncretic edifice of concepts and practices which only in its entirety may be called Chinese Medicine. And while I emphasize the social and ideological environment variables as responsible for shaping the spectrum of individual and often antagonistic conceptual systems of health care forming, in their syncretic union, the edifice of Chinese Medicine, I should also like to emphasize that there appear to be some basic differentials separating this complex and heterogeneous edifice of Chinese Medicine on the one hand from European (and that includes, as a recent outreach, American) approaches to the formation of knowledge on health care.

ON THE ORIGINS OF PHARMACEUTICAL KNOWLEDGE
IN CHINA AND EUROPE

In this paper I wish to point out how cultural differentials influenced the formation of pharmacological systems in ancient Europe and medieval China. Pharmacology, in a modern sense, is the science concerned with the reaction of the living organism to stimuli exerted by chemical agents.[4] Although the term 'pharmacology' represents a modern concept and was not introduced prior to the seventeenth century,[5] I shall extend it, with a slightly modified definition, to an analysis of events that occurred many centuries earlier. The term pharmacology, as I shall use it in this paper, refers to knowledge concerned with the explanation of drug effects in the living organism by linking certain drug properties to a perceived physiology of the body.

A precondition for the emergence of pharmacological systems is an accumulation of extensive pharmaceutical knowledge. In ancient China such knowledge may have been developed and transmitted for a long time before it was documented in literary form. The earliest texts on Chinese pharmaceutics available today are also the earliest records known on Chinese drug lore. They consist of prescriptions and appear to have been compiled around 200 B.C.; they were discovered in the famous Ma-wang-tui tombs near Ch'ang-sha, Hunan province, in the early 1970s. Another three hundred years elapsed before the first known Chinese herbal was compiled in the first century A.D. Whereas the prescriptions had focused on illness and disease, this herbal concentrated on a description of numerous individual substances. The *Shen-nung pen-ts'ao ching* ('Shen-nung's Scripture on Materia Medica') is said to have contained, in correspondence to the number of days in a solar year – a total of 365 drug monographs.[6]

Both the prescriptions of the Ma-wang-tui texts and the drug descriptions in the *Shen-nung pen-ts'ao ching* are basically pragmatic; that is, although in numerous instances we may hypothesize that criteria based on demonological or magical reasoning supported the selection of a particular substance for the treatment of a particular ailment, the texts themselves do not contain any explicit references to such considerations.[7] The *Shen-nung pen-ts'ao ching* lists names, places of origin, drug qualities, and indications; the Ma-wang-tui prescriptions provide but indications and drug names, as well as references to dosages and suitable pharmaceutical processing of raw drugs. The drug qualities listed in the *Shen-nung pen-ts'ao ching*, i.e., various flavors and thermo-qualities associated with individual substances, correspond to abstract qualities (possibly of food) listed in the classics of the theory of the medicine of systematic correspondence, that is, the *Huang-ti nei-ching* of the second and first century B.C. However, a linkage of drug application with the theoretical foundations of systematic correspondence was not attempted, in China, until the 12th through the 14th century, during a period, that is, which proved favorable to the union of the hitherto antagonistic traditions of pharmaceutics on the one hand and of the medicine of systematic correspondence (favoring the therapeutic technique of needling) on the other hand. The socio-political and ideological context that kept these traditions apart for more than a millennium and brought them together only one and a half thousand years after their formation, has been described and analysed in detail elsewhere, and need not be repeated here.[8]

Before we take a closer look at the 'pharmacology of systematic correspondence' resulting from this union, I should like to trace corresponding developments in ancient Europe.

The origins of pharmaceutical literature were somewhat different here than in China. The earliest European herbals known to us and transmitted, at least in fragments, to the present time were compiled by Diokles of Karystos and by Theophrastos of Eresos in the fourth century B.C. They, too, were part of a much older tradition – the epic of Homer of the second millennium B.C. provides the earliest European literary data on an application of therapeutic drugs – but they appear to have emerged from an Aristotelian interest in botany, that is, from a general interest in herbs and other plants, some of which were known to possess therapeutic properties, and were described accordingly.[9]

A long series of herbals is known to have followed the works of Diokles and Theophrastos, and prescriptions were recorded in some of the texts of the 'Corpus Hippocraticum' during the final four to five centuries B.C., until the first European herbal was compiled that has come down to us in full length, that is, the *Materia Medica* of Dioscurides of the first century A.D.

Similar to its Chinese contemporary, the *Shen-nung pen-ts'ao ching*, the *Materia Medica* of Dioscurides was pragmatically oriented and contained no explicity theoretical pharmacology even though some of the drug qualities referred to could easily have been employed as links to the physiology and pathology of systematic correspondence dominating the 'Corpus Hippocraticum'.

The step from an empirical justification of drug use to a theoretical or 'scientific' understanding of why drugs achieve certain effects in the living organism was undertaken in Europe rather early, that is, in the second century, by the Greek physician Galen of Pergamon who preferred to practice in the capital of the Roman empire for many years of his life.

Galen and the Chinese scholars of the 12th through the 14th century had similar tasks at hand, namely, to integrate a vast body of pharmaceutical knowledge gained through observation and 'pre-scientific' speculation, and described in the existing literature in empirical terms, into a theoretical framework that had been applied, for centuries already, to the normal and abnormal workings of the living organism.[10]

The differences in the contents and structures of the epistemic edifices construed in ancient Europe and medieval China can hardly have originated from differences in the drugs – not a few substances were identical – or from differences in Chinese and European physiological reactions to the effects of these drugs. The differences between Chinese and European pharmacological systems result from differing cultural contexts shaping the formation of knowledge.

COGNITIVE TENDENCIES IN THE FORMATION OF CHINESE AND
EUROPEAN PHARMACOLOGICAL DOCTRINES

In the following I wish to point out some basic differences between cognitive tendencies in European culture and China. My hypothesis is that in the history of European knowledge, for more than two thousand years, a tendency may be identified, and appears to have dominated, to build cognitive systems permeated by one homogeneous paradigm. This paradigm is preferably internally stringent and free of any internal antagonistic contradictions; it claims truth but for itself, and cannot accept any other truth besides it. This European attitude towards knowledge entails that all those concepts and ideas cannot be accepted as knowledge, and cannot be accepted as 'true', that cannot be integrated into a dominating cognitive system without apparent contradictions. The tendency thus described applies both to knowledge gained through transcendental revelation, i.e., religious knowledge, and to knowledge gained through an observation of and hypothesizing about nature, i.e., 'scientific' knowledge.

A rather different tendency, it seems to me, has influenced – to a significant degree – the formation of knowledge in China for the past two and a half millennia. In China, as in Europe, many authors, in the course of time, have offered comprehensive and partial paradigms and world-views, contradicting existing explanatory models. And, as in Europe, heated and lengthy debates occurred in Chinese history on the 'truth' or 'adequacy' of conflicting paradigms. However, in contrast to Europe, Chinese culture, be it in philosophy or 'science', appears to have favored, after an initial phase of fierce confrontation, an inclusion of various paradigms within one complex syncretic structure of knowledge. This way, the former antagonists were each granted a certain degree of – limited – truth, or at least a certain competence to solve some specific issue. As a result, extremely complex and highly impressive cognitive edifices emerged that could not be free of internal contradictions between their integrated parts, but that may be called logical and contingent since all these parts could be traced – despite their mutually antagonistic nature – to a common basic paradigm.

This rather generalized characterization of the Chinese structuring of knowledge needs to be modified immediately. The combination of various – (in Western eyes) even mutually contradictory – paradigmatic patterns into one epistemic edifice occurred within one and the same more encompassing paradigm, and transcended this basis only rarely. That is to say, the yinyang and the Five Phases doctrines, to name but one prominent example, represent two mutually antagonistic world views within the more encompassing paradigm of systematic correspondence. A Western observer would favor an 'either – or' decision between the two because many of their conceptual consequences appear to him mutually exclusive. In China, however, bridges were built to link the two schools of thought, and, already during the Han dynasty, a union occurred that made the yinyang and the Five Phases doctrines appear as constituents of one system of thought.

Such a conciliatory tendency towards speculative interpretations of one commonly accepted basic paradigm differs from cognitive approaches in the history of Western knowledge where internal stringency was favored over logical contingency. More research on European and Chinese history of knowledge may be necessary, though, before we can make definitive statements as to whether the differences pointed out above represent reality or reification. This applies, in particular, to an initial impression that even in cases where social or political barriers prevented a syncretic union between two antagonistic world views (such as Confucianism and Taoism; or demonology and Buddhism on the one side and systematic correspondence on the other side), Chinese culture appears to have permitted – tacitly, and more persistently than European culture – a mechanical perspective on paradigms or ideologies, in that antagonistic paradigms or world views were utilized as suitable tools by one and the same individual, and, possibly, by society in general, for coping with different aspects of daily life and of a perceived reality.

A continuity of one dominant school of thought or orthodox world view or paradigm – as both European sciences and religions have striven for with great efforts (although the ideal result was reached only rarely) for the past two millennia – seems to have been alien to Chinese culture. The concept of 'Scientific Revolutions' propagated by Thomas Kuhn, as well as Hegelian ideas concerning a dialectic solution of social and cognitive contradictions – these epistemological models could be conceived, obviously, only upon the background of European traditions in the formation of knowledge; their claims to a comprehensive explanatory value may have to be reconsidered when Chinese traditions are taken into account as well.

The two differing tendencies that I have outlined here seem to have influenced the formation of European and Chinese pharmacological systems in the same manner as many other realms of knowledge, as can be demonstrated by a comparison of essential features of Galenic and medieval Chinese efforts to provide an explanation for invisible links, in the living organism, between visible substances and their intake on the one side, and visible or, at least, perceivable drug effects on the other hand.

CHARACTERISTICS OF ANCIENT EUROPEAN PHARMACOLOGY

Georg Harig has pointed out, in his studies on Galenic pharmacology in the 1970s, that Galen intended to construe a purely theoretical system of drug effects, but, at the same time, was forced to take into account empirical categories that had been associated with drug therapy and drug effects during preceding centuries.[11]

Galen's starting point was the ancient European version of the paradigm of systematic correspondence, that is, the so-called doctrine of the Four Humors (corresponding to the doctrine of the Four Elements) with its notion of four basic drug qualities, i.e., warm, cold, dry, and moist. The issue to which Galen directed his attention was the replacement of time-honored empirical descriptions of drug effects – such as 'draining pus', 'purging', 'eliminating pain', or 'causing one to sleep', and many others – by scientific, that is, theoretical criteria of categorization. These theoretical criteria were not to be based, primarily, on a sensual perception of specific drug properties but on the position of a drug within the system of the four basic drug qualities.[12]

Of course, Galen was aware of the fact that a complete exchange of 'unscientific', empirical criteria of drug evaluation with the 'scientific' categories derived from the doctrine of the four humors would have meant construction of a system of ideas so far removed from daily clinical reality that most physicians could not have made any use of it.[13] The pharmacology construed, finally, by Galen, and published in his *De simplicium medicamentorum temperamentis ac facultatibus*, represents a quite sophisticated union between theoretical claims and sensually perceptible reality. Galen created a system that was sufficiently open to integrate any future results from empirical observation; at the same time, from a theoretical perspective, it was sufficiently homogeneous to remain free of internal contradictions. A survey of the structural components of Galen's pharmacology may clarify this statement.

The theoretical premise on which Galen built his system was rather simple. (Table I)
The four humors, the four elements, and further fourfold categorizations, such as annual seasons and body organs, were seen as corresponding to the four basic qualities warm, cold, dry, and moist. All drugs were supposed to contain these four basic qualities in varying proportions; that is, these basic qualities are contained in all drugs in specific mixtures (*krasis*) and are, therefore, responsible for the medicinal effects of these drugs. The medicinal effects, in turn, represent an empirical category comprising altogether 17 groups that were adopted, by Galen, from the descriptive literature of former

TABLE I
The four basic drug qualities within the system of the Four Humors and Four Elements

Humors	phlegm	blood	yellow bile	black bile
Elements	water	air	fire	earth
Basic Qualities	moist	dry	warm	cold
Seasons	winter	spring	summer	autumn
Organs	brain	heart	liver	spleen

centuries, and that ranged from 'remedies generating pus' to 'remedies suppressing the generation of semen'.[14]

To achieve the intended connection between the basic theory of the Four Elements/Four Humors, on the one side, and the empirical category of the 17 groups of drug effects, on the other side, a mediating link was necessary. Galen introduced here what he called the 'secondary qualities' of drugs, and these 'secondary qualities' comprised, in turn, an empirical and a theoretical category themselves.[15]

Galen took over, from Plato, seven flavor qualities, and from Theophrastos one (i.e., fatty). He himself added 'astringent' as ninth.[16] These nine sensually perceivable qualities were supposed, in the eyes of Galen, to produce altogether six pharmacological functions. Since each drug was assumed to contain a specific mixture of flavor qualities, and, hence, of pharmacological functions, the latter provided a theoretical link between the two empirical categories of nine taste qualities and 17 drug effects.

Surveying Galen's pharmacological system in its entirety, we recognize a structure that, firstly, combines – through two total intersections and one partial intersection – altogether two theoretical and two empirical categories, and that, secondly, enables a far-reaching harmonization in a theoretical system acknowledging but four basic categories of all phenomena, on the one side, and the manifold reality of observed phenomena, on the other side.

It should be emphasized here that the four-fold categorization along the lines of the Four Elements/Four Humors theory remained but a limited basic pattern in ancient Greek/Roman medicine; it was understood as but the nucleus of a multiplicity of phenomena that could transcend the number four in many ways. The four basic qualities warm, cold, dry, and moist, within the six primary qualities, constitute the sole nexus with the fundamental paradigm of the doctrine of systematic correspondences. To the four basic qualities were added two others – 'course-grained; and 'fine-grained' – qualities that were essential for an explanation of drug effects that were identified as slow or fast, as occurring near the surface or in the depth.

Of central importance is the concept of 'mixture', or *krasis*; it was pivotal in the linkage between theoretical and empirical data. Whether a substance is

TABLE II
The seventeen groups of drugs according to their effects

1. Pus moventia	remedies generating pus
Emollentia	softening remedies
2. Indurantia	hardening remedies
3. Laxantia	relaxing remedies
4. Emplastica	lubricating remedies
5. Poros repurgantia, etc.	remedies cleaning pores
Extergentia	cleansing remedies
6. Urinam cientia seu moventia	diuretic remedies
7. Rarefacientia	remedies opening pores
Aperientia	remedies opening vessels
Condensantia	remedies closing pores
8. Urentia	remedies causing a burning
9. Putrefacientia	remedies generating putrefaction
Cathaeretica	cleansing remedies
10. Ad cicatricem ducentia	remedies generating scars
11. Attrahentia	remedies drawing together
Repellentia	remedies that repel
12. Alexeteria seu alexipharmaca	protective remedies, antidotes
13. Dolorem sedantia	remedies killing pain
Dolorem lenientia	remedies decreasing pain
Dolorem mitigantia	remedies mitigating pain
14. Somnifera	remedies causing sleep
15. Lactem creantia seu laedantia	remedies stimulating or harming the generation of milk
16. Menses provocantia seu sedantia	remedies stimulating or stopping menstruation
17. Semen generantia seu extingentia	remedies stimulating or suppressing the generation of semen

TABLE III
The secondary qualities of drugs

Empirical	Theoretical
Sensually perceivable flavor qualities	Assumed corresponding pharmacological functions
Astringent	drawing together; densifying
Sour	same as above
Acrid	same as above
Pungent	cutting; diluting
Sweet	dissolving; smoothing; softening
Fatty (oily)	same as above (+ moistening)
Salty	drawing together; drying; roughening
Bitter	diluting; dissipating; cleansing
Biting	diluting; cleansing; dissipating; breaking up scars; generating scurf

acrid, pungent, sweet, or salty, depends on the specific mixture of primary qualities it contains; and, similarly, a specific mixture of inherent pharmacological functions is responsible for the appearance of a substance in one of the 17 groups of drug effects.

With his pharmacological system, Galen created a cognitive structure that was, according to the standards of European science aesthetics, both elegant and typical. It linked theoretical and empirical elements on the basis of homogeneity and internal stringency, and needed no further amendment until the transformation towards modern science about two centuries ago.

Galen's pharmacological system may now be compared to corresponding Chinese efforts.

CHARACTERISTICS OF MEDIEVAL CHINESE PHARMACOLOGY

In various respects, Chinese scholars who undertook to create a theoretically founded pharmacological system were confronted with issues similar to those faced by the physician and author from Pergamon – even though they were separated from each other not only by obvious cultural boundaries but also by vast geographic distances and by a time-span of one thousand years. Like Galen in the second century, the Chinese physicians of the twelfth through fourteenth century had to take the empirical data of an already quite sizeable descriptive literature on materia medica and prescriptions into account, and they had to find a way to conclusively link a rather unflexible theoretical premise with the manifold observations gained from the reality of varying drug effects.[18]

Contrary to an assumption widespread in the West, Chinese medicine is not senior to European medicine by millenia – not even by centuries. The oldest known medical and pharmaceutical texts of China were compiled not earlier than during the third century B.C., and they cannot be compared with the texts of the 'Corpus Hippocraticum' – written, in part, centuries earlier – as far as the breadth of topics treated and the depth of reflections on the foundations of health care are concerned.[19]

The Chinese texts of the third to first centuries B.C. contain many data on pharmaceutics (suggesting a lengthy, albeit undocumented prior development), but a first herbal that concentrated on cataloging and describing therapeutically effective substances appears to have been compiled in China only at the same time as the materia medica of Dioscurides, that is, during the first century A.D. Another twelve centuries had to pass before the times allowed for a linkage of a by then very rich pharmaceutical knowledge with a theoretical superstructure that had been limited, until then, to an explanation of physiological processes and how these processes could be manipulated through an insertion of needles. Notions of a systematic correspondence of all phenomena appeared in China not much later than in ancient Greece. The beginnings of Chinese thinking in terms of such laws of nature may be found in the fifth century B.C. In contrast to the Greek development though, there appear to have emerged, in China, almost simultaneously, two antagonistic schools. One of them, the yinyang school, explained all coming into being, all change, and all passing away through the dualism of two complementary categories of all being; the second school propagated the so-called Five-Phases doctrine which saw the sum of all phenomena, and all of their mutual relationships, as resulting from interactions among five categories of all being. The situation appears to have become even further complicated by the fact that the yinyang school itself seems to have split into two sub-doctrines, one of which held a two-fold sub-categorization while the other advocated a three-fold sub-categorization of both yin and yang.[21]

The complete range of Chinese concepts of systematic correspondence included, therefore, patterns based on the numbers two, four, five, and six for a categorization of all phenomena of perceived and assumed reality, and for an explanation of the relationships and interactions among these phenomena.

TABLE IV
The pharmacological system of Galen

Primary qualities	*krasis*	Secondary qualities	*krasis*[17]	Therapeutic effects
4 Basic qualities + 2 Additional qualities		9 sensually perceivable taste qualities		6 groups of pharmacological functions		17 groups of drug effects
Theoretical		empirical		theoretical		empirical

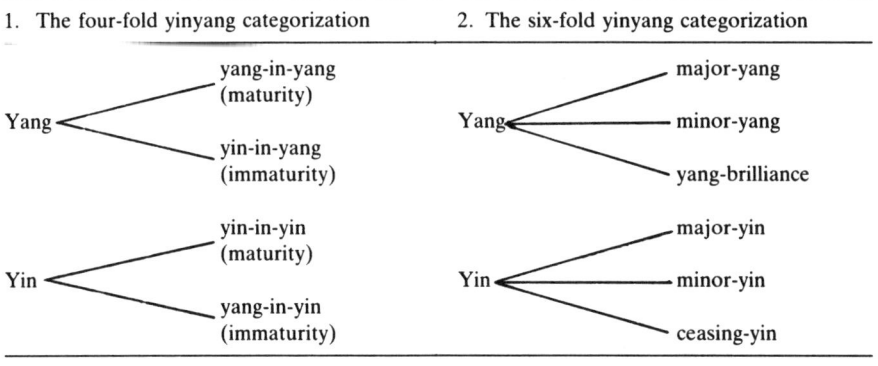

TABLE V
Yinyang categorizations

1. The four-fold yinyang categorization

Yang
  ├─ yang-in-yang (maturity)
  └─ yin-in-yang (immaturity)

Yin
  ├─ yin-in-yin (maturity)
  └─ yang-in-yin (immaturity)

2. The six-fold yinyang categorization

Yang
  ├─ major-yang
  ├─ minor-yang
  └─ yang-brilliance

Yin
  ├─ major-yin
  ├─ minor-yin
  └─ ceasing-yin

In contrast with European traditions in science, none of the competing patterns of categorization remained victorious and became dominant for some time. On the contrary, following an initial period of antagonism, all the patterns mentioned found entrance, into a rather complicated system of ideas, each structural part of which was attributed a certain, limited, degree of truth. Where Western modes of thought demanded an 'either – or' decision, Chinese tradition appears to have preferred, again and again, an 'as well as' approach.[22] Hence, when, in China, during the Sung-Chin-Yüan era of the twelfth through fourteenth century the available pragmatic knowledge on drugs and their effects was to be given theoretical foundations, inevitably a system was generated that differed, in its structure, greatly from that of Galen – despite similar premises and contents.

A number of Chinese authors participated in the development of the pharmacology of systematic correspondence. Typical for the outcome of their efforts are the theoretical sections of the *T'ang-yeh pen-ts'ao* of Wang Hao-ku of the late thirteenth century. The following discussion will be concentrated on Wang's work.[23]

Generally speaking, the integration of the entirety of perceived and assumed phenomena into the numeric patterns of systematic correspondence was carried through, in China, more rigidly and more persistently than in ancient Europe. The possibility of bridging the problematic intersections between an empirical diversity of observations and a theoretical rigidity of categories by means of the concept of a 'mixture' of primary qualities was not made use of in China, although the descriptive pharmaceutical literature had occasionally attributed two or more primary qualities to a single substance.[24]

If one considers, as an example, the integration of drug qualities into the pattern of a four-fold yinyang categorization, some of the consequences resulting from the Chinese approach become obvious.

Yin and yang here represent the basic theoretical categories to which are correlated the flavor and the temperature qualities of drugs as basic empirical categories. The pattern of a four-fold sub-categorization appears with the splitting of both yin and yang into a 'mature' and an 'immature' phase, each of which is correlated with one of two sub-divisions of flavor and temperature. Although, basically, flavor and temperature represent sensually perceivable qualities, the definition of sour, bitter, and salty as 'strong flavors' in contrast to a definition of acrid, sweet, and neutral as 'weak flavors' denotes a domination of theoretical considerations in column three of Table VI. 'Strong' corresponds to 'maturity'; 'weak' corresponds to 'immaturity'.

The seemingly unambiguous correlation of primary qualities with the four theoretical and empirical yinyang sub-categories in columns three and four of Table VI, is supplemented by a second correlation (column five) superseding that first correlation significantly. Here, even more than in the first correlation, the attribution of primary qualities to one of the four yin and yang

TABLE VI
The four-fold yinyang categorization of drug qualities

Yang	Temperature	Yang-in-yang (mature yang)	Strong temperature	Warm hot balanced	Warm-acrid warm-sweet hot-acrid hot-sweet	Heating
		yin-in-yang (immature yang)	weak temperature	cold cool	cold-acrid cold-sweet cold-neutral cool-acrid cool-sweet cool-neutral	dissipating
Yin	flavor	yin-in-yin (immature yang)	strong flavor	sour bitter salty	cold-sour cold-bitter cold-salty	purging
		yang-in-yin (immature yin)	weak flavor	acrid sweet neutral	balanced-sour balanced-bitter balanced-salty	penetrating
Theoretical	Empirical	Theoretical		Empirical	Theoretical	Empirical/Theoretical

TABLE VII

The six-fold yinyang categorization of the locations, paths, and hours of drug effects

	Location	Path	Time
	Palace	Channel	Hours
Yang	Large intestine	Hand-yang-brilliance	5 – 7
	Stomach	Foot-yang-brilliance	7 – 9
	Triple burner	Hand-minor-yang	21 – 23
	Gall-bladder	Foot-minor-yang	23 – 1
	Small intestine	Hand-major-yang	13 – 15
	Bladder	Foot-major-yang	15 – 17
	Depot	Channel	Hours
Yin	Lung	Hand-major-yin	3 – 5
	Spleen	Foot-major-yin	9 – 11
	Heart-enclos. network	Hand-ceasing-yin	19 – 21
	Liver	Foot-ceasing-yin	1 – 3
	Heart	Hand-minor-yin	11 – 13
	Kidneys	Foot-minor-yin	17 – 19

sub-categories is guided by theoretical criteria; it is achieved by combining flavor and temperature qualities taken from the two basic categories set against each other before. For instance, a 'weak flavor' is defined here by a combination of a mature, i.e., strong, temperature quality, that is balanced, with mature, i.e., strong flavor qualities, that are sour, bitter, and salty. Considering the first (in column four) and the second correlation (in column five) within this pattern of a four-fold categorization of drug qualities, it will be obvious that the four pharmacological functions – attributed to the drugs as secondary qualities – were each correlated with almost all flavor and temperature qualities, thus transcending the initially rigid four-fold categorization – a result achieved in ancient Greece by the concept of 'mixture' (*krasis*).

The empirical data in column four demonstrate, furthermore, that the pattern of 'four' was left behind here. In a structural asymmetry, altogether six flavor qualities were set against only five temperature qualities.

However, the patterns of six-fold and of five-fold categorization were represented in Wang Hao-ku's pharmacology as well. For instance, it was known that drug effects in the body may move, via differing paths, to different locations, and, also, that drug effects may manifest themselves at varying times of the day. Such notions were expressed through a pattern in which the hours, the locations, and the paths of drug effects in the body were correlated with a six-fold yinyang sub-categorization.

Here, too, a certain structural asymmetry is hidden. Since the six functional units called 'palaces' had to be correlated with six so-called 'depots', the original pattern of five depots was supplemented by a 'heart envelope' to

TABLE VIII
The five-fold categorization of drug qualities

Five Phases	Depots	Palaces	Flavor	Temperature	Yinyang
Wood	liver	gall	salty	warm	yang-in-yin
Fire	heart	small intestine + triple burner	sour	hot	yang-in-yang
Soil	spleen	stomach	sweet	balanced	- - -
Metal	lung	large intestine	bitter	cool	yin-in-yang
Water	kidneys	bladder	acrid	cold	yin-in-yin

reach the number six. Similar adaptations enabling linkages between basic patterns of four, five, or six appear in this system quite regularly. Some situations may require one to speak and think in terms of a sum of five depots in the organism; other circumstances may demand a consideration of altogether six depots. The acceptance of such alternatives is quite characteristic of patterned knowledge; the choice between such alternatives would create difficulties, however, for a scientist raised in the Western tradition and, hence, obliged to demand a decision as to the existence of five *or* six functional depot units in the organism.

As a final example of a categorization of drug qualities in the work of Wang Hao-ku, a pattern of a five-fold categorization is reproduced in Table VIII. In this pattern, the depots and the palaces are correlated with the flavor and temperature qualities of drugs, and also with a four-fold sub-categorization of the yinyang pattern. It should be pointed out that, for instance, 'warm' is defined here as yang-in-yin, whereas it is categorized, in Table VI, as yang-in-yang. Similar inconsistencies appear in the definition of other qualities as well.

Considering all the patterns together now, the total structure of Wang Hao-ku's pharmacological system may be illustrated graphically as follows in Table IX; it represents a typical example of 'pattern science'.

With this structure, different patterns could be employed for explaining different relationships between such pharmacological dimensions as drug qualities and pharmacological functions, as well as locations, paths, and times of drug effects. Additional yinyang and Five Phases patterns, not quoted here, made possible, for instance, an integration of drug effects into the course of the annual seasons with their corresponding climatic changes. All these patterns may be called contingent with each other because all of them are logically derived from the basic paradigm of systematic correspondence. The dotted lines in Table IX indicate the kind of links between the individual patterns as they appear, for instance, in Table VIII.

TABLE IX
The structure of the pharmacology of Wang Hao-ku

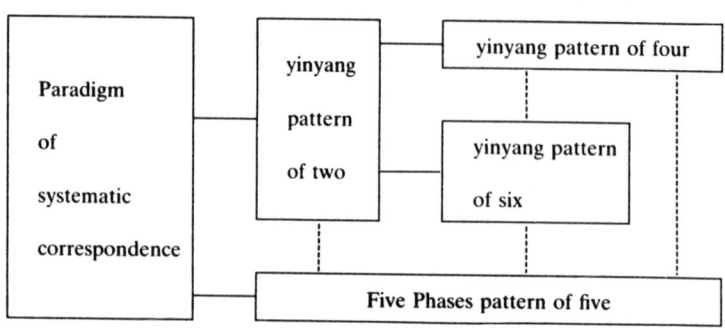

The cognitive edifice of Wang's pharmacology cannot be called homogeneous in the sense outlined in the beginning of this essay, because the individual patterns are, among themelves, incongruent and often contradictory. The attitude, apparent in this structure, of accepting 'as well as' solutions may have been the key not only to harmonizing the accepted rigidity of theoretical categories with the multiplicity of perceived and assumed phenomena, but also to harmonizing, within certain limits, antagonisms among hypothetical explanatory models in general. Further research is needed though, to strengthen or refute this statement.

IMPLICATIONS

The realm of pharmaceutics is, like many other aspects of medicine and health care, conditioned culturally. In this essay, I have pointed out but one facet of cultural differences in pharmaceutics by contrasting Greek and Chinese pharmacological systems. The comparison presented here may add strength to the argument that one ought to be quite cautious in applying even time-honored occidental epistemological concepts to non-Western cultures. One may still speak of a 'system' in the case of both ancient European and medieval Chinese pharmacology, because the term 'system' refers to but the intellectual process of 'combining' or 'causing (here: ideas) to stand together' (and that is what both Galen and Wang Hao-ku intended to do). But one should be aware that not only the structures but the very nature of these 'systems' are entirely different. We should also be cautious, though, not to separate, in this case Chinese and European, cultures too deeply. Chinese and European/Western medicine have many levels, some of them being surprisingly close to their cultural counterparts others being rather different.

Galen's pharmacology was complete and remained useful for one and a half millennia. Wang Hao-ku represented, in the history of Chinese pharmacology, but one author; others followed, partly adopting the contributions of their predecessors, partly introducing notions of their own. One would be misled if one were to search for a 'final', for a 'complete' outcome here; with the decline of Sung-Neoconfucianism – the socio-philosophical ideology accompanying the union between pharmaceutics and the paradigm of systematic correspondence – the interest in a pharmacology of systematic correspondence faded away too. But the 'system', or, more adequately, the varying patterns constituting the system of Chinese pharmacology, remained in – at least literary – use until recent times.

In contemporary China, traditional Chinese medicine and pharmaceutics continue to be utilized by significant segments of the population, but the political issue of how to structure the coexistence of China's medical-pharmaceutical heritage with so-called Western medicine has not been solved yet. In fact, little progress seems to have been made in comparison with the debates on the future role of traditional Chinese medical theories of sixty years ago. The enthusiasm of the 1960s and 1970s – when general political considerations and ideological support on the basis of dialectical materialism added strength to the practice and to some selected concepts of traditional Chinese medicine, and fostered attempts to unite it with Western medicine – this enthusiasm appears to have given way to a renewed confrontation. The *fu-ku* ('restore the ancient origins') movement of so-called 'veteran doctors' of Chinese medicine is directed – explicitly – against any reinterpretation of traditional Chinese therapeutic practices on the basis of modern scientific insights. If one takes the very different cognitive structures of the pharmacology of Wang Hao-ku and of modern Western pharmacology into account, it should become obvious that a merger is quite unrealistic if both are to retain their respective conceptual background. One may, however, wonder to what degree the practice of traditional Chinese pharmaceutics was based on the ideology of systematic correspondence in the past anyway. There is strong evidence that a very pragmatic, symptom-oriented application of drugs has continued throughout the centuries, and there is little reason why such substances whose usage had never been fully integrated into the concepts of systematic correspondence should not continue to be used either without theoretical basis at all or legitimized through modern pharmacological and clinical investigations.

In personal discussions with physicians trained in Western medicine and with health administration personnel in China, one is frequently told that both systems should develop further. However, at this point in time it appears unclear how traditional Chinese pharmaceutics could be developed further – if not on the basis of modern scientific thought. An assumption of a future development strictly along the lines of systematic correspondence is – if we take anthropological considerations into account – rather unrealistic because the social and cultural environment legitimizing the dynamics of a pharmacology of systematic correspondence during the imperial age has faded away entirely. There may exist numerous 'veteran doctors' supporting the ancient concepts for many years to come, but Chinese children passing through the contemporary educational system and being raised, without exception, in a society based on modern technology and science will become – irrevocably – representatives of a culture that is distinctly different from a socio-cultural environment that could keep the medicine and pharmacology of systematic correspondence not only in use but also alive. Hence there is no question that traditional Chinese medicine and pharmaceutics will continue to play an important and useful role in future Chinese health care – as an alternative and complement to so-called Western medicine – but I believe it is safe to expect that future generations will become increasingly alienated from its theoretical background.

NOTES

1. Artelt, W. Studien zur Geschichte der Begriffe 'Heilmittel'und 'Gift'. Ambrosius Barth Verlag. Leipzig. 1937. Unschuld, P. U. Ma-wang-tui Materia Medica. A Comparative Analysis of Early Chinese Pharmaceutical Knowledge. Zinbun: Memoirs of the Research Institute for Humanistic Studies. Kyoto University 18. 11–63. 1982.
2. Unschuld, P. U. Medicine in China. A History of Ideas. p. 115. University of California Press. Berkeley, Los Angeles, London. 1985.
3. Unschuld, 1985, p. 259.
4. Domenjoz, R. Zur Geschichte der Pharmakologie. Antrittsvorlesung zur Übernahme des Lehrstuhls für Pharmakologie an der Rhein. Friedr. Wilhelm-Univ. Bonn. Dec. 13, 1958, p. 5.
5. Heischkel, E. Pharmakologie in der Goethezeit. Sudh. Arch. 42. 302–311. 1958.
6. Unschuld, P. U. Medicine in China. A History of Pharmaceutics. p. 17. University of California Press. Berkeley, Los Angeles, London. 1986a.
7. Harper, D. The Wu Shih Erh Ping Fang. Translation and Prolegomena. Ph.D. thesis. University Microfilm Services. Ann Arbor. 1983.
8. Unschuld, P. U. 1985, pp. 154 ff.
9. Jaeger, W. Diokles von Karystos. pp. 181–186. Walter de Gruyter & Co. Berlin. 1938. Kudlien, F. Probleme um Diokles von Karystos. Sudh.Arch. 47. 456–464. 1963.
10. For Galen, see Harig, G. Verhältnis zwischen Primär- und Sekundärqualitäten in der theoretischen Pharmakologie Galens. NTM Schriftenreihe 10. 64–81. 1973.
11. Harig, 1973, p. 66.
12. Harig, 1973, p. 67.
13. Harig, 1973, p. 66.
14. Harig, 1973, pp. 76–77.
15. Harig, 1973, p. 69.
16. Harig, 1973, pp. 70–75.
17. Galen did not employ the term krasis for this intersection. It appears to me, though, that it may be applicable here – with all necessary caution – in the sense of 'mixture of pharmacological functions'.
18. Unschuld, U. Traditional Chinese Pharmacology. An Analysis of its Development in the Thirteenth Century. Isis 68. 224–248. 1977.
19. Unschuld, P. U. Die Bedeutung der Ma-wang-tui Funde für die chinesische Medizin- und Pharmaziegeschichte. Perspektiven der Pharmaziegeschichte (P. Dilg et al. eds.). pp. 389–417. Akademische Verlagsanstalt Graz. 1983.

20. This was the Shen-nung pen-ts'ao ching, mentioned above, of unknown authorship. Although this work is generally attributed to the first century A.D., a definite date can be given only for a later edition of it, prepared by T'ao Hung-ching around the year 500. Cf. Unschuld, P. U., 1986a.
21. Yamada, K. Kyū-ku hachi-fu setsu to shōshiha no tachiba. Tōhō gakuhō 52. 199–242. 1980.
22. For detailed examples of such 'as well as' structures see Unschuld, P. U. Nan-ching. The Classic of Difficult Issues. University of California Press. Berkeley, Los Angeles, London. 1986b.
23. Three of the following tables have been discussed, from a different perspective, in Unschuld, U. 1977 already.
24. The Shen-nung pen-ts'ao ching defined drugs, for instance, as 'bitter and slightly sour'. Chu Chen-heng (1281–1358), the last scholar contributing original ideas to the development of a pharmacology of systematic correspondence, was the first, though, to correlate systematically two or three flavor and temperature qualities to one single substance. This enabled him to explain different effects of one single substance that could not be understood through the common rigid correlation of one quality per substance only. See Unschuld, P. U. 1986a, pp. 117–118.

LINDA K. SUSSMAN

THE USE OF HERBAL AND BIOMEDICAL PHARMACEUTICALS ON MAURITIUS

Medical beliefs and practices are clearly both products and integral parts of the sociocultural systems in which they occur. Thus, much of medical anthropology has been devoted to the understanding of traditional medical systems within their sociocultural contexts.

Until the second half of this century, there was no distinct subdiscipline of 'medical anthropology' that focused upon matters of health, illness, and healing in non-Western societies. The study of indigenous medical beliefs and practices was, rather, usually conducted by general ethnographers and in conjunction with research on 'primitive' religion and magic. In these studies the traditional healer was depicted as routinely engaging in ceremonies and rituals to restore patients to states of spiritual, social, and psychological harmony. Accompanying the focus on magic, religion, and ritual was an emphasis on the supernatural aspects of traditional medical beliefs and the importance that is placed on spiritual, psychological, and social, as well as physical, well-being in traditional beliefs and practices (e.g., Evans-Pritchard 1937; Spencer 1941). Such studies usually emphasized those aspects of traditional medicine that differ from Western views of illness causation and treatment (e.g., Fortune 1932; Evans-Pritchard 1937; Harley 1941; Carstairs 1955).

It is only recently that specialists in medical anthropology have attempted to study the full range of medical beliefs and practices in non-Western societies and with this trend it has become increasingly noted that 'naturally' caused illness, requiring only 'natural', physical treatment, is, indeed, a category of illness recognized by most peoples. There is a growing body of literature that at least makes note of the enormous pharmacopoeias of some cultures and the propensity of peoples to use relatively straightforward, non-ritualized, physical treatment for some types of illness – especially those that are common, minor, and short-term (e.g., Maclean 1971; Ahern 1975; Kunstadter 1975; Spiro 1975; Lewis and Elvin-Lewis 1977; Ngubane 1977; Janzen 1978; Nichter 1978; Sussman 1980; Feierman 1981; Janzen and Prins 1981; Mahaniah 1981; Bibeau 1982; Reid 1982; Etkin and Ross 1983; Welsch 1983; Etkin 1986).

Few societies today remain culturally isolated and free of the influence of biomedicine. Societies in which biomedicine has been introduced and Western countries to which immigrant groups have brought their own healing systems have provided anthropologists with opportunities to study the ways in which non-Western and Western medical beliefs and practices interact (e.g.,

Saunders 1958; Read 1966; Schwartz 1969; Maclean 1971; Landy 1974; Woods 1977; Janzen 1978; Welsch 1983). Some researchers have focused on the interactions between the indigenous and biomedical systems and have found a number of relationships to occur when the two systems coexist. These include competition, compartmentalization, and exploitation (Press 1969) along with complementarity (Garrison 1977) and a hierarchy of resort (Schwartz 1969). Moreover, as a result of the interaction, new medical roles – 'emergent roles' – may be created (Landy 1974). In short, it is common in such societies for patients to have different expectations regarding the various systems and either to choose different types of healing specialists for different types of problems or to utilize them simultaneously, each to deal with a different aspect or symptom of the same problem (Jahoda 1961; Benoist 1975; Garrison 1977; Woods 1977). Moreover, individuals frequently have different expectations concerning the medicines which they receive. A common pattern is to expect biomedical pharmaceuticals to act quickly and traditional herbal treatments to act more slowly. Thus, there are distinctions in the ways in which the different forms of treatment are used by patients (e.g., the length of time a particular medication will be taken) and evaluated by them.

While most research on traditional healing has focused on healers or the patients of healers, another relatively recent trend has been to conduct household surveys, to focus on entire illness episodes as units of analysis (e.g., Woods 1977; Janzen 1978; Kleinman 1980; Roberts 1981; Yoder 1981), and to collect quantitative data on the utilization of practitioners and on decision-making during illness episodes (Woods 1977; Nichter 1978; Kleinman 1980; Young 1981). As a result there is a growing body of literature on the treatment practices of individuals who have not consulted healing specialists for their illnesses, and it appears as if most illnesses are initially treated at home and the majority of these never come to the attention of a medical practitioner (see, e.g., Kleinman 1980). Herbal and over-the-counter Western pharmaceuticals play major roles in self-treatment.

THE RESEARCH SETTING AND DESIGN

In this chapter I shall examine the utilization and cultural context and meaning of both Western and local herbal pharmaceuticals on the Indian Ocean island of Mauritius. Mauritius is a polyethnic society with a plural medical system. It represents a type of society that has rarely been studied by ethnographers in that all of the people and all of the healing systems arrived on Mauritius in relatively recent times. The island was uninhabited until the seventeenth century when the Dutch briefly settled there. However, it was not until the 1720s that French traders and privateers, with their African and Malagasy slaves, first established a permanent settlement on the island. Indian indentured laborers and Indian Muslim traders arrived in the mid-nineteenth century, and Chinese merchants (Hakka and Cantonese) arrived in the late nineteenth and early twentieth centuries. Today the majority of the population (68%) is of Indian origin (Indo-Mauritian), 3% are of Chinese origin (Sino-Mauritian), and 29% are of European origin and 'creoles' (of African or mixed origin).

A wide range of healing resources are found on Mauritius. These include biomedicine – in the form of Government Medical Service which provides free medical care, dispensaries at sugar estates and other large industries, private physicians and hospitals, and nurses and pharmacists – Ayurveda, homeopathy, traditional Chinese medicine, professional Tamil herbalists, folk herbalists, traditional midwives, specialized Creole healers, and sorcerers. Religious specialists – Hindu *maraz*, Tamil *poussari*, Buddhist sisters, Muslim *miadee*, and Christian clergymen and shrines – are also visited in times of illness. In addition, a number of different types of pharmaceuticals may be obtained directly by patients without resort to healing specialists. The most widely distributed are biomedical pharmaceuticals, local herbal remedies, and patent Chinese herbal remedies.

In order to determine how Mauritians conceptualize illness and utilize the multiple healing systems, I conducted a 21-month field study which included an island-wide survey of healers (including biomedical practitioners) and their patients and a 14-month longitudinal study of medical beliefs and treatment-seeking by 32 households (198 individuals) or approximately 10% of the population of two adjacent villages in the rural southwest. In the survey of healers and patients, I interviewed and observed 32 practitioners from eleven different healing systems to discover the theoretical foundations and therapeutic procedures associated with the various healing systems. A sample of patients of these practitioners was also interviewed concerning their symptoms, previous treatments sought for the illness, and general demographic information such as sex, age, ethnic group, and occupation.

The household sample consisted of 60% Creoles and 40% Indo-Mauritians.[1] Most respondents were manual laborers of low socio-economic status with little formal education. In an initial interview I obtained information on demographics, socio-economics, past and present health problems, diet, beliefs about illness causation, and knowledge, opinions, and past use of healing resources. Respondents were also asked which treatment(s) they would choose for a list of forty ailments and symptoms. I then conducted monthly follow-up interviews on the nature and severity of all illnesses experienced by household members since the last interview, the steps that were taken to treat the illnesses, and the outcomes of the treatment. Additional data were collected on the knowledge of medicinal plants. (See Sussman 1983 for a more detailed discussion of methodology.)

ACCESSIBILITY OF BIOMEDICAL AND HERBAL PHARMACEUTICALS

Biomedical pharmaceuticals are highly accessible on Mauritius. They are dispensed free of charge at local government dispensaries and hospitals. Common remedies such as painkillers (e.g., Panadol), decongestants (e.g., Thermogène), and antiseptics can be found in most local general stores. Both general stores and a government dispensary were located in one of the villages in which I worked. These two sources of medicines were, thus, readily available to villagers. Pharmacies, on the other hand, were found only in the major towns and, thus, were less accessible to village residents who would have to take a bus to the nearest town. While the town is only approximately 10 miles away (20 minutes by car), it would require at least one half day away from home for village residents to go buy medicine at a pharmacy.

In terms of economic accessibility, medicines dispensed at the local dispensary are free and common, over-the-counter, non-prescription remedies at general stores are relatively inexpensive while medicines bought at pharmacies are considerably more expensive. I found little evidence of illegal trade in medicines requiring prescriptions. However, some health care personnel employed by the government medical system (e.g., nurses) do give private consultations and dispense both prescription and non-prescription medications inexpensively – presumably medications taken from the hospital storerooms.

Herbal remedies that contain either plant species that grow wild in the area or that are cultivated in home gardens are also readily available and cost-free. While the herbal remedies sold by professional herbalists are much less expensive than pharmaceuticals sold at pharmacies (Sussman 1980), herbalists are located in only a few large towns and village residents would still have to take the time and expense to travel to them to buy their remedies.

UTILIZATION OF PHARMACEUTICALS

Individual households had utilized from three to seven different types of practitioners prior to the longitudinal study, and both Creoles and Indo-Mauritians had consulted a mean of five different types of healers. The majority had utilized a government physician, private physician, specialized Creole healer, either a Christian priest or Hindu *maraz*, and either a Tamil *poussari* or a sorcerer. Slightly under one half of the households (43%) had consulted a professional herbalist. The reason most frequently cited for not having consulted an herbalist was that illnesses that had been treatable by herbal remedies had been treated at home with easily obtainable wild herbs and had not required those sold by the herbalists.

When asked which types of treatment they would use for a list of forty symptoms and ailments, respondents stated that they would use Western pharmaceuticals (either by consulting a biomedical practitioner or by buying patent medicines themselves) for a mean of 55% of the ailments and that they would use home herbal remedies for a mean of 22% of the ailments.

During the longitudinal study, eight different healing systems were utilized, represented by ten different types of resources (including self) (Table I). They consisted of (1) biomedicine (government practitioners, private doctors and nurses, and self-treatment by patent medicines);[2] (2) home treatment by herbs and miscellaneous techniques (e.g., rest, change of diet); (3) traditional midwives; (4) professional Tamil herbalists; (5) specialized Creole healers; (6) Catholic priests; (7) Hindu *maraz*; and (8) sorcerers.

Moreover, biomedical and herbal pharmaceuticals played major roles in the treatment of illness episodes (Table II). Indeed, Western pharmaceuticals,[3] herbal remedies, and 'no treatment' were used initially and at some time in the quest for cure to treat 90% of all of the illness episodes. They were used as second resorts[4] for 82% of the episodes for which two or more practitioners had been consulted. Biomedical pharmaceuticals were used initially to treat 67% of all of the illness episodes and were used at some time during the quest for cure for 72% of all episodes. They were used as second resorts for 54% of the illness episodes for which more than a single practitioner was consulted. Herbal remedies were used less frequently but ranked as the second most frequent form of treatment used. They were initially used for 7% of all illness episodes and were used at some time for 9% of all episodes. They were used as second resorts for 13% of the episodes for which more than a single type of treatment was chosen.

CHARACTERISTICS OF ILLNESSES TREATED BY PHARMACEUTICALS

In order to determine whether biomedical and herbal pharmaceuticals were being chosen for different types of illness, each illness episode was categorized by illness type (acute, recurrent, chronic), duration, and disability. This analysis yielded no distinctions between illnesses for which biomedical treatment was sought and those for which herbal remedies were utilized (Table III, columns 1 and 2). Both were used predominantly for acute illnesses, either of short duration (less than one week) or of long duration (over three weeks), with little or no disability associated with them. The use of herbal pharmaceuticals was associated with a greater number of treatment resorts (p≤.05).

However, if the occurrence of treatment by oneself or by a healing specialist is controlled for, some distinctions are found in treatment choice. Self-treatment by biomedical pharmaceuticals is used more frequently for acute, short-lived illnesses and self-treatment by herbs and treatment by biomedical and herbal specialists[5] are more frequently used for chronic, longer-lasting episodes of illness. Therefore, the greatest distinction does not appear to lie

TABLE I
Treatment choices during longitudinal study

Type of treatment	Percentage of illness episodes		
	First resort	Second resort	All resorts[a]
Government facility	42.8%	21.6%	47.6%
Private doctor/nurse	5.5	15.9	8.8
Professional herbalist	0	2.3	0.4
Traditional midwife	0.2	1.1	0.4
Specialized Creole healer	0.7	2.3	1.3
Self-treat (total):	(30.7)	(35.3)	(38.2)
Biomedicine at general store	10.5	4.6	11.4
Biomedicine at pharmacy	7.9	11.4	10.1
Home herbal remedies	6.6	10.2	9.0
Other treatment	5.7	9.1	7.7
Religious specialists	0	1.1	0.8
Sorcerer	0	1.1	0.2
No treatment	16.2	15.9	19.5
Missing information	3.9	3.4	4.8
(N)	(456)	(88)	(456)

[a] The sum of this column is greater than 100% because multiple treatments were used for 19% of the 456 illness episodes.

TABLE II
Use of pharmaceuticals during longitudinal study
(recall period one month)

Type of treatment	Percentage of illness episodes		
	First resort	Second resort	All resorts[a]
Western pharmaceuticals	66.7%	53.5%	71.5%
Herbal remedies	6.6	12.5	9.4
No treatment	16.2	15.9	19.3
Total	89.5%	81.9%	90.4[a]
(N)	(456)	(88)	(456)

[a] This represents the percentage of illness episodes treated by any of the three types of treatment at any time during the episode. It does not equal the sum of the column since multiple treatments may have been utilized.

in the choice between the biomedical and herbal systems of medicine but rather in that between self-treatment by biomedicine and treatment either by herbal medicine or biomedical practitioners.

The use of biomedical practitioners is also associated with episodes resulting in greater disability. Data collected on treatment preferences for the list of forty ailments and symptoms also supports this finding. While biomedical practitioners and self-treatment (either by herbs or biomedicine) were chosen for 40% and 38% of the minor ailments respectively, biomedical practitioners were preferred for 91% of the serious ailments.

Herbal and biomedical treatment were used for many of the same illness episodes. Of those episodes treated by herbal remedies, 56% were treated with herbs exclusively while the remainder (44%) were treated with both herbs and biomedicine: 35% were treated with herbs and a biomedical practitioner and only 9% were treated with herbs and biomedical self-treatment.

THE USE OF PHARMACEUTICALS FOR SPECIFIC ILLNESSES

Many of the same illnesses accounted for the majority of those treated by biomedical practitioners, herbalists, and self-treatment by herbs and biomedicine (Table IV).

Gastro-intestinal disorders, coughs, colds, fever, and influenza accounted for many of the illnesses treated by all of these resources. However, the data from the longitudinal study on treatment utilization and on treatment preferences for the list of hypothetical illnesses along with informal observations all indicate that patients do tend to prefer different types of treatment for a set of specific illnesses.

Self-treatment by biomedical pharmaceuticals is generally preferred for coughs, colds, fever, intestinal parasites, and headaches. Panadol is usually bought at local general stores for fever, headaches, and colds while cough syrups and parasite medication (e.g., Mintezol) is frequently bought at pharmacies.

Self-treatment by herbs is usually preferred for gastro-intestinal disorders and vomiting, while both treatment by home herbal remedies and by biomedical specialists are preferred for rheumatism, hypertension, nerves and palpitations, and diabetes. Commonly used remedies for indigestion include seeds of *Salvia* sp., *Linum usitatissimum*, and *Hordeum vulgare* that may be purchased at the general stores in addition to leaves of *Mentha* sp. and *Litsea glutinosa* and roots of *Cocos nucifera* which are either cultivated in backyard gardens or grow wild in the vicinity of the village. *Eupatorium ayapana* is an herbal remedy for vomiting known by virtually all of the village respondents, and camomille flowers are a well known remedy for vomiting in infants. These species are cultivated in gardens. *Cassia alata* and *Bryophyllum pinnatum*, remedies for hypertension and rheumatism, respectively, are likewise widely known and frequently raised in gardens. Herbal remedies for diabetes and palpitations are less widely known and less readily available. These consists of the leaves of *Faujasia flexuosa*, the heart of *Ravenala madagascariensis*, and the roots of *Bruguieria gymnorhiza* and *Rhizophora mucronata* for diabetes and the leaves and stems of *Selaginella* sp., *Mimosa pudica*, and *Potamogeton chamissoi* for nerves and palpitations (Sussman 1980). These are usually bought from professional herbalists.

TABLE III
Characteristics of illnesses treated by herbal and biomedical pharmaceuticals

Illness characteristic	Pharmaceutical		Practitioner		Self-treatment	
	Herbal (N=43)	Western (N=319)	Herbalist (N=2)	Physician (N=241)	Herbs (N=41)	Biomedicine (N=97)
Illness type						
Acute	62.8%	67.1%	0%	61.8%	65.9%	78.4%[a]
Recurrent	14.0	16.3	50.0	17.4	12.2	15.5
Chronic	23.3	16.6	50.0	20.7	22.0	6.2
Duration						
<7 days	46.7	42.9	0	31.5	50.0	63.5[b]
1–2 weeks	3.3	13.9	0	15.5	3.6	11.8
2–3 weeks	0	6.4	0	8.0	0	3.5
>3 weeks	50.0	36.8	100.0	45.0	46.4	21.2
Disability						
None	64.7	50.4	50.0	42.0	65.6	69.0[c]
Mild	23.5	29.3	50.0	33.5	21.9	19.5
Moderate	0	11.1	0	14.2	0	5.8
Bedridden	11.8	9.3	0	10.4	12.5	5.8
# Resorts						
One	55.8	74.2	0	69.0	58.5	73.2
Two	37.2	20.6	100.0	24.2	34.1	21.6
Three or more	7.0	5.2	0	6.9	7.3	5.2
Mean # resorts	1.51	1.31[d]	2.00	1.38	1.49	1.32

[a] $X^2 = 13.12$, df = 4, p < .02. Because of the small number of cases, herbalists are not included in any of the statistical tests.
[b] $X^2 = 31.01$, df = 6, p < .01.
[c] $X^2 = 25.09$, df = 6, p < .01.
[d] t = 2.02, p < .05 for biomedical vs. herbal pharmaceuticals.

It is generally believed that biomedical pharmaceuticals are stronger than herbal remedies. This is a positive characteristic in that biomedical pharmaceuticals act quickly and forcefully to relieve symptoms and cure infectious diseases. The negative aspect associated with them is that because they are so potent they may 'shock' the body and produce unwanted side effects (cf. observations in India by Nichter 1980). Herbal remedies, on the other hand, are believed to act more slowly and naturally without producing undesirable side effects.

Illnesses such as coughs, colds, and parasites along with other serious infectious diseases require strong medicine that will give rapid relief of symptoms and kill the germs causing them. These illnesses are usually short-lived and treatment is required for only a short period of time. Therefore, there will be no long-term side effects and patients usually prefer

TABLE IV
Percentage of illness episodes treated by each type of treatment (ranked)

Illness	Herbalist[a] (N=180)	Self-treat with herbs (N=41)	Biomedical practitioner (N=257)	Self-treat with biomedicine (N=98)
Gastrointestinal disorders	20%(1)	44%(1)	8%(3)	6%
Coughs, colds	2%	15%(2)	18%(1)	36%(1)
Fever, influenza	8%(4)	2%	9%(2)	11%(2)
Parasites	0%	0%	8%(3)	7%(4)
Rheumatism	1%	7%	5%(4)	3%
Skin problems	10%(2)	7%	3%	3%
Headache	0%	7%	1%	9%(3)
Conjunctivitis	0%	0%	8%(3)	0%
Accidents, wounds	1%	0%	5%(4)	5%
Diabetes[b]	9%(3)	NA	NA	NA
Palpitations/Nerves[b]	8%(4)	NA	NA	NA

[a] This column includes 178 patients of herbalists who were observed during the survey of practitioners.
[b] There were no cases of diabetes or palpitations/nerves during the longitudinal study.

biomedical pharmaceuticals. Indeed, patients will attempt to obtain the strongest medications they can for these illnesses. It is generally believed that medicines supplied by government dispensaries are not as strong as those bought at pharmacies. Therefore, patients prefer medicines for coughs and parasites that are purchased at pharmacies rather than obtained at dispensaries.

Alternatively, illnesses such as rheumatism, hypertension, palpitations, and diabetes are either recurrent or chronic and, thus, require the long-term use of medication. While biomedical pharmaceuticals do relieve the symptoms or control the illnesses, it is believed that they are too strong to be taken for long periods of time. Herbal remedies can also control the symptoms but do so in a more mild manner. For these illnesses, patients prefer those medicines that are effective but also as mild as possible. Therefore, herbal remedies are frequently preferred over biomedical pharmaceuticals for these illnesses. They may also be alternated with biomedical remedies so as to 'give the body a rest from the [Western] medicine'. Herbal remedies are also frequently used for gastro-intestinal disorders and vomiting. They are especially used for vomiting in children because they are less potent than biomedicine. Gastro-intestinal disorders are quite common. Many of these are simply indigestion believed to result from eating spicy food. Herbal remedies for such complaints are commonly known, readily available, and frequently used.

KNOWLEDGE AND USE OF HERBAL REMEDIES

Until the twentieth century there were few medical doctors and biomedical facilities on Mauritius, especially in the rural areas (Colony of Mauritius Annual Report on the Medical Department 1885; Population Census of Mauritius 1881, 1901; Titmuss and Abel-Smith 1968). Moreover, although the island is quite small, and there were roads and some railroads connecting major towns and cities in the nineteenth century (Pike 1873), transportation from rural areas to facilities in the major cities was slow (Twain 1897). Some Mauritians recalled that in the 1930s and 1940s travel from the central highlands to coastal areas in the southwest constituted a major day-long voyage. Furthermore, village residents in the southwest reported that twenty years ago there was only one bus per day to the capital and other highland cities. There are still some villages in the district today to which there is no bus service.

It is probable, therefore, that until the increase in the number of hospitals and dispensaries and the improvement in public transportation and roads, health problems were treated at home with herbs and the use of local herbalist-healers. Today, a substantial percentage of illnesses are still treated with herbs but biomedicine appears to have supplanted herbal medicine as the treatment of choice for most illnesses. Biomedicine is used to treat a greater variety of ailments. During the longitudinal study, some form of biomedicine was used to treat 50 of the 54 different ailments or symptoms reported while herbal medicine was used to treat only 18 of these. As noted above, herbal remedies are generally preferred for chronic ailments and are also used to treat some common, minor illnesses.

Village residents tended to be familiar with a relatively consistent but very small set of herbal remedies. Out of a list of 110 medicinal plant species, the uses of only 19 of these were known by the majority of village respondents. Those that they knew and used most were for indigestion (*Mentha* sp., *Cocos nucifera* roots), vomiting (*Eupatorium ayapana*), hypertension (*Cassia alata*), rheumatism (*Bryophyllum pinnatum*), and coughs (*Cymbopogon citratus*).

Professional herbalists and Chinese pharmacists, as well as village residents, all believe that the use of herbal remedies is declining. I found a considerable amount of individual household variation in the knowledge and use of medicinal plants. However, in general, younger Mauritians tend to prefer biomedicine. In comparing the knowledge of medicinal plants among mothers and daughters, I found a mean loss of 38% from one generation to the next. Factors that appear to be contributing to the popularity of biomedicine include: (a) the widespread distribution of biomedical resources as compared to the relatively localized concentration of herbal medical resources (i.e., professional herbalists, the small ranges of some of the indigenous plant species, and also the declining availability of some of these species); (b) the availability of free biomedical care; (c) the relative convenience of biomedical forms of treatment, such as tablets and injections, as opposed to the inconvenience of herbal remedies which must be made into infusions, decoctions, or bathing solutions; and (d) the legal status accorded to biomedicine and the inability of other types of practitioners to issue sick leave certificates and utilize diagnostic services available at hospitals.

THE CONTEXT OF PHARMACEUTICAL USE

Medical belief system

The treatment-seeking behavior, and especially the frequent use of biomedicine, by Mauritians must be understood within its sociocultural context. The frequent, and almost sole, use of straightforward, physical remedies, the high rates of utilizing biomedicine, and the decline in the use of herbal medicine may lead one to believe that Mauritians have been completely 'converted' to Western medicine and have fully adopted the biomedical model of health and illness. This, in fact, is not the case.

Indeed, all of the village respondents held multicausal medical belief systems. Illnesses are grouped into several major etiological categories which include: 'Illnesses of God'; 'Fright' or 'Illnesses of Dead Souls'; 'Sorcery' or 'Illnesses of Man'; and 'Illnesses of Saints'.

'Illnesses of God' (*malades Bondieu*) may be caused by a variety of physical factors such as germs, diet, weather, and weak constitutions. It is 'normal' to get sick periodically. *Malades Bondieu* exist and are part of the natural order of the universe as God created it.

'Illnesses of Dead Souls' (*mauvaise air*) and 'Fright' (*gayn père*), result from encounters with spirits of individuals who have died prematurely. It is believed that individuals who die early – usually by violence or accident – will stay on earth until their predetermined time to die. Some spirits are malign and intentionally harass or possess the living. Others are benign but nevertheless unwittingly frighten individuals who encounter them.

Illnesses from sorcery (*mésanseté, gayn diab*) or 'Illnesses of Man' (*malades dimun*), usually result from the harnessing of evil powers by men to make individuals ill or insane. Evil powers include the devil along with other evil spirits and demons. While there is widespread belief in the existence of 'Evil', the lay population has limited knowledge about the actual powers that can harm people and the methods by which this is accomplished.

'Illnesses of Saints' (*malades saints*) result from offending a saint, either intentionally or unintentionally. This type of illness is usually attributed to Hindu saints or gods and may occur if promises to saints are not fulfilled or purification rites are not appropriately observed.

The causes of illness described by the heads of both Creole and Indo-Mauritian households were strikingly uniform, regardless of ethnic or religious affiliation. The only major difference between ethnic groups concerned *malade saints* which is a religiously based category. Creoles cited a median of three illness categories while Indo-Mauritians described a median of four illness categories; *malade saints* accounted for the difference.

Appropriate healers for each illness category

No single healing system was believed to be capable of diagnosing and/or curing all of the etiological categories of illness. Illnesses of God are treatable by biomedicine, home herbal medicine, and professional Tamil herbalists. A small subset are curable by specialized Creole healers, and Christian clergymen may aid the healing process through prayer. Illnesses caused by dead souls and saints are curable by sorcerers, Christian priests and ministers, Hindu *maraz*, and Tamil *poussari*.[6] Those caused by sorcery are curable by sorcerers and Tamil *poussari*. Hindu *maraz* are believed to be capable of diagnosing the causes of all types of illness but are able to treat only those caused by dead souls and saints. In general, except for Hindu *maraz*, practitioners are expected to assign illnesses to etiological categories that they are able to treat. It is expected, for example, that biomedical physicians will diagnose ailments as illnesses of God and that sorcerers will diagnose them as caused by sorcery or dead souls. Each ethnic group tended to prefer different practitioners for some types of illnesses although variation between households was quite high.

Relationship between symptoms and cause

In general, choice of an appropriate healing system is dependent upon the illness category to which the illness is assigned. However, while some symptoms tend to be associated with particular etiologies, there is, in general, no clear correlation between symptom and cause. Behavioral changes, insanity, spells of irrational behavior, sudden paralysis, loss of consciousness, and delirium are the symptoms most frequently cited as being associated with possession by dead souls or sorcery. It is believed, however, that these may also be symptomatic of naturally caused diseases. If one becomes ill shortly after undergoing ritual purification or participating in a Hindu religious ceremony, one might suspect that the illness is caused by offended saints. If an individual succumbs to one illness after another, or has a string of misfortune, which may include illness, then sorcery might very well be suspected.

In general, however, any set of symptoms may be caused by any agent. Moreover, even illnesses that appear to be naturally caused and whose symptoms are recognized and diagnosed by biomedicine may ultimately be caused by other, biomedically unrecognized, causes. Dead souls, saints, and sorcery may cause an individual to be afflicted either with an ailment recognized by biomedicine (e.g., peptic ulcers caused by a magical thorn) or with one that does not correspond to any biomedically known disease.

Assignment of illness to etiological categories

Given the lack of general diagnosticians and the apparent lack of symptomatic guidelines for assigning causes to illness episodes, it seems that patients faced with illness episodes would find it difficult to decide upon the general etiological category to which to assign their illnesses. Given the lack of correspondence between symptom and cause, Mauritians cannot classify their illnesses by symptomatology and then choose an appropriate practitioner or treatment. Nor is there a universally recognized specialist to whom they may turn to diagnose the cause of their illness. This problem is solved by Mauritians by designating the causes of illness and using the various types of healing resources in a specific pattern in the quest for cure.

When asked the type of treatment they would use initially for the list of forty symptoms and ailments, respondents most frequently chose government biomedical facilities and self-treatment by herbs, patent medicines, and miscellaneous techniques (e.g., change of diet, rubbing with alcohol). For all of the ailments and symptoms listed, most individuals chose either biomedical practitioners or self-treatment, which accounted for 80–97% of the treatments chosen by each respondent. In no case did respondents indicate that they would initially consult a priest, *maraz*, *poussari*, or sorcerer despite the fact that the list included symptoms frequently associated with illnesses caused by dead souls, fright, and sorcery such as convulsions, sudden paralysis, bizarre behavior, and loss of consciousness. All initial treatment choices were appropriate only for illnesses of God.

The use of pharmaceuticals in the quest for cure

Mauritians, thus, tend to classify all illness episodes initially as *malades Bondieu* and utilize treatments appropriate for such illnesses. There is, therefore, a hierarchy of resort in which biomedicine and herbal medicine are used first, as are the most accessible and least expensive types of treatment. Self-treatment by herbs or biomedicine and treatment at the local government dispensary are usually followed by treatment at pharmacies and by private biomedical physicians. Patients tend to exhaust all of these resources before suspecting that an illness is supernaturally caused, reclassifying it, and consulting appropriate religious specialists or sorcerers. Indeed, one of the major criteria for believing that an illness is caused by dead souls or sorcery is that it does not respond to treatment appropriate for illnesses of God. Therefore, by initially classifying all illnesses as illnesses of God, patients can eliminate what is believed to be the most 'simple' cause of illness, they can utilize some of the least expensive healing resources, and they can also obtain information relevant to the appropriate classification of the illness (i.e., whether or not it responds to biomedicine or herbal medicine).

The high rates of utilization of both biomedical and herbal pharmaceuticals must, therefore, be understood within the context of the medical belief system, the diagnostic process, and the resultant structure of the quest for cure. Biomedicine and herbal medicine are alternate forms of treatment appropriate for *malades Bondieu* which is the first etiological category to which illness episodes are assigned. Since most illnesses are of relatively short duration and quickly cured, it is in only relatively few cases that individuals go on to reclassify their illness during the quest for cure and consult religious specialists or sorcerers for ritual treatment. Furthermore, it is mainly problematic illnesses – either those that are difficult for biomedicine to cure or those that tend to recur – that are likely to be brought to the attention of these practitioners.

ACKNOWLEDGEMENTS

The field research and writing of this manuscript was supported in part by an International Doctoral Research Fellowship from the Social Science Research Council, a Dissertation Improvement Award from the National Science Foundation, a postdoctoral traineeship in epidemiology from the National Institute of Mental Health, a University Fellowship from Washington University, a Biomedical Research Support Grant from the Biomedical Support Program, Division of Research Resources, National Institutes of Health, and by a Grant-in-Aid of Research from the Society of Sigma Xi.

NOTES

1. The results reported here are generalizable only to rural Creoles and Hindu Indo-Mauritians. Hence, my subsequent use of the term 'Mauritian' is here meant to refer only to this group. However, informal observations and interviews with more urbanized Creoles, Hindu and Muslim Indo-Mauritians, and Sino-Mauritians suggest that the conclusions reached in this study are, indeed, applicable to Mauritius as a whole.
2. For this analysis, individuals who bought medicine at a pharmacy are included in the self-treatment category although they may have asked a clerk to suggest a medicine to treat their illness (e.g., a cough medicine or a medicine for parasites).
3. Individuals who consulted biomedical practitioners are considered here to have been treated with Western pharmaceuticals because with very few exceptions all such patients expected and were given some type of medication.
4. A change in level of resort here signifies a switch *initiated by the patient* either (a) from one healing system or mode of treatment to another or (b) from one practitioner to another within the same healing system. For example, all of the following would be counted as two levels of resort: government dispensary to private doctor, pharmacy to private doctor, self-treatment by herbs to self-treatment by patent Western medicine, private doctor to another private doctor, and sorcerer to *poussari*. However, if the change of practitioner resulted from a referral from one practitioner to another and represented the following by the patient of an ongoing diagnostic and treatment process, a change in level of resort would not be recorded. This situation usually occurred when patients were referred by the local dispensary to the government hospital for diagnostic tests, consultations, and, in some cases, treatment (e.g., surgery).

5. Since village respondents consulted herbalists on only two occasions, no conclusions can be reached concerning the use of professional herbalists.
6. Homeopathic, Ayurvedic, and traditional Chinese practitioners, Buddhist sisters, and Muslim *miadee* were unknown to the village respondents and are, therefore, not included in this discussion.

REFERENCES

Ahern, E. M.
    1975 Sacred and Secular Medicine in a Taiwan Village: A Study of Cosmological Disorders. *In* Medicine in Chinese Cultures: Comparative Studies of Health Care in Chinese and Other Societies. A. Kleinman, P. Kunstadter, E. R. Alexander, J. L. Gale, (eds.) pp. 91–113. Washington, DC: John E. Fogarty International Center for Advanced Study in the Health Sciences, US Dept. of Health, Education, and Welfare, DHEW No. (NIH) 75-653.

Benoist, J.
    1975 Patients, Healers and Doctors in a Polyethnic Society. African Environment 1(4): 40–64.

Bibeau, G.
    1982 A Systems Approach to Ngbandi Medicine. *In* African Health and Healing Systems: Proceedings of a Symposium. P. S. Yoder, (ed.) pp. 43–84. Los Angeles: Crossroads Press.

Carstairs, G. M.
    1955 Medicine and Faith in Rural Rajasthan. *In* Health, Culture and Community: Case Studies of Public Reactions to Health Programs. B. D. Paul, (ed.) pp. 107–134. New York: Russell Sage Foundation.

Colony of Mauritius Annual Report on the Medical Department.
    1885 London: Her Majesty's Stationery Office.

Etkin. N. L. (ed.)
    1986 Plants in Indigenous Medicine and Diet: Biobehavioral Approaches. Bedford Hills, N.Y.: Redgrave Publishing Co.

Etkin, N. L. and Ross, P. J.
    1983 Malaria, Medicine, and Meals: Plant Use Among the Hausa and its Impact on Disease. *In* The Anthropology of Medicine: From Culture to Method. L. Romanucci-Ross, D. E. Moerman, L. R. Tancredi, (eds.) pp. 231–259. South Hadley: J. F. Bergin.

Evans-Pritchard, E. E.
    1937 Witchcraft, Oracles, and Magic Among the Azande. Oxford: Clarendon Press.

Feierman, S.
    1981 Therapy as a System-in-Action in Northeastern Tanzania. Soc. Sci. Med. 15B: 353–360.

Fortune, R. F.
    1932 Sorcerers of Dobu: The Social Anthropology of the Dobu Islanders of the Western Pacific. London: George Routledge & Sons.

Garrison, V.
    1977 Doctor, Espiritista or Psychiatrist?: Health-Seeking Behavior in a Puerto Rican Neighborhood of New York City. Medical Anthropology 1(2): 65–180.

Harley, G. W.
    1941 Native African Medicine: With Special Reference to its Practice in the Mano Tribe of Liberia. Cambridge: Harvard University Press.

Jahoda, G.
    1961 Traditional Healers and Other Institutions Concerned with Mental Illness in Ghana. Intl. J. Soc. Psychiatry 7(4): 245–268.

Sumahatmaka
    1981   Rinkasan Centini (Suluk Tambang Glaras). Jakarta: Balai Pustaka.
Janzen, J. M.
    1978   The Quest for Therapy in Lower Zaire. Berkeley: University of California Press.
Janzen, J. M. and Prins, G.
    1981   Issues and Findings: Causality and Classification in African Medicine and Health. Soc. Sci. Med. 15B: 429–437.
Kleinman, A.
    1980   Patients and Healers in the Context of Culture: An Exploration of the Borderland Between Anthropology, Medicine, and Psychiatry. Berkeley: University of California Press.
Kunstadter, P.
    1975   Do Cultural Differences Make Any Difference? Choice Points in Medical Systems Available in Northwestern Thailand. *In* Medicine in Chinese Cultures: Comparative Studies of Health Care in Chinese and Other Societies. A. Kleinman, P. Kunstadter, E. R. Alexander, J. L. Gale, (eds.) pp. 351–383. Washington, D.C.: John E. Fogarty International Center for Advanced Study in the Health Sciences, US Dept. of Health, Education, and Welfare, DHEW No. (NIH) 75–653.
Landy, D.
    1974   Role Adaptation: Traditional Curers Under the Impact of Western Medicine. Am. Ethnol. 1(1): 102–127.
Lewis, W. H. and Elvin-Lewis, M. P. F.
    1977   Medical Botany: Plants Affecting Man's Health. New York: John Wiley & Sons.
Maclean, U.
    1971   Magical Medicine: A Nigerian Case-Study. London: Penguin Books.
Mahaniah, J. K. M.
    1981   La Structure Multidimensionnelle de Guerison Chez les Kongo du Zaire. Soc. Sci. Med. 15B: 341–349.
Ngubane, H.
    1977   Body and Mind in Zulu Medicine: An Ethonography of Health and Disease in Nyuswa-Zulu Thought and Practice. London: Academic Press.
Nichter, M.
    1978   Patterns of Resort in the Use of Therapy Systems and Their Significance for Health Planning in South Asia. Medical Anthropology 2(2): 29–56.
    1980   The Layperson's Perception of Medicine as Perspective into the Utilization of Multiple Therapy Systems in the Indian Context. Social Science & Medicine 14B; 225–233.
Pike, N.
    1873   Sub-Tropical Rambles in the Land of the Aphanapteryx. Personal Experiences, Adventures and Wanderings in and around the Island of Mauritius. New York: Harper & Bros.
Population Census of Mauritius
    1881   Census of Mauritius and Its Dependencies Taken on 4th April 1881.
Population Census of Mauritius
    1901   Report of the Commissioners Appointed to Take a Census of the Island of Mauritius and Its Dependencies.
Press, I.
    1969   Urban Illness: Physicians, Curers and Dual Use in Bogota. J. Health and Soc. Beh. 10(3): 209–218.
Read, M.
    1966   Culture, Health, and Disease: Social and Cultural Influences on Health Programmes in Developing Countries. Philadelphia: Tavistock Publ., J. B. Lippincott

Reid, M. B.
  1982 Patient/Healer Interactions in Sukuma Medicine. *In* African Health and Healing Systems: Proceedings of A Symposium. P. S. Yoder, (ed.) pp. 121–158. Los Angeles: Crossroads Press.
Roberts, C. D.
  1981 *Kutambuwa ugonjuwa*: Concepts of Illness and Transformation Among the Tabwa of Zaire. Soc. Sci. Med. 15B: 309–316.
Saunders, L.
  1958 Healing Ways in the Spanish Southwest. *In* Patients, Physicians, and Illness. E. G. Jaco, (ed.) Glencoe, Illinois: Free Press.
Schwartz, L. R.
  1969 The Hierarchy of Resort in Curative Practices: The Admiralty Islands, Melanesia. J. Health and Soc. Beh. 10: 201–209.
Spencer, D. M.
  1941 Disease, Religion and Society in the Fiji Islands. Monographs of the American Ethnological Society No. 2. Second printing 1966. Seattle: University of Washington Press.
Spiro, M. E.
  1975 Supernaturally-caused Illness in Traditional Burmese Medicine. *In* Medicine in Chinese Cultures: Comparative Studies of Health Care in Chinese and Other Societies. A. Kleinman, P. Kunstadter, E. R. Alexander, J. L. Gale, (eds.) pp. 385–399. Washington, D.C.: John E. Fogarty International Center for Advanced Study in the Health Sciences, US Department of Health, Education, and Welfare, DHEW Publication No. (NIH) 75-653.
Sussman, L. K.
  1980 Herbal Medicine on Mauritius. J. Ethnopharmacology 2(3): 259–278.
  1983 Medical Pluralism on Mauritius: A Study of Medical Beliefs and Practices in a Polyethnic Society. Ph.D. dissertation, Washington University.
Titmuss, R. and Abel-Smith, B.
  1968 Social Policies and Population Growth in Mauritius. Report to the Government of Mauritius. Second Edition. London: Frank Cass & Co., Ltd.
Twain, M. (Samuel L. Clemens)
  1897 Following the Equator: A Journey Around the World. Hartford, Conn.: The American Publishing Co.
Welsch, R. L.
  1983 Traditional Medicine and Western Medical Options Among the Ningerum of Papua New Guinea. *In* The Anthropology of Medicine: From Culture to Method. L. Romanucci-Ross, D. E. Moerman, L. R. Tancredi, (eds.) p. 32–53. South Hadley: J. F. Bergin.
Woods, C. M.
  1977 Alternative Curing Strategies in a Changing Medical Situation. Medical Anthropology 1(3): 25–54.
Yoder, P. S.
  1981 Knowledge of Illness and Medicine Among Cokwe of Zaire. Soc. Sci. Med. 15B: 237–246.
Young, J. C.
  1981 Medical Choice in a Mexican Village. New Brunswick: Rutgers University Press.

SUSAN REYNOLDS WHYTE

THE POWER OF MEDICINES IN EAST AFRICA

In East Africa, as elsewhere in the developing world, Western pharmaceuticals have been readily accepted and widely disseminated. But the 'drugging' of East Africa is not limited to an enthusiasm for Western medications. It is part of an increasing interest in 'medicines' of all kinds, both as explanations of misfortune and as modes of treatment. The awareness of medicines is evident in African concern about increases in the use of sorcery medicines. That concern has in turn stimulated an enormous growth in anti-sorcery medications and movements. More recently, the new consciousness of 'traditional' healing has been characterized by a pharmaceutical emphasis, clearly visible in the pharmacological analyses of herbal medicines upon which a number of the new Institutes of Traditional Medicine have concentrated. African healing is being seen as a medicinal exercise.

This heightened consciousness about all kinds of medicines suggests that, in order to understand the cultural appropriation of Western pharmaceuticals, we must begin by asking some questions about medicines as a general category. What is their significance within the context of East African culture, and how shall we explain the apparent increase in their popularity?

Recently several studies have examined indigenous conceptualizations of medicines. Research in India (Nichter 1980) and Sierra Leone (Bledsoe and Goubaud, this volume) has shown that semantic analysis can provide important insights into the ways people perceive and utilize medications. Indigenous and Western medicines are significant and comparable in terms of color, size, strength, habituation and dietary requirements. This research has emphasized meaningful dimensions *within* the category of medicines. The approach I take here is a broader, relational one; I assume that medicines as a category have meaning in relation to other categories of therapeutic power. Rather than focusing on the particular characteristics attributed to different types of medications, I shall stress the common features of all 'medicines', as they contrast with the healing powers of elder kin, ancestors and spirits. 'Medicines' in a wider cosmological sense have to do with people's conceptions of morality, social relations, and their own identity in the world. The appropriation of Western drugs is part of a general trend towards treating suffering by the application of substances rather than the ritual manipulation of relationships.

This chapter examines medicinal ideas and practices among the Nyole of Eastern Uganda, where my husband and I carried out fieldwork from 1969–71. (Although we left Bunyole four months after Amin's coup, the material refers generally to the relatively more stable conditions obtaining before Amin came to power.) Since some of the points I want to make seem to have general relevance, I shall refer to other African examples as well.

WHAT IS MEDICINE?

In Bunyole, medicine was many things. The term could be applied to all kinds of substances, both healing and harmful, which were thought to have an inherent capacity to achieve an effect upon a person or thing. To transform an ordinary dog into a good hunting dog, medicine (not training) had to be given. To get a good cash crop, 'cotton medicine' (DDT) was sprayed on the plants. In the Nyole language, one can speak of 'bicycle medicine' (the rubber cement used to patch tires), sorcery medicine (*obulesi bw'obulogo*), as well as curative 'hospital medicine' (*obulesi bw'edwaliro*) and African medicines (*obulesi bw'ehimali*) in their various forms. On occasion Nyole distinguished medicines according to their functions (protective, curative, offensive) or according to their modes of preparation and application, rather as Bellman (1975) reports that the Fala Kpelle do. But the point is that all this variety is subsumed under the category of medicine.

Medicine seems to be a broad semantic category in many African languages. Among the Abron of the Ivory Coast, Alland notes the conflation of magical items and medicines. 'The semantic class *sino* includes magical devices and real medicine, either of which may be native or Western' (Alland 1970: 177–8). The Zinza of northwestern Tanzania include Western and indigenous remedies together with protective and destructive substances in the category of medicine (Bjerke n.d.: 93–94). Among the Zezuru of Zimbabwe, the term for medicines (*muti*) can refer to 'any substance or technique which is used to bring about change in the human condition, whether it be aspirin or a love potion made out of pubic hairs and sweat' (Fry 1976: 23). The Safwa of Tanzania conceive of medicines as capable of enhancing and repairing relationships and conditions as well as spoiling them (Harwood 1970: 62–3). The Swahili word *dawa* seems to have the same breadth; note the usage *dawa ya viatu*, 'shoe medicine', for the substance used to restore the condition of skuffed shoes.

Medicine is a substance that transforms something – for better or worse. How does it do so? In Nyole thought, medicine achieved its effects through some power inherent in itself, without reference to morality, relationships or intention. In this it differed from other major modes of transforming conditions – curing through prayer, ritual and sacrifice, and harming through cursing or the power of spirits.

A sorcerer could use medicines to harm anyone, whether related to him or not, and even though his motives in doing so were immoral. The power of the medicine might even work independently of his intentions. Medicine buried to harm one person could be unwittingly 'jumped' by someone else, who then fell ill instead. A love potion might make the object of desire run mad instead of turning affectionate. Medicine could even be 'turned back' by more powerful medicine, striking the sorcerer with the affliction he intended for his victim.

By contrast, in the curse of senior relatives, or the effects of ancestors and spirits, Nyole conceived of the power to transform as being inherent in a relationship, rather than a substance. Senior relatives, ancestors and clan spirits affected only their own kin. Unrelated spirits established a relationship with their victims that had to be regularized or broken. A curse or a spirit's displeasure could never fall on the wrong person by mistake, nor could it work in a way the agent did not intend. (The biblical story of Jacob tricking his father into blessing him instead of Esau goes quite against Nyole principles in this respect.) The power of such agents could not be turned back upon them. In speaking of these causes of suffering, Nyole said, 'Do not argue with something that looks over its shoulder at you, but that you cannot see'.

While the response to sickness caused by medicine was more medicine, misfortune caused by senior relatives or spiritual agents required negotiation, gift giving and sacrifice in a public ritual. Words had to be spoken so that all, including agent and victim, were conscious of the nature of the suffering, the relationship involved and the transformation desired. If the agent was a spirit, one addressed it openly and asked it to accept an offering. By contrast the counter-action of sorcery by other medicines was a private, usually secret affair. If relationships and intentions were specified, words were spoken 'in the heart', not out loud. Open confrontations between presumed sorcerers and their victims were extremely rare. Suspicion and the secret application or manipulation of powerful substances were the rule. The individual nature of sorcery treatment, and the idea that the power to transform lies in a substance rather than in openly dealing with a relationship, put this form of treatment closer to Western bio-medicine. These are common characteristics of medicines.

Another essential quality of medicines is that they are transactable. As substances, they can be acquired and exchanged, diffused and adopted in ways that ritual relationships cannot. As objects, they can become commodities; as powers they can be transferred – they are not bound to particular social statuses and role relationships. David Parkin, writing of anti-sorcery movements, has suggested that this characteristic of medicines as 'physical commodities subject to transaction' makes them appropriate means of challenging authority, especially by younger people who have contacts to a world beyond the local society. 'The point should not be missed . . . that it is people living or working outside the society or having major external contacts who import medicines; and it is often these same people who challenge established authority within the society' (Parkin 1968: 428–9).

The transactable nature of medicines is fundamental to Harwood's analysis of Safwa witchcraft and sorcery as well, though his errand is a somewhat different one. He contrasts witchcraft as a mode of expressing conflict in incorporative relations with sorcery, which is associated with relations of transaction (Harwood 1970). In Bunyole the transactable nature of medicine contrasted most clearly not with witchcraft, but with the incorporative character of a person's relation to senior relatives, ancestors and clan spirits.

In order to understand the meaning of medicines, we must grasp their logical opposition to ritual forms of transformation. This contrast is not simply a logical one however. Medicines and ritual were actual alternative choices which Nyole faced in daily life. Choosing medicines – whether Western pharmaceuticals or 'African medicine' – might be a way of avoiding ritual obligations and inconveniences. To see this clearly, we must examine the types of medicinal practice that existed in Bunyole.

TREATMENT BY MEDICINES

Many individuals in Bunyole knew herbal remedies. These were usually symptom specific and a person might know only a few. He or she might treat family members or neighbors for diarrhea or leg pain, perhaps, but would go to someone else to get medicine for stomach ache. In every neighborhood, people knew who was a curer (*omugangi*) for which particular symptoms. The actual ingredients of the herbal remedies were not revealed; the one who knew the remedy was paid a small sum for 'going in the bush' (*ohwingisa mwisugu*) to get the medicine. Herbal medicines were also sold at the weekly markets; these too were symptom specific.

In every neighborhood, there was also at least one curer who specialized in injections. He might give no other type of treatment, and have no training in Western medical techniques. His fees were higher than those of other neighborhood curers, but like them, he dispensed one kind of medicine thought effective against certain symptoms. The 'needle men' (*ab'epishyo*) I knew, injected procaine penicillin. Some bought their supplies at the markets in nearby towns. It was rumored that medicine was sold privately by some people working in government dispensaries and this may have been a source for needle men.

A vigilante movement called '99', which was active while we were in Bunyole, was said to be against the practice of the needle men. Their motives were not necessarily pure; they had been known to declare against certain activities in order to extract protection money from those involved. In any case, it would have been extremely difficult to stop village injections. Like the Thai 'injection doctors' of whom Cunningham (1970) wrote, Nyole needle men provided a popular service in making the 'best' of Western medicine conveniently available. They charged a fee, but they called at home in a friendly manner. Trained staff gave injections free at the local dispensary when prescribed, but one risked walking many miles, waiting in line several hours, and then being given tablets instead.

There was another reason too for the success of the local needle men.

Venereal disease was quite common in Bunyole, and it was said that government health facilities demanded that one name or even bring along for treatment the sexual partner from whom one had contracted the disease. I do not know what the actual policy was at the clinics, but treatment there was widely perceived as a very delicate matter. A friend, who came asking us whether we had medicine for gonnorhea, explained his difficulties. His wife had been away for some time attending funeral ceremonies at her home. A 'guest' had kept him company in the meantime, and given him the disease. His wife was due home, and he felt it would be indiscreet to go to the dispensary with his 'guest', who was married to someone else. So he had gotten a village injection and was looking for more medicine. (Apparently the problems continued; some time later he confided that both he and his wife had been given injections by a needle man because they both had gonnorhea.)

During the period of our fieldwork, Bunyole County was served by a health centre at the county headquarters, first established as a dispensary in 1926. The man in charge claimed that they sometimes had as many as five hundred out-patients a day. The maternity and general wards were also heavily used. In addition, two aid posts (later up-graded to dispensaries) also served the needs of the county's 90,000 inhabitants. These were the major sources of Western medications.

A person attending these facilities for treatment always took a bottle, for patients were supposed to supply their own containers for liquid medicine. From the point of view of local people, dispensaries provided three kinds of medication: tablets (*amakarenda*), medicine for drinking (*obulesi bw'ohunywa*), and injections (*epishyo*). Most people spoke of Western medicines in terms of their forms rather than their ingredients. This did not necessarily show naivité; it corresponded well with the cultural construction of local medicines. Medicinal content was the secret of he or she who 'goes in the bush' to gather the remedy. What was discussed was the way the medicine was administered. On this dimension, Western medicine was far less differentiated than African medicine, which could be used in bath water, smoked in a pipe, rubbed into incisions, worn in amulets, inhaled under a make-shift steam tent, smeared on various parts of the body or mixed with specified kinds of food or drink (to mention only the varieties of medicines applied directly to persons).

Curers, needle men and national health facilities all provided treatment which may be characterized as symptomatic in nature. That is to say, they administered medicines which were thought to affect the signs and symptoms of a disorder, rather than to address its cause. The distinction between symptomatic and etiological treatment was important in Nyole medical practice. The etiological level was dominant both in terms of the perception of sickness and conception about treatment. This level had enormous ideological importance; images of social identity were articulated and reproduced through explaining and treating the causes of sickness in certain ways (Whyte 1981). But the point I want to make here is not so much the difference between symptomatic and etiological levels, as the relation between them.

In practice, causal explanation and treatment were not usually thought to be necessary if symptomatic measures proved effective. Concerning a certain condition for instance, I was told that it used to be caused by a spirit but that now people just got it cured at the dispensary. It was not invariably the case that symptomatic relief obviated the need for rituals addressed to supernatural causes. It was often said that the symptoms would return or that another misfortune would strike if identified causes were not dealt with. But there was definitely a tendency to put off expensive, complicated rituals and uncomfortable confrontations if possible. What made it possible – in many cases – was medication to relieve symptoms. An example will illustrate my point.

Samwiri had been married to Jani for some years, and they had three children. Early in 1971, the middle child, a boy, fell very ill with what looked like pneumonia. Fearing for his life, we offered to drive the child and his parents to the hospital in Tororo, 25 miles away. Samwiri agreed immediately, but Samwiri's mother hesitated, pointing out that her grandson had already been given an injection at the dispensary, which had not helped. She and the neighbors suspected that Samwiri's father-in-law had cursed Jani to lose the children. His curse had been diagnosed in connection with earlier troubles, and relations between him and Samwiri had been poor for some time. He claimed that Samwiri had never visited him when he was in jail, never gave him gifts though he had a steady job, had still not paid the last cow on Jani's bridewealth, and was generally a bad son-in-law. Samwiri said openly that he disliked his wife's father, that he was greedy, drank too much, and did not deserve the satisfaction of the goat he would receive for removing the curse. Not to mention the matter of the cow.

That time Samwiri's wishes prevailed and the child was taken to the hospital for treatment. But then the next child fell ill almost immediately. Jani's father sent a message saying that Samwiri should come and make arrangements about how he could help the sick children (implying a curse removal ceremony), but Samwiri refused saying, "I do not want to see that man". He accepted our offer to drive this child to the hospital, but it was Jani's turn to refuse. With tears streaming down her face as she held her feverish, trembling child, she declared that there would be no medical treatment until Samwiri went to see her father to arrange for him to remove the curse.

In this case, Samwiri's motives for seeking Western medicines were surely not simply that they were effective. In fact the opposite had been demonstrated; an injection had failed to cure the one child, and even after his hospitalization and recovery, sickness still threatened the lives of Samwiri's other children. Samwiri insisted on Western medicine because he wanted to avoid what Nyole custom required – that he go humbly to his father-in-law.

Much has been written of the efficacy of Western medicines and the pragmatism of people who adopt what is seen to have such powerful effects (Foster 1977: 530). But this view of 'the practical patient' may be a bit too simple. Certainly people appreciate that Western medicines cure some symptoms. But there may be push as well as pull factors in their attraction. What pushes people towards medicines are the dynamics and difficulties of the non-medicinal solutions to health problems.

Anthropologists and health planners have often seen 'traditional' medicine as an alternative that prevents full adherence to Western bio-medicine. While the latter is attractive in some ways, the former continues to draw people in other ways. Gonzalez (1966: 125) expresses this view when she suggests that the efficacy of scientific medicines in relieving symptoms is what is valued in Western medicine, while indigenous practices aimed at relieving the basic cause of the disease attract people towards traditional therapy. It is undeniable that Nyole people are concerned to address the cursers, ancestors and spirits who are defined as agents of affliction. Yet there are situations, and there are probably an increasing number of them, when some people would rather avoid the kin and community involvement which such therapeutic rituals entail. Then ritual practices actually make Western medicine more attractive. And not only Western medicine. In Bunyole, certain types of African medicine were also popular because they obviated ritual inconveniences.

While the medicines offered by curers, needle men and dispensaries were used symptomatically, those offered by another type of specialist were more directed towards the causes of sickness. The medicinal specialists *par excellence* in Bunyole were the *abang'eng'a*, literally the 'protectors'. Elsewhere (Whyte 1982) I have called these experts 'medicine men' because the verb *ohung'eng'a* has the sense of protecting by means of medicines. These men were particularly knowledgeable about dealing with sorcery. They provided both prophylactic and curative medicine, protecting people and property, and treating those who believed themselves affected by sorcery. Because cure and cause were so closely related in Nyole thought, the medicine men were also believed to be able to work sorcery themselves and to provide sorcery medicines to their clients for use against enemies. Their medicines were not only for sorcery however; they claimed to be able to deal with all kinds of problems by the manipulation of medicines – unemployment, legal cases, school examinations, marital difficulties and love affairs. Their principle seemed to be that an individual could cope with life's crises and obstacles through the proper application of powerful substances.

Many medicine men were diviners as well. I worked closely with two such specialists, and was able to compare their approach with that of more 'traditional' Nyole diviners, who worked through spirit possession. All diviners diagnosed the same basic causes of misfortune, although the medicine men tended to find sorcery more frequently, while the spirit diviners more often diagnosed spirits as a cause. However, the most striking differences between the two kinds of diviners was not their explanations of misfortune, but their prescriptions for treatment. The medicine men often prescribed medication as the remedial measure even in cases where the cause was found to be cursing or possession by spirits. This goes against the principle that the agent who causes a misfortune must be addressed in order to relieve it. Perhaps we may see it as a step toward the breakdown of the distinction between etiological and symptomatic treatment. For the medicine man's remedies, while 'recognizing' an etiological agent, provided a cure for symptoms without the trouble of dealing directly with the presumed cause.

This can be illustrated with respect to cursing, which was a common explanation of misfortune in Bunyole, requiring public reconciliation and remedial ritual. A diviner working through spirit possession prescribed curse removal rituals in all of the 35 recorded cases where he found cursing to be a cause of misfortune. But a medicine man diviner for whom 23 divinations of cursing were recorded, suggested curse removal ritual for only six of them. For one other he proposed treatment at the dispensary, and for another, that a student having problems change schools. For thirteen cases, he offered to 'tie' the curse through medication, so that the cursed person did not have to approach the presumed curser for the rituals of removal. In two other cases he told the client that the curse could either be 'tied' or removed 'in the Nyole way', as the client liked.

On February 28, 1971, for example, a young man came with his father to divine about why he could not get a job. The divination revealed that he was cursed by his father's brother who was annoyed at his father over a matter of bridewealth. The two clients said they did not want to go for the ceremony of removal. It was inconvenient because the curser was living in Jinja. So arrangements were made to have the medicine man 'soften' the curser and help the youth get a job – through medication.

There is clearly a parallel between the preparations of the medicine men and Western medication in that both provided a way around the obligations of ritual therapy. The more individualistic application of transactable substances was perceived as 'liberating' in relation to the obligations and expenses of Nyole kinship and rituals. There is not only a parallel between these kinds of medicines, but a convergence in some cases: the medicine man might inquire whether a sick person had been sent to the dispensary – and recommended it sometimes.

This by-pass aspect of medicines has been noted by Alland who writes that medicine ' . . . provides an alternate set of means for the attainment of certain social ends' and ' . . . may be drawn upon by individuals to by-pass or overcome social and/or economic restrictions' (Alland 1970: 138). Alland seems partly to associate this characteristic with the inclusion of magical items and what he calls 'real medicine' in the same category. But it is not simply the case that medicines are magical ways of attaining the goal of health and well-being. The point is that medicines permit the detachment of therapy from the social and spiritual relationships in which it is usually embedded. Medicines are potentially an individualistic means to an end. Alland recognizes this in discussing the way Western medicines may be utilized without the supervision of a Western doctor. Van der Geest (1982: 212) speaks of the large scale circulation of pharmaceuticals on the free markets of developing countries, which patients utilize quite independently of doctors. He speaks of the 'social utility' of medicines which 'can be acquired and used without becoming dependent on others' (personal communication).

THE POWER OF FOREIGN MEDICINE

One of the most striking characteristics of the Nyole medicine men was that they so frequently had foreign experience and used exotic techniques. Often they had spent years at distant places or as apprentices to people from faraway. It was said that many of the men who served abroad in World War II worked as medicine men when they returned to Bunyole. Muslims, a minority in Bunyole, were thought to be powerful medicine men. They used medicines first introduced by Arab and Swahili traders – especially 'prayers' (*eduwa*), which consisted of Koranic texts dissolved in water for drinking or bathing (also called *kombe*). The majority of those who bought such medicines were Christians; it was not the religious content that interested them, but the power of an exotic medicine. One medicine man sold Zandu, a medicine manufactured in Bombay and 'useful in the treatment of one hundred diseases', and bicarbonate of soda. Another sold special amulets made by a technique he had learned in Tanzania.

The use of exotic substances and techniques was not only recognized, but emphasized. The experts themselves contrasted their methods with 'the Nyole way' and demonstrated their special 'gimmicks' with a certain amount of pride. The exotic, extra-ordinary nature of this medicinal practice has implications which can best be grasped by returning to the general contrast between medicine and ritual.

Treatment by ritual, in which relationships were openly stated and acted upon, also involved the manipulation of objects and substances. These items had symbolic meaning which could be traced through various rituals. They were usually common items known to everyone, such as spears, winnowing trays, beer, staple food or domestic animals. In removing a curse, water was poured or sprinkled on the cursed person or millet porridge, formed into balls called *ebigwasi*, was given to the victim to eat. *Ebigwasi* were also eaten by the living when any sacrifice was performed for the ancestors. But these substances were not medicine; their efficacy was not inherent, but derived from the beings and relationships activated in the ritual.

Medicine contains a power which is not public and social in the same sense. Knowledge of it is restricted; its content tends to be secret. Its source is outside of morally regulated human relationships. Conceiving of it as foreign and difficult to obtain underlines these aspects. Even neighborhood herbalists spoke of their modest fees as payment for 'going in the bush'. If we understand the bush as the conceptual contrast to the familiar, domestic homestead, then we can draw a cosmological parallel between the bush and the faraway places from with other kinds of medicine come. They are both in symbolic opposition to what Lewis (1971) calls the 'central morality cult', the set of rituals and relationships which define Nyole as kinsmen and moral persons. All medicines, in a sense, come from outside, so that it may be misleading to make too strong a contrast between Nyole medicine and foreign medicine, or between African medicine and hospital medicine.

In thinking about the foreign nature of medicine, we must stress once again the transactable nature of powerful substances. When power is not tied to particular relationships, it becomes cosmopolitan in a way that kin-specific powers never can be. It can be transacted over great distances, between people who have different though overlapping, symbolic universes. The belief in the innate power of certain substances, and the tendency to attribute special capacities to more esoteric medicines create the basis for lively experimentation and entrepreneurial activity.

There is a stereotype of the African medicine man as a local resident, embedded in his own tribal culture, serving the needs of his neighbors by manipulating the symbols with which they are familiar. The traditional healer is 'a co-member of his patient's social group' whose treatment ' . . . reinforces and gives legitimacy to time honored beliefs' (Green 1980: 499). While it is true that Nyole diviners and medicine men addressed 'traditional' notions of etiology, medicine men in particular were cosmoplotian and innovative, rather than 'traditional' in their orientation. The successful medicine man drew his clientele from a large area and a variety of ethnic groups. Out of 101 people who visited one well-known Nyole specialist for divination and treatment, only 37 were Nyole. Some Nyole specialists travelled all over Eastern Uganda.

Likewise Nyole sought out foreign experts, especially when the problem was difficult and dangerous. For example, a man accused of having misappropriated funds from the cotton cooperative society sought medicine from a specialist in Mbale, 35 miles away, to make the case against him die. The specialist was a Ganda Muslim who had lived ten years in Nairobi; his wife, who also treated people, dressed like a coastal Swahili.

Speaking of the importance of medicines, a Nyole acquaintance also expressed their cosmopolitan character. 'Ministers and big men use medicine men from Pemba and Kenya. Even the most religious people must go to medicine men to protect themselves. No one can be safe without going to them. Even Dr. Obote must do so'. Nyole saw the growing importance of medicine as part of a general situation in Eastern Africa, where life was dangerous and where improved communication had increased awareness of and access to new kinds of foreign medicine, both Western and African. Although Nyole had not been heavily involved in labor migration, they were very much integrated in the cash economy and were in touch with other parts of the country through road and railway. Cotton was the universal cash crop and the primary source of income at the time fieldwork was carried out in Bunyole; land was at a premium, and the power of senior males, who controlled land, livestock, and rights in women, may well have been enhanced after cotton was established at the time of the first world war. This power was expressed and accepted through the interpretation of misfortune in terms of cursing, clan spirits and ancestral ghosts. In this context, I believe that medicines and medicine men had a particularly strong appeal to women and younger men. Elsewhere I have elaborated on the attractions of medicine men as diviners and their potential for challenging authority (Whyte forthcoming).

THE PHARMACEUTICAL INVASION

Ivan Illich (1977) uses the term 'pharmaceutical invasion' to describe the flooding of Third World countries by multi-national drug companies. One approach to this subject is to focus upon the companies themselves and their aggressive marketing strategies. While this is extremely important, it is insufficient from an anthropological point of view. We must also examine the terrain being conquered, and the cultural and historical processes which form the local context of the intrusion. In Africa, the power of foreign medicines was already established long before Western pharmaceuticals began to circulate on a large scale. The increased use of medicinal substances in general seems to have been partly a result of improved inter-regional communication facilitated by colonialism.

One of the most famous anthropological studies of religion in Africa speaks of a medicinal invasion among people who professed to have had very little in the way of medicines in earlier times. In 1930, when Evans-Pritchard lived among the Nuer, fetishes, 'medicines which talk', were being brought into eastern Nuerland. He writes that: 'Fetishes are amoral in their action. They are acquired in the first instance by purchase, though they may later be inherited, for private ends and personal aggrandizement . . . Nuer told me that European administration has made it easier for men to acquire and exercise these powers . . . new fetishes frequently appear, they become well-known in one district and are unknown in others, and they wax and wane in popularity' (Evans-Pritchard 1956: 100–103).

In the introduction to their anthology on witchcraft and sorcery in East Africa, Middleton and Winter (1963) discuss the belief common in many African societies that sorcery is increasing. They relate this to increases in hostility, insecurity and anxiety, to an increasing conflict between African traditional and modern individualistic norms, and to the fact that changes have created situations and statuses for which there were no indigenous precedents. Several of the articles in the collection report that sorcery medicines and techniques were supposed to have originated outside the local society. LeVine notes that Gusii sorcerers were usually trained by Luo (*Ibid.*: 133) and Middleton speaks of a kind of medicine which Lugbara men buy 'either in the Congo or in southern Uganda where Lugbara meet Congolese as fellow labour migrants' (*Ibid.*: 265).

The perceived threat of new sorcery techniques was and is met by new counter-medicines, whose efficacy is also associated with foreign provenance. In addition to the steady individual diffusion of medicines, there have been anti-sorcery movements which have swept over large areas. The medicines administered in the Kamcape anti-sorcery movement in southern Tanzania were said to have originated in Malawi (Willis 1968: 5) and Field (1940) reports that people from the southern Gold Coast travelled to the Northern Territories to bring back powerful anti-sorcery medicines for the new cults being established everywhere.

More recently, several studies have established the receptivity of African societies to all kinds of new medicines. Alland writes of the Abron: 'New medicines are accepted from the outside at a startling rate. While the average Abron tires of a therapeutic technique which does not produce rather immediate effects, the Abron pharmacopaeia is open and in a state of constant change' (Alland 1970: 120). Murray Last, writing about a Hausa area in northern Nigeria, stresses the extremely eclectic nature of the medical scene, which he describes as a 'non-system'. Healers often travel and work among foreign communities. 'The value of their remedies lies in their very strangeness, in their *not* being part of a known system of medicine' (Last 1981: 389). Last relates inventive and entrepreneurial uses of Islamic, Western and various African medical elements to the disintegration of traditional medicine as a system; the breakdown of kinship groups has forced individuals to rely upon their own medical defences. He finds that people no longer 'know' what the proper therapeutic response to sickness is, and in this atmosphere of 'not-knowing' secrecy and skepticism thrive. The foreign, little-known provenance of medicines fits with the general uncertainty of the times.

An excellent example of the increasing use of medicines is to be found in Keller's study of women's reliance upon love and luck medicines in a small, mostly Tonga-speaking Zambian town. A woman in a socially and economically vulnerable situation may use medicines to get and keep a husband, to prevent him beating her, to bring him directly home after work, to make him help in the house and even – on the 30th of each month – to make him hand over a sufficient portion of his pay! Keller says that the medicines, far from being ethnic-specific, are of foreign origin. 'In fact, consistent with the prevalent idea that foreign diviners or spirit mediums are more powerful than local ones is the belief that exotic medicines are more potent than local ones' (Keller 1978: 498). But the increased availability of medicines from other ethnic groups, due to greater mobility, cannot alone explain the more common use of medicines today. Keller attributes it to women's greater isolation in monogamous households, especially in towns, and to the loss of support of older relatives. In the past, young women were given medicines by their elders, but this was accompanied by instruction to both sexes on proper behavior and by 'other institutional supports for marriage which do not function today' (*Ibid.*: 504).

Thus, although the pharmaceutical invasion may be the work of the drug companies, the capitalist system did not create the demand for foreign medicines. That is based on the dynamic relationship between indigenous concepts of medicines and of other sources of transformative power. Presumably medicines are an ancient concept in Africa, and perhaps in their most powerful forms they have often been seen as coming from beyond the domestic circle of familiar culture. In the last hundred years or so, two important kinds of changes have shifted the balance in the relation between medicines and other powers. First, there has been a great increase in people's experiences with 'otherness', entailing among other things the greater availability of foreign medicines in any locality. Second, the kinds of social relationships in which spirit and kinship powers were embedded have themselves changed in various ways, increasing the attractions of medicines, for some people at least.

THE NEW 'TRADITIONAL MEDICINE'

Having suggested that there has been a change in the balance between medicines and other powers within local society, I would like to leave the local ethnographic scene to glance briefly at a conceptual development at the national and international levels. I refer to the new consciousness of traditional medicine which can be seen in the media, in the pronouncements of African governments and in the stated concerns of international agencies dealing with health development. A pharmacological bias is evident here, which parallels in its way the fascination with medicines seen in many local societies.

The medicine man is regaining his lost honor, according to an article in a Tanzanian newspaper (Van Amelsvoort 1976: 55). But other articles made it clear that in the new traditional medicine, the dross of superstition must be separated from the gold of scientific truth: ' . . . it must be understood that the root or leaf of a tree with medicinal content cures a disease purely because of the medicinal content and not because of the superstitious words that are uttered when administering it or the taboos and paraphernalia that is associated with its administration' (*Ibid.*: 70). Here African healing is being measured by the standard of Western bio-medicine. Interest is focused on the content of substances, not on symbols and relationships. Medicine men are seen as experts; they are the sources of healing medications, comparable to Western specialists. Little attention is paid to the therapeutic community of kinsmen and spirits, and there is no place here for etiological explanations and therapeutic rituals.

Pharmacological research predominates in the steps taken by international organizations to initiate research on African medicine and in most institutes of traditional medicine (Bibeau 1979). At least some indigenous healers are aware of this interest and may redefine their own practice accordingly. In

1982 and 1983, when I interviewed healers in Tanzania, a number had had contact with the Traditional Medicine Research Unit in Dar es Salaam and knew of the investigations of herbal medicines being carried out there.[1] Like the Nyole medicine men, many of these practitioners tended to emphasize medicinal therapy, sometimes combining elements of Western and African medicine. One district organization of 'traditional healers' had established a hospital for traditional medicine (*hospitali ya dawa ya jadi*) which was actually a cooperative herbal apothecary. Healers brought roots, bark and leaves, which were mixed, bottled and labelled with scientific-sounding names. This organization was hoping to gain government support, and the form and content of its practice fit well with the Western-derived model of 'traditional medicine' mentioned above. African traditional medicine had been redefined as African medicines. Relations to kin, community and spirits are quite irrelevant to the application of powdered herbs with labels like Na 15 A.U.K. In this case a government-supported model of healing, which emphasized medicines, had been appropriated and used to shape the form that therapy took.

Medicines are an area where Western and African conceptions of healing seem to meet. Just as Western drugs are easily incorporated within the African conception of therapeutic powers, African herbalism can be made acceptable to the bio-medical model. Because of this overlap, there is a tendency to place a great deal of emphasis on the medicinal aspect of African 'traditional' healing, without properly appreciating either the breadth of the African conception of medicines or the relation of medicines to other forms of healing. This image of 'traditional' medicine is being propagated at a time when other factors have contributed toward an emphasis on medicines in relation to other types of powers. Thus the medicinal bias is over-determined.

CONCLUSION

I have been suggesting that medicines assume significance in relation to other possible forms of healing. In this chapter Nyole ethnography has stood model for a system in which the private application of substances is an alternative to rituals in which relationships are openly articulated and transformed. Examples from other African cultures show that this approach is useful elsewhere too.

Over much of Africa, medicines are seen as substances having an inherent power to transform a condition; as objects they can be detached from relationships and transacted over great geographic and cultural distances. These characteristics are, I believe, potentials which can be realized in different ways in different societies and at different points in time. The Nyole context, which I know best, was one where medicines were an alternative to therapeutic rituals involving relations to kinsmen, ancestors and spirits. The availability of medicines was 'liberating' in the Marxist sense that it freed therapy from the social relations in which it would otherwise be embedded. This does not mean that medicines in themselves actually broke down relationships to kinsmen. In 1970 kinship was certainly the dominant structuring principle in Nyole society and the framework within which misfortune was interpreted. Cursing, and affliction by ancestors and clan spirits were very much in evidence. It was because relations to kin and spirits were so important that medicines assumed a special significance as an alternative. Their meaning and implications were determined by the context in which they existed.

Obviously medicines have different implications for African urban elites or for Christian fundamentalists; a proper analysis requires a careful elucidation of the whole range of therapeutic powers in each African context. For medicines are never simply substances, nor are they merely infrastructure in a technology of therapy. They are always a part of a total configuration of alternatives, and they assume meaning in relationship to this context; they are elements of consciousness and cosmology, as well as technology. Only through such a broad perspective can we hope to understand why, in some circumstances, foreign substances are seen as particularly attractive and powerful modes of dealing with suffering.

ACKNOWLEDGEMENTS

I would like to thank Sjaak van der Geest and Robert Welsch for their helpful comments on my plans and first draft for this article. The fieldwork on which it was based, supported by the US National Institute of Mental Health, was carried out together with Michael A. Whyte. He has contributed many suggestions and useful criticisms to the paper, for which I thank him very much.

NOTES

1. These interviews were part of a baseline study of the current treatment of mental health problems, carried out in connection with the Tanzania Mental Health Programme which is supported by the Danish International Development Agency and the World Health Organization.

REFERENCES

Alland, Alexander
    1970   Adaptation in Cultural Evolution. New York & London: Columbia University Press.
Amelsvoort, V. Van
    1976   Medical Anthropology in African Newspapers. Oosterhout: Anthropological Publications.
Bellman, Beryl Larry
    1975   Village of Curers and Assassins. The Hague & Paris: Mouton.

Bibeau, Giles
    1979 The World Health Organization in Encounter with African Traditional Medicine. *In* Ademuwagun et al. (eds.) African Therapeutic Systems. Waltham, Mass.: Crossroads Press.
Bjerke, Svein
    n.d. Religion and Misfortune. Oslo: Universitetsforlaget.
Cunningham, Clark E.
    1970 Thai 'Injection' Doctors: Anti-biotic Medicators. Social Science & Medicine 4: 1–24.
Evans-Pritchard, E. E.
    1956 Nuer Religion. London: Oxford University Press.
Field, M. J.
    1940 Some New Shrines of the Gold Coast and their Significance. Africa 13: 138–49.
Foster, G. M.
    1976 Medical Anthropology and International Health Planning. Social Science & Medicine 11: 527–534.
Fry, Peter
    1976 Spirits of Protest. Cambridge: Cambridge University Press.
Gonzalez, Nancie Solien
    1966 Health Behavior in Cross-cultural Perspetive. Human Organization 25: 122–5.
Green, Edward C.
    1980 Roles for African Traditional Healers in Mental Health Care. Medical Anthropology 4, 4: 489–522.
Harwood, Alan
    1970 Witchcraft, Sorcery and Social Categories among the Safwa. London: Oxford University Press.
Illich, Ivan
    1977 Limits to Medicine: Harmondsworth: Penguin.
Keller, Bonnie B.
    1978 Marriage and Medicine: Women's Search for Love and Luck. African Social Research 26: 489–505.
Last, Murray
    1981 The Importance of Knowing about Not-knowing. Social Science & Medicine 15B: 387–92.
Levine, Robert A.
    1963 Witchcraft and Sorcery in a Gusii Community. *In* Middleton and Winter (eds.) Witchcraft and Sorcery in East Africa. London: Routledge & Kegan Paul.
Lewis, I. M.
    1971 Ecstatic Religion. Harmondsworth: Penguin.
Middleton, John
    1963 Witchcraft and Sorcery in Lugbara. *In* Middleton and Winter (eds.) Witchcraft and Sorcery in East Africa. London: Routledge & Kegan Paul.
Middleton, John and Winter, E. H. (eds.).
    1963 Witchcraft and Sorcery in East Africa. London: Routledge & Kegan Paul.
Nichter, Mark
    1980 The Layperson's Perception of Medicine as Perspective into the Utilization of Multiple Therapy Systems in the Indian Context. Social Science & Medicine 14B; 225–233.
Parkin, David J.
    1968 Medicines and Men of Influence. Man 3: 424–439.
Van der Geest, Sjaak
    1982 The Illegal Distribution of Western Medicines in Developing Countries: Pharmacists, Drug Pedlars, Injection Doctors and Others. A Bibliographic Exploration. Medical Anthropology 6, 4: 197–219.

Whyte, Susan Reynolds
   1981   Men, Women and Misfortune in Bunyole. Man 16, 3.
   1982   Penicillin, Battery Acid and Sacrifice: Cures and Causes in Nyole Medicine. Social Science & Medicine 16: 2055–2064.
   n.d.   Knowledge and Power in Nyole Divination. *In* Philip M. Peek (ed.) African Systems of Divination: Ways of Knowing. forthcoming.
Willis, R. G.
   1968   Kamcape: an Anti-sorcery Movement in South-west Tanzania. Africa 38, 1: 1–15.

ANKE NIEHOF[1]

TRADITIONAL MEDICATION AT PREGNANCY AND CHILDBIRTH IN MADURA, INDONESIA

INTRODUCTION

In Madura as in other parts of Indonesia, herbal cures are important to folk medicine. Medicinal herbs are used for a large variety of physical disorders and conditions. Most village women are familiar with the composition and preparation of a large number of medicinal potions and ointments. The *materia medica* mainly consists of vegetable substances, partly collected fresh from one's own garden and nearby fields and bushes, and supplemented with dried ingredients from the shop. Lixiviated chalk and ashes are the most frequently used mineral products.

There are four domains where the use of herbal medicine is prominent: (a) for minor ailments; (b) for febrile skin diseases, known as *tombuwan*; (c) in the field of sex and eroticism; (d) during pregnancy and the postpartum period. In this chapter we will focus on the last. The reason for doing so is the importance of these events in Madurese culture and social life. Because of the significance attached to them, traditional medication in this field clearly reflects the basic principles of order in Madurese folk medicine.

When, as in Madura, mortality rates are high,[2] childbirth is even more important. The perception of mortality risks is integrated into people's views on birth and death. People are aware of the hazards of childbirth for mother and child, and take culturally appropriate precautions to ward off dangers.

In this chapter we want to describe what measures the Madurese take to shield mother and child from the real and perceived dangers involved in pregnancy and childbirth. These measures are of several kinds. They include the application of all kinds of medicines, rules for behavior, and ritual. We intend to demonstrate that these measures are viewed as one complex. Some are directed towards more general purposes of maintaining or achieving a certain health condition, while others serve more specific ends. The latter, however, cannot be understood in isolation from the more general aims of the traditional medication process and the notions which underlie it. These notions are part of an indigenous cognitive framework which provides explanations and guidance for action in all kinds of matters: arranging a marriage, building a house, treating the sick, or giving birth.

RESEARCH SETTING

According to the latest census (1980) the island Madura counted about 2.7 million inhabitants. Many more Madurese live outside Madura, especially in mainland East Java. Conditions on the dry and infertile island have stimulated a flow of emigration that has been going on for centuries. The island Madura is administered by the governor of the province of East Java. The Madurese are a distinct ethnic group with a language of their own. They are known as devout Muslims, extravert and hardworking people, who do not take an insult lightly.

Modern medical facilities have also been introduced in the Madurese countryside. Spread all over the region, but usually near the sub-district offices, there are 85 health centres. Madura counts 66 general practitioners, 12 dentists, and 205 nurses or midwives. In each of the four regency capitals there is a small general hospital (cf. Provincial Health Services 1984). Madura's main health problems are primarily due to its low standards of living: poor sanitation and hygiene, prevalence of protein-energy malnutrition (in the interior more than in the coastal areas), hypovitaminosis A, and nutritional anaemia (cf. East Java Nutrition Studies 1977–1979). Compared to East Java as a whole the health condition fo Madura's population is poor, as is the case with the socio-economic situation in general.

The research on which this chapter is based took place in two villages in central Madura: the first is a fishing village on the northern coast, the other an agricultural village in the interior. Though differing in more aspects than main means of subsistence,[3] with respect to the present theme we did not find significant differences. Apparently, medication and ritual surrounding pregnancy and childbirth strike a common chord in Madurese culture. Even the fact that in the fishing village people have access to a health-centre and a resident modern midwife, did not lead to fundamental differences in the way people cope with the hazards of pregnancy and childbirth and did not basically alter their views on the processes involved.

Islam is a factor of importance in Madurese society and Islamic elements have been incorporated in Madurese rituals, including those surrounding childbirth. But the people themselves do not distinguish between elements of Islamic and non-Islamic origin. Islam is blended into 'how ordinary people . . . order and articulate categories, symbols and the relations between them in the pursuit of comprehending, expressing and formulating social practice' (Ellen 1983: 54). In any case, the specific Islamic elements that could be detected are not very prominent in the sphere on which this discussion focusses. Pregnancy and childbirth are essentially a women's affair, where formal Islam retreats in favour of Madurese custom, of which women are the guardians (Niehof 1985: 218).

A SYNOPSIS OF MADURESE FOLK MEDICINE

The point of departure in Madurese thinking about health and illness is the notion that the 'normal' state of being is one of balance or harmony in the individual's relation to the natural and supernatural order (Jordaan 1985: 228 ff). This state of balance is intermediate between misfortune and well-being, which are symbolically equated with respectively 'hotness' and 'coolness'. Thus, the balance may be offset in two ways. While 'hotness' always has negative implications, 'coolness' is essentially positive. Persons in special conditions or with special attributes may be in such a 'cool' state. Examples are: children who are born with a caul, or with a physical handicap, or people who possess extraordinary talents or objects. In the next section we shall demonstrate how the thinking in terms of 'hot' and 'cold' is applied more specifically with regard to the processes of gestation and childbirth.

Here, it is important to note that the balance concept of health yields a three-dimensional model, in which there are two states of imbalance: a positive and a negative one. This contrasts with models built on an all too narrow interpretation of binary oppositions (e.g. Hiroko Horikoshi 1980: 160–164). Because in such two-dimensional representations 'hotness' is considered a disturbance equated with illness, health has to be equated with 'coolness'. Disturbance of the balance may be brought about by all kinds of circumstances: either by natural or supernatural factors, or, for instance, by violating basic principles in the socio-cultural order.

For a person afflicted with illness or misfortune, there are several options open in order to regain the state of balance. Home-remedies are the first alternative to turn to, unless there is acute danger which calls for more drastic action. Home-remedies include herbal drinks, ointments, purgatives, fumigation, bathing, massaging, cupping, and the like. Sometimes it is sufficient to follow dietary restrictions. These kinds of remedies may be used for both therapeutic and prophylactic purposes. Herbal drinks and poultices may be home-made, bought from the vendor, or bought in the shop. There are two kinds of vendors: a Javanese vendor who sells her medicines ready-made in bottles, and a Madurese vendor who prepares the medicine in front of the client from the ingredients she carries in a basket on her head. Preference for the one or the other is a matter of personal taste, and depends on the kind of remedy one is looking for. The village shops offer a variety of Indonesian-made prefabricated *jamu*. Sometimes one can freely buy antibiotics at the local market.

When self-treatment fails, or is expected to be ineffective, people seek medical assistance from others. 'Outside' medical assistance (called *ètambha lowar*) ranges from the indigenous magico-medical specialists to the health-center auxiliary or physician. In serious cases people may consider bringing the patient to the hospital in town. The indigenous specialists are of two kinds. First there is the *dukon*, a word that is used for a motley assembly of part- and full-time practitioners. Secondly, there is the *kiyai*, the religious teacher who, by virtue of his religious knowledge and experience, is ascribed healing powers. Although all Madurese *dukon* are Muslims, the main difference between the *kiyai* and the *dukon* is that the first is primarily a representative of the Islamic Faith, while the second represents custom and tradition, however interwoven with Islam. The *kiyai* hardly ever uses herbal medicine, while *dukon* generally do. There are many kinds of *dukon* (see Jordaan 1985: 161–174). The specialist in the field of pregnancy and childbirth is the *dukon rèmbi'*, who is always a woman.

The choice of a particular healer or a representative of modern health care is based on a number of considerations. It largely depends on how the patient and his relatives interpret the symptoms. If there is a pattern of general misfortune or if one is convinced of the involvement of supernatural powers, it is no use going to the health-center . In such cases there are *kiyai* and certain kinds of *dukon*, dependent upon the circumstances at hand, to turn to. On the other hand, in case of stab wounds, accidents and the like, a doctor or a paramedic is consulted. Similarly, the doctor is considered more effective in treating bodily disorders like gastro-enteritis. In the other cases, the course of the illness and its duration will be closely watched when deciding on the measures to be taken. As for 'outside' medical assistance, it is believed that there should be a 'good fit' (*juddhu*) between healer and patient for the therapy to be effective. Madurese are convinced that the results of exactly identical treatments by equally gifted *dukon* (or doctors, for that matter) differ according to this mysterious 'fit'. If a healer has proved to be *juddhu*, he or she will be consulted by preference, even if this implies travelling. Interestingly, the healer or doctor who is considered *juddhu* often does not live in the same village, but at some distance. It follows that considerations of geographical distance and costs play only a secondary role in the decision-making process.

NOTIONS ABOUT HUMAN REPRODUCTION AND CHILDBIRTH

Madurese women's understanding of the physiology of human reproduction differs from the Western perception. In general, they think that the seed contains the micro-foetus, the womb being only needed to accomodate it. Sterility is thought to result from a womb that is too dry and hot. To regain the optimal balance, one should take 'cooling' drinks (such as coconut water). Sterility is seen as a failure for which only women can be responsible, because they are the child-bearers. No explanations are given if men marry many times without making their wives pregnant.

Notions about feminine sexual attraction are in some respects the reverse of those about female fecundity. In order to please her husband or lover, a woman should have a vagina that is fragrant and dry. Packaged *jamu* which are said to achieve this end, are popular items in the shop (see also Afdhal and Welsch, in this volume).

Most village women do not regard their menstrual cycle as consisting of fertile and infertile days. And those who do, think they are most likely to conceive on the days just before and just after menstruation, the 'safe period' according to Western medicine. They believe the mid-period of the cycle to be sterile.[4] These ideas are based on the association of dry with sterile and moist or wet with fertile. The womb is thought to be driest in the middle of the cycle. Just before menstruation it is thought to be moist and swollen with blood, providing an ideal host environment for the seed. After menstruation the womb is thought to be like an open wound, facilitating penetration and settling of the seed. During menstruation sexual intercourse is prohibited. Violating this taboo is believed to result in the birth of a child suffering from leprosy.

Pregnancy as a physiological event is viewed by the Madurese as a process, not as a state.[5] For an understanding about how they conceptualize the process, we have to take a closer look at some important classificatory associations in Madurese thinking. These are the association of 'coolness' with fecundity and growth, and of 'hotness' with infecundity, abortion, and check of growth.

The Madurese say that the 'cool' drinks and *jamu* to induce conception have three closely related but distinct properties: coagulation of the woman's blood and the man's sperm, increased viscosity of the mixture to prevent easy extrusion, and stimulation of fetal growth. 'Hot' food and medicines have the opposite qualites: they liquify the mixture to prevent its adhesion to the womb, they hamper or slow down fetal growth, and they are abortive (Jordaan 1985: 210). This picture is surprisingly similar to the Malay version as provided by Laderman (1983: 78): ' . . . operating on the theory that coolness is necessary for conception, some women drink "hot" medicines for their supposed contraceptive qualities and some use them as an abortifacient. The fetus is considered to be a clot of blood, and hot medicine is thought to liquify the blood, and to make the womb uncongenial for the child.'

One aspect which can be discerned clearly in the ritual surrounding pregnancy and childbirth is that of transition. For the child, these processes imply a transformation from an anonymous fetus, a mere clot of blood in the beginning, to a member of society. This transformation is achieved gradually, and is only completed when the baby, about forty days after birth, is taken out of the house and shown to the neighbors for the first time.

For the mother pregnancy and childbirth imply gradual social isolation before birth, and social re-integration thereafter. Especially for women who are pregnant for the first time the accompanying ritual takes on the character of a rite of passage. Interwoven in rite-of-passage symbolisms, are symbols which are thought to avert danger and which point to well-being and fertility.

Conditions of uncleanliness and impurity are thought to be inherently dangerous, for the woman and child involved as well as for their environment.

The crucial point is that perceptions about gestation and birth as physiological processes and notions about them as social processes and cultural events run parallel courses. In customs and beliefs concerning pregnancy and childbirth they are intertwined, forming – as it were – knots at significant moments in the process.

PREGNANCY UNFOLDING: MEDICATION AND RITUAL

Since Madurese women are very concerned about the regularity of their menstruation, every pregnancy is dubious in the beginning. The fact that it is common to take medicine if menstruation is not on time (the so-called *jamu telat bulan*, for instance), provides a way out when pregnancy is suspected and unwanted. A similar attitude[6] is reported to prevail among women in two Chinese communities in Malaysia: 'The ambiguity in folk beliefs about when a developing fetus becomes human makes the period between a missed menses and the positive identification of pregnancy a time in which menstrual induction cannot be subjected to negative legal sanctions or labelled medically as abortion' (Ngin 1985: 40). In Madura, any woman who takes her body seriously should start drinking herbal medicine some days or even a week before menstruation is due. The herbal medicine should contain ingredients that are classified as 'hot', such as vinegar, yeast, ginger, and the like. A woman who is eagerly awaiting pregnancy should refrain from these measures.

When in spite of all medication the menstrual flow does not start, pregnancy becomes probable. If it is unwanted, the woman may look for more drastic means, such as induced abortion by massage. In the area of research this was done by some elderly women, who were known as illicit abortionists. The local traditional midwives did not want to have anything to do with these practices. If anything went wrong it was usually the modern midwife who was called in. When massage fails to produce the desired effect, pregnancy has to be accepted. The *dukon rèmbi'* will be called or visited for a first examination. During the first months of pregnancy 'hot' food and drinks are forbidden. The early months of pregnancy, called *andhek*, which refers to the ceasing of menstruation, are accompanied by the familiar physical signs and complaints. The whims of a woman's appetite in such circumstances (getting sick from one type of food, while craving for particular snacks) are explicitly acknowledged. The husband is expected to see to it that his wife gets what she wishes. It is the only situation in which women are allowed, and even expected, to make explicit demands on their husbands.

If a woman sticks to the dietary rules, her pregnancy should develop well. Still, incidence of pregnancy wastage appeared to be quite high. In the research area about 10% of all pregnancies resulted in miscarriage or stillbirth (Niehof 1985: 229). After the immediate risk of abortion is over, during the second period of the pregnancy, which lasts from the third to the seventh month, some women reported having a missed abortion which they called *èkakan sambhilang*. The fetus is thought to have been consumed in the womb by a malicious spirit which materializes as a snake-like creature. The womb expels only blood and dead tissue, sometimes pieces of bone.

The most significant moment in the second period of the pregnancy is when the movements of the baby are felt for the first time, because this means that the soul or *roh* has entered. Usually then, an offering of food is sent to the *kiyai*. In some parts of Madura a special ritual is staged for the occasion. 'Ensoulment' marks the fetus as a developing human being. From now on the *dukon rèmbi'* will visit the pregnant women regularly. The course of action is now focused on strengthening the baby. This implies that food and drinks classified as 'cool' are preferred to those classified as 'hot'. The discontinuity between the two periods is in the status of the fetus, deniable in the first period, positively identified in the second. During the first period the woman refrains from taking 'hot' food for fear of abortion, during the second period she takes 'cool' food in order to promote the baby's growth.

When pregnancy has lasted for seven months there is another turning point in the course of gestation. While in the first seven months attention is focussed on the stability, position, and growth of the fetus, during the last months of the pregnancy the overriding concern is to facilitate birth. This is dramatically demonstrated by the fact that the expectant mother will now abstain from 'cool' food and drinks, because these would stimulate the baby's growth too much and impede a smooth delivery.

Besides the change in food and drink habits, the last period of gestation shows an increase in behavioral rules for the expectant mother and father, which fall into a pattern described in detail for South-East Asia as a whole (Hart et al. 1965). Many of the rules are aimed at preventing a complicated and prolonged delivery. One of the complications most feared is a retention of the placenta. Other rules are to protect the expectant parents in their vulnerable condition. The fact that the same type of rules apply, for example, to persons on the verge of their first marriage and for newlyweds, is in accordance with the perception of pregnancy and childbirth as a transition process.

The last turning point in the course of gestation is ritually and ceremonially emphasized. On a suitable day in the seventh month a ritual is held. It is referred to as *rasol pellet kandong*, 'ritual for the massage of the belly'. In conjunction with the actual massage treatment by the *dukon rèmbi'* several activities are staged. The ritual should take place in the house of the expectant mother (where the young couple will usually live, given the rule of uxorilocality). The family of the expectant father has to be invited formally; both families contribute food for the meal to be offered to the guests at the end, money, and other attributes necessary for the ceremony. Usually, a *kiyai* is invited to lead the recital of Islamic texts with the male guests.

The expectant mother is massaged, and showered with water containing flower petals. The main attributes and acts in the ceremony point to the concern with the coming end of the gestation process. Symbolically, a smooth delivery is anticipated.[7] The *dukon rèmbi'* leads the ceremony. At the end she is rewarded for her services with food, money, and the piece of white cloth which was used in bathing the expectant mother. She has now committed herself formally to assist at the delivery. The pregnancy, which was hitherto a more or less private affair, has acquired wider social significance.

CHILDBIRTH

When the birth pangs announce that the moment of delivery is near, the *dukon* is fetched. The woman in labor is placed on a mat in the inner room of the house. She is put in a semi-upright position, head and shoulders leaning against the wall, and is covered with a piece of cloth. A towel is put over her shoulders. The *dukon* usually refrains from internal manipulation and delivers the baby more or less by the touch.

After the baby has been delivered safely, the *dukon* awaits the birth of the placenta before cutting the umbilical cord with a bamboo knife. The baby is cleansed with kitchen soot and tamarind fruit, and carefully bathed. The navel wound is treated with an embrocation of turmeric root and mashed leaves, but sometimes only wetted with water heated in a potsherd held in the fire. To promote the drying of the wound, ground coffee beans, or the pulverized earthen nests made by a specific sort of wasp, are put on it as well. Usually some kitchen soot is added. The wound is dressed with a *sirih* (*Piper betle* L.) leaf, and all this is covered with a piece of cloth tightly wound around the baby's waist. The baby is given some honey or coconut water; the colostrum is thought unfit for the baby to drink. Then it is brought to the father, who has to whisper the Islamic confession of faith in the baby's ear. After that, the baby may rest. It is put to sleep on a bed between pillows, or on an upturned rice winnow. A knife with a chalk-cross on it, and a native broom, made of the nerves of coconut palm leaves,[8] are put alongside, to protect the child from evil spirits.

The placenta also receives careful treatment. It is regarded as one of the baby's siblings. In case of twins with one placenta, it is cut in half. The placenta is thought to be the material form of one of the four invisible siblings, who accompany the baby at birth, and who will reappear before their earthly companion at the end of his or her life. This belief in the four invisible siblings is not only found in Madura, but all over the Indonesian archipelago. In this article we will not elaborate the theme.[9] I mention it to point to the importance of the placenta. The placenta is cleansed with the same ingredients as the baby was washed with. It is salted, and seasoned with all kinds of spices, both of the 'hot' and the 'cool' type. Then it is wrapped in white cloth, and put into an earthenware jar together with some rice, maize, coins, a piece of script (Arabic or Javanese), and a needle or a pencil. The jar is kept in or near the house for some time (for a reason explained below), and after that it is thrown into the sea, buried, or suspended from the eaves.

The mother is also washed with water which contains kitchen ashes, tamarind fruit, and salt. After that she is allowed to stand up and have an ordinary bath. Then she is given a drink of water containing the lixiviated ashes of coconut shell and kitchen soot (called *landhana batok*). Starting immediately after birth, and to be continued during the whole forty-day period (see below), she is expected to drink her *jamu* (herbal medicine) three times a day. A long piece of cloth (*bangkong*) is wrapped tightly around her waist and belly, so that she is hardly able to walk.

During the period just after childbirth, mother, baby, and afterbirth are considered very close, almost as if the same blood still runs through their veins. The mother's well-being will directly affect that of the baby. Illness of the mother (puerperal fever, for example) is thought to be caused by an inadequate treatment of the afterbirth. As a therapy for the mother, salt and spices will be added to the placenta.

It appears that kitchen soot or ashes play an important role in the treatments of and ceremonies for mother and baby at and after childbirth. These elements are not only regarded as purifying, but they also serve the purpose of linking mother and child more closely to the earth. The kitchen with the hearth (traditionally consisting of three hearth-stones) symbolizes the earthly and the domestic context. It makes sense if one keeps in mind that the period of childbirth and the first forty days after it, is regarded a transitional and hazardous one.

THE FIRST FORTY DAYS AFTER CHILDBIRTH

Because the baby is almost entirely dependent upon its mother's milk during the first months of its existence, the mother has to take care that her supply is sufficient and the milk is of good quality. This is one of the ends served by regularly drinking *jamu* (*jhamo* in Madurese). There are, however, other reasons as well. The mother's body should be freed from all contamination and pollution, both internally and externally, and should regain its normal shape. To these ends, she has to drink daily herbal potions, and is rubbed with herbal ointments. Just as in pregnancy there are also specific behavioral rules which should be observed.

As regards the last, these are based on two principles. In the first place the mother and baby are thought to be in a state of transition which makes them very vulnerable to supernatural evil forces. Secondly, they are not only contaminated, but also contaminating. The mother should therefore confine herself to the house and compound, and should not come near the kitchen or participate in cooking and cleaning activities.

The application of ointments follows a simple basic pattern. The woman's body is thought to consist of two parts: from the waist up, and from the waist down. The latter part is called *poro baba*, the 'lower sore'. It is regarded as a sore wound, which has to heal by expelling the pollution. For this part of the body the ointment, called *parem*, contains 'hot' ingredients. The so-called *parem baba* is thus classified as 'hot', while the *parem* for the upper part should be fragrant.

The *parem baba* is particularly meant to expel the lochia, the 'dirty blood', from the body. This blood is supposed to consist of white and red blood. Retention of the 'red dirty blood' will cause the mother to feel unwell and look unhealthy, while it also enhances susceptibility for a quick next pregnancy. The consequences of retention of the dirty white blood are even more unfavourable. This polluting substance is believed to disperse throughout the body, causing the woman to become pale and thin, finally leading to death. The lixivium of burnt coconut shell, which was usually administered in the interior village to women after childbirth, serves the same purpose. So does the *jhamo* of the 'hot' type. This shows again that the interpretation of the hot-cold dichotomy should take into account the ascribed qualities of the categories, in this case the supposed liquifying effect of 'hot' medicine.[10]

Just as the extrusion of the lochia is thought to be stimulated by 'hot' medicine, the flow of milk is thought to be stimulated by it as well. The supply of milk should be kept up by drinking medicine of the 'bitter' type, the so-called *ababeddjha*, which consists of an extract of particular leaves. In the village in the interior it was known as *jhamo ronronnan*. This type of *jhamo* is also thought to enhance femininity. It is never taken by men. The whole complex of medication, rules, and practices to be followed during the postpartum period is summarized in Diagram I (see p.245); in Diagram II (see p.246ff.) are listed the names and the ingredients as well as the therapeutic purposes of the main herbal drinks and ointments to be taken by pregnant and post-parturient women.

During the period of forty days after childbirth, it is customary to visit mother and child, bringing a gift in kind. Only female guests are expected. Formerly, they were requested to hold their feet over a smouldering woodfire which was kept burning in front of or on the front porch especially for this purpose. This was to prevent the visitors from inflicting illness and adversity upon the vulnerable baby. Nowadays, few people keep to this custom. When there are guests, the young mother keeps in the background, letting her relatives, or a neighbor do the honors. It is a relaxed social occasion, which allows for leisurely gossiping.

Although this last stage of the gestation and childbirth process is referred to as the forty-day period, actually the closing ceremony may take place when the baby is between 38 and 42 days old. For the selection of the day of the final ceremony the sex of the child is also taken into account: an odd number of days after birth for a boy, an even number for a girl. The occasion is called *molang arè*, which could be translated as the 'turning point day'. The day

DIAGRAM I
Treatment of the mother during forty-day period after childbirth

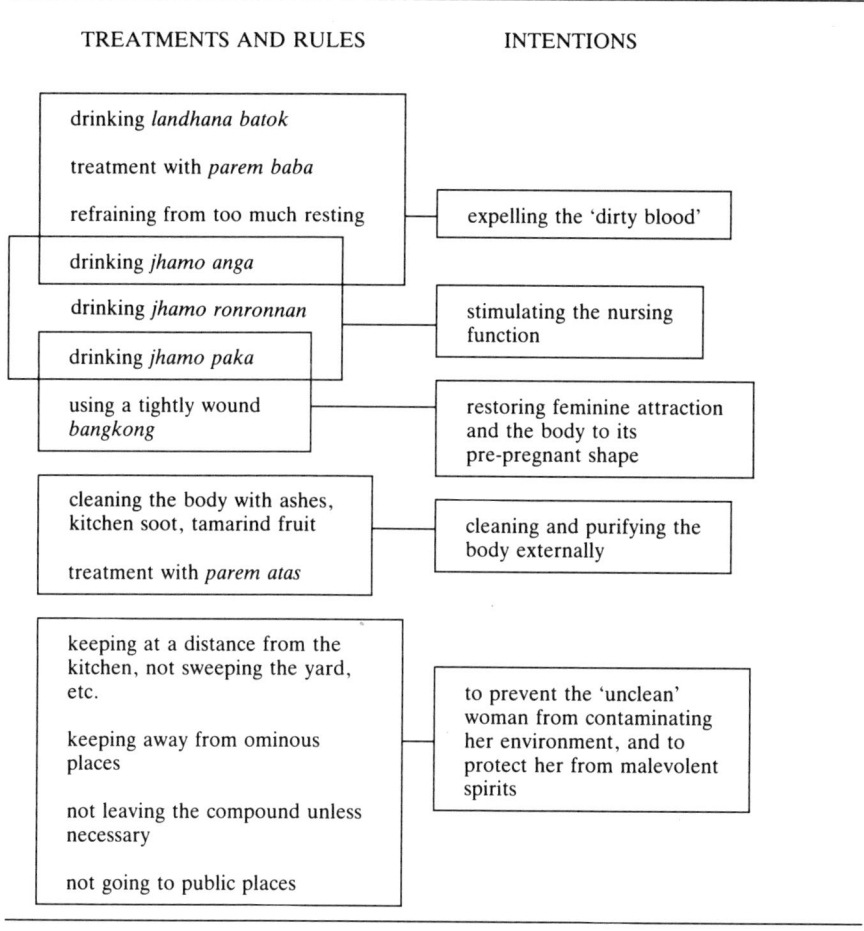

(adapted from Niehof 1985: 244)

should be a good one according to Madurese time reckoning and divination.

Mother and baby are showered with water containing flower petals. All women who had assisted at the delivery join in the showering. Because the hair of the baby is thought to carry the uncleanness of the mother's womb, it is shaved. (For the same purpose a hairlock was cut or burned when the baby was seven days old). Girl babies are given a perfunctory scratch on the clitoris, either at the age of seven days or at *molang arè*. Also, a baby girl's ears are pierced. The *dukon rèmbi'* massages the mother 'to put the womb back into place'. Incense is burned, over which the mother has to stand with parted legs, while the *dukon* mutters an incantation. The *dukon rèmbi'* is in charge of all these proceedings.

DIAGRAM II

Herbal drinks (*jhamo*) and/or ointments (*parem*) during gestation and the post-partum

Name of herbal drink or ointment	Common ingredients		Therapeutic purpose
	Local name	Scientific name	
jhamo rang-rang ana' ('birth control jamu)	sèntok mosè sa'ang bunto' cabbhi alas jhai laos	*Cinnamomum sintok* Bl. *Carum copticum* Benth. *Piper cubeba* L. *Piper retrofractum* Vahl. *Zingiber officinale* Ros. *Alpinia galanga* Sw.	One of several 'hot' herbal potions commonly used for regulating the menses. It may be regarded as the Madurese equivalent of the factory-made *Jamu Telat Bulan* (see text). In fact, it can also serve contraceptive or rather abortive purposes (hence its name rang-rang ana').
jhamo cellep ('cool' jamu)	sère temmo ora' koncè pèt koncè konèng jhintèn èreng aeng landhana kapor sènnam bluntas paspasan	?*Piper betle* L. *Kaempferia rotunda* Linn. *Gastrochitis panduratum* Ridl. *Nigella sativa* L. water from lixivated chalk. ?*Tamarindus indica* L. *Pluchea indica* Less. *Coccinia Cordifolia* GLGN.	These ingredients make up one of the 'cool' herbal potions to be taken during the first months of gestation. Apart from its 'cooling' effects, the herbal potion should have adhesive properties lest the ovum should be expelled too easily. This herbal potion is taken for three months and then replaced by herbs which belong to the basic ingredients of 'cool' herbal potions, like *sènnam, bluntas, paspasan*
jhamo anga' ('hot' jamu)	jhai daun jerruk kerrès mènya' nyèor	*Zingiber officinale* Ros. *Citrus* spec. (unidentified) *Cocos nucifera* Linn.	At about the sixth month of gestation women should avoid 'cool' herbal drinks lest the fetus should grow too large, thus impeding a normal delivery. To facilitate delivery one may take herbal potions which contain both 'hot' and lubricating substances, as is shown in the composition.

247

jhamo marèna lahèr (post-partum jamu)	1. temɔn labak daun bluntas accem telo: ajam buja aeng landana batok	Curcuma longa L. Pluchea indica Less. Tamarindus indica L. egg (yolk) salt water from lixivated ashes of coconut	These herbal potions are taken during the forty days after parturition. In combination they serve a three-fold purpose: to stimulate lactation, to clean the body of 'dirty' blood and other polluting substances, to restore or enhance the health of the mother.
	2. kaju konyèngal bhabang potè aeng landana abu tomang	Cinnamom spec. Allium sativum Linn. water from lixivated kitchen soot	
parem baba ('lower' ointment)	klabhet kastorè klèmɔa' kaju candana kembang konanga kemɔang ramo' kencor sa'ang potè bunto' jhai laos	Trigonella foenum graecum Lam. Hibiscus abelmoschus L. Rheum officinale Baill. Santalus album Z. Cananga odorata Hook & Thoms. flower (unidentified) Kaempferia galanga L. Piper cubeba L. Zingiber officinale Ros. Alpinia galanga SW.	A 'hot' type of herbal ointment, which is to be applied to the lower part of the body. Its main purpose is to expel the lochia and to prevent abdominal swellings.
parem atas ('upper' ointment)	koranga ghaddung klabhet kastorè mɔsojè poɔok klèmba' kalabistu candana	Cananga odorata Hook & Thoms. Dioscorea hirsuta Bl. Trigonella foenum graecum Lam. Hibiscus abelmoschus L. Massoia aromatica Saussurea lappa Clark. Rheum officinale Baill. Andropogon muricatus Retz. Santalum album L.	This ointment, which is both fragrant and 'cool', is to be applied to the upper part of the mother's body (including the face). Its main purpose is the stimulation of lactation.

continued on p. 248

DIAGRAM II continued

Herbal drinks (*jhamo*) and/or ointments (*parem*) during gestation and the post-partum

Name of herbal drink or ointment	Common ingredients		Therapeutic purpose
	Local name	Scientific name	
ababeddjha (a bitter drink)	kasêmbu'an daun jabbau ga'saya'an lang-alang rèbbha pèna'an daun kamonèng nèr-mennèran daun bluntas daun lambibing salangkèng daun blimbing bulung	*Paederia foetida* L. unidentified *Hydrocotyle asiatica* L. *Imperata arundinaceae* Cyrill. *Ehretia microphylla* Lamk. *Murraya exotica* L. *Phyllanthus nururi* Linn. *Pluchea indica* Less. ?*Stenochlaena palustris* Bedd. *Anisomeles ovata* R. Br. *Averrhoa bilimbi* L.	This is a herbal potion to stimulate lactation and simultaneously promote the health of mother and child.
jhamo ronronnan (a lactative jamu)	daun kasêmbu'an daun mangkamang rebbha sèbu daun ka'sèka'an daun nèr-mennèran daun prèngtalè buwa koddu' moda daun lanas duri daun komangaè konco'na daun rokkem ngoda	*Paederia foetida* L. *Hyptis suaveolons* Poit. ?*Oplismus Burmanni* R. Br. *Euphorbia reniformis* Bl. *Phyllanthus nururi* Linn. *Bambusa* spec. *Morinda citrifolia* L. *Agave vivipara* L. *Ocimum basilicum* Linn. *Flacourtia Rukam* Zoll. & Mor.	To stimulate lactation.

jhamo paka' (an aphrodisiac)	majha kellèng	*Terminalia chebula* Retz.
	sontè	*Zing. offic.* L. var. Hassk.
	ghantè	*Ligusticum acutilobum* S. & Z.
	jlabi	*Terminalia laurinoides* T. & B.
	concong pandan	
	cangkok	*Rhus Semialata* Murr.
	majhakanè	*Schima noronhae* Rnw.
	pèkok	*Quercus infectora* Olv.
	samarantok	unidentified
	kadabung	*Sindora sumatrana* Miq.
	klemba'	*Parkia intermedia* Hassk.
	masoji	*Rheum officinale* Baill.
	prabas	*Massoia aromatica*
	katombhar	*Tetranthera brawas* Bl.
	jhinten èreng	*Coriandrum sativum* L.
	bidhara ghunong	*Nigella sativa* L.
	konyè'	*Strychnos ligustrina* Bl.
	pocok	*Cur. longa* L. var. Hassk.
	addas	*Saussurea lappa* Clar.
	palasarè	*Foenicum vulgare* Gaertn.
	koncè pèt	*Alyxia stellata* R. & S.
		Kaempferia rotunda Linn.

After *molang arè*, the end of the post-partum period, the woman is allowed to resume sexual intercourse. For that purpose she may take *jhamo paka'*, an aphrodisiac herbal potion. This drink not only makes her vagina shrink, but also prevents unpleasant odors.

The *kiyai*, who is also invited, leads the male guests in the singing about the life of the Prophet. In the village in the interior, the bathed and dressed-up baby is put on a tray with flowers and handed over to the men, who are sitting together in the *langgar*. They hold the baby in turns, while singing and taking a flower from the tray. Thus, it is welcomed into the community of believers. Finally, everybody is given a meal. The *dukon rembi'* is rewarded for her services in money and in kind. She is also given a chicken which is the same as the one the pregnant woman held on her lap as a baby chicken at the occasion of the 'ceremony of the massage of the belly'. The chicken is referred to as *rèp-orèp* ('being alive'), to signify the fact that the baby has survived the first critical weeks of its existence.

After the *molang arè* ceremony, the baby may be carried out of the house. It is shown to neighbors and relatives, and given coins. As the people say, in this way they 'share in the coolness of the baby'. The mother is now considered clean. She is supposed to take up her social duties and get to work again. The couple may resume sexual intercourse. The process of transition is completed.

SOME CONCLUDING REMARKS

The use of medicines plays a prominent role in the Madurese management of gestation and birth. Although Western pharmaceuticals are available here and are part of the context of choice, they are not perceived as relevant for this area of health care. Instead locally produced herbal medicines and packaged *jamu* available in the shops are taken by Madurese women. As the paper by Afdhal and Welsch in this volume shows, manufactured *jamu* has developed as an important industry in the historical context of pharmaceutical pluralism in Indonesia. Here I have developed a more local perspective on *jamu* by showing how it is interpreted within a Madurese understanding of physiological processes. Such an approach elucidates the way meaning is attributed to medicines and guides their use.

Several points have been made about the Madurese logic concerning gestation and medication. The most important one is that the Madurese view the events as processes with distinctive phases. The beginning of a new phase, such as when the pregnancy has lasted for seven months, is marked by a combination of ritual and changes in dietary rules and medication for the woman concerned. This holds for the whole sequence, and lasts till the transition which mother and child are perceived to undergo, ends at *molang arè*.

Another striking point is the complexity of the medication customs. One type of *jhamo* may serve more than one purpose, while on the other hand a specific end may require several actions, medical and non-medical (that is, from our point of view) at the same time. An example of the first is the 'hot' *jhamo* to be taken after childbirth. It has to drive out the 'dirty blood' and stimulate the flow of mother's milk. An example of the second is provided by all measures taken to clean or purify the young mother, both externally and internally.

The Madurese herbal medicines are suited to these complex ends. The birth attendant is expected to know about these matters. If she does not, for instance because she is not a daughter (or granddaughter) of a *dukon rèmbi'*, she will turn to someone who does, to provide her with the necessary herbs and advise her on their use. The *jhamo* vendor is also familiar with the medicines required during pregnancy and after childbirth. She knows where to find the herbs and how to prepare them. Much of the knowledge about traditional medicine is shared among the elderly women anyway. It has been passed on from generation to generation and this process continues, in spite of the introduction of modern medicine. Also the packaged *jamu* sold in the shop has not replaced traditional herbal medicine. It has become an alternative for parts of it. Thus, a woman may use a 'hot' postpartum *jamu* from the shop, while relying on the *dukon* or some other elderly expert for the *jhamo ronronnan*.

It is clear that opposition 'hot-cold' plays an important part in Madurese traditional medicine. However, it should be emphasized that any attempt to reduce the basic principles in traditional medicine to this opposition leads the researcher astray. Such mechanical thinking ignores the complexities involved. By focusing on a specific field of traditional medication, I hope to have demonstrated this.

NOTES

1. The author did fieldwork in Madura for two years, during the years 1978–79. The doctoral dissertation based on this fieldwork was published in Leiden in 1985 (see References below). The research was subsidized by the Indonesian Studies Programme. A substantial part of the data in the present article is taken from a study of Madurese traditional medicine by my husband R. E. Jordaan, who conducted his own field work in Madura during the same period (see Jordaan 1985).
2. The rates for infant mortality and mortality of children under five, which were calculated on the basis of Fertility Survey data from the two villages of research, were significantly higher than comparable figures for rural East Java. Infant mortality rates for both sexes, computed for the birth cohorts of 1967–76 were 197 and 191 (per thousand) in the two Madurese villages, while the rural East Java figure is 121 per thousand live births for a comparable period. Figures of children who died before reaching the age of five, of the birth cohorts 1957–72 were 296 and 317 per thousand live births in the Madurese villages, while the rural East Java figure declines from 192 to 117 during about the same period. See Niehof 1985: 288–290.
3. The position of women and the level of fertility appeared to be strikingly different for the two types of villages (cf. Niehof 1985).
4. These ideas are not uncommon in Asia. See, for instance, Hunte (1985: 53) on indigenous methods of fertility regulation in Afghanistan.
5. Manderson's (1981: 510) observation that 'Malays regard pregnancy as a hot state' does not apply to the Madurese. As we shall see in the next section, in Madura the notions of hot and cold are applied throughout the processes of gestation and childbirth in a differential manner,

which refutes a static perception of pregnancy. Another researcher reporting on Malay birth customs (Laderman 1983: 41) actually denies that the Malay view pregnancy as a persistently hot state.
6. See also Browner (1985) on pregnancy control in Cali, Colombia, and Hunte (1985) on indigenous fertility regulation in Afghanistan.
7. For a description of the ceremony see Niehof 1985: 232–235.
8. This broom is called *panebbha* (Indonesian *sapu lidi*). It features in many ceremonies and is regarded to have an auspicious influence.
9. More information about the 'four invisible siblings' can be found at several places in Jordaan 1985.
10. Explanations such as that 'with parturition heat is lost and the woman moves to a state of excess cold' (Manderson: 1981: 511), or that 'after child-birth a woman enters a "cold" state because her body has been depleted of blood, the "hot" body fluid' (Laderman 1983: 41), do not take these into account.
11. For a more detailed list of recipes of herbal medicine to be taken during gestation and the postpartum period, see Jordaan 1985: Appendix E, pp. 332–342.

REFERENCES

Browner, C. H.
 1985 'Traditional Techniques for Diagnosis, Treatment, and Control of Pregnancy in Cali, Colombia', *In* Women's Medicine L. F. Newman (ed.), pp. 99–125, New Jersey: Rutgers University Press.
East Java Nutrition Studies (Report I, II, III)
 1977– Surabaya/Amsterdam: Universitas Airlangga/Koninklijk Instituut voor de Tropen.
 79
Ellen, R. F.
 1983 'Social Theory, Ethnography and the Understanding of Practical Islam in South-East Asia', *In* M. F. Hooker (ed.), Islam in South-East Asia, pp. 50–92, Leiden: E. J. Brill.
Hart, D. V. et al.
 1965 Southeast Asian Birth Customs. Three Studies in Human Reproduction. New Haven, Conn.: Human Relations Area Files.
Hiroko Horikoshi-Roe
 1980 'Asrama: An Islamic Psychiatric Institution in West Java'. Soc. Sci. & Med. 14B (3): 157–167.
Hunte, P. A.
 1985 'Indigenous Methods of Fertility Regulation in Afghanistan'. *In* L. F. Newman (ed.), Women's Medicine, pp. 43–77, New Jersey: Rutgers University Press.
Jordaan, R. E.
 1985 Folk Medicine in Madura (Indonesia). Leiden: Ph.D. thesis.
Laderman, C.
 1983 Wives and Midwives: Childbirth and Nutrition in Rural Malaysia. Berkeley: University of California Press.
Manderson, L.
 1981 'Roasting, Smoking and Dieting in Response to Birth: Malay Confinement in Cross-cultural Perspective'. Soc. Sci. & Med. 15B: 509–520.
Niehof, A.
 1985 Women and Fertility in Madura. Leiden: Ph.D. thesis.
Ngin, Chor-Swang
 1985 'Indigenous Fertility Regulation Methods Among Two Chinese Communities in Malaysia'. *In* L. F. Newman (ed.), Women's Medicine, pp. 25–43, New Jersey: Rutgers University Press.

CAROLINE H. BLEDSOE AND MONICA F. GOUBAUD

THE REINTERPRETATION AND DISTRIBUTION OF WESTERN PHARMACEUTICALS: AN EXAMPLE FROM THE MENDE OF SIERRA LEONE

INTRODUCTION

Western pharmaceuticals have the dubious distinction of being as popular and available around the world as Coca-Cola. In the smallest villages in many countries, one can purchase an antibiotic capsule as easily as a bottle of Coke. International alarm increases over the importation to developing countries of drugs banned in the US and Europe, including highly toxic medicines. Increasing attention is focusing on the distribution of pharmaceuticals within developing nations through the illegal activities of drug peddlers, market women, and even licensed pharmacists and medical personnel (see van der Geest 1982a, 1982b, 1984). Medicines are sold in the streets and open-air markets with no information – or wrong information – on the dosage or even on the type of illness that should be treated (e.g., Wasunna and Wasunna 1974). However, there is little research on how people have actually incorporated these pharmaceuticals into their treatment regimens – whether 'appropriately' or not. Moreover, we believe that even when local people do have reasonably accurate information, the ways in which they actually perceive and use Western pharmaceuticals are not always in congruence with assumptions of medical personnel and drug manufacturers about how the drugs should be used and the illnesses they should be used to treat.

Most practitioners and manufacturers of Western medicine make two assumptions about their medications. One is that access to Western pharmaceuticals is available only through appropriate practitioners. Second, a patient will take a medication as prescribed or recommended: at the proper time, in the proper dosage, and for the illness at hand – not for another illness, for which it might be useless or even harmful, but which the local culture defines as an appropriate application.

The research on this problem of misuse of Western pharmaceuticals was conducted in a rural chiefdom of Sierra Leone during an ethnographic study among the Mende. Like many anthropologists, the investigator[1] found herself cast into the role of Western medical expert and medicine supplier by the people with whom she worked. Local people recognized her as a potential source of *puu-hale*, 'white people's medicine', in the local English gloss. They also assumed she would know a great deal about these medicines, so they brought individual pills to her, usually unlabelled, and asked what they were for. She noticed, however, that the ways in which local people, even many well-educated ones, were perceiving and using Western pharmaceuticals rarely corresponded with manufacturers' assumptions – although these were often explained on containers – about the chemical composition of the medicines and what illnesses they should be used to treat. People asked if she had any capsules they could break open and pour on open sores. Antibiotics were among those locally available, but people would have been happy with any capsules. Others asked for her red-coated One-A-Day vitamins (containing no iron) to replace blood they felt had been lost during debilitating illnesses. Even her assistant, a well educated man, bought a large bottle of Catholicon, a European manufactured laxative, to alleviate his malaria. Realizing the significance of the problem, the investigator began to examine Mende beliefs about illness and curative practices, and, in particular, how these beliefs structured people's uses of Western pharmaceuticals.

This problem has many facets. We first outline some of the ways in which researchers have examined the intersection between native healing systems and Western medicine, suggesting that the cultural issue surrounding the 'inappropriate' use of drugs merits fuller attention. We propose a framework for viewing the issue, employing the notion of *cultural reinterpretation*, in which old meanings are ascribed to new elements (Herskovits 1948). After describing some of the local problems of access to health care facilities and pharmaceuticals, we describe some traditional beliefs about illness and curative measures among the Mende of Sierra Leone. In doing so, we show that many of the Mende uses of modern pharmaceuticals follow logically from these more traditional beliefs.[2] Finally, we draw international health implications for the Mende uses of Western medicines and place them in the larger context of pharmaceutical problems in developing countries.

PREVIOUS RESEARCH

The relationship of traditional medical systems to Western scientific medicine is a longstanding concern in medical anthropology. Rivers (1924) asserted early that like other social institutions, indigenous medical practices are rational in the context of local causation beliefs. As such, indigenous health practices are part of a rationally motivated, structured system of medicine, rather than manifestations of ignorance, illiteracy, or cultural inferiority.

Beginning in the 1950s, the concerns of the international public health movement spurred medical anthropologists to examine the relationship of indigenous medical practices to Western scientific medical systems. Because traditional people often preferred their own healers' advice to that of Western practitioners, research concerns shifted to peoples' underutilization of, or noncompliance with, the Western scientific medical system. The assumption frequently underlying this effort is that the two medical systems are discrete and that they conflict or compete with each other (see also Wellin 1977, and Good and Good 1981). As Welsch (1983) notes, such studies describe the classifications and categories of traditional medical systems and 'identify areas where local belief, values, practices, role relationships, and economic requirements conflict with those of the Western medical system' (p. 35). In this light, Western medicine has been viewed as an introduced medical system which is, at best, awkwardly integrated into the society and culture of its users.

In many cases, however, it may be possible to ask how Western medicine *does* meet the perceived needs of traditional people (Welsch 1983). Adopting a pragmatic perspective, Foster (1976) argued that people empirically observe the advantages of pharmaceutical medicine and 'situationally' select the more efficacious therapies. We point out, however, that they do not always have adequate information to select the appropriate medicine. Nor do they necessarily restrict their applications of the medicines to illnesses for which they may have used the same medicines previously. People often take medication that has no effect (at least from a demonstrated pharmacological point of view) on the illness, which may take its course without – or in spite of – the use of these drugs. Alland (1970), on the other hand, argued that traditional peoples' use of Western pharmaceuticals is governed by the medicines' often random availability in shops and from travelling salesmen, rather than from any belief in or systematic use of health care. These approaches correctly point out that people are pragmatic and use what is available. But we press further, asking if people actively seek Western pharmaceuticals because certain qualities they perceive in the medicines fit with their own categories.

More recent studies have explained traditional people's uses of the Western-style medical system in terms of 'pluralistic' medical systems, in which discrete elements of both Western and traditional practices have evolved into a system of therapeutic choices (for example, Logan 1973, Romanucci-Ross 1969, Welsch 1983). Janzen's (1978) study of BaKongo (Zaire) responses to Western medicine demonstrates that people may utilize drugs, surgery, and hospital care, but they also seek out native doctors, prophets, and traditional consultations among kinsmen. He argues that these 'different forms of therapy play complementary rather than competitive roles in the thoughts and lives of the people' (p. 3), as patients and their families make decisions among alternative therapy choices.

Logan's (1973) cognitive analysis of pluralistic medicine in Guatemala proposes that indigenous people may combine notions of diseases and medications that stem from conflictual medical systems in a complementary manner (see also Mitchell 1983). Logan shows that the highland Maya incorporate modern scientific notions of diseases and cures into their traditional classifications of hot and cold. He points out, for instance, that the Indians classify fever as a hot symptom. Consequently, they have placed its treatment, penicillin, into their 'cold' category to acknowledge its efficaciousness for fever. In this way the Indians render Western medicines acceptable.

Logan's work is an important step, for it asks how indigenous beliefs may affect perceptions of more modern treatment regimens, rather than *vice versa*. However, it assumes that left to their own choices, the Maya will find other uses for penicillin that are appropriately indicated in the native system as 'hot' or 'cold', and that penicillin will be used as its manufacturer intended: for the eradication of certain strains of bacteria. We would ask, in addition, whether the Maya use penicillin, a 'cold' medicine, to treat other 'hot' illnesses for which modern practitioners might insist the drug has no effect. We would also ask if patients attempt to treat 'hot' illnesses with unprescribed medicines they regard as 'cold'.

At any rate, a new framework seems to be emerging, asserting that for the user, Western medicine and the native medical system are not analytically discrete, and that treatment choices can often be explained by reference to indigenous illness beliefs (e.g., Gunaratne 1980). Like Logan, we examine the cultural logic by which people have incorporated medicine that *did* originate from a different medical system. We move on, however, to ask how this cultural integration affects the use of these originally alien therapeutic agents.

It is important to lay out a framework for understanding how this transformation in meaning can take place. One of the most useful notions that can explain how the Mende view Western pharmaceuticals is the idea of cultural reinterpretation, as elaborated by Herskovits (1948). Herskovits drew on Ralph Linton's idea that elements of culture contained four qualities: form, meaning, use and function, and on H. G. Barnett's insight that these can vary independently as culture changes. That is, new meaning could be read into an old form, or a new principle could be applied to an object whose previous function differed. Herskovits called this 'cultural reinterpretation: the process by which old meanings are ascribed to new elements or by which new values change the cultural significance of old forms' (p. 553).

Herskovits has been superseded in subsequent years in the development of culture theory. However, he was among the first to ask why some innovations were acceptable and others were not, from what he termed a 'psychological' (what we might call 'cognitive') approach, instead of a purely utilitarian perspective. In elaborating the notion of reinterpretation as a cultural phenomenon, he drew attention to the fact that the meaning with which certain people imbue objects or rituals is not necessarily the same that people in another culture attribute to it. Hence, although objects may look the same to both groups, their meanings cannot be understood out of context.

Herskovits was interested in this process primarily from the perspective of social change, the phenomenon this paper also addresses. He attempted to show that cultural traits were rarely borrowed intact from other cultures. However, the process of reinterpretation can be applied logically to any process by which individuals reinterpret the meaning of things in varying contexts.

Recent work by Nichter (1980) seems to stem from a similar framework.

Examining local uses of traditional Ayurvedic versus 'cosmopolitan' or 'english' medicine in India, Nichter shows that 'villagers demand from practitioners the kinds of medicine they want' (p. 227), and that these demands are based on indigenous notions of power gradients in 'cosmopolitan' vs. traditional medicine. For instance, injections are seen as quite powerful curative agents, but are said to overheat the body. Hence, they must be balanced by cooling agents such as milk. As such, 'The villager listens, watches, and interprets what transpires in the clinical experience in terms of an existing cognitive framework . . . . the perceived action of a medicine causes the villager to extend, invent, or reinterpret notions of physiology and bodily processes' (p. 230). Nichter then considers various qualities of medicines, such as physical characteristics, color, and taste, and shows how the willingness of a patient to take them is related to notions of ethnophysiology.

Our interests parallel those of Nichter. He begins with kinds of medicines and asks how Indian villagers interpret them in the light of local medical beliefs. We ask similar questions, but we begin at the other end, with indigenous notions of sickness and cures. We then ask how the Mende have reinterpreted certain kinds of Western pharmaceuticals as appropriate to treat these sicknesses. We also touch on the issue of how individual actors not only reinterpret meaning, but do this strategically at times, using cultural meanings for pragmatic gain.

Finally, we stress the public health dangers that can accrue from such cultural reinterpretations. This problem of inappropriate use of pharmaceuticals stemming from native categories is obviously of interest not only to anthropologists but also to development practitioners. Until recently, however, there was little convergence of focus between the two fields. For the most part anthropology has focused on indigenous medicine and practice or on underutilization of Western medical innovations. On the other hand, past development advocates tended to regard traditional medical practices as having minimal physiological efficacy, or even being harmful. Hence, although some recent development practitioners advocate retaining traditional healing practices in conjunction with Western practices (WHO Report 1978), the bulk of development efforts focused on ways to convince traditional peoples to adopt Western medical practices and pharmaceuticals and to make their use economical (e.g., Gunaratne 1980).

It is important to emphasize, in any case, that although anthropology and development practitioners differ widely, both have tended to view, at least in the past, the two medical systems – the 'traditional' and 'modern' (Western) – as discrete and generally incompatible. Thus, they have sought to discover the conditions under which indigenous people use one or the other system, or how people select elements of both. Research has been interested in *whether* indigenous people adopt Western medicines, but has paid little attention to *how* they actually use them.[3]

The 'inappropriate' uses of pharmaceuticals, when noted, have often been attributed to ignorance or illiteracy. We suggest that the problem is much deeper. It is a cultural one. The Mende, for example, rarely expressed conflicts in accepting one system or rejecting the other. Indeed, the Mende have readily, and even eagerly, embraced Western medicine as a supplement or even an alternative for many of their traditional medicines.[4]

Hence, we believe that people's perceptions of pharmaceuticals cannot be divided *a priori* into discrete categories of traditional versus modern medicines. Rather, it is more useful to consider all available medicines as potentially part of a unitary cultural whole, and *then* to ask what kinds of criteria people use to select from it. We ask how the entire system of local health beliefs – traditional as well as modern – influences decisions about what remedies to use, and how to use them, for particular illnesses.

An examination of data from the Mende of Sierra Leone offers preliminary answers for these questions. We will show how Mende uses of Western medicines are logically consistent with Mende beliefs about illnesses and therapy choices, which, when viewed from the Western perspective, are inappropriate and even harmful.

BACKGROUND

Sierra Leone, located in the equatorial lowlands of West Africa, has a population of about 3 million people. The majority live in rural areas, in small villages or larger towns. The Mende, living primarily in rural southern and eastern chiefdoms of the country, comprise the largest ethnic group: estimates vary from 30% to 40% of the total population. Traditionally slash-and-burn rice agriculturalists, many now engage in cash cropping, diamond mining, trades, and wage labor.

Problems in access to Western health care

Before we examine the local perceptions and uses of pharmaceuticals, it is useful to understand who distributes pharmaceuticals, and how these medicines integrated into the local society and economy. Public health services in Sierra Leone are in poor condition. MacCormack (1984) notes that the Sierra Leone economy has suffered recently because of low world demand for the commodities and minerals it relies upon to generate external income. This means, for example, that although certain vaccines must be kept cold before injection, petrol and kerosene shortages in many parts of the country necessitate leaving the vaccines in warm storage areas with no refrigeration for long periods. Moreover, she points out that despite extraordinarily high morbidity and mortality rates, especially among children, the government – in theory the main health care provider in the country, with an elaborate system of hospitals, clinics, dispensers, and other subsidiary workers – assigns low priority to health care: 8.2% of the total budget in 1980–81.

Distribution of, and access to, pharmaceuticals

Several factors lie behind the widespread reinterpretation of Western pharmaceuticals. One is the high value placed on medicines from Europe and the US. *Puu-hani* ('white people's things') are generally accorded considerable respect and awe, and medicines are viewed similarly. The Mende know that white people tend to live long, healthy lives, and view their medicines and doctors as powerful instruments of this longevity. Although these medicines and the practitioners who distribute them have by no means replaced traditional healers and medicines, they are seen increasingly as acceptable, and, at times, preferred alternatives.

However, some aspects of Western medicine are more accessible to the Mende than others. Hospitals are valued for their facilities and skilled personnel, but are beyond the budgets of many Mende. Not only are doctors and beds expensive by local standards, but many local nurses, concerned with the image of their jobs, insist that patients bring fine towels, thermoses, clothes, and vaseline. Besides these expenses, patients must also provide tips to nurses who administer injections and find admissions cards, to technicians who perform laboratory analyses, and so on.

Given all these problems with formal hospital institutions, people find the simple purchase of pharmaceuticals an easier way to gain benefits from Western medicines. In addition, local dispensers who sell pills and tablets are usually sensitive to the monetary constraints of their clients and amenable to adjustments. One salesman reported that people usually tell him how much they can spend, and he tailors his recommendations accordingly, selling them what he believes would be the best remedy within their means or the first stage for a treatment. Local salesmen, moreover, because they are salesmen, are easy to approach, and will sell to anyone. One man reported that on one of his trips to a rural village to sell medicines, an unaccompanied nine-year-old girl came up to him complaining of stomach aches. He sold her a 20 cent adult size packet of worm medicine.

These examples suggest that a multitude of factors lie behind the phenomenon of cultural reinterpretation. They also suggest that the medicines are often divorced from contexts that would facilitate the adoption of more 'appropriate' ideas about their purposes and uses. Medications are easily removed from government and mission medical institutions, which might instruct people on their appropriate uses. One of the most lucrative sources of income for health middlemen is taking the funds marked for purchase of medicines by the government, or even taking the medicines themselves from government hospitals or from the shipping docks in Freetown for private sale.

Medications end up for sale on the street or in private drug stores and clinics of private practitioners. A 'secondary' system of medical practice has arisen in which medical personnel who work in major hospitals and clinics also set up private practices in their own homes with these supplies and sell them at discounted rates (see also van der Geest 1982a and 1982b).

For these reasons, a sick person is unlikely to find many Western pharmaceuticals at government hospitals or clinics. More likely sources are private pharmacies owned by doctors who work in the major government hospitals, locally trained nurses, licensed – and unlicensed – dispensers, shop keepers, market women, and often illiterate and unlicensed drug salesmen who walk or bicycle into rural villages with drugs bought from large stores in town. (Mission hospitals, however, usually have better supplies than government hospitals.) One man with no medical training reported that his wife, a nurse at a local hospital, had her own 'private practice' and sold medicines out of her home. If she was out of the house or busy when patients came, he himself would diagnose the illnesses, sell the patients medicines, and advise them on dosages.

Despite the dearth of medicines in government hospitals, almost any Western drug that gets into Sierra Leone can be purchased from these alternative practitioners and dispensers, or over the counter in private pharmacies. One Peace Corps volunteer reported that some of her students were falling asleep during class. She finally confiscated some narcotic tablets from a boy who had supplied them to his classmates, and found that they were a variety that had been banned in the US. People also acquire drugs readily from friends or relatives with unused supplies, who are frequently called upon for advice. Even drugs that were acquired through controlled prescriptions are easy to get through an acquaintance who decides not to complete a treatment, but to save the rest of a prescribed dosage for his own or someone else's future need. Such drugs, in fact, may be seen by people as more desirable to try, because the initial requirement of a prescription made them more difficult to obtain, and thus heightened their aura.

Many possibilities for inappropriate use of pharmaceuticals, then, do stem simply from lack of information. For example, pills are usually sold without containers or directions, other than those the salesman gives – often wrongly. This occurs because practitioners acquire most drugs in large quantities, whereas their customers can seldom afford to buy more than a few doses at a time. Also, because of the general lack of containers in the area, a person may put all his pills together in one jar or in a small bit of plastic, and soon forget what the original purpose of each pill was said to be. When literate Mende visit villages, they are frequently approached by residents with jars containing different kinds of pills and asked to identify them. One teenage school boy related that the way he generally dealt with this problem was by asking what the sufferer's complaint was when he or she was given the pills. When an elderly woman, for example, brought him some tablets to identify, she recalled that she was not eating well when she was given the tablets at the hospital clinic. Since eating well is an important attribute to the Mende, the young man naturally concluded that the tablets must be intended to improve her appetite, and told her so.

If widespread availability of medications and lack of knowledgeable surveyors lead to greater possibilities of interpretation, another factor compounds the problem. Because imported pharmaceuticals are valued goods and are seen as effective for a wide range of sicknesses, it is not surprising that individuals strategically reinterpret and exploit the meaning of these valued new elements. Injections, for example, are given for a wide range of maladies, though they often have no physiological justification from a Western perspective. They are widely touted by practitioners who play upon their customers' beliefs in the power of injections in order to boost cash flows. Van der Geest (1982b: 270) cites an even more apt example in Ghana, wherein a young boy attempted to sell him some capsules which, the boy said, were for piles. Later, to other customers (presumably Ghanaians), the boy cast the same capsules as remedies for sexual impotence. It is clear that the boy had sized up the likely worries of the two kinds of customers, and pitched his efforts accordingly.

Our findings clearly point to such tendencies. Pill traders in Sierra Leone develop a keen sense of who their potential customers are and of their likely complaints. When traveling to rural villages, traders are apt to call out, 'Medicines for aches and pains!', whereas in an urban setting they will advertise the same medicines to secondary school students as agents combatting sleepiness and inability to concentrate. In general, they try to ask customers' complaints, rather than wait for customers to ask if they have certain kinds of pills. In this way, the traders draw attention to attributes of the pills they *do* have that are culturally compatible with their customers' perceptions of the causes of their afflictions.

Not only can the meaning of the medicines be manipulated: it can also be hidden deliberately. Because medicines comprise the basis of many individuals' livings, accurate knowledge about cheap and effective pharmaceuticals and remedies is not always transmitted to people. Employees of a mission hospital periodically drove out to a rural village to give public talks on cheap and simple malarial remedies involving chloroquin sequences, and to explain WHO – recommended treatments for child diarrhea using boiled water, salt and sugar. However, the local licensed government dispenser, who derived most of his income from the private sales of medicines, realized he would lose a good deal of money from the sale of painkillers and dysentery medicines if such information were spread widely. Consequently, he successfully pressured the town leaders to forbid the hospital employees to return.[5]

Besides the blatantly exploitative uses of medicines, even when the manufacturers' instructions and warnings are known, a major reason why the Mende do not necessarily accept the rationales that outsiders present for how the medicines work is that some of these alleged functions are contrary to the

Mende logic of sickness and cures. That is, pharmaceuticals may be used inappropriately because of how the Mende attempt to reinterpret outside drugs with powerful, mysterious potentials into locally comprehensible cultural categories. In such cases, we would predict that only if these medicines are culturally reinterpreted will they be accepted. We turn, then, to this more cognitive aspect of Mende views and uses of pharmaceuticals.

METHODOLOGIES

Most of the material for the study was collected in a town around 4,500 in Eastern Sierra Leone. The population was predominantly Mende, although it contained people belonging to several other ethnic groups. The methodologies employed in the study included making observations and conducting interviews on local uses of Western medicines, common illnesses and their etiology and treatment, the local health care delivery system, and the diagnosing and prescribing practices of drug sellers. Those interviewed included local health practitioners such as store keepers, an itinerant drug salesman, several hospital workers who had private practices, as well as laymen. At times, formal interviews were conducted in the researcher's house; but she also went to stores and clinics to obtain a sense of the contexts in which illnesses were diagnosed and medicines dispensed. One of the most valuable methods was simply walking through the town and asking questions when sick people were observed and while medicines were being taken.

Besides these more open-ended methods, the investigator also constructed a large plastic packet as an elicitation device that displayed locally available pharmaceuticals. Several vertical and horizontal seams were sewn into the plastic to create 30 pockets, each containing a pill, capsule, or other Western preparation such as a small tin of Mentholatum. Included were antimalarials, vitamins, analgesics, worm medications, digitalis, ephedrine compounds, steroids, antibiotics, and so on.[6] The packet also contained a few drugs such as a Contac cold capsule and a One-A-Day vitamin that were not available locally. These provided variety in shapes, sizes, and color which might elicit interesting responses.

The investigator then asked ten people if they had ever seen the medicines before, and if so, how they or other people had used them: for what illnesses or symptoms, in what kinds of dosages, and why those particular ones had been chosen. She also asked individuals what else they would do or take for the maladies they had mentioned, even if these remedies were not included in the packet. A few people queried were illiterate, and one could speak no Krio or English – the lingua franca of Sierra Leone. But most people interviewed had at least a secondary school education, and several had been through three years of Teacher Training college. One man had been sent to Nigeria by the Sierra Leonean government for extensive training in hematology and later worked for a mission hospital.

This sample was not intended to be statistically significant or even representative of the local population. The method was used simply to elicit cultural notions of disease etiologies and appropriate treatments. It is interesting to note, in this light, that although educated people tended to know more of the 'proper' uses of Western medicines, they seemed to use traditional criteria, with few apparent cognitive conflicts, for identifying and using the medicines. In actual practice, these people used the medicines much like the illiterate people did.

THE FINDINGS

Forms and quantities of medicine

The results indicate that although the ways in which the Mende use Western medicine appear random – and even dangerous, according to Western criteria – their choices have logic. One criterion people use is the reputed success of the drug in curing an ailment of a friend or relative that seems similar to their own. Generally, though, the physical characteristics of the pharmaceuticals are most important to the Mende view of Western pharmaceuticals. And although the forms of the pharmaceuticals have not changed from one context to another, cultural reinterpretation has transformed their meanings in ways that manufacturers might find surprising.

Size is one factor. One man said that small pills were the most powerful. When this man was shown the plastic pouch containing the variety of Western pharmaceuticals and asked to pick which he thought was the most potent, he pointed to a small yellow pill, folic acid, that was widely available in the area. Most people, however, believed larger pills were most powerful and that they yielded the best cost returns.

The form of the medicine is an important criterion, as Nichter (1980) has also pointed out. Injections are seen as the most potent remedy, apparently because the pain associated with them must indicate efficacy. People like to receive injections because of their power as well as their perceived widespread effectiveness for all kinds of maladies.

Local dressers and druggists, anxious to please, often give their patients unnecessary injections of penicillin and antibiotics – or sometimes simply water – on a weekly basis. This, of course, can lead to antibiotic-resistant micro-organisms. Moreover, most people can recall deaths from infections from unsterilized needles or apparently from allergic reactions. Some months after she returned, the investigator learned that the town chief where she had lived died of an infection contracted from the unsterilized needle used by a local dresser.

Not only do people decide which ailments warrant which treatments: they also decide which ailments preclude certain treatments. Because injections, for example, are powerful, they can also be a dangerous force. For some illness conditions, injections are seen as fatal. One man conducting a survey of child mortality found that women whose children were thought to be suffering from yellow fever did not bring them to the hospital, for fear that they would receive injections and die.

Pills and tablets are seen as less effective than injections, though their potency is not to be underestimated. People usually chew pills thoroughly before swallowing them, because they fear that the tablets will settle in the stomach and cause pain. Moreover, people fear that the pills' effectiveness will be reduced if swallowed whole, making them act very slowly, if at all.

Capsules are seen as among the strongest remedies that vendors of Western medicines can offer. Capsules are preferred for the treatment of wounds because the contents are in powdered form; people break the shells and pour the powder on wounds or open sores. However, capsules are also swallowed for a variety of ailments, and their perceived value is high. Said the head of an under-fives' clinic for children:

The clinics we run do not have capsules [since antibiotics can be dispensed in other forms]. When we go, they [patients' mothers] ask us, 'Did you bring capsules?' We say, 'No'. In fact, I tell them that capsules cannot be swallowed by a young baby, so that means the [medicine] is out of our list. So they just move up [go away].

When asked why the Mende like capsules so much, one young man replied that the medicine must be powerful because the manufacturers took the trouble to seal it tightly in plastic. He also pointed out that because Western practitioners told patients the taste would be very unpleasant if they chewed it first (and thus urged them to swallow the capsule quickly), this was also a sign that it must be a powerful medicine.

Interestingly, the logic of this can be extended to remedies with which people are unfamiliar. The investigator showed two people, independently, a Contac cold capsule, which they had never seen, and asked them what they noticed about it and what they thought it might be useful in treating. Both drew attention to the fact that the capsule actually contained many smaller capsules or plastic balls that contained the medicine. One man pointed out further that because capsules are seen as powerful, then this form of capsule – a capsule within a capsule – must be highly potent indeed. The two also drew attention to the fact that these smaller balls were of three different colors. Although both dismissed the Contac capsule as efficacious for open wounds because the little balls would fall off, one of the two commented that people would use the capsules for diarrhea (often attributed to worms) because of the white medicine balls (white being associated with a bitter taste), and perhaps for blood problems, because of the red balls.

Colors are critical attributes by which the Mende interpret the functions of medications. White and red colors are important signifiers of certain kinds of physiological effects, as the following section will amplify. One woman reported that a big yellow tablet that is sold as an all-purpose worming medicine (although it is manufactured specifically for bilharzia) is commonly used by people also for malaria because, she said, when you have malaria your urine is very yellow. In this case, the perceived effect is to purge the sickness from the body by 'fighting fire with fire'.

Taste is an important Mende criterion of medical effect. Pungent tasting and smelling medications are said to soothe the throat, and anything bitter must be for fever (see below). Anything bitter that is sucked or drunk is for coughs. Hence, Mentholatum is viewed as an appropriate substance to drink for sore throats and coughs, besides its effectiveness for fever.

Temperature is another quality that concerns the Mende. People generally worry about cold substances in the body, including that of their medications. A hospital nurse complained that elderly grandmothers in particular often negate the effects of injections. When a child gets a 'cold' injection, an old woman will often put a hot compress on the immunization spot, making it swell up and spoiling the effects of the medicine. Consequently, even if medications last through a carefully preserved cold chain, their effects may be negated through purposive heating.

In terms of quantities ingested, people frequently take drugs in quantities different from those prescribed either on the label or by health professionals. The itinerant drug salesman stated that he usually prescribed dosages lower than those recommended on the packages, especially during the rainy season, since he felt his patients were weaker then because of food scarcities. He also pointed out that many medicine packages called for administration before meals, and since most Mende eat only one meal a day during the rainy season, multiple doses during the day would be ineffective.

Cost is another factor. People usually see little reason to take many pills of the same variety, reasoning that if they begin to feel better, they need not continue a complete prescription sequence. Consequently, for example, most people who received antibiotic capsules through prescription or from local salesmen rarely took more than a few capsules of the complete dosage. The drug salesman reported that he gauged his recommendations of how many capsules to take on the perceived gravity of the disease: he told his patients to take only a few if the disease was a mild one, and for the entire ten days, if the patient had an illness that was seen as particularly serious. On the other hand, if people do not feel better, they see little reason to continue a sequence of medications that apparently are not working.

However, especially when people feel very ill, they tend to take too much medicine because they are trying to reduce their misery and speed up the curative process. Other times in which people overdose are when drastic action is needed: pregnant school girls are said to take large amounts of chloroquin, nivaquin, or codeine to try to induce abortions.[7]

MENDE ILLNESS ETIOLOGY AND CONSEQUENT REINTERPRETATIONS OF WESTERN PHARMACEUTICALS

The most important factors that governed people's choices of remedies for specific ailments seemed to revolve around qualities such as shape, color, taste, and consistency. These choices reveal that fundamental transformations in meaning have taken place as the Mende adopt certain pharmaceuticals. Yet their choices often reveal remarkable consistency with traditional interpretations of the causes and cures of various types of illnesses. To illustrate this, we describe three maladies that people mentioned most frequently and some of the Western pharmaceuticals they used to treat them.

Fever

Fever is a common Mende complaint. In Western etiology it is associated with a host of illnesses, with malaria perhaps the most predominant cause. Many people, particularly the well educated ones, understand that mosquitoes carry malaria. But virtually everyone expressed a humoral theory of its ultimate causation: exposure to excessive cold or wind is said to cause the chills that precede high temperatures. Some people report malaria attacks after drinking cold liquids, and politely refuse drinks that have been refrigerated. Fever is also said to result from hard work, because sweat is produced, which cools the body. Sweat is harmless during the warmth of the day, but if not washed off thoroughly in the evening with warm water, it will cause fever because of its cooling elements. (Hard work may also produce body aches which the Mende associate with malaria.)

Because the body is said to be suffering from too much cold, traditional remedies have been those that people believe will make the body warm. Dressing warmly, of course, is the most immediate remedy, and one commonly sees small children as well as adults who are suffering from fever bundled in heavy caps and layers of clothes.

Foods provide other fever remedies. Indeed, just as the Mende do not rigidly separate traditional from Western medicines, neither do they necessarily separate food and drink from medicine (see also Etkin and Ross 1982). People say they eat rice, the staple food, to fill up the body, alleviate hunger, and (for children) to grow. But they view the other foods such as sauces, condiments, and palm oil that go with the rice as medicinal agents that help maintain the body's health. A salient ingredient of West African food dishes is spicy hot pepper. To Westerners, peppers are a type of food or condiment, but the Mende insist that peppers have strong medicinal properties: they produce heat in the body, which can combat fevers. During the 'cold season' from November to February, some people add even more peppers to their sauces, along with other traditional bitter remedies, using them prophylactically to give the body additional protective warmth.

A commonly used traditional remedy for fever that is applied externally is a white chalk that is found in clay deposits near stream beds. When rubbed on the skin, it is said to cause a prickly warm sensation, and it is still common today to see feverish children with white chalk smeared on their bodies. However, for adults, this traditional chalk is seen as indicative of backwardness or poverty. Much more desired are Western pharmaceuticals, which have posed no conflicts with traditional notions of how to treat fever. Instead, they have provided new options. Some people are familiar with medications such as chloroquin and what they are supposed to do for malaria. But many people choose white medicines to treat fever, because of their analogies to the traditional white chalk, and their assumed bitterness which, in turn, is said to produce warmth. This means that medicines such as chloroquin are acceptable if they are white or if their bitterness is not disguised by sugar coatings. But it also means that heart stimulants, low blood pressure medications, and anti-diarrheals can be as acceptable as chloroquin or aspirin if their color and taste are consistent with the traditional Mende logic of treating fever with white or bitter medicines.

Local dispensers reportedly attract business by prescribing bitter white pills that their customers feel are appropriate to fevers. The fact that they are willing to cater to customer preferences in tablets gives them a competitive edge over hospitals, which do not always prescribe medicines and remedies that the Mende would consider efficacious. Such actions may include putting children who are convulsing dangerously with high fever under a cold water tap, an act the Mende feel could kill them. That such children survive after these treatments is said to be in spite – rather than because – of the cold water dousing, and their recovery is attributed to the tablets administered afterward, which often happen to be bitter or white.

However, the Mende reinterpretation of Western medicines is not limited to pills and tablets. When people saw the small tin of Mentholatum in the investigator's experimental packet, they reported that they smeared it on their faces and hair to produce heat to combat the cold that they feel causes fever. Several people, including a well-educated school teacher, said that they also drank Mentholatum because in the Mende ethnophysiology, fever lodges in the stomach. One woman demonstrated how she would dip her finger into the tin, pull out a large dab of Mentholatum, swirl it in a cup of hot water, and drink it. However, one man remarked that one of the best remedies nowadays for fever is alcohol because of the warmth it seems to impart: 'People who are advanced drink brandy or whiskey, although Muslims don't do this so much'.

Although fever is primarily attributed to cold, the Mende say it can be caused also by constipation. The causal reasoning goes like this: constipation leads to stress and straining, which leads to headaches and then to fever. This explains, then, why some people buy laxatives to combat malaria: to relieve the stress which was causing the fever.

Worms

The Mende say that worms and small organisms called *fulu-haisia* (literally, living things') in the body can cause a multitude of conditions. 'Big worms' that can often be seen in the stools cause diarrhea, vomiting, dysentery, and cholera, with consequent weight loss and malnutrition, especially among young children. Most diarrhea and vomiting, in fact, is attributed to worms, making worm medicine a frequent accompaniment to a variety of remedy sequences. People also attribute conditions such as kwashiorkor to worms, because a child's skin may become light, which indicates to the Mende that worms have been sucking the blood. Also the stomach becomes bloated which suggests the presence of worms.

'Small worms (organisms)' that cannot be seen but can be felt are said to cause conditions such as sore throats and coughs, including diseases such as tuberculosis, because the scratchiness in the throat is said to result from the worms crawling up and down as the sufferer breathes in and out.

Although the Mende believe that worms can be acquired from drinking water that is visibly dirty, worms are said to thrive on 'sweet' things that the sufferer has eaten, or even to spontaneously generate in the body, from too many 'sweet' things. 'Sweet', here, implies either sugary sweet, such as papaya, oranges or Western-inspired candy, or good tasting, such as chicken, meat, etc.

In Mende logic, because *fulu-haisia* thrive on sweet things, they may be killed in the body, or at least discouraged, by eating or drinking bitter things. Tuberculosis, for example, may be treated by drinking the juice of bitter limes or lemons, which trickles slowly down the afflicted throat. Intestinal worms can be treated by eating extra helpings of peppers.

To help prevent worms, on the other hand, children should be given little meat, chicken, eggs, or fish, all of which are considered 'sweet'. In Mende logic, in fact, these 'sweet' protein foods should be the last things to feed a child with *kwashiorkor*, because the worms that are said to cause this condition would simply be encouraged to grow and spread. When asked, however, why adults can eat 'sweet' foods that are considered harmful, one man explained that adults willingly eat bitter things to counteract the effects of the sweet foods. But children are too young to be coaxed to inject bitter foods or medicines that would counteract the bad effects of sweet foods. Western-trained medical workers in Sierra Leone report widespread non-compliance with their recommendations about proper foods for *kwashiorkor* patients. They complain that small children are commonly given little more than bones to chew on, implying that adults do this out of greed. It is true that meat is considered a luxury rather than a necessity; thus, adults – particularly men, who command the most privilege – deserve most of it. These appear to be important factors in many *kwashiorkor* cases among Mende children, although declining access to sources of animal protein is probably equally important. But the Mende also say that bone marrow, which children are commonly given, is one of the best parts of the meat; more importantly, marrow is safe for young children because it is surrounded by solid bone which *fulu-haisia* cannot penetrate.

Although the Mende traditionally used bitter peppers, leaves or roots to treat cases of *fulu-haisia*, Western medicines that taste bitter are quite acceptable alternatives. Therefore, although people do take pharmaceutical worm medication that is sold expressly for the purpose, they may take as worm antidotes any pills that are bitter. Indeed, it is likely that many people actually avoid the large sugary worm tablets manufactured by Western companies for children, preferring to use any pills that are bitter. And, as with fever, the preferred pills for treating worms and diarrhea are white, not because of the color *per se*, but because white is associated with bitter pills, which kills worms. For sore throats, coughs, or tuberculosis, anything harsh smelling such as Mentholatum or harsh tasting such as certain kinds of cough drops are said also to kill worms.

Blood

The Mende say that blood is vital yet difficult, if not impossible, to replace. It may be lost through injuries or debilitating sicknesses, which are said to make the blood dirty or drain it. Blood is also lost during bouts with *fulu-haisia*, which are said to suck it, or by having blood samples and donations drawn at the hospital. The Mende view with great fear the attempts of hospital workers to induce them to give blood. Hospital workers in Sierra Leone – as in much of West Africa – report enormous difficulties in getting people to donate blood, even for the use of close relatives who may be dying.

Nonetheless, people do try to replace or purify blood. Traditionally, the Mende have relied on certain foods and medicinal substances. Greens such as spinach and potato leaves used in sauces are commonly used for these purposes. However, palm oil is the favorite remedy for dirty or inadequate blood. In fact, young children may be fed only soft rice and palm oil until well into their second year: rice develops the body, while palm oil makes it produce blood. Unfortunately, though, some of the foods that might be richest in iron are seen as potent medicines that are too strong for a young child's stomach. Although Western trained medical personnel try to urge mothers to feed greens to their children, they report limited success in this.

Like the traditional Mende remedy, Western medicines that are red in color are widely used to build or purify the blood. Hence, all the red medicines in the display packet were said to be suitable for blood. These included iron tablets, diuretics, pile tablets to relieve constipation, and folic acid to promote healthy pregnancies. In fact, the man trained in hematology in Nigeria for hospital work, now working as an independent drug seller, expressed great interest in obtaining the investigator's bottle of One-A-Day vitamins, even after he was told there was no iron in the tablets, because he knew how eagerly his customers would buy red medicines. When asked if people would actually take pills of different colors, the salesman replied that they probably would, but if they did not feel better after a day or two from the effects of what they perceived as blood problems, they would probably abandon these other pills. However, they would be more likely to stick to red pills.

Besides these remedies in the packet, people pointed out that there are other red remedies for blood problems. Blood tonics manufactured abroad that are red or brown in color – undoubtedly, intentionally – are extremely popular. Other blood remedies include red soft drinks and even orange-colored drinks such as orange Fanta. A favorite remedy is Guiness Stout, a beer that is deep reddish brown in color. Several of the Mende hospital workers were said to recommend it 'for blood'. Such uses question standard assumptions of the Westerner that what is a non-nutritious luxury item will be viewed by local people in the same ways. The researcher commonly offered Mende visitors soft drinks such as Coke, Sprite, and Fanta, However, one man finally explained that although her guests chose politely among these, most would really prefer Vimto, a bright red carbonated beverage, for health reasons, or brown Guiness Stout, neither of which she bought because she disliked their taste.

Health maintenance

Besides treating symptoms of diseases, the Mende are concerned with maintaining a healthy body, and view foods such as greens and palm oil as useful for this. They are also impressed by the health maintenance potentials of Western medicines. Several different medicines can help maintain good health. According to one old woman, small orange junior aspirin can give good health and strength, and can be taken every day or whenever extra strength is needed.

The Mende particularly value capsules for preventive medicine. As noted above, they perceive capsules as highly potent. Moreover, capsules with different plastic colors on either end are seen as particularly efficacious because the two colors suggest that the capsules contain different kinds of medicine. A secondary school graduate reported he took a 'red and black' capsule, which he knew to be the antibiotic Ampicillin, after a hard day of work on the farm, to prevent a sore body the next day and to wake refreshed for the next day of work. They are also used on a more regular basis. A clinic worker reported that because capsules are seen as a potent Western medicine, they are highly valued as daily preventive medicines. Hence, people with wealth often buy capsules – which usually happen to be antibiotics – and take them once a day, like vitamins. The clinic worker explained:

Some [people], when they come to sell their coffee or cocoa, they buy these drugs . . . as a sort of [prevention] kit. They take it every morning, like antibiotics. They make it as something usual. Every morning, when they are eating their food, they will take one. They feel it is prevention against further sicknesses. In fact, some people say that is why you [white, foreign] people live longer: because every day you eat (take) medicine . . . They say every *pumoi* [white, foreign person] has got a small stock of drugs which they use every day. This makes them active and strong.

IMPLICATIONS FOR DEVELOPMENT AND INTERNATIONAL HEALTH

Our description of Mende uses of Western pharmaceuticals is not meant to imply that the Mende use these medicines only according to how taste, color, and so on fit into their traditional notions of sickness and disease. Aside from their own decisions about self-medication of pharmaceuticals purchased from local vendors, it is true that people take medicinal remedies as prescribed by health personnel. However, if they feel no improvements within a short time, they will more quickly abandon the treatment if the nature of the pharmaceuticals does not meet their cultural notions of the etiology of a sickness and the kinds of medications appropriate to treat it, than if the treatment does coincide with their beliefs.

These ways in which the Mende sometimes reinterpret and use Western medicines pose public health problems, because the ways in which they extend their cultural beliefs about sicknesses and remedies to Western medicines can cause harmful physiological consequences. As many Mende people themselves pointed out on occasion, the misuse of Western medicines has sometimes led to problems larger than the original malady.

A particularly fearsome aspect of the availability of drugs is that many of the drugs that Western countries ban or strictly control are exported with few restrictions to countries like Sierra Leone. Drugs such as chloramphenicol, lincocin, Depo-Provera, and clioquinol (which a local pharmacist reported was widely available over-the-counter) can cause neuropathy, blood disorders, or death, even under the best of medical supervision. Given the conditions under which even prescription drugs in Sierra Leone become available to people, the consequences may be serious indeed. Nor is the danger simply from inappropriate use of these highly toxic drugs. Commonly available drugs in Sierra Leone have specific contraindications and can have serious side effects when taken indiscriminately.[8] Overdosage, the widespread desire for apparently potent 'injections', the use of multiple doses of widely available medicines for abortifacients, and so on, have resulted in toxic poisoning, infection, and sometimes death.

A Sierra Leone clinic attendant reported that instead of taking a recommended dosage of aspirin every four hours for fever, many of his patients took it every hour, resulting later in gastric ulcers. A prominent man died soon after taking eight pills of unknown origin during self-medication for an illness. Another reported that his six-month-old daughter got sick with malaria when she was taken with her mother to visit the mother's village. The mother and the relatives gave her 'all sorts of tablets' and had the local dresser inject her. She died, the father reported, probably because of all this medication: not because of the malaria. Not surprisingly, children suffer many of the more serious consequences of inappropriate uses of pharmaceuticals. Several cases of toxic poisoning and death were reported among children who were fed whole packages, or even bottles, of worm medicine. Nor are the Mende alone in such mistakes. A hospital supervisor noted that the baby of a local Lebanese merchant family had died because its mother had dosed it with many different drugs on her shelf, attempting to cure it of what was initially a minor ailment.

There may also be a large number of disguised cases of pharmacogenic maladies. During an interview with a local nurse about the uses of Western medicines, an elderly woman came in with her small grandson who was suffering from a severe case of malaria. Perhaps because she was being queried about the subject, the nurse probed the grandmother and discovered that she had given the boy a large dose of worm medicine to cure his stomach ache, but this had apparently made him sicker, further depressing his appetite and weakening his resistance. This, in turn, intensified and prolonged his malaria.

These findings have important implications for development professionals and for medical practitioners seeking to apply their knowledge and introduce pharmaceuticals into societies that have cultural assumptions that differ widely from their own. However, the reinterpretation of pharmaceuticals has implications for our own society, because practitioners may assume too readily that they and their patients share understandings and assumptions about illnesses and how medicines affect them. It is probable that people in all societies engage to a greater or lesser extent in reinterpreting medications they have borrowed from other people or especially from other societies. For example, American patients' occasional 'noncompliance' with physicians' treatment instructions have been a persistent concern to medical sociology. In fact, a group of nurses at a US hospital, hearing the results of the Mende study, declared that they repeatedly encountered patients in their own wards who refused medications or asked for other kinds of treatments the nurses were convinced had no medical basis.

Another public health problem that can result from the reinterpretation of medicines is that the effectiveness of certain drugs for the outside world depends on sparing yet thorough application. Nonessential use of antibiotics as well as using antibiotics in dosages that are too small to effectively kill the target bacteria encourage the development of resistant dangerous bacterial strains, and lower the effectiveness of antibiotics, a problem of growing international concern.[9]

Limiting access to medications would be only a partial solution, as would attempting to regulate multinational drug firms. We also feel that color-coding medications to correspond with local beliefs about the purposes of certain drugs might help. But there would be enormous packaging and marketing difficulties involved in tailoring drugs to many different cultural areas. Moreover, even if the drugs were color-coded, this system would be even more susceptible to 'counterfeiting' by salesmen who sought to boost sales by presenting a drug of a particular color as efficacious for a disease for which it has no pharmaceutical relevance.

Certainly the misuse of drugs and efforts to procure drugs from ignorant pill traders are inseparable from an inability to afford medications in licensed urban pharmacies. More basically, reliable information is either unavailable to local people or impossible for them to distinguish from unreliable information. Hence, we cannot blame the victims for their own misfortune.

Paradoxically, it is easy to see the differences between our own and other people's cultural beliefs when examining material items that are very different from our own. But it is harder to appreciate the strength of those different traditional beliefs when the materials they involve originate from our own culture, and have been reinterpreted in another cultural setting. Such items or ideas may be imbued with completely different assumptions and meanings, but because of our familiarity with the objects, we fail to perceive this shift in meaning that has taken place. Yet in the case of drugs, the potential consequences of this reinterpretation are enormous.

ACKNOWLEDGEMENTS

We thank the following people for their assistance during the research as well as helpful comments on earlier drafts: Hermann Dornieden-Müller, Renata Dornieden-Müller, Evelyn Early, Sister Hilary Lyons, Carol MacCormack, William Murphy, Robert Welsch, and Sjaak van der Geest.

A previous version of this paper appeared in Social Science and Medicine, Vol. 21(3), pp. 273-282. We are grateful to the editors for permission to revise and publish this version.

NOTES

1. The paper is based on Bledsoe's field investigations in Sierra Leone.
2. The Mende usually attribute serious illnesses and death to God or to evil spiritual beings. Because of space limitations, a thorough analysis of the social and spiritual nature of Mende beliefs and behavior cannot be attempted. Also in this context, although we refer to 'the' Mende, regional variations and exposure to different cultural influences obviously affect people's belief systems. Hence, even within the population we refer to, there were obviously some differences of opinion on medical matters. Nonetheless, we have tried to distill the most salient beliefs for the present purposes.

3. Self-medication is usually the first and most common form of treatment, yet it is one of the least studied. Research has focused on behaviors in clinical situations, whereas few systematic observations have been made on the role and prevalence of self-medication by sick people: for example, asking family members, friends, and neighbors for medical advice, and evaluating the effects of self-treatment and therapy from different sources. See, however, Arya and Bennet (1974), A. Young (1976), Taussig (1978), Cosminsky and Scrimshaw 1980, Kleinman (1980), Nichter (1980), Ferguson (1981), J. Young (1981), Melrose (1982), Silverman et al. (1982), van der Geest (1982a), Good (1977), and Kroeger (1983). Attention to self-medication and the acquisition of pharmaceuticals in developing nations provides information on the networks and resources for health care outside 'official' channels; the roles of innovators and cultural interpreters that drug peddlers, 'injection doctors', and others play; and, so on.
4. For related discussions, see Simmons (1955), Gonzales (1966), Press (1971), and Logan (1973).
5. However, hospital personnel themselves do not always adhere strictly to Western notions of moral practice. The same hospital employees who were evicted from town created 'private practices' out of the opportunities created by their jobs. When they arrived in a village, they stipulated that patients pay an additional 20 cents as a 'service fee' for the expenses of running the clinic and the vehicle that had brought them, all of which the mission hospital had already paid for. They also prescribed more medicines than were necessary to patients, and overcharged for their medicines, thus pocketing the profits. Although it can be argued that local hospital personnel are poorly paid and need to make a bit of money through 'private practice', some become quite wealthy by local standards from the 'private practices' they create.
6. Although the investigator sometimes inserted the small paper container that came with the medicine, usually the medicines had no labels on them, other than what was printed on individual tablets by the manufacturer. But often it was not important what the package said about how to use the pill; most people had been using pills without package labels, and usually professed familiarity with the medicines displayed.
7. Maitai et al. (1981) report that chloroquin is responsible for over half the fatal poisonings in Kenya.
8. We have not dealt here with the problem of drug 'dumping' by Western pharmaceutical companies, in which drugs that are banned or limited in Western countries are sold abroad with few or no warning labels (e.g., Silverman et al. 1982).
9. One example of this is when approximately 20,000 Mexicans died from typhoid because of the bacteria's built up resistance to chloramphenicol, which had been used indiscriminately in the area (see also Mintz 1979). Moreover, studies of the widespread use of antibiotics in animal feed in the US have found that bacteria resistant to a particular drug in one animal can transmit that resistance (through fecal and other contamination) to the same bacteria which are drug sensitive in another animal (Schell 1984). This means that drug resistance is communicable in the same way as the infectious disease the drug is designed to cure.

REFERENCES

Alland, A., Jr.
    1970 Adaptation in Cultural Evolution: An Approach to Medical Anthropology. New York: Columbia University Press.

Arya, O. P. and Bennett, F. J.
    1974 The Use and Misuse of Medicines in Relation to some Sexually Transmitted Diseases in Uganda. *In* The Use and Abuse of Drugs and Chemicals in Tropical Africa. A. F. Bagshaw et al., (eds.) Nairobi: East African Literature Bureau.

Cosminsky, S. and Scrimshaw, M.

1980 Medical Pluralism on a Guatemalan Plantation. Social Science and Medicine 14B: 267–278.
Etkin, N. L. and Ross, P. J.
1982 Food as Medicine and Medicine as Food; an Adaptive Framework for the Interpretation of Plant Utilization among the Hausa of Northern Nigeria. Social Science and Medicine 16: 1559–1573.
Ferguson, A. E.
1981 Commercial Pharmaceutical Medicine and Medicalization: a Case study from El Salvador. Culture, Medicine, and Psychiatry 5: 105–134.
Foster, G.
1976 Medical Anthropology and International Health Planning. Medical Anthropology Newsletter 7: 12–18.
Gonzales, N. S.
1966 Health Behavior in Cross-cultural Perspective: a Guatemalan Example. Human Organization 25: 122–125.
Good, B.
1977 The Heart of What's the Matter: the Semantics of Illness in Iran. Culture, Medicine, and Psychiatry 1: 25–58.
Good, B. and Good, M. J.
1981 The Meaning of Symptoms: a Cultural Hermeneutic Model for Clinical Practice. In The Relevance of Social Science for Medicine. L. Eisenberg and A. Kleinmen, (eds.) pp. 165–96. Dordrecht, Holland: D. Reidel Publishing Company.
Gunaratne, V. T. H.
1980 Bringing Down Drug Costs: the Sri Lankan Example. World Health Forum 1: 117–122.
Herskovits, M. J.
1948 Man and His Works. New York: Knopf.
Janzen, J.
1978 The Quest for Therapy in Lower Zaire. Berkeley: University of California Press.
Kleinman, A.
1980 Patients and Healers in the Context of Culture. Berkeley: University of California Press.
Kroeger, A.
1983 Anthropological and Socio-medical Health Care Research in Developing Countries. Social Science and Medicine 17: 147–161.
Logan, M. H.
1973 Humoral Medicine in Guatemala and Peasant Acceptance of Modern Medicine. Human Organization 32: 385–395.
MacCormack, C. P.
1984 Primary Health Care in Sierra Leone. Social Science and Medicine 19: 199–208.
Maitai, C. K. et al.
1981 Self Medication in Management of Minor Health Problems in Kenya. East African Medical Journal 58: 593–600.
Melrose, D.
1982 Bitter Pills: Medicines and the Third World. Oxford: Oxfam.
Mintz, M.
1979 The Dump that Killed Twenty Thousand. Mother Jones, Nov.
Mitchell M. F.
1983 Popular Medical Concepts and their Impact on Drug Use. Western Journal of Medicine 139: 841–847.
Nichter, M.

1980 The Layperson's Perception of Medicine as Perspective into the Utilization of Multiple Therapy Systems in the Indian Context. Social Science and Medicine 14B: 225–33.

Press, I.
   1971 The Urban Curandero. American Anthropologist 73: 741–756.

Rivers, W. H. R.
   1924 Medicine, Magic and Religion. New York: Harcourt Brace.

Romanucci-Ross, L.
   1969 The Hierarchy of Resort in Curative Practices: the Admiralty Islands, Melanesia. Journal of Health and Social Behavior 10: 201–209.

Schell, O.
   1984 A Kind of Commons. New Yorker Magazine. April 23, pp. 50–73 and April 30, 1984, pp. 50–79.

Silverman, M. et al.
   1982 Prescriptions for Death: the Drugging of The Third World. Berkeley: University of California Press.

Simmons, O.
   1955 Popular and Modern Medicine in Mestizo Communities of Coastal Peru and Chile. Journal of American Folklore 68: 57–71.

Taussig, M.
   1978 Nutrition, Development, and Foreign Aid: a Case Study of U.S. Directed Health Care in a Colombian Plantation Zone. International Journal of Health Service 8: 101–21.

Van der Geest, S.
   1982a The Efficiency of Inefficiency: Medicine Distribution in South Cameroon. Social Science and Medicine 16: 2145–2153.
   1982b The Illegal Distribution of Western Medicines in Developing Countries: Pharmacists, Drug Pedlars, Injection Doctors and Others: a Bibliographic Exploration. Medical Anthropology 6: 197–219.
   1984 Anthropology and Pharmaceuticals in Developing Countries. Medical Anthropology Quarterly 15: 59–62, 87–90.

Wasunna, A. E. O. and Wasunna, M.
   1974 Drugs in the Wrong Hands. In The Use and Abuse of Drugs and Chemicals in Tropical Africa. A. F. Bagshaw et al., (eds.) pp. 161–163. Nairobi: East African Literature Bureau.

Wellin, E.
   1977 Theoretical Orientations in Medical Anthropology: Continuity and Change over the past Half Century. In Culture, Disease and Healing. D. Landy, (ed.) pp. 47–58. New York: Macmillan.

Welsch, R. L.
   1983 Traditional Medicine and Western Medical Options among the Ningerum of Papua New Guinea. In The Anthropology of Medicine: From Culture to Method. L. Romanucci-Ross et al., (eds.) pp. 32–53. New York: Praeger.

WHO
   1978 The Promotion and Development of Traditional Medicine: A Report of a WHO Meeting. WHO Technical Report Series 622. Geneva: World Health Organization.

Young, A.
   1976 Internalizing and Externalizing Medical Belief Systems: an Ethiopian Example. Social Science and Medicine 10: 147–56.

Young, J.
   1981 Medical Choice in a Mexican Village. New Brunswick, N.J.: Rutgers University Press.

CULTURAL MEANINGS OF ORAL REHYDRATION SALTS IN JAMAICA

ORAL REHYDRATION THERAPY AND ORAL REHYDRATION SALTS

Oral rehydration therapy is the replacement of fluids lost in diarrhea with drinks of water in which have been dissolved glucose (sugar), sodium bicarbonate, and sodium and potassium chlorides. Pharmaceutical firms manufacture packets of these chemicals. The packets contain mostly sugar, but they are usually labelled as Oral Rehydration Salts. The therapy was first used on a large scale among refugees from the 1971 India-Pakistan war where deaths from diarrhea dropped from 30% to 1% (Elliot and Cutting 1980a).

In the first issue of *Diarrhea Dialogue* the question of whether guardians of young children should be taught to make a simplified solution from home supplies of sugar and salt, or whether manufactured packets should be promoted, was raised. One author suggested that 'packeted chemicals are regarded more highly as "medicine" while salt and sugar are regarded as food' (Hirschorn 1980). Hirschorn, assuming the manufactured packet approach, calculated that the cost of supplying packets for all episodes of children's diarrhea in developing countries might be $300 million per year, so as a cost-cutting alternative packets might be given only to children coming to a health centre (10–50% of cases), or only to children under age three (Hirschorn 1980: 5). From the beginning of world-wide promotion of oral rehydration therapy there was a tension pulling in opposite directions. The appropriate technology group who did so much to promote this therapy were interested in saving lives by spreading knowledge of this new simple technology through the use of simple language (in translation where appropriate) and pictures. They wanted primary health care workers to teach guardians of young children (Elliot and Cutting 1980b). The other approach was professional. Qualified people should prescribe a carefully quality-controlled remedy through recognized health facilities. Ironically, today in industries countries where few children die of diarrhea the packets can easily be bought over-the-counter, but in many developing countries they are not available in shops.

In point of fact, for the vast majority of diarrhea cases dehydration is mild and any sweet drink, cereal gruel or soup made by the guardian is adequate therapy (Elliot and Cutting 1987: 1). Only in the small minority of severely dehydrated children are the precise balance and concentrations of sugar and salts important as an alternative to intravenous rehydration in hospital. The original purpose in promoting this appropriate technology was that it be so widely available that an ever decreasing number of children reached the severely dehydrated stage where a quality-controlled drink of balanced electrolytes was needed.

PRIMARY HEALTH CARE AND DIARRHEA MANAGEMENT IN JAMAICA

Jamaica has been in the forefront of the primary health care movement. Before primary health care workers had been identified in the WHO/UNICEF declaration of 1978 as essential for equitable health coverage, Jamaica had trained Rural Medical Aides and deployed them with nurses in small health centres all over the island. By 1981 D. Ashley had published an important paper on the success of oral rehydration therapy for Jamaican children with acute diarrhea (Ashley 1981). In the pediatric hospital in Kingston the number of children admitted for intravenous rehydration dropped dramatically as guardians with sick children were taught oral rehydration skills in an outpatient clinic. Oral rehydration clinics have now been extended to some parish hospitals and all categories of health workers should be able to teach guardians the therapy.

METHODS

This chapter results from a multi-disciplinary evaluation of the Jamaican national health service done with the collaboration of the Ministry of Health. It recommends ways in which a good health service, given severe economic constraints, might become even better.

For this study on diarrhea we had conversational interviews with 263 guardians of sick children. Interviews were guided by a brief schedule of open-ended questions augmented by some coded questions for factual information. Guardians were interviewed in three categories. One group were guardians who had brought a sick child to the diarrhea clinics in Kingston and St. Ann's Bay hospitals. The children had been examined by a doctor and the guardians had received a talk from a nurse on what oral rehydration therapy was and how to use it. Guardians were interviewed as they sat in clinic feeding the liquid by spoon into the sick child. A second group were guardians who had brought a child for either preventive or curative care to a rural health center in Black River, Lacovia, Newell, Newmarket, Appleton, Bohemia, Borobridge, Clarkson Ville, Alexandria, Brownstown and Lime Hall. Since clinic attenders were a self-selected sample that could introduce bias, we interviewed a further 156 adults at random in fruit and vegetable markets in Kingston, Black River, Newmarket and Brownstown. As many guardians in the health center and market samples did not have a child currently sick with diarrhea we asked what they had done the last time one of their children had diarrhea. The hospital and health center sample was 44% urban and 56% rural. Of the guardians, 89% were mothers and most of the others were relatives. Guardians ranged in age from 15 to above 45; 63% were between the ages of 20 and 29. Eighty-three percent had between 7 and 12 years of school (39% had 10-12 years). Sick children ranged in age from infancy to 10; 72% were under the age of 24 months. We used housing as a proxy for social class and found that 65% of the diarrhea children live in very crowded conditions, in houses with twice as many residents as rooms in the house. In the random sample of people interviewed in markets only 54% lived in very crowded conditions.

GUARDIANS' STRATEGIES FOR MANAGING CHILD'S DIARRHEA

We sought to understand the threshold of symptoms that stimulate a guardian to seek help for a child with diarrhea. We asked the guardian of sick children in hospital clinics and health centers how they knew this current episode of diarrhea was serious. Increased frequency of bowel movements was most salient, but vomiting, fever and mucous ('cold') in the feces were also important (Table I).

TABLE I
Signs of serious diarrhea (multiple responses).

Criteria	Number	%
Frequent	155	21
Watery	89	12
Mucous	107	14
Blood	27	4
Vomit	125	17
Fever	107	15
Worms	16	2
Persistent	51	7
Cold symptoms*	34	5
Wasted (dry)	19	3
Other	6	1
Total	736	101

* May include mucous in the feces.

Guardians were asked what they had done first to help their child. Most tried to cope with the condition at home (Table 2). We assume that most diarrheas are successfully managed at home, but in this sample of clinic attenders we saw more seriously ill children. Only 1% gave the therapy officially recommended in nurses' health talks: drinks made from packets of Oral Rehydration Salts. Of the other remedies most are very good for a mildly dehydrated child, and the water from the center of a coconut is an excellent rehydration fluid. We were puzzled by the ten mothers (2%) who said they used to give coconut water or mint tea, but now they gave 'salt water'. Strong salt solutions draw water into the gut, away from vital organs, and can kill an already dehydrated child.

TABLE II
First treatment (multiple responses – some remedies used in combination)

Treatment	Number	%
Glucose and water	49	9
Coconut water	89	17
Fruit juice or fruit syrup and water	81	16
Mint tea*	45	9
Other bush tea	28	5
Home sugar and salt solution**	28	5
ORS Packet	6	1
Breast milk	27	5
Bottle milk	10	2
Parched flour porridge	9	2
Corn meal porridge	37	7
Laxative	5	1
Other OTC medicine (e.g. Infant Preservative)	18	3
Salt water	10	2
Private doctor	3	1
Health centre	21	4
Hospital out-patients	26	5
Other	25	5
Total	517	99

* Usually blackmint or peppermint with sugar added.
** Sometimes with fresh lime juice.

Sixty-eight percent (179) of the guardians said they sought a second treatment for their child (Table III). Forty-nine percent (128) said they sought a third treatment. Of those, only 1% tried a further home remedy (laxative) and the rest went to a private doctor (10%) or to a government clinic or hospital outpatient facility. Five percent (14) sought a fourth treatment. Only one went to a private doctor and the rest went to clinic or hospital outpatients.

To get some idea of the proportion that may have had chronic diarrhea we asked how long the child had had symptoms (Table IV). If we consider those having diarrhea symptoms for more than ten days as having chronic diarrhea (Ross Institute 1983), about a quarter of this sample had chronic diarrhea. They were being treated with an oral rehydration drink which is not adequate treatment. For example, those with giardiasis should have had a fecal sample examined, followed by the correct drug to kill the gut parasite causing the diarrhea. None of the mothers of children with chronic diarrhea said that the doctor had asked for a fecal sample after examining the child and taking a case history. We can only speculate on reasons why: (1) doctors were

TABLE III
Second treatment mothers tried

Treatment	Number	%
Came to place of interview (e.g. Bustamante Hospital)	78	43
Went to other clinic or health centre	74	41
Went to a private doctor	17	9
Went to other practitioner	6	3
Gave coconut water	2	1
Gave fruit juice	1	½
Gave home sugar-salt solution	1	½
Gave corn meal porridge	1	½
Gave laxative	1	½
Gave other OTC medicine	1	½
Total	182*	99½

* Three mothers reported giving a different home drink of porridge *and* going to clinic or hospital.

TABLE IV
Interval between onset of symptoms and this interview

Interval	Number	%
1 day	65	25
2 days	40	15
3 days	29	11
4 days	33	13
5 days	13	5
6 days	5	2
7–13 days	48	18
14–20 days	8	3
21–27 days	4	1
28–89 days	3	1
90 days or more	3	1
Not recorded	9	3
Total	263	100

screening too many children to take case histories; (2) laboratory services were overstretched given the health budget; or (3) 'faith' in Oral Rehydration Salts as the new wonder drug for diarrhea.

GUARDIANS' CONCEPTS OF DIARRHEA: CAUSE AND CURE

As a protective device to help guardians explain their concepts of child physiology, we gave them an outline of a child's body and asked prompting questions to encourage them to draw the digestive system as they visualized

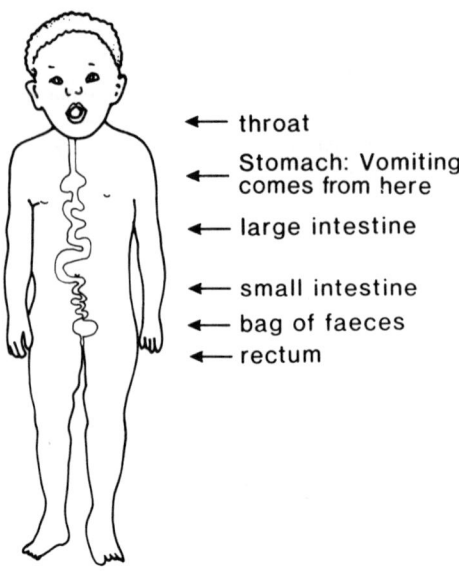

Fig. 1

it, and explain what happened when the child had diarrhea. Some made quite detailed drawings (Figure I), but most were not very interested in the digestive system. This was in marked contrast to a parallel study where we asked women to draw their reproductive system and explain its function and the action of contraceptives (MacCormack and Draper 1987). There was far more emotional involvement with the reproductive system. Pregnancy produces a child that enables a woman to grow in social power, whereas diarrhea produces only waste. However, both systems are similar in that people were concerned that matter move freely through them. Constipation was a greater concern than diarrhea, and some guardians used a laxative during diarrhea to help the system flush out the 'bad do do' so the body could cleanse itself and become healthy. Similarly, women do not like contraceptives that stopped or diminished regular menstrual flow, so that they could not 'see their health'. Some used alaxative to help clear out a burden of contraceptive pills threatening to 'block them up'. Although a few women thought of the reproductive and digestive systems as a single system, we concluded that most thought of them as being in a metaphoric relationship with each other.

Diarrhea is referred to as 'running belly' in Jamaica, and as women drew, they explained that 'the belly gets loose and the food comes through too fast'. Most drew a round stomach (Figure 2) where food is ground. Some said diarrhea resulted when food 'wasn't digested; it went through the belly without being adequately ground'. But others said it 'gets ground up too soft and runs out of the belly'. When we asked what caused diarrhea in a

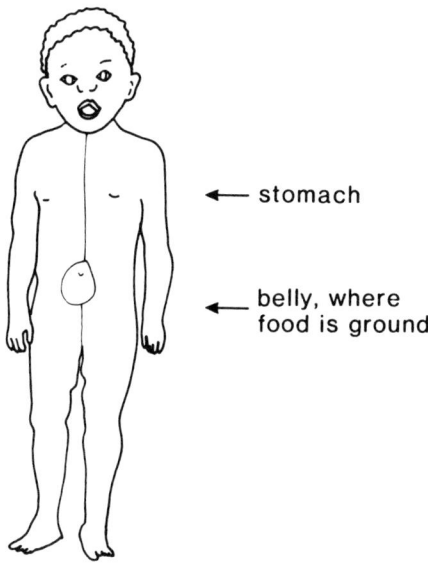

Fig. 2

questionnaire format we received more medical-type answers: such as dirt and germs (Table V).

This Table compares responses from the hospital/clinic sample with responses from people interviewed in fruit and vegetable markets. The latter seemed more aware of the hazards of polluted water and spoiled food, whereas mothers in clinics had much to say about 'teething water'. Most of the sick children were of teething age. In all developing countries, episodes of diarrhea tend to peak in the post-weaning months when children are teething. The Jamaican explanation was that teething children drool, food mixes with too much saliva ('teething water') and therefore runs through the body too quickly. One mother explained that Oral Rehydration Salts made the body 'still', so that the food did not run through too quickly.

CONCEPTS OF ORAL REHYDRATION SALTS

Part way through this diarrhea study we realized that some guardians were understanding the nature of oral rehydration salts in a way that was not intended by the health service. The study design was flexible enough to include questions about 'salts' in the latter part of the study. Table VI gives responses to an open-ended question about how the therapy worked. This question was asked only to guardians sitting in a diarrhea out-patients clinic, spooning rehydration fluid into their sick child immediately after hearing a health talk from the nurse on oral rehydration therapy. If we consider 'puts

TABLE V
Mother's explanation for cause of diarrhea: clinic and community samples compared

Cause	Clinic No	Sample %	Community No	Sample %
Dirty things (including feeding bottles and feeds)	132	39	62	27
Germs or viruses	50	15	42	19
Food that is spoiled or doesn't agree with you	37	11	47	22
Swallowing teething saliva	66	20	10	5
Cold on the stomach (exacerbated by hunger or measles)	11	3	9	4
Polluted water	0	0	28	13
Worms	4	1	0	0
Other	36	11	3	1
Don't know	0	0	16	7
Total	336	100	217	100

TABLE VI
The meaning of salt in oral rehydration salts

Meaning	Number	%
Laxative (similar to Epsom Salts etc.)	30	19
Medicine	23	15
Similar to food salt	14	9
Other (e.g. electrolyte)	8	5
Don't know	80	52
Total	155	100

back strength or substance' and 'replaces fluid' as correct answers, less than a third of the guardians were understanding the message that had just been given to them.

When we realised the importance of such remarks as 'I used to give coconut water but now I give salt water', we began to ask systematically what mothers thought was in the packets labelled Oral Rehydration Salts.

Guardians who thought of Oral Rehydration Salts as laxative salts explained that it 'cleans out the belly', it 'loosens her, and the runs out the cold (mucous)', or 'cleans out the child to get rid of the germs'. Pharmacies gave much shelf space to a wide range of laxative salts and a newspaper article advised parents to give their children a mild preparation with Epsom Salts (magnesium sulfate), Andrews Salts (magnesium sulfate) or Glaubers Salts (sodium sulfate) rather than harsh castor oil. The idea of purging with salts for a 'wash out' even in cholera therapy has been popular in Jamaica at least since the last century when Mary Seacole treated cholera patients with laxative salts and plenty of good food in the Caribbean, and in the Crimean War (Seacole 1984).

For at least a century many Jamaicans have treated diarrhea in two stages: first a 'wash out', then plenty of liquid and food, especially mint tea and foods such as porridge and banana that 'make the do do firm'. Recently Oral Rehydration Therapy took on, for many people, both functions at once. One guardian explained 'it cleans her stomach, it prevents her from getting worse by feeding her, it prevents her from getting too dry, it is like Andrews Salts, not strong like Epsom Salts'. Others said 'it kills germs', 'stops vomiting', or 'makes his do do f.rm'. One said 'this new salt water makes them thirsty and so they drink more which is good'.

We asked a sub-sample of guardians attending clinic with a sick child what kind of salt the packets contained. Some did not know what kind it was, some said it was like laxative salts, a few said it was the same as cooking salt and an equal number said it was different but did not know how it differed. Two said it was a special salt that 'helps to fight germs', and one said it was medicine 'like oxygen or glucose' (see Table VI).

We found it disconcerting to learn that some guardians stopped giving children coconut water which is an adequate natural rehydration fluid containing electrolytes and enough sugar to speed their absorption. We were especially concerned to learn that the 'cost' of sitting in clinic for half a day to be given only one packet of Oral Rehydration Salts was too expensive in time, child care and transport, so mothers were buying look-alike packets of Epsom Salts done up locally by pharmacies. But lest we conclude that the 'natural' treatment with coconut water is 'good' folk knowledge which was led astray by allopathic professional and commercial pharmacies, we must know how guardians thought about 'natural' treatments. Four guardians said quite explicitly that coconut water 'washed out the system beginning with the stomach'.

What no one ever asks is what the child likes to drink when it is sick with diarrhea. Most guardians said that the child likes breasmilk best. Coconut water, or sweet lime juice or other fruit juices and sweet blackmint or peppermint tea were also popular. Some mentioned Pepsicola or other bottled soda drinks. One said quite explicitly that the child liked *anything* better than the oral rehydration fluid. Might fruit flavourings be added to the packets, as they are in Britain? What are breastfeeding mothers to make of the clinic nurse's message to 'resume half-strength milk feeds? Nurses were quite explicit in warning guardians never to give traditional remedies again; they must only use the packets mixed with water.

ANTHROPOLOGICAL ANALYSIS

Economics

Much of the primary health care planning literature is concerned with scarcity of essential drugs, and the equitable distribution of drugs that are available (see for example WHO 1983, 1987; Mamdani and Walker 1985). These are morally correct concerns, but they reflect an excessively 'top-down' perspective which ignores useful self-help remedies people already use. If Jamaicans were encouraged to continue using coconut water, mint tea with sugar, and other popular remedies for mild dehydration from diarrhea, Jamaica would not have to use foreign exchange for packets imported from Switzerland. This 'essential drug' makes even less economic sense when we realize that the Jamaican economy has been based on sugar production for centuries, and the main ingredient in the imported packets is sugar.

Bilateral and international aid agencies have given much effort and money to finance packet production and publicize their use. They are reluctant to let private firms cash in on this created market. Therefore, many developing countries only have packets that come into the country through aid agency channels, and are distributed through the national health service. This restricts supply and ignore costs to the guardian in travelling to a clinic and waiting in a queue most of the day. In this Jamaica case study, 63% (165) of guardians spent between 1 and 10 Jamaican dollars in transport to come to the clinic, 57% (149) spent between 1 and 10 dollars on snack food as they travelled and waited, and others lost their wage for the day or had to pay for a minder to look after other children left at home. Given these costs there was quite a good economic reason for the guardian to nip into a nearby shop and buy a look-alike packet of Epsom Salts instead.

Sociology of Professional Medicine

Doctors and nurses spoke to us of mothers giving children 'bush teas' that damaged the liver or kidneys. So far as we know, no one has ever asked the mothers what they did give. In our survey, when a herbal tea was mentioned we asked exactly what herb, and quite safe mints were overwhelmingly preferred. The tea was served with sugar and perhaps a little salt could be added to make a good rehydration fluid. However, nurses were instructed to tell guardians never to use traditional remedies. Nurses validated their professional status by using words such as 'electrolytes' when explaining the therapy, and it is therefore not surprising that 52% of the guardians who had just heard the nurse's talk did not have any idea – correct or incorrect – of what the 'salts' were. We were observing the process of mystification that guarantees secrecy which underpins professional status. People were being told never to use the traditional therapies they understood and could make at home, and therefore were being made dependent upon medical services provided by 'qualified' personnel who commanded secret knowledge. Nurses, especially, enjoyed the power of 'gatekeepers' to the therapy, sometimes berating the guardians in a verbal show of power.

Symbolic meaning of 'salts'

The packets were presented as medicine. One nurse commented to us: 'if they knew it was just sugar and salt they wouldn't come to the clinic'. They were also presented as a precise, quality-controlled chemical formula. Perhaps even doctors were swayed by this symbolic presentation to the extent that they did not attempt more appropriate therapies for children with chronic diarrhea.

Guardians who travelled by public transport or walked to clinics carrying a sick child, and sat for hours waiting to be seen, substituted this ordeal for the calm caring attention they might have given the child at home. To some extent, 'medicine' was substituted for comforting. Also lost was the possible placebo effect of mint tea that 'warms the stomach' or tea made from gizzard, the chicken's strong stomach, that stops a child from vomitting. Traditional remedies fitted with indigenous ideas of hot and cold. They also gave optimism through the analogical transfer of qualities in nature (strong gizzard) to the sick child (queasy stomach). We were observing a shift from this holistic understanding of diarrhea to a medicalized response.

REFERENCES

Ashley, D.
    1981 'Oral Rehydration Therapy in the Management of Acute Gastroenteritis in Children in Jamaica.' *In* Acute Enteric Infections in Children, ed. by T. Holme, J. Holmgren, M. Merson and R. Mollby, pp. 389–394. Elsevier/North Holland: Biomedical Press.
Elliot, K. and Cutting, W. A. M.
    1980a 'Diarrhea Need Not Kill', Diarrhea Dialogue, Issue 1: 1
    1980b 'Agents of Change' Diarrhea Dialogue, Issue 3: 1
    1987 'Time for Action' Diarrhea Dialogue, Issue 28· 1
Hirschorn, N.
    1980 'Issues in Oral Rehydration' Diarrhea Dialogue, Issue 1: 4.
MacCormack C. and Draper, A.
    1986 'Social and Cognitive Aspects of Female Sexuality in Jamaica'. *In* The Cultural Construction of Sexuality ed. by P. Caplan, pp. 143–165. London: Tavistock.
Mamdani, M. and Walker, G.
    1985 Essential Drugs and Developing Countries: A Review and Selected Annotated Bibliography. E. P. C. Publication No. 8. London: London School of Hygiene and Tropical Medicine.
Ross Institute
    1983 Coping with Diarrhea. London: London School of Hygiene and Tropical Medicine.

Seacole, M.
   1984   The Wonderful Adventures of Mrs. Seacole in Many Lands (reprint). London: Falling Wall Press.

World Health Organisation
   1983   Report of a Workshop on Essential Drugs. Action Programme on Essential Drugs, OAP/84.2 Geneva: WHO.

RICHARD BURGHART

PENICILLIN: AN ANCIENT AYURVEDIC MEDICINE

In the early history of its commercial and administrative presence on the Indian subcontinent British servants of the East India Company treated native healers of south Asia with as much respect as they treated English physicians. In part, this respect was provoked by the European belief that certain illnesses were caused by the airs and water of a country (Jones 1967); hence treatment of such illnesses required the diagnostic skill as well as pharmacological knowledge of the physicians of that country, in this case the hakims and vaidyas. To this personal view must be added the Company's considerable interest in the discovery of useful native plants, such as medicines and dyes, the knowledge of which was published in the early issues of Asiaticke Researches, later the Journal of the Asiatic Society. The journal, and indeed the Society, was founded by a group of Englishmen, trained in the classics, who developed an interest in the ancient languages and civilizations of the Indian subcontinent. Even though in some cases these Englishmen, dubbed Orientalists, might have thought the Brahmans of Bengal to be poorly qualified, indeed degenerate, inheritors of a glorious civilization, this did not diminish their respect for the civilization itself. 'Native doctors' were attached to regiments and civil stations; and ayurvedic medicine was taught in conjunction with English medicine at the Calcutta Sanskrit College, founded with Company support in 1824 (Gupta 1976: 369).

Although Orientalism remained a force in Company, and later British, administration of the subcontinent, by the mid-1830s their influence was eclipsed by the Anglicists who sought to administer India on rational, utilitarian lines. The dominance of the Anglicist faction and extension of government policy to medical education and public health together with the rise of scientific medicine and its professionalization in Great Britain formed a matrix of specifically imperial relations constraining the practice of medicine on the subcontinent. In the context of these relations some Ayurvedic practitioners began to professionalize their ranks, taking their healing tradition to be the medical science of India, equivalent in value to western medicine. The outcome was the emergence of two institutional forms of ayurveda on the subcontinent: modern ayurveda with its state-supported colleges, professional registers and massive pharmaceutical interests; and traditional Ayurveda practised by Brahmanical families in which the healer is both doctor and compounder, deriving his livelihood not from a fee system but from the medicines which he prepares and sells to his clients in the locality.

Throughout the late colonial period one important influence of Western bio-medicine upon Ayurveda was the practice of *injeksan cikitsa*, or injection therapy. There is no precedent for injection therapy in the classic formulation of Ayurveda, yet injections have virtually become a standard mode of treatment. Indeed, even ayurvedic pharmaceutical firms now prepare medicines in a form suitable for injection. Bhatia et al. (1975) in a survey of hakims and vaidyas in three states of northern India reported that 87% of the healers in their sample possessed syringes and needles. In spite of being subject to government regulation, the practice of injection therapy has, for the most part, remained beyond the control of the state. Most pharmaceutical items – if they are available at the chemists – can be purchased over-the-counter without prescription. Hence patients appear at chemists not only with valid prescriptions written by medically qualified doctors, but also with others sorts of prescription written on scraps of paper by traditional healers, locally known as 'rustic doctors'. Instructional booklets describing injection procedures and detailing drugs available for injection can be purchased at roadside bookstalls in the market towns of upper India and Nepal. The supply of materials is matched by the demand. Indeed, injection therapy has been so readily taken up by south Asian peoples that it seems as if a niche awaited it, long before the method was discovered and the materials actually arrived from the West. The aim of this paper is to describe how injection therapy has been integrated within Ayurveda. I shall focus on the clinical practice of one particular healer, under whom I trained in 1984–85.

THE QUALITIES OF PENICILLIN

The clinic of Sri Hari Narayan Misra Vaidya operates out of his household in a small provincial town of northern Mithila. Vaidya Ji is Brahman by caste; and his patriline have been vaidyas in the Bhojpur region of Western Bihar for several generations. He was the first in his family to be sent for training at the Ayurvedic Medical College in Patna, Bihar. Thus he is a product of both ayurvedic traditions: the modern, professional one and a Brahmanical family tradition. Following his graduation he set up practice in a village just across the Bihar frontier in the Nepalese Tarai. Throughout the 1950s he built up a clientele and, by his own account, incorporated within his practice the pharmacopoeia and diagnostic procedures of Western bio-medicine. The nearest hospital at that time was some thirty miles away, or nearly a day's journey by bullock cart and train; hence his clinic was a popular one as a primary medical resort for the peasants of the region. In the 1960s, however, he began to react against Western medicine, developing his own Ayurvedic patent medicines which he sought to market in the region. One particular tonic, called *abal pippli*, was a sovereign remedy. In his sales campaign he claimed that this medicine was like an arrow from Lord Ram's quiver – capable of destroying all enemies. He also stressed to prospective buyers that his tonic was made from the herbs of the countryside, not from foreign products; and in piques of pride he challenged Western-trained doctors, with their foreign medicines, to come up with anything better. In the early 1970s, in order to market his sovereign medicine more effectively, he quit the village and re-located his clinic in the nearby market town.

Although Vaidya Ji has weeded most bio-medical products from his dispensory, he still keeps two on hand: penicillin and coramine. The latter, of course, is essential in cases of allergy to penicillin, but it would seem that its use is more generally as a 'life-giving' medicine, capable of reviving from near-death those who have collapsed from heart attacks and asthmatic attacks. In fact, coramine was infrequently used. Penicillin injections, however, were commonplace, being used in the treatment of serious infections, skin ulcerations and for pulmonary tuberculosis and 'asthma' (including tropical pulmonary eosinophilia. Vaidya Ji also applied penicillin externally in the treatment of abscesses and conjunctivitis. This does not exhaust the range of illnesses for which he believed it could be used, but it does exhaust much of what I saw at his clinic.

The quality of penicillin was largely understood in terms of its ability to heat and dry the body. Hence its efficacy in the treatment of certain pulmonary illnesses. The lungs are thought to be a cool, damp organ and various pulmonary illnesses, such as asthma, tuberculosis and 'cough' result from the immoderate presence of these two qualities. The term 'asthma' includes tropical pulmonary eosiniphilia, and the term 'cough might include an early misdiagnosis of tuberculosis. In its advanced stages, however, pulmonary tuberculosis would be recognized as a separate illness. As for 'coughs', there are both hot, dry coughs (e.g. whooping cough) and cool, wet ones (e.g. chronic bronchitis and pulmonary tuberculosis). It is only the latter kind which concern us here. Penicillin, by virtue of its heating and drying qualities, restores equilibrium, to overly wet and cool lungs; hence its efficacy in the treatment of asthma, eosiniphila, tuberculosis and bronchitis.

In addition to its heating and drying qualities, penicillin was also thought to possess an antiseptic power which was apparent in the procedures which Vaidya Ji used in giving injections. He knew that boiling the syringe and needle in water for fifteen minutes was standard practice among Western doctors, but he adopted a different procedure. Attaching the hypodermic needle to the syringe, he draws clean water from the neighborhood tubewell. After rinsing both syringe and needle in the water, he breaks off the cap of the distilled water ampoule, inserts the needle and draws up distilled water to rinse again the inside of the syringe. After ejecting this water, he draws fresh, distilled water into the syringe which he then ejects into the phial of penicillin powder. After shaking the phial vigorously, he draws the liquid penicillin into the syringe. Next several drops of penicillin are expressed onto a tuft of cotton wool, which is rubbed on both the exterior of the needle as well as the site of injection. Vaidya Ji explained to me that since penicillin was powerful enough to destroy all illnesses in the body, it was also powerful enough to purify the needle and syringe of contamination. From a Western, clinical point of view one can see that penicillin takes on the antiseptic function of alcohol. From a Hindu point of view penicillin takes on the purifying function of Ganges water; that is, it is not only pure but it is also capable of purifying all other waters, without itself becoming impure.

The power of penicillin was also seen to stem from its being injected directly into the body, bypassing thereby the preliminary stages in the body's assimilation of food. Here it must be explained that in ayurveda the body is integrated by a seven-stage digestion process. The process begins in the stomach, likened to a cooking pot, which digests the food, converting it to a nourishing juice which is then transferred to the liver. In the liver the juice undergoes a further 'digestion', transforming it into blood. The heart drives the blood to the extremities of the body where it is digested further and transformed into flesh. The flesh is subsequently transformed into fat, the fat into bone, bone into marrow and marrow into 'seed'. The seed – that is semen or menstrual blood – is the source not only of one's fecundity but also of one's mental and physical energy. The progressive refinement of food entails the production of a dross at each stage: excrement, urine, bile, etc. Health and longevity entail as much the accumulation of energy as it does the elimination of this dross.

To my knowledge, Vaidya Ji never prescribed penicillin tablets; the implication here is that the tablet form of medicine is 'cooked' in the stomach and then transferred to the liver where it passes into the blood; and thence to the heart from where it is pumped to the extremities of the body to nourish the flesh. The first two stages of digestion last at least one full day; hence there is considerable delay before the medicine can begin to combat the illness. Injections, however, shortcut the entire process, although at the cost of disenabling the body to assimilate the poweful and potentially dangerous qualities of the drug. Hence the notion that weak, vulnerable people, and especially infants, should be given tablets rather than injections. In practice, however, even children who had not yet been fully weaned, received injections at his clinic.

Vaidya Ji also applied liquid penicillin externally to skin ulcerations, boils and abscesses. He reasoned that if penicillin, administered intramuscularly, was effective in destroying illness then it should be effective when applied superficially to the infected areas and the surrounding tissue. Skin has the power to absorb liquid penicillin, which it does through the pores into the hair follicles and then into the flesh. In cases of serious infection Vaidya Ji would give an injection then, with whatever penicillin remained in the syringe, he re-moistened the tuft of cotton wool and dabbed it on the infected area. Similarly a batch of penicillin might be made up in order to treat conjunctivitis. A few drops administered in the corner of the eye morning and evening would clear up the illness in the matter of a day or two. This external use of penicillin was a discovery for which Vaidya Ji took credit. He claimed that he had extended the frontiers of medical knowledge beyond that known by Western doctors.

THE HEALER AS A SOURCE OF MEDICATION

It is generally recognised in upper India and Nepal that injection therapy is derivative of bio-medicine – or what is referred to locally as 'English medicine' or 'Doctor medicine'. These two terms do not designate so much a system of healing as a source (be it 'England' or 'Doctors') of medication. Many ayurvedic healers, including Vaidya Ji, say that they eschew injection therapy; yet their patients demand it and they know that without patients they cannot survive. In rural areas, at least, local autonomy from bio-medicine would spell bankruptcy for the healers. But in taking up injection therapy, Ayurvedic healers run the risk of being seen to have no professional identity or integrity. They become mere dispensers of Western medicines. Vaidya Ji's discomfort in this was considerable. Our discussions about injection therapy were always marked by ambivalence, prevarication, hypocrisy and braggadocio.

In comparing his own ayurvedic practice with allopathy, Vaidya Ji had recourse to two key metaphors. The first was that of illness being a tree, the various limbs of which are different illnesses. Allopathy, with its concept of specific causation, attacks one illness at a time by sawing off its limb. But illnesses are often inter-related; or they may be manifestations of an underlying problem. In either case cutting of the limb is no more effective than pruning a tree. After a short while the limb sprouts new and more vigorous growth. By contrast, ayurvedic medicine goes straight to the roots; and by attacking the problem at root, all the sick limbs wither and die. The second metaphor conceives of illness in an administrative mould. Here illnesses are seen to exist at ministerial level – to each ministry a disease. One can treat each ministry of its specific disease; alternatively one can treat the problem at the level of kingship, thereby ridding all ministries of illness. According to Vaidya Ji allopathy offers ministerial cures; ayurveda royal ones. Whether as a 'root' cure or as a 'sovereign' cure, ayurveda is superior to allopathy which, from Vaidya Ji's point of view, neither gets to the 'bottom' of an illness nor does it get on 'top' of it. It treats the symptoms; it brings relief to the patient, but it does not achieve a lasting cure.

Vaidya Ji himself was very much interested in sovereign cures; and he believed that *abal pippli*, which he had developed twenty years earlier in the village, was a sovereign cure. An impression of his claims about the virtues of *abal pippli* can be gained from a promotional leaflet which he distributed in the region in the 1970s.

Sri Patuh

MAKE NATIONAL INDUSTRY STRONG BY USING MEDICINES
MANUFACTURED IN YOUR OWN COUNTRY

Abal Pippli is beneficial for everyone: children, youth, the elderly and pregnant women

When water drips from your nose and eyes, your head aches; your entire body is tight, a dry cough pierces your throat and you have a fever of 98.5 to 99 F. then make use of *Abal pippli* together with several *tulsi* leaves [*Ocimum basilicum*] or with honey or tea or in hot milk or water; otherwise in betel leaf or in anything at hand. Within only two hours whatever ailment, pain, sickness, or distress that you feel will be far removed. If you complain of asthma or cough, then take two or three doses daily of *Abal Pippli* with honey or *Sitopaladi Curn* [a cough medicine] and at once – like the arrow of Ram [capable of killing all enemies] – it will restore you to good health. This Pippli has been prepared from a mixture of gold, ground coral, ground borax and mother-of-pearl ashes together with peepli ashes. *Abal Pippli* can be taken at anytime by anyone; it may also be taken with homeopathic, yunani, and English medicine. Women from their third or fourth month of pregnancy, who take daily a portion in honey or hot cow's milk will make their child strong. When you leave your village on a journey, take a few packets with you. Consume a portion every day and your body will put on weight. Because this medicine contains ashes of coral and mother-of-pearl, there is abundant calcium in each portion. This is a scientific medicine which nourishes at the time of one's daily meal the unborn infant, small children and adults. *Abal Pippli* is your very own medicine sold near at hand and available in shops.

Virtues: By means of this medicine small children will find rest from every kind of illness, such as sudden fever, jaundice, diarrhea, vomiting, cough, whooping cough, pneumonia, malnutrition (including rickets), illness at the time of cutting teeth, etc.

Dosage: Give a one-quarter dose to babies from one to three months old, a half portion from three months to one year. From one to fifty years of age give a full portion three times daily. For children medical opinion recommends that the medicine be mixed with honey or breastmilk and given three times daily.

Note: *Abal Pippli* has been praised by thousands of people and doctors. For you also this medicine will perform a reliable service in removing the above-mentioned illnesses. In the Rasayana Sala [the name of Vaidya Ji's clinic] even incurable illnesses receive medical treatment and many people have benefited from this. The test of this has already taken place. The Rasayana Sala has been serving the people for the last forty years, just as much as it continues to serve them today.

From my discussions with Vaidya Ji I learned that two notions of sovereignty informed his cure-all. First, he referred to an alchemical notion of pure and base substances; the pure ones having transformative powers *vis-à-vis* the base. Among the ingredients of *abal pippli* is the sovereign metal gold, the power of which for Vaidya Ji seemed equal to its price. Second, the medicine includes numerous ingredients, each of which acts as a cure for a specific complaint: ashes of iron to cure anaemia, ashes of calcium to cure rickets, etc. Hence his medicine was a sovereign cure because it contained within it the totality of all specific cures. To revert to the administrative metaphor: *abal pippli* contains within it not only a medicine for each ministry but also a royal medicine which has power of agency over all ministries.

Yet in penicillin Vaidya Ji seems to have met his match. The virtue of this powerful antibiotic is described in a booklet entitled *The Modern Allopathic*

Injection Book, which I purchased from a bookstall a few hundred yards down the road from Vaidya Ji's clinic. The book, written in Hindi and aimed at a rural readership, lists 307 drugs and tonics and explains the procedures of intradermal, subcutaneous, intramuscular, intravenous and intraspinal injection. The passage on penicillin reads (pp. 67–8):

Penicillin

Dose According to personal experience and the needs of the ill person.
Virtues This medicine is useful in hundreds of illnesses: in particular, urinary diseases, pneumonia, blood-poisoning, inflammation of the bones and marrow, recurrent fever, ear inflammations, puerperal fever, venereal disease, syphilis, rheumatic fever, boils and abscesses, skin diseases, eye illnesses, encephalitis, gas gangrene, pulmonary infections, degenerate heart disease, broken bones, smallpox, tuberculosis, and cough.
Caution This medicine is as dangerous as it is beneficial.
 1. Always store in a cool place.
 2. Always mix with distilled water or with normal saline.
 3. Always use a syringe which has been boiled in water.
 4. Clean one's hands before administering the injection.
Side-effects Loose bowels, vomiting, increase in fever, skin rashes, giddiness.
Remedy Stop penicillin treatment. Inject coramine or anthisan. Inject benadryl.
Warning Do not inject intravenously by mistake. Only inject intramuscularly.

The passage goes on to list twenty-five varieties of penicillin available. Readers will recognize the names from their Hindi transliterations: *proken penisilin, pronapen, dyumesilin, elprosin, kris phor, seklopen, peniken, yusilin, hostasilin, omnosilin, repidosilin*, etc. From the passage there can be no doubt that penicillin is a sovereign cure, and that coramine, like the royal guru, comes to the king's rescue from an even higher source of authority.

Vaidya Ji thought that *abal pippli* was as effective as penicillin, but he recognized that it worked differently and more slowly. *Abal pippli* was absorbed through the digestive system; penicillin went straight to the flesh. Thus the power of penicillin could not be controlled. If by mistake one injected penicillin intravenously, the medicine would go straight to the heart; the patient would be almost dead by the time one got the coramine injection ready. But even without mistakes, penicillin was dangerous because the patient might already be in a weakened condition, unable to tolerate such a strong medicine. The dosage for *abal pippli*, though, is lower; and it takes more than a week for its effect to build up within the body. But each case of illness has urgency; and these days, admitted Vaidya Ji, patients want a rapid treatment. They ask for penicillin; and in some cases they even buy it themselves before coming to the clinic. One man, who had devised his own cure for asthma, simply arrived with ten phials of penicillin – five for the left arm and five for the right. All he wanted from Vaidya Ji was to give one injection per day to 'dry' out his asthma. Another man arrived with several phials of penicillin in treatment of gonnorhea. Colloquially penicillin is known as the *barah lakhwala*, or the 'twelve hundred thousand' [medicine], after the number of international units of penicillin mentioned on the label on the phial. From his mates he had heard that the *barah lakhwala* destroys this illness; and that's what he asked for at the chemists, who duly supplied it to him on the strength of his self-prescription. He was unable to understand the label on the phial because it was written in English, but he could read the numbers 1,200,000 and hence reassure himself that he had been sold the right medicine.

INJECTION THERAPY AND THE AUTONOMY OF INDIGENOUS HEALING

In spite of the institutional differences between modern, professional Ayurveda and local traditional practice, there is an overall unity in Ayurveda and this unity is seen by its practitioners to stem from their textual sources. All Ayurvedic practitioners subscribe to the knowledge contained in two key texts, the *Carak Samhita* and *Susruta Samhita*, which were compiled roughly two millennia ago. These texts do not, however, have quite the same relevance for practitioners as they might in a positivistic medical science. In Hindu society traditional knowledge is divine, both in its conception and its mode of perpetuation. Celestial gods conceived this knowledge and revealed it millennia ago to mundane gods – namely members of the Brahman caste. Such knowledge includes not only 'religious' knowledge, such as the codes of practice and ascetic self-discipline, but also the arts and sciences, such as grammar, dance, architecture, astrology, music and 'longevity' otherwise called Ayurveda. It follows that the members of various Brahmanical schools did not see themselves as discoverers of medical knowledge, for the knowledge pre-existed their awareness of it. Indeed, according to Ayurvedic historiography, the gods knew the science of medicine even before the appearance of illness in the world. Later on in the cosmic cycle, when illness spread and life expectancy decreased, several Brahman sages appealed to Indra – King of the Gods – for instructions in this knowledge. Out of compassion for mankind, Indra transmitted this knowledge to the sages. This was subsequently compiled by Caraka, Susruta and others. Thus Carak and Susruta were neither authors of texts nor discoverers of knowledge, but recorders of texts and interpreters of knowledge.

From the point of view of the exponents of tradition, the texts were not based on practice; indeed they preceded clinical practice. Practice is not derivative of text; rather each serves to inform the other. Hence the Brahmanical tradition is not a rigid one, and over the centuries prestigeous alien medical traditions have been assimilated within Ayurvedic practice. In the same way that certain aspects of yunani medicine were assimilated within Ayurveda during the Mughal period (Leslie 1976; Hume 1977) so also in the modern period certain notions and practices of allopathy have been taken up by Ayurvedic healers (Tabor 1981). The question of Greek influence during the ancient period is, in some respects, a more hotly contested issue (see

Kutumbiah 1962). Neither the traditional practitioner of ayurveda, believing in its divine origin, nor the modern practitioner, believing in its national origin, would want to accept alien – and indeed 'barbarian' – influence at the outset of his tradition. But regardless of how the question of ancient influences is settled, it would seem that Ayurveda has perpetuated itself throughout history by interpreting its textual basis in the light of current practices – be they prestigious alien forms of medicine or simply the health practices of the regional culture of patient and practitioner.

In view of patient demand Vaidya Ji was unable to eliminate penicillin from his practice; nor was he able to persuade his patients to take abal pippli instead. All that he could do was to interpret penicillin in such a way that it become a part of Ayurveda. Here he had recourse to the tree methaphor of medical pluralism. There are four major branches of medicine – modern Ayurveda, allopathy, homeopathy and 'natural therapy' (*prakrticikitsa*) – but there is only one trunk. Since the *Carak Samhita* and *Susruta Samhita* are the source of all medical knowledge, then allopathic knowledge must also come from that source. Thus all forms of medicine have their roots in ancient ayurveda. Similarly the pharmacopoeia of 'Doctor' medicine must also come from Ayurveda. The so-called discoveries of western science appear as discoveries simply because Europeans have forgotten the original source of their knowledge. 'The more forgetful they are', said Vaidya Ji, 'the more wondrous appear their discoveries'. Coramine is not 'new'; it is simply the English word for the Ayurvedic elixir *makardhvaj*. As for penicillin, Vaidya Ji was less certain of its Ayurvedic equivalent. In this respect he complained that his task was not made easy for him by the use of brand names by Western pharmaceutical companies. He saw this as deceit, hiding the 'real' name by which the substance could be known. But Vaidya Ji was certain that penicillin must have been known to Indra, when he instructed Brahmanical sages millions of years ago. Hence he believed that penicillin was as much part of Ayurveda as it is of 'Doctor' medicine. Modern Ayurveda and allopathy are merely different limbs of the same tree, modern Ayurveda being somewhat superior by virtue of its having a better memory of its ancestor.

In returning to the divine source and traditional mode of all medical knowledge, Vaidya Ji asserted the autonomy and centrality of his own therapeutic practice. In this way he was able to integrate bio-medicine on terms which were reassuring to him, namely his own terms. Yet he knew, and we knew, that the world was not being written up on his terms. The Western-trained doctors in the market town had thriving practices. Some also had large town houses and country estates. Their sons commanded high dowries. But Vaidya Ji lived in a small house in a poor, disreputable neighborhood where his wife struggled to make ends meet. He is a proud man, but his penurious circumstances perpetually remind him of just how marginal his totalizing vision of the world has become.

ACKNOWLEDGEMENT

A somewhat different version of this paper was previously published in *Holistic Medicine* vol. 2 (1987). I am grateful to John Wiley & Sons for permission to reproduce this modified version in the present volume.

REFERENCES

Bhatia, J. C., Dharam Vir, Timmoppaya, A. and Chattari, C. S.
    1975   Traditional Healers and Modern Medicine. Social Science & Medicine 9: 15–22.

Gupta, Brahmananda
    1976   Indigenous Medicine in Nineteenth–and twentieth–century Bengal. *In* Asian Medical Systems. Leslie, C. (ed.) pp. 368–78. Los Angeles & Berkeley: University of California Press.

Hume, J.
    1977   Rival Traditions: Western Medicine and Yunan-i-tibb in the Punjab, 1849–1889. Bulletin of the History of Medicine 51: 214–31.

Jeffery, R.
    1979   Recognizing India's Doctors: the Establishment of Medical Dependency: 1918–1939. Modern Asian Studies 13: 301–26.
    1982   Policies towards indigenous healers in Independent India. Social Science & Medicine 16: 1835–41.

Jones, M. O.
    1967   Climate and Disease: the Traveller Describes America. Bulletin of the History of Medicine 41: 254–66.

'Kokca', Harnarayan.
    Adhunik Elopaithik Injeksan Buk [The Modern Alopathic Injection Book] Delhi: Dehati Pustak Bhandar, n.d.

Kutumbiah, P.
    1962   Ancient Indian Medicine. Madras: Orient Longmans.

Leslie, C.
    1976   The Ambiguities of Medical Revivalism in Modern India. *In* Asian Medical Systems. Leslie, C. (ed.) pp. 356–67 Los Angeles & Berkeley: University of California Press.

Tabor, D.
    1981   Ripe and Unripe: Concepts of Health and Sickness in Ayurvedic Medicine. Social Science & Medicine 15: 439–455.

NINA L. ETKIN

CULTURAL CONSTRUCTIONS OF EFFICACY

INTRODUCTION

Healing should be understood as a process, comprised of stages to which are ascribed different meanings and for which the outcomes expected at each stage of prevention and therapy may vary from one medical system to another. Thus it follows that the efficacy of medical treatments can be properly evaluated only by multidimensional approaches that take into account this processual nature of healing, distinguish among emic and etic criteria that determine efficacy, and comprehend an interrelatedness among the biological and behavioral aspects of healing. The intent of this chapter is to demonstrate the implications of using such an approach, through review of recent literature in the areas of ethnopharmacology[1] and cross-cultural studies in health care. Examples are drawn from the author's research on Hausa (northern Nigerian) indigenous medicine (Etkin 1979, 1980, 1981; Etkin and Ross 1982, 1983) and from selected references.

The following discussion is organized to explore the extent to which efficacy is considered in studies of indigenous medicines, the criteria used in evaluating that effectiveness, and how a biomedical bias in research has distracted researchers from a better comprehension of medical efficacy as a cultural construct that has both biological and behavioral dimensions. Somewhat more emphasis (space) is given the discussion of biomedical bias, insofar as that is clearly one of the most cogent – and more problematic – features of studies of therapeutic and preventive efficacy.

IS EFFICACY IMPORTANT?

Various studies have examined the persistent role of indigenous healers in societies in which the introduction of Western medicine and other forms of culture change have challenged the continued viability of those healers (e.g., Leslie 1980; Elling 1981; Janzen and Feierman 1979; Kroeger 1983; Landy 1977). For the most part these have focused on such variables as: the socio-economic strategies used by healers (Russell 1984); changes in the emphasis of treatment – as, for example, transformation from healing generalists to increasingly specialized healers (Weisberg 1984), or the perception of certain disorders as treatable only by indigenous therapy (Mo 1984); inclusion of traditional healers in primary health care programs (Bloom and Reid 1984; Berman 1984; Oswald 1983); professional rivalries among different categories of healers (Karim 1984); political and economic factors influencing the status and power of healers (McCauley 1984); and ideologic dimensions of disease definition and perception (Finerman 1984; Bastien 1982). Social science research on medical pluralism is thus overwhelmingly concerned with the social and political contexts in which health care choices are made. This exclusive focus on such issues belies the possibility that the continued success of indigenous healers in medically pluralistic contexts is due in part or even primarily to their efficacy.

A few studies do in fact report preference for one medical system or another based on efficacy. For example, Ho and co-workers' (1984) study of health-seeking behavior in culturally pluralistic Singapore cites 'effectiveness' as the principal reason for choosing traditional Chinese medicine and for switching between Western and Chinese healers. In this case 'effectiveness' clearly refers to patient's perceptions, but in this and other such studies the specific *criteria* used to establish that efficacy are not explicated.

DEFINITIONS OF EFFICACY

Differences in medical ideologies notwithstanding, all human societies share a general understanding of medical efficacy as some combination of symptom reduction and other physical and behavioral transformations that indicate restoration of health. But this generalization obscures a wealth of meanings and expectations that are encoded within the complex patterns of medical behaviors that characterize different medical systems. In order to comprehend the diverse uses of indigenous plant medicines and judge the outcomes of such behaviors, it is necessary to clarify what one means by such terms as 'effectiveness', 'therapeutic benefit', 'efficacy', and the like – i.e., to establish what precisely is meant by the contention that something 'works'.

Emic and etic interpretations

Key to consideration of efficacy is the distinction between emic and etic interpretations. The emic (local) perspective is a culture-specific one that is consistent with the ideology of the society under study and that presents health-related (and other) phenomena through reference to indigenous understandings of the universe and the intended outcomes of plant use and related practices. On the other hand the etic (outside) perspective uses concepts and theories that are grounded in some other ideology in order to create a framework on which to project and interpret medical beliefs and behaviors. Reflecting the very nature of the research conducted by western scientists, etic interpretations of indigenous medical practices are informed by a western scientific or biomedical paradigm.

Taking into account emic and etic perspectives, Young (1983: 1208) defines efficacy as 'the perceived capacity of a given practice to affect sickness in some desireable way', with distinctions drawn between: curing, which 'refers to practices which are efficacious *from the point of view of biomedical science*; and healing, which refers to practices which are efficacious *from the point of view of these people [being studied]*' [emphasis in the original]. While this distinction helps to clarify some of the differences, it also implies that Western biomedical and ethnomedical understandings of efficacy cannot be the same. But of course they can be, and to ignore that advances the western stereotyped view that other medical systems are fundamentally 'irrational' and based on the precepts of magic and religion rather than on empirical observation of the biological universe.

Similarly, in their consideration of whether and how indigenous treatments are efficacious, Kleinman and Sung (1979: 8) conclude that biomedicine successfully treats 'disease' (disorders of biological and physiological processes), while indigenous medicines treat 'illness' (secondary, affective and subjective reactions to disease). This view assumes that ethnomedicines have no biological efficacy against 'disease', although a growing literature in ethnopharmacology attests to the fallacy of that presumption.

Plant use and other medical behaviors are effective if they effect or assist in producing the requisite, culturally defined outcomes. By so doing, these actions confirm shared beliefs about the nature of health and illness (Young 1976, 1977), in the same way that the expected outcomes of such western practices as surgery and antibiotic therapy reaffirm belief in biomedicine. It merits note that the failure of a medicine to produce cure or another requisite outcome does not necessarily undermine one's faith in the medical system. Among the Hausa, for example, this is taken as sign that the medicine and the individual were not 'right' (suited) in that particular instance. As do their biomedical counterparts, Hausa practitioners call on alternative diagnoses and/or medicines when preventive and therapeutic efforts fail to yield desired results.

Western biased interpretations obscure these key behavioral dimensions of medical treatment. For the first, pharmacologic evaluations that determine that plant medicines have outcomes different from those considered appropriate by biomedicine are critical of ethnomedical practices. For the second, the ostensible 'failure' of some treatments is generalized to all indigenous medicines, and the subsequent resort to other diagnoses and treatments is deplored, at least as built-in rationale, if not as processual sham. Both of these outlooks have the effect of trivializing nonwestern ideologies and denying the capacity of indigenous populations to observe and act on the outcome of their behaviors.

One of the most formidable obstacles to full comprehension of efficacy and other characteristics of indigenous medical systems is the failure to understand healing as *process*.

Proximate and ultimate outcomes

In its totality, medical treatment should be understood as a complex and processual ordering of biological and behavioral expectations which can to varying degrees be differentiated from one another. Thus, efficacy might mean a number of things, ranging from full symptom remission to some physical sign (e.g., fever, salivation, emesis, etc.) which is interpreted as a requisite *proximate* effect that indicates that the curing/healing *process* is under way and can be expected to proceed to the *ultimate* outcome – i.e., restoration of health with, perhaps, other proximate effects anticipated along the way. In addition to such physical signs, efficacy might lie in determination of who or what caused the illness and why that particular person was affected. All of these different (emic) signs of efficacy – diagnosis, change in physical state, partial remission, full cure – are likely to be differently interpreted and valued in biomedical investigations of efficacy. In order to adequately evaluate efficacy – using either emic or etic criteria – we need to understand cultural expectations and biological outcomes at various stages of the therapeutic process. An examination of indigenous pharmacopoeias sheds further light on such cultural construction of efficacy.

INDIGENOUS PHARMACOPOEIAS

What do the content, size, internal consistency, variability, and potential for change of a given pharmacopoeia *mean*? Does a large and varied herbal pharmacopoeia reflect the skilled elaboration of a broad-based and effective therapeutic regimen, a botanically rich environment, the occurrence and symbolic rendering of many illnesses, the ability of a population to develop numerous effective means of dealing with only a few diseases, a group's dependence on many marginally effective medicines, or some constellation of these (and other) circumstances? Studies of biologic taxonomies inform some of these questions.

Taxonomies are generally considered to reflect how people structure their knowledge of the physical universe, but the specific interpretation of those classifications varies with philosophic or theoretical orientation. Morris (1984) distinguishes among three predominant views in his discussion of folk classifications: (1) Lévi-Strauss (1966) embodies the structuralist approach that perceives folk taxonomies to be the outcome of a group's intellectual, non-pragmatic interaction with their physical universe – a process through which different aspects of culture are symbolically unified. (2) Born of a theoretical tradition in Anglo-Saxon empiricism, ethnoscientists (e.g., Berlin et al. 1974) similarly focus on classificatory terminology, seek universals, and view ethnotaxonomies as intellectual, non-pragmatic perceptions of the biological world. Where structuralists emphasize symbolic logic, ethnoscientists view form and structure as the fundamental classificatory criteria. (3) Different from these two approaches, the utilitarian view stresses serviceability as a key criterion for classification (Morris 1984; Hunn 1982; Alcorn 1981). These (and other) approaches inform our comprehension of indigenous medical systems by advancing an understanding of how different biological and behavioral variables, including efficacy, influence the content and character of herbal pharmacopoeias.

Plant selection

Although ecological variables have been demonstrated to be important in influencing human-plant interactions, for no population studied can the selection of plants be explained merely by the availability and diversity of the ambient flora (Moerman 1979). Analogously, the use of those plants as medicines is not a simple function of epidemiologic patterns (e.g., Davis and Yost 1983; Wilbert 1983). How those plants are selected and used and the intended outcome of that use have direct bearing on questions of efficacy.

While most of the plants that comprise herbal pharmacopoeias are wild species, a good deal can be learned about the criteria used in plant selection from study of the evolutionary development of domesticated and semi-cultivated plants. These are species whose reproduction is a least partly controlled by human agency, a process greatly accelerated and intensified since the advent of agriculture. Color, size, potency, texture, taste, availability, toxicity, susceptibility to disease, storage, pharmacologic activity, and other characteristics have resulted from interactions among cultural and biological phenomena in such a way that these plants represent a distillation of desired traits. Thus, understanding the dynamics of such developments sheds light on how human populations identify, select, and maintain different plant characteristics. A number of ethnobotanical and anthropological studies have incorporated such questions into their study of food crops. (e.g., Brush et al. 1981; Harlan 1975, 1976; Rindos 1984; van Zeist and Casparie 1984), but little research of this nature has been applied to plants used as medicines. (See Johns [1986] for an interesting combination of both uses.)

Despite admonishments regarding the paucity of detailed information about the features of plant use that can affect therapeutic outcome (e.g., Croom 1983), works published in such journals as *Lloydia, Journal of Natural Products, Planta Medica*, and *Journal of Crude Drug Research* – and to a lesser extent *Economic Botany*, and the *Journal of Ethnopharmacology* – often report results of pharmacologic analyses devoid of cultural context or with mere mention that the plants under investigation are 'used in folk medicine' or 'used for intestinal disorders', without knowledge of what the specific expectations of such uses are – i.e., mode of use, (preparation, dose, etc.), expected influences on prevention, proximate outcome, symptom abatement, and/or cure. One can deduce from the titles of some such works that the analyses were inspired by folk tradition – e.g., '. . . Screening of

Saudi Medicinal Plants' (Al-Yahya et al. 1984), 'Traditional Medicinal Plants of Thailand' (Mukhopadhyay et al. 1983) – but these still lack the relevant behavioral data with which to develop informed judgements of efficacy.

The intended use of a plant may be encoded in its name, as in case of plants called by the disease they are used to treat. For example, *Guiera senegalensis* is called 'sabara' in Hausa, as is one of the diseases (skin sores) that it is used to treat. Similarly, *Glaucium oxylobum*, *Hypericum lanuginosum*, *Marcurialis annua*, and *Ceterach officinarum* are called 'wound's herb' in Israeli folk medicine (Dafni et al. 1984). Crosscultural comparisons reveal that such descriptive or functional names are in many cases the same or similar in culturally and geographically disparate populations, a phenomenon that some researchers use (at a low level of confidence) as 'confirmation' of that plant's efficacy (American Herbal Pharmacology Delegation 1975: 68; Ortiz de Montellano 1975; Lewis and Elvin-Lewis 1977). But it is not clear from such names *how* that plant is expected to affect that particular disease process, and it is entirely plausible that different populations use the same plant for the same disease but to effect different outcome. More information regarding expectation is revealed by plants named for their anticipated activity – e.g., the Paraguay name 'anestesia' (anaesthesia) for *Ottonia frutescens* which is taken to reduce the pain of sore throat and toothache (Makapugay et al. 1983).

Throughout the world medicinal (and other) plant use is influenced by various humoral theories of disease in which disease etiologies are ascribed to imbalances, prevention takes the form of maintaining balance, and therapy is designed to restore balance. The idioms of contrasting symbolic qualities that inform these theories include hot-cold, sweet-bitter, sweet-sour, wet-dry, clean-poison, yin-yang, and others. Bastien's (1981, 1983, 1985) symbolically rich accounts of the Qollahuayan (Bolivia) pharmacopoeia illustrate well such interrelations between ethnopharmacology and ethnophysiology. The Qollahuaya are informed by a physiologic model that perceives the body as a 'humoral system characterized by a muscular-skeletal framework and conduits through which air, blood, feces, milk, sweat, and phlegm flow' (1983: 99). Consistent with this model, medical treatment involves: maintenance and repair of the supporting framework; assurance of flow of the primary humors – fat, blood, air, and water; and regular cleaning of the conduits to avoid or reduce the toxic accumulation of the secondary humors – phlegm, sweat, gas, urine, feces, and bile. The formulation of medicines is a metaphor for this body – e.g., in the preparation of decoctions and infusions the medicinal properties are solubilized and dispersed in the water, just as consumption of these preparations ensures the transfer of those properties via the stomach to the blood.[2]

Meaning and efficacy are afforded through the symbolic manipulation of these binary oppositions, but for most of these constructs, the establishment of an efficacy that is consistent with biomedical criteria is neither possible nor particularly meaningful. For example, in Ramanamurthy's (1969) effort to determine whether the 'hot-cold' classification of Indian plants has 'any reasonable explanation' (p. 190), he compared plants of both categories on such criteria as nutrient (protein, calorie, etc.) content and post-consumption urine values for pH, urea nitrogen, and minerals. He also elicited from study participants 'subjective feeling[s] of burning eyes, burning micturation and a feeling of warmth all over the body . . .' Methodologically flawed in any case, this study implies that such classification can be understood devoid of cultural context and that one can make sense of such phenomena by reference to biomedical concept and theory.

In other studies, McCullough and McCullough (1974) and Logan (1972) have shown that maintenance of 'hot-cold' balance in Mexican and Guatemalan populations can be described as adaptive by the criteria of biomedicine. This overlap between indigenous and biomedical paradigms is interesting, but one should avoid the mistake of conflating biomedical and ethnomedical understandings. In the case of McCullough and McCullough's work, the maintenance of electrolyte balance and the avoidance of dehydration that apparently result from 'hot-cold' balancing behaviors are not conceptually analogous to maintaining an emically defined balance between those two symbolic constructs; and even the regulation of physical temperature that occurs as a result of balancing behaviors is not the same as the symbolic manipulation of the 'hot' and 'cold' qualities (that have the same name as, but a different reality from, a hot and cold that can be measured by thermometer). In the case of Logan's study, maintenance of dietary nutrient variability through use of a wide range of foods in order to maintain balance is not conceptually analogous to manipulation of symbolic 'hot' and 'cold'. Similarly, Ahern's (1975) study of ethnodietetics and medicine in Taiwan notes that 'hot' foods tend to be viscous, oily, or of animal origin, and they are considered to be the most nutritious. Consumed in order to build the body's resources and on social occasions, their viscosity and nutritive value are a metaphor for physical and social cohesion and growth. The biomedical efficacy of these food-related behaviors is implied insofar as protein is generally 'good for growth' and the consumption of high protein foods on social occasions may serve to redistribute protein among a broader population than what might otherwise afford such foods. But again, although there is more conceptual overlap in this case, the understandings of efficacy that are encoded in these ethno- and biomedical models are different.

Researchers commonly invoke the Doctrine of Signatures to explain the selection and use of plant medicines in populations throughout the world. For example, the Hausa explicitly cite color as the criterion for use of yellow *Cochlospermum tinctorium* in treatment of a symptom complex for which the principal diagnostic indicator is jaundice and which biomedicine recognizes as hepatitis. Dafni et al. (1984) report the same use in Israel folk medicine for the yellow extracts of *Rhamnus alaternus* and *Ecbalium elaterium*. Similarly, the nomadic Turkana (Kenya) use a yellow product from *Vahlia viscosa* for jaundice, with both plant and illness termed 'longyang' (yellow) (Morgan 1981: 101). Analogously, for Hausa and other medicines, plants of phallic shape are used as aphrodisiacs, Native Americans use red-sapped *Sanguinaria canadensis* and red-rooted *Phaseolus* spp. as hemostatics and to treat blood disorders, while plants with multi-lobed leaves are used in the treatment of liver disease (Moerman 1977; Nabhan et al. 1980; Lewis and Elvin-Lewis 1977).

In other cases the physical attributes of a plant are associated with certain uses. The Hausa avail themselves of strong smelling plants to contend with witches and spirits (e.g., *Allium* spp., *Zingiber officinale, Eugenia caryophyllata*), using the sweet smelling plants to appease them and the foul ones to prevent their coming or to chase them away. Davis and Yost (1983) report similar associations in the use of aromatic plants (*Guatteria, Siparuma, Renealmia*, and *Philodendron* spp.) by the Waorani (Ecuador). By another association, *Ficus iteophylla* is used in Hausa medicines to prevent witches from causing disease, the expectation being that the witch will be overcome with a choking cough resulting in death, in the same way that this plant grows on and kills other plants.

While western interpretations frequently dismiss such medical behaviors as 'merely symbolic', it is important to note that the mnemonic identification of medicinal plants may be related to empirical observations of activity and physiologic outcome. Delaveau (1981), for example, contends that the use of red plant substances for skin disorders may advance healing in view of the presence of red quinones which have antimicrobial and hemostatic activities. The Doctrine of Signatures in any case cannot explain all uses of a given plant – e.g., those yellow- and red-producing plants noted above are used as well for other disorders in which the color association does not hold. The persistent highlighting of this Doctrine and invoking sympathetic magic as explanation may reflect more the inability of Western researchers to otherwise 'make sense' of plant selection than it does the reason for that selection.

In other cases selection includes also, or instead, choice for a particular activity. For example, Australian Aborigines distinguish at least two varieties of *Duboisia hopwoodii*: the nonaromatic variety has as its principal alkaloid toxic nornicotine and is used as a poison in animal trapping; the aromatic variety (containing the aromatic metanicotine) contains nicotine as its principal alkaloid and its various uses are consistent with the properties of that alkaloid (Watson et al. 1983). With different outcomes expected, in different healing episodes or as part of a single healing process, a quid prepared from the leaves and terminal stem of the aromatic variety is chewed as a stimulant to mitigate the effects of physical stress, and in larger doses as an analgesic in preparation for painful initiation rites. While Watson and co-workers propose that these observations suggest that the criteria for selection are 'nicotine as the major alkaloid, a low nornicotine content and the presence of metanicotine' (1983: 309), a more accurate interpretation is that the selection criteria are the *effects* of the relative concentrations of these constituents: analgesia in high dose and stimulation (due to the presence of high nicotine levels), the absence of toxicity (low nornicotine concentration), and aromaticity (from metanicotine). While the intent and outcomes of ethno- and biomedical behaviors may be identical, the former cannot be explained with reference to 'alkaloids' and comparable language of biomedicine.

Plant selection and processual healing

The selection of medicinal plants for one or another color, smell, activity. etc. may be directed at one or more culturally patterned stages of a preventive or therapeutic process. For many medical systems, and for a wide variety of disorders, one of the requisite proximate effects is some indication that disease causing entities (cold, dirt, spirits, etc.) leave the body. In Hausa medicine, treatment for gastro-intestinal disorders includes the administration of plant medicines to induce purgation, emesis, diuresis, and other tangible signs of disease egress, followed later by medicines taken for the ultimate effects which should be stomachic, costive, emollient, and antispasmodic (Etkin and Ross 1982, 1983). Similarly, Green (1985 reports the use of plant medicines to effect emesis or purgation in the treatment of some forms of diarrhea in Swaziland. This is consistent with a disease model that understands diarrhea as caused by the accumulation of foods unsuited for one's digestive system, and it finds parallels in the medical systems of Bangladesh (Shahid et al. 1983), Honduras (Kendall et al. 1984), New Mexico Zuni (Camazine and Bye 1980), Mexican Americans (Kay 1977), Huastec (Mexico) (Dominquez and Alcorn 1985), and others.

One of the proximate effects that the Hausa expect in the process of treating infected wounds is the expulsion of 'dirt' (in the general sense of something unclean, causing illness). For the initial stages of wound treatment plants are deliberately chosen for caustic, irritating, and other qualities which induce bleeding and suppuration, a practice likely to be misjudged by biomedical criteria as 'only exacerbating' the problem. In later stages of wound treatment the expected outcomes are hemostasis, reduction of inflammation and swelling, and scar formation. Similarly, in Taiwanese medicine 'clean' plants are used to wash wounds in order to draw out poisons and, metaphorically, to remove unfriendly spirits from the social group (Ahern 1975).

In Bangladesh *Azadirachta indica* and *Lagenaria vulgaris* are applied externally to promote rash eruption; and *A. indica* and *Momordica charantia* are taken internally so that the rash erupts on the skin rather than on the intestinal walls (Shahid et al. 1983). In this and analogous examples (e.g., Axton 1975), loose stools and mucus are signs of disease egress. Similarly, the Hausa treatments for measles, chicken pox, and other rashes include the consumption of plant preparations to hasten the eruption of the rash from within the body (e.g., *Bauhinia reticulata, Centaurea calcitrapa*), external application of these and other plants to reduce the rash (e.g., *Guiera senegalensis, Citrus* spp.), and the burning of still other plants (e.g., *Tamarindus indica*) to produce a crackling sound that is metaphor for disease egress through the skin. These various phases of the treatment process have different expected outcomes, and any investigation of efficacy must take into account this processual nature of healing.

This is relevant again in Hausa therapies for cough which include the burning of plants and inhalation of the smoke. The desired proximate effect in this case is the discomfiture and chasing of the cough inducing agent (spirit, witch) or the dislodgement of the disease substance (natural product). Similarly, Wassen (1979) describes Amerindian treatments in which the smoke of burning medicines is inhaled and the expired air-plus-smoke is viewed as evidence that disease causing 'aire' (air) leaves the body. The Hausa (and presumably others who use such treatments) expect as later outcomes in the sequence of treatments antitussive, inflammation suppressive, and decongestant effects. Thus, if we understand treatment and healing as *processual* and recognize that only a *series* of outcomes will fulfill expectations, then we need not dismiss as 'irrational', as have others (e.g., Disengomoka et al. 1983), such behaviors as inhaling smoke for cough.

In some cases the Hausa facilitate disease egress by application of medicines to the site of discomfort, followed by cupping with a hollow cow's horn. By sucking air through the horn, the healer creates a vacuum and causes the skin and underlying tissues to rise in a welt, indicating accumulation of disease substance at that locus. Incision of the welt effects disease egress, after which the site may be treated with other plants to continue the therapeutic process. Scarification – creating small, superficial incisions, usually in the area of the torso or upper arms – is similarly part of an annual or biannual general preventive against disorders caused by the accumulation of old blood and other bodily substances. Moxibustion, phlebotomy, cicratization, and other forms of minor surgery are analogous behaviors that appear throughout the world. For example, Sargent et al. (1983) describe the suction technique used in Khmer medicine as treatment for various discomforts such as stomachache, headache, and fever. Placing a lit candle covered with a jar upon the body creates a visible bruise that signals that the pain has been localized at this site, thus facilitating its departure. Flogging with nettles (*Dendrocnide, Laportea*, and other spp.) has been reported for a variety of treatments of fever, headache, or general pain – e.g., in New Guinea (Johannes 1986), Ecuador (Davis and Yost 1983). These examples illustrate the role that expectations of proximate outcomes play in *healing processes*. Various indigenous medical models explain that such treatments expel disease substances or chase the pain of fever, while biomedical interpretation might describe this as efficacious due to counterirritant effects.

STUDIES OF EFFICACY: THE BIOMEDICAL BIAS

The Western bias that pervades studies of efficacy in ethnomedical behaviors takes two general and related forms: (1) the outright ignoring of non-Western medical ideologies, and (2) the conflation of ethno- and biomedical models. Both of these presume that medicines 'work' only in ways in which bioscience understands 'efficacy'. By ignoring illness models other than those of biomedicine one obscures and vitiates the consistent logic of those medical systems. Similarly, a conflation of Western and non-Western medical models presumes that if indigenous medical behaviors are judged effective by bioscientific criteria, than it must be because the indigenous model is not only functionally, but also conceptually, like that of biomedicine.

A statement from the work of Nasser and Court (1984) is illustrative of a lack of appreciation for other than biomedical understandings of disease processes: 'The bitter bark [of *Rauvolfia caffra*] is strongly purgative and said to produce severe abdominal pains; *nevertheless* the Pondos use the bark for abdominal disorders' (emphasis added). This particular South African use of *R. caffra* is consistent with many ethnically disparate treatment models that interpret purgation, emesis, and the like as evidence that the disease entity leaves the body, a sure sign that the healing *process* is underway (*vide supra*).

Not unexpectedly, Nasser and Court in the same publication imply that they understand non-Western motivations when expectations appear to be the *same* as or similar to those of Western scientists: 'The pharmaceutically important 18-hydroxyyohimbine alkaloids reserpine and rescinnameme were not detected; *therefore* the stem bark is not used as a hypostensive or tranquillising agent in tribal medicine, although it is used as a poisoning agent which probably *acts because* of the high yield of the cardiac slowing alkaloids norajmaline and ajmaline' (emphasis added). Quite likely their interpretation is partly accurate, but only partly. The reason that the stem bark of *Rauvolfia* is not used as a hypostensive is not because certain *alkaloids* are absent, but because of some other meaning that the plant conveys and/or because of a lack of observed hypotensive *effect*. Similarly, indigenous understandings of how poisoning agents 'work' rest not on understanding cardiotropic *alkaloids*, but on observed effects and other meanings such as 'power', 'toxicity' (in a sense similar to that comprehended by biomedicine), and the like.

Malone (1983) too demonstrates this superficial approach to behavioral data when he states that 'Medicine men are frequently *wrong* about how their plant drugs [sic] work' (p. 134, emphasis added), and that 'No person wittingly will take an *inactive* drug when he or she is ill' (p. 146, emphasis added). What criteria are applied in determining 'correct' explanations and definitions of activity? With a similar biomedical bias, but with considerably more sensitivity to cultural variables, Abebe (1984: 43) contends that 'healers do not have any knowledge of the mechanisms of the occurrence of side effects'.

The value of an otherwise comprehensive study of the genus *Tabernaemontana* L. (Apocynaceae) also is diminished by the authors' failure to address the issue of indigenous expectations. One entire issue of the *Journal of Ethnopharmacology* (1984, 10: 1) is devoted to this genus and includes extensive information on taxonomy, geographic distribution, constituents, and studies of pharmacologic activity. Also, ethnobotanic data are presented in more detail than in many other works, and include the listing of plant parts used, form of preparation, and disease/symptoms against which it is used. It is implicit in this work that one can use these data to pursue questions of efficacy using *biomedical* criteria, and that estimations of efficacy using indigenous paradigms have no meaning. The 'ethnobotanic conclusions' (van Beek et al. 1984: 128–129) are in any case very tentatative, only summarizing by most common use, general mode of preparation, and plant part used. One of the authors' statements is particularly illustrative of the point I wish to make. In stating that 'Of the medicinal uses reported, *those which rely on antimicrobial action* are the most common' (emphasis added), the authors ignore that peoples who employ these plants may not have concepts of germ, contagion, and the like. Medicinal use may rely on something altogether different (healing power, spirit propitiation, color, astringency). From the authors' implication that medicines containing 'antimicrobials' are likely to be effective when used against 'infections' must we extrapolate to conclude that peoples who do not share a biomedical understanding of infective processes and antimicrobial activity cannot have developed medicines effective in treating infectious diseases?.

A similar criticism can be levied against Banerjee and Sen (1980: 296) who conclude their survey of ferns used in various indigenous medical systems by stating that there is 'considerable agreement between the observations recorded by us regarding the antibiotic activity of the pteridophytes and their uses in folk medicine'. Medicinal use is drawn from secondary and tertiary sources and is addressed summarily by noting that many of the disorders against which pteridophytes are used are caused by viruses, bacteria, protozoa, and helminths. Against a paucity of cultural information are juxtaposed detailed botanical and pharmacologic data indicating the presence of antimicrobial activity in many of the species tested. Until the depth of detail is matched in the behavioral realm (providing data on plant selection, preparation, administration, and intended outcome), Banerjee and Sen's conclusion is unwarranted.

Chagnon's (1984) assessment of Rwanda ethnomedicines provides more information regarding the particular symptoms or disorders in whose treatment these plants are used, but such data are not combined with pharmacologic data in any way that affords credibility to indigenous disease models and therapeutic expectations.

Watson et al. (1983: 310) also presume a consistency between western and other medical models where it is not demonstrably warranted. Noting that Australian Aborigines do not collect *Duboisia hopwoodii* leaves until the fire for their drying is considered hot enough, they conclude that 'enzyme action *must have* ceased moments after picking with little loss of alkaloid content' (emphasis added). Why 'must have'? Presumably because the biochemical activity of the constituent alkaloids is consistent with what they report as indigenous expectations. But such consistency, while interesting, is not *necessary* for the credibility of medical behaviors. Such associations (method of preparation and influence on biochemical activity) are best presented after confirmation through empirical study or as hypotheses, and in any case they cannot be properly appreciated without consideration of the expectations of the individuals whose medical behaviors are the object of study.

Similarly, Basker and Negbi's (1983) careful review of the literature on medicinal and other uses of saffron (*Crocus sativus*) reports an antiatherogenic (cholesterol lowering) effect on *intramuscular* administration. Albeit an interesting observation, particularly in view of the possible relationship of this action to a low incidence of cardiovascular disorders in parts of Spain where saffron is consumed in appreciable quantities (Grisiola 1974), it is not clear how such activity is related to ethnomedical expectations, although their reference to a 12th century use of saffron as a 'cheering cardiac medicament' (p. 229) might be invoked to make that association (only slightly) less tenuous.

In an analogous case, Capasso et al. (1983a, b) investigated the actions and phytochemistry of *Tamus communis*, the root decoction of which is applied topically by Italian indigenous healers for various inflammatory disorders. These researchers report the anti-inflammatory and analgesic activity of *orally* administered *ethanol* extracts of the plant and suggest that such action may be ascribed to one or more of several known constituents (campesterol, stigmasterol, and B-sitosterol) determined by (nonaqueous) extraction. Clearly their implied conclusion is that this medicine is effective. But an orally administered ethanol extract is neither a conceptual nor a functional equivalent of a topically applied aqueous preparation. Would topical application produce the same or similar results? Further, what are the expectations of the user? Should this medicine only relieve inflammation or is some other action(s) required, in addition, in order to indicate that healing is in process.

Contrast this with Carlini et al.'s (1983) study of *Licaria puchurymajor*, a plant used in Brazilian folk medicine as a stomachic and calmative for various disorders. Analyses included examination of both the (nonaqueous) essential oil fraction and an aqueous extract (comparable to that used in folk preparations), and revealed that both included activities consistent with the indigenous medical model. And the work of Ampofo (1977), Elvin-Lewis (1986), and Iwu (1986) include a clinical component as well as taking into account indigenous expectations, modes of preparation, and administration.

Shanmugasundaram et al. (1983a, b, c) also have demonstrated how one can use a biomedical paradigm to more thoroughly understand the hypolipemic and hypocholesterolemic activities of a traditionally prepared Indian (Sidha-Ayurveda) antiatherosclerotic medicine, Anna Pavola Sindhooram (APS), containing *Corallium rubrum*, *Vinca rosea*, *Lawsonia alba*, *Cynodon dactylon*, *Acalypha indica*, *Lippia nodiflora*, *Hibiscus rosasinensis*, *Phyllanthus emblica*, *Citrus aurantifolia*, and ferrous sulphate. The indigenous disease model understands 'arterial thickening' to be an age associated disorder that is magnified by lack of exercise, obesity, and over-eating. Treatment includes changes in diet and exercise as well as ingested medicines that are expected to (proximally) act as cholagogues, diuretics, expectorants, laxatives, hematinics, and 'tonics'. Ultimately, such treatments should mobilize fats and other wastes that have collected in the body and effect their removal in order to restore the hot-cold balance and harmony among the body's humors (dosha). This is in part consistent with a biomedical understanding of atherosclerosis which emphasizes elevated levels of plasma cholesterol, triglycerides, phospholipids, and circulating lipoproteins and which prescribes treatments that reverse these elevations. Shanmugasundaram and coworkers' (1983a, b, c) investigations demonstrate the likely effectiveness of APS while at the same time illustrating a case of overlap in the paradigms of a biomedical and an Indian medical system.

The use of toxic plants has been held as an indicator of the 'irrationality' of non-Western beliefs and practices. However, attention to indigenous modes of plant preparation and the expected sequellae of these behaviors illustrates again that a biomedical understanding of phytochemistry is not requisite for the manipulation of plants for certain desired outcomes. Western scientists have marvelled at the 'skill' (or, more cynically, the 'good luck') of populations throughout the world who have developed a variety of preparatory techniques which reduce the content of toxic hydrogen cyanide in cassava (*Manihot esculenta*) (Lancaster et al. 1982). The use of toxin containing plants in health related activities has not been afforded the same respect – non-Western peoples are presumably acute enough observers of their physical universe to render their foods safe for consumption, but not their medicines. That this latter implication is not true is evident in, for example, studies of *Aconitum* spp., plants whose common use in Oriental medicines has been criticized as being 'irrational' or 'unknowing' in view of the toxicity of aconitine alkaloids. Since *Aconitum* spp. are used as arrow poisons by these same populations, it seems safe to conclude that they are indeed well aware of this toxicity. With more attention paid to indigenous expectations in using these plants in medical treatment – reduction of fever, pain, and infection – we learn that indigenous modes of preparation (aqueous decoctions) eliminate toxicity (Hikino et al. 1977) and antipyretic, analgesic, and antimicrobial activities are present (Bisset 1981). Thus, simple knowledge of presence of toxins – or, for that matter, of any active constituents – is insufficient basis for the evaluation of efficacy.

This is illustrated as well by biomedical criticism of the use of pungent substances in the treatment of inflammations – e.g., the Hausa application of such plants as *Capsicum annum* and *Eugenia caryophyllata* to treat eye and skin disorders. The efficacy of such treatments can be understood on two levels. First, the Hausa treatment of (eye or skin) inflammation should be understood as a *process*, with one of the proximate expectations being some evidence that the disease substance is surfacing and leaving the body – reddening of the eye and skin inflammation confirm Hausa expectations that healing is in process, while the biomedical understanding of this is only of symptom exacerbation. Both the proximate effect and the ultimate effect – relief of pain and irritation – also can be understood as consistent with the principles of biomedicine: capsaicin (from *Capsicum* spp., chile pepper) and eugenol (from *Eugenia* spp., clove) cause immediate inflammation of the affected area, followed by longlasting local analgesia (Isaacs 1983; Anonymous 1983).

Similarly, Turner's (1984) review of Native American uses of the Ranunculaceae notes that the widespread medicinal application of these plants has been criticized in view of their containing the irritant and vesicant protoanemonin. Particularly insofar as the Ranunculaceae are commonly employed in the form of poultices applied (externally) for wounds, boils, and other skin disorders, and for respiratory disorders, the vesicant action of these plants is inconsistent with western biomedical models of healing. A closer reading of Turner's work shows that this can be understood on two levels. First, we should not be surprised to learn that the irritant and sometimes poisonous qualities of the Ranunculaceae are known to these Native Americans – likely they are as keen observers of their actions as Western practitioners pride themselves to be. Turner records that these species were judiciously used to achieve the effects desired with minimal harmful consequences and, although she does not detail the underlying medical ideology and expected sequelae, it merits attention that the inducement of irritation with resultant change in skin color and vesication can be understood as being consistent with illness models that require tangible evidence that 'something' happens to the body in the *process* of cure and/or that healing involves physical evidence that disease entities surface and then leave the body. On another level, one can 'confirm' the efficacy of these uses of the Ranunculaceae in a way that is consistent with biomedical models of healing. Specifically, Turner (1984) suggests that the efficacy of these plants in treating skin disorders might be attributed to fluid being drawn from surrounding tissues and blood flow increased to the affected area, and that the effectiveness of these plants in treating respiratory illnesses might be ascribed to the decongestant action of protoanemonin.

Studies of efficacy are compromised as well by investigations that group plants for study in such a way that indigenous expectations are, if not completely ignored, obscured by use of some bioscientific or other categorization. De Smet's (1983, 1985) reviews of 'intoxicating' enema and snuff rituals', albeit detailed treatments of taxonomic and pharmacologic data, fail to convey the depth of meaning and rich cultural contexts within which the uses of 'snuff' or 'enemas' occur cross-culturally. The use of the terms 'intoxicating' and 'rituals' in the title serves to sensationalize behaviors which – to judge by de Smet's brief ethnographic descriptions and other, more detailed anthropological accounts – vary a great deal cross-culturally and, more importantly here, are not conducted with the intention of intoxicating or other psychotropic outcome, and are not always (sometimes never) conducted in the context of 'ritual' in the sense that that term ordinarily conveys (Turner and Turner 1982: 201; Myerhoff 1982: 131). For example, *Acorus calamus* rhizome has been used by Native Americans in nonceremonial contexts as a stimulant and nonpsychotropic medicine (Morgan 1980). Intranasal use of *Capsicum* spp. among the Tukano of Colombia is likely to have irritating and local anaesthetic (Anonymous 1983), but not psychotropic, effects.

By apparently implying that the ceremony accompanied by intoxication is the most cogent or meaningful common denominator, de Smet collapses a potentially enormous variety of ethnographic detail into categories of use (like 'tea', 'tonic', etc.) which carry limited if any analytic power. Is the mode of application/administration of plant substances here – or ever – of key importance? De Smet's discussions are not necessarily sensationalizing, however through his use of bioscientific concepts for categorization he presents the data in an inefficient – and in some cases uninformed and disinforming – way. Might we not reach a better understanding if we take into account indigenous categories, definitions, and expectations? Certainly, some of de Smet's data *are* best (that is, consistent with indigenous perceptions) grouped as plant medicines or substances applied as snuff or enemas, perhaps used ritually, but in any case used for purposes of intoxication. But is it sufficient to stop there? What meaning does intoxication itself carry? Is it the ultimate desired effect (then why?), or is intoxication a proximate outcome in the healing *process*, requisite to achieve some other or ultimate end – for example, to experience dreams or other means of divining, to induce clarity of vision in preparation for hunting, or for some other end?

Side/secondary effects

Failure to differentiate (or show overlap) between indigenous and Western biomedical meanings is illustrated as well by the poor differentiation between primary and secondary effects and the ethnocentric view that biomedical researchers bring to consideration of 'side effects'. For example, the published reports on coca chewing (*Erythroxylum* spp), are inconsistent in explaining why indigenous patterns of coca leaf chewing involve addition of alkaline substances such as lime or ash. Many explanations (e.g., Burchard 1975) have emphasized the drug potentiating effect of an alkaline environment – specifically, increase in pH results in hydrolyzation of cocaine into benzoylecgonine and ecgonine which, on absorption, account more than cocaine does for the pharmacologic effects of coca chewing. More recently, the assumption that lime is used to enhance psychotropic activity has been questioned. Rivier (1981), for example, noted that experimental simulation of natural coca chewing indicated neither rapid nor extensive hydrolysis of cocaine under alkaline conditions, and reports that coca chewers have relatively high levels of cocaine in plasma and experience central nervous system stimulation also suggest against alkaline induced hydrolysis of cocaine to the metabolites benzoylecgonine and ecgonine. Further, the oral anaesthesia noted by enured coca chewers (de Smet 1985) suggests the presence of cocaine (Ritchie and Cohen 1975) rather than the metabolites, which effect little or no local anaesthesia (Novak et al. 1984). An alternative explanation, still emphasizing enhancement of drug activity, is that the absorption of cocaine by the oral mucosa is enhanced in an alkaline environment (Holmstedt et al. 1979; Rivier 1981; Siegel 1982). A similar interpretation has been offered for the inclusion of alkaline plant ash in the preparation of betel nut (*Areca catechu*), kola nut (*Cola acuminata, C. nitida*), and other 'chews' (Watson et al. 1983; Lewis and Elvin-Lewis 1977) and in snuffs (de Smet 1983), although an equally plausible explanation – particularly in the case of snuffs – is that this prevents humidity-induced clumping of the finely pulverized plant material (Schultes 1967). Explanations that are more consistent with indigenous perceptions, and that do not ignore the pharmacologic data, suggest that the recognition of organoleptic properties is more important in the prescribed patterns of coca use – specifically, that increased alkalinity through addition of lime or ash alters the taste of the coca leaves from bitter and disagreeable to sweet. This view is reinforced by consideration of other, plant materials that are added to the coca quid – e.g., the Chimane Indians of eastern Bolivia add the bark of *Mussatia hyacinthina* or *Clytostoma sciurpabulum* which, with the addition of lime, significantly sweetens the quid (Davis 1983: 225).

This does not deny that coca chewers would likely also note an enhanced psychotropic effect. That indigenous populations have (most likely wittingly) enhanced cocaine content (and are thus cognizant of its effects) is illustrated by the observation that cocaine does not occur in appreciable quantities in most wild species of *Erythroxylum* (Plowman and Rivier 1983; Plowman 1981; Holmstedt et al. 1977).

It is important to note that the localized oral anaesthesia experienced by practised coca chewers is an anticipated/expected reaction. It is not perceived as a 'secondary' or 'side effect' but instead a measure of the amount of active substance (i.e., cocaine alkaloid) that is extracted during the chewing (Antonil 1978; in: de Smet 1985). To the extent that knowledge and regulation of dosage is important, this analgesia could be perceived as primary, not secondary.

Abebe (1984: 43) suggests a similar dose regulating role for the 'side-effects' of traditional medicines used in Ethiopia and notes that healers view these outcomes as evidence of the therapeutic activity of the medicine. If such pharmacologic activities are expected, then the Western researcher's designation of 'secondary' or 'side effect' is ill placed. Secondary by whose standard? The Western biomedical model based in the germ theory of disease perceives cure or symptom remission as the prime goal. Thus, other outcomes are aptly 'side' effects. That this is not necessarily consistent with other medical models is important for considerations of efficacy. This categorization of 'side effects' is frequently cause for devaluation of indigenous medicines.

In the same vein, Rodriguez and co-workers' (1982) interpretation of the use of psychotropics both offers a novel perspective on the significance of these plants and underscores a tendency of western researchers to be attracted by, and to exaggerate, the more 'exotic' features of cultures other than their own. Rather than concentrate as so many others have on the hallucinogenic and related qualities of psychotropic plants, Rodriguez et al. have suggested that other activities better inform their use in indigenous medicine. They note for some psychotropic species antimicrobial and other antiparasitic effects, due in part to strong purgative and emetic activity; and they suggest these as the principle criteria for selection, marshalling as 'evidence' repeated ceremonial reference to the 'cleansing' qualities of these plants, and proposing that the psychotropic effects were used as dosage indicators. Thus we can ponder the possibility that psychoactivity was perceived as 'side effect' to emesis, whereas the conventional view considers diarrhea and vomiting as 'side effects' of psychotropic plant use.

EFFICACY AND THE MULTICONTEXTUAL USE OF PLANTS

Too little attention has been paid to the use of medicinal plants in more than one context. Perhaps most significant among other uses is the role that some medicinal plants play in indigenous dietaries (e.g., see Etkin 1986a, b). These categories of use – medicine, food – are in many cases clearly distinguished (although commonly interrelated through metaphors of nurturance, growth, and the like), so that medicinals and foods have different meanings and are prepared, applied, and consumed with different intended outcomes. However, to the extent that such plants are pharmacologically active, their consumption in various contexts merits closer attention.

In Chinese medicine, seemingly more so than in the case of other medical systems, diet is inextricably linked to both preventive and therapeutic dimensions of medical care (e.g., Ahern 1975; Ho 1985; Anderson and Anderson

1975; Koo 1984). Studies of efficacy become increasingly complex as one must both distinguish between and conflate the conceptual and functional categories of 'food' and 'medicine'. And the problem is further exacerbated by lack of consensus regarding definition of such related terms as 'tonics', 'patching medicines' (Gould Martin 1975), 'teas', 'health foods', 'tisanes', and 'medicinal foods'. Koo's (1984) discussion of the use of food in Chinese preventive and curative medicines is a particularly exaggerated confusion of such concepts.

Such confusion is illustrated as well in Morton's (1983) promotion of the South African beverage 'Rooibos tea' (*Aspalathus linearis*) as a more 'healthy' substitute for 'conventional tea and coffee' in view of its being caffeine free, low in tannins, high in ascorbic acid and (anti-cariogenic) fluoride, containing the antispasmodic quercetin. Is this then a tea or coffee 'substitute', a food, a medicine, or something else altogether? While such beverages may be or become conceptual near equivalents of 'tea' (and perhaps coffee, for which 'tea' itself frequently serves as 'substitute') – witness the great proliferation of 'herbal' teas available in increasing variety in urban centers worldwide – they are explicitly and deliberately *not* functional equivalents. As regards definitional murkiness, Morton jumps into the fray to suggest that since the 'healthful' character lies more in what is absent rather than in what it contains, ' . . . it should not be classified as a medical infusion. It is, rather, a salubrious beverage' (p. 169). Any progress toward definitional clarity is rapidly dissolved in Morton's two closing sentences which describe the potential for using Rooibos *tea* 'in gelatin desserts . . . tarts . . . cookies, aspics . . . and in meat sauces', and which conclude that 'The possibilities are endless, thus greatly enlarging the potential role of rooibos *tea* in the diet of infants, children and adults' (emphasis added).

The inclusion of pharmacologically active plants in diet is particularly significant in view of the relatively larger quantities in which foods are generally consumed relative to medicines, thus suggesting important implications for estimating effects based on relative dosages. For example, among the 107 Hausa plants commonly used in the treatment of a variety of gastro-intestinal disorders, most contain constituents that are likely to be beneficial in the treatment of gastro-intestinal disorders (from the points of view of both Hausa and western medicine), and half appear as well as elements of diet (Etkin and Ross 1982; 1983). From a pharmacologic perspective, this suggests that narrowly directed studies of plant medicines that neglect the consumption of botanicals in other contexts may significantly underestimate the extent to which these species influence the occurrence and expression of illness. (And from a nutritional perspective, knowledge of the pharmacologic activity of dietary elements provides a broader base from which to study dietary quality.)

Studies of indigenous medicinal plants and dietaries have been constrained by a bioscientific perspective that circumscribes as appropriate inquiry for medicinal plants only pharmacologic investigations, and for dietary plants only conventional nutrient analyses for protein, calories, vitamins, etc. This obscures other meanings and expectations – i.e., other contexts of use – and thus provides insufficient basis from which to formulate judgements of efficacy.

CONCLUSION

Many of the recommendations from world health assemblies concerned with ethnopharmacologic research are at least implicitly guided by practical ends – e.g., the development and incorporation of indigenous medicinal plants that have been determined to be efficacious in order to decrease the cost of pharmaceutical products and to advance primary health care in populations where synthetic drugs are not available (Velimirovic and Velimirovic 1980; Balandrin et al. 1985; WHO 1978; Oberender and Diesfeld 1983; Oyeneye 1985; Young 1983). Determination and specification of 'efficacy' are central to this task. Beyond these applied concerns, questions of efficacy are relevant as well for advancing the comprehension of human-plant interactions and other issues of concern in ecological modelling. Whereas the applied programs are interested in 'efficacy' as understood by the western paradigms of physiology and pharmacology, ecological inquiries of more conceptual and theoretical rigor must be concerned with 'efficacy' in its broadest definition, including any number of etic and emic understandings.

This attention to emic (local) and etic (other, outside) perspectives in evaluating medical efficacy speaks to one of the integrating themes of this volume – good anthropological studies of therapeutics (or any other cultural construct, for that matter) require that researchers be both insiders (who 'contextualize', or embrace the 'circumstantiality' of their observations) and outsiders (who 'denaturalize' those same observations in order to understand them though reference to other organizing principles or frameworks). Particularly in the case of evaluating efficacy, we have argued, it is important to recognize when and how inside and outside perspectives can be conflated or distinguished, and to understand how such similarities and differences affect the criteria applied in judging efficacy.

We have tried in this chapter to illustrate the cultural construction of efficacy and to emphasize the importance of recognizing the processual nature of healing in judging such effectiveness. While the focus has been on indigenous medicines, our perspective casts light on Western medicines as well. Obviously, Western medicines are no less cultural than the medications of other pharmacopoeias. Studying the efficacy of Western medicines requires stepping out of biomedicine and viewing it as a cultural system. It allows us to see that biomedicine 'works' because it is more than the pragmatics of biomedicine. A cultural interpretation provides a more satisfactory 'explanation' of the efficacy of western medicines.

The main theme of this volume, Western pharmaceuticals in developing countries, poses a special challenge to those working towards a cultural understanding of efficacy. The suggestions made here regarding how people perceive the effects of indigenous medicines may serve as guidelines for research in how they evaluate the efficacy of Western medicines.

NOTES

1. The prefix 'ethno-' and the term 'indigenous' are used throughout to designate understandings – of health, disease, plants, etc. – other than those informed by the precepts of Western science and biomedicine. This is to imply neither that Western biomedicine and other medicines are always (or ever) categorically different, nor that one should understand by the term 'ethnomedicine' (or 'indigenous medicine') a single, homogeneous system of knowledge any more than one should understand Western biomedicine to be always and everywhere the same regardless of the context in which it appears.
2. Such metaphors, as well as the use of dietary elements in the prevention and treatment of illness, blur the distinctions between foods and medicine – e.g., see the discussion in this chapter on the multicontextual use of plants [page 316].

REFERENCES

Abebe, Worku
  1984 Traditional Pharmaceutical Practice in Gondar Region, Northwestern Ethiopia. Journal of Ethnopharmacology 11(1): 33–47.
Ahern, Emily M.
  1975 Sacred and Secular Medicine in a Taiwan Village: A Study of Cosmological Disorders. *In* Medicine in Chinese Cultures: Comparative Studies of Health Care in Chinese and other Societies. A. Kleinman, P. Kunstadter, E. R. Alexander, and J. L. Gale, (eds.) pp. 61–75. Washington, DC: US Department of Health, Education, and Welfare, NIH.
Alcorn, Janis B.
  1981 Factors Influencing Botanical Resource Perception among the Huastec: Suggestions for Future Ethnobotanical Inquiry. Journal of Ethnobiology 1(2): 221–230.
Al-Yahya, Mohammed A., Khafagy S., Shihata A., Kozlowski J. F., Antound, Mikhail D. and Cassady, John M.
  1984 Phytochemical and Biological Screening of Saudi Medicinal Plants, Part 6. Isolation of 2a-Hydroxyalantolactone the Antileukemic Principle of *Francoeuria crispa*. Journal of Natural Products 47(6): 1013–1017.
American Herbal Pharmacology Delegation
  1975 Herbal Pharmacology in the People's Republic of China. Washington, DC: National Academy of Sciences.
Ampofo, Oku
  1977 Plants That Heal. World Health (November): 26–30.
Anderson, E. N., and Anderson, Marja L.
  1975 Folk Dietetics in Two Chinese Communities, and Its Implications for the Study of Chinese Medicine. *In* Medicine in Chinese Cultures: Comparative Studies of Health Care in Chinese and Other Societies. A Kleinman, P. Kunstadter, E. R. Alexander, and J. L. Gale (eds.) pp. 143–175. Washington DC: US Department of Health, Education and Welfare, NIH.

Anonymous
    1983 Hot Peppers and Substance P. Lancet I: 1198.
Axton, J. H. M.
    1975 Measles: a Protein-losing Enteropathy. British Medical Journal 3: 79–80.
Balandrin, Manuel F., Klocke, James A., Wurtele, Eve Syrkin and Bollinger, Wm. Hugh
    1985 Natural Plant Chemicals: Sources of Industrial and Medicinal Materials. Science 228: 1154–1160.
Banerjee, R. D. and Sen, S. P.
    1980 Antibiotic Activity of Pteridophytes. Economic Botany 34(3) 284–298.
Basker, D. and Negbi, M.
    1983 Uses of Saffron. Economic Botany 37(2): 228–236.
Bastien, J. W.
    1981 Metaphorical Relations between Sickness, Society and Land in a Qollahuaya Ritual. *In* Health in the Andes. J. W. Bastien and J. Donahue, (eds.) pp. 19–37. Washington, DC: American Anthropological Association.
    1982 Exchange between Andean and Western Medicine. Social Science and Medicine 16: 795–803.
    1983 Pharmacopeia of Qollahuaya Andeans. Journal of Ethnopharmacology 8(1): 97–111.
    1985 Qollahuaya-Andean Body Concepts: A Topographical-Hydraulic Model of Physiology. American Anthropologist 87: 595–611.
Berlin, Brent, Breedlove, D. E. and Raven, P. H.
    1974 Principle of Tzeltal Plant Classification. New York: Academic Press.
Berman, Peter A.
    1984 Village Health Workers in Java, Indonesia: Coverage and Equity. Social Science and Medicine 19(4): 411–422.
Bisset, N. G.
    1981 Arrow Poisons in China. Part II. *Aconitum* – Biology, Chemistry, and Pharmacology. Journal of Ethnopharmacology 4(3): 247–336.
Bloom, Abby L. and Reid, Janice (eds.)
    1984 Anthropology and Primary Health Care in Developing Countries. Social Science and Medicine 19(3): 183–303.
Brush, Stephen B., Carney, Heath J. and Huaman, Zosimo
    1981 Dynamics of Andean Potato Agriculture. Economic Botany 35(1): 70–88.
Burchard, Roderick E.
    1975 Coca Chewing: A New Perspective. *In* Cannabis and Culture. V. Rubin, ed. pp. 463–484. The Hague: Mouton.
Camazine, S. and Bye, R. A.
    1980 A Study of the Medical Ethnobotany of the Zuni Indians of New Mexico. Journal of Ethnopharmacology 2: 365–388.
Capasso, F., Mascolo, N., Autore, G., Simone, F. de and Senatore, F.
    1983a Anti-inflammatory and Analgesic Activity in Alcoholic Extract of *Tamus communis* L. Journal of Ethnopharmacology 8(3): 321–325.
Capasso, F., Simone, F. de and Senatore, F.
    1983b Sterol Constituents of *Tamus communis* L. Journal of Ethnopharmacology 8(3): 327–329.
Carlini, E. A., Oliveira, A. B. de and Oliveira, G. G. de
    1983 Psychoparmacological Effects of the Essential Oil Fraction and of the Hydrolate Obtained from the Seeds of *Licaria puchury-major*. Journal of Ethnopharmacology 8(2): 225–236.
Chagnon, M.
    1984 Inventaire Pharmacologique General des Plantes Medicinales Rwandaises. Journal of Ethnopharmacology 12(3): 239–251.

Croom, Edward M.
  1983 Documenting and Evaluating Herbal Remedies. Economic Botany 37(1): 13–27.
Dafni, Amots, Yaniv, Zohara and Palevitch, Dan
  1984 Ethnobotanical Survey of Medicinal Plants in Northen Israel. Journal of Ethnopharmacology 10(3): 295–310.
Davis, E. Wade
  1983 The Ethnobotany of Chamairo: *Mussatia hyacinthina*. Journal of Ethnopharmaoclogy 9(2, 3): 225–236.
Davis, E. Wade and Yost, James A.
  1983 The Ethnomedicine of the Waorani of Amazonian Ecuador. Journal of Ethnopharmacology 9(2, 3): 273–297.
Delaveau, P.
  1981 Evaluation of Traditional Pharmacopoeias. *In* Natural Products as Medicinal Agents. J. L. Beal and E. Reinhard (eds.) pp. 395–404. Stuttgart: Hippokrates Verlag.
de Smet, Peter A. G. M.
  1983 A Multidisciplinary Overview of Intoxicating Enema Rituals in the Western Hemisphere. Journal of Ethnopharmacology 9(2, 3): 129–166.
  1985 A Multidisciplinary Overview of Intoxicating Snuff Rituals in the Western Hemisphere. Journal of Ethnopharmacology 13(1): 3–49.
Disengomoka, Ina, Delaveau, Pierra and Sengele, Kaba
  1983 Medicinal Plants Used for Child's Respiratory Diseases in Zaire. Part II. Journal of Ethnopharmacology 8(3): 265–277.
Dominguez, Xorge, and Alcorn, Janis B.
  1985 Screening of Medicinal Plants Used by Huastec Mayans of Northeastern Mexico. Journal of Ethnopharmacology 13(2): 139–156.
Elling, Ray, (ed.)
  1981 Traditional and Modern Medical Systems. Social Science and Medicine 15A(2): 87–192.
Elvin-Lewis, Memory
  1986 Therapeutic Rationale of Plants Used to Treat Dental Infections. *In* Plants in Indigenous Medicine and Diet: Bio-Behavioral Approaches. N. L. Etkin, (ed.) pp. 48–69. Bedford Hills, New York: Redgrave Publishers.
Etkin, Nina L.
  1979 Indigenous Medicine among the Hausa of Northern Nigeria: Laboratory Evaluation for Potential Therapeutic Efficacy of Antimalarial Plant Medicinals. Medical Anthropology 3: 401–429.
  1980 Indigenous Medicine in Northern Nigeria. I. Oral Hygiene and Medical Treatment. Journal of Preventive Dentistry 6: 143–149.
  1981 A Hausa Herbal Pharmacopoeia: Biomedical Evaluation of Commonly Used Plant Medicines. Journal of Ethnopharmacology 4: 75–98.
  1986a Multidisciplinary Perspectives in the Interpretation of Plants Used in Indigenous Medicine and Diet. *In* Plants in Indigenous Medicine and Diet: Bio-Behavioral Approaches. N.L. Etkin, (ed.) pp. 2–29. Bedford Hills, New York: Redgrave Publishers.
Etkin, Nina L., (ed.)
  1986b Plants in Indigenous Medicine and Diet: Bio-Behavioral Approaches. Bedford Hills, New York: Redgrave Publishers.
Etkin, Nina L., and Ross, Paul J.
  1982 Food as Medicine and Medicine as Food: An Adaptive Framework for the Interpretation of Plant Utilization among the Hausa of Northern Nigeria. Social Science and Medicine 16: 1559–1573.
  1983 Malaria, Medicine, and Meals: Plant Use and its Impact on Disease. *In* The Anthro-

pology of Medicine. L. Romanucci-Ross, D. E. Moerman, and L. Tancredi,(eds.) pp. 231–259. New York: Praeger.

Finerman, Ruthbeth D.
1984 A Matter of Life and Death: Health Care Change in an Andean Community. Social Science and Medicine 18(4): 329–334.

Gould Martin, Katherine
1975 Medical Systems in a Taiwan Village: *Ong-ia-kong*, the Plague God as Modern Physician. *In* Medicine in Chinese Cultures: Comparative Studies of Health Care in Chinese and Other Societies. A. Kleinman, P. Kunstadter, E. R. Alexander, and J. L. Gale, (eds.) pp. 115–141. Washington DC: US Department of Health, Education and Welfare, NIH.

Green, Edward C.
1985 Traditional Healers, Mothers and Childhood Diarrheal Disease in Swaziland: the Interface of Anthropology and Health Education. Social Science and Medicine 20(3): 277–285.

Grisiola, S.
1974 Hypoxia, Saffron, and Cardiovascular Disease. Lancet 2: 41–42.

Harlan, J. R.
1975 Crops and Man. Madison, Wisconsin: American Society of Agronomy
1976 Genetic Resources in Wild Relatives of Crops. Crop Science 16: 329–333.

Hikino, H., Sato, H., Yamada, C., Konno, C., Ohizuei, Y., and Endo, K.
1977 Change of Alkaloid Composition and Acute Toxicity of *Aconitum* roots During Processing. Yakugaku Zasshi 97: 359–266.

Ho, Suzanne S. Y. C.
1985 Dietary Beliefs in Health and Illness among a Hong Kong Community. Social Science and Medicine 20(3): 233–230.

Ho, Suzanne C., Lun, K. C. and Ng, W. K.
1984 The Role of Chinese Traditional Health Care in Singapore – III. Conditions, Illness Behaviour and Medical Preferences of Patients of Institutional Clinics. Social Science and Medicine 18(9): 745–752.

Holmstedt, B., Jäätmaa, E., Leander, K., and Plowman, T.
1977 Determination of Cocaine in Some South American Species of *Erythroxylum* Using Mass Fragmentography. Phytochemistry 15: 1753–1755.

Holmstedt, B., Lindgren, J.-E., Rivier, L. and Plowman, T.
1979 Cocaine in Blood of Coca Chewers. Journal of Ethnopharmacology 1: 69–78.

Hunn, Eugene S.
1982 The Utilitarian Factor in Folk Biological Classification. American Anthropologist 84: 830–847.

Isaacs, G.
1983 Permanent Local Anaesthesia and Anhidrosis after Clove Oil Spillage. Lancet I: 882.

Iwu, Maurice M.
1986 Empirical Investigations of Dietary Plants Used in Igbo Ethnomedicine. *In* Plants in Indigenous Medicine and Diet: Bio-Behavioral Approaches. N. L. Etkin, (ed.) pp. 131–150. Bedford Hills, New York: Redgrave Publishers.

Janzen, John M. and Feierman, Steven (eds.)
1979 The Social History of Disease and Medicine in Africa. Social Science and Medicine 13B: 239–356.

Johannes, Adell
1986 Medicinal Plants of the New Guinea Highlands: An Ethnopharmacologic and Phytochemical Update. *In* Plants in Indigenous Medicine and Diet: Bio-Behavioral Approaches. N.L. Etkin, (ed.) pp. 186–210. Bedford Hills, New York: Redgrave Publishers.

Johns, Timothy A.
  1986 Chemical Selection in Andean Domesticated Tubers as a Model for the Acquisition of Empirical Plant Knowledge. *In* Plants in Indigenous Medicine and Diet: Bio-Behavioral Approaches. N. L. Etkin, (ed.) pp. 266–288. Bedford Hills, New York: Redgrave Publishers.
Karim, Wazir-Jahan
  1984 Malay Midwives and Witches. Social Science and Medicine 18(2): 159–166.
Kay, Margarita A.
  1977 Health and Illness in a Mexican Barrio. *In* Ethnic Medicine in the Southwest. E.H. Spicer (ed.) pp. 99–166. Tucson: University of Arizona Press.
Kendall, Carl, Foote, Denniss and Martorell, Reynaldo
  1984 Ethnomedicine and Oral Rehydration Therapy: a Case Study of Ethnomedical Investigation and Program Planning. Social Science and Medicine 19(3): 253–260.
Kleinman, Arthur and Sung, Lilias H.
  1979 Why Do Indigenous Practitioners Successfully Heal? Social Science and Medicine 13B: 7–26.
Koo, Linda C.
  1984 The Use of Food to Treat and Prevent Disease in Chinese Culture. Social Science and Medicine 18(9): 757–766.
Kroeger, Axel
  1983 Anthropological and Socio-medical Health Care Research in Developing Countries. Social Science and Medicine 17(3): 147–161.
Lancaster, P. A., Ingram, J. S., Lin, M. Y., and Coursy, D. G.
  1982 Traditional Cassava-based Foods: Survey of Processing Techniques. Economic Botany 36: 12–45.
Landy, David
  1977 Role Adaptation: Traditional Curers under the Impact of Western Medicine. *In* Culture, Disease, and Healing. D. Landy, (ed.) pp. 468–481. New York: Macmillan.
Leslie, Charles, (ed.)
  1980 Medical Pluralism. Social Science and Medicine 14B(5): 381–460.
Lewis, Walter H. and Elvin-Lewis, Memory P. F.
  1977 Medical Botany. New York: Wiley.
Lévi-Strauss, C.
  1966 The Savage Mind. London: Weindenfeld and Nicolson.
Logan, Michael H.
  1972 Humoral Folk Medicine: A Potential Aid in Controlling Pellagra in Mexico. Ethnomedizin 4: 397–410.
Makapugay, Helena C., Soejarto, Djaja D., Kinghorn, A. Douglas and Bordas, E.
  1983 Piperovatine, The Tongue-numbing Principle of *Ottonia frutescens*. Journal of Ethnopharmacology 7(2): 235–238.
Malone, Marvin H.
  1983 The Pharmacological Evaluation of Natural Products — General and Specific Approaches to Screening Ethnopharmaceuticals. Journal of Ethnopharmacology 8(2): 127–147.
McCauley, Ann P.
  1984 Healing as Sign of Power and Status in Bali. Social Science and Medicine 18(2): 167–172.
McCullough, J. M. and McCullough, C. S.
  1974 Las Creencias del Sindrome de 'Calor-frio' en YucataPH'n y Su Importancia para la Antropologia Aplicada. Anales de Antropologia 11: 295–305.
Mo, Bertha
  1984 Black Magic and Illness in a Malaysian Chinese Community. Social Science and Medicine 18(2): 147–157.

Moerman, Daniel E.
 1977 American Medical Ethnobotany. New York: Garland.
 1979 Symbols and Selectivity: a Statistical Analysis of Native American Medical Ethnobotany. Journal of Ethnopharmacology 1: 111–119.
Morgan, G. R.
 1980 The Ethnobotany of Sweet Flag among North American Indians. Botanical Museum Leaflets, Harvard University 28: 235–246.
Morgan, W. R. W.
 1981 Ethnobotany of the Turkana: Use of Plants by a Pastoral People and Their Livestock in Kenya. Economic Botany 35(1): 96–130.
Morris, Brian
 1984 The Pragmatics of Folk Classification. Journal of Ethnobiology 4(1): 45–60.
Morton, Julia F.
 1983 Rooibos Tea, *Aspalanthus linearis*, a Caffeineless, Low-Tannin Beverage. Economic Botany 37(2): 164–173.
Mukhopadhyay, Sibabrata, Cordell, Geoffrey A., Ruangrungsi, Nijsiri, Rodkird, Supreeya, Tantivatana, Payom and Hylands P. J.
 1983 Traditional Medicine Plants of Thailand. IV. 3-(2', 3'-Diacetoxy- 2'-Methylbutyryl)-Cuauhtemone from *Pluchea indica*. Journal of Natural Products 46(5): 671–674.
Myerhoff, Barbara
 1982 Rites of Passage. *In* Celebration: Studies in Festivity and Ritual. V. Turner, (ed.) pp. 109–135. Washington, DC: Smithsonian Institution Press.
Nabhan, G. P., Berry, J. W. and Weber, C. W.
 1980 Wild Beans of the Greater Southwest: *Phaseolus metcalfei* and *P. ritensis*. Economic Botany 34(1): 68–85.
Nasser, A. M. A. G. and Court E. W.
 1984 Stem Bark Alkaloids of *Rauvolfia caffra*. Journal of Ethnopharmacology 11(1): 99–117.
Novak, M., Salemink, C. A. and Khan, I.
 1984 Biological Activity of the Alkaloids of *Erythroxylum coca* and *Erythroxylum novogranatense*. Journal of Ethnopharmacology 10: 261–274.
Oberender, Peter, and Diesfeld Hans Jochen
 1983 Health and Development in Africa. Social Science and Medicine 17(24): 1945–1946.
Ortiz de Montellano, Bernard
 1975 Empirical Aztec Medicine. Science 188: 215–220.
Oswald, I. H.
 1983 Are Traditional Healers the Solution to the Failure of Primary Health Care in Rural Nepal? Social Science and Medicine 17(5): 255–257.
Oyeneye, O. Y.
 1985 Mobilizing Indigenous Resource [sic] for Primary Health Care in Nigeria: a Note on the Place of Traditional Medicine. Social Science and Medicine 20(1): 67–69.
Plowman, T.
 1981 Amazonian Coca. Journal of Ethnopharmacology 3: 195–225.
Plowman, T. and Rivier, L.
 1983 Cocaine and Cinnamoylcocaine Content of *Erythroxylum* species. Annals of Botany 51: 641–659.
Ramanamurthy, R. S. V.
 1969 Physiological Effects of 'Hot' and 'Cold' Foods in Human Subjects. Journal of Nutrition and Dietetics 6: 187–191.
Rindos, David
 1984 The Origins of Agriculture: an Evolutionary Perspective. New York: Academic Press.

Ritchie, J. Murdoch, and Cohen, Peter J.
  1975 Local Anesthetics. *In* The Pharmacological Basis of Therapeutics. 5th edition. L. S. Goodman and A. Gilman, (eds.) pp. 379–403. New York: Macmillan.
Rivier, L.
  1981 Analysis of Alkaloids in Leaves of Cultivated *Erythrozylum* and Characterization of Alkaline Substances Used during Coca Chewing. Journal of Ethnopharmacology 3: 313–335.
Rodriguez, P., Cavin, J. C. and West, J. E.
  1982 The Possible Role Amazonian Psychoactive Plants in the Chemotherapy of Parasitic Worms – a Hypothesis. Journal of Ethnopharmacology 6: 303–309.
Russell, Susan D.
  1984 Curing and Commerce: Changes in an Indigenous Medical Practice in a Highland Philippine town. Social Science and Medicine 18(2): 129–137.
Sargent, Carolyn, Marcucci, John and Elliston, Ellen
  1983 Tiger Bones, Fire and Wine: Maternity Care in a Kampuchean Refugee Community. Medical Anthropology 7(4): 67–79.
Schultes, R. E.
  1967 The Botanical Origins of South American Snuffs. *In* Ethnopharmacological Search for Psychoactive Drugs. D. H. Efron, B. Holmstedt and N. S. Kline, (eds.) pp. 291–306. Washington, DC: US Department of Health, Education and Welfare, Publication No. 1645. Government Printing Office.
Shahid, Nigar S., Mizanur Rahman., A. S. M., Azia, K. M. A., Faruque, A. S. G. and Bari, M. A.
  1983 Beliefs and Treatment Related to Diarrhoeal Episodes Reported in Association with Measles. Tropical and Geogragphical Medicine 35: 151–156.
Shanmugasundaram, K. R., Seethapathy P. G. and Shanmugasundaram, E. R. B.
  1983a Anna Pavala Sindhooram – An Antiatherogenic Indian Drug. Journal of Ethnopharmacology 7(3): 247–225.
Shanmugasundaram, K. R., Marita, R., Rajagopal, C., Shanmugasundaram, E. R. B. and Misra, K. P.
  1983b Plasma Cholesterol and Lipoprotein Lowering Effect of Anna Pavala Sindhooram. Journal of Ethnopharmacology 8(1): 19–34.
Shanmugasundaram, K. R. and Parthasarathy, R.
  1983c Lipids and Cholesterol Esterifying Enzyme Changes by Anna Pavala Sindhooram Therapy in Experimental Rat Hyperlipaemia. Journal of Ethnopharmacology 8(1): 35–52.
Siegel, R. K.
  1982 Cocaine Smoking. Journal of Psychoactive Drugs 14: 271–299.
Turner, Nancy J.
  1984 Counter-irritant and Other Medicinal Uses of Plants in Ranunculaceae by Native Peoples in British Columbia and Neighboring Areas. Journal of Ethnopharmacology 11(2): 181–201.
Turner, Victor and Turner, Edith
  1982 Religious Celebrations. *In* Celebration: Studies in Festivity and Ritual. V. Turner, (ed.) pp. 201–219. Washington, DC: Smithsonian Institution Press.
van Beek, T. A., Verpoorte, R., Baerheim Svendsen, A., Leeuwenberg, A. J. M. and Bisset, N. G.
  1984 *Tabernaemontana* L. (Apocynaceae): A Review of its Taxonomy, Phytochemistry, Ethnobotany and Pharmacology. Journal of Ethnopharmacology 10(1): 1–156.
van Zeist, W. and Casparie W. A.
  1984 Plants and Ancient Man: Studies in Palaeoethnobotany. Rotterdam: A.A. Balkema.

Velimirovic, Helga, and Velimirovic, Boris
   1980   Do Traditional Plant Medicines Have a Future in Third World Countries? Curare 3: 173–191.
Wassen, H. S.
   1979   On Concepts of Disease among Amerindian Tribal Groups. Journal of Ethnopharmacology 1(3): 285–293.
Watson, P. L., Luanratana, O. and Griffin, W. J.
   1983   The Ethnopharmacology of Pituri. Journal of Ethnopharmacology 8(3): 303–311.
Weisberg, Daniel H.
   1984   The Practice of 'Dr' Paep: Continuity and Change in Indigenous Healing in Northern Thailand. Social Science and Medicine 18(2): 117–128.
WHO
   1978   Promotion and Development of Traditional Medicine. World Health Organization Technical Report Series 622. Geneva: WHO.
Wilbert, Johannes
   1983   Warao Ethnopathology and Exotic Epidemic disease. Journal of Ethnopharmacology 8(3): 357–361.
Young, Allan
   1976   Some Implications of Medical Beliefs and Practices for Social Anthropology. American Anthropologist 78(1): 5–24.
   1977   Order, Analogy, and Efficacy in Ethiopian Medical Divination. Culture, Medicine and Psychiatry 1: 183–199.
   1983   The Relevance of Traditional Medical Cultures to Modern Primary Health Care. Social Science and Medicine 17(16): 1205–1211.

CONCLUSION

SJAAK VAN DER GEEST[1]

PHARMACEUTICAL ANTHROPOLOGY: PERSPECTIVES FOR RESEARCH AND APPLICATION

This collection of papers offers an anthropological perspective on pharmaceuticals in developing countries. It assembles contributions that describe the context of medicines and stress the cultural relativity of their transaction and meaning. We hope that the volume will be seen as a beginning – a first step in the development of a new and exciting research field in medical anthropology. Therefore, it seems appropriate to end the book with a preliminary stocktaking and some suggestions for future research in pharmaceutical anthropology. The final section of this chapter will discuss the possibilities of using this research for improving conditions of drug consumption in developing countries.

THE LATE APPEARANCE OF PHARMACEUTICAL ANTHROPOLOGY

Until very recently, most anthropologists failed to 'de-naturalize' their own cultural conventions and products. They regarded familiar Western phenomena in the field as 'natural' and unfit for anthropological scrutiny. Only non-Western customs and artifacts drew their attention as possible study objects. Only the exotic was seen as 'cultural'; the familiar things were just 'natural'.

It should be emphasized, however, that some anthropologists did not take their own culture for granted. They attempted to question certain traditions at home by showing examples of other traditions that proved successful solutions to the problems of life. Or they wanted to gain a deeper understanding of their own way of life by confronting it with alternatives in other cultures. This applies for example to early anthropologists such as Mead and Benedict, and also to some extent to people as different as Lévi-Strauss, Diamond and Harris. The wish to know oneself by knowing other people was a primal inspiration to anthropology, as expressed in the title of Kluckhohn's (1949) book *Mirror for Man*. The net result, however, was that even anthropologists who did not take their own culture for granted, took little interest in Western phenomena abroad. They were looking for an alternative way of life and an alternative way of thinking: *the other culture*.

This also explains why Western biomedicine was seldom studied by anthropologist working outside their own culture. Until about 1975, probably even later, ethnographic work by medical anthropologists was almost entirely devoted to 'traditional' medical phenomena. Early reviews of medical anthropological research (Caudill 1953; Polgar 1962; Scotch 1963; Fabrega 1971; Colson and Selby 1974) underscore this unambiguously. At first these phenomena were studied within the framework of religion (cf. Whyte n.d.), belief system or politics. The most conspicuous examples are 'witchcraft', 'sorcery', and 'magic'. Most authors did not even regard these as 'medical' and the term 'medical anthropology' was not coined until much later. When medical anthropology as a separate field of study came into existence research focused on 'indigenous' beliefs and practices. Around that time the term 'ethnomedicine' was coined referring exclusively to the study of non-Western medicine. It is significant that the aspect of being 'ethnic' (cultural) was not extended to Western medicine. This myopia continued when the distinction between 'disease' and 'illness' was introduced. 'Disease', the Western scientific definition of a health problem, was exempted from cultural questions; 'illness', on the other hand, tended 'to be viewed as a cultural category and as a set of culturally related events' (Fabrega 1971: 167).

I am not saying that the Western-type public health programs in the colonies and – later on – 'developing countries' entirely escaped the attention of social scientists. I do however contend that Western medicine in the non-Western world was not studied as a cultural phenomenon. Applied anthropologists who carried out research for the benefit of public health programs did not examine these programs but studied indigenous ideas and practices which were seen as 'barriers' to the acceptance of Western medicine (cf. Paul 1955; Foster 1976).

Only recently have medical anthropologist turned towards biomedicine as an object for cultural research, both in non-Western and Western societies. Hahn and Kleinman (1983: 305) have called the exploration of biomedicine 'a new frontier in medical anthropology'. Studies of biomedicine in a non-Western context often deal with themes such as medical pluralism, therapy choice, and the cultural hegemony of biomedicine. It is significant that, in spite of the interest in biomedicine as a cultural tradition open to anthropological research, anthropologists have hardly begun to look at 'the hard core' of biomedicine: pharmaceuticals. Until very recently the delusion that biomedicine was 'beyond culture' still hovered around its therapeutic substances. Now at last anthropologists are beginning to direct their unsettling questions at what used to be entirely taken for granted, their medicines.

FIVE THEMES IN PHARMACEUTICAL ANTHROPOLOGY

The contributions to this volume have been arranged aroung two broad themes, transaction and meaning. The former comprises studies that stress the more tangible events concerning drugs and view them in their social, economic and political context. Contributions assembled under the latter theme focus on more hidden aspects of pharmaceuticals: their symbolic value, the way they are perceived by those involved in their transaction. The distinction transaction versus meaning is artificial; both move together throughout the 'life' of a drug. Together they constitute, as it were, the outside and the inside of the cultural context.

Here I propose a somewhat different division of research themes. Following, more or less, the 'biography' of a drug we could perhaps distinguish five themes that lend themselves to anthropological research. These do not refer to well-defined and separate fields of study, but rather indicate prominent themes in pharmaceutical anthropology that are closely interrelated and overlap one another considerably. The five themes to be discussed here are: (1) production and marketing; (2) prescription; (3) distribution; (4) use; and (5) efficacy.

Production and marketing

The most busily researched theme is without doubt the production and marketing of Western pharmaceuticals, but little of this research has been done from an anthropological perspective. Most of it is economic. Numerous studies have tried to provide an 'anatomy' of the pharmaceutical industry showing how its transnational character allows better control of the market, transfer pricing, dumping and other practices that enhance profits. Of special interest are the patent system, the transfer of technology, biased information on drug use, and promotional activities by sales representatives.[2]

The overriding – and rather obvious – conclusion is that pharmaceutical production has a commercial character that is concealed behind images of scientific research and medical concern. But investigating the structure and practice of the pharmaceutical industry does not always provide the necessary context for making its existence and successes intelligible. Several questions remain unanswered: how is the industry able to continue certain harmful practices; why do the governments of importing or exporting countries not put a stop to these practices; how does the medical system at large relate to the pharmaceutical industry; how do legal systems and insurance programs support the commercial interests of the industry; and, how does the promotion and supply of medicines 'work' in concrete situations. Economic analysis can be revealing (for example the finding that the term 'Research & Development' covers on the average about twice as many expenses for advertising as for research, but usually it provides only a fragmentary picture of this complex industry.

It is precisely this lack of information about the context in which drugs are manufactured and sold to developing countries that allows the continuation of dubious marketing practices. Companies (and others who share in their profits) are not interested in such information and may, consciously or not, suppress the scanty, but rapidly growing, social research about pharmaceutical distribution in developing countries. At the same time, however, critics of existing drug policies have insufficient anthropological field evidence at their disposal to be able to persuade policy makers to introduce drastic changes.

The activities of sales representatives are a case in point. There is increasing evidence that 'sales reps' are particularly numerous and active in a number of developing countries where they exert considerable influence on doctor's prescribing patterns. Drug representatives provide doctors with drug information and free samples. They often reward doctors for prescribing particular drugs. Yudkin (1980: 459) reports that in 1977 there was one representative for every four doctors in Tanzania as compared with only one for every twenty in Britain.

Drug representatives visit not only physicians but also pharmacists and traditional practitioners, since these 'prescribe' pharmaceuticals as well. Boeken et al. (1981: 16) write that reps in the Philippines visit pharmacies where they can check doctors' prescriptions to find out what drugs they prescribe. Some case material on reps is presented by Melrose (1982: 63), Boeken et al. (1981: 122), Nichter (1981, 1983: 962) and Giovanni (1980). But on the whole little is known about them with certainty and anthropological research on them will be difficult as this is likely to interfere with their commercial activities.

The international pharmaceutical industry receives considerable support from a world-wide ideology concerning the importance of development and a firm belief in the blessings of technological progress, capital investment and employment. These allow drug companies to justify their role in the developing world as assisting in development and technological advancement. These concerns also allow companies to disregard their failures and their critics and to advance unsupported claims which fit with the ideology of development in both the developed and 'underdeveloped' world. It is striking that with regard to pharmaceuticals this development ideology is strongest where its failure is most conspicuous: in the Third World.

The culture of pharmaceutical production and marketing is amenable to anthropological research. In the description above I may have given the impression that the pharmaceutical industry is an evil institution fully conscious of its harmful practices. I am sure it is not. Mercantilism is a cultural phenomenon with its own ideas and institutionalized practices. In every culture people have their blind eyes and techniques to justify their ways of life and to prove their superiority over other cultures. The culture of pharmaceutical production is usually little understood by its critics. It seems only logical that anthropologists also apply their call for an 'emic approach' to research on the pharmaceutical industry. Why not grasp 'the native's point of view' when it comes to the capitalist entrepreneur?

It becomes clear from this sketch that research into other themes, such as prescription, distribution and consumption of medicines partially provides the context of drug production and marketing. I am referring both to the social conditions of drug supply and to the more hidden assumptions and intentions of producers and suppliers, the visible and invisible context, the transaction and meaning of medicines.

In this volume only scanty attention has been devoted to the context of production and marketing. Afdhal and Welsch discuss the ambiguous cultural convergence of the production of Indonesian *jamu* and Western pharmaceuticals. Wolffers describes the activities of a self-styled drug manufacturer in Sri Lanka and the marketing practices of drug representatives in two villages. Ferguson too reports about drug representatives and explains that the pharmaceutical self-help sector in El Salvador has emerged under the commercial pressure of the international industry.

On the ground research about the marketing of medicines is perhaps the most conspicuous gap in studies analysing the role of pharmaceutical firms in developing countries.

Prescription

There would be good reasons to place drug prescription by medical doctors and paramedics in the same category as the distribution of drugs by pharmacists and vendors, but it is presented here as a separate theme because doctors and paramedics are usually thought of as a distinct category.

Studies on the role of doctors in the prescription and distribution of drugs in developing countries have mainly been carried out by medical and pharmacological researchers. They have produced information on a number of the more hidden aspects of drug prescription, some of which are clearly disturbing. As we shall see momentarily, the purchase of prescription drugs without a doctor's prescription is a major problem in many developing countries. This does not imply, however, that where prescriptions *are* used, drug distribution functions well. I shall present four issues from the literature that cast serious doubt on the appropriateness of much prescribing and plead for a sociocultural analysis. Some of these issues obtain also in Western societies.

One of the most interesting aspects of drug prescription is its symbolic meaning. Smith (1980) identified 17 'latent functions' of prescribing, some of which are communicative and symbolic. The prescription entails a confirmation and tangible proof of the patient's illness that allows him to assume the social role of 'being sick'. But at the same time the prescription also confirms the doctor's social role. Melville and Johnson (1982: 180–1) summarize Smith's views as follows:

Prescribing has clear advantages for doctors and they cooperate with patients to produce this mutually desired outcome. It is a display of the doctor's power and privilege . . . In exchange for the acknowledgement of this position of power and trustworthiness, he gives a token, a symbol of his concern: the prescription.

The fact that the prescription (and the medicine!) and not something else (for example the conversation) has become the focus of medical symbolism is no coincidence. Prescribing reflects the curative thrust of Western medicine. Moreover, as Melville and Johnson (1982: 181) remark, 'it is easy to prescribe, it requires less thought[3] and effort than a carefully explained suggestion about life style change'. And finally, there are clear time-saving (read: financial) advantages to prescribing. It is more quickly finished than a discussion of life problems and it is a subtle but effective device to announce the end of the consultation and send the patient away to make room for the next customer. But because prescribing is such a powerful symbol it is also likely to be overused; overprescription seems an obvious consequence.

A second point raised by some authors is that physicians are not always well informed about the most appropriate drugs (cf. Speight 1975). This is partly due to the fact that many physicians in the Third World rely on information materials provided by the industry, and these may be biased to suit the industry's interests.[4] Senturias et al. (1984), who conducted a preliminary survey among 135 physicians in Manila, report frequent prescription of doubtful drugs for four common ailments. Similar observations were made by Group DCP (1984) and Hardon (1987). Silverman et al. (1982: 91) quote seven drug experts in the Third World who 'label much of the prescribing in their countries as irrational'. They mention several types of 'irrational prescribing',[5] one of which is the preference for injections. This preference has been widely reported, also in medical journals. Greenhalgh (1987) provides quantitative data on injections in India and Kleinman (1980: 287–8) in his Taiwan study suggests that this professional preference is based on a mix of science, psychology and commerce:

As odd as it sounds, of the 300 cases we observed in the clinics (private and public) of Western-style practitioners, fewer than one-fourth failed to receive injections of one sort or another. There is a strong financial motive here . . . If a practitioner gives the patient medicine to take orally, he gets paid, but less than if he gives the patient an injection. Furthermore, giving an injection is giving the patient the message that you are offering him the best treatment you possess. Consequently, almost all medicinal agents that can be given by injections are so administered . . . Many Western style doctors told me this was dangerous, quite unnecessary practice, but one they could not relinquish given the 'realities' of clinical care in Taiwan. They feared the loss of income and patients.

This practice shows that the transmission of medical concepts not only goes from professional to layperson, a type of medicalization which De Swaan (1983: 216) calls 'proto-professionalisation', but also in the opposite direction: doctors comply with their patients' expectations and ideas. This remarkable phenomenon has been little noticed.[6] The view that drugs are an essential element in any treatment is common not only among large groups of patients,[7] but also among doctors. It may be enlightening to study this belief as a symptom of doctor's compliance.

The opposite is also discussed in the literature: the lack of concern physicians sometimes have for the conditions in which their patients live. This leads to another kind of 'irrational prescribing', i.e. prescribing drugs which people cannot buy. As a result patients may select just some of the prescribed drugs that they can pay for and leave the others. Muller (1982: 45–61) rightly points out that even though such drugs are 'effective' they are not 'efficient'. For economic reasons people are not able to use them. Some authors who refer to the socio-psychological gap between prescribing doctors and poor patients are Melrose 1982, Senturias et al. 1984, and Shatrughna n.d.[8]

These observations are, of course, related to the fact that physicians themselves have commercial interests in prescribing. This is the case if they sell the medicines they prescribe or if they have connections with pharmaceutical distributors. What I have called 'irrational prescribing' above may be irrational according to medical standards and also from the patients' point of view, but 'rational' in other senses because it serves the physician's economic interests. Kleinman (1980: 287) reports that most doctors in Taiwan sell their own medicines in order to receive the maximum profit from their prescriptions. In such situations, overprescribing obviously yields considerable benefits. Similarly, Melrose (1982: 86–89) gives striking examples of overprescribing in North Yemen, Burkina Faso and Bangladesh, which she refers to as 'sledge-hammer therapy'. Overprescribing seems to occur worldwide, but there can be little doubt that it is least controlled in developing countries.

It should be noted, that overprescription for economic reasons occurs not only in commercial health services. 'Non-profit', usually church-related, institutions often make considerable profits by selling medicines. Hospitals and health centers with little or no government subsidy have often found that the easiest way for them to obtain an income lies in the sale of drugs. Overprescription of course is likely to ensue in such a situation (cf. Barnett et al. 1980: 495).

A last problem to be mentioned is that patients tend to imitate prescriptions in self-medication. Overprescribing or otherwise irrational prescribing by doctors may thus lead to dubious methods of self- medication. Hardon (1987) reports this for the Philippines, Group DCP (1984) for Brazil, and Greenhalgh (1987) for India.

Distribution

Drug distribution tends to be extremely complex in most developing countries. Comparison with distribution in the Western world is misleading. The situation is often paradoxically marked by both shortage and abundance. The shortage concerns essential drugs, cheap and useful; the abundance non-essential drugs, usually expensive, often superfluous and sometimes harmful. Moreover, prescription drugs tend to be readily available without a prescription, even in countries that require a prescription for their purchase.

The most typical situation is that legal and illegal distribution are intertwined. Ferguson (this volume) speaks of a 'two-tier delivery system', but the 'illegal' practice is usually socially accepted and 'normal'. Parallelling this, one often finds an articulation between public and private distribution. In Cameroon (Van der Geest, this volume), the private sale of drugs tends to be made possible by the failure of free public distribution, and, inversely, the private sale renders distribution in the public sector inefficient. There is strong evidence that the two-tier system described for El Salvador and Cameroon occurs widely in the Third World.

Anthropological research should describe and analyze the linkages between the various kinds of drug distribution. The informal, often illegal, character of these linkages also requires an informal research approach. Thus, the anthropological tradition of participant observation and unstructured interviewing seems particularly apt for studying this topic.

Research could also focus on one or more of the various types of distributors. The following have been mentioned by a number of authors: pharmacists, health care workers such as doctors, nurses and non-medical personnel, traditional healers, and unqualified drug vendors.

The role of pharmacists in developing countries is increasingly under study, usually from a critical perspective. Researchers have often found that pharmacists routinely give medical advice and prescribe drugs.[9] They also find that much of the actual work in pharmacies is carried out by unqualified personnel.[10] To understand people's visits to pharmacies and their use of pharmaceuticals recommended by the pharmacy staffs, there is a great need for more research into what drugs are being suggested and what information passes from pharmacists (or their assistants) to clients and also into how patients are using these medicines as a result of such consultations. The chapters in this volume by Ferguson, Kloos et al. and Logan provide examples of what can be achieved by examining the role of pharmacists in local contexts.

Personnel in health centers and hospitals are important drug distributors. Their formal role as prescribers is discussed above, but it is clear that they also play a role as informal distributors of drugs. The two-tier delivery system often allows them to function as private practitioners alongside their official tasks in health care institutions. This practice seems extremely wide-spread; it involves doctors as well as nurses and non-medical workers.[11] Their access to pharmaceuticals and other necessities enables them to provide medical services in their homes (or private clinics). Often patients may look in vain for these services in the public institutions. This is a delicate topic for social research, since these practices are likely to be illegal and may be regarded as criminal if they involve theft or medical harm to patients. But in some instances 'moonlighting' practices of this kind are highly appreciated by patients and constitute the best services available. For obvious reasons the informal practices of formal health personnel (cf. Van der Geest 1982b) have as yet hardly been studied and anthropologists should pursue this topic with greater vigor.

Another pattern that is beginning to receive considerable attention is the involvement of indigenous practitioners in the distribution of modern drugs. These may be practitioners of all kinds, from an Indian Ayurvedic doctor (Burghart, this volume) to a Mexican *h'iloletik* (Fabrega and Silver 1973).[12] These practices seem to be a logical outgrowth of what has come to be called medical pluralism, though they are also encouraged by attractive commercial benefits for the practitioners. As Landy (1978) has suggested, anthropologists should study the activities and position of these traditional practitioners within the context of pluralistic and rapidly changing health care situations. Unfortunately, most studies have tended to study indigenous medical practices in isolation from and in contrast to Western medicine. This has often resulted in a biased picture, either romanticizing or deprecating indigenous medicine. The contributions of Wolffers and Burghart to this volume provide a more realistic approach to the sorts of development actually occurring among 'traditional healers'.

A fourth category consists of drug vendors without any formal pharmaceutical training. Their widespread occurrence in developing countries seems to be largely due to inefficiencies in the formal drug delivery system, but there can be little doubt that they are also encouraged by the great demand for drugs among the population. Drug vendors fill in gaps in the formal health care system, particularly when health services are unevenly spread throughout the country resulting in shortages of drugs, especially in rural areas. While private pharmacists are usually found only in urban centers, drug vendors tend to spread very widely, even in rural areas. Despite what one might expect, there are some remarkable examples of their efficiency.[13] It is therefore no wonder that their services are eagerly sought and their practices, though illegal, are often tolerated. Surprisingly, the illegal sale of drugs even occurs where drugs are readily available through legal avenues, sometimes where drugs are free of charge. Drug vendors are not restricted to the remote villages, but are found in the markets and shops of major towns that have hospitals and pharmacies. They can even be found on the doorsteps of hospitals and health centers. The most likely reason that they can conduct an active trade in such situations is that they are more approachable than physicians or nurses. Some authors (e.g. Alland 1979; Bleek 1979; Gonzalez 1966) have suggested that sick people in their area of research were really after Western pharmaceuticals and regarded the Western trained health worker as an 'unnecessary adjunct' to the pharmaceuticals. Buying drugs directly from a shop or vendor, saved them much time, inconvenience and embarrassment.[14]

Drug vendors constitute an enormously variform category. Some are merely merchants, while others add some medical practice to their trade, for example giving injections; some specialize in pharmaceuticals and tend to have a substantial assortment of drugs, while others sell only a few of the most needed together with other essentials for daily life such as bread, rice, cigarettes, sardines and batteries; some have a fixed place for their trade, a shop or a booth, others are mobile and travel from village to village.

Although it is generally recognized that illegal drug vendors are common in the Third World, research about them is virtually non-existent. A host of studies can be cited which briefly mention the drug vendor,[15] but I know only four studies that more or less focus on them. Cunningham (1970) describes the Thai 'injection doctor' as a mediator between popular and professional medicine and provides case material on two injection doctors. One of them had first worked as a 'doctor's assistant' in a government health center. Such links are often reported[16] and it seems probable that some informal drug providers started their careers while attached to a health institution, for example, as a lowly ranked nurse, a laboratory assistant, a cleaner or a porter. Two other studies by Kloos (1974) and Nordberg (1974) describe drug vendors in Ethiopia. Kloos as a geographer is mainly interested in spatial and economic aspects of their trade. Nordberg studies the types of pharmaceuticals sold in 25 rural drug shops, the number of clients and the amount they spent. Fassin (1985), who did research on markets in the capital of Senegal, explains why the Senegalese society and the authorities tollerate the illicit trade in medicines. One of his answers is that the society cannot do without this informal distribution as the state's provisions are insufficient. Moreover, the clandestine business produces attractive fringe benefits for various groups of people among whom the police. Fassin also has interesting things to say about the careers and 'training' of medicine vendors.

Little is known about the social context in which drug vendors operate and, as far as I am aware, there has hardly been any participant observation in their shops (however, my investigation in South Cameroon, reported in this volume, and Fassin's work in Senegal suggest that such research is quite feasible). Even less is known about drug vendors' beliefs and medical knowledge or the financial aspects of their trade.[17] As a result, one finds contradictory statements about drug vendors in the literature; some authors regard them as extremely dangerous while others have suggested that they be given some training and included in the formal health care system. It is high time we had a clearer and more complete picture of this recent but very common provider of popular health care. Two studies in this volume try to fill this gap: Kloos et al. and Van der Geest.

Use of medicines

In Western society the use of medicines has been mainly studied from a medico-centered perspective, as 'compliance' and 'non-compliance'. Only recently is it beginning to be studied through a patient-centered approach, as 'self-regulation' (see for example Conrad 1985). In non-Western societies it has never been very useful to regard patients' use or non-use of drugs as non-compliance, although the majority of health workers in these countries probably continue to do so. The role of doctor's prescription has been marginal in most developing countries (despite the importance health care administrators have placed on the role of physicians in the health care systems) and self-medication has probably been the predominant feature of pharmaceutical use in all non-Western societies. Self-medication in such societies traditionally consisted largely of taking home-made, usually herbal, medications. This practice has, however, increasingly been complemented or replaced by the use of industrially manufactured pharmaceuticals, either Western products or drugs from non-Western manufacturers such as Ayurveda, Unani, Jamu and the like.

Although self-medication is probably the dominant therapy even in Western societies (often accounting for 75 percent or more of all treatments), it has received little research attention. Researchers have characteristically considered self-medication trivial and uninteresting. Moreover, since self-medication lies outside the domain of formal health care services it was easy to overlook it. Informants tend to take self-medication as a matter of course and may forget instances of self-treatment in their own lives. Here again, the use of patent medicines and self-administered drugs are so much a part of the researcher's own life, that it often goes unnoticed in the study community. Only in the past few years has the interest in self-medication grown.[18] This is probably related to the attention given to primary health care and the increasing recognition that most health care occurs in the home. Self-medication is coping with health problems at the most primary level. It should be an extremely important theme in pharmaceutical anthropology.

To understand patients' use of drugs the anthropological approach of contextualization and de-naturalization looks particularly fruitful. 'Contextualization' is partly – but *only* partly – provided by analyzing the several research themes discussed above: the role of the industry, the distribution and marketing system, and prescription by doctors or other individuals. But the context of drug use is not limited to the pharmaceutical themes alone. It also includes wider socio-economic data, kinship, religion, medical pluralism and the integration of new ideas or practices with more traditional ones. It is important that patients' drug use not be approached as a process that exclusively concerns the patient (i.e. a strictly patient-centered approach) or is merely a social process of doctor-patient interaction (what is typically a practitioner-centered approach). As Janzen (1978) and a number of others have shown, the family or domestic unit and the community are often centrally involved in making health decisions for the patient as a 'therapy management group'. Indeed, in many cases the family's input may be as important or more significant than that of a doctor or patient.[19]

The use of pharmaceuticals must be understood within the total health seeking process of the individual as part of a social group and a wider community. It is impossible to draw the boundaries of this *relevant* context apriori, and thus it is the task of the anthropologist to assess what aspects of the broader context are relevant, based on his empirical knowledge of the community under study.

There is one context feature which seems particularly relevant to the study of drug consumption: the social control which is felt most acutely during periods of sickness. Western pharmaceuticals can be bought privately (with money that can be earned individually) and they allow a sick person to bypass those who otherwise might have used his sickness to exert social pressure upon him. Whyte (this volume) sees medicines as a 'liberating' force in contrast with ritual and relational therapies that confirm the patient's place in relation to others. It seems likely, therefore, that where self-medication with Western medicines increases, the importance of the family-based 'therapy management group' will diminish.

The common observation that people often prefer to purchase medicines without consulting a physician (e.g. Alland 1970; Ferguson this volume) should be seen in that light; doctors are no less agents of social control than lineage elders. The urge to bypass others will be the greatest when the sickness is embarrassing and threatens to impair a person's reputation, for example in the case of venereal disease (see Kloos et al. this volume) or induced abortion. Indeed the increase of venereal disease in Africa may well have fueled the demand for Western drugs (oral communication S. Whyte), and so may the growing practice of clandestine abortion.

'De-naturalization' also depends partly on the themes discussed above, but even more so on the theme yet to be considered: the concept of drug efficacy. De-naturalization of pharmaceuticals can only be achieved by stepping outside the context of pharmaceutical use in the study community, but it also requires that the researcher step outside his own cultural context. Taking medicines is not a *natural* act *per se*; it appears so to the social actors concerned (and often to the researcher) because of their culturally imposed premises. No matter how natural drug taking may initially seem it is always supported by arbitrary cultural conventions. Ideas about when to take drugs and what kinds of drugs are the correct ones or the most effective ones are inevitably part of an individual's cultural heritage (it should be noted that this is as true of the physician, whose cultural heritage includes his or her medical training, as of the rural patient).

Moreover, underlying these ideas about medicine use are subconscious symbolizations that can be elucidated only with great care. One of the most important of these symbolizations is that medicine use affirms and legitimizes the patient as being sick. Clearly, the symbolic aspects of pharmaceutical use will differ from culture to culture and from situation to situation, but this merely demonstrates the cultural arbitrariness of these underlying concepts about medicines.It is thus the anthropologist's task to examine these concepts and symbolizations in order to 'de-naturalize' patients' drug use. This brings us to people's concepts of pharmaceuticals, perhaps the most important part of the context of medicine use.

In spite of the keen interest in the cognitive and symbolic aspects of culture that has long been present in anthropology (and is very much in vogue in medical anthropology), people's concepts and ideas about pharmaceuticals have remained little studied. Indigenous ideas, classifications and medical beliefs became popular topics for research, but in most cases these ideas were regarded as almost static, intra-cultural phenomena. 'Ethnomedicine' in particular, which became a dominant theme in medical anthropology, was defined as referring to beliefs and practices that were products of (almost exclusively) indigenous cultural development (Hughes 1978: 151), thus contrasting these beliefs with Western medical thought. In most cases this research has concentrated on constructing static and overly systematized descriptions of the traditional medical system often using the ethnographic present (and thus ignoring the numerous changes in local medical practices that have come with colonization). Moreover, despite the assertion that local people do not present their medical ideas and beliefs in such a systematic fashion, the majority of such studies strive to describe such medical beliefs as a consistent and coherent belief system. Indeed, it can be argued that the oversystematization of traditional beliefs has in itself created an artificial problem for analysis (cf. Unschuld, this volume). When traditional medical beliefs are depicted as unchanging, it becomes difficult to understand why so many Third World communities readily seek imported pharmaceuticals.

Only gradually has the study of indigenous medical beliefs begun to shed its static character and some anthropologists have begun to examine how foreign ideas and practices are conceptualized by users to make them fit existing cultural concepts. Welsch (1983: 35), for example, argues that anthropologists are too quick to describe local beliefs as *conflicting* with Western medical thinking, and goes on to show that among the Ningerum of Papua New Guinea Western medicine is instead 'highly integrated into the local setting' (1983: 36). Judging from the wide-spread popularity of Western medicines, it is indeed plausible that the cultural 'integration' or 'reinterpretation' of Western medical thought and practice has been taking place far more frequently than is reported by anthropologists.[20]

Some examples of such a 'reinterpretation' may be briefly mentioned here. Alland (1979) shows that the Abron in Ivory Coast interpret the activities of Western-trained medical doctors and nurses by classing them with indigenous analogues. Lewis (1981) describes how people in Papua New Guinea use Western disease terminology for an indigenous classification system. Van Luijk (1981: 53) gives the example of a Kamba herbalist in Kenya who uses Western teaching material about the life cycle of the schistosoma fluke in his practice, explaining every sickness as coming from the gall bladder.[21] Examples of research into the 'reinterpretation' of Western pharmaceuticals in a non-Western culture are particularly hard to find. One outstanding example, however, is M. Logan's (1973) study of the hot-cold classifcation of pharmaceuticals by Guatemalan peasants. It is significant that for a long period of time Logan's research did not inspire colleagues working in other cultures. Nichter (1980) was one of the first to attempt a similar approach in southern India, but did not refer to Logan's example. The same applies to Kleinman's

(1980) voluminous study of medicine in Taiwan, to Mitchell's (1983) publication on pharmaceutical concepts in Jamaica and to an article by Herxheimer and Stimson (1983) which scrutinized the literature about lay views on medicine use. It seems clear that for more than ten years medical anthropologists did not perceive the reinterpretation of pharmaceuticals as a relevant research topic.

Bledsoe and Goubaud (this volume) have rediscovered Logan's study.[22] Their discussion of Mende reinterpretation of Western medicines in Sierra Leone deals with people's perception of qualities such as form, color and taste. Medications for three common ailments are studied. At the same time the authors emphasize that medications reinterpreted by the Mende are sometimes of dubious benefit or even dangerous from a Western pharmacological point of view, thus reflecting at the same time Western medical concerns. Another example of reinterpration of Western pharmaceuticals is provided by Del Vecchio Good (1980) who reports that women in Iran translate the working and side-effects of the contraceptive pill into their own cultural concepts of physiology. The most drastic case of reinterpretation I know of is reported by Burghart (this volume): an Ayurvedic healer asserts that injectable penicillin *is* an Ayurvedic medicine. Confiscation is the ultimate form of reinterpretation.

I expect that pharmaceutical concepts will be an active research theme in a few years time. Both the growing interest in pharmaceuticals, and the popularity of a cognitive/symbolic perspective point in this direction. There are, however, two caveats that should be noted.

In the first place we should beware of a too cultural view of indigenous culture. There is a danger that, in their zeal to 'find' cultural concepts, anthropologists will construct them.[23] Anthropologists sometimes expect clear-cut, articulate, ideas where their informants may be inarticulate and vague. They are trained not to be satisfied with the answer 'I don't know', but to press further until the informant tells what he 'knows'. Last (1981) has drawn attention to the possibility that the informant really does not know and that the most important cultural 'concept' may be the absence of clear concepts: simply 'not knowing'. Last writes that in Northern Nigeria many Hausa medical terms have no standard meaning (1981: 390). He suggests that it would perhaps be more appropriate to speak of a non-system, although he is aware that people systematize even in the context of such a 'non-system'. Last's main point, however, is well taken: people's thinking and acting upon health problems may be considerably less well-defined than anthropologists, hunting for meaning and rationality, may want to admit. This suggestion could well be applicable to the reinterpretation of pharmaceuticals. Decisive motives for taking specific medicines may be ambiguous and even unconscious. Views of the difference between particular medicines may constitute a non-system in Last's sense. What *is* systematic is the ritual of drug taking which, as I have suggested earlier, provides a symbolic marking of the fact that a person is ill or that he is being treated and will thus recover. Viewed in this way, not the type of drug, but drug *taking* as a culturally defined act, seems of primary importance.

A second note of caution is that we should beware of a too 'natural' view of our own culture. In pharmaceutical anthropology this would imply an exclusive interest in non-Western concepts about drugs and a neglect of drug concepts in Western countries. There is, however, another more hidden form of 'ethnocentrism': regarding only lay people's concepts as objects of anthropological research and overlooking the 'culturalness' of professional ideas. This bias underlies the original formulation of the 'disease-illness distinction'. But the same ethnocentricism repeatedly appears in studies that accept without question the pharmacological conclusions about the benefits or dangers of pharmaceuticals.[24]

An example of this bias can be found in Helman's (1984) otherwise excellent introduction in medical anthropology. He provides 'exotic' examples of folk-concepts about anatomy, food, illness and medicines in Western society, but hardly pays attention to the ideas of physicians. Kleinman (1980) similarly presents 'colorful' descriptions of patient explanatory models of physiology that conflict with those of the physicians. But while the patients' models are closely scrutinized, those of the nurses and physicians are very much taken for granted. The growing literature on overprescribing suggests that their ideas about drugs merit anthropological research as well. A point deserving special attention is the high preference for injections that has been observed world-wide. This preference exists not only among lay people/ patients (cf. Wyatt 1985),[25] but also among physicians, as we have seen when we discussed drug prescription.

Efficacy

The fifth and last research theme in pharmaceutical anthropology discussed here is drug efficacy. Etkin's contribution to this volume criticizes the biomedical bias of most studies of efficacy in non-Western cultures. She points out that these studies either fail to take local medical theories seriously, or coopt them by conflating them with the biomedical model. She pleads for an interdisciplinary approach which attempts to combine etic and emic viewpoints and takes into account the cultural dimension of efficacy. A similar plea is implied in the growing literature on the placebo effect[26] which suggests that the efficacy of drugs cannot be understood when we limit ourselves to medical-pharmacological explanations. If we make the somewhat artificial distinction between the actual effect of drug taking and the perception of the effect, we can discern a twofold contribution of anthropology to the study of efficacy.

Helman (1984: 106), following Claridge, speaks of a 'total drug effect' which is brought about by various aspects, only one of which is the pharmacological substance of the drug. The other aspects are:

1. the attributes of the drug itself (such as taste, shape, colour and name); 2. those of the patient receiving the drug (such as experience, education, personality, socio-cultural background); 3. those of the person prescribing or dispensing the drug (such as personality, professional status or sense of authority); and 4. the setting in which the drug is administered – the 'drug situation' (such as a doctor's office, laboratory or social occasion).

By studying the context of drug taking we may gain a fuller understanding of efficacy. The various research themes mentioned above present a great deal of that context: the patient's ideas and expectations, the distribution situation, the identity of the drug dispenser, etc. At the same time it should be stressed that it is not known *how* these cultural factors are related to the healing process. The most probable hypothesis is that the patient in a particular context and using the semantic resources available to him 'creates meaning'. It is this meaning which may be either wholesome (placebo) or noxious (nocebo; with the ultimate consequence of 'voodoo death') (cf. Hahn and Kleinman 1983b).[27] Moerman (1983a: 158) says it neatly: 'Meaning mends' and 'Metaphor can heal'. But, again, how this takes place we can only guess at present.

It should be noted that the placebo effect has mostly been regarded as a troublesome disturbance in pharmacological testing. Slowly it has dawned upon some medical scientists that the placebo may be one of the most exciting and promising discoveries in the entire history of medicine. Surprisingly, however, systematic research into the 'roots' of placebo is still minimal. A possible explanation may be that there is little commercial attractiveness in placebos; they cannot be patented and sold by the pharmaceutical industry. The placebo can be likened to 'orphan drugs', pharmaceuticals that are treated in a stepmotherly fashion by the industry because they yield no profit.

There are also, however, good medical reasons that may discourage placebo research, since such research may be counterproductive in terms of effect. Placebo research is likely to destroy its own findings. Placebos seem to be especially effective when patients do not recognize them as placebos. Metaphors thus seem to heal best when they are taken literally, as long as their symbolic identity is not recognized. De-mystification could have the same devastating effect on medicine as it has had on religion.

The most prominent explanation for the reluctance to enter into placebo research is, however, that placebos lie outside the biomedical paradigm and are hardly 'seen' by medical researchers. It is no wonder that the term 'placebo' has been predominantly used in a pejorative sense in biomedicine. It indicated the imperfection of pharmaceuticals, or 'explained' the success of alternative medical practices.[28] 'Placebo', one could say, is often used to mark the boundaries of biomedicine, to express the difference between 'we' and 'they'. Thus, one often finds physicians resistent or even hostile to the idea that when they prescribe drugs with few likely benefits to a patient they are in effect using these as placebos. Instead, physicians generally discuss such practices in terms of the 'known' efficacy of certain pharmaceuticals against particular diseases, ignoring the small probability that this particular illness is the result of the previously identified pathogen for which the drug is known to be effective. This is not to say that the placebo is completely neglected, but that those conducting placebo research find themselves somehow at the fringe of biomedicine.

One short remark should be made about the studies on placebo which *have* appeared. The placebo effect in biomedical practice has been exclusively studied in Western societies. The few existing observations of placebos in a non-Western context apply entirely to indigenous medical practices. The most classic examples are probably Lévi-Strauss' (1963) essays 'The sorcerer and his magic' and 'The effectiveness of symbols'.[29] The Ndembu ethnographic work by Victor Turner has also frequently been cited for its presentation of efficacious therapeutic symbols (see for example Douglas 1975). Non-Western healing practices have often been described as effective because of their histrionic and persuasive character (such as singing, dancing, praying, excorcism, trance, etc.) (cf. Rubenstein 1984). Thus, the effectiveness of placebos, writes Moerman (1981: 257), is underrated in modern and overrated in 'primitive' medicine. The study of Western medicine's placebo in a non-Western context constitutes a special challenge to medical anthropologists and others. It could improve the understanding of placebo in general.

There is a second aspect to the anthropological study of drug efficacy which I will mention only briefly. Anthropologists have pointed out occasionally that efficacy is not a concept that can be measured ojectively. Healing, like beauty, is in the eye of the beholder, it is a cultural concept, that does not lend itself easily to intercultural codification (cf. Hansluwka 1985).

The concept of 'health' (which is the desired result of a drug's efficacy) tends to be inchoate even within local cultures. People, including medical practitioners, find it easier to define illness (or disease) than to describe health. And some societies may even lack an ideal construct of health that corresponds closely to the meaning of 'health' in Western countries. Welsch (1982), for example, makes this point for the Ningerum in Papua New Guinea. Many anthropologists nevertheless have tried to provide a sketch of what people in 'their' culture understand by health.[30] Such sketches often contrast sharply with narrow biomedical definitions. They emphasize that 'health' is a holistic concept, including not only the body but also psychic, social, religious and even economic aspects, referring not only to the individual, but also to his kin, his cattle, his natural environment and his business.[31] There is, however, no *apriori* reason to assume that any society should have a clear concept of health that can be understood in terms of a Weberian 'ideal type'. Thus attempts to define what people understand as 'health' may be a misguided and poorly advised endeavor.

Kleinman (1980: 311–74) who studied the efficacy of various medical systems in Taiwan discusses the 'vexing yet basic question: What is healing?' (p. 354):

Successful treatment (can mean) . . . success in treating the female family member (s), rather than the sick person . . . (or) appropriately treating the fate or expelling the god or ghost possessing the client . . .

Kleinman then seeks shelter in the distinction 'disease' – 'illness'. From an etic biomedical point of view a disease may be treated effectively, even though from an emic cultural point of view, the illness is not, and vice versa (p. 360). Even if this explanation were intellectually satisfying, it would pose a dilemma in practical policy. Should 'charlatans' and 'quack doctors' be tollerated if people regard them as effective? Do 'charlatans' and 'quack doctors' exist at all in the light of an emic definition of efficacy? And what should be done with dubious and dangerous pharmaceuticals when people say they 'work'?[32]

If there is so much variety and vagueness in cultural definitions of health and if the concept of healing is so elusive, an intercultural discussion about the efficacy of medicines becomes problematic, if not impossible. Should streptomycin be called efficacious if it does not appease the ancestors? There are no intercultural standards for health or drug efficacy. In Kleinman's terminology, the perception of effective healing, is part of the Explanatory Model, which may vary from (sub)culture to (sub)culture. The concept of efficacy is itself a cultural artifact. It is the thankless task of the anthropologist to point this out to health planners, without being able to show them an easy way out of the dilemma.

Of course, international criteria for health and healing can be established, but they are bound to be based on cultural dominance, most likely the dominance of biomedicine. Anthropological research should reveal the pitfalls of such an international definition, by emphasizing emic views. But they themselves run the risk of falling into another pitfall, that of overemphasizing the difference and viewing them as static, the trap of exoticism. Research into concepts of drug efficacy is faced with the same challenge mentioned with regard to medicinal concepts in general: it should have an eye open to the transitional, pluralistic and syncretic character of those ideas; it should also take seriously the absence of clear ideas.

PRACTICAL RELEVANCE

It would be gratifying to end this survey of themes in pharmaceutical anthropology with some clear-cut examples of how its insights can be put to practical use. Various authors in this volume do in fact discuss the practical relevance of their research (e.g. Ferguson, Wolffers, Ugalde and Homedes; Kloos et al.; Logan, Bledsoe and Goubaud; and MacCormack and Draper), but unrestrained optimism about such possibilities would be naive. Getting to know and understand the context of medicines in developing countries makes one hesitant to prescribe simple practical suggestions. Whole-hearted applied anthropology seems feasible only for those anthropologists who are able or willing to close their eyes to a part of social reality.

Anthropologists are best at pointing out the mistakes that have already been made. McElroy and Townsend (1979: 408) remark that anthropologists are often called in too late. As a result they can give only 'a postmortem analysis of what went wrong'. I would rather say, however, that anthropology *is* 'postmortem discipline'. It is not called in too late, it prefers to arrive late. Before things go wrong it does not offer much advice. It does little more than describe the complexity of the problem.[33]

Foster and Anderson (1978: 205–301) optimistically devote a hundred pages to practical roles that anthropologists can fill *in* medicine. But it must be reckoned to their credit that they do not let themselves be enticed to give ready-for-use prescriptions. They summarize the anthropologist's role in health development in four areas: (a) offering a holistic view; (b) emphasizing cultural relativism: 'a willingness to look sympathetically on the cultural forms of other societies and not judge them against the "normal" of our own' (1978: 211); (c) warning against misunderstanding in cross-cultural communication; and (d) suggesting a more appropriate research methodology to explore the problems encountered in medical programs. These four points can be summed up in one: making health technicians more sensitive to people's problems. I would not be surprised if some of the technicians lack the sensitivity to get the message. They are instead looking for concrete solutions. In a recent publication Foster (1987) has chastized the WHO for the low standard of its behavioral research. His pessimism about present applied health research implies however optimism about better possibilities. Foster pleads among other things for more recognition of qualitative research.

The major practical relevance of pharmaceutical anthropology is probably its *suspicion* of solutions. Anthropologists are awkward consultants in development work and wavering critics of the industry. They are a nuisance to policy makers who think that they have solved the problem, and they spoil the pleasures of action groups.

To illustrate my point I will sum up a number of common solutions to the problems of supply and use of pharmaceuticals in developing countries, adding some anthropological comments to each. Solutions have been suggested by many authors and organizations. Comprehensive overviews are provided by Melrose (1982: 129–99), Beardshaw (1983), HAI (1982b) and Medawar (1984). From these lists of solutions I consider only a few examples and these have been chosen somewhat selectively, because they suit my purpose.

The best known and most widely documented policy measure is the WHO's (1977, 1983) proposal for *essential drugs program*. Briefly, the proposal entails ensuring that populations in Third World countries have access to essential drugs at reasonable prices. The plan was remarkable in two respects.

It was designed very late although it seems the most obvious solution one could think of. Secondly, although it was unanimously applauded, only a handful of countries have effectively implemented it.[34]

A (more or less postmortem) anthropological analysis would stress at least three points which (with local variations) can be derived from a contextual description of the essential drugs program. They are: (1) the obstacles to implementation raised by various groups with vested interests in the old situation;[35] (2) the 'irrational' preference for non-essential drugs among lay users of medicines; and (3) the observation that public and private health care are so intertwined (cf. Ferguson and van der Geest in this volume) that it is impossible to introduce essential drugs in the public sector alone. An additional observation, no less pertinent, is that effective implementation of an essential drugs scheme is unlikely to prevent harmful misuse of drugs. Dubious lay practices of drug use will almost certainly continue after its implementation, leading to 'inessential' and even harmful use of drugs which are meant to be essential.[36]

Another important initiative for improving access to useful drugs in developing countries has been an attempt to introduce essential drugs in conjunction with *primary health care*. Primary health care involves a comprehensive program for better health, emphasizing the primal importance of prevention and self-reliance. Drugs are thus introduced in a context discouraging their use. I am not denying that this is a very sensible way of improving access to medicines, but again some marginal notes from the anthropologist's point of view seem in order.

By now we have overwhelming evidence that the basic idea of primary health care, viz. self-reliance, is missing in most so-called 'primary health care programs'. These programs are usually initiated by national or regional authorities with the help of outside financing. The very start of such programs implies a denial of their basic tenet. 'Development from below' is introduced from above. The net result is often an increase in dependency instead of self-reliance (cf. MacCormack and Draper in this volume). If medicines are supplied through the program, they will add their momentum to the loss of self-reliance, because medicines are the most desired and sought after products of Western medicine and they can only be obtained from outside the community.

It is, however, not so certain that medicines will in fact become more available through primary health care. Designers of primary health care often had a far too harmonious picture of local communities. It is naive to expect that communities have no conflicts and that their members will unanimously work for common goals, particularly when they may find it hard to survive privately. In actual practice individual members often see primary health care as an opportunity to improve their own position, and use its supplies for private consumption. One of the most desired supplies is, of course, medicines. I have seen numerous unpublished evaluation reports mentioning this problem. I have also had quite a few conversations with planners and fieldworkers confirming the disappearance of medicines from primary health care facilities.

Another suggestion frequently offered is to *improve the quality of the drug distribution* services that are *already in existence*, rather than starting entirely new experiments. The four most common distributors of drugs, as we have seen, are physicians (prescribing and selling), pharmacists, traditional health practitioners and unqualified drug vendors. The improvement of the physician's role in drug distribution has, of course, been the most common recommendation. One of the ways to achieve this would be providing them with 'balanced drug information' and 'guidance on cost-effective treatments' (Melrose 1982: 195). The improvement of the pharmacist's role has been suggested by, among others, Gish and Feller (1979: 88) and Mitchell (1985). The contribution to this volume by Logan makes a similar proposal. The idea here is that pharmacy workers are often expected to advise clients on drug use. Informing them about correct drug consumption and the dangers of drug misuse could have a beneficial effect on the quality of drug use. It is evident that this recommendation would be pointless without prior anthropological investigation into the actual practices going on in local pharmacies.

Another suggestion, that many will regard doubtfully, is the training of indigenous healers to improve their knowledge about Western pharmaceuticals and to enable them to prescribe and distribute these drugs more correctly. One author proposing this solution is Dunlop (1975). Numerous commentators have recommended a general integration of traditional practitioners into the formal health care system (because they 'are there already') (Pillsbury 1979). This would certainly also include accepting their role in prescribing and supplying drugs.

The idea of giving training to drug vendors is mentioned by Nordberg (1974) and Buschkens and Slikkerveer (1982: 121) for Ethiopia, by Casey and Richards (1984) for Nepal and by Sural (1985) for Bangladesh. Undoubtedly this idea will be rejected by a large number of health workers, who regard the unqualified drug vendor as a serious health hazard in Third World countries.

Although I sympathize with all the above suggestions, I want to draw attention to one formidable factor that is likely to hinder the intended measures quite seriously: the commercial one. Training will certainly be helpful in so far as the problems derive from lack of information. But there are indications that, from Western-trained physicians to unqualified vendors, it is the commercial aspect of pharmaceuticals that leads most directly to maldistribution, overprescription and misuse. Fieldwork at the spot should reveal whether the commercial factor is likely to become an obstacle in particular cases.

Another suggestion has been aimed directly *against the commercialization* of medicines. Marxist oriented authors in particular have proposed that the state regulate the supply of medicines. Pharmaceuticals, they argue, should be de-commercialized and be made available free of charge to everyone who needs them.

Anthropological reports in various developing countries make one wary of the feasibility and effectiveness of state regulation. My own research in Cameroon, for example, dealt directly with problems of gratis drugs in public health care. The absence of the commercial factor proved as problematic as its presence elsewhere. Drugs tended to be in short supply both for patients and health care workers. Bureaucratization and illegal private use of medicines (petty corruption) took the place of commerce, or rather became a new type of commerce.[37] A study of the social context of drug distribution could provide suggestions as to how much commerce is needed to keep the system running. The experiment in the Dominican Republic reported by Ugalde and Homedes in this volume shows the value of research for tackling these problems.

A very specific suggestion is to *tighten the 'controls on private drug distribution* to prevent sales of prescription drugs by untrained and unlicensed drug sellers' (Melrose 1982: 195). Anthropological research shows how problematic this advice is. In the first place, drug sellers are so much in demand *because* the official system cannot guarantee a sufficient and evenly distributed supply of drugs. Earlier in this chapter I have said that drug vendors tend do be ubiquitous, even in rural areas. They provide drugs where the government fails. Putting a stop to their practices would cause serious problems for villagers who have no alternative ways to purchase certain prescription medicines they need. Another problem lies in the idea of 'control'. Lack of control is usually not a technical failure but a structural characteristic of young soft states, one that has been extensively described by political anthropologists such as Huntington, Leys, Scott and Wertheim. Strengthening control over public goods would require structural societal change. Without such a change 'more control' could mean 'less control' because more people privately benefit from their position as controller.

Again another suggestion, heard from the consumer movement, is *to mobilize consumers of medicines* in the Third World. The question of the innocent anthropologist would be: who are these consumers? The existing studies of pharmaceuticals in the Third World, as we have seen, are mainly concerned with the macro-structures of drug distribution. We know virtually nothing about the people who actually *use* the medicines. We do not know their needs, their expectations, their ideas about medicines, how they are entangled in political or economic relations, etc. As long as so little is known about them it seems ill-advised to 'mobilize' them, if this were possible at all. Consumer action could even turn out to be harmful to consumer interests.

This problem poses a considerable dilemma to consumer groups. Not being able to know, let alone reach and assist, these consumers, they help most those who need their help least. A spokesman of the pharmaceutical industry has, with anthropological wit, observed a similar paradox in Western society:

... those patients who might be thought most at risk of suffering poor treatment are probably those least likely to be represented by the more active consumerists. Desirably or otherwise, older, sicker and less-educated people probably want to be able to put their trust in their doctors and avoid being confronted with too many difficult choices related to their treatments (Taylor 1983: 26).

Action and consumer groups in the industrial world have also pleaded for a *tighter control of the export of pharmaceuticals* from their own country to the Third World. One problem with this suggestion is easily recognised by anyone: the multinational structure of the pharmaceutical industry makes it easy to circumvent restriction on its export from one country. More information about the conditions of drugs procurement in Third World countries will probably teach activist groups that the political, commercial and medical elites there, eventually determine what medicines are delivered, although it must be admitted that their choices are heavily influenced by the industry. 'Solutions' which overlook the local elite factor are not likely to have much effect at all.

The pharmaceutical industry has its own 'solutions'. One has been a voluntary *'Code of Pharmaceutical Marketing Practices'* (IFPMA 1981) which, it claims, meets the complaints of its critics concerning misleading advertising and other dubious marketing practices in the Third World. In actual fact the code has been a successful attempt to prevent the imposition of a harsher and 'involuntary' code composed by the international consumer organization, Health Action International (HAI 1982).

One need not be an anthropologist to see that such a voluntary code is a sham, to allow the continuation of old marketing practices in a more watchful world. The code as such, therefore, does not call for anthropological comment, but its content does, in particular the general thrust that the industry is fully aware of its special responsibility, that it produces high quality medicines and sincerely tries to safeguard optimal use of those medicines.

Research into the conditions of medicine distribution and use in developing countries reveals that the industry cannot be serious when it says that its products 'have full regard to the needs of public health'. Its optimistic assessment of the use of its products seems unwarranted in most developing countries. Although it purports to be concerned about public health, it is uninterested in Third World conditions that encourage wrong use of its medicines and subsequently cause serious health hazards. When the industry is informed about these conditions it ignores or even denies them (for two examples see Medawar and Freese 1982; Wolffers 1983). The industry attempts to continue its business with the help of some 'myths' that vaguely imply that conditions in the Third World are the same as in the industrialized world of the West. Three of those myths are: (a) that the industry can guarantee the safety of its products and the adequacy of its information; (b) that it is able to withdraw misinformation about its drugs when necessary; and (c) that prescription-drugs are purchased with a doctor's prescription.

It is not difficult for an anthropologist to show that in a particuar society these claims are untenable. A description of the context in South Cameroon, for example, reveals that drugs are taken in completely different ways than prescribed by the industry and that those who do so have no possibility of discovering this because the industry's information on correct use is not available. My research also makes clear that misinformation about drugs is wide-spread and that the industry can do very little about it. It finally shows that prescription drugs can be obtained everywhere without a doctor's prescription.

Pharmaceutical anthropology may not have many 'prescriptions for change' but the above examples will underscore my claim that such analyses can be useful in pointing out the weaknesses and contradictions in solution which are being proposed. Furthermore, insights derived from anthropological field research make one wary about the possibility of improving drugs use by 'talking to' the authorities. Anthropologists have pointed out that authorities often have a direct interest in maintaining the existing conditions. Providing information and suggestions to those who are the 'victims' of present circumstances seems a more realistic lever for change.

CONCLUSION

The primary purpose of this chapter was to present themes for anthropological research on pharmaceuticals in developing countries by taking stock of what has been done so far and suggesting new research that should be undertaken to gain a deeper understanding of pharmaceuticals. The second aim was to discuss the practical relevance of pharmaceutical anthropology.

The conclusion is that anthropological research on Western pharmaceuticals in a non-Western context is still scarce. To date, the overwhelming majority of studies have been undertaken from a biomedical or economic point of view. Contextualization is hardly applied and the authors rarely manage to 'de-naturalize' their own medical and pharmacological concepts.

At present, policies for the improvement of drug use in developing countries are being initiated while the cultural complexity of drug use is but poorly understood. There is a greater-than-ever need for an anthropological analysis that views pharmaceuticals in their 'natural' context and, at the same time, divests them of their 'naturalness'. Such anthropological research should deal with the social and cultural aspects of the entire life history of pharmaceuticals, their production and marketing, their prescription, retail distribution and consumption and their efficacy. During their 'lives' pharmaceuticals move from hand to hand and from head to head. Both the transaction and the meaning of medicines deserve the anthropologist's attention.

This collection of studies makes a beginning by viewing medicines in their cultural context. The authors show how medicines as commodities are produced, sold and consumed. They elucidate the roles of drug company salesmen, pharmacists, street vendors and 'traditional' practitioners and finally they describe how Western pharmaceuticals are understood in terms of local medical cultures. Their findings are not only relevant for health care policy in developing countries; they also provide us with a fresh perspective on the cultural dimension of the use of medicines in the West.

NOTES

1. This chapter owes very much to Robert Welsch who commented extensively on its earlier versions and provided numerous suggestons for change. I also thank my co-editor Susan Whyte for her help and comments.
2. Some publications analysing the working of the multinational industry are: Beardshaw 1983; Blum et al. 1983; Bühler 1982; Gish and Feller 1979; Haslemere Group n.d.; Heller 1977; Lall 1977; Ledogar 1975; Melrose 1982; Muller 1982; Patel 1983; Turshen 1976; Unctad 1975 and 1982. Research on the biased drug information in developing countries was carried out by (among others): Medawar and Freese 1982; Osifo 1983; Silverman 1976 and 1977; Silverman et al. 1982a and 1982b.
3. Some doctors, I was told, may first prescribe a drug and then add a 'fitting disease' to it. As some doctors know very few drugs this method greatly simplifies the diagnosis. Prescribing reassures the patient *and* the doctor (oral communication, David Lee, Panama).
4. There is abundant literature on biased information by the industry. Some of the most prominent publications are: Greenhalgh 1987; Medawar 1979; Melrose 1982; Osifo 1983; Peters 1983; Rolt 1985; Silverman 1976; Silverman et al. 1982; Yudkin 1980.
5. The examples of 'irrational' prescribing cited by Silverman et al. (1982: 91–2) are:
   – prescribing multiple hormones, multiple antibiotics, and similar combinations when only a single drug is clinically indicated;
   – prescribing any antibiotic in the treatment of 'flu' or the common cold;
   – prescribing a newly-introduced drug solely on the grounds that it is new;
   – declining to prescribe or dispense a high-quality, low-cost generic-name product in place of a costly brand-name product – which may or may not be of high quality – on the grounds that 'the generic firms can't be trusted' (such prescribers and pharmacists are apparently unaware that the generic and the brand-name versions may be made by the same firm);
   – giving a drug by injection rather than by mouth because 'our people prefer it that way – we belong to an "injection culture".' (Patients and physicians alike have been duped by rumors and hush-hush campaigns suggesting that aspirin is too dangerous for most children – 'You doctors in Europe and America do not seem to know this' – and should be replaced with a costly and more hazardous substitute, preferably given by injection.)
6. Two examples of doctors' compliance are reported by Sich from Korea. She describes how she was induced by a woman in labor to do a cesarian section, although this was against the medical criteria she adhered to. The other example was an old man with a common cold who made a doctor comply with his request to give him an injection of Kanamycin (Hinderling and Sich 1985: 8). Doctors' compliance to patients' demands is particularly prone to occur when doctors compete for clients on a free market basis. Wolffers' contribution to this volume provides a case in point. Sri Lanka traditional practitioners use Western medicines in

order not to lose patients. A Dutch study (Krol 1985) has shown that general practitioners frequently refer patients to a specialist because the *patients* want it. Referring children to a pediatrician happens in 46% of all cases on request of the parents. Helman (1978) makes the point that physicians in Britain sometimes use concepts that closely parallel the concepts of their patients rather than those of their medical training.
7. Haak (1987) reports from two Brazilian villages that 48 out of 62 households were of the opinion that every consultation with a doctor should end with a prescription.
8. A typical example of harmful overprescribing is reported by Hardon (1987: 281) in the following case occuring in a Filipino village:

> Emma complains. Her child has diarrhoea. And she consulted a private doctor. She wants the best she can get for her child. The doctor prescribed five medicines. She cannot buy them, as her husband is jobless this month. She has borrowed money from relatives . . . . I ask her how severe the diarrhoea is. I categorise it as simple diarrhoea: according to the recommendations in the Primary Health Care manuals oral rehydration is the best therapy. The doctor prescribed: a drug to prevent vomiting, an antidiarrhoeal, an antibiotic, a multi-vitamin, and an analgesic. Total price: 120 peso (one week salary).

9. For studies discussing therapeutic practices by pharmacists see for example: De Walt 1977; Dressler 1982; Ferguson 1981; Group DCP 1984; Haak 1987; Igun 1987; Kloos et al. (this volume); K. Logan (this volume); Mitchell 1983 and 1985; Nichter 1983; Sussman 1981; Weisberg 1982.
10. The following studies refer to the role of unqualified personnel in licensed pharmacies: Ferguson (this volume); Haak 1987; Igun 1987; Jayasena 1985; Unschuld 1976; Van der Geest 1985; Weisberg 1982; Wolffers 1987b.
11. Some studies reffering to informal private practices by health personnel are: Bledsoe and Goubaud 1985; Janzen 1978; Lasker 1981; Maclean 1974; Nichter 1978; and 1983; Thomas 1975; Van der Geest 1982b and 1985; Wolffers (this volume).
12. Studies referring to the distribution of Western drugs by non-Western healers do so only briefly. Some examples are: Alexander and Shivaswamy 1971; Alger 1974; Bhatia et al. 1975; Brown 1963; De Walt 1977; Dobkin de Rios n.d.; Dressler 1982; Fabrega and Silver 1973; Golomb 1985; Messenger 1959; Minocha 1980; Nichter 1983; Taylor 1976; and Waxler 1984. A more substantial discussion is found in Burghart (this volume) and Wolffers (this volume and 1987a).
13. Anne Laurentin told me in 1979 that during her work as a physician in Burkina Faso and the Central African Republic she sometimes ran out of drugs, especially antibiotics. She then informed the local chief who often managed to bring in a trader with the required drug. Not infrequently the drugs were in bottles with hand-written labels, which made it impossible to check them.
14. For a more elaborate discussion of illegal drug sale, see Fassin 1985 and Van der Geest 1982a.
15. Some studies referring to drug vendors are: Bagshawe et al. 1974; Bledsoe and Goubaud 1985; Buschkens and Slikkerveer 1982; Dressler 1982; Fabrega and Silver 1973; Janzen 1978 and 1979; Kleinman 1980; Kloos 1974; McEvoy 1976; Nichter 1983; Nordberg 1974, Schulpen and Swinkels 1980; Thomas 1970; Unschuld 1976; Van der Geest 1987. Some publications that mention the administration of injections by vendors are Cosminsky and Scrimshaw 1980; Cunningham 1970; Ferguson 1981; Maclean 1974; Taylor et al. 1968; Van der Most van Spijk 1982; Whyte 1982 and this volume.
16. Authors who mention a – sometimes peripheral – medical background of drug vendors are: Buschkens and Slikkerveer 1982: 54; Cominsky and Scrimshaw 1980: 271; Igun 1987; Maclean 1974: 107; Taylor 1976: 298; Van der Most van Spijk 1982: 47. The Underwoods (1981) give the example of an 'injection doctor' in South Yemen who had spent one month as

a hospital cleaner. In Ghana I heard about a hospital gate keeper who trained himself by 'checking' and studying the patients' prescriptions. After some time he set up a private practice of his own in a village at some distance from the hospital.
17. The observation concerning pharmaceutical companies' primary interest in profits may apply equally to many drug vendors, who seem to be little hindered by knowledge of the dangers of wrong drug use. Ferguson (this volume) writes that the owners of two pharmacy shops in El Salvador 'engaged in their own forms of dumping', and Last (1981: 392) makes mention of vendors who 'extended normally specific illness terms to cover arbitrarily a wider range of symptoms in order more easily to sell off a specific remedy'. I witnessed similar practices during research in South Cameroon.
18. Some publications which discuss self-medication in a non-Western context are: Abosede 1984; Greenhalgh 1987; Haak 1987; Hardon 1987; K. Logan 1983; Kleinman 1980: 179–202; Nitschke et al. 1981; Ohnuki-Tierney 1981; Parker et al. 1979; Van der Geest 1987; J.C. Young 1981: 104–8; and various contribution to this volume. An overview of literature on self-medication is provided by Kroeger 1983.
19. See also Kleinman 1980; Lewis 1975; and Welsch 1982. An early study focusing on the role of the family in treatment involvement is Boswell's (1965) research in a Zambian hospital.
20. Re-conceptualization of Western ideas and practices was mentioned very early by Paul (1955) in the introduction to his classic study. Few researchers, however, have taken up his call for further study in this field.
21. 'Translation' from professional to layperson also takes place within Western culture. Blumhagen (1982) for example shows how patients in the USA translate bodily sensations into medical terms as 'hypertension'. Helman (1984) quotes some British studies which describe lay perceptions of physiology and disease that are partly derived from professional theory. They use its terminology and yet differ sharply from it. Kleinmans's (1980) Explanatory Model is an attempt to account for such 'translations'. It would be short-sighted to see only the translations from Western to non-Western, and from professional to non-professional. Translations in the opposite direction are equally common, but seldom recognized. Cultural anthropology, in spite of its emic claims, could be regarded as a continuous attempt to understand foreign phenomena in Western terms. By the same token, medicine reformulates lay experiences into professional language.
22. In the meantime Logan's study had been reprinted in Landy (1977) and Logan and Hunt (1978). A revised version of the article by Bledsoe and Goubaud is found in this volume.
23. The 'construction' of culture by anthropologists has been a recurrent theme in recent anthropological self-reflection. Goody (1977) has suggested that the dichotomous view of cognitive aspects of human cultures (advanced versus primitive, modern versus traditional, logico-empirical versus mythopotic, etc.) should be regarded as an ethnocentric attempt by the Western academic to express the 'we-they experience'. Hobsbawm and Ranger (1983) have collected essays in which it is argued that 'tradition' is not simply there, but is 'invented' by dominat social groups, often for very practical purposes, for example in a colonial context. The idea of 'tradition' often produced a platform for symbolic forms and ceremonies to legitimize political power. From there it is only a small step to 'Culture as camouflage' (Schrijvers 1983), hiding social and economic oppression behind cultural phrases and images.
24. See also Etkin (this volume) on the concept of efficacy in non-Western pharmaceuticals on this latter point.
25. Mburu (1973: 94) writes about the Kenyan situation: 'Cognitive orientation towards the use of injection is so intense . . . that many people regardless of their educational level think it is the only valid type of modern therapy'. Studies mentioning the popularity of injections abound; see for example Bledsoe and Goubaud 1985; Burghart (this volume); Cunningham 1970; Igun 1987; Kleinman 1980; Nichter 1980.
26. The placebo effect can be – negatively – understood as the total drug effect minus the pharmacological effect of the drug.

27. The concept 'nocebo' ('I shall harm') is sometimes used to indicate a negative placebo effect, for example by Herzhaft (1969). Illich (1977: 121–2) uses the term to describe the process of 'social iatrogenesis'. Medical procedures, according to Illich, have a nocebo effect when 'instead of mobilizing his self-healing powers, they transform the sick man into a limp and mystical voyeur of his own treatment'. For an ethnographic account of 'voodoo death' see Lewis 1987.
28. In a WHO discussion Polunin (1982: 20) has said that 'reliance on the placebo effect . . . is characteristic of charlatans'. Some 'hard' biomedical statements on placebo are also quoted by Brody (1983). As Lisbeth Sachs pointed out to me, the fact that the placebo has not been included in the WHO's list of essential drugs epitomizes biomedicine's suspicion of it (personal communication). In some countries, however, vitamins are included as placebos.
29. Laderman (1987) has criticized the somewhat apocryphal status of the shaman's words cited in Lévi-Strauss' latter article. Lévi-Strauss never witnessed the events nor heard the words which were to become the classic anthropological example of symbolic healing. His argument is entirely based on a text transcibed by others.
30. It is remarkable, however, that anthropologists rarely present indigenous *terms* used by their informants to describe those experiences which the ethnographer believes should be translated as 'health'. An exception is Ohnuki-Tierney's (1981: 34) analysis of the Ainu term *ramu pirika* which literally means 'soul-beautiful', and, according to the author, refers to the essential unity of body and mind in the Ainu concept of health.
31. Publications that stress a holistic view of health in various non-Western cultures are (to mention only a few): Fabrega and Silver 1973; Morley and Wallis 1979: passim; Hinderling 1981 and Katz 1982. Some anthropological observations are tinged with a dose of romanticism, reflecting the desire for 'lost values' in their own culture. A typical example of such a romanticizing view is the following quotation from Katz (1982: 34) about the Kung Bushmen in Southern Africa:

Healing seeks to establish health and growth on physical, psychological, social and spiritual levels; it involves work on the individual, the group, and surrounding environment and cosmos. Healing pervades Kung culture as a fundamental integrating and enhancing force.

The well-known WHO definition of health comes close to it: 'A state of complete physical, mental and social well-being'. This definition has been widely criticized as too static, too soft, too broad and too idealistic (for an overview of the comments see Hansluwka 1985). Lewis (1976: 100–2), who worked as a physician and anthropologist among the Gnau in Papua New Guinea, rejects the holistic definition, at least for illness: '. . . illness is a misfortune sensed by the sick person in ways which other misfortunes, like his house burning down, are not'. Lewis suggests that this must be a 'universal recognition'.
32. For more discussion on emic concepts of the efficacy of medical treatment and on the difficulties of comparison, see Lévi-Strauss 1963; Thomas 1973: 242–51; A. Young 1977; Foster and Anderson 1978: 123–6.
33. Heggenhougen (1985: 133) criticizes anthropologists for their passive attitude in health development:

Anthropologists should not only show why something should not be done in a certain way but should make suggestions for alternative approaches . . . We must persist in presenting a broader definition of progress and development and in cautioning impatient developers to consider the socio-cultural, economic, and health ramifications a program may have. But a concern for complexities should not prevent action altogether.

34. About 40 countries report that they have implemented an essential drugs program (1987), but I regard most of these programs as little effective; doctors are still able to prescribe 'non-essential' drugs and patient continue purchasing them in the private sector. The

publications on essential drugs are numerous. Most of them are from a medical-pharmacological, economic and political point of view. Extensive bibliographies are provided by Bannenberg 1985, Mamdani and Walker 1985 and WHO 1985.

35. Observations about the obstruction of essential drugs programs now abound, but – understandably – precise and 'hard' data on this sensitive issue are difficult to come by. One of the first observations is by Lall and Bibile (1978) in Sri Lanka. Descriptions of Bangladesh's attempts to reorganize drug supply are manfold (see e.g. Rolt 1985). In a note about three East African countries Korn (1984: 35) is outspoken and vague at the same time:

> It is a strange experience speaking to the doctors in Eastern Africa. You will not find one you would suspect of accepting bribes or of excessive prescribing, let alone one who would admit to such practices. However, the national import statistics, the shelves of the pharmacy stores, and the rarely available records of the international drug companies will convince you that you are dealing with Jekyll/Hydes who are likely to raise silent and obstinate political pressure against any attempted drug policy in their country.

Referring to Tanzania the author turns almost cynical:

> The philisophical and political platform for a national drug policy existed in Tanzania. The economic disaster situation would also help to justify to the population a restrictive drug list. Anyone would agree that some essential drugs would be better than no drugs at all. Nothing but the implementation was lacking in Tanzania (Korn 1984: 36).

36. A collection of papers (Sterky 1985) on essential drugs, published by the Dag Hammarskjöld Foundation in Uppsala, Sweden, illustrates this point. Concepts like 'rational use' of medicines and 'needs', why take a prominent place in many of the papers, are only used in a biomedical sense. A more cultural definition of 'rational' and 'need' would have made the discussion far more complex!
37. Some countries seem to be an exception to this 'rule'. It is reported that Botswana and Zimbabwe, for example, have an efficient public system of drug distribution which leaves few opportunities for informal private trade in medicines (various oral communications).

REFERENCES

Abosede, O. A.
    1984   Self-medication: an Important Aspect of Primary Health Care. Soc. Sci. & Med. 19(7): 699–703.
Ademuwagun, Z. A. et al. (eds.)
    1979   African Therapeutic Systems. Waltham, Mass.: Crossroads Press.
Alexander, C. A. and Shivaswamy, M. K.
    1971   Traditional Healers in a Region of Mysore. Soc. Sci. & Med. 5(6): 595–601.
Alger, N.
    1974   The Curandero-Supremo. *In* N. Alger (ed.) 'Many Answers': A Reader in Cultural Anthropology. St. Paul: West Publ., pp. 282–91.
Alland Jr, A.
    1979   Native Therapists and Western Medical Practitioners among the Abron of the Ivory Coast. *In* Ademuwagun et al. 1979: 171–5.
Bagshawe, A. F. et al. (eds.)
    1974   The Use and Abuse of Drugs and Chemicals in Tropical Africa. Nairobi, etc.: East African Literature Bureau.

Bannenberg, W. J.
  1985 Implementation of Essential Drug Policies in Eastern Africa. Unpublished Thesis, London School of Hygiene and Tropical Medicine.
Barnett, A. et al.
  1980 The Economics of Pharmaceutical Policy in Ghana. Internat. Jl. of Health Serv. 10(3): 479–500.
Beardshaw, V.
  1983 Prescription for change. The Hague: IOCU.
Bhatia, J. C. et al.
  1975 Traditional Healers and Modern Medicine. Soc. Sci. & Med. 9: 15–22.
Bledsoe, C. H. and Goubaud, M. F.
  1985 The Reinterpretation of Western Pharmaceuticals among the Mende of Sierra Leone. Soc. Sci. & Med. 21(3): 275–82 (revised version in this volume).
Bleek, W.
  1979 The Doctor and the Herbalist: Views by Ghanaian School Pupils. In Van der Geest and Van der Veen 1979: 91–110.
Blum, R. et al. (eds.)
  1983 Pharmaceuticals and Health Policy. International Perspectives on Provision and Control of Medicines. London: Social Audit & IOCU.
Blumhagen, D.
  1980 Hyper-Tension: A Folk Illness with a Medical Name. Culture, Medicine & Psychiatry 4: 197–227.
Boeken, L. et al.
  1981 De Medicijnmarkt. The Hague: Novib.
Boswell, D.
  1965 Escorts of Hospital Patients. Rhodes-Livingstone Communication 29: 1–19.
Brody, H.
  1983 Does Disease have a Natural History? Med. Anthr. Quart. 14(4): 3, 19–22.
Brown, J.
  1963 Some Changes in Mexican Village Curing Practices Induced by Western Medicine. America Indigena 23: 93–120.
Bühler, M.
  1982 Geschäfte mit der Armut: Pharma-Konzerne in der Dritten Welt. Frankfurt/M: Medico International.
Buschkens, W. F. L. and Slikkerveer, L. J.
  1982 Health Care in East Africa: Illness Behaviour of the Eastern Oromo in Hararghe, Ethiopia. Assen: Van Gorcum.
Casey, M. and Richards, R. M. E.
  1984 A Training Programma for Drug Retailers in Nepal. Pharmacy International 5(5): 114–6.
Caudill, W.
  1953 Applied Anthropology in Medicine. In A. L. Kroeber (ed.) Anthropology Today: An Encyclopedic Inventory. Chicago: University of Chicago Press, pp. 771–806.
Colson, A. C. and Selby, K. E.
  1974 Medical Anthropology. Annual Review of Anthropology 3: 245–62.
Conrad, P.
  1985 The Meaning of Medications: Another Look at Compliance. Soc. Sci. & Med. 20(1): 29–37.
Cosminsky, S. and Scrimshaw, M.
  1980 Medical Pluralism on a Guatemalan Plantation. Soc. Sci. & Med. 14B: 267–78.
Cunningham, C. E.
  1970 Thai 'Injection Doctors': Antibiotic Mediators. Soc. Sci. & Med. 4: 1–24.

DelVecchio Good, M. J.
  1980   Of Blood and Babies: the Relationship of Popular Islamic Physiology to Fertility. Soc. Sci. & Med. 14B: 147–56.
De Swaan, A.
  1983   De Mens is de Mens een Zorg. Amsterdam: Meulenhoff.
De Walt, K. M.
  1977   The Illnesses No longer Understand: Changing Concepts of Health and Curing in a Rural Mexican Community. Med. Anthrop. Newsletter 8(2): 5–11.
Dobkin de Rios, M.
  n.d.   An Amazonian Urban Healer's Pharmacopoeia. In Press.
Douglas, M.
  1975   The Healing Rite. In Implicit Meanings. London: Routledge & Kegan Paul, pp. 142–52
Dressler, W. W.
  1982   Hypertension and Culture Change. Acculturation and Disease in the West Indies. South Salem NY: Redgrave.
Dunlop, D. W.
  1975   Alternatives to 'Modern' Health Delivery Systems in Africa: Public Policy Issues of Traditional Health Systems. Soc. Sci. & Med. 9: 581–6.
Etkin, N. L. and Ross, P. J.
  1983   Malaria, Medicine and Meals: Plant Use among the Hausa and its Impact on Disease. In Romanucci-Ross et al. 1983: 231–59.
Fabrega, H. Jr.
  1971   Medical Anthropology. Biennial Review of Anthropology 1971: 167–229.
Fabrega, H. Jr. and Silver, D. B.
  1973   Illness and Shamanistic Curing in Zinacantan. An Ethnomedical Analysis. Stanford: Stanford Un. Press.
Fassin, D.
  1985   Du clandestin à l'officieux: les réseaux de vente illicite des médicaments au Sénégal. Cahiers d'Etudes Africaines 25(2): 161–77.
Ferguson, A. E.
  1981   Commercial Pharmaceutical Medicine and Medicalization: A Case Study from El Salvador. Culture, Medicine & Psychiatry 5(2): 105–34 (also this volume).
Foster, G. M.
  1976   Medical Anthropology and International Health Planning. Medical Anthropology Newsletter 7(3): 12–8.
  1987   World Health Organization Behavioral Science Research: Problems and Prospects. Soc. Sci. & Med. 24(9): 709–17.
Foster, G. M. and Anderson, B. G.
  1978   Medical Anthropology. New York, etc.: J. Wiley & Sons.
Giovanni, G.
  1980   A Questao dos Remedios no Brasil: Producao e Consumo. Sao Paulo : Livraria e Editora Polis.
Gish, O. and Feller, L. L.
  1979   Planning Pharmaceuticals for Primary Health Care: The Supply and Utilization of Drugs in the Third World. Washington DC: APHA.
Golomb, L.
  1985   An Anthropology of Curing in Multiethnic Thailand. Urbana & Chicago: Un. of Illinois Press.
Gonzalez, N. S.
  1966   Health Behavior in a Cross-Cultural Perspective: A Guatemalan Example. Human Organization 25: 122–5.

Goody, J.
  1977   The Domestication of the Savage Mind. Cambridge, etc.: Cambridge Un. Press.
Greenhalgh, T.
  1987   Drug Prescription and Self-medication in India: an Exploratory Survey. Soc. Sci. & Med. 25(3): 307–18.
Group for Defense of Consumers on Pharmaceuticals (GDCP)
  1984   Antibiotics, Analgesics and Vitamins: Use and Abuse in Recife, Brazil. Recife: GDCP (mimeo).
Haak, H.
  1987   Moderne Geneesmiddelen in Santa Rita en Salomao: een Case Study. Unpublished Thesis, Groningen.
Hahn, R. A. and Kleinman, A.
  1983a Biomedical Practice and Anthropological Theory: Frameworks and Directions. Annual Review of Anthropology 12: 305–33.
  1983b Belief as Pathogen, Belief as Medecine: 'Voodoo Death' and the 'Placebo Phenomenon' in Anthropological Perspective. Med. Anthrop. Quarterly 14(4): 3, 16–9.
HAI
  1982   An International Code of Pharmaceutical Marketing Practice. Penang: HAI.
Hansluwka, H. E.
  1985   Measuring the Health of Populations: Indicators and Interpretations. Soc. Sci. & Med. 20(12) : 1207–24.
Hardon, A. P.
  1987   The Use of Modern Pharmaceuticals in a Filipino Village: Doctor's Prescription and Self-Medication. Soc. Sci. & Med. 25(3): 277–92.
Haslemere Group
  n.d.   Who Needs the Drug Companies? London: War on Want.
Heggenhaugen, H. K.
  1985   The Future of Medical Anthropology. In Hill 1985: 130–6.
Heller, T.
  1977   Poor Health, Rich Profits: Multinational Drug Companies and the Third World. Nottingham: Spokesman Books.
Helman, C.
  1978   'Feed a Cold, Starve a Fever': Folk Models of Infection in an Engish Suburban Community, and their Relation to Medical Treatment. Culture Medicine & Psychiatry 2: 107–37.
  1984   Culture, Health and Illness. Bristol: Wright-PSG.
Herxheimer, A. and Stimson, G. V.
  1983   The Use of Medicines for Illness. In Blum et al. 1983: 36–60.
Herzhaft, G.
  1969   L'Effet Nocebo. Encéphale 58: 486–503.
Hill, C. E. (ed.)
  1985   Training Manual in Medical Anthropology. Washington: Am. Anthrop. Association.
Hinderling, P.
  1981   Kranksein in 'primitiven' und traditionalen Kulturen. Norderstedt: Verlag für Ethnologie.
Hinderling, P. and Sich, D.
  1985   The Cultural Integration of Illness. Korpilampi: Conference Paper.
Hobsbawm, E. and Ranger, T.
  1983   The Invention of Tradition. Cambridge: Cambridge Un. Press.
Hughes, C. C.
  1978   Medical Care: Ethnomedicine. In Logan & Hunt 1978: 150–8.
IFPMA
  1981   Code of Pharmaceutical Marketing Practices. Zürich: IFPMA.

Igun, U. A.
  1987 Why we Seek Treatment here: Retail Pharmacy and Clinical Practice in Maiduguru, Nigeria. Soc. Sci. & Med. 24(8): 689–95.

Illich, I.
  1977 Limits to Medicine. Medical Nemesis: The Expropriation of Health. Harmondsworth: Penguin.

Janzen, J. M.
  1978 The Quest for Therapy in Lower Zaire. Berkeley: Un. of Calfornia Press.
  1979 Pluralistic Legitimation of Therapy Systems in Contemporary Zaire. In Ademuwagun et al. 1979: 208–16.

Jayasena, K.
  1985 Drugs: Registration and Marketing Practices in the Third World. Development Dialogue 1985 (2): 38–47.

Katz, R.
  1982 Boiling Energy. Community Healing among the Kalahari Kung. Cambridge, Mass.: Harvard Un. Press.

Kleinman, A.
  1980 Patients and Healers in the Context of Culture. Berkeley: Un. of California Press.

Kloos, H.
  1974 The Geography of Pharmacies, Druggist Shops and Rural Medicine Vendors and the Origin of Customers of such Facilities in Addis Ababa. Jl. of Ethiopian Studies 12: 77–94.

Kluckhohn, C.
  1949 Mirror for Man. New York: McGraw-Hill.

Korn, J.
  1984 Eastern Africa: Perspectives of Drug Use. Danish Medical Bulletin 31, Supplement 1: 34–6.

Kroeger, A.
  1983 Anthropological and Socio-Medical Health Care Research in Developing Countries. Soc. Sci. & Med. 17 (3): 147–61.

Krol, L. J.
  1985 De Consument als Leidend Voorwerp in de Gezondheidszorg-Dissertation, University of Amsterdam.

Laderman, C.
  1987 The Ambiguity of Symbols in the Structure of Healing. Soc. Sci. & Med. 24 (4): 293–301.

Lall, S.
  1977 Medicines and Multinationals: Problems in the Transfer of Pharmaceutical Technology to the Third World. Monthly Review 28 (10): 19–30.

Lall, S. & Bibile, S.
  1978 The Political Economy of Controlling Transnationals: The Pharmaceutical Industry in Sri Lanka, 1972–328.

Landy, D.
  1977 (ed.) Culture, Disease and Healing. Studies in Medical Anthropology. New York: Macmillan.
  1978 Role Adaptation: Traditional Curers under the Impact of Western Medicine. *In*: Logan & Hunt 1978: 217–41.

Lasker, J. N.
  1981 Choosing among Therapies: Illness Behavior in the Ivory Coast. Soc. Sci. & Med. 15A (2): 157–68.

Last, M.
  1981 The Importance of Knowing about Not Knowing. Soc. Sci. & Med. 15B (3): 387–92.

Ledogar, R. J.
   1975   Hungry for Profits. U.S. Food and Drug Multinationals in Latin America. New York: IDOC.

Leslie, Ch. (ed.)
   1976   Asian Medical Systems. A Comparative Study. Berkeley: Un. of California Press.

Lévi-Strauss, C.
   1963   The Effectiveness of Symbols. In Structural Anthropology. Harmondsworth: Penguin, pp. 186–205.

Lewis, G.
   1976   A View of Sickness in New Guinea. In Loudon 1976: 49–103.
   1981   Cultural Influences on Illness Behavior: A Medical Anthropological Approach. In L. Eisenberg and A. Kleinman (eds.). The Relevance of Social Science for Medicine. Dordrecht: Reidel, pp. 151–62.
   1987   Fear of Sorcery and the Problem of Death by Suggestion. Soc. Sci. & Med. 24(12): 997–1010 (reprint).

Logan, K.
   1983   The Role of Pharmacists and Over-the Counter Medications in the Health Care System of a Mexican City. Medical Anthropology 7(3): 68–89 (revised version in this volume).

Logan, M.
   1973   Humoral Medicine in Guatemala and Peasant Acceptance of Modern Medicine. Human Organization 32(4): 385–95.

Logan, M. and Hunt Jr., E. E. (eds.)
   1978   Health and the Human Condition. Perspectives on Medical Anthropology. North Scituate: Duxbury Press.

Loudon, J. B. (ed.)
   1976   Social Anthropology and Medicine. London, etc.: Academic Press.

Maclean, U.
   1974   Magical Medicine: A Nigerian Case Study. Harmondsworth: Penguin.

McElroy, A. and Townsend, P. K.
   1979   Medical Anthropology in Ecological Perspective. North Scituate: Duxbury Press.

McEvoy, J.
   1976   The Bus-stop Dispenser. East African Medical Journal 53(3): 193–5.

Mamdani, M. and Walker, G.
   1985   Essential Drugs and Developing Countries. A Review and Selected Annotated Bibliography. London: School of Hygiene & Tropical Medicine.

Mapes, R. (ed.)
   1980   Prescribing Practice and Drug Usage. London: Croom Helm.

Mburu, F. M.
   1973   A Socioeconomic Epidemiological Study: Traditional and Modern Medicine among the Akamba Ethnic Group of Upland Machakos, Kenya. Unpublished M.A. Thesis, Makerere.

Medawar, C.
   1979   Insult or Injury? An Enquiry into the Marketing and Advertising of British Food and Drug Products in the Third World. London: Social Audit.
   1984   Drugs and World Health. The Hague: IOCU.

Medawar, C. and Freese, B.
   1982   Drug Diplomacy. London: Social Audit.

Melrose, D.
   1982   Bitter Pills: Medicines and the Third World Poor. Oxford: Oxfam.

Melville, A. and Johnson, C.
   1982   Cured to Death. The Effects of Prescription Drugs. London: Secker & Warburg.

Messenger, J. C.
1959 Religious Acculturation among the Anang Ibibio. *In* W. R. Bascom and M. J. Herskovits (eds.) Continuity and Change in African Cultures. Chicago: Chicago Un. Press, pp. 279–99.

Minocha, A. A.
1980 Medical Pluralism and Health Services in India. Soc. Sci. & Med. 14B (4): 217–23.

Mitchell, F. M.
1983 Popular Medical Concepts in Jamaica and their Impact on Drug Use. Western Journal of Medicine 139: 841–7.
1985 Improving Pharmacy Practice in the Third World. The Jamaican Experience. Möbius 5(3): 129–34.

Moerman, D. E.
1981 Edible Symbols: The Effectiveness of Placebos. *In* Th. A. Sebeok and R. Rosenthal (eds.) The Clever Hans Phenomenon: Communication with Horses, Whales, Apes, and People. New York: New York Academy of Sciences, pp. 256–68.
1983a Physiology and Symbols: The Anthropological Implications of the Placebo Effect. *In* Romanucci-Ross et al. 1979: 156–67.
1983b General Medical Effectiveness and Human Biology: Placebo Effects in the Treatment of Ulcer Disease. Med. Anthrop. Quarterly 14(4): 13–16.

Morley, P. and Wallis, R. (eds.)
1979 Culture and Curing. Anthropological Perspectives on Traditional Medical Beliefs and Practices. Pittsburgh. Un. of Pittsburgh Press.

Moshaddeque Hossain, M. et al.
1982 Antibiotic Use in a Rural Community in Bangladesh. Intern. Jl. of Epidemiology 11(4): 402–5.

Muller, M.
1982 The Health of Nations: A North-South Investigation. London: Faber & Faber.

Nichter, M.
1978 Patterns of Curative Resort and their Significance for Health Planning in South Asia. Med. Anthrop. 2(1): 29–58.
1980 The Layperson's Perception of Medicine as Perspective into the Utilization of Multiple Therapy Systems in the Indian Context. Soc. Sci. & Med. 14B: 225–33.
1981 Toward a Culturally Responsive Rural Health Care Delivery System in India. *In* R. Gupta (ed.). The Social and Cultural Context of Medicine in India. Ann Arbor: South Carolina Press, pp. 223–36.
1983 Paying for what Ails you: Sociocultural Issues Influencing the Ways and Means of Therapy Payment in South India. Soc. Sci. & Med. 17(14): 957–65.

Nitschke, C. A. S. et al.
1981 E Studo Sobre o Uso de Medicamentos em Quatro Bairros de Porto Alegre. R. AMRIGS 25(3): 184–9.

Nordberg, E.
1974 Self-Portrait of the Average Rural Drug Shop in Wollega Province, Ethiopia. Ethiopian Med. Jl. 12(1): 25–32.

Ohnuki-Tierney, E.
1981 Illness and Curing among the Sakhalin Ainu. A Symbolic Interpretation. Cambridge, etc.: Cambridge Un. Press.

Osifo, N. G.
1983 Overpromotion of Drugs in International Product Package Inserts. Tropical Doctor 13(1): 5–8.

Parker, R. L. et al.
1979 Self-Care in Rural Areas in India and Nepal. Culture, Medicine and Psychiatry 3(1): 3–28.

Patel, S. J. (ed.)
    1983   Pharmaceuticals and Health in the Third World. Special Issue of World Development 11(3).
Paul, B. (ed.)
    1955   Health, Culture and Community: Case Studies of Public Reactions to Health Programs. New York: Russell Sage.
Pelto, P. J. and Pelto, G. H.
    1978   Anthropological Research. The Structure of Inquiry. Cambridge, etc.: Cambridge Un. Press.
Peters, G.
    1983   Information and Education about Drugs. In Blum et al. 1983: 93–121.
Pillsbury, B.
    1979   Reaching the Rural Poor: Indigenous Health Practitioners are there Already. Washington DC: US/AID.
Polgar, S.
    1962   Health and Human Behavior: Areas of Interest Common to the Social and Medical Sciences. Current Anthrop. 3: 159–205.
Polunin, I.
    1982   Traditional Medicine is a Predominantly Social Activity. World Health Forum 3(1): 19–21.
Rolt, F.
    1985   Pills, Policies and Profits. London: War on Want.
Romanucci-Ross, L. et al. (eds.)
    1983   The Anthropology of Medicine. From Culture to Method. New York: Praeger.
Rubenstein, J.
    1984   Ritual Healing and Performance. Anthropology and Humanism Quarterly 9(2): 3–7.
Schrijvers, J.
    1983   Cultuur als Camouflage: Westerse Weerstanden tegen Vrouwen als Ontwikkelingsrelevant Onderwerp. Internationale Spectator 37(1): 556–62.
Schulpen, T. W. J. and Swinkels, W. J. A. M.
    1980   The Utilization of Health Services in a Rural Area of Kenya. Trop. & Geograph. Medicine 32: 340–9.
Scotch, N. A.
    1963   Medical Anthropology. Biennial Review of Anthropology 1963: 30–68.
Senturias, E. N. et al.
    1984   A Preliminary Study on the Prescribing Habits of Physicians in Manila, Philippines. Quezon City: NEHCC (unpublished).
Shatrughna, V.
    n.d.   Drug Prescription: Service to Whom? In A. Bang and A. J. Patel (eds.). Health Care: Which Way to Go. Pune: Medico Friend Circle, pp. 25–9.
Silverman, M.
    1976   The Drugging of the Americas. Berkeley: Un. of California Press.
    1977   The Epidemiology of Drug Promotion. Intern. Jl. of Health Services 7(2): 157–66.
Silverman, M. et al.
    1982a   Prescriptions for Death: The Drugging of the Third World. Berkeley: Un. of California Press.
    1982b   The Drugging of the Third World. Intern. Jl. of Health Serv. 12(4): 585–96.
Smith, M. C.
    1980   The Relationship between Pharmacy and Medicine. In Mapes 1980: 157–200.
Speight, A. N. P.
    1975   Cost-effectiveness and Drug Therapy. Tropical Doctor 5:89–92.
Sterky, J. (ed.)
    1985   Another Development in Pharmaceuticals. Development Dialogue 1985/2.

Sural, P. N.
 1985 Orientation Course for Drug Retailers and Wholesalers, Nepal. Kathmandu (unpublished paper).
Sussman, L. K.
 1981 Unity in Diversity in a Polyethnic Society: The Maintenance of Medical Pluralism on Mauritius. Soc. Sci. & Med. 15B (3): 247–60.
Taylor, C.
 1976 The Place of Indigenous Medical Practitioners in the Modernization of Health Services. *In* Leslie 1976: 285–99.
Taylor, C. et al.
 1968 Health Manpower Planning in Turkey: An International Research Case Study. Baltimore: Hopkins.
Taylor, D.
 1983 Medicines and the Consumer. Pharmacy International 4(2): 23–6.
Thomas, A. E.
 1970 Adaptation to Modern Medicine of two Kamba Communities. Unpublished Ph. D. Thesis, Stanford University.
 1975 Health Care in Ukambi, Kenya: A Socialist Critique. *In* S. R. Ingman and A. E. Thomas (eds.). Topias and Utopias in Health. The Hague/Paris: Mouton, pp. 267–81.
Thomas, K.
 1973 Religion and the Decline of Magic. Harmondsworth: Penguin.
Turshen, M.
 1976 An Analysis of the Medical Supply Industries. Intern. Jl. of Health Services 6(2): 271–94.
UNCTAD
 1975 Major Issues in the Transfer of Technology to Developing Countries: A Case Study of the Pharmaceutical Industry. Geneva: Unctad.
 1982 Guidelines on Technology Issues in the Pharmaceutical Sector in the Developing Countries. Geneva: Unctad.
Underwood, P. and Underwood, Z.
 1981 New Spells for Old: Expectations and Realities of Western Medicine in a Remote Tribal Society in Yemen, Arabia. *In* N. F. Stanley and R. A. Joshe (eds.). Changing Disease Patterns and Human Behaviour. London: Academic Press, pp. 271–97.
Unschuld, P. U.
 1976 The Social Organization and Ecology of Medical Practice in Taiwan. *In* Leslie 1976: 300–16.
Van der Geest, S.
 1982a The Illegal Distribution of Western Medicines in Developing Countries. Med. Anthrop. 6(4): 197–219.
 1982b The Efficiency of Inefficiency: Medicine Distribution in South Cameroon. Soc. Sci. & Med. 16(24): 2145–53.
 1984 Anthropology and Pharmaceuticals in Developing Countries. Med. Anthrop. Quarterly 15(3): 59–62; (4): 87–90.
 1985 The Intertwining of Formal and Informal Medicine Distribution in South Cameroon. Canadian Jl. of African Studies 19(3): 596–87 (revised version in this volume).
 1987 Self-care and the Informal Sale of Drugs in South Cameroon. Soc. Sci. & Med. 25(3): 293–306.
Van der Geest, S. and van der Veen, K. W. (eds.)
 1979 In Search of Health: Essays in Medical Anthropology. Amsterdam: CANSA, Un. of Amsterdam.
Van der Most van Spijk, M.
 1982 Who Cares for her Health? An Anthropological Study of Women's Health Care in a Village in Upper Egypt. Leiden: Women & Development, State Un. of Leiden.

Van Luijk, J. N.
  1982   Traditional Medicine among the Kamba of Machakos District, Kenya. Part II. Unpublished manuscript, Royal Tropical Institute, Amsterdam.
Waxler, N. E.
  1984   Behavioral Convergence and Institutional Separation: An Analysis of Plural Medicine in Sri Lanka. Culture, Medicine & Psychiatry 8: 187–204.
Weisberg, D. H.
  1982   Northern Thai Health Care Alternatives. Soc. Sci. & Med. 16(16): 1507–17.
Welsch, R. L.
  1982   The Experience of Illness among the Ningerum of Papua New Guinea. Ph. D. Dissertation, University of Washington.
  1983   Traditional Medicine and Western Medical Options among the Ningerum of Papua New Guinea. In Romanucci-Ross et al. 1983: 32–53.
WHO
  1977   The Selection of Essential Drugs, TRS 615. Geneva: WHO.
  1983   The Use of Essential Drugs, TRS 685. Geneva: WHO.
  1985   Annotated Bibliography on Essential Drugs. Geneva: WHO/DAP.
Whyte, S. R.
  1982   Penicillin, Battery Acid and Sacrifice: Cures and Causes in Nyole Medicine. Soc. Sci. & Med. 16(23): 2055–64.
  n.d.   Anthropological Approaches to African Misfortune: From Religion to Medicine. Unpublished Paper.
Wolffers, I
  1983   Druppels tegen de Armoede. Organon in de Derde Wereld. Baarn: Fontein.
  1987a Changing Traditions in Health Care, Sri Lanka. Leiden: Ph. D. Dissertation.
  1987b Drug Information and Sale Practices in Some Pharmacies of Colombo, Sri Lanka. Soc. Sci. & Med. 25(3): 319–21.
Wyatt, H. V.
  1984   The Popularity of Injections in the Third World: Origins and Consequences for Poliomyelitis. Soc. Sci. & Med. 19(9): 911–5.
Young, A.
  1977   Order, Analogy and Efficacy in Ethiopian Medical Divination. Culture, Medicine & Psychiatry 1(2): 183–200.
Young, J. C.
  1981   Medical Choice in a Mexican Village. New Brunswick: Rutgers Un. Press.
Yudkin, J. S.
  1980   The Economics of Pharmaceutical Supply in Tanzania. Intern. Jl. of Health Services 10(3): 455–77.

LIST OF CONTRIBUTORS

Ahmad Fuad Afdhal
  Jurusan Farmasi, Fakultas Matematika dan Ilmu Pengetahuan Alam, Institut Sains dan Teknologi Nasional, Bumi Srengseng Indah, Jakarta 12640, Indonesia

Solomon Belay
  City Council Pharmacies, Addis Ababa, Ethiopia

Caroline H. Bledsoe
  Department of Anthropology, Northwestern University, Evanston, Illinois 60208, USA

Richard Burghart
  Department of Anthropology, School of Oriental & African Studies, University of London, Malet Street, London WC1 7HP, UK

Alizon Draper
  London School of Hygiene & Tropical Medicine, University of London, Keppel Street, London WC1 7HT, UK

Nina Etkin
  Department of Anthropology, University of Minnesota, 215 Ford Hall, 224 Church Street S.E., Minneapolis, Minnesota 55455, USA

Anne Ferguson
  Bean/Cowpea CRSP Management Office, 200 Center for International Programs, Michigan State University, East Lansing, Michigan 48824, USA

Kefalo Gebre Tsadik
  City Council Pharmacies, Addis Ababa, Ethiopia

Berhanu Getahun
  Department of Geography, Addis Ababa University, P.O. Box 31609, Addis Ababa, Ethiopia

Monica F. Goubaud
  Department of Anthropology, University of New Mexico, Albuquerque, New Mexico 87131, USA

Nuria Homedes
School of Public Health, University of Texas, Austin, Texas 78712-1088, USA

Helmut Kloos
Department of Geography, Addis Ababa University, P.O. Box 31609, Addis Ababa, Ethiopia

Charles Leslie
Center for Science and Culture, University of Delaware, Newark, Delaware 19716, USA

Kathleen Logan
International Studies Program, University of Alabama at Birmingham, 338 Ullman Building, Birmingham, Alabama 35294, USA

Carol MacCormack
London School of Hygiene & Tropical Medicine, University of London, Keppel Street, London WC1 7HT, UK

Anke Niehof
Netherlands Ministry of Foreign Affairs.
Home address: Galileistraat 3, 2561 SX The Hague, The Netherlands

Linda K. Sussman
Department of Psychiatry, Medical School, Washington University, P.O. Box 8134, St. Louis, Missouri 63110, USA

Asregid Teferi
Department of Geography, Addis Ababa University, P.O. Box 31609, Addis Ababa, Ethiopia

Antonio Ugalde
Department of Sociology, University of Texas, Austin, Texas 78712-1088, USA

Paul U. Unschuld
Institut für Geschichte der Medizin der Ludwig-Maximilians-Universität, Lessingstrasse 2, 8000 München 2, West Germany

Sjaak van der Geest
Antropologisch-Sociologisch Centrum, University of Amsterdam, Oude Zijds Achterburgwal 185, 1012 DK Amsterdam, The Netherlands

Robert L. Welsch
Department of Anthropology, Northwestern University, Evanston, Illinois 60201, USA

Susan Reynolds Whyte
Institut for Etnologi og Antropologi, University of Copenhagen, Frederiksholms Kanal 4, 1220 Copenhagen K. Denmark

Ivan Wolffers
Freelance Primary Health Care and Health Education Consultant, Middellaan 11, 3721 PG Bilthoven, The Netherlands

INDEX OF NAMES

Abebe, W. 309, 316
Abel-Smith, B. 206
Abosede, O.A. 51, 355
Adisasmita, K.S. 169
Afdhal, A.F. xii, 8, 10, 17, 250, 333
Ahern, E.M. 199, 305, 307, 316
Ahmed Zein, Z. 102
Alcorn, J.B. 303, 307
Alexander, C.A. 70, 354
Alger, N. 354
Alland Jr, A. 58, 119, 218, 224, 228, 255, 337, 340–341
Al-Yahya, M.A. *et al.*, 304
Amat, B. 132
Amelsvoort, V. van *see* Van Amelsvoort
Ampofo, O. 311
Anderson, B.G. 347, 356
Anderson, E.N. 316
Anderson, M.L. 316
Anderson, T.H. 42
Antonil 316
Arragie, M. 95
Artelt, W. 196
Arya, O.P. 274
Ashley, D. 278
Axton, J.H.M. 307

Bagshawe, A.F. *et al.*, 354
Balandrin, M.F. *et al.*, 318
Balasubramaniam, K. 50
Ball, R.A. 110
Banerjee, R.D. 310
Bannenberg, W.J. 356
Barnett, A. *et al.* 335
Barnett, H.G. 230
Barth, F. 54
Basker, D. 311
Bastein, J.W. 300, 304
Beals, A.R. 119
Beardshaw, V. 347, 353
Bedassa, A. 83
Bellman, B.L. 218
Benedict, R. 329
Bennett, F.J. 274
Benoist, J. 200
Berliner, H.S. 23

Berman, P.A. 299
Bertero, C.O. 19, 38
Bhatia, J.C. *et al* 47–48, 70, 290, 354
Bibeau, G. 199, 229
Bibile, S. 19, 50, 146–147, 356
Bisset, N.G. 312
Bjerke, S. 218
Bledsoe, C.H. 7–8, 176, 217, 342, 346, 354–355
Bleek, W. 337
Bloom, A.L. 299
Blum, R. *et al*, 353
Blumhagen, D. 355
Boeken, L. *et al.*, 332
Boswell, D. 355
Breman, J. 133
Brody, H. 356
Brown, J. 27, 107–108, 119, 125, 354
Brown, K.H. 82
Browner, C.H. 252
Brush, S.B. *et al.* 303
Bühler, M. 353
Burchard, R.E. 315
Burghart, R. 8, 177, 337, 342, 354–355
Buschkens, W.F.L. 349, 354
Bye, R.A. 307

Camazine, S. 307
Canedo, L., 107, 109
Capasso, F. *et al.* 311
Carlini, E.A. *et al.* 311
Carroll, C.R. 119
Carstairs, G.M. 199
Casey, M. 349
Casparie, W.A. 303
Castleman, B.I. 38
Caudill, W. 329
Chagnon, M. 310
Chavira, J.A. 111, 118, 125
Chen, L.C. 47
Chinas, B. 108
Claridge, G. 343
Cohen, P.J. 315
Colson, A.C. 119, 329
Conrad, P. 338
Cortadellas, T. 132

Cosminsky, S. 22, 27, 36, 274, 354
Court, E.W. 309
Croom, E.M. 303
Cross Beras, J. 76
Cunningham, C.E. ix, 47, 67, 220, 338, 354–355
Cutting, W.A.M. 277

Dafni, A. et al., 304–305
Davis, E.W. 303, 306, 308, 315
De Guevarra, C.C. 42
Delaveau, P. 306
DelVecchio Good, M.J. 342
De Smet, P.A.G.M. 314–316
Desta, A., 102
De Swaan, A. 334
De Walt, K.M. 108, 110, 125, 354
Dharma, A.P. 169
Diamond, S. 329
Diesfeld, H.J. 318
Disengomoka, I. et al., 308
Dobkin de Rios, M. 354
Dodge, R.W. 94
Domenjoz, R. 196
Dominguez, X. 307
Dotsenko, A.P. 82
Douglas, J.D. 133
Douglas, M. 345
Draper, A. 4, 177, 282, 346, 348
Dressler, W.W. 354
Dubos, R. 38, 41
Dukes, M.N.G. 119
Dunlop, D.W. 57, 349
Durham, W.H. 41

Echols, J.M. 168
Edgerton, R.B. et al., 118, 125
Ellen, R.F. 236
Elling, R. 299
Elliot, K. 277
Elvin-Lewis, M.P.F. 199, 306, 311, 315
Eoff, G.M. 57
Erasmus, CH. 111, 119
Etkin, N.L. 7, 177, 199, 266, 299, 307, 316–317, 343
Evans, P. 19–20, 38
Evans-Pritchard, E.E. 199, 227

Fabrega, H. Jr. 107–108, 125, 329–330, 337, 354, 356
Fassin, D. 338, 354
Feierman, S. 199, 299

Feller, L.L. 19–20, 37, 147, 349, 353
Ferguson, A.E. 15, 47, 58–59, 147, 274, 335–336, 340, 346, 348, 354–355
Fernando, J. 50
Field, M.J. 228
Finerman, R.D. 300
Foege, W.H. 38
Fortune, R.F. 199
Foster, G.M. 222, 255, 330, 347, 356
Fraser, H.S. 90
Freese, B. 351
Freij, L. et al., 82
Friedman, P.S. 82
Fry, P. 218

Gagon, J.F. 101
Garrison, V. 200
Gebre-Medhin, M. 82
Gedebou, M. 94
Geertz, C. 167
Geest, S. van der see Van der Geest
Gereffi, G. x, 59
Geschiere, P.L. 133, 144
Giel, R. 102
Gilman, R. 82
Gimlette, J.D. 169
Giovanni, G. 332
Gish, O. 19–20, 37, 147, 349, 353
Gobezie, A. 82
Golomb, L. 354
Gonzalez, N.S. 223, 274, 337
Good, B. 254, 274
Good, CH. et al., 47
Good, M.J. see DelVecchio
Goody, J. 355
Goubaud, M.F. 7–8, 176, 217, 342, 346, 354–355
Gould Martin, K. 317
Green, E.C. 226, 307
Greenhalgh, T. 47, 334–335, 353, 355
Griffenhagen, G. 118
Grisiola, S. 311
Gunaratne, V.T.H. 256–257
Gupta, B. 289

Haak, H. 354–355
Hahn, R.A. 330, 344
Hailu, B. 81
Hansluwka, H.E. 345, 356
Haragewoin, M.D. 82
Hardon, A.P. 47, 57–58, 334–335, 354–355
Harlan, J.R. 303

INDEX OF NAMES

Harley, G.W. 199
Harper, D. 196
Harris, M. 329
Harrison, P. 27
Hart, D.V. *et al.*, 241
Harwood, A. 218, 220
Harig, G. 185, 196
Haslemere Group, 353
Heggenhaugen, H.K. 356
Heischkel, E. 196
Hellegers, J.F. 19–20
Heller, T. 353
Helman, C. 343, 354–355
Herskovits, M.J. 113, 254, 256
Herxheimer, A. 342
Herzhaft, G. 356
Higgins, C.M. 108
Hikino, H. *et al.*, 312
Hinderling, P. 353, 356
Hiroko, Horikoshi-Roe 237
Hirschorn, N. 277
Ho, S.S.Y.C. 316
Ho, S.S.Y.C. *et al.*, 300
Hobsbawm, E. 355
Holmstedt, B. *et al.* 315
Homedes, N. 8, 16, 76, 346, 350
Hughes, C.C. 341
Hume, J. 296
Hunn, E.S. 303
Hunt Jr., E.E.355
Hunte, P.A. 251–252
Huntington, S.P. 350
Hyma, B. 47

Igun, U.A. 354–355
Illich, I. 15, 22–23, 35, 40, 227, 356
Isaacs, G. 313
Iwu, M.M. 311

Jaeger, W. 196
Jahoda, G. 200
Janzen, J.M. 119, 199–200, 255, 299, 339, 354
Jayasena, K. 354
Johannes, A. 308
Johns, T.A. 303
Johnson, C. 333
Jones, A.D. 70
Jones, M.O. 289
Jordaan, R.E. 150, 167, 169–170, 237–239, 251–252

Karim, W.-J. 299

Katz, J.M. 38, 76
Katz, R. 356
Kay, M. 126, 307
Keefe, S. 118, 125–126
Keller, B.B. 228
Kelly, I. 108, 119, 125
Kendall, C. *et al.*, 307
Kewitz, H. 20
Kiev, A. 111
Kitaw, Y. 89–90
Kitaw, Y. *et al.* 82
Kleinman, A. 119, 169, 200, 274, 301, 330, 334–335, 341, 343–346, 354–355
Kleinman, A. *et al.*, 169
Kloos, H. 84–85, 90, 102, 338, 354
Kloos, H. *et al.*, 8, 16, 76, 83–84, 90, 100–102, 147, 336, 338, 340, 346, 354
Kluckhohn, C. 329
Koo, L.C. 317
Korn, J. 356
Kristanto, J.B. 153–154, 162, 170
Kroeger, A. 86, 100, 274, 299, 355
Krol, L.J. 354
Kunstadter, P. 199
Kutumbiah, P. 297

Laderman, C. 239, 252, 356
Lall, S. 19, 38, 50, 59, 146–147, 353, 156
Lancaster, P.A. *et al.*, 312
Landy, D. 36, 47, 200, 299, 337, 355
Lasker, J.N. 354
Last, M. 228, 342, 355
Laurentin, A. 354
Ledogar, R.J. 19–20, 22, 27, 29, 38, 353
Lee, Ph. R. 117, 353
Leon-Portilla, M. 109
Lesbow, R. *et al.*, 57
Leslie, Ch. 41, 169, 296, 299
Lester, F.T. 82
Lévi-Strauss, C. 302, 329, 345, 356
Levine, R.A. 227
Lewis, G. 341, 355–356
Lewis, I.M. 225
Lewis, W.H. 199, 306, 315
Leys, C. 350
Linton, R. 256
Loewe-Reiss, R. 109–112
Logan, K. 47, 336, 346, 354–355
Logan, M.H. 8, 16, 27, 255–256, 274, 305, 341, 355
Lopes Acuna, D. 57
Lundin, S. 102

McCauley, A.P. 300
McClain, C. 111
MacCormack, C. 4, 177, 258, 282, 346, 348
Maclean, U. 119, 199–200, 354
McCullough, C.S. 305
McCullough, J.M. 305
McDermott, W. 38
McElroy, A. 347
McEvoy, J. 354
McGee, T. 133
McKeown, Th. 41
Madsen, C. 107
Mahaniah, J.K.M. 199
Maitai, C.K. et al., 274
Makapugay, H.C. et al., 304
Malone, M.H. 309
Mamdani, M. 147, 286, 356
Manderson, L. 251–252
Manzur, J. 82
Maran, C. 153–154, 159–161, 167–168, 170
Mardisiswojo, S. 169
Martin, H.W. et al., 113, 118, 122, 125
Martin, P. 57
Mburu, F.M. 355
Mead, M. 329
Meche, H. 83
Medawar, C. 347, 351, 353
Melrose, D. 42, 47, 58–59, 147, 274, 332, 335, 347, 349–350, 353
Melville, A. 333
Menéndez, E.L. 57
Mercier, J. 102
Messenger, J.C. 354
Messing, S.D. 102
Middleton, J. 227
Minas, M. 101
Minocha, A.A. 354
Mintz, M. 274
Mitchell, F.M. 116, 121, 255, 342, 349, 354
Mo, B. 299
Moerman, D.E. 303, 306, 344–345
Morgan, G.R. 314
Morgan, W.R.W. 306
Morley, P. 356
Morris, B. 302–303
Morton, J.F. 317
Mudakir, K. 169
Muji, M. 169
Mukhopadyay, S. et al., 304
Muller, M. 147, 334, 353
Mulugeta, S. 82
Murray, G. 27

Mustika, R. 153
Myerhoff, B. 314

Nabhan, G.P. et al 306
Nasser, A.M. 309
Navarro, V. 23, 43
Nchinda, T.C. 146
Negbi, M. 311
Neumann, A.K. et al., 47
Ngin, C.S. 240
Ngubane, H. 199
Nichter, M. 48, 199, 206, 217, 256, 263, 274, 332, 341, 354–355
Niehof, A. 10, 176, 236, 240, 251–252
Nitschke, C.A.S. et al., 355
Nolesco, M. 109
Nordberg, E. 94, 102, 338, 354
Novak, M. et al., 315

Oberender, P. 318
Ohnuki-Tierney, E. 355–356
Olsson, B. 82
O'Nell, C.W. 109, 122, 125
Ortiz de Montellano, B. 304
Osifo, N.G. 353
Osterwald, R. 82
Oswald, I.H. 299
Oyeneye, O.Y. 318

Pankhurst, R. 91
Parker, R.L. et al., 355
Parkin, D.J. 219
Parry, E.H.O. 82
Patel, M.S. 58, 76
Patel, S.J. 353
Paul, B. 330, 355
Pausewang, S., 100
Pelto, G.H. 110
Pelto, P.J. 110
Pérez Mera, A. 59, 76
Peters, G. 353
Peters, W. 42
Pike, N. 206
Pillsbury, B. 349
Plorde, D.S. 82
Plowman, T. 315
Poerwadarminta, W.J.S. 168
Polgar, S. 110, 329
Polunin, I. 356
Press, I. 27, 118, 125, 200, 274
Prins, G. 199
Purcell, J.F,H. 111–112

INDEX OF NAMES

Rajakmangunsudarso, H. 169
Ramanamurthy, R.S.V. 305
Ramesh, A. 47
Raney, M. 117
Ranger, T. 355
Read, M. 200
Reid, J. 299
Reid, M.B. 199
Rianggoro, K. 169
Richards, R.M.E. 349
Rindos, D. 303
Ritchie, J.M. 117, 315
Rivers, W.H.R. 254
Rivier, L. 315
Roberts, C.D. 200
Rodinson, M. 102
Rodriguez, P. et al., 316
Rokos, L. 95
Rolt, F. 353, 356
Romanucci-Ross, L. 119, 141, 255
Ross, P.J. 199, 266, 299, 307, 317
Rubel, A.J. 109, 111, 122, 126
Rubenstein, J. 345
Russell, S.D. 299

Sachs, L. 356
Sahly, S. 168–169
Sarasti, H. 20
Sarder, A.M. 47
Sargent, C. et al., 308
Sastroamidjojo, A.S. 154–158, 168–170
Saunders, L. 200
Schaller, W.E. 119
Schell, O. 274
Schendel, G. 109
Schrijvers, J. 355
Schulpen, T.W.J. 354
Schultes, R.E. 315
Schwartz, L.R. 200
Scotch, N.A. 329
Scott, J.C. 350
Scrimshaw, M. 22, 27, 36, 274, 354
Seacole, M. 285
Segall, M. 19, 37–38, 57
Sekhar, C.C. 102
Sekhar, C.C. et al., 102
Selby, K.E. 329
Sen, S.P. 310
Senturias, E.N. et al., 334–335
Sesser, S. 19
Shadily, H. 168
Shahid, N.S. et al., 307

Shanmugasundaram, K.R. et al., 312
Shannon, G.W. 101
Shatrughna, V. 335
Shiferaw, T. 82
Shivaswamy, M.K. 354
Sich, D. 353
Siegel, R.K. 315
Siler, W. 43, 337
Silver, D.B. 107–108, 125, 254, 356
Silverman, M. 19–20, 31, 95, 117, 138, 354
Silverman, M. et al., 59, 138, 274, 334, 353
Simandjuntak, E.S. 153, 160, 161, 165–166, 168
Simeonov, L.A. 48
Simmons, O. 274
Simoni, J.J. 110
Slater, P.E. et al., 90
Slikkerveer, J.L. 102, 349, 354
Smith, C.E.G. 38
Smith, M.C. 333
Soedibyo, M. 153, 169
Soeparto, S. see Suparto
Soleh, M. 169
Speight, A.N.P. 334
Spencer, D.M. 199
Spiro, M.E. 199
Starr, P. 76
Sterky, J. 356
Stinzing, G. et al., 82
Sumahatmaka 169
Sung, L.H. 119, 301
Suparlan, P. 167, 169
Suparto, S. 167, 169
Sural, P.N. 349
Surindo Utama, P.T. 162, 163
Sussman, L.K. 8, 10, 175, 199–200, 202, 354
Swinkels, W.J.A.M. 354

Tabor, D. 296
Takulia, H.S. et al., 47
Tassew, A. 94
Taticheff, S. et al., 82
Taussig, M. 274
Taylor, C. 20, 22, 41, 354
Taylor, C. et al., 354
Taylor, D. x, 351
Tekle-Haimanot, M. 86
Teklu, B. 82
Teller, C.H. 110, 118, 125
Thomas, A.E. 354
Thomas, K. 356

Thomson, H.W. 169
Tilaar, M. 153
Titmuss, R. 208
Townsend, P.K. 347
Trotter, R.T. II, 111, 113, 118, 122, 125
Tsega, E. 82
Tsega, E. et al., 95
Tunön, C. et al., 57
Turner, E. 314
Turner, N.J. 313
Turner, V. 314, 345
Turshen, M. 353
Twain, M. 206

Ugalde, A. 8, 16, 57–58, 61, 76, 346, 350
Ugalde, A. et al., 61, 67
Underwood, P. 354
Underwood, Z. 354
Unschuld, P.U. 6, 8, 41, 175, 196–197, 341, 354

Van Amelsvoort, V. 229
Van Beek, T.A. et al., 310
Van Binsbergen, W. 133
Van Dijk, M.P. 133
Van der Geest, S. 17, 47, 57, 59, 65, 90, 135–136, 146–147, 224, 253, 260–261, 274, 336, 338, 348, 354–355
Van der Most van Spijk, M. 354
Van Luijk, J.N. 341
Van Zeist, W. 303
Velimirovic, B. xi–xii, 318
Velimirovic, H. xi–xii, 318
Visser, M. 146

Waitzkin, H. 23
Walker, G. 286, 356
Wallace, C.K. 94
Wallis, R. 356

Wanninayaka 49
Wartensleben, A. 59
Wassen, H.S. 308
Wasunna, A.E.O. 253
Wasunna, M. 253
Watson, P.L et al., 306, 310, 315
Waxler, N.E. 47, 52, 54, 354
Weaver, Th. 111, 113
Weisberg, D.H. 299, 354
Wellin, E. 254
Wells, H.G. ix
Welsch, R.L. xii, 8, 10, 17, 199–200, 250, 254–255, 333, 338, 345, 355
Wertheim, W.F. 350
Westheim, P. 33
White, A. 41
Whiteford, M. 119, 122, 125
Whyte, S.R. 5, 7, 168, 176, 222–223, 227, 330, 240, 354
Wilbert, J. 303
Willis, R.G. 228
Winarno, B. 153–154, 159–161, 166–168, 170
Winter, E.H. 227
Woldeab, M. 83
Wolffers, I. 10, 48, 51–52, 147, 333, 337, 346, 351, 354
Woods, C.M. 27, 36, 200, 353
Workneh, F. 102
Wright, D.J. 82
Wyatt, H.V. 70;, 341

Yoder, P.S. 200
Yost, J.A. 303, 306, 308
Young, A. 37, 94, 102, 274, 300–301, 318, 356
Young, J.C. 107–108, 110–111, 113, 119, 200, 274, 355
Yudkin, J.S. 146, 332, 353

INDEX OF SUBJECTS

Abbott 28, 38
abdominal
 – obstruction 53
 – pain 199
 (*see also* gastro-intestinal; stomach)
abortifacient 239, 271
abortion 43, 53, 89, 240–1, 265, 340
Abron 218, 288, 341
abscesses 53, 291–2
absenteeism 63, 68
abundance of medicines 335
 (*see also* shortage of medicines)
abuse of medicines 63
 (*see also* inappropriate use; misuse)
accessibility
 – of herbal medicines 202
 – of medical services 57, 60, 84, 90, 109, 110, 117
 – of new 'foreign' medicines 226–7
 – of pharmaceuticals 59, 73, 81, 99, 202, 239, 253, 255, 273
 – of treatment for diarrhea 286
 – of Western health care 208, 258–61, 290
aceitas, *see* oils
acetylsalicylic acid 51
acetominophen 51, 53
activity space 101
adaptation 47
advertising x, 37, 125, 138, 141, 160–1, 163, 164
advice on the use of drugs by relatives 92–95, 99, 107, 339
 (*see also* choice of drugs; information about medication; inserts; personnel in medical institutions)
Afghanistan 251–2
Africa 20, 47, 57, 82, 340
 – Eastern– 357
 – West– xi
 – Southern– 356
African medicine 223, 228
 – relation to western medicine 228–30
aguas, *see* mineral water
aid agencies 286
Ainu 356

Air-Mankur 152, 153, 161–3
Algon 89
alkaloids 306, 309, 311
Alka-Seltzer 119, 121
allergic reaction 38–9
allopathy in relation to Ayurveda 293–7
alternative healer, *see* indigenous practitioner
American, Native
 – treatments for blood disorders 306
 – treatments for cough 308
 – uses of the Ranunculaceae 313
Amharic
 – concepts 94, 95
 – language 100
Ampicillin 39, 51, 96, 98, 270
amulets 225
Anacin 121
anaestesia 304
analgesics 51, 59, 71, 89, 90, 120, 136–7, 149, 262
ancestors in Nyole treatment of sickness 223, 225, 231
Andrew Salts 284–5
anemia
 – aplastic– 30
 – medicines 136–7
Anna Pavola Sindhooram 312
antacid 90
anthropology 107–8, 119, 125, 257, 331, 336, 355
 – as postmortem discipline 347
 – awareness of pharmaceuticals in– 9–11
 – exotic bias of– 9, 11
 (*see also* medical anthropology)
antibiotics ix, 20, 27, 32, 38–9, 43, 47, 51–3, 59, 62, 71, 84, 89, 90–1, 94–5, 99–101, 136–8, 154, 177, 237, 253–4, 262–5, 270–2, 274, 354
anti-diarrheals 267
antimalarials 262
antimicrobials 310
antipyretics 89
antiseptics 202
anti-sorcery medicines and movements 219, 28

377

antipasmotics 71, 94
aphrodisiacs xii, 166–7, 306
articulation
  – of formal and informal medicine 17,
    54, 22, 82, 85, 108, 125, 131–47, 152,
    335–6, 349
  – of modes of production 133, 143–5
Asawin 38
ascariasis 98
ascaricide 95, 96, 98
Asia ix–x, 20, 57, 149, 153, 165
Aspirin 38, 63, 89, 115, 120, 267, 270–1,
  353
asthma 86, 94, 98, 155, 291, 295
atacado pel pecho 27
Australian Aborigines 306–7, 311
availability of medicines, see accessibility
Ayurveda 49, 53–4, 339, 342
Ayurvedic medicine 11, 201, 257, 289–97
  – modern – 289–90
  – patent medicines x, 290
  – pharmaceutical firms ix, xii, 289–90
  – practitioners of – 15, 177, 213, 289–97
  – relation to biomedicine 293–7
  – textual sources of – 296–7
  – traditional – 289–90
Azarcon 124

bacteria 82
bactrim 28, 38, 99
bandages 98
Bangladesh xi, xii, 47, 307, 335, 349, 357
banned drugs 253, 271
barefoot doctor x
barrida see ritual treatment
Bayer, 33, 37, 42
beef consumption 91
behavorial changes 210–1
behavorial rules 235, 241, 243, 245
benzyl benzoate ointment 51
betel nut 315
bicarbonate of soda 225
bicycle medicine 218
bilharzia 265
Binotal 39
biomedicine
  – bias of – 177, 299, 309–18
  – hegemony of – 330, 346
  – influence of – 199
  – legal status of – 209
  – relation to Ayurveda 293–7
  – relation to ethnomedicine 200, 300–1,
    305–7

bipenicillin 140
Bintang Toedjoeh 155
blood
  – at childbirth in Madura 244
  – Mende views and treatment of – 176,
    254, 264, 268–70
  – Native American treatment of
    disorders of – 306
blood pressure medications 267
boils 292
Bolivia 304
bone setter 85
bonificaciones, see sales incentives
botica 71
Botswana 357
brand-name medications 28–9, 34–5, 63,
  71–2, 84, 99, 119, 353
brand names x, 50, 152
Brazil 20, 27, 335, 354
Brazilian folk medicine 311
Breacol 119, 121
Bristol Myers 38
British
  – medicines ix
  – pharmacopeia 51
bronchitis 39, 43, 86, 291
Broncovinotal 39
buda, see evil eye
bureaucratization 350
Burkina Faso 335, 354
burns 51, 121
bush-homestead opposition 225
butter 89
by-passing
  – health centres 62–3
  – physicians 115

Cameroon 6, 17, 58, 65, 131–47, 336, 338,
  350, 352
Campolon B–12 28
capsules viii, xii, 17, 89, 100, 149, 151,
  159–63, 253–4, 264–5, 270
  – power of – 264
cardiogram 63
cardiovascular disorders 311
cartel 38
castor oil 284
catarrh 52
Catholicon 254
causes of illness, see etiology
Central African Republic 136, 354
Central America 47
Central American drug reference 30

ceremony *see* ritual
cesarian section 353
charlatans 346
chemists, *see* pharmacies
chicken pox 307
childbirth
    – traditional Madurese medication at– 176, 235–52
    – as transition in Madura 243, 250
China 179–97
    – co-existence of Chinese and Western medicine in– 194–5
    – origins of pharmaceutical knowledge in– 181–3
    – syncretism of cognitive systems 183–5
Chinese in Malaysia 240
Chinese medicine x, 316–8
    – syncretism of - 180–1
    – traditional - 201
    – practitioners of - 213
Chinese pharmaceutical companies xii, 154, 155
Chinese pharmacology 175, 179–97
    – drug hierarchies in - 180
    – heterogeneity of - 180–4
chloramphenicol 30, 32, 51, 95, 271, 274
chloroquin 261, 265, 267, 274
choice
    – of drugs 81, 92–102, 114
    – of treatment 52, 85, 87–8, 90, 115–24, 203–7, 255–6, 330
    (*see also* doing-nothing)
cholera 268, 284–5
Christian clergyman 201–3, 210–211
chronic illnesses 82, 86, 89, 110, 207
church
    – healers 85
    – related institutions 134, 335
cicratization 308
cigarettes as medicine 155
cirrhosis of the liver 110
    (*see also* liver diseases)
clean blood 169
clinics 260, 262, 278
clioquinol 271
coca 315
cocaine 315
code of pharmaceutical marketing practices x, 142, 351
codein 95, 265
cognitive analysis 255–6
colds 27–8, 31–2, 37–9, 82, 86–7, 96, 98, 136–7, 205–6, 353

colmaditos 59
colmados 73
colonialism 227, 289
colostrum 242
Columbia 27, 252
commercial
    – aspects of drugs 349–50
    (*see also* price of drugs; profit on drugs)
    – reasons for the use of pharmaceuticals 48, 54–5
commercialization 15, 59, 349
commerciogenesis 15, 23, 35–40, 42
commodity nature of medicines vii, 5, 219
community participation 82, 77, 83
compliance 334, 338, 353
concepts of pharmaceuticals 340–3
conceptualizations
    – about the nature and treatment of illness 22, 31, 36–7, 39, 123
    – about the use of medications, lay- 31, 342–3
    – about the use of medications, professional- 343
    – of medicines, recent studies of - 217
concreteness of medicines 3–4
Confucian pharmaceutics 180
Congo 227
conjunctivitis 115, 291–2
constipation 89, 267, 269, 282
consumer
    – groups 350–1
    – movement 350
consumption of drugs 58
Contac cold capsule 262, 264
context ix, xiii
    – and research methodology 8, 262, 303, 305, 314, 318–9
    – in which medicines are obtained and used 6, 250, 259
    – definition of - of medicines 3, 8
    – local - vii, xiii
    – meaning of medicines in relation to– 231, 256
    – national culture 8
    – of drug distribution 350
    – of drug purchase 96–101
    – of health care 339
    – of plant use 316–8
    – of use of drugs 344
contextualization 352
contraceptives 342
control of medicines 6

convenience of biomedical pharmaceutical 208–9
convenience of health care service by pharmacist 124
convulsions 211, 267
cooking oil 121
coramine 291, 297
Corpus Hippocraticum 182, 187
corruption 350
corticosteroids 47, 51–2
cosmetics 149, 151–3, 159–60, 163, 165–
cost
 – of medicines 265
 – of treatment (*see also* economics) 285
cough 16, 89, 119, 120–4, 168
 – Mauritian views and treatment of - 205–7, 212
 – medicine 136
 – Mende views and treatment of - 265, 268–9
 – Native American treatment of - 308
 – syrup 39, 120
counter-indications 20, 28, 30–1, 39
creams 17, 149, 151–2, 163
 (*see also* oils)
credit system for the purchase of drugs 65, 67–8, 72, 90
Creoles 175, 201, 209, 212
cross-cultural communication 347
Cuba 76
cultural appropriation of Western medicines 177, 217
cultural concepts 342–3, 345
 – of healing 345–6, 356
 – of health 345–6, 356
cultural hegemony of biomedicine 330
cultural reinterpretation
 – definition of - 256
 – of Western pharmaceuticals 253–76
cultural relativism 347
Cultural Revolution 180
cultural syndrome 87, 89
culture, construction of - 355
cupping 308
curanderos 108, 111, 114–5, 118, 125–6
 (*see also* indigenous practitioners)
curing, definition of - 256
cursing among Nyole 223–4, 231
 – tying of curse by medicine 224

dangerous medicines 124–5, 164, 170
dead souls 209–11

debtera, *see* church healers
deception in selling drugs 139, 146
decisions about treatment 111
 (*see also* choice of treatment)
decongestants 90, 202
dehydration 28, 138, 277
delirium 210
deliveries 48
demystification 344
denaturalization of cultural conventions 329, 339–40, 343, 352
dentists on Madura 236
dependence on medicines 19–46, 58–9
Depo-Provera 271
dermatological disorder 34
descuido 32
Desenfriol 119, 121
deterioration of quality of health 41
Dexadrina 107
diabetes 86, 110, 123, 205, 207
diagnosis 211–212
 – by pharmacist 107, 124
diagnostic examinations as reason for choice of health care 118
diarrhea 16, 32, 51, 53, 89, 91, 96, 110, 119–24
 – concepts of - 281–4
 – home remedies for 285–7
 – Mende views and treatment of - 264, 268
 – and oral rehydration therapy 177, 261, 277–87
 – and psychotropic plant use 316
 – symptoms of - 279–81
 – and teething 283
 – treatment of - by emetics and purgatives 307
Diazepam 30
dichlorophen 91, 97
diet 53, 109, 316–9
 (*see also* food)
dietary rules 240, 250
diethylstilbestrol (DES) 43
digitalis 262
dillution of medicine 43
dimenhydrinate 30
disease
 – definition of - 301
 – egress 307–8, 313
 – illness dichotomy 330, 343, 346
 – substance 308
disinfectant 89

dispensaries
- government- 111–2, 114, 118, 120
- in Bunyole 220
- on Mauritius 201–2, 207–8, 211
dispensers 260, 267
distance to health resources 16, 90–1, 100–2, 110, 116
distribution of Western pharmaceuticals 17, 33–4, 47, 50, 54, 65, 73, 131–47, 159, 253–76, 333, 335–8, 349–51, 357
(*see also* drug representatives)
distribution of medical services, *see* accessibility of medical services
diuretics 94, 269
diviners in Bunyole 223–4, 228
doctors, *see* physicians
Doctrine of Signatures 305–6
doing-nothing in case of illness 87–8, 120, 123,
Dominican Republic 6, 16, 57–77, 350
Dorze 100
dosage
- of coca 316
- in diet 317
- different from prescribed 265, 271–2
Dramamine 30
dressers 85
drug
- biography 331, 344
- total- effect 343–4
- obsolete meaning of- 7
- poisoning 95
- representatives 15, 22, 28, 31, 33, 50–1, 115, 117, 255, 260, 262, 270, 331–3, 353
- resistance 20, 39, 94
- revolution 41
dry-wet balance concept of health 238–9
dukun 149, 169
dumping of drugs x, 20, 331, 355
dysentery 15–6, 268

ear
- infection 86
- problem 86
East Africa 7, 176, 217–31
ecological
- factors and health problems 109
- inquiries 318
economics
- of diarrhea treatment 286
- of medicine use 177, 202

Ecuador 306, 308
educational level 16, 24, 29, 31, 51, 61, 86–7, 89, 90, 101, 121–2
effects of medicines 176
- anaesthetic 315
- analgesic 306–7, 312, 316
- antiatherogenic 311
- antimicrobial 312, 316
- antiparasitic 316
- antipyretic 312
- antispasmodic 307
- antitussive 308
- calmative 311
- caustic 311
- cholagogue 312
- concepts of - in Chinese and European pharmacology 180–2, 185–8, 190–4
- costive 307
- counterirritant 307
- decongestant 308, 313
- diuretic 312
- emetic 316
- emollient 307
- hematinic 312
- hypocholesterolemic 312
- hypolipemic 312
- hypotensive 309
- inflammation suppressive 308
- irritant 307, 313
- lack of effect 255
- laxative 312
- proximate and ultimate 307–8, 313
- psychotropic 315–6
- purgative 316
- stimulant 306–7
- stomachic 307, 311
- vesicant 313
(*see also* efficacy of medicines)
efficacy of medical treatment 356
efficacy of medicines 7, 90, 94–5, 100, 115, 155, 157–8, 164, 335, 340, 343–6, 355
- criteria for evaluating 99 326
- cultural constructions of - 299–326
- definitions of - 300–2
- and equilibrium theory of illness 177
- of indigenous medicines 177, 299–326
- of injections 263
- of penicillin 291
- of Western medicine xii, 177, 222–3, 272
efficiency of medical service 58, 83
El Salvador 6, 15, 19–46, 333, 336

elixer 166, 169
emergencies and choice of health care 118
emesis 307, 309
emetics 95
emic approach 332, 346, 355–6
emic and etic interpretations 330–1, 318
enemas 314
enteritis 109
entrepreneurs 54–5, 332
environmental sanitation, see hygiene, public-
eosinophilia 291
ephedrine compounds 262
epidemics 82
epidemiology 82
epilepsy 87
Epsom Salts 284–6
esencias, see essences
essences 36
essential drugs x, xi, 16, 20, 58, 62, 65–7, 72–4, 76, 84, 125, 146, 286, 335, 347–8, 356–7
Ethiopia 6, 16, 41, 81–102, 338, 349
ethnic affiliation 90, 100, 153, 163, 165–6, 169
ethnocentrism 343, 355
ethnomedical beliefs 117
ethnomedicine 330, 341
 – definition of- 319
 – relation to biomedicine 300–1, 305, 309–18
ethnopharmacology 3, 299, 301, 304, 318
ethnophysiology 267, 304
etic approach 346
etiology of illness
 – Mende reinterpretation of Western pharmaceuticals and- 266–70
 – Nyole treatment and- 221–4
 – Mauritian treatment and- 175–6, 209–212
Europe 149–50, 165, 353
 – ancient pharmacological system 179–197
 – origins of pharmaceutical knowledge in- 181–3
 – homogeneity of cognitive systems 183–7
evil eye 89
exotic bias in research vii, 131, 316, 346
 (see also anthropology)
exotic substances and techniques, see foreign medicine

expectorant 51, 90
expenditures, drug- 20, 57, 60, 64–6, 72–3
experiments with drugs x
expertise, trust in- 150
expiry date 138
Explanatory Model 346, 355
eye
 – disorders 313
 – drops 89
 – infections 86, 89

faith in medication 43
Fala Kpelle 218
family health care 111
family planning 25
fatigue 170
female headed households 111
fertility 239
fetishes 227
fetus 241
fever 89, 94, 156
 – Khmer suction treatment for- 308
 – Mende perception and treatment of- 176, 265–7
 – Mauritian treatment of- 205
 – Mayan treatment with 'cold'penicillin 255
Five Phases doctrine 180, 184, 189, 193
folic acid 263, 269
folk medicine, Madurese 237–8
food 32, 89, 99
 – as medicine 122–3, 152
 – biomedical views of efficacy of- 305
 – and Jamaican views and treatment of diarrhea 282, 285
 – and Mende prevention and treatment of illness 266, 268–70
 – relation to medicine 266, 277, 316–8, 266
 (see also diet)
foreign medicine
 – as vehicle of cultural change 175
 – contrast to indigenous 33, 290–1
 – power of- viii, 7, 225–9, 231, 259, 262
formal and informal medicine distribution 131–47
formal sector 133–5
forms of medicine 16, 221, 263–6
 (see also qualities)
France 20
Franol 98
free medicines 16, 60, 62–8, 72–3, 83, 115

fumatory 95
Gabon 136
gall 341
garlic 99
gasoline 89
gastric ulcers 53, 271
gastritis 53, 86, 89, 96
gastro-intestinal disorders 25–6, 32, 34, 53, 89, 205, 207, 238, 307, 317
gastro-intestinal infections 37–8
general practitioners, *see* physicians
generic drugs x, 98–9, 102, 353
 (*see also* restricted list of drugs)
Gentamycin 99
Germany ix, xi, 20
Gesterra 33
Ghana 355
Glauber Salts 284–5
Gnau 356
gonnorhea 86, 94, 96–8, 221, 295
government control
 – on drugs 59, 81, 83, 350
 – on export of drugs 351
 (*see also* legislation)
government health facilities 201, 221, 227, 278
Great Britain xi, 53, 138, 332, 354
Guatemala 27, 42, 341
Gusii 227

H.A.I. (Health Action International) 347, 351
hair oil xii
Hausea
 – eclectic nature of medicine 228–9
 – reaction to failure of therapy 301
 – plant medicines 304–8, 313, 317
hawkers of medicines, *see* informal sale of drugs
headache 16, 34, 39, 88–9, 99, 119, 120–4, 205, 207, 267, 308
healer
 – as source of medication 293–7
 – choice of 210–211
 – Creole 201–3, 210
 – Madurese (dukon) 237–51
 – role of - 299–300
healing
 – as process 299, 301–2, 307–11, 313–4, 318
 – definition of - 301
health certificates 118

health centres 23–5, 29, 109–2, 120, 157, 236–8, 278, 338
 – quality of - 109
 (*see also* government health facilities)
health development, *see* health planning
health maintenance, Mende concern with 270–1
health planning 176–7, 271–3
health posts, *see* health centres
health problems on Madura 236
health risks of injecting medicines 70
heart
 – attacks 291
 – conditions 86, 94, 110
 – stimulants 267
helminthiasis 137
hemostatics 306
Henley's toothache remedy 51
hepatitis 86, 306
herbal medicine 52–4, 85, 89, 91, 108
 – accessibility of - on Mauritius 202, 208
 – African - 229–30
 – Ayurvedic 290
 – characteristics of - on Mauritius 206–9
 – Chinese patent - 201
 – domains of use of - in Madura 235
 – knowledge and use of - on Mauritius 208–9
 – Madurese 235–52
 – Mauritian 175, 199–215
 – Nyole 220, 225
 (*see also* jamu; plant medicines)
herbalists 85, 201–3, 205, 208, 210, 213
herbals
 – Chinese - 181, 187
 – European - 182
hierarchy of resort 141, 211–2
'high-tech' viii
Hindu maraz on Mauritius 210–3, 210–1
Hindu saints on Mauritius 209–10
Hingua Steca 53
histrionism 345
hoarding of drugs, *see* storage of drugs
holism 167, 345, 347, 356
holy water 87–88
home remedies
 – for susto 16
 – Jamaican - for diarrhea 285–7
 – Madurese 237
homeopathic
 – companies xii
 – medicine 99–100

homeopathy on Mauritius 201, 213
honey 168, 152
hospitals vii, 110, 143, 201–2, 208, 213, 259–60, 267, 269, 278
 – for traditional medicine 230
 – medicine 218
 – personnel, *see* personnel in medical institutions
 (*see also* government health facilities)
Hostacilina 39
hot-cold dichotomy 305, 341
 – Madurese- 237–42, 244, 246–7, 250–2
 – Mayan- 255–6
 – Mende- 265–7
 – Indian- 257, 312
 – Jamaican- 287
 (*see also* humoral theories)
household remedies 85, 87, 89, 111–2, 115, 118, 120–3, 339
 (*see also* home remedies)
Huastec 307
humoral theories of disease xii, 304, 312
hygiene, public 37, 41, 83
hypertension 66, 86, 94, 123, 205, 207, 355
hypothetical questions 112–3

iatrogenesis 22, 35, 40, 65, 356
ideal type 332
identity and medicines 217
ideology 332
idóneos 23, 29, 37, 39
illegal
 – clinics 84
 – distribution of medicines 335
 – private use of medicines 350
 – sale of medicines, *see* informal sale of drugs
illness
 – definition of- 301
 – duration of- and treatment 203–4, 206–7, 238
 – 'of God' 209–12, 273
 – treatment of episodes on Mauritius 207
imodium 53
importation of medicines xi, 149, 152, 155–9
improper use of medicines, *see* inappropriate use of pharmaceuticals
inappropriate medicines 124
inappropriate use of pharmaceuticals 16, 59, 94–5, 116, 138, 176, 253–4, 257–8, 262, 271–3, 349, 351
incense 245
income 24, 31, 36, 90, 100, 108–9, 121–2
 – and choice of treatment 110
 – family- 111
 – physician's income 334
incorrect use of medicines, *see* inappropriate use of pharmaceuticals
India ix–x, xii, 21, 41, 47–8, 119, 145, 177, 217, 289–97, 305, 334–5, 341
 – overlap of Indian and biomedical paradigms 312
indications 31, 39
indigenous healer, *see* indigenous practitioner
indigenous healing, *see* indigenous medicine
indigenous medicine
 – autonomy of- 296–7
 – commercially produced- ix
 – definition of- 319
 – efficacy of- 177, 299–326
 – interaction with biomedicine 10, 200
 (*see also* ethnomedicine)
indigenous practitioners using Western medicines 21–2, 27–9, 41–2, 47–55, 64, 108, 125, 177, 332, 337, 349, 353–4
indigestion 53
individual nature of medicinal treatment 219, 224
individualization vii
Indo-Mauritians 175, 201, 209, 212
indomethacine 53
Indonesia xi, xii, 10, 17, 145, 149–70, 176, 235–52, 333
infant formulas 38
infants 25
infections xii, 34, 39, 41, 82, 86, 88–9, 121, 291
 – acute and chronic respiratory 82, 86–8
 – intestinal- 86
 – intestinal parasitic- 82, 88
 – upper-respiratory- 25, 37–9, 86–9, 91, 98
 – uro-genital- 25, 98–9
 (*see also* respiratory disorders)
 (*see also* uro-genital disorders; venereal disease)
inflammatory disorders 311, 313
influenza 71, 87, 95, 109, 205
informal medicine distribution 17, 131–47
informal modern health care 132

informal sale of drugs vii, 15, 17, 59, 84–5, 111, 135–6, 139–44, 150, 152, 157, 164, 169, 202, 205, 220, 235, 237, 237, 251, 253, 255, 260–2, 333, 337–8, 349–50, 354–5
informal sector 133, 135–6, 139–41
information on drug use 29–31, 42, 53, 92, 95–6, 100, 114–5, 117, 119, 124–5, 138, 145, 152, 158, 253, 331–2, 334, 336, 349, 352–3
(*see also* advertisements; advice on use of drugs by relatives; intructions; inserts; media broadcasts)
injection doctors ix, 22, 43, 83–5, 87–8, 98, 102, 220, 338, 354
injections vii, ix, 32–3, 35–6, 38, 47, 70–1, 73, 84, 89, 96, 98–9, 118, 135, 138, 140, 334, 337, 343, 353, 355
 – compared to tablets in India 292
 – death from– in Sierra Leone 263–4
 – heating qualities of– in India 257
 – Mende views and use of– 261, 263, 271–2
 – penicillin– by Ayurvedic doctors 177, 290–7
 – penicillin– by Nyole needle men 220–1
 (*see also* health risks)
innovation of culture 55
insanity 210
insecticides 42
inserts 22, 30–1, 39, 138
instructions about drug use 6, 94, 102, 259–61, 265, 272, 274, 290
 (*see also* information about medicines)
integration of western and alternative medical practitioners, *see* articulation of formal and informal medicine
Inter-American Development Bank 59
interweaving of formal and informal 141–5
 (*see also* articulation)
intestinal helminths 42, 53
intoxication 314
intravenous rehydration 277–8
iodine 154
Iran 342
iron tablets 269
Islam 236, 238
Islamic medicine 228
Israel folk medicine 304–5
Italy 20
Italian indigenous healers 311
Ivory Coast 218, 341

Jamaica 121, 177, 277–87, 342
Jamu Iboe 154
Jamu industry 149–70
Jamu Jago 152, 154, 160, 163, 168
Jamu medicine x, xii, 17, 339
 – packaged– 10, 17, 149–51, 158, 161, 237–8, 250–1
 – ready-to-drink 150
 – relation to Western medicine 10
 – use in pregnancy and childbirth 10, 176, 239–40, 243–9, 251 Jamu Pasuka Ambon 154
Japan x, 20
jargon, biomedical 31
jaundice 305–6
Java 149–70, 251
jhamo, *see* jamu

Kamcape anti-sorcery movement 228
kaopectate, 119, 121
kaloin pectin ointment 51
Kamba 341
Kanamycin 353
kebele, *see* urban dwellers' associations
keftegna, 91–3, 102
Kenya 306, 341
Kerala 47
key informants 110
Khmer medicine 308
knowledge
 – of household remedies 122
 – of traditional medicine 150, 157
Koranic texts as medicines 225
Korea 353
Kossopharm 91
Kung bushmen 356
kwashiorkor 268

Laboratorio Lopez 30
labour pains 53
Latin America 20, 29, 41, 57–9, 63, 68, 111
laws, *see* legislation
lay health reporting systems 86
laxative xii, 136–8
 – Indian– 312
 – Jamaican treatment for diarrhea 279, 282, 284–5
 – Mende treatment for malaria 254, 267
lead poisoning 124
legal cases, medicines for– 223
legislation
 – on drug distribution 50, 136, 141, 144

– on traditional medicine 117, 151–2, 156–9, 168, 170
leprosy 86
liberating nature of medicines 176, 224, 230, 340
Lilly 38
lincocin 271
Lisalgil 39
liver diseases 82, 306
   (see also cirrhosis of the liver)
liquid forms of medication 32–3, 163
local context vii, xiii
loperamide 53
loss of consciousness 210–1
lotion 151, 152
   (see also creams, oils)
love and luck medicines 223, 228
Lugbara 227
Luo 227

Ma-wang-tui texts 181
Madura 10, 176, 235–52
magic 199, 330
Maka 143
malaria 48, 156, 254, 261, 265–7, 272
Malawi 228
Malays 251–2
Malaysia, 119, 156
maldistribution of drugs 349
   (see also abundance; distribution; shortage)
males 36
malnutrition xii, 25, 37–8, 43, 82, 86, 268
   (see also kwashiorkor; nutritional disorders)
manufacturers of Western pharmaceuticals 15, 253–4
Manus 119
Mao x
marital difficulties, medicines for– 223
marketing of drugs, see promotion of drug sales
markets, see informal sale of drugs
Marxism 349–50
massage 240–2, 245, 250
materia medica 3
   – ancient Greek– 6
   – Chinese– 6
   – Chinese descriptive literature on– 187
   – Madurese– 235
   – of Dioscurides 182, 187
   – Shen-nung's scripture on– 181–2, 197

Mauritius 6, 10, 175, 199–215
meaning of medicines vii, xiii, 4, 6–7, 175–326
measles 307
medhaniyd awaki, see herbalists
media broadcasts 124–5
medical anthropology vii, 10, 179, 199, 330
   – applied– 73, 329–57
medical personnel, see hospital personnel
medical pluralism 223–7, 229
medical self-help books 153
medicalization 15, 17, 19–46, 48, 334
medication errors 39, 43
medication induced illness 38
mediums 42
Mejorales 119, 121
Mende 7, 176, 253–76, 342
menstrual irregularities 33, 169
menstruation 239–40
mental illness 87, 94, 123
menthol 168
Mentholatum 262, 265, 267, 269
Mercantilism 332
mercury 154, 170
Merek 38
Mestizo 23
metaphor 344
methodology of research 110–1, 133, 137, 262–3, 278–9
   (see also contextualization; hypothetical questions; key informants; participant observation; qualitative research; quantitative research; questionnaires; research design; surveys; static character; unstructured interviews)
methods of contextualizing medicines 8
Metronidazole 95
Mexico xi, 6, 8, 16, 20, 27, 31, 39, 43, 107–25, 307
midwives 201, 203, 236, 240
migration 57, 59, 81
mineral water 36
Mintezol 140, 205
misdiagnosis 101, 116, 124
misfortune 221, 223
misinformation about drugs 351
   (see also information)
misuse of pharmaceuticals, see inappropriate use
mixture, concept of– in Greek pharmacology 185–7, 189, 196
Mkesson 30, 42

INDEX OF SUBJECTS

mode of production 144
modern medical services 131
modernization 149, 152, 159, 160–1
modification in use of drugs 100
morality 217
morality cult, central– 225–6
mortality 39, 41, 94–5, 109–10
 – infant - 48, 49
 – maternal - 48, 49
mortality rates 251
 – Madurese - 235
 – Sierra Leonese - 258
mother-and-child health care 83
moxibustion 308
Mustika Ratu, 153

narcotic tablets 260
national identity 149, 160
nationalization of health care 81–3
'natural' character of medicines 3, 9–11
'natural' treatment 199
'natural' view, see denaturalization
naturally caused illness 199, 210
Ndembu 345
need of medicines 357
needle men, see injection doctors
Nembutal 107
Nepal 290, 293, 349
nerves 205
Nestlé 38
nettles, flogging with– 308
network, social 99
New Guinea 308
Nigeria xi, 119, 135–6, 138, 228
Ningerum 341, 345
nivaquin 265
nocebo 344, 356
noncompliance 272
non-infectious diseases 88, 89
non-profit institutions 134, 335
non-system 342
North American 109
Nuer 227
number of consultations 62–3, 67–8, 72
nurses
 – in Jamaica 278, 286–7
 – in Madura 236
 – in Sierra Leone 259–60
 – on Mauritius 201
nutrition 41, 317
nutritional
 – disorders 34, 86–9, 110

(see also malnutrition)
 – supplements 28, 47, 99
(see also vitamins)
Nyole 217–31
Nyonya Meneer 152–4, 163, 168
Nystadin 30, 38

obat 154–69
Obat Karuhun 154
oils 36
ointments 51, 243–4, 246–9
One-A-Day vitamins 262, 269–70
Optalgin 96
Optotonico 38
oral rehydration salts 177, 277–87
orphan drugs 344
out-of-date medicines 124
outcome 304, 308,
 – proximate and ultimate 302, 314
over-the-counter medicines 21, 27, 31, 47,
 59, 69, 83, 100, 107–25, 277, 290
overmedication 63, 65, 100, 124
overutilization of drugs 73

packaging of medicines viii, 7, 16, 17, 72–3,
 98, 138, 144, 260, 273
(see also Jamu)
packets
 – of jamu medicines 238, 250–1
 – of oral rehydration salts 277, 279,
 284–7
painkillers 47, 51–2, 202, 261
Palmicetina 30
palpitations 205
panaceas xii
Panadol 202, 205
Pantomicina 28, 30
paper, burned– 121
Papua New Guinea 341, 345, 356
parallel, see: two-tier
paralysis 210–11
paramedics 333
paramparika 49, 52
Paraquay 304
parasite infestation 37
parasites 82, 89, 115, 206–7, 212, 279
parem 162
participant observation 8, 125, 336
patent control x
patent medicines ix, 146, 203, 211
 – Ayurvedic - 290
P.D.R. 30, 39

INDEX OF SUBJECTS

peddlers of drugs, *see* informal sale of drugs
pedralyte 28, 30
penacine 98
penicillin 11, 39, 89, 95, 98, 177, 220, 255–6, 263, 289–97, 342
  – dangers of - 295
  – power of - 291–2, 5
  – qualities of - 291–2
pepper 89
Pepto-Bismol 121
perception
  – of disease 81, 90
  – of use of drugs 99, 102
personnel in medical institutions 35, 142–3, 21–2, 29, 93, 116, 260, 262, 274, 336, 338, 354
Pfizer 30
pharmacopeias, indigenous - xi, 302–8
pharmaceutical anthropology ix, 3, 5, 179
pharmaceutical firms 19–46, 125, 134, 141, 146, 154–5, 158–9, 277, 331, 333, 351, 355
  – multinational - ix–xii, 273–4
  – national - 38
(*see also* manufacturers)
pharmaceutical industry 15, 19–46, 142, 144–5, 332
  – multinational - 19–21, 29, 30, 36, 38–40, 42, 50, 59, 331, 353, 357
pharmaceutical invasion 9, 19–46, 175–6, 227, 229
  – economic consequences of - 19–21, 331
pharmaceutical pluralism 10, 250
pharmaceutical, definition of - 5
pharmaceutics
  – and culture 179–97
  – cognitive basis of - 179–81
pharmacies xii, 17, 19–46, 50–1, 59–77, 107–25, 133–4, 139–43, 154, 158, 202, 205, 207, 211–2, 260, 284–5, 290, 355
  – communal - 16, 64
  – government - 16, 81
  – wholesale - 33, 34, 35, 36
pharmacists 15, 16, 135–6, 141–6, 150, 201, 208, 253, 332–3, 353
  – as health care practitioner 107–25, 113–7, 336, 354
  – diagnosis by 107, 124
  – pro - 141, 146
  – professional organization 110
  – training of - 116–7, 124

pharmacy clients, case histories of - 96–100
pharmacy owners 30, 32–3, 42, 50
pharmacy personel 30–4, 37, 40, 47, 51, 84, 95, 98, 99, 102, 354
pharmacogenic maladies 271–2
pharmacology
  – analyses 303
  – bias 229, 318
  – Chinese, medieval 179–97
  – definition of - 181
  – European, ancient 179–97
  – Galenic 185–7, 190, 193
  – historic textual sources on - 179, 181–2, 187
  – origins in China 181–3
  – origins in Europe 181
  – research 229–30
  – Wang Hao-Ku, of 189–196
Pharmacopeias
  – cultural nature of - 318
  – indigenous - 302–8
  – literature on - 199
Philippines 57–8, 332, 335, 354
phlebotomy 308
physicians 15, 26, 28–9, 39–40, 43, 47, 49–51, 57, 59–65, 68–9, 110, 114, 123, 125, 146, 150, 157, 169, 201–3, 205, 211–2, 236–7, 259–60, 286, 332, 336, 340, 343–4, 349, 353, 357
  – and manufacturing medicines 154
  – and traditional medicine 156–7, 167, 170
  – compulsory service by - 60
  – patient relationship 116, 335, 339
  – private - 111–2, 118, 120–2, 157
physiology, Western paradigms of 318
pile tablets 269
pilfering of medicines 62
pills, *see* tablets
Piperazine 43
placebo 343–5, 355–6
  – and commerce 344
placenta 241–3
plant medicines xi, 17
  – qualities of - 303–8
(*see also* herbal medicines)
plants
  – descriptive or functional names of - 304
  – selection of - 303–8
  – smell of - 306
P.L.M. 30, 39

pneumonia 109, 156
poison 5, 306–7
  (*see also* toxicity)
policy, national - on drugs 59, 72, 102, 331, 357
politicians 146, 331, 352
politics 330
pollution 243–4
pomadas, *see* pomades
pomades 36
Pondo 309
popular
  – health care 338
  – sector 19–46
popularization
  – of biomedical terminology 43
  – of medical traditions 36
possession 89
poverty 25, 109
  (*see also* socio-economic factors; income)
powder 17, 149, 151, 159, 161–3
power of medicines 176, 217–31
practical relevance viii
pragmatism 222
pregnancy
  – and counter indication of drugs 28
  – and modern diagnosis 53
  – traditional medication at- in Madura 176, 135–52
  – transitional nature of - in Madura 239, 241, 250
prepackaging of medications 23, 27, 35, 37, 39–40
  (*see also* packaging)
prescription(s) 115, 117–8, 333–5, 142
  – and financial advantages 35, 334
  – by pharmacist 107, 124
    (*see also* over-the-counter)
  – by physician 107, 332, 338, 354
  – (*see also* prescription medicines)
  – historical texts on Chinese - 181–2, 187
  – irrational- 334–5, 353
  – medicines 27–9, 31, 37, 43, 84, 94, 96, 101, 157, 335, 350, 352
  (*see also* preventive measures)
  – over - 334–5, 343, 349, 354
  – purchasing medicines without- 143, 147, 202, 260, 253, 265, 271, 290,
  – symbolic meaning of prescription 333
prevention 37, 348
preventive
  – health 48, 82, 83

  – measures, use of prescription medication as - 27–8
  – medicine 118
price of medicines x, xi, 16, 34–5, 38, 59, 63–5, 67, 69, 71, 73–76, 84, 90, 98, 102, 115, 117, 124, 139, 152, 347
  – cost - 65, 72, 75
  – retail - 66–7, 75
  – wholesale - 67, 75
primary health care xi, 57, 77, 82, 84, 117, 177, 278, 286, 299, 318, 339, 348
private commercial institutions 134
private non-profit institutions 134
privatization 48, 50
production of drugs 19–20, 50, 83, 331–3
  (*see also* pharmaceutical firms; pharmaceutical industry)
professional status
  – of nurse in Jamaica 286
  – of Ayurveda in India 289
profits on drugs 35, 84, 139, 331, 335
promotion of drug sales 42, 50, 73, 125, 161, 163–4, 273, 331–3, 351
propharmacies 141, 146
proto-professionalization 334
psychiatrist 123, 125
psychological disorder, *see* mental illness
psychotropic drugs 84
public health 257
  – care 350
  – measures, *see* hygiene, public -
  – movement 254
  – problems posed by Mende use of Western medicine 271
  – programs 330
public medical institutions 29, 43, 57, 133–6
public sector 348
public traditional facilities 49
Punjab 47
Pure Food and Drug Act ix
purgation 307, 309
purgatives 95
purification of mother 243, 251

qollahuaya 304
quack doctor 346
qualitative research 347
qualities of medicines 255, 257
  – color 7, 264–5, 269, 273
  – taste 7, 265
  – temperature 265
  (*see also* forms, commodity, foreign,

INDEX OF SUBJECTS

liberating, secrecy, substantial, transactable, transformative)
quality
 – of medical service 57–8, 115–6
 – of packaging of drugs 71
qualude 107
quantitative research 81–102
quantities of drugs 32–3, 70–2, 84, 89, 95, 115
quest for cure 211–2
questionnaire 110–1
quinacrine 140
quinine 154

rashes 307–8
rational use of medicines 357
reasons for use of health care facility 113–6
 (*see also* choice of treatment)
recall of illness events 100
recurrent illnesses 207
Red Cross 111–2, 114, 118, 120
reinterpretation
 – of Western medical thought 341–2
 – of Western pharmaceuticals 253–76
 – of pharmaceuticals 342
reliance on medications 37, 39–40, 42
 – over– on over-the-counter drugs 124
religion 199, 330
religious specialists 212, 238, 250
remedies, sovereign– 290, 293–5
'reps' *see* drug representatives
research viii, 73, 158, 164–5, 329–57
 – and development x, 331–2
 – design 200–1
 (*see also* methodology)
 – of traditional medical phenomena 329
 – themes 331–46
respiratory disorders 34, 155, 313
restricted list of drugs 50
 (*see also* generic drugs)
retail of medicines 17, 29, 135
retired health officers 84
rheumatism 34, 53, 89, 205, 207
ringworm 86
rite of passage 239
ritual treatment 123, 125
rituals
 – contrast to medicine 7, 176, 219–20, 222–6, 229–30
 – enema and snuff 314
 – healing– 199, 212
 – Madurese– for pregnancy and childbirth 239–42, 244–5, 250, 252
Rooibos tea 317
rural clinics 57
rural health service 57–77
Rural Medical Aides 278
Rwanda 310

safety of drugs 352
 (*see also* dangerous drugs)
Safwa 219–20
sales incentives 33
salesmen, *see* drug representatives
sanitation 37, 109
Saudi 304
scabies 86, 156
scarification 308
schistomiasis 341
school examinations, medicines for– 223
seasonal variation in drug purchase 91
secondary effects 314–6
secrecy
 – of medicine 219, 225, 228
 – surrounding drug purchase 94
sedatives 47, 52, 63
self-care vii, 4–5
self-diagnosis 97, 99, 101, 107–8, 110
 see also medical self-help books)
self-medication 15, 26, 28, 38, 43, 47, 51, 59, 63, 65, 67, 74, 87–90, 92–3, 101, 107–8, 110, 115, 118, 120–2, 124, 138–41, 175, 200, 203–7, 211, 237, 335, 339, 355
self-reliance 82, 348
sellers of medicines, *see* informal sale of drugs
semantic analysis 217
semantic catergory of medicine 218
Senegal 338
sexual performance 166, 169
sexuality 238
shampoo 151
Shen-nung's Scripture on Materia Medica 181, 182, 197
shop keepers, *see* informal sale of drugs
shopping around for drugs 100
shops, *see* informal sale of drugs
shortage of medicines 134, 135, 156, 335
 (*see also* abundance; distribution)
sick role 333
side effects 21, 51, 94–6, 99, 114, 160, 176, 206, 271, 310, 314–6, 342
Siddha medicine 49

Sierra Leone 7, 176, 217, 253–76, 342
Simona 155, 170
Singapore 165
skin
  – disease 82, 86
  – disorders 313
  – sores 291–2, 304
smuggling of medicines 135
snuff 314–5
soap xii
social class 73, 116
social control 340
social distance 116, 141
social identity 221
social relations 217, 228–9, 231
social security 111–2, 114, 118, 120
socialism 81–2
socialized health care system 65
socio-economic class, see income
socio-economic factors and health problems 109
sorcery 202–3, 209–12, 218–20, 223, 227–8, 330
sore, septic– 156
sore throat 268–9, 304
South Africa 309, 317
Spain 311
speed of health service 124
spirits
  – Hausa- 306, 308
  – Madurese- 242
  – Mende- 273
  – Nyole - 223, 231
  – Taiwanese- 307
Squib 30
Sri Lanka xi, 6, 15, 47–55, 177, 333, 353, 357
state-owned facilities 133–4
static character of research 341
statistics, official (health)- 41, 61, 161–3
Steclin 30
sterility 238–9
steroids 262
Stetlin 38
stigma, social- 87, 94, 102
stomach-ache 16, 308
stomach conditions 32, 89, 96, 119–24
  (see also gastritis; gastro-intestinal disorders; infections)
storage of medicines 87–9, 90, 138
stores, see shops
substances as medicines 3

sulfa products 27, 41, 99
sulfamethoxazole 28, 38
supernatural powers 238
surgery, minor- 308
surveys 8, 200–1
  – household - 81, 85–92, 100
susto 16, 113, 119–24, 126
Swadeshi movement ix
Swahili 218
Swaziland 307
Switserland xi
symbolic
  – healing 356
  – marking 342
  – value of pharmaceuticals 330, 340
symbols 344–5
symptom(s) 175, 238
  – relationship to cause 210–212
  – relief 124
  – treatment of - 195, 204–7, 220–4, 293
syncretism 15
synthetic drugs 154
syphilis 86, 94
syringes 70–1, 73
syrup 32
system, definition of– 193
systematic correspondence, doctrine of- 180, 182, 184–96

T'ang-yeh pen-ts'ao of Wang Hao-ku 189–96
tablets vii, 17, 32–3, 43, 51, 149–52, 160–3, 264, 267
  – size of - 263
taenia passin 96
taenicide 91, 95–7
Taiwan 41, 334, 342, 345
Taiwanese medicine 307
Tamil poussari 201–2
Tanzania 218, 228–31, 332, 357
Taoist pharmaceutics 180
Tawon Jaya, 154
taxonomies, folk– 302–3
technological advancement 332
Terrabron 30, 38
Terramycina 30, 121
tetracycline 28, 30, 32, 38, 89, 96, 98, 140
Texas 108, 118, 122
textual sources
  – Ayurveda 296–7
  – Chinese and Greek medicine 179, 181–2, 187

Thailand ix, 145, 304, 338
therapeutic consequences 177
therapeutic purposes of herbal medicines 246–9
therapy choices, *see* treatment choices
therapy management group, 339–40, 355
Thermogene 202
Tonga 228
tonic 151, 166, 169, 290
tonsilitis 87
tooth paste xii, 121
toothache 51, 304
toxicity (*see also* poison) 309
 – of plants 312
traders, *see* peddlers
traditional healer vii, 199, 226, 230
 (*see also* healer)
traditional knowledge 121, 149, 153–4, 169
traditional medicine 10, 131, 223, 229–30
 – institutes of– 229–30
 – relations to 'modern' (Western) medicine 10–11, 223, 254–6, 258
 (*see also* indigenous medicine)
traditional practitioners, *see* indigenous practitioners
traditional remedies 287
training
 – of pharmacists 116–7, 124
 – of traditional practitioners 49–50, 52–3, 82, 349
 – of vendors 338, 349
transactable nature of medicines 4, 219–20, 226, 230, 330–1
transaction of medicines vii, 15–172
transfer of technology x–xi
transformative powers 229
 – of medicines 3, 218–9
 – of relationships and rituals 219
transitional medicine 82, 85
transportation 57, 59, 66, 76, 87, 90–1, 101–2
trauma 34
treatment
 – choices, *see* choice of treatment
 – of illness episodes 203–7
 – of mother after childbirth 245
 – strategies 279–81
trimethoprim 28, 38
tuberculosis 84, 86, 87, 94, 110, 123, 156, 268–9, 291
tumour 53
Turkana 306

turnover of drug inventories 90
two-tier delivery system for medical care 29, 335–6
Tylenol 119, 121
typhoid 274

Uganda 217–31
ulcer 43
umbilical cord 242
Unani 339
 – companies xii
 – medicines x, 49
underemployment 24
underutilization of medical facilities 57–8, 330
unemployment, medicine for 223–4
Unipar 95
United States of America ix–xi, 20, 30–1, 41, 76, 108–9, 117, 119, 150, 168, 353, 355
unstructured interviews 336
urban context of drug purchase 81–102, 107–125
urban dwellers' associations 81–83, 86, 90–92, 100, 102
urbanization 90
 – influence of– on health 82
 (*see also* migration)
uro-genital disorders 34, 169
 (*see also* infections; venereal disease)
US AID 59
use of medications 338–343
 – inappropriate– 20
utilization of medical facilities 57, 59–65, 69, 71–2, 86–90, 101–2, 110–1, 113–8

vaccination 38, 41, 83
valium 63
vector 82
 – control 48
vendors, *see* infomal sale of drugs
venereal disease 82, 86–7, 94, 96, 340, 221
vermifuges 37
veterinary products 42
viajeros, *see* drug representatives
Vicks Vaporub xii
vinetas, *see* sales incentives
viruses 82
visitadores, *see* drug representatives
vitamins 28, 37–8, 47, 94, 96–7, 136–7, 262, 270
 – One-A-Day 254

vomiting 96, 205, 207, 268, 316
Voodoo death 344, 356

water
 – consumption 82
 – supply 37
Waorini 306
Western medicine 330
Whateroga 53
Whitfield ointment 51
WHO xi, 20, 86, 132, 134, 261, 347, 356
 – Essential Drugs Programme 9
WHO/UNICEF declaration of 1978 278
wholesale of medicines 17, 135–6
 (*see also* pharmacies, wholesale)
witch 5
witchcraft 36, 39, 176, 268–9, 330
woggesha 85
women 16, 110–1
World Bank 59

worms 156, 176, 268–9
 – medications for 96, 98, 136, 262, 265, 272
wounds 89, 307

yellow fever 264
Yemen
 – North 335
 – South 354
yin-yang doctrine 180, 184, 189–94
Yomesan 91
Yunani medicine 296

Zaire 119
Zambia 228, 355
zar, *see* possession
Zezuru 218
Zimbabwe 218, 357
Zinza 218
Zuni 307